St. Giles's

PROCEEDINGS IN THE PARLIAMENTS OF ELIZABETH I

Proceedings in the Parliaments of Elizabeth I

VOLUME II 1584–1589

Edited by T. E. Hartley

LEICESTER UNIVERSITY PRESS

London and New York

LEICESTER UNIVERSITY PRESS
A Cassell imprint
Wellington House, 125 Strand, London WC2R 0BB, England

First published in 1995

British Library Cataloguing in Publication Data
A catalogue record for this book is available from the British Library

ISBN 0 7185 1890 X

Library of Congress Cataloging-in-Publication Data
Card Number: 81–80390

Typeset by Best-set Typesetter Ltd., Hong Kong
Printed in Great Britain by The Bath Press, Avon

Contents

The Sixth Parliament: 29 October 1586–23 March 1587

The Seventh Parliament: 4 February–29 March 1589

Abbreviations

Add.	Additional
BL	British Library
CJ	*Journal of the House of Commons*
Commons	*The House of Commons, 1558–1603* (ed. P. W. Hasler, The History of Parliament Trust, 1981)
CSPD	*Calendar of State Papers, Domestic*
Dean	D. M. Dean, 'Bills and Acts 1584–1601,' (Cambridge PhD, 1984)
D'Ewes	Sir Simonds D'Ewes, *The Journals of all the Parliaments during the Reign of Queen Elizabeth, both of the House of Lords and House of Commons* (1682)
DNB	*Dictionary of National Biography*
EHR	*English Historical Review*
EP	J. E. Neale, *Elizabeth I and her Parliaments* (2 vols., 1953, 1957)
Harl.	Harley, Harleian
HMC	Historical Manuscripts Commission
Hughes and Larkin	P. L. Hughes, J. F. Larkin, *Tudor Royal Proclamations*, (3 vols., 1964, 1969)
Lansd.	Lansdowne
LJ	*Journal of the House of Lords*
LP	*Letters and Papers, Foreign and Domestic, of the Reign of Henry VIII*, ed. J. S. Brewer, J. Gardiner, R. H. Brodie et al. (21 vols. and *Addenda*; 1862–1932)
PRO	Public Record Office
Procs, i	*Proceedings in the Parliaments of Elizabeth I, 1558–81*, ed. T. E. Hartley (Leicester, 1981)
SP Dom	State Papers Domestic
SR	*Statutes of the Realm*, 12 vols. (1810–28)
Strype, *Annals*	J. Strype, *Annals of the Reformation* (Oxford, 1842 edn.)
Strype, *Whitgift*	J. Strype, *The Life and Acts of John Whitgift* (Oxford, 1822 edn.)
Strype, *Grindal*	J. Strype, *The Life and Acts of Edmund Grindal* (Oxford, 1821 edn.)
Woodworth	A. Woodworth, 'A Purveyance for the Royal Household in the Reign of Queen Elizabeth', *Transactions of the American Philosophical Society*, new ser., xxxv, part I (Philadelphia, 1945)

Preface

My first debt of gratitude here, as before, is to the late Professor Sir John Neale who suggested that I assume the responsibility of publishing documents on Elizabethan parliamentary history, a task which he himself had originally intended to undertake. Helen Miller and Patrick Collinson were mainly responsible for producing for him the original transcripts, to which I was allowed access by the History of Parliament Trust. I am grateful to them for the enormously beneficial starting point this gave me. Thanks are also due to those with whom I have discussed this project; but I am especially thankful to Mr J. D. Cloud and Dr G. H. Martin, former colleagues at Leicester University. Among present colleagues, Mr N. S. Davidson, Dr G. A. Harrison and Professor A. N. Newman were generous with their time and advice when I asked for them.

My debt to Dr David Dean is substantial. I was able, as a result of a generous grant from the British Academy, to benefit from his skills in checking many of the transcripts against the original manuscripts. But over and above what I could legitimately ask of him he was prepared to discuss many of the problems associated with the material: since he had already worked with many of the manuscripts while writing his doctoral thesis on the parliaments of the second half of Elizabeth's reign this was an important bonus. Perhaps even more valuable to me personally was his constant friendship and encouragement throughout a long undertaking, one which eventually occupied more time and demanded greater patience than was originally envisaged.

The format adopted in the first volume of *Proceedings in the Parliaments of Elizabeth I* – as explained in the preface there – has generally been retained in this second part; and the editorial approach is also broadly similar. Square brackets enclose matter which is not part of the text, either words supplied, or indications of problems in the manuscript itself. I have tried to provide information about variant readings which indicates changes of significance from manuscript to manuscript, rather than noting every change: I have not noted small variations – mispellings, minor changes in word order, or the omission of single words – which seem to be slips of the pen, unless a real change of meaning occurs. Though I have included some discussion of diary writing in particular (especially with regard to 'anonymous' manuscripts), the whole subject of journal keeping in the sixteenth century – and beyond – is one which deserves closer and more extensive treatment than was possible, or even advisable, here. Though the policy of concentrating on providing reliable transcriptions and avoiding lengthy editorial comment and apparatus has also been maintained here, I am conscious as before of being unable to trace many of the textual allusions which occur, especially in speeches: many frustrating hours were spent attempting to locate the sources of these, and I also encroached on the precious time of colleagues in various fields. I hope that the fact that quotations and citations have not always been traced does not disappoint too greatly, and I am confident that others will be able to find answers which have eluded me. I also remain responsible for any errors which may remain in this book.

I wish to thank the following for their co-operation, and for their permission to print transcripts of manuscripts in their collections: the British Library; Lambeth Palace Library; the Marquess of Bath at Longleat; the Marquess of Salisbury at Hatfield House; Trinity College Dublin; Northamptonshire County Record Office and the representatives of the late Earl Fitzwilliam; the Public Record Office; the Inner Temple Library; Cambridge University Library; the Bodleian Library, Exeter College and Queen's College, Oxford; Hertfordshire County Record Office; the Huntington Library, San Marino, California; and the Pierpont Morgan Library, New York. As already mentioned, the British Academy gave generous financial support for the research associated with this project, and the former Research Board of the University of Leicester also provided grants at various times. I am also grateful to Professor Collinson, who – since this book went to press – tells me that Jane Ladley has located further copies of the account of Whitgift's response to the Commons' petitions, as well as the latter's reaction to it, which form part of the compilation known as Fitzwilliam's journal (for 1584–5): they are in the Surrey Record Office (Loseley MSS LM 1961 and 1962).

My wife has been constant in supporting my efforts. A statement of my gratitude at this point is no mere formality, an obligatory closing part of a preface: it is a heartfelt recognition of the incalculable worth of her own contribution.

Introduction

This collection of documents is a further stage in the publication of material relating to proceedings in Elizabeth's parliaments, and follows the first volume of *Proceedings* covering the sessions up to and including that of 1581. Two considerations have led to the publication of this section now. In the first place, the quantity of material to be included for the six sessions from 1584–5 to 1601 is more extensive than that which appeared in the first volume, and made a single volume a less feasible proposition. One consideration may illustrate this: the Hayward Townshend journal for 1601 alone extends to about 70,000 words, without any commentary or footnotes. Secondly, it is some time since the appearance of the first volume and it seemed right to divide what remained rather than prolonging the interval even further while work on the last three sessions of the reign is completed.

The manuscripts printed here were chosen by Sir John Neale and formed part of the collection which he had himself originally intended to edit. The characteristic common to all the documents included is simply that they are concerned with matters arising in Parliament, or were intended for use there. Thus there are, as in the earlier volume of *Proceedings*, two broad categories of printed manuscript: firstly, accounts of individual speeches or proceedings on a particular issue – the separates; and secondly, journals, or diaries, which cover proceedings generally, either for part or all of a parliamentary session. It remains true here, as it was for the earlier volume, that in some cases there is no firm corroborative evidence that a 'speech', which exists in manuscript form, was actually delivered, though an indication that it was at some time destined for Parliament explains its inclusion.[1]

In many respects the format of this second part of the project is consistent with that adopted in the first.[2] In particular, the problem of explaining all the allusions and all the historical, legendary or mythical references which appear in the body of the documents remains a substantial one, as it does with Latin quotations and legal citations with which members apparently peppered their speeches on occasions, however inaccurately recorded. The basis on which footnote information about variant readings were provided is also maintained in principle, namely that a note has been supplied where the sense of the adopted text is affected, that is where there is a change of 'significance'. The integrity of documents has also been preserved: running accounts of the events of more than one day which journals provide have not therefore been divided up and printed with sections of other documents so as to consolidate all available accounts of particular days' business. The latter approach clearly has advantages for the reader who wishes to discover all that the sources can say about what occurred on a specific day; and the former means that, although several

1. See for example the speech on the succession in 1586–7: Doc.9.

2. *Procs*, i pp.xxvi–xxviii.

treatments of the same topic may appear, they are dispersed among other material. On the other hand, it does seem to be important that readers be able to appreciate the character of a particular narrative or journal, and this would clearly be more difficult if sections were to be scattered throughout a composite account of proceedings. A carefully constructed index will, it is hoped, help the hard-pressed reader who may find it frustrating to have to search through the text for the several versions of the same episode, or speech, which may from time to time be available: bracketed 'signposts' in the index will indicate where material occurring in more than one place is to be found. However, long undifferentiated index entries can clearly bewilder and waste time, so sub-division of entries (where appropriate) by session and by document may ease the problem considerably.

This volume does differ, however, from the earlier one in an important respect. In all but two instances the volume covering the period from 1559 to 1581 was made up of evidence which had been used directly in writing *Elizabeth I and her Parliaments*, the exceptions being documents which came to light subsequently and which concerned the succession to the throne, a matter which was central to proceedings in the 1560s. Moreover, Neale obviously adhered broadly to the principle that he would publish the main sources on which his second volume of *Elizabeth I and her Parliaments* was based, yet his later selections include a number of documents which found no place in his account of proceedings in Parliament. They are mostly concerned with matters which Neale did not fully address in his political account of Parliamentary affairs, though the document concerning the succession to the English throne is a notable exception: they deal with a broad range of legislative business and provide glimpses of those areas of parliamentary endeavour which continued against the background of threats to the security of the throne and nation at home and abroad. Users of this volume will also notice that documents which are strictly speaking accounts of what happened in the House of Lords have now been treated as Lords' documents: opening and closing proceedings, though involving orations by the Speaker of the Commons, were events which occurred in the Upper House. Beyond this, however, the rate of survival of evidence has not favoured the Lords in comparison with the early part of the reign, and we still lack substantial accounts of debates among the peers of the realm.

The diaries or journals covering proceedings in these three sessions are varied in length and nature. Generally they are less comprehensive accounts of daily proceedings than Thomas Cromwell's earlier accounts of the 1572 session, or perhaps of 1581, were and by the same token they cannot match Hayward Townshend's record of the 1601 session. A large proportion of Thomas Cromwell's account of the 1584–5 session is devoted to recording bill readings, though there are instructive comments on proceedings from time to time. The so-called Fitzwilliam diary for the same session is much more obviously de-voted to recording speeches and proceedings on a number of themes, especially the Queen's safety and religion, and is perhaps more accurately described as a compilation, even an edited account, of selected major events. And the anonymous journal for the same session is again largely devoted to speeches, or summaries and snatches of debate, on a variety of bills, seemingly arranged without clear chronological order.[3] Fleetwood's brief account of the events of the first few days of the session is the fourth of these very different 'journals' which have survived for the first session covered in this volume. Two documents for 1586–7 which are described here (largely for convenience) as journals, one for the Lords and the other for the Commons, are almost *sui generis* in that their purpose is to record the progress of solid blocks of opinion in the respective Houses as they moved inexorably to one simple conclusion about the fate of the Scottish Queen. They present a picture of total, even inevitable, consensus, so that no one could be left in doubt about what should happen. The anonymous journal for the same session deals with only a two-week period beyond that covered by the Lords and Commons. It is perhaps the most truly 'journalistic' account of proceedings printed here, since it looks like an attempt at a daily record of events, and it may well have been written in the House of Commons itself: it is interesting that it covers part of a session which had initially been planned as a much shorter one, and which would have ended before the journal began. Finally, for 1589 there is a very brief account of some of the Commons' proceedings which Neale attributed to Henry Jackman.

The different perspectives and ranges of these journals and the fact that four, that is half, of them deal with the 1584–5 session alone means, incidentally, that the extent to which the same business is covered in more than one journal is limited. In turn the potential benefit accruing from constructing accounts of business on a day-to-day basis from entries extracted from more than one source – rather than retaining the integrity of individual journals – is also limited.[4] Despite the fact that these journals, like many historical documents, do not tell us all we would want to know we clearly do benefit from having a range of particular contemporary perspectives. Taken together they represent a comprehensive view of the multi-faceted work of Elizabeth's parliaments at this time.

The fact that the approach to compiling journals could be so various is necessarily connected with the question of authorship, as well as the purpose for which accounts of proceedings were written. Neale was happy to attribute two of the journals included here to William Fitzwilliam and Henry Jackman, though it must be said that there is a degree of speculation in this judgement.[5] The Fitzwilliam journal is to be found among the family papers in Northamptonshire, yet nothing in the manuscript itself ties it exclusively to William, Mildmay's son-in-law, who was a member at the time. The handwriting, a neat and compact clerical script, differs from that used to record some committee deliberations in 1587 and which may be his own.[6] Of course, it is not inherently unlikely that Fitzwilliam himself was instrumental in some

3. See session introductory remarks.
4. See pp. 1–2.
5. *EP*, ii.24, 207, n.1, 209, n.1.
6. See 1586–7: Doc.23.

way in the composition of both documents as a participating member of the House of Commons. Equally, his role may simply have been that of manuscript collector; the way the journal is put together supports this to some extent because important sections of it exist in their own right in other manuscripts. Since his father-in-law features prominently, however, it is easy to believe that Fitzwilliam was responsible for the journal's composition.

Henry Jackman appears in Neale's accounts of the parliaments of 1589, 1593 and 1597, though there is some doubt about his contribution in 1589.[7] Neale attributed two manuscript accounts of speeches which belong to the session to him, as well as an account of some of the proceedings which he described as a 'fragmentary diary'. All these items appear in a Lansdowne manuscript – number 55 – in the British Library, though none of them bears any information, for example an endorsement, which specifically attributes them to Jackman. There are some notes of sayings or quotations on fos.186–7 of the manuscript, apparently marshalled for possible use in the speeches on the subsidy and on foreigners.[8] Another Lansdowne manuscript – number 105 – has a speech from the 1597 parliament, and it alone has an indication of its origin: it has as an endorsement, in a contemporary or near contemporary hand, the words 'speech conceived by H.J.' The words 'Henry Jackman' have been written below this, though in another hand, possibly Strype's. Lansdowne 83, f.206v is endorsed 'Henry Jackman', though the document is a draft of the husbandry and tillage bill of 1597 and not a speech as Neale appeared at one point to have believed.[9] This endorsement has been crossed out, possibly because it ought to belong to fos.98–98v, which contain notes on the tillage bill, again which Neale assumed to be Jackman's. Lansdowne 88, f.21 is also relevant: it is a copy of a bond signed 'Henry Jackman'. This signature is not identical with the endorsement on Lansdowne 105 and differs from the secretary hand used to write the three documents in Lansdowne 55, and from that used in Lansdowne 105. It is not clear, however, that the bond could not therefore have been signed by the writer of these items. The crucial point seems to be the relationship between the three items in Lansdowne 55 with the speech in Lansdowne 105, and with the notes in Lansdowne 83: these last two, as we have seen, are linked with Jackman – no other member with the initials 'H.J.' has been identified as sitting in 1597. Comparison of the hand used in these five documents reveals a secretary hand which, while not consistently identical, is similar. The three items in Lansdowne 55 are also clearly related. There is a possibility therefore that all these five documents were written by the same hand, and the endorsement on Lansdowne 105 may be telling us that the speech was not just 'conceived' by Jackman – and copied by a clerk – but that it was Jackman's own working document. If this is so, then it is plausible to suggest, as his biographer does, that Jackman's various speeches and jottings found their way into the Lansdowne collection by way of his friendship with Michael Hickes.

Is it possible to say why these documents, particularly the journals, were written in the first place? In the case of the Lords and Commons documents relating to Mary Stuart in 1586–7 the answer may seem obvious enough; but generally there is probably no easy answer to this question. It may be that there is a case for looking at all the Elizabethan journals together (or all the early Stuart ones as well) in the hope that some common characteristics or answers emerge. Such a task promises to be a considerable undertaking in its own right, and one which could prove to be relatively unfruitful. We are perhaps dealing with a kind of document here whose being and initiation is particularly shrouded in mystery, and never more so than in the case of those journals whose authorship is unknown.

If we take the 1584–5 Cromwell journal, for instance, we must consider the suggestion, plausible enough, that this account was written for Lord Burghley, Cromwell's patron. As yet the suggestion is merely hypothetical. If Burghley was relying on Cromwell at this stage, however, he would have received a product which differed from his earlier efforts: this one was less concerned with recording debate, more involved with recording titles, summaries and readings of bills. At the close he commented that he had not been able to hear the Queen's oration – odd perhaps if he was compiling a record for someone like Burghley who would have heard it, or of it, himself. Then again it is interesting to remember that this was, as far as we know, the last journal Cromwell compiled, though he continued to sit in Parliament until 1589. By this time he was involved extensively in committee work and perhaps diary keeping was a luxury he could no longer indulge in. By this time too, Burghley's son Robert had taken up his first seat in the Commons. The so-called anonymous journal, or account of various speeches in the parliament of 1584–5, might have supplied some of what Cromwell missed. The fact that its entries are not dated might not have mattered to someone like Burghley, and the fact that it is apparently written in the same hand which was responsible for other documents among Burghley's papers in the Lansdowne collection leads to the reasonable suggestion that this 'journal' also owed its existence to the Lord Treasurer. Fleetwood's own version of the opening days' events certainly seems to have arisen from a desire to provide Burghley with a descriptive account; and perhaps the anonymous journal for 1586–7 was also meant for him.[10] In the case of the Lansdowne manuscript we have just been considering, as well as the other anonymous journal, for 1586–7, there are no obvious clues on which to base suggestions about authorship: however, further speculation about the phenomenon of anonymous journals will be reserved for the next volume (which deals with the last three sessions of the reign) when the extensive anonymous journal for 1593 is considered.

These three sessions span that part of the 1580s when England's rift with Spain fast developed into open conflict, so the major background preoccu-

7. See *EP*, ii.206–7, 341–3, 349–51; *Commons, sub* Jackman, Henry.
8. BL Lansd. 55, fos.180–3, 188–9.
9. *EP*, ii.206–7 and n., 339 n.

10. See M. A. R. Graves, 'Managing Elizabeth's Parliaments' in *The Parliaments of Elizabethan England*, ed. D. M. Dean and N. L. Jones (1990), p.60 and n.40.

pations for these parliaments were obvious and stark. To many it seemed that England and its society were at risk from invasion and plots. Catholic foes were at work inside and outside the realm, and it was necessary to guard against them constantly. Money and special laws were the main official requirements, and Elizabeth remained unwilling to concede demands which from time to time appeared in the course of parliamentary business: for her Parliament was an occasion for her subjects' co-operation with her. The willingness of many to co-operate in efforts to preserve her life were abundantly clear. The threat presented by Mary Queen of Scots had become so great as to precipitate the Bond of Association before the first session assembled in 1584. From the point of view of those who sat in Parliament, the attempts to protect Elizabeth from plots and provide a justification in the end for executing Mary often meant a thorough, if not tedious, rehearsal of her misdeeds, alleged or real, many of which would have been familiar to members who had been present in the 1570s.[11] Intimately connected with this theme was the suspicion of Catholics and the possibility of their involvement in plots against the Crown. Discussion of these problems showed that many were keen to stress the merits of Elizabeth's regime in England in contrast to the tyrannies of Europe which offered nothing but threats to peace and prosperity. So the English queen's importance as a symbol of Protestant stability, security and liberty was a powerful one throughout these years. Other princes were more or less explicitly open to condemnation as falling short of the virtues she possessed, though sometimes as in the case of Job Throckmorton it was possible to make the point too strongly.[12]

Elizabeth, despite all this, did not escape criticism from time to time because of her apparent unwillingness to conform fully to the logic of this position as some saw it, most notably by assuming sovereignty in the Low Countries or by pushing on with the reformation of the English Church with the vigour many demanded of her. These years were an important stage in the development of a politico-religious ideology which saw parts of Europe as areas of struggle between Protestant light and Catholic darkness, and where vigilance was necessarily constant.[13] Two points must be made though. In the first place, the awareness that Protestantism was under attack must not be stripped of the practical context which clearly underpinned it. Law and 'liberty', which were valued so much by Elizabeth's Protestant supporters, were guarantees of property and peace for the subjects of the realm which seemed to be at obvious risk from Spanish invasion and a return to Roman Catholicism. Similarly, as the documents relating to Low Countries' sovereignty in 1587 show, the feeling of solidarity for Protestant co-religionists abroad contained significant elements of concern about trading rights and routes, and about the strategic importance of the area because of its geographical position *vis-à-vis* England.

The other point is that Protestant denunciations of Catholicism and the need to prevent its creeping into the Church at home led, as we know, to calls for further reform of the Church, some of which required a structural redefinition on Presbyterian lines. Though this proposal for major change only appealed to a minority, it provided part of the justification for the Queen's wholesale rejection of any moves for ministerial reform in the Church which appeared from time to time as they had done in the recent past. The Protestant would-be reformers, whose motivation was drawn in part from a desire to reform in order to strengthen and unite the realm and its people, were seen by Whitgift and others as subversive, even as worse than the enemy. The defenders of the Church as it stood seemed to be prepared to argue that the desire for change, however modest and limited it might be, was fundamentally wrong and misguided. At best the mere spectacle of some English Protestants calling for reform and seemingly divided from others about their Church provided a propaganda weapon for the Catholics and thereby played into their hands. There was an apparent willingness throughout these years to use requests for reform as proof that the worst kind of religious extremity was close at hand and that the appropriate religious and political answer was therefore to retreat into a rigid upholding of the *status quo*. The pre-eminence of Whitgift and Hatton, even of Bancroft[14] is clearly reflected in the documents included here, and the views propounded were obviously consonant with Elizabeth's own political instincts which reacted strongly against anything which threatened the statutory supremacy Parliament had recognized in her in 1559. In a way then, any hopes which Protestants may have entertained about playing on fears of Catholicism and the subversion it threatened rebounded intellectually, for it was they who were painted as enemies of the *status quo* and sometimes in very direct language.[15]

Some comments have already been made about collectors of manuscripts, as well as the preponderance of copies, rather than originals, among the material which is assembled in these collections of parliamentary papers. Something has also been said of the general historical value of separates and journals, and what they may reveal about the nature of the law and perceptions of the relationship between Queen and subject.[16] The range of topics in the documents presented here is full, as will already be clear from what has been said about the journals for 1584–5 alone. Lofty discussion about the safety of the realm, Fleetwood's complaints about members laughing at him, Elizabeth's messages about religion, and bills about timber and iron, for example, all find a place here. And the documents which Neale did not employ are in their varying ways all comments on the practicalities of government and administration which continued while threats to the regime at home and abroad came and went.

This collection is also rich in fine speeches. Nicholas Bacon's absence from the scene is readily compensated for by the outstanding contributions of Hatton and Throckmorton in particular, and even the unknown author of a speech on Mary in the 1586–7 session: these would have provided rich rewards for those

---

11. See *Procs*, i.
12. See, in particular, Mildmay and Hatton on Spain and the Pope in 1586–7.
13. See speeches for supply in particular.

14. See 1586–7 introduction.
15. See, for example, Whitgift's calumnies in 1589.
16. *Procs*, i. pp.xii–xiii, xvii–xxv.

who chose to listen to them. It may be simply that the passionate concerns of men who were anxious about the state of their country and their faith naturally resulted in what are undoubtedly a number of oratorical gems. Job Throckmorton's efforts in 1586–7 are perhaps all the more interesting if we subscribe to the belief about his prominence in the Martin Marprelate controversy.[17] But it is hard to deny that these men were possessed of rare speaking skills. Burghley was presumably no less concerned about the safety of England than anyone else, and Elizabeth's own passion about the sanctity of her royal authority was unsurpassed. Yet where we have the opportunity to examine Burghley's efforts to compose a speech the results seem drab in comparison with Hatton's. The Queen's speeches continue to demand close analysis in their own right: though the passion clearly is present, there is often – perhaps inevitably – a starchy quality which militates against sheer brilliance. The amendments she frequently made may have been merely stylistic, yet it is impossible to avoid the temptation to weigh the possible political significance of alterations of word and phrase. Additionally there was clearly considerable concern about producing public versions of speeches initially delivered to a group of members of Parliament – ostensibly private occasions – yet inevitably perhaps destined at these crucial times to become public. Elizabeth was obviously able to produce magical turns of phrase on occasion, delicious morsels which may genuinely have helped to enthral her audience. But often there persists an element of opacity in parts of her convoluted prose, and the reader may be confronted at times with sections which are not easily digested.

No less interesting is the content of Elizabeth's accumulated utterances to Parliament. The usual ingredients duly make their appearance: her subjects' love for her, the assurance that her care for them was unsurpassable, but also the equally unsurpassable conviction that her authority must not be compromised. The realm and the Church were hers to rule as far as she could, and there could be no doubt that her love for her subjects would be given on her terms. We may never know precisely how ready she was to allow the law to take effect against Mary in 1587, but the *message*, pondered and amended, was unambiguous. Diplomatic considerations and public decency themselves probably dictated that Elizabeth should assume the role of reluctant participant in her cousin's death. But it is also legitimate to wonder whether acceding, however formally, to a parliamentary request also played its part. Her love for her subjects could not be freely available, especially when it necessitated the execution of a prince.

17. Leland H. Carlson, *Martin Marprelate Gentleman: Master Job Throckmorton Laid* *Open in his Colors* (San Marino, Huntington Library 1981).

THE FIFTH PARLIAMENT:
23 NOVEMBER 1584–
29 MARCH 1585

Documents

A new parliament was needed in 1584 to deal with the crisis presented by the activities of Catholics at home and abroad. William of Orange's death in July, and the rupture of diplomatic links with Spain because of involvement in the Throckmorton plot, pointed to the need for further security for Queen and realm. Lords 1 is an account, not used by Neale, of the procession of Queen, Lords and Commons to St Peter's in Westminster before moving on to the Lords for the opening ceremony. It includes a summary of Whitgift's sermon, though it is impossible to know how widely his words about the wicked and the laws were meant to be interpreted. Others were certainly concerned about the continuing threat from Catholic activities, including those of Mary Queen of Scots. Whitgift's images of God sweeping away the wicked like spiders and cobwebs was powerful, as was his reference to possessions being wasted. However, when he spoke of 'many orators' he may have had others in mind.

The major official business for the session was set out by Mildmay and Hatton, while Lord Chancellor Bromley had already ruled out discussion of religion when replying to the Speaker's request for privileges. On 28 November, Mildmay and Hatton spoke at great length against Spain and the Pope, of the dangers facing England, and of the need to provide measures for Elizabeth's safety and against Jesuits and seminary priests. Anxious to establish a firm legal, moral, and political basis for further legislation, Mildmay in particular stressed the Queen's mercy against Catholics in this country in contrast to what Protestants abroad might expect from the hands of Catholics: 'never called, never harde, never iudged accordinge to lawe'. Moreover, Jesuits and seminary priests in England were, he said, keen to 'stirr sedition' rather than to save souls.[1] The documents which Neale assembled for this session (not all of which were used in *Elizabeth I and her Parliaments*) offer perspectives on important lawmaking business other than that of the Queen's safety and Catholic priests. And despite Elizabeth's wish, and Bromley's statement, the subject of religion was not kept off the agenda, not least during the closing proceedings.

The four journals or diaries known to have survived for this session display a range of radically different approaches to recording proceedings in the Commons. The first of them, Fleetwood's, is more precisely an account of the

1. See in particular Fitzwilliam's diary,
    fos.3v–4.

first days (from 23 to 28 November), and is therefore concerned mainly with opening proceedings and the major speeches of Mildmay and Hatton on the need for action to deal with Spain. Fleetwood sent this to Burghley, though it is not known whether he composed it on instruction (Journals 1). Whatever the case, there are some interesting observations from a man who was presumably a seasoned observer of the parliamentary scene, because he had sat in every session of the reign thus far. New members and the relative infrequency of parliamentary sessions no doubt accounted in large part for the confusion about opening procedures which he reported. His comment about the committee on the Sabbath bill is also important. He noted that approximately a third of those present one afternoon spoke. Though it was his view that 'nothing' was done, the apparent willingness of members to speak may modify the view that parliamentary business was dominated by a minority of speaking members as represented in many of the surviving diaries where, indeed, men like Fleetwood himself are often represented as taking a leading role in debate. Certainly this is the case in the journal to which no author can yet be safely ascribed (Journals 3). It is written in a difficult secretarial hand – with a number of readings remaining uncertain – and the organization of the material, both in terms of chronology and the identification of speakers and speeches is problematic: as the journal is arranged, its contents appear to be out of order. The lack of internal references to days, and the incomplete, or ambiguous, attribution of what may be either summaries of, or quotations from, speeches is tantalizing. It is not possible, for example, to identify speakers on the Shoemakers bill.[2] It may be that the scribe was himself the author of the journal and that he wrote on separate folios while in the House itself. The apparently incomplete nature of reporting may indicate as much.[3] Neale was inclined to believe that the author was indeed the scribe and that he was also responsible for the four draft speeches on bills which appear in this volume of the Lansdowne papers. The point is though that this journal is preoccupied with speeches, in strong contrast to Cromwell's journal for the session (Journals 2), and indeed the document is described in its endorsement as a 'report on diverse speeches'. It is not therefore a journal in the way Cromwell's earlier efforts were, or indeed as Fleetwood's albeit incomplete account was. Nevertheless, it is still invaluable. This anonymous journal gave prominence to the contributions of men like Alford and Digges; and the commanding position of a seasoned speaker like Fleetwood is well indicated, though he complained of a group of men who were always laughing at him. There are important accounts of members' views on specific measures, some of which clearly caused earnest debate and threw up sharp differences of opinion. Not the least significant was the objection made by one member about the clash of loyalties arising from subscribing to the Bond of Association.[4] Potentially just as rewarding, however, are the indications scattered throughout which reveal members' general attitudes, for example on procedural matters, on precedent and the need for accuracy in citing evidence in speeches.[5] At the heart of all this was perhaps a concern, publicly adhered to at least, that members ought to do their work well.

Fleetwood himself was scornful of poorly drafted-bills which demanded much time to put them right, and he seems to have complained about members who voted without hearing the issues at stake properly.[6] He also argued that members should act independently of fees and inducements which could come their way: 'I am not feed; I speak my conscience, and I think so of every man here', he said.[7]

The remaining two journals, Cromwell's and Fitzwilliam's, are substantial. The first (Journals 2) is the last apparently kept, or at least surviving, by Thomas Cromwell, although this was not his last parliament. Unlike Fitzwilliam's journal, Cromwell's does not spend much time at all reporting speeches. Though Parliament met on 23 November, Cromwell notes his absence till 1 December, thus missing the three working days of 27, 28 and 30 November, and he was also absent through sickness from 11 to 22 February. He does, however, provide information on bills which would otherwise be lost to us.[8] Even so, his committee work was extensive and sometimes meant his missing bill readings in the House[9], though he did sometimes try to supply what he had missed.[10] Neither did he record all his appointments to committees.[11] Sometimes his record is disappointingly laconic: Cromwell, like most compilers of accounts of parliamentary business in Elizabeth's reign, cannot provide answers to all questions which might be asked. He notes, for instance, that the Stationers bill was disliked, though he does not explain why.[12] And Turner and his bill and book are not mentioned. Neither did he comment on the new bill for the Queen's safety on 3 March, though he had recorded the contents of the bill introduced on 14 December (including the distinction between invasion and rebellion), and Hatton's message from the Queen on 18 December.[13] His description of the petitions on the Church is brief[14] and, as a member of one of the committees involved, he was apparently as much concerned to record the steps whereby Lords and Commons discussed the matter.[15] In these respects the journal may reflect the particular interests of the experienced committee man that he had by now become. None the less, he gave extensive, and exceptional, coverage to Hatton's account of Parry's case and its background on 24 February – he had already noted Parry's attack on the bill against Jesuits, and registered what seems to have been a generally felt sense of outrage and insult that Parry had refused to explain himself to the

2. F.171.

3. e.g. f.174v.

4. F.173v.

5. Fos.167v, 168, 170v.

6. F.173v.

7. F.174v.

8. D. Dean, 'Bills and Acts', p.21, and Appendix, pp.256–61, which gives details of bill readings provided from the journals or diaries for the six sessions from 1584 to 1601.

9. Fos.88, 89.

10. See f.91.

11. Cf. e.g. D'Ewes, p.335 for 4 Dec.

12. F.81; see Doc.3.

13. Fos.78, 79, 87v.

14. Fos.77, 79v.

15. See also fos.80, 80v for lack of comment on the long adjournment until February, and on fraudulent conveyances, though his description of it is extensive, fos.77v–8.

House.[16] Elizabeth's reactions to the petitions on 22 February and 2 March also appear, and Cromwell's rendering of the latter in particular is sharp: it encapsulates the heart and soul of her objections to independent parliamentary action.[17] It was not the appearance of the petitions alone which troubled the Queen, but the fact that they signified a 'diffidence' in her reformation.[18] His account of concern in the Commons over subpoenas and privilege also reveal a degree of scrupulous and responsible scrutiny of these matters by a House which was, as a matter of course, always enjoined to act with care and circumspection.[19] In these ways Cromwell emerged as an active participant in the business of Parliament, as well as an astute observer of the Commons' activities and sensitivities.

The Fitzwilliam journal (Journals 4) is a compilation of speeches and points made by, and to, Commons' members. It is written in a neat secretary hand, though a different script is used to record the parliamentary precedents cited at the beginning, and another hand is obvious in a marginal comment that these had been gathered from the parliament rolls. The journal clearly owes much to separate copies of items which make up important parts of its contents. The compiler's access to these documents allowed a degree of editorial comment to be added to the section on the petitions on religion, and it seems clear therefore that the journal was composed after the events recorded.[20] Speeches are not always attributed, though the major contributions of Mildmay and Hatton are notable exceptions. The MS is, therefore, an account rather than a journal or daily record of major matters, principally the Queen's safety and religion. It is a representation of argument and counter-argument, and individual speakers often do not appear, their identities subsumed in accounts of general feeling in the House. The gaps in the MS, especially on folios 11v–13, 28v–29v, may indicate an intention to include other material gathered subsequently. At one point the compiler even commented on some forgetfulness in organizing the account: 'I should have shewed you . . . howe there was a bill presented. . . .'[21] If William Fitzwilliam was indeed the author or compiler of this journal, then it is tempting to believe that the 'you' was Sir Walter Mildmay, Fitzwilliam's father-in-law, though there can be no certainty that this was so.

Much time was devoted to the Queen's safety and the need to provide as much security as possible, and to the question of the action on petitions for reform of the Church, which Mildmay stressed was a continuation of earlier requests for action.[22] This in any case took place in the context of some surprise that Elizabeth had banned discussion on religion, and which the compiler of the journal made much of.[23] The nature of the petitions themselves may have reinforced this apparent bewilderment, for at several points it was clear that the active co-operation and participation of the establishment – the bishops – was being solicited: part of the complaint was simply that the disciplining of ministers did not always involve the bishops themselves.[24] The journalist's account of the reaction to Elizabeth's quashing of the agitation over religion is well known, though its significance needs to be re-examined in view of newer approaches to the nature of discontent over religion in Elizabeth's parliaments.[25]

The journal also provides extensive coverage of the discussion surrounding the bill for the Queen's safety, and the Bond of Association naturally figured in this debate. It is important to stress Fitzwilliam's comments at various points which reveal the worries that surfaced from time to time, both in this matter and elsewhere, about the effectiveness and intent of bills as well as the appropriateness of proposed penalties: these were the natural and constant concerns of men who were actively engaged in the business of making law, whatever it concerned. For example, discussion of the proviso for the safety bill concerning the heirs of offenders provoked the idea that the Oath of Association with which it conflicted could not be set aside, though others argued that the *intent* of the Oath was to save Elizabeth's life and that it ought not to be done *unlawfully*, for example by killing the innocent: 'ill parentes have manye tymes good children'.[26] Others said the conflict was more apparent than real because the Oath was stricter in the letter than in 'equity', which was to punish the offender only. As the debate unfolded it was also clear that some were worried about the strictness of other provisions in the bill.[27] And some practical limitations to any anti-Catholic fanaticism which may have been apparent in the House were also evident when the question of a double subsidy for Catholics emerged.[28] It was also apparent that members could become concerned about the scope of their freedom to legislate: should laws be made which were retrospective, and could precedents in effect be altered, or should members be 'in subiection to their predecessors' orders'?[29]

Concern with religion and the state of the Church is illustrated in a number of documents here, as well as in Fitzwilliam's account. Doc.4 charts the proceedings of 15 February 1585, well into the session, in connection with the presentation of petitions on the state of the ministry, a matter which had first been raised before Christmas on 14 December. It also marks the continued involvement of Mildmay and attempts to work with the Lords which had been apparent almost from that day.[30] It is practically identical with what appears in D'Ewes, and may therefore be a copy of part of the Commons journal from which D'Ewes worked. Mildmay's recalling of the recent history of the petitions provided a correct framework for action, and he said that news would come from the Lords within 24 hours. Doc.5 may be the petition, or supplication, offered by Stoughton on 15 February and referred to in the first part of

16. Fos.78v–9.
17. Fos.82v, 87. Fitzwilliam also comments pertinently on this (f.32v).
18. F.87v.
19. Fos.81v–2, 92v–3.
20. See f.23v.
21. F.35.
22. F.21v.
23. See *EP*, ii.26–7.
24. F.20v.
25. *EP*, ii.72–8.
26. F.8.
27. F.14v.
28. F.34–v.
29. F.35–v; see also Anonymous Journal, f.166 and Cromwell, fos.91v, 92 for recoveries.
30. *EP*, ii.61–5.

Doc.4. The Commons were called upon to take action: they were to consider the complaints about the clergy, and in 'godlie wisdome to provide redresse' for clerical activities contrary to the laws of the realm. Included among these was the allegation that counsel was sometimes denied in cases of discipline, and that there was probing into 'the secret thoughtes of men's hartes'. Action was not taken in public, but in a private chamber where the 'dore is kept shutt'. However, the anti-clericalism in this document ranges more widely into traditional areas of complaints about excessive fee-taking and the use of excommunication.

Whitgift's response (Doc.6) to the petitions which had been drawn up by the Commons before Christmas was probably compiled, for or by him, from notes used in the meeting with members of the Commons on 22 February. They should be compared with the report which appears in Fitzwilliam's journal: this version does not carry as much of the acerbity which is apparent in that journal, though in some respects it is a fuller account.[31] Generally, it is in accord with it. What is striking is the moderation of the tone relative to that which ran through another version which Whitgift evidently compiled for Elizabeth's eyes.[32] The 'Queen's version' is in places much more obviously suffused with expressions of fear for the fabric of the state, either genuine, or calculated to ensure the Queen's alarm at what the petitioners were attempting. Most notably, the manuscript includes a damning indictment in response to the fourth petition, though publicly, that is to the Commons themselves, Whitgift refused, as here, to explain his reasons for rejecting the petition.[33] The notion of the petitioners as religious radicals and subverters of Church and state, which is unmistakably at the heart of Whitgift's explanation of his position to the Queen, did not then, as far as we can tell from Fitzwilliam, emerge as starkly in what he had told the Commons' delegation, though he had been far from emollient.

There is no evidence to show how Whitgift came to hear of the members' speeches which are noted in Doc.7, or what he intended to do with the information. It is assumed that these gleanings were part of the reaction to his reply, and it is not surprising that he should hear of what had been said. Naturally, all four members appear to have been antagonistic to the Archbishop's answers, and between them they attacked his demeanour as well as the substance of what he had said. More than this, a degree of more generalized anti-clericalism appeared in the notion that the Bishops had not been true reformers. Puckering (Doc.8) set out his notes of the Queen's message to be conveyed to the Commons on 2 March about the petitions and the bill concerning bishops' oaths of allegiance.[34] He apparently consulted both Walsinghamn and Hatton and produced two sets of notes, neither of which offered any hope of a positive outcome to the Commons' petitions or the bishops' bill. She took her stand on her own power as Supreme Governor, and discounted any role for the Commons in the matter. It was her duty to admonish them 'as a mother over the commen welthe must warne them as her children'. She claimed to recognize a general antipathy to the clergy, and hoped that this trait would be reformed as the bishops were 'the principall members of this state'. The Commons' excesses in this matter were attributed to slackness among Privy Councillors who ought to have moved the House 'to some other course'. The document has a third section, written by Puckering in law French, though this was done in a column formed after the paper had been folded into four. It may therefore not be connected with the notes for the speech: the subject matter is not sufficiently clear to establish a definite connection.

Other work did not, of course, cease in the wake of the important and grave business of this session. The first bill to be dealt with by the Commons was in fact the Sabbath bill on 26 November, and by the end of 28 November, when Mildmay and Hatton spoke, a bill concerning hue and cry, and two others, were also on the agenda: in the Lords the bill on fraudulent conveyances was one of three being handled at the same time.[35] Doc.1 (not used by Neale) is a speech on the bill concerned with fines and recoveries in Wales, though we cannot say for certain if, or when, it was delivered. Perhaps it was part of the committee deliberations of 19 December, though it was still being handled by the Commons on 8 March 1585.[36] The author was probably a lawyer – there are specialist legal citations – but there are important observations on the need for a careful, considered and consistent approach to making law. In this particular case it was also argued that part of the bill which eventually became an act was unnecessary as it had been adequately covered in 1581. Further it was said that this aspect had been 'conynglie intruded to serve some especiall mane' to others' hurt, and that it ought, therefore, to be excised. Four other documents here (Docs 2, 3, 9 and 10) are all in the same hand which wrote the anonymous journal, and Neale assumed that the speech on fraudulent conveyances and the stationers' bill were the journalist's own draft speeches prepared for debate: he did not use the other manuscripts.[37] In a variety of ways these four documents throw light on the care and attention devoted to considering bills before the House and also to some of the guiding principles, or even prejudices, which shaped the process of legal review. Doc.2 bears no title, though its references to conveyances and Star Chamber must link it with the debate on the fraudulent conveyances bill. Much of it, however, is devoted to the importance of members speaking audibly in debate so that matters before the House could be considered properly, and consented to 'apon knowleg and

31. Fos.22v–23.
32. Strype, *Whitgift* (1822), i.360–1; iii.124–30. The MS used by Strype now appears to be part of the Fairhurst papers in Lambeth Palace Library (MS 2002, fos.53–7: another version at fos.72–8v varies slightly, principally by running together responses to petition numbers 7, 8, 9, 10 and 11, as does Fitzwilliam's account).
33. Fitzwilliam, f.22v.
34. *EP*, ii.73–5, 77.
35. D'Ewes, pp.314, 333.
36. D'Ewes, p.364.
37. *EP*, ii.85–6.

conscience'. In a matter of great weight such as this, there were many dangers to avoid; and one of them was giving too much scope to the informer, 'who will find a hole in a man's cote and not leave him till he pull his cote over his ears'.[38]

Doc.3 was probably drafted for the debate on the stationers bill on 10 February, though it seems to be a series of three working drafts rather than a finished product. The author speaks of the benefits which all would derive from controlling the availability of slanderous books. His belief in the social and political potency of books was obvious, and he wanted to avoid the corruption which he said was threatened by 'leud and wanton discourses of love'. People should be encouraged to read good books rather than 'sitt idell in ther howses apon rayny dayes'. Perhaps his purpose, most clearly revealed in the third attempt to draft the speech, was to remove the suspicion that the bill was simply a means of enforcing the Queen's grant of extensive powers to the stationers. The speech on the bill for the government of Westminster (Doc.9) may have been drafted for the debate on 8 March, though the Commons had first read the bill on 11 December, and it had been the subject of inter-House discussion on 3 March.[39] The difficulty here was to devise a means of enforcing a law on some, but not on others; how best, in other words, to target the weight of the law so as not to pervert its intention. Westminster had become, the author said, a 'harborag and host[el]ry of the basest and baddest sort of persons', including what he described as 'idle housewyves'. These were to be punished, but not the poor who lived honestly by lawful trade, though justices of the peace were too stretched already. The best means would be to appoint a number of officers with specific responsibilities. This is a repetitive speech as it stands, and it may be an early draft.

An endorsement on the fourth MS (Doc.10) describes it as a speech on the bill against starch-making: this probably indicates that it was connected with discussion of the bill against abuse of corn and grain which the House agreed to engross on 13 March. Again, we seem to have an evolving speech here, for there are two drafts.[40] The main concern was 'superfluous, wastfull, and unweldy ruffes' which demanded excessive use of starch when corn was not in abundance. It was underpinned by the argument, more fully developed in the second version, that man was merely a steward of the earth and its resources, and the view that exporters and ingrossers of corn acted selfishly, rather than with social responsibility.

The closing speeches for this parliament appear to have caused some concern to Burghley and Puckering, and examination of their drafts of speeches for the Speaker's address to the Queen on 29 March suggest that this was especially true of references to religion. Lords 2 is Burghley's version: the MS is not dated or given a title, but comparison with Lords 3 and Fitzwilliam's report[41] leaves no doubt that it belongs to this parliament. Puckering seems to have based his speech largely on his own draft rather than Burghley's, so the *precise* function of Burghley's draft is not clear.[42] Burghley followed a conventional, self-deprecatory opening with a statement that the Commons had done as commanded in considering the advancement of God's cause and Elizabeth's safety, but had not wished to offend the Queen's commandment on religion. The importance of remedying abuses in the Church was nevertheless under-lined, and the changes to the MS at this point strengthen the request that reform be undertaken. The speech concluded with the request that Elizabeth assent to the bills agreed by the two Houses, including the bill for the Queen's safety, an amendment at this point removing a possibly implied reference to Mary of Scotland. Many of these elements appear in Puckering's own version (Lords 3), though the Speaker did not emphasize Elizabeth's own supreme powers of Church governorship in the way Burghley had done. At the same time he did not include the idea that she might have to press on to remove abuses in the Church, unlike Burghley and Fitzwilliam's report of what Puckering actually said on the day. According to Fitzwilliam, Puckering also mentioned explicitly the disappointment members felt, both over the petitions on the Church and the eventual scope of the safety bill (also alluded to in Burghley's draft). But Puckering's draft has a substantial section on the Sabbath bill and the support it had attracted from both Houses, from men who had thought it 'theire partes' to ground the laws of men on God's commandments.

Neale was right to draw attention to the typically 'Elizabethan' style of John Stow's account of the Queen's speech on this occasion (Lords 4). She spoke after the Lord Chancellor's speech reproving the excesses of 'some particular persons' during the session: the Church was perfect, he said, so further action by the Commons was redundant. Elizabeth seems to have expressed her usual gratitude to her subjects for their love for her, but she too pointed to those who found fault with the state of the Church: the clergy would rectify this situation, under threat of losing their jobs. One of the Queen's chief concerns at this point appears to have been the need to avoid 'open exclamations' about the state of the Church, and she purported to offer comfort to her audience by pointing out that God had a better place for them in heaven. There was also a promise that she would, with 'God's holy trew rule' deal with both Romanists and 'new-fanglenesse': perhaps reflecting some of Whitgift's pro-fessed concern about the political order, she was also at this point explicitly linking Catholics and radical Protestants as 'dangerows to a kyngely rule'. If this speech was balm to the sting of Bromley's speech, as Neale suggested, it was not reported thus by Fitzwilliam. The Queen, he says, 'used some speache hir selfe, much tendinge to the foresayde poyntes'.[43]

38. See *EP*, ii.84–8 for this bill.
39. Cromwell, 11 December; D'Ewes, pp.348, 361, 362, 364.
40. D'Ewes, p.366.
41. Fos.36–7v.
42. See *EP*, ii.95–6.
43. F.39v.

1. [House of Lords] Herald's account of opening proceedings, 23 November 1584

Text from BL Add. 5758, original
(The account in Thomas Milles, *Catalogue of Honour* (1610),
pp.64–8 (referred to by D'Ewes) is a full account of the
procession and proceedings, except that no text of the sermon or
speeches is given. See also 'Von Wedel's Journey through
England', *Transactions of the Royal Historical Society* (1895), pp.259–
62: an account of opening proceedings, though without speeches.)

Add. 5758, fos.75–7.

The procedinge of the Quene's Majestie from White Hall to the churche of
St Peter in Westminster at the begininge of the parliament on Mondye the 23
of November 1584.[1]

f.76v.   The canopie borne by vj: Sir William Fitzwilliam, Sir Edward Hastinges, Sir
Thomas Layton, Sir Thomas Myldmay, Sir John Peter[2]

This canapy was so borne[3] by these knightes over the Quene only after she had
kneled downe without the north dore of the churche, and she received of the
Deane the long cepter with the dove after she had redd certayne prayers in a
book kneling and so arose with the cepter delivered into her handes and was
conveyed under the canapy and the Quene's chappell singing in copes, and so
went towardes the west dore and passed certyene 4 pyllers and then turned to
the quier and so to the upper quier, and there her Majeste departed from her
canapy to her travers. And the lordes toke places prepared of long duble
benches lyke as is in the parliament howse, the lords on the southe syd and
the bushopes and some lords on the north syde, with[4] where above the
f.77   archebishops / was the pulpit and above the pulpit the canapy was sett ageynste
the wall.

After the sermon taken owte of the xth of Proverbes[5], *Qui fodit foveam in
epsum*[6] *cadit, qui dissipat sepem mordebit eum serpens*, of which the Archbushope of
Canterbury made a breefe speche tending to the respect for good lawes, for the
lawes of the wycked tend to overthrowe the just but God revelethe theyr
secrettes and [they] are together swept awaye lyke the spider in his cobwebe;
and of *qui dissipat sepum mordebit eum serpens*, comparing lawes to the hedges
which broken the possession lyethe wasted, saying owt of the Greek
Demostenes, '*Lex est anima civitatis*', alleaging *quod non est regnum ubi leges non*

observantur, and the three causes of troubles in kingedoms: many orators, no execution of lawes, and contempt, *quod est inditium[7] ruinae proximum.*

Wchiche[8] sermon ended then the lordes arose and proceded on in order. Then the Queen cam forthe of her travers, and the gentlemen that stood by the canapye toke up the same and her Majeste cam under and went out at the southe dore where her Majeste delivered the cepter to the Deane, and the Bushope of Sarum was in a cope also and assisted the Deane as Deane of the Queen's Chappell now so appoynted. All the lords went on foote and the Queen also on foot under the same cannapie for uppon her comandement the other canapy was sett asyde, and so went to the stayres of the parliament all on foote, and the fote men claymed to have the canapie according to custom.

---

1. There follows an account of the correct order of proceeding to Parliament, starting with gentlemen, esquires and knights. The way the Queen was to enter and leave the Church is briefly described, as is her subsequent transit to the Lords. For part of this journey the practice was to carry a canopy over her.

2. *Sic.*
3. MS repeats 'was borne'.
4. *Sic.*
5. *Sic; recte* Eccl. 10:8.
6. *Sic.*
7. *Sic.* i.e. *indicium.*
8. *Sic.*

2. [House of Lords] speaker's speech at close of Parliament, drafted by Burghley, 29 March 1585

Text from BL Lansdowne 104, original amended draft, in Burghley's hand.
Other MSS Lansdowne 43 (some words missing or unclear at margins) *Printed.* Strype, *Annals*, 3.ii.356–61

Lansdowne 104, fos.150–4.

'Most excellent prynce, and graciouss Quene.

'The last tyme of my being in this place[1] befor your most excellent Majesty and this honorable assembly of your 3 estates, I did mak my most humble submission and request uppon your knolledg of my dishabilite and unworthynes, that I might have bene forborn to have occupyed this place; but such was your Majestie's graciouss opinion as it semed conceaved of me uppon the election of your faythfull and obedient subiectes representyng the whole 'comminalte of your realme, that I was therto directed, and as than I, best knowyng myn own insufficiencyes, did for my excuse desyre your Majestie's graciouss acceptation of that which was only in my power, which was of my good will, dilligence and indevor to be bestowed / in this service. So now if I shuld not acknolledg in this place, havyng here in my company so many wytnesses ageynst me, the multitude of imperfections that I have found in my self duryng the tyme of this my service, I shuld shew my self to be over-partiall in myn own case, and in some sort to be voyde of modesty; but knowyng your Majestie's accustomed goodnes, to accept the good wills and endevors of all men in your services, without any strayt regard or accompt of the eventes or successes of ther actions, and therwith havyng also had all this tyme of this session of Parlement dayly proves of the favorable tolleration of my lackes by the grave, wise and experiensed persons and the good will generally of the whole body of your commens towardes me, in ther quiet allowance of my service, I am the bolder, throwyng behynd my back these my lackes and wantes as thynges not now to be imputed to / me, and am to present my selff in your Majestie's sight accordyng to myn office, as a person allowed by your Majestie's goodnes only, and not by my desert, and so to procede to present to your Majesty in the names of all your commens, first our most humbly[2] thankes for the benefittes that we have receaved by your Majestie's permission to have this assembly so long contynewed, secondly our lyk humble requestes of

v.

f.151

pardon for any thynges which thrugh ignorance without any intention of offence[3] in our consultations might be by your Majestie's gret wisdom imputed to us, and lastly I am also in ther names to exhibit our most humble and ernest petitions to your Majesty to gyve liff to / the workes not of our handes but of our myndes cogitations and hartes, which otherwise than being lightened with the beames of your favor shall be but vayne, domm[4] and dead.

    'For the first I do confes, and that do I in the name of all your commens here assembled, and so I may presume to add the lyk for the lordes here assembled in your Majestie's presence, that we can not imagyn how your Majesty can bestow a gretar benefitt that can deserve more thankes of your subiectes universally, than that your Majesty as yow have hertofor at many tymes so now specially in this tyme whan our necessite for many respectes required the same, summoned your whole realme by callyng your estates to gether to this parlement, to consult frely and at gret lesure, what war first mete for the furtherance and avancement of Gode's service by which we only have our being; and what war also necessary for the preservation of your Majestie's person, by whose long liff / and contynuance we ar kept fre from all tyranny and subiection of forrayn oppression; and lastly to devise amongst our selves and provide, not only what shuld[5] be both in generall and particular good and proffitable for our own [?] estates but also to seke how to avoyd thynges hurtfull to the same. Which good endes we do acknolledg that by your Majestie's goodnes and permission our assembly hath now tended, and for the good that we ar to receave therby we do yeld to your Majesty our most humble thankes, besechyng God to graunt your Majesty many happy yeres above the term of our lyves, that as we have allredy so after us our posterite may receave the lyk benefittes of your goodness, from tyme to tyme as cause shall require, to procure to them selves by good lawes under your government lyk meanes to lyve in such peace, happynes and welth, as we have done from the begynning of your reign and as our forfathers never did the lyk with such contynuance. Secondly, after these our thankes most humbly presented uppon our knes, we do both in generall and particular humbly beseche your Majesty to gyve your accustomed gratiouss interpretation to all our procedynges, wherin if any speches, motions or petitions / have passed from us that might have miscontented your Majesty in your gret wisdom above our capacites I can assure your Majesty that in this assembly wherin I was allweiss present, ther was never found in any speche privat or publyck, any argument or token of the mynd of any person that shewed any intention to be offensyve to your Majesty. And for prooffe hereof whan it pleased your Majesty to direct me to declare your plesure[6] to the commen houss, in what sort yow wold they shuld stey any

v.

f.152

v.

---

1. These words are deleted here: 'wherunto which now I have occupied by your Majestie's direction'.
2. *Sic* (not Lansd.43).
3. These words are added: 'without . . . offence'.
4. Lansd.43: 'donne'.
5. Lansd.43 omits.
6. These words are deleted: 'though unworthy to utter your princely speches'.

furder procedyng in debatyng of the manner of reformation of such thynges as they thought might be reformed in the Chirch, I found them all generally and particularly redy to obey your Majestie's plesur therin, which as it semed to me and so I have cause to perswade with my self they did for that it was well understood that your Majesty, as having by Gode's ordonnance a supreme authority for that purpouss, had straytly charged the archbishops, bishops and your whole clergy now assembled in ther convocation to have due regard to see to the reformation of dyvers abuses in the government and disciplyn of the chirch. And so our firm[7] hope is that your Majesty will by your streyt comandment to your clergy[8] contynew your care to se and command that[9] such abuses as ar crept in to the Chirch by the neglygence of the ministers may be spedely reformed to the honor of almighty God, and to your owne immortall prayse, and comfort of your subiectes.[10] /

f.153   'The next matter wherof I have to spek is, most humbly to offer to your Majesty our most humble request, wherin I must ioyne to us your commens, the state of the lords here of this highar houss of Parlement, that is, that it may please your Majesty to yeld your royall assent to such petitions both generall and particular, as have bene uppon long deliberations determyned and conceaved in wrytynges with on uniform consent of the lordes spyrituall and temporall and us your commens of this your parlement assembled, wherin your Majesty shall do no less than perteyneth to the authorite which yow have lyk to God almighty, who as he gyveth lyff and being to all his creatures gret and small, so your Majesty shall gyve lyff and contynuance to the fructes of our consultations, as well to the small as to the great, without which your royall assent by your own breath, the same shall become without liff and sence, and all our labors therin lost and our expectations made frustrat. And though in your Majestie's princely sight many of these our petitions may seme to be of meane vallew ether becausse they ar some of them particular, or because the matters of some of them may seme to be of low or bass degre, yet consideryng, to them for whom they belong, the same ar of as gret importance and benefitt

v.   as to gretar estates, gret matters ar, / and the lack of the benefittes which to them may grow therby shall be as grevouss as the lack of gretar in gretar bodyes, and that in every naturall body the meanest partes and membres ar by the head regarded as beneficiall for on meanes or other to the rest of the whole body, so we with all humblenes in the name of the whole body besech your Majesty as our only head and fountayne of our lyff to accept the meanest petitions for the comfort of the partes of the body to whom the same may belong, as we know your Majesty of your clemency is accustomed with your most graciouss eies and countenance to comfort dayly your basest[11] poure subiectes sekyng releff at your fete.

'Next to this we do offer to your Majesty with our whole hartes our bodyes and lyves to be servisable to the savety of your Majestie's most noble person, for defence wherof and for revendg of any act or imagin[ation] ageynst your Majesty,[12] we have by a form of law, if it shall lyk your Majesty to assent therto, gyven a testymony to the whole world how deare the savetie of your liff is to us. And this I do assure your Majesty, that we your most lovyng subiectes, war most willyng to have extended this ordonnance to a furder streytar courss as we thought the same mete for your savety and for terrefyeng of all persons not well willyng to you, if otherwise we had not understand, that your Majestie's plesure was that it shuld not be extended to any straytor poyntes than it is. /

'And as your Majesty hath a manifest demonstration herby of our hartes and myndes, so also we have added for a furder outward declaration therof by our dedes, offred to your Majesty of our voluntary myndes a small portion out of those wor[l]dly goodes which God hath gyven us, and by the long peace under your blessed government we have increased, by way of a subsydy and of twoo fiftens to be used by your Majesty, as in former tymes yow have allweiss doun, for the defence of this your realme and us your humble subiectes, which though we know it shall not amont to that vallew that percase shall be nedefull for defence of your realmes, dominions and subiectes ageynst all attemptes that may be ministred by the ennemyes of God and of your Majesty, yet your Majesty may mak an assured accompt that besydes this our offer, yow can not lack a furder supply of the rest that we have to be spent or committed to your direction as cause shall require.

f.154

'Lastly uppon our knees we do most humbly yeld our harty thankes for your most gratiouss and fre generall pardon wherby a gret multitud of your subiectes ar to be releved of / dyvers paynes and penalties which by the order of your lawes your Majesty might most justly have inflicted uppon them, by which your clemency we all shall tak occasion, beside our thankfullnes for so great a benefitt, to endevor our selves more carefully to observe your lawes, both to the honor of God, and to the comfort of your Majesty, and finally to the mayntenance of peace, tranquillite and concord amongst our selves.'

The pardon.

v.

---

7. Added.
8. These words are added: 'by your . . . clergy'.
9. These words are added: 'and command that'.
10. The words 'spedely reformed' and 'own immortal' are added to the sentence

which originally ran: '. . . may be to . . . your subiectes reformed.'
11. Lansd.43 has 'and poorest' rather than 'poure'.
12. These words are deleted: 'wherof ageynst all the persons of what estate so ever the same shall be, and to revendg all'.

3. [House of Lords] Speaker's speech at close of parliament, 29 March 1585

Text from BL Lansdowne 115, copy in the hand of a secretary, endorsed by Burghley.
Printed. Strype, *Annals*, 3.i.427–32 (in part, and in reported speech; from Lansdowne).

Lansdowne 115, fos.33v–46

[Endorsed by Burghley: '1585. The oration of Serieant Pukeryng, Spekar of the Commen Howss in the end of the session of Parlement . . .']¹

f.33v. 'If I did find in my self (most graciouse and redoubted Sovereigne) a concourse of all those partes which be requisite to accomplishe a man to speake, not onely in the behalf of those (a great manie grave and discreete persons for whome I was chosen as theire mouth unworthy) but also in the presence and before the majestie of your self, a most wise, lerned and mightie prince (as the Lord knoweth, and I to myne owne sorrowe doe feele, howe emptie I am even of any meane furniture towardes so weightie a service), yet shold I of necessitie be compelled to confesse that all those powers whatsoever weare too weake and insufficient, either to expresse the singuler goodnes of your Majestie towardes us, in callinge and hitherto contynuynge this present assemblie of Parliament, or to sett forth the incomparable joye and due thankfullnes that wee all and everie one doe conceave and acknowledge for the doeing of the same; ffor as
f.34 the kingly care and most watchfull love of your Majestie to / procure the common good of us all, hath in this part appeared, not inferior to the affection in likelood of a most tender and kind mother towardes her naturall children, even so proporcionablie on our partes the ioye and comfort that we receave thereof is infinitly greate, and the debt of thankfullnes that we doe owe to your Majestie therefore is utterly unspeakeable. And therefore since I cannot render to your Majestie those thankes which in office I ought, I most humblie beseech your Highnes to vouchsafe (by my mouth onely) [to accept] the most willinge and readie humble and hartie thankes of a multitude representinge the whole state of the commons of your realme offered unto youe in the greatest measure
v. of theire most loyall and bounden duties, that your / Highnes may be best pleased to comprehend in that most rare and singuler wisdome wherewith the Lord hath bewtified and blessed youe.

'First, for that it hath liked your Majestie with greate care of mynde, to take
so good and seasonable opportunitie for the summonynge of this assemblie,
whereby we have gained the comoditie to deliberate of matters tendinge noe
lesse to the glorie of God, and preservacion of your Majestie, then to the
common utilitie and welfare of oure selves and all our fellowe subiectes.

'Secondly, for that it hath pleased your Majestie to cheere us therein with
the presence of your most royall and gladsome person, then the which
nothinge (under God) can be more comfortable unto us, and without the
which all our consultacion wold have ben heavie and displeasaunt.

'Thirdlie, for your Majestie's most graciouse, free, and generall pardon
whereby both wee doe feele our selves delivered of sondrie paines, that your
Highnes might have justlie inflicted uppon us, and are also most graciouslie
incited (by this your Majestie's / clemencie) to a more dilligent and carefull   f.36
observacion of your Highnes' lawes then heretofore wee have accustomed.[2]
Howbeit suffer me I beseech your Majestie to crave some enlargment in this
behalf aswell for my self perticulerlie, as also generally for all the whole
companie of your commons that kneele before your Highnes. For my self I saie
who, besides a readie obedience, faithfull mynd, and willinge endevoure have
performed nothinge that belonged to my place and have therefore great neede
of your Majestie's furder pardon, which also I most humblie crave and desire,
and hope your Majestie will the rather graunt me, because (the conscience of
myne owne wea . . .)[3] I both foresaw and foretold my wantes, and was neverthelesse chardged with . . .[4] service by your Highnes. To this whole companie
I beseech your Majestie also to / pardon and remitt whatsoever hath duringe   v.
this cession of Parliament fallen out to your Majestie's discontentment,
assuringe your Highnes in the obligacion of that faith and alleageaunce which
I doe beare unto your Highnes that howsoever some thinge have escaped by
humane infirmitie, I have seene nothinge either willfully or contemptuouslie
comitted, to anie purpose of offence to your Majestie. Yea, rather, the truth
draweth me to report that they have with all zealous and dutifull myndes
towardes your Majestie, and with great moderacion and wisdome, dilligence
and paines takinge spent the whole cession in devisinge lawes, which (if it shall
like your Majestie to ratifie them) will (as I suppose) greatlie availe towardes
the honor and glorie of God, the safetie of your Majestie's most royall person
and estate, and the publique comoditie and benefitt of your Highnes' people
and contrie: the cheife and onelie markes whereat all good and Christian lawes
ought to ayme and levell. /

'In which part also I am most humblie to recomend unto your princely   f.38
consideracion and iudgment thease whereuppon your Majestie's nobles and
comons have after greate and mature deliberacion condiscended. First, an act
for the more reverent and better observacion of the Sabaoth day. Secondlie an
act devised for the safetie of your Majestie's most royall person, and the

1. There is an illegible word (date?) here.
2. *Sic.*
3. MS mutilated.
4. MS mutilated.

preservacion of the realme in peace. Also an act to ridd and keepe out of your Majestie's domynions all Jesuytes, semynarie priestes . . .[5] beinge utter enemies to the realme, seducers of soules from the trewe faith . . .[6] dewe obedience, and divers other actes which to avoid tediousnes I will forbeare . . . laritie[7] leavinge the same to be redd unto your Highnes. /

v.   'First, beinge persuaded that all good lawes of men ought to be grounded uppon the eternall lawe of God expressed in the second table of his tenne comaundementes, and callinge to theire remembraunce what godlie and Christian lawes youre Majestie hath alreadie published in former parliamentes, both for the worshippinge of the onelie true God, and the worshipping of him aright as himself hath prescribed, and also for the abolishinge and punishment of all devilish coniuracion, popishe idolatrie, and supersticion, fantasticall prophesieinge, and falsehood in forswearinge (offences against the first, second and third comaundment of the first table), theie have thought it theire partes to goe forwardes, and (by providing for the rest, and right use of the Sabaoth daie) to provoke your Majestie to give lawe, concerninge the iiij[th] and last comaundment of the same table also.

'Secondly, theise your Highnes' nobles and commons, knowinge (that next after the service of God him self) the honor of parentes is comaunded by the

f.40   first precept of his lawe (being both the first and / formost of the second table, as having a promise annexed to the same), and consideringe on the one syde that all the blesse[8], ioye and securitie of this most happie estate of the realme is layd upp and reposed (next under God) in the life and safetie of your Majestie's royall and most preciouse person (which God graunt us yet manie moe yeres to enioye), and beholdinge on the other syde the maliciouse plottes pr . . .[9] abroad and at home, both by the professed ennemyes of her Majestie and the . . .[10] ambicious frendes and favourers of some that pretend title to youre Majestie's most [undoubted title][11] of the crowne, they have thought yt the bounden duties of them all ([being the subjects of][12] your Majestie, theire naturall prince and common parent) to honor your royall [person and consulting the best][13] and most provident meane of preservacion that theire wittes cold

v.   devise / and have therefore laid downe a most prudent and pollitique forme of lawe which they entitle "An act for the saftie of the Quene (your Majestie's) most royall person and contynuaunce of the realme in peace", by the which they doe indevoure to cut of all hardinesse of anie wicked attempt against your Majestie by, or for, anie pretended successor, showinge thereby theire most bounden and loyall dutie and affection towardes your Majestie.

'Thirdly, your Majestie's nobles and comons here, perceavinge well that all the evilles entended against the religion of God, the royall person of your Majestie, and the welfare of your Highnes' realmes and domynions, are ment to be prepared, and sett on foote, by a certeine sect of Romishe prelates (calling themselves Jesuites and semynarie men), have thought it therefore most expedient to offer unto your Majestie some meane of a lawe for the banishment of theise seedmen of sedicion furth of your Highnes' domynions, entitled "An act

f.42   against Jesuites, semynarie preestes and other such like disobedient / persons",

besides divers other formes of lawes for the pollitique benefitt *etc*, which to
avoid tediousnes I forbeare to recite, leavinge the same to be red to your
Highnes.

'But for . . .[14] are but deade elementes, except some influence from the
heade (which hath the . . .)[15] be derived into them; and because also, that life
cannot long last . . .[16] contynually fedd and maintayned with fitt nowrishment
for the same: wee most . . .[17] Majestie (our sole and supreame head under God)
first that by the breath of your Majestie's royall . . .[18] life of lawe may be
inspired into them, and furthermore that it [might please][19] your Majestie to
geve in chardge to your judges and iusticers, that the same may be / dilligentlie   v.
put in execution, the onely nutryment of all lawes, and without the which they
must starve at the last, what life of authoritie so ever be at the first bestowed
upon them.

'And nowe that your Majestie may also receave some signification of our
gratefull hartes towardes your Highnes, as we have inumerable markes of your
most lovinge and carefull goverment over us: I am lastlie with all humylitie to
present your Majestie with this gift of a subsidie and twoe fifteenes and tenthes
most willinglie graunted, and as redilie agreed uppon, by all your Highnes'
nobles and commons in this present parliament, who seeing not onelie the
vyperous natures of some unnaturall subiectes, that strive to make ther waye
through a[20] verie bellie of the realme theire owne contrie and mother, but also
the envious disposicions of some forreine popishe potentates that awaite all
advauntages to undermyne your most godlie, happie and blessed estate, have
thought it most expedient and necessarie that your Majestie have before hand
some masse of treasure in a readines against all necessities and / eventes. To the   f.44
end that (by the favourable protection of God) your Highnes may the rather
thereby both prevent the mischeife of the one sort, and countermyne the
malice of the other. And this wee offer unto your Majestie not as anie
sufficiencie to serve for so weightie and chardgeable tornes; [but as an earnest][21]
penny and pledge of all the rest that remaines with our selves, which also
(together [with our faithful service of][22] bodie and mynd even to the endes of

5. MS mutilated.

6. MS mutilated.

7. MS mutilated.

8. *Sic.*

9. MS mutilated.

10. MS mutilated.

11. MS mutilated. Strype has these words.

12. MS mutilated. These words are from
Strype's reading, though 'the subjects'
are supplied by him (in square brackets)
in his printed version.

13. MS mutilated. These words are from
Strype's reading, though 'and consulting'
are supplied by him (in square brackets)
in his printed version.

14. MS mutilated.

15. MS mutilated.

16. MS mutilated.

17. MS mutilated.

18. MS mutilated.

19. MS mutilated: supplied from Strype.

20. *Sic.*

21. MS mutilated. These words are from
Strype's reading, though 'as an earnest'
are supplied by him (in square brackets)
in his printed version.

22. MS mutilated. These words are from
Strype's reading, though 'with our
faithful service' are supplied in square
brackets in his printed version.

our lives) we devote and dedicat [to your Highness: throughly sensible,][23] by a longe and an assured experience of your Majestie's most frugall [and thrifty disposition and care][24] for oure selves, and laid up in a most sure and safe treasury for our best [advantage. May the King of][25] kinges and God of glorie that so brightlie shineth and sheweth himself . . .[26] government as well by the

v.   presence of his holly word, as by / the full fruicion of all earthlie blessinges; assist your Majestie's counsels, contynue his favourable spyrite with youe, establish your royall seate and estate, preserve youe from all your ennemyes, reveale and frustrate all theire wicked practises and devices, and graunt youe long to live and reigne over us and ours here, and take youe late (but at length) from us furth of this mortall kingdome unto himself into his heavenlie kingdome, there to reigne with him in glorie for ever. Amen.'

23. MS mutilated. These words are from Strype's reading, though 'throughly sensible' are supplied in square brackets in his printed version.
24. MS mutilated. These words are from Strype's reading.
25. MS mutilated. These words are from Strype's reading.
26. MS mutilated.

4. [House of Lords] Queen's speech at Close of Parliament, 29 March 1585

Text from BL Harley 540, copy in the hand of John Stow.
Other MSS. London: BL Harley 4888, Harley 1877, Add. 15891, Add. 38823. Oxford: Bodley, Tanner 79 (not headed). Cambridge: University Library Ee.v.23. Scotland: Scottish Record Office, Warrender Papers, vol.B.
Printed. Stow, *Annales* (1631) 702–3; D'Ewes 328–9 (from copy in Stow's hand); Holinshed iv.588–9; Scottish History Society (1931) 174–6 (from the Warrender Papers).

Harley 540, f.115.

The Qwene's Maiestie's oration, made in the Parliament Howse, at the breakyng up there of, the xxix day of Marche, in *anno Domini* 1585.

'My lords, and ye[1] of the Lower Howse, my scillence must not iniurie[2] the owner[3] so mocche as to suppose a substitute sufficient to rendar yow the thanks that my harte yeldethe yow: not so moche for the safe kepinge of my lyfe, for which yowr care apperes so manifest, as for the neglectinge yowre private future perill not regardyng otherway[4] then my present state.

'No prince herein I confesse can be surar tyed or fastar bound then I am with the lynke of yowre good will, and can for that but yelde a hart and heade to seeke for evar all yowr best. Yet one mattar towchethe[5] me so nere, as I may not ovarskype:[6] religion, the grownd[7] on which all othar mattars[8] owght to take roote, and beinge corrupted maye mare all the tree.[9] And that there be some faulte findars with the ordar of the clergye, which so maye make a slaundar to my selfe and the Churche, whose ovar rular God hath made me, whose negligance can not be excused yf any scismes or errours hereticall were suffered.[10] Thus much I must say, that some faultes and neglygences may grow and bee, as in all othar great charges it[11] happenethe,

1. Harl. 4888: 'yow that be'.
2. Cam: 'iniure' (+ Harl. 1877, Warrender)
3. Harl. 1877: 'your honnours' (+ Cam), Add. 38823: 'your honnor' rather than 'the owner'.
4. Harl. 1877: 'other thing'; Cam: 'of any other thing'.
5. Harl. 1877: 'touchinge'.
6. Harl. 1877: 'overslipp' (+ Add. 15891, Cam, Warrender); Add. 38823: 'overslipp

yt' (+ Tanner) rather than 'ovarskype'.
7. Add. 38823 omits 'the grownd'.
8. Harl. 4888: 'actions' (+ Add. 15891, Tanner, Warrender) rather than 'othar mattars'.
9. Add. 15891 repeats this sentence in the margin.
10. Tanner omits.
11. Cam: 'as'.

and what vocation[12] without? All which yf[13] yow my lords of the clergye do not amend, I meane to depose yow. Loke ye therefore well to yowr charges: this may be amended without heedlesse or open exclamations. I am supposed to have many stoodies, but most philosophicall. I must yelde this to be trwe: that I suppose fewe[14] (that be no professors) have reade more. And I nede not tell yow that I am so symple[15] that I undarstond not, nor so forgetfull that I remembar not. And yet amydst my many volumes I hope God's booke hath not bene my seldomest lectures, in which we finde that which by reason[16] (for my parte) we owght to beleve: that seinge so greate wickednes and greves in the worlde, in which we lyve but as wayefaringe pilgrymes, we must suppose that God wold nevar have made us but for a bettar place and of more comforte then we find here. I know no creature that breathethe whose lyfe standeth howerly in more perill[17] for it then myne owne; who entered not into my state without syght of manyfold daungers of lyfe, and crowne, as one that had the mightiest and greatest to wrestle with. Then it folowith that I regarded it so much as I lefte my selfe behynd my care. And so yow se that yow wronge me to much (yf eny suche there be) as dowbt my coldnes in that behalfe. For yf I were not[18] perswaded that myne were[19] the trewe way of God's will, God forbyd I shuld lyve to prescribe[20] it to yow. Take yow hede lest Ecclesiastes say not to trwe, they that feare the horye frost, the snowe shall fall upon them.[21] I see many ovarbold with God almightye, makynge to[22] many subtill[23] skannyngs of his blessed will, as lawyers do with humayne testaments. The presumption is so greate as I may not suffar it. Yet mynd I not hereby to animate Romanists, (which what advarseryes they be to myne estate is suffi- ciently knowne) nor tollerate new-fanglenesse.[24] I meane to guyde them both by God's holy trew rule. In both parts[25] be perrylls and of the latar[26] I must pronounce them daungerows to a kyngely rule, to have every man accordinge to his owne sensure to make a doome[27] of the[28] validitie and privitie[29] of his princis governement, with a comon vaile and cover of God's worde, whose folowers[30] must not be iudged but[31] by pryvate men's exposition. God defend yow from suche a rular that so evill[32] will gwyde yow.

'Now I conclude that yowr love and care neythar is nor shall be bestowed uppon a carelesse prince; but suche[33] as but for yowr good will[34] passeth as[35] litle for this worlde, as who carethe leaste: with thanks for yowr fre subsidye,[36] a manyfest show of the aboundance of yowr good wills. The which I assure yow: but to be imployd to yowr weale[37] I cold be bettar pleased to / returne then receyve.'[38]

v.

12. Harl. 4888: 'of what' rather than 'what vocation'.
13. Cam omits.
14. Harl. 1877: 'many' (+ Cam).
15. Harl. 4888 adds 'not' (+ Tanner); Warrender; 'I am no am not so simple'.
16. Add. 38823 omits 'by reason'; Cam has 'finde in this worlde' rather than 'finde that ... in the worlde'; Harl. 4888 has 'of ryght' that than 'which by reason (for my part)'.
17. Harl. 1877 omits 'in more perill'.
18. Harl. 1877 omits (+ Cam).
19. Cam adds 'not'.
20. Harl. 1877: 'subscribe' (+ Cam).
21. The saying is not apparently Biblical in this form. Add. 15891 repeats the saying in the margin.
22. Harl. 1877 omits.
23. Add. 38823 omits.
24. Harl. 1877: 'new fanglers' (+ Add. 15891, Add. 38823); Tanner: 'newe fangles' (+ Cam).

25. Harl. 4888: 'sortes' (+ Add. 15891, Add. 38823, Tanner, Warrender).
26. Warrender: 'in the laste' rather than 'and of the latar', Harl. 1877: 'laste'.
27. Harl. 1877: 'doubt' (+ Cam).
28. Tanner: 'his owne'.
29. Harl. 4888: 'pietie' (+ Add. 15891, 38823, Tanner, Warrender).
30. Add. 38823: 'flowers'; Add. 15891 has a marginal sentence repeating the sense of 'In both parts ... God's word'.
31. Harl. 1877 omits (+ Harl. 4888, Cam).
32. Harl. 4888 omits.
33. Add. 38823; 'but uppon such a one' rather than 'but suche'.
34. Harl. 4888 omits (+ Add. 15891, Add. 38823).
35. Cam: 'all'; Tanner has 'good and passeth' rather than 'good will passeth'.
36. Harl. 1877: 'and' (+ Cam).
37. Harl. 1877: 'wealthes' (+ Cam).
38. Add. 38823: 'retourne to you then receive from you'.

1. [House of Commons] Speech on bill for reformation of Errors in fines and recoveries in Wales, 19 December(?) 1584

Text from PRO SP Dom.Eliz.176/73, ? fair copy of original.

SP Dom.Eliz.176/73.

[Endorsed in another hand 'Consideration uppon the bill for Wales'.]

'This bill I doe well commende as a necessary lawe for Wales.[1] But as in that respecte I doe well like of it so doe I greatlie doubte that I may as much dislike one especiall braunch theirin inserted, which eyther I take it to be needelesse by reason that the same was sufficientlye provided for by the statute of $23°$ of the Quene's Majestie[2] and by the common lawes before that also, or els gracelesse as karyinge theirin some secret meaninge or rather myscheif to help some private or particuler case to the great displeasure of some other.

'The bodie of the acte is in generall pretence sett forthe for Wales, and theirof I make allowaunce as a thinge not before provided for. But the especiall matter whereof I doe compleyne to be nedlesse or perilous is this.

'It is amonge other thinges desired to be enacted, that the exemplificacion under the great seale of Englond made or to be made accordinge to the teanor and effecte of the said statute made in the said 23 yere of her Majestie's reigne of eny recovery or fyne levied, had or passed in the courte of Common Pleas shalbe of as good force and validitie in the lawe to all intentes, respectes, and purposes so exemplified as the verie originall recorde it self beinge extante and remayninge were or ought by lawe to be.

'Nowe I wolde learne what neede there is of this braunch to enacte that an exemplificacion of a fyne or recovery levied or had in the Common Pleas under the broode seale of Englond shalbe good.

'This, as I said before, is needelesse, for the statute of $23°$ of the Quene's Majestie amonge other thinges provideth that recoveryes *etc.* extante and remayninge or that shalbe extant and in beinge maye upon the request of the partie be inrolled, and that the said inrollement shalbe of as good force and validitie in lawe to all intentes and purposes as the same beinge extant and remayninge were or oughte in lawe to be.[3]

'Is not this sufficient to provide that the inrollement of a fyne or recoverye shalbe of as good force as the originall recorde? Trewelie it is in forme, sense and substaunce all one with this braunch that is here inserted. For this braunch sayeth that the exemplificacion of a fyne or recovery shalbe as good as the originall record and even so sayeth the statute of *23°* of the inrollement therof. Then yf both these tende to one purpose as they be in deede, what need is there of it?

28 *Liber Assisarum*, p. 14

'Besides I tolde yowe it was sufficientlie provided for by the common lawe. It is truth, it is so. By the common lawe yf a fyne or recoverye or eny record or acte of Parliament beinge once exemplified under the broode seale of Englond, yf the same be sett downe in better forme of lawe then before the originall record was, yet agaynst this exemplificacion there is no averment to say that *nul tiell record etc.*, and so be the aucthoritie of our bookes as in 26 Henry 6 and 8 Henry 7.

26 Henry 6
8 Henry 7
16 Henry 7, 11
22 Henry 8
M. Brook
ti.record[4]

In the case of premunire upon the statute of *25°* Edward 3 where the archebuyshopes wolde not assent unto it, but made protestation agaynst it which was also entered in the parliament roll.[5] After upon a premunire brought, the defendant pleade *nul tiell acte*. And the Lord Chauncelor certified such an acte and so the defendant condempned, for that he colde have no averement agaynst it. And so this appeareth needelesse by the common lawe as a thinge alreadie provided for both by statute lawe and common lawe.

'Then must I thinke this braunch gracelesse for that it seameth to be conynglie intruded to serve some especiall mane and some especiall purpose whome it cane not pleasure but to some others' great hurte and that deserveth no favoure in this place. And theirfor yf eny such person have neede of this braunch let his case be especiallie opened here that such on th'other parte as are to be greived and towched thereby maye come in to defend their case so as thereby we may proceade to the makinge of a lawe accordinge to the equitie of their cases. And thus much towchinge this braunche which may be well in my opynion omytted.

'And nowe to retorne to the bodie of the byll, as I said before I doe commend of it as a needefull lawe for Walles. But yet ther is some thinge to be added to it and that is this. This byll is patronized by the said statute of *23°* of the Quene's Majestie and beinge so in pretence, it ought to be so in matter. But in this byll I doe not fynde that equalitie and proporcion of justice as is in the former acte of *23°*. For in the said former acte there is a generall proviso and a speciall proviso: the generall proviso is that none shalbe by that acte debarred

---

1. This bill was committed on 19 December: it emerged as a new bill on 18 February, apparently passing the House on 8 March, though Vernon's proviso was agreed on 9 March (D'Ewes, pp.343, 353, 354, 364, 365; Cf Cromwell's journal, f.89).
2. 23 Eliz, c.3 (1580–1) in *SR*, iv.661–3.
3. This follows word for word the first clause of the 1581 act.
4. This seems to refer to Brook's New Cases under the title 'Record' (*English Reports*, 73. 917).
5. 25 Ed.III, stat.4 was the statute of provisors; the praemunire act was 27 Ed.III, stat.1. For objections by the clergy, cf. *Rot. Parl*, ii.285 for the 1365 statute, and iii.264, 341 for 1390 and 1397.

yf he suythe his writt of error within five yeres, which five yeres be not yet expired; the especiall proviso for the Earle of Kente. And both these provisoes by this byll desired to be enacted are eyther in parte omytted or els verie fare[6] different from the provisoes in the former statute, which yf they be then is there not that good consideracion used that was in the former statute; besides yf there be eyther omition or difference yt taketh away the benifite that was geven to the subiectes in the former provisoes, for that the five yeres geven and lymited to bringe the writt of error in *23°* be not yet expired.[7]

'And howe unseemlye it is to make a lawe and to reverse it agayne in the next parliament in eny parte without great consideracion I leave it to your judgement.

'Theirfor to conclude, I thinke it necessarye that these provisoes be compared and reduced to the former provisoes and that the former braunch be omytted unlesse there may be some especiall good cause shewed to mayntayne the same.'

6. *Sic* (far).
7. The bill was passed (*SR*, iv.715–17) and contained no mention of Common Pleas, though the provisos cited here were included.

2. Speech on bill against fraudulent conveyances, 8 February(?) 1585

Text from BL Lansdowne 43, original amended draft in the same hand as the other 1584 speeches and journal in this volume.

Lansdowne 43, f.178v.

'I am bold to move yow for my self and those that sitt about me in the lower f.178v. part of the House that it would please yow to move such as mean to speak to any bill that they would speak as loud as reasonably they can and for so short tyme rather take some paynes and not respect ther owne ease and as it were to enforce them and strech their voyces, thought[1] it [be] to their payne, rather then that we should lose the profitt of their speach.

'I doubt not but they that speak to any bill[2] their meaning is to draw the hole Howse to their mynde, which they can hardly bring to passe except we heare them, for without hearing we can not understand them, nor without understanding can not give our consentes, but shalbe like those that hear service in a strange tonge, and say Amen to that they understand not, when they think they pray to our Lord they shall saye Amen to a prayer made to our Lady. For suerly if we give our consentes, we muste rather do it apon a strong faith then any certane knowlege.

'We se by experience that we are dryven many tymes to rise both to our disease and distorbance of those that sitt beneth us. We see also we ar constrayned many tymes, as seems against good manner and not without parent offenc, to crye "Speak out, speak out", wherunto as it hath bene sayd that we must bring our eares with us, so we[3] may better bring ther tonges with them.

'It was moved that[4] to know how farr men might tell the secrettes of the Howse: it is nedlesse to us for we can tell none for we hear none.

'I speak it now apon thes occasion of this bill which being very long and of great waight, would be well understood before it go to passage. It hath bene told us that it was drawne, perused, considered and passed, that it is a bill of great necessity and consequen[ce] to the common wealth; agane it hath bene told us by other som that [it] is very dangerous full of inconveniences, impossibillity, great burdens to the subiectes, overthrow of the common lawe, to bring as it were West[minster] hall into the Starr Chamber, to lay every

---

1. The final 't' is characteristic of this scribe.
2. There are several amendments or additions between the lines, most of them illegible. At this point 'not only to declare their' appears to have been written in.
3. *Sic.* i.e. 'they'.
4. *Sic.*

man's conveyanc which may be done honestly though secretly into the world, open a gape woork for promoters; not woork for the tynker, for he will stopp a gapp,[5] but for the enfor[mer] who will find a hole in a man's cote, and not leave him till he pull his cote over his ears.

'Wher the truthe is that I trust every man desires to know, for if knowleg must grow apon argumentes which I would be[6]

'That we may give our consent apon knowleg and conscience and not at a ventur nor for any respectes whatsoever.

'And for my particular satisfaction be glad to hear that I might give my voyce both apon knowleg and conscience.'

5. The word 'hole' is superscript.   6. *Sic.*

3. Speech on bill for ban on printing certain books, 10 February? 1585

Text from BL Lansdowne 43, three original amended drafts, in the same hand as the other 1584 speeches and journal in this volume.

Lansdowne 43, fos.181–3.

[Endorsed (f.180) '*anno* 27 Eliz. Towching an bill exhibited for repressing of prynting of certein bookes *etc*'.[1]]

'And please yow Mr Spe[aker], I hard ones an old Parlyment man[2] saye ones, that statutes many tymes are made to cach crowes and take pigeons.[3] I do remember apon what occasion he spake it than, and this bill of prynting puttes me in remembrance therof now and I percyve some ar aferd that if this bill go forward ther will follow the like effect.   [i.] f.181

'But for myne owne part as I am not of that iudgment, understanding from whence it came, so neither would I wishe that it should passe with this preamble; not for that all the partes of the preamble are not good to be reformed, but because, except the iudges of such bookes be mervylous men of great . . . [illegible] and knowleyge, that booke may be sayd a disturber of the churche which tends to the propagation of the Churche. It was sayd by Achab to Elias that he trobled and disturbed Israel; he answered, "Nay, it is thee and thy father's howse that disturbe Israell."[4]

'Therfor, because the meaning of the bill tends but to suppresse certain persons that use the art of prynting, to the hyndranc of her Majestie's privelege

---

1. See Cromwell's journal, f.81.
2. The words 'and one of . . . [illegible] good experience' and other illegible words are apparently crossed out.
3. There are some amendments or corrections between the lines of this manuscript, mostly in these opening sentences. There are also several marginal comments which are difficult to read, one at this point being almost wholly illegible. This is also true of the interlinings, though 'our penall' and 'are like nettes' seem to be superscript at the appropriate

point, and probably therefore reflect the opening passage of the second draft of the speech. The hand of this scribe, never easy in the 'anonymous journal' or the other speeches included here, becomes impenetrable at times in this first draft. Even so, what is decipherable makes sense most of the time though the impression is of the first stages of the evolution of a speech rather than the 'finished' drafts encountered elsewhere.
4. 1 Kgs. 18:17–18.

by her letters patentes and . . . [illegible] to the freedom of the corporacione, without lycenc,[5] this preamble may be clean left out, and[6] some other face putt to it, fitter for the body.

'Now as thowching[7] the substance of the bill I think it very fitt that the corporation and patente[e]s, but I could wishe withall that some further order then is here[8] sett downe might be taken for the suppressing of leud and yll bookes to be prynted herafter as also for the calling in of such bookes as be already abroad *cum privelegio* nay[?] of them in their forhed, as her Majeste hath done with her base coyne, not currant.

'I will not speake of bookes sclanderous to the stat, pernicious in every way[?], because ther be statutes to lay hold on them, and for that all or the greatest part of such come from beyond the seas and ar not prynted here.

'But I meane of unprofitable and idell pamphlettes, leud and wanton discourses of love, propha[ne] ballades, lying historyes, which all tend to the corruption of manners and expence of tyme which otherwise men would bestow in reading of the scripture and other good treatises of morallite or wytt, for men would read good bookes rather then sitt idell in ther howses apon rayny dayes, and albeit he read it not to the entent to take any frut therby yet it may be he shall, as he that walks in the sone is sone burnt albeit his meaning. /

v.

'Ill speaches corrupt good manners: how much more doth yll bookes, considering a thing read is a deper impression then thinges recyved in by the ear.

'Ther is no man I think that thinkes not but that yll scholemasters do much hurt to the youth of England, but the wurst scholemasters of all other ar yll bookes, both to persons of all ages and of all degrees and condicions.

'Amongst all the blessinges of God ther is none greater then the art of prynting, that hath advanced and spread the kingdom of the gospell and battred the kyngdom of Antichrist then it; so agayne, no thing agayne hath more mightily sett up the kyngdom of the devill then it, either by the ignorance and corruption of former tymes and the negligenc of this tyme.

'I shall not nede to name any particulers.

'I would a visitation, as the phisitions do visit the potecary shoppes for ill drugges, so prynters' shoppes were surveyed for these kinds of drugges withe which our youth is poysoned.[9]

'Is it not strang that Ovid, *De arte amandi*, is not only sold openly and read in the scholes for the which the aughtor was punished by exile by a heathen.

'Is [it] not strange[10] that the tymes of popery forbad the prynting and reading *Colloquies* of Erasmus, a notable learned man, because he did touch and discover the treacherys of that tyme, and shall we suffer in the tyme of the gospell so many leud bookes as do teache plainly?

'I am verely persuad that both good bookes and preaching both together do as much hurt as yll bookes alwaie.

'It is complynd of the pulpitt, and sync there is no reformation it wer good it wer redressed by parlyment.

'To which end, Mr Speaker,[11] I have gotten here a bill drawne the last parlyment by a godly discreet gentleman, which I have thought good to offer[12] to be considered of with the other bill, that of both on good on might be framed to help both the greifes /

'And please yow I remember I hard a good old Parliment man say ones that [ii.] f.182 many penall statutes ar very like unto nettes, which being made to cache crowes do often tymes take pigeons. And as I do remember apon what occasion he spake it than, so I see now that some ar afrayd that if this bill should go forrward that a like effect would followe.

'Of whose iudgment thought[13] I be not for that we hard it testified that it was drawne to a nother purpose and as I understand was preferred by a nother kynd of person, yett I would wishe that it should not go forrward with this preamble in his forhead.

'Not for that I think not him woorthy of severe punishment who shall offend in dede against any of the partes of the preamble, but for that if the iudges in such cases be not men of great knowlege and conscience, Elias may be counted to distorb and troble the peace of Israell, when in dede it is Achab and his father's howse. Our owne chronicles amongst others do aforde us a notable example of a certane honest marchant of the cittie of London, who sayd he would make his sonne heir to the crowne. We se in experience that the coulor of a tytle is enought for him that sets to clymb to a kyngdome, and the bare letter of a lawe for him maks no conscienc to wrest a lawe, contrary to the meaning of the makers of that lawe.

'Therfor, since the body of the bill recheth no further then to preserve the priveleges of the company of the prynters and the prerogatyf of her Majestie's patente[e]s I would have this quareling head cutt clear of and some other framed fitter for the body.

'But withall I am to move to this honorable Howse 2 thinges. The first is that som order might be taken also, for the callinge in of a multitude of unprofitable, leud and lascivious discorses, by the reading wherof what hinderance hath growne to the church of God, and what an encrease in the corruptions, it is very lamentable to considder, and very strange that it is suffrable in a Christian common wealth. That scholemaster of love Ovid was banished of a heathen emperor for writing that booke and shall the same booke be salable and suffrable to be read openly in scholes, in the tyme of the

5. 'I think it meet that' apparently crossed out before 'this preamble'.
6. The following words are apparently crossed out: 'that nothing of the body of the bill taken awaye and some other putt in that place that is more agreeable with the matter and meaning of the bill'.
7. *Sic.*
8. The words 'yet by lawe' superscript at this point.
9. Marginal entry: 'and burnt like coyne and current called in. Contribution.'
10. Marginal entry: '. . . [two illegible words] bookes burnt to the valewe of a thowsand markes'.
11. Marginal entry: 'a gent[leman] well knowne to this Howse which for the . . . [illegible] in effect . . . [illegible]'.
12. MS repeats 'to offer', and continues 'to if that is go[od] to . . .'.
13. This final 't' is characteristic of this scribe and appears in the 'anonymous journal'.

gospell?[14] I confesse in the tyme of ignorance and under the goverment of [the] Churche of Rome it was and is a good pollecy to allow of all such books, wherby the people may be occupied and so not[15] and hyndred from the reading of the scripture, but it is a shame and a synn it should be so now.

'And therfore I besech yow let us tak som order for it. Let us do [as] her Majeste hath most graciously donn by the base coyne of the realme in making it pure sylver, or at the least take a pattern of the phisition[s] who, yearly I think at their discretions, do visit the poticaryes' shoppes and do burn all druges that they fynd defectif (yea, and lett us have more care here then they because the poticaryes' druges do but poyson the body, but the prynters' drugges do poyson the soule). The losse of which books may be borne by a generall contribution. /

v.　'Thus much I thought good to say for bookes already prynted.

'And now (because it is to litle purpose except ther be also restraynt for the tym to come for the prynting of such and the lik) I have thought good also to offer to the consideracion of this honorable Howse a bill tending to that effect framed by a very godly learned and discret gentleman I think the last parlyment, but for want of tyme.[16]

'It is not long if it please may be read and either considered of to be added to the other or els to passe as a bill by it self.'

[iii.] f.183v.　'[I] remember I hard an old Parlyment [man] say ones that many penal statutes . . .

'I remember apon what occasion he spake it then and I am sory as often as I remember the occasion.

'But that which makes me remember it now is the feare which I see some conceyve that if this bill go forward that the lik effect would follow.

'Of whose iudgment though I be not, because both the body of the bill importes no such matter and besides, it was declared unto us the last daye by a gentleman of good understanding and credytt who sems to be privy both to the purpose and preferring of the bill, that it was drawn to no other purpose but to preserve the prerogatif of her Majestie'[s] patentees and the priveleges of the company of the prynters; yet to take away all suspicion and to make the bill have the better passage in som matters most nedfull of reformacion, I could wishe that the hole preamble wer cutt of and som other shaped more suitable to the body of the bill.

'Howbeit I would not be taken that I do not think him woorthy severe punishment that shall offend against any part of the preamble, but for that if the iudges be not competent ther is great danger for them that be accused, for whom the issu shalbe wither they conteyn matter of heresy, error, or to the disturbance of the peace and government of the Churche.

'St Paul sayd to this[?], I[f] the highe prestes may be iudge,[17] after this [way] that yow call heresy I woorship.

'If Achab may be iudg it is Elias that trobles the peace of Israell.

'If *omnium* in the Church be *bene*, as I have hard out of Paule's Crosse, then he that shall say *omnium* is not *bene* in the Church must nedes be on that was . . . [illegible][18] a disturber of the Church.

'Our iust and godly peticions exhibited for the reformacion of that high and shamfull abuse [of the] censur[?] of the Church to have it reduced to his first is a dist[urbance].

'To bring in a learned ministry, according to the expresse commandment of[19]

'To spirit wrytt[20] against pluralit[ies] and non-residences.

'To him that will pervert . . . [illegible][21] the bare letter of the law is enough.

'To him that clayms a crown, a coulour of tytle to claym it. /

'The art [of] printing is one of the most excellent invention[s] most profitable that ever was. Want a number of . . . [illegible] want . . . [illegible]. For want of it in former ages stone, brasse, pillers, barkes of trees perished.   f.183

'God never gave any thing that gave such a blowe to them and made such a battry to the bullwarkes of popery.

'If that tym could have but imagyned, dreamed of . . . [illegible] they would have burnt all the presses and made it treason.

'It hath enlarged the kingdom of the gospell and Christ.

'I speake it to this end that yet I think as faith and knowlege hath ben encreased of God by good bookes, so, by yll bookes, corruption of manners, wantones: that I may compare it to the tre that was placed in the myddest of Parridise, the knowleg of good and yll.

'That I am of opynion ther hath ben as much hurt on way as ther hath come good another.

'I speake it to this end that ther would be a straight care of the prynting of bookes.

'The number is infinit and they dayly encrease. It wer better we had fewe and good, as it is sayd of penall statutes, it wer better if we had fewe, better executed.

'It is not masked[?] of all men what poyson yll bookes do in their youthe. Maydens and wemen, that litle reading they have must use it to the reading of wanton Italian discorses and tales, which be nothing els but very scholmasters of wantones and uncleannes.

'What a number of shamfull bookes wrytyng not only unprofitable but leud, as Court of Venus *etc.*, which if all wer cutt of, men would rather read good bookes when they had nothing els to do on a rayny day then sitt idell in their howses.

'Wherby it may happen to them as it did to the old[22] woman that Mr Latymer makes mencion of that went to a sermon to slepe, and was taken napp.

'Men that walke in the sone.

'Therfore, as this statute would remedy that every body shall not be a prynting, so every body a writer.'

---

14. There is a largely illegible marginal entry at this point which mentions Erasmus: see the first draft of the speech.
15. *Sic.*
16. *Sic.*
17. The words 'maye be iudge' are crossed through.
18. ? 'against'.
19. *Sic.*
20. *Sic.*
21. ? 'against'.
22. MS appears to read 'wold'.

4. *Presentation of petitions on abuses in the ministry, 15 February 1585*

Text from PRO SP Dom.Eliz.176/55, copy,
? of Commons' Journal.
Printed. D'Ewes 349.

SP Dom.Eliz.176/55

[Endorsed '27° *Elizabethae*. Proceeding of the House upon the [petitions]']

27° *Elizabethae. Die Lune xv° Februarii.* 1584.

Mr William Staughton offred unto this House a certein supplicacion in parchment of certein abuses in the ministerie within the countie of Leycester. And also a note of certein articles in paper concerning some disorder in the bishops' ministerie.

Mr Edward Lewknor offred also another peticion in parchment touching lyke abuses in the ministerie on the behalf of the inhabitantes of the east partes of the countie of Sussex.

These peticions were presently read, as also another lyke peticion in paper from the inhabitantes of the parish of Folkston in the countie of Kent, which was delivered into the House sythence the last adiournment by Mr John Moore.

After sundry speeches and mocions touching these peticions Mr Chancellor of the Exchequer, putting the House in mynd of the lyke peticions in effect offred to the House before the last adiournment and imparted to the Lords by a committee of this House, with suit unto their lordships that they would therin be a meane unto her Majestie, moveth nowe to forbeare any further dealing therin until the House have first receyved answere from the Lords of the other peticions, alledging further that he had very latelie putt some of their lordships in remembrance therof on the behalf of this House. And that yt was answered we should heare from their lordships to morowe next.

Therupon yt was thought good to expect answere accordingly from the Lords before any further proceeding.

5. *Petitions against the bishops' government (the petition offered by Stoughton, 15 February 1585?)*

Text from BL Add.48064 (Yelverton 70), copy.
Other MS PRO SP Dom.Eliz.176/72 (a late copy).

Add.48064 (Yelverton 70), fos.42v.–43

[Headed by Beale 'Offred to the parlament 27 *Regine Eliz.*']

Wheras divers and sondrie thinges[1] practised by the archbishopps, bishopps and other ecclesiasticall officers contrary to the act of Parlament and lawes of this realme, and contrarye to their owne canons, to the greate dishonour of almightie God, hinderaunce of the gospell, endangeringe of her Majestie's most excellent estate, and the encrease of manifolde and intolerable grievaunces of her Highnes' most faithfull and obedient subiectes: maye it therfore please this honorable House to take knowledge of the same, as they here followe, and in godlie wisdome to provide redresse.

Disorders against actes of Parlament.[2]

In primis they make ministers which are not able to render an accompt of their faythe in Latin accordinge to the articles of religion agreed uppon in the convocacion 1562, contrarie to an act of Parlament 13 *Reginae Elizabethae.*[3]
Item they make, promulge and execute articles and iniunctions without her Majestie's writt and royall assent, contrarie to two actes of Parlament 25 Henry 8[4] and 1 Elizabeth, and contrarie to their owne vowes which they have made unto her Highnes and all estates of the lande *in verbo sacerdotii.*[5]
Item they sweare ministers unto canonicall obedience to the archbishops, bishops and their successors contrary to the othe which they have taken to the Queene's prerogative.
Item they observe not the booke of King Edwarde 6 confirmed by act of Parlament made for consecratinge bishopps and ordering priestes and deacons,[6] *viz* they make and[7] ordeine ministers without a sermon in private places as in

---

1. SP Dom adds 'are'.
2. SP Dom numbers the disorders 1–8.
3. 13 Eliz, c.12 (1571) in *SR*, iv.546–7.
4. 25 Hen VIII, c.19 (submission, 1533–4) in *SR*, iii.460–1.
5. *Recte* '*sacerdotis*', as in SP Dom.
6. i.e. the ordinal authorized with the Second Prayer Book.
7. SP Dom omits 'make and'.

their chambers and chappells, where skarse anie at all are present but their owne servauntes.

Item they make ministers not in the presence of vj other ministers required by an act of Parlament that so manye should be present at the orderinge of everye minister, 21 Henry 8.[8]

Item they forbid a minister to preache within his owne cure beinge licenced therunto by act of Parlament *anno* 8 Elizabeth.[9] /

f.43   Item they urge a subscription at the handes of the ministers unto more thinges then the statute doethe require which was made 13 Elizabeth to limit how farre subscription should be required of everye minister, and contrarie to the tenor, forme and intent of the same statute they suspende and putt from execucion of their function such as refuse not in anye wise to subscrybe in maner and forme as the sayd statute doethe prescrybe.

[Item][10] they dispense for banes askinge contrarie to the Booke of Common Prayer.

Disorders against lawes and customes in force.

1. *In primis* they urge men under paine of imprisonment to take an othe to accuse them selves in causes criminall, and such as refuse to take the said othe they imprison.
2. Item the interrogatoryes which they minister uppon the same othe beinge captious, they denie the examinate anie copie to aunswer with deliberacion[11] and counsell, but he must answer uppon the sodaine for matters don or spoken certaine yeres past.
3. Item in their interrogatoryes ministred uppon the said othe they enquire into the secret thoughtes of men's hartes to knowe what they thincke of such and such ceremonyes, and what opinion or iudgment they minde to be of for the same herafter.
4. Item when they have thus extorted a confession out of anie against them selves they proceade uppon the same unto suspencion and deprivacion, which is not don in a publyke place where there is free accesse, but in a private chamber where the dore is kept shutt.
5. Item they holde such out of the ministerie as they have thus deprived, denyinge them the copie of those crymes for which they are suspended and deprived.
6. Item they imprison men for prayinge in their houses at due tyme and[12] due maner, and with convenient and laufull number.
7. Item they cite into their courtes, molest, trouble, and excommunicate men for goinge abroad to other parishes to heare the worde of God preached when they have no teachinge at home. /
v.   8. Item they [and] their chauncelors, commissaries, officialls, registers, summners and servauntes exacte and take excessive fees for and about lettres of orders, licences to preache, suspencions, excommunications, absolutions, probates of testamentes, and manie other such lyke, also for institucions and inductions, which put those that receyve them unto 3 or 4[13] charges.

Disorders against their owne canons.

1. *In primis* they suffer their chauncelors, commissaryes, and officialls to excommunicate contrarie to their owne canons.
2. Item they suffer them to commute[14] penaunce contrarie to their owne canons.
3. Item they make ministers without a tytle contrary to their owne canons.
4. Item they make ministers where no place of ministracion is voyd contrary to their owne canons.
5. Item they make ministers such as are not of their owne diocesse contrarye to their owne canons.
6. [Item][15] they make ministers not exercysed in holie scriptures contrary to their owne canons.
7. [Item] they make handycraftesmen ministers, contrarie to their owne canons.
8. [Item] they confirme leases of parsonages for terme of many yeres contrarye etc.[16]

8. 21 Hen VIII, c.13, sect xiii (1529) in *SR*, iii.294.
9. ? 8 Eliz, c.1 (1566) in *SR*, iv.485–6; SP Dom continues 'and *anno* 2 Henry 4, and by their provinciall constitutions.'
10. Supplied from SP Dom.
11. SP Dom: 'deliberance'.
12. SP Dom adds 'in'.
13. SP Dom adds 'pound'.
14. SP Dom: 'committ'.
15. Supplied from SP Dom (and for nos.7, 8).
16. SP Dom: '. . . contrary to their owne canons'.

6. *Whitgift's answer to the Commons' petition, (his own version), 22 February 1585*

Text from Inner Temple, Petyt 538 / 38, copy in the hand of a secretary, endorsed by Whitgift.
Other MSS BL Lansdowne 120 (in hand of Whitgift's secretary, endorsed by Burghley), Add.29546 (in hand of Whitgift's secretary, endorsed by Whitgift 'My answere to the Nether Howsse of Parlament'); PRO SP Dom.Eliz.177 / 36 (in hand of Whitgift's secretary); Lambeth Palace 577.
Printed. Strype, *Whitgift*, i.354–60 (from Lansdowne).

Petyt 538 / 38, 79–82

[Endorsed by Whitgift 'An answer to the petitions'.]
1584

The first petition desireth that those ministers which were ordered synce *13°* and not qualified according to the act of Parlement then made shoulde bee suspended from their ministery untill they were qualified accordingly.

The second petition desireth that such unlearned ministers as have been admitted unto benefices since *anno* 1575 might be deposed, *etc.*

To theis two I aunswered thus in effect, first that I knewe not how many of theis unlerned ministers there were: but wished that they were knowne, together with the bishoppes that ordered them, lest the falt and negligence of some fewe might peradventure be imputed to all. For mine owne part I signified that since my coming to this place, I had omitted nothing that might perteyn to the reforming of that abuse. It was one of the first things I did, and is sett downe amonge those articles that are so greatly mislyked of some:[1] hopinge that since that time there hath bene no great cause to complayne.

But touching theis two petitions: I sayd[2] we could not assent unto them (especially yf such ministers were not otherwise criminouse) for the causes following.

1°: lest diverse thinges might be called into needelesse questions, as doon by unlawfull ministers, as mariages which they have celebrated, and sacramentes which they have ministred.

2°: lest also diverse parishes might be lefte destitute of ministers to say divine service, celebrate the sacramentes, read the scriptures, and the learned and godly homilies appointed for that purpose, for we thought yt much better to have some to reade the service *etc* without a sermon, then that the people like brute beastes should be left without prayers, sacramentes, reading the scriptures and homilies, and without sermons also.

3º: We thought yt ageinst charitee to send such ministers together with their families a begging which had dedicated them selves to the ministery, and had not otherwise any trade wherby to lyve.[3] /

Notwithstanding, for the better enforcing of such unlearned ministers to studie *etc*, we were purposed to devise some kinde of exercise for them, not like unto that which they called prophecies (which had bene the cause of some trobles in the Church) but some other more privat, such as shall seeme best to our selves both for the peace of the Church, and their better instruction, wherby I hoped that their xij[th] petition also was satisfied.

The third petition desireth that none be admitted hereafter but such as are qualified according to the statut, which I said we willingly yeelded unto, and had therfore taken order more then a xij moneth since. Adding that hereafter they should rather finde falt with lack of ministers, then with too great a nomber of unlearned ministers.[4]

The fourth petition seemeth to prescribe a manner how the third might be perfourmed, which manner we liked not of, for diverse causes to us knowne, and then needelesse to be rehersed, trusting that having the thing they would not contend with us aboute the manner: and that we were determyned to observe the lawes therin establyshed.

The vth petition desireth that none be admitted into the ministery but eyther to a benefice with cure, or else to some preachershipp, or unlesse he were eyther fellow or scholler in some colledge of one of the universitees. To this I aunswered that yf the meaninge of the petition were that none should be admitted into the ministery *sine titulo*, that is without some certeyne stay of livinge, we did very well lyke therof, and had already taken ordre therin, longe before the exhibiting of theis petitions, being a thing which the lawe yt selfe doth require.[5] But the petition yt selfe as yt is sett downe we thought to be very short, and to tende to the abridging of the nombre of preachers and especially of the gravest and best, contrary to that which by the sayd petitions seemeth to be pretended, ffor / yt secludeth from the ministery deanes, prebendaries, and other ministers of cathedrall churches, masters of colledges also in the universitees, against the foundations of the sayd colledges, arch-deacons lykewyse and diverse others, all which heereafter must be meere lay men, yf the petition should be graunted in manner and fourme.

The vj[th] petition desireth that the pastor which ys to be admitted to a cure might be tried and allowed by the parish *etc.*, wherunto I aunswered, we had

v.

f.80

---

1. i.e. Whitgift's recently promulgated articles.
2. Lambeth 577 adds '2ly'.
3. These three reasons are differently ordered in Fitzwilliam's journal, f.22v.
4. Lansd., SP Dom and Lambeth 577 omit.
5. Cf. Fitzwilliam's journal, f.22v.

before taken ordre that none should be admitted into the ministerye but such as had a sufficient testimoniall of their behaviour eyther from the colledge wherin they were, or from the place wherein they made their most abode. But the petition we could not yeelde unto because,

1. yt savoureth of popular elections longe agoe abrogated in the Church for diverse inconveniences therof;
2. it wold breede variaunce and dissention betwixt the parishioners and the patron and oftentimes devide the parish among them selves;
3. it would preiudice the patrone's right, and alter many lawes;
4. and finally, yt would not worke the effect pretended, the partie presented being altogether unknowne to the parish as in most places yt must of necessitee come to passe.

The v petitions following, *viz*: the vij[th], viij[th], ix[th], x[th] and xj[th] I sayd did tende to such a libertee and freeing of ministers from all kinde of subiection, as no subiect in this lande did enioy: and as in deede is most intollerable in any setled state or well governed church.

Likewise that they did tende not only to the continuing of the contentions which are allready, but also to the encreasinge of them and that mightely.

To the utter frustrating also of the statut made for the uniformitee of common prayer.

v.   For the vij[th] petition wold not have them to be urged / to any other oath or subscription than that which ys expressed in the statutes of the realme, except yt bee the oath against simonie, wherby yt wold have them freed from the oath of canonicall obedience, which they take to the ordinaries *in omnibus licitis et honestis*, which also the law now in force, though not the statutes, requyreth of them, and which every bishopp by statut is bounde to take to his metropolitan, and hath not hetherto bene excepted ageinst by any.

It also freeth them from subscribing to the orders and rites of the Church by lawe establyshed, contrary to the use and manner of all reformed and well-governed churches in Christiandome, and contrary also to the practise of this Church, both in the time of King Edward and since the beginninge of her Majestie's raigne: wherein subscription hath beene requyred to the selfe same articles that are now sett downe and that in more streite termes and wordes penned then now they are.

The viij[th] petition would have them freed from the temporall magistrate, and also from the ecclesiasticall. For yt desiereth that neither of them both may intermeddell with them or call them to accompt for omissions or chaunges of some portions or rites in the Booke of Common Prayer *etc*, so that they may omitt what they will, and alter and chaunge what pleaseth them without controllment, which beinge suffred yt will shortly come to passe that we shall have *tot altaria quot schismata, etc*.

The ix[th] doth simply exempt them from commissaries and officialls, and in effect from the bishop also, for his authoritee ys so restrayned that he shall not be able to doo any thinge. Wherunto yf a portion of the xj[th] petition be added, the ecclesiasticall commissioners also are restrayned from dealing with them. So that in effect they are freed from all kinde of subiection and authoritee. /

The xth requireth that those which are suspended or depryved for want of   f.81
conformitee might be restored, *etc.* Wherunto I aunswered that in iustice we
could not so doo, forasmuch as that which we had done against them we had
done yt iustly, neverthelesse yf they would yeeld them selves to conformitee,
I promised in mine owne name, and in the name of the rest, that we would
shewe unto them all manner of humanitee.

The xjth would not have them examined *ex officio*: wherby should be taken
from us an usuall lawfull and ordinarie kinde of proceeding without which we
can not perfourme that which ys looked for at our handes, beinge also used in
sundry other courtes of the greatest accompt in this lande, and evermore
practised in the ecclesiasticall courtes and by the high commissioners: never
gaynsayed or mislyked till of late by the Jesuites and seminarie preistes, of
whom I thought that our men also had borrowed their exceptions against that
manner of proceedinge.

The xijth petition is aunswered before.

The xiijth and xiiijth concerne excommunication, which censure wee can not
alter without alteration of many lawes, and without bringing into the Church
a newe censure, which in short time would breed greate offence and quarrelles,
as no warranted by the worde of God.

The xiiijth petition seemeth to mislyke the cause of excommunication, and
also the persons which exercise the same as lay men. The cause which is so
misliked is contumacy, which in our opinion is a fault deserving excommunication, neyther ys yt materiall upon what small valew contumacye proceedeth,
be yt xij^d or lesse. The smallnesse of the value doth not diminish but augment
the crime. No man ys excommunicated for the value / of xij^d: nor for any   v.
somme, but for contemning authoritee, for disobeyinge of processe, for refusing to aunswer according to lawe.[6] Neither ys this censure more hadde[7] in thee
Church then the like is in the common wealth, for upon the selfe same causes
and like contempt men are proclaymed rebelles, and oftentimes outlawed,
wherby they live without goodes and libertee and are, as yt were, without
protection.

As for chauncelers *etc* termed to be lay men, in truth they do not excommunicate, but pronounce the sentence of lawe *contra contumaces*, which sentence
notwithstanding is not of force till yt be denounced by the minister openly in
the church.

Neverthelesse for satisfieinge of some men's scrupulositee in this behalfe, we
are purposed to be more streite in that censure, and to ioyne some preacher in
commission with other of the officers for that action and in matters of
importaunce to take the knoweledge thereof our selves.

The xvth ys agaynst facultees for non-residence and pluralitees. I signefied I
had not graunted one facultee for non-residence since my comming to this
place, but onely one to a man of lxxx yeares of age, and that for a xij moneth
only. Neverthelesse I thought that ffacultee to be necessarie, because men in

---

6. **Lansd.** adds 'etc'.   7. Lansd.: 'hard' (+ Add. 29546, Lambeth
                                          577).

respect of sicknesse, suites of lawe, or other occasions may be forced to be longer from their cures then the lawe will permitt, which they can not doo without danger, unlesse they be dispensed with. I sayde I was therin but her Majestie's officer.[8]

Pluralitees I tould them could not be taken away without discouraging the best sort of ministers, and taking away the reward of learninge. /

f.82   The xvj[th] I thought to be reasonable, yf the place were able to meynteine such a curat.

---

8. Lansd. adds 'etc' (+ Add. 29546, Lambeth 577); cf. Fitzwilliam's apparently more acerbic version of this section on non-residence and pluralism (f.23).

7. Whitgift's notes of sayings of four MPs, 25 February(?) 1585

Text from PRO SP Dom.Eliz. 175 / 51, original.
Written by Whitgift in the column made by the paper having
been folded twice.

SP Dom.Eliz.175/51

Mr Blage: the cardnall and metropoliticall answere.

Beale: that there was nether law of God nor man, learning nor witt in the answere to the petitions.
And that the bishops had abused the Queen's lawes and the comission this 26 yeares.

Thomson: that yt was rather a discowrse then anie resolution of a divine.
And that subscription was not used in anie Church.

Lukenar:[1]   speaking of bishops sayd that they were rather deformers then reformers.

---

1. Henry Blagge, Lawrence Tomson and Edward Lewknor were appointed committee members to consider the petitions on 16 December 1584 (*Commons, sub* Blagge, Lewknor and Tomson).

8. Speaker's notes for his speech conveying the Queen's inhibition of proceedings on religion, 2 March 1585

Text from BL Harley 6853, two original sets of notes, in Puckering's hand.

Harley 6853, fos.285, 286–7

[Endorsed by Puckering 'The message from the Queen to the House touching the petitions and byll of bishops.']

[i.] f.285v.　My colleccion with Mr S[ecretary] of my spech from her Majestie to the House.

Cause of my absens yesterday.[1]

Not for any[2] slothe or necligens[3] or any want of goodwill to be present,

for I assur you I am not better pleasyd in this parlyament then whilest I ame occup[ied] in Parlyament matters.

I think no tyme to erly to come hither, nor to long to tarye.

So as I trust you will accept my absens *etc*,

craved with your favor and paciens to wynne me better healthe *etc*, to make me more hable to serve you.

But at noone I received a message from her Majestie to come presentlye to the court.

My meaning was to be heare this day, and lothe to go to the court as this.

Message　As she well understoode I was your mowth, so she well knew I was your mouthe by her allowans and with cawcion and excepcion, to deale in all causes ffyt, but not in causes forbydden or restrayned to her lycens; and blamed me for reading suche bylles *etc*, and allowing the reading of suche articles and mocyons *etc*.

To you all she willed me to saye:

she knowes and thinkes you know she ys suprem governor of this Churche next under God,

hathe full power and aucthoritye bothe as Queen by law of the crowne as by law posityve by statute to reforme anye disorders in the same,

and hopes you doubt not but as she hathe power, so hathe she good will to cause examination[?] and to redres whatsoever may be found amysse.[4]

And by sundry complaintes which she hathe hard of she ys of opynion that ther ys some cause of redresse to be had yn some thinges touching the churche goverment.

But her Majestie cannot choose but marvayles of these courses of your procedinges,[5] that geving you so loving comaundment not to meddle with these matters of rightes[6] and disciplyne of the Churche (wherin by her owne mowthe she declared to you that she thought somthing was amisse and she in her princely aucthoritye wold see reformacion),

that this notwithstanding, you wold attempt to deale by receipt of petycions and publik reading of the same and with suche kynd of proceding as hathe folowed touching the same: /   f.285

1. b. to distrust her promes,
2. a. to break her comandment,
3. c. to derogate her aucthoritye,
    as not having suffic[ient] power to reforme and as thoughe insuffyc[ient] law for 27 yeres for yt,
4. or having law, that she wanted good will and good dispocycion to be myndfull of so wayghtie a cause to execut her aucthoritye in that behalfe or to be found necligent therin.

Wherof consequentlye dothe folow these great enormyties:

That th'adversarye may saye

that eyther we want yet suffycient lawes to maynt[ain] our churche doctryne and disciplyen,

or having yt, that you mistrust her Majestie's good execucion of yt,

or els that you shew your selves very undutiffullye to use these meanes to call her ecclesiasticall goverment into these suspyci[ons].

Wherin her Majestie is greatlye greved that she hathe occasyon to cause this thus to be delyvered unto [you] whom she dothe know and affyrmethe to be as loving subiectes as any prynce in the world hathe.

And therfore of her great and tender ffavor she could not choose but as a mother over her children eftsones to warne you to forbeare any further procedinges in this course.

The rather for that she takes yt pertayned least unto them being the lowest of the iij estates,

and the rather because conferryng herin with the Lords they received suche answer fyrst from my Lord Treasorer and after by my Lord Archebishop.

Her resolute pleasure, she will receive no motion of alteracion or change of any law wherby the religion or Church of England standes established at this daye; but yet upon dew course of complaint see th'execucion of any law alredy made, or whatsoever els she may do by her supreme aucthoritye to reforme what shalbe found amisse.

---

1. 'Yesterday' replaces 'today'.
2. The words 'want of good will or for' are deleted here.
3. The words 'but for [?] cawse, or to recover perfit healthe' are deleted here.
4. These words have been deleted here: 'And as she nothing doubtes but

something ys amisse for manners and disciplyne in some particulers or particuler places, but not in generall'.
5. The words 'against her commandement by the Lord Chancellor' are deleted here.
6. i.e. rites.

[ii.] f.286   ij *Martii*. The note that Mr Vicechamberlayne and I conceyved of her Majestie's speache to be delivered to the House.

Sent for me.
She had accepted me ther mowth,
with this cawcyon or excepcion
set downe with same command to them selves:
that we shold not medle with matters of the Churche neither in reformacion of religion or of disciplyne.
That contr[ary] to this they have received petyc[ions] and conceyved dyvers addycions to the same,
which she hoped she had well aunsweryd bothe by the mowthe of my Lord Treasurer and by th'Archbishop of Canterbury.
Albeyt understanding they procede contr[ary], she cannot but let them know that they have proceded without that dew consyderacion as she thought to fynd in suche men.
Th'auctoritye of the reformacion ben[?][7] in her selfe bothe by th'aucthoritye of her crown, by comone law, and by statute well knowen to them selves,
wherin yf they medle above that that dothe become them she must let them playnly know that suche wrong course wyll rather preiudyce the cause then do any good at all, or to them selves. /

v.   And that her Majestie ys most sory in respect of ther zealous love towardes her that th'adversarye shold take suche advantage as to charge them with suche an undutifull kynd of dealing.
Wherin she ys grevyd that of necessitye she must offer them this course of admonycion, but that she as a mother over the commen welthe must warne them as her children.
Resolutlye she will receive no motyon of innovacion nor alter or chaunge any lawe wherby the religyon or Churche of England standythe established at this daye.
And yet will upon any motyon to be made see th'execucion of lawe alredye made and whatsoever she may by her supreame aucthoritye do for th'amendment of the same.
Wherin fyrst to the bishop of the dyoces, next to the metropolitan, then to the counsell, and at lengthe to the Queen.
She findes not onlye a discontentacion in the third state of the realme against the clargye in generall, but that they have with most undecent termes used the chefe bishops, the principall members of this state, which she thinkes fyt to be reformed in the particuler offenders therin.[8] /

f.287   And thinkethe the complaintes being to the parlyament and the lords being movyd made suche answer as might satisfye us.
Yet we alone seke further, which we ought not to do. That this kynd of dealing seamyd to derogat her aucthoritye and to touche her with some empechment of slaknes in suche dutye as she would be lothe to be found neclygent yn.
And for thus far proceding she dothe gretlye blame my masters of her counsell,

who have suffryd thus far proceding and hathe not movyd the House to some other course more agreable to the furtherans of the cause and to ther dutye. Touching the bill of bishops and the visytacions her Majestie's pleasure ys that I should gyve yt no further reading nor any you shold any further call upon yt.

Message del Erle Leyc[ester].
Accordant a votre appointment
jeo wayt sur Seigneur Steward[9]
et [?][10] le message nous avons recu de luy
quel nous plus acceptablement recu
et que nous bien croiace que fut report
et que [?][11] sans tiell report nous croy nyt lesse de luy
s'il fut son plesur a nomm le person
nous ferr[ons?] comme serroit meete.
Il one[12] grand thankes recomend eftsones
sa bon entent pour le commen wele
et one le credyt de son honor
et grand affirmacion que peut etre fait
quel jeo ne poy expresser
cibien comme jeo voy son affeccion ultre ce
qu'il n'entend unque, ne par ascun sache
que peut etre profyt a luy
et ce peut [?][13] qu'il unque parle al ascun del
message comment . . . [illegible] ad amyes entre eux s'il veut avoir en tiell
matter compas a que veut avoir parle overtement
ou al meins secretment avoir parle one ascun.
Auxi recomend son desyer
si tiell bon matter serra hinder
en ascun opinion de son charge al subiect
que pour tant que peut ascun voie
etre imagyn a venir a luy on[14] son offyce et profyt
que peut etre proviso a redres ce
pour le person que parla il ne desier reformacion del man
mes del matter en le man
que tiell qu'il est, peut luy ne[15] satisfyer de tiell ymagyned
entent de profyt
mes a tant comme jeo poy collect
fut parle hors de ce message
et parle en le court
al ascun person de grand account.

7. Word illegible.
8. Altered from 'state, as must be callyd to be aunswered in an other place'.
9. i.e. Lord Steward of the Household, Leicester.
10. MS unclear: 'une'.
11. MS unclear: 'iss'.
12. i.e. 'with'.
13. MS unclear: 'app'.
14. MS unclear: 'ou[?]'.
15. MS unclear: 'η'.

9. Speech on bill for the good government of Westminster, 8 March(?) 1585

Text from BL Lansdowne 43, original amended draft, in the same hand as the other 1584 speeches and journal in this volume.

Lansdowne 43, fos.178, 179

[Endorsed (f.178) '27 Elizabeth. Bill towching reformation of disorders in Westminster'.][1]

f.179   'I mervyle not a litle that such a bill as this is, grounded apon so iuste causes, and considered of with so long and good deliberation, should travayl thus long in childbed, befor it come to his birth. But I mervyl the lesse that it bredes such troble here amongst us, when I considder, how troblesom a kynd a people they be whom it doth concerne. Besides I have noted from my litle experience in this place that those best billes do passe comonly, as I may say, throught[2] the piks[3] and purgatory.[4]

'Towching the matters conteyned in the bill, wither if any man doubt ther be such cause of complant as the bill pretendes I refer them to the honest creditt of such persons as have profed and feld the complaintes, who ar men of the best sort of the inhabitantes of that place, and I refer them further also to the reportes which have bene made here unto us by ij justices of peace. And lastly I refer them to the voyce of the people, which is that the cittie of Westminster is a common harbourag and host[el]ry of the basest and baddest sort of persons both of men and women, which being so, I think ther is no man her that doth not think it fitt that both the place should be purged of such persons and such persons punished according to ther demerittes.

'But now, wither it be convenient that such persons as are aucthorised by this act have the punishment of such offenders, that is doubted of many and hath bene denyed by some and therfor sufficient procese[?]. It hath bene said, by som, that ther be justices of peace already which have auchtority and may reform all this geare. It hath ben answered for them by them selves, that they ar more trobled with Westminster causes then with all the matters of their owne proper iurisdiction, that by reason of them, they ar drawn hither from their proper attendance; and therfore do desire that other[s] may be ioyned to bear the burden with them.

'As towching that some would have, thatt some great men should have [jurisdiction], I think it is an authority that they will not well accept of, and

I think it very unfitt that such men should have the examination of such causes as ar conteyned in [this bill] and I think they will thank us but litle to bestow such office apon them. /

'Synce, then, neth[er] the justices of peace can intend to reform it and that   v. it is not fitt for [great men] ther is none left fitter to be chosen then amongst them selves. The persons that is required to be chosen by this act ar in number xij according to the xij several divisions and wardes. They are to be chosen by the dean and high steward of whom we nede not to doubt but that they will make ther choise of xij of the fitt men of the cittie both for ther welth and honesty and understanding.

'Now, the power which they hav by this act, that is restreyned to the auchtority of an alderman's dignity of London, not what they do but what they lawfully may do, and not in all causes neither, but in a few such as [are] mencioned in this act and in dede fittest to be examyned and punished by such persons.

'But for myn part I am of opynion that if this bill may passe ther will followe good and spedy reformation of the abuse mentioned in the bill.

'First for the persons that ar to mak the choise ar the Deane of Westminster, or the High Steward for the tyme being, either of whom we nede not to doubt but that they will make their choise of men both of the ablest for their wealth and of the fittest for their honesty and understanding.

'The number appoynted ar xij according to the xij severall wardes and divisions and are few enough for a place so pestred with such pestilen[ce]. The which may seme a great many for so smale a precinct, but considering many handes mak light work.

'For the power that they shall have it is not absolut nor over all offendors but it is reserved and restreyned to the iurisdiction of an alderman deputy of London, how, as he may lawfully do, and that not of all kynds of fault but of a few, mencioned in the bill, so that apon the matter it falles ow[t] to be no more but a kynd of enquest of enquiry as is yearly in London, which hath bene declared unto us doth more good in the cittie in such causes then all the courtes besides.

'The citie of London which is as well governed a citie as any is is[5] Christendom; who sees not what advantag it hath therto by the aldermen and ther depute in ther severall wardes for the reason they ar the fittest men to fyn[d] out and the readiest at hand to apprehend all suspected persons and such as shall lurke and loyter, within ther severall iurisdictiones. /

'Now, towching removing of inmattes, God forbyd that it should extend to   f.178 expell out any honest poore man be he never so poor lyving orderly and apon

---

1. Cromwell's journal, f.75v has first reading, and there was much argument on 8 March (D'Ewes, p.364. See *SR*, iv.763–4; HMC *Third Report*, 5).
2. The added 't' is characteristic of this scribe: see 'anonymous journal', and

other documents here.
3. i.e. trial of the pyx.
4. There is a deleted paragraph at this point, but it seems to be a version of the following paragraph.
5. *Sic.*

som lawfull trade out of their habitations. It is only ment to mete with masterles men and idell howswyves, who, as it hath bene sayd, do gather up their rentes under heges and in high wayes, who are here to daye and gone to morrowe.

'And yet this must I say withall that thought they be never so poore nor never so honest, ther is good care and regard to be had by the officers that thes places of habitate be not over pestred, which we [see] to be the cause of contagion and infection in such places, because we see that here is the repayre of all sortes of persons out of all partes of the realme, to terms and parlymentes. Her is the pallice of the princes of this lande, wher oftentym.[6]

'And we can remember that this cittie of Westminster being cleare from the plag although some reasonable number have died in the cittie of London, yet the term hath ben kept her, wheras if ther dye but a fewe her and thought ther should dye non at all in London.[7]

'Therfor, for these reasons and many other that might [be given] I think this thinges in the bill [a]re fitt to be reformed and the persons requir[ed] fitt persons to have the reformation of them. And yet as it hav ben moved I could like very well that this statut be lymited to a reasonable certaine tyme, to mak tryall wither this good will ensu of it as is wished and expected, which if it do, it is easly contynued and if not, it is as easly repelled.'

6. *Sic.*   7. *Sic.*

10. *Speech on bill against making of starch, 13 March(?) 1585*

Text from BL Lansdowne 43, two original amended drafts, in the same hand as the other 1584 speeches and journal in this volume.

Lansdowne 43, fos.176v, 177

[Endorsed (f.176) '27 Elizabeth. Towching a bill exhibited againste making of starche'.]

'And please yow for myn own part I neither myslike very much of the [i.] f.176v. meaning of him that preferred this bill,[1] nor yet of the matter conteyned in the bill. For it tendes to the taking aweye of a very foule and shamfull abuse of the good creatures of God, ffor the mayntenance and encrease wherof so many profitable and holsome lawes have bene hertofore made in divers parlymentes, and in this present parlyment we see it hath ben very carefully considered of and provided for.

'But in my poore opynion we might go a nearer waye to the woode, and mete both with this mischief and a nother as yll as this [and] so make one bushe that should both stopp this gapp, and a nother as nedefull to be stopt as this. And that is, to sett downe some convenient and reasonable sise for owr, I will not terme them as some do outragious, monstrous and abhominable ruffes, but I may truly saye superfluous, wastfull and unweldy ruffes.

'The excesse wherin is no doubt no lesse sinfull then the abuse in the other is both foule and shamfull. For is it not a very lamentable thing that we should bestowe that about the bettering (as we wene) of Gode's woorkmanship in our selves by art, the which being rightly spent on the on side and reasonably sparde on the other, would both stanche the hunger and cloth the nakednes of a great many poore soules that want of both the on and the other?

'And albeit it hath pleased God of his great goodnes under her Majeste's moost gracious and happy goverment to blesse this land both with peace and the fruites of peace now by the space almoost of 27 yeres, yet let us not forgett that within those 7 yeares next going before, ther was such a scarscitie of corne within the realme of England, as the common people in moost partes of the lande wer glad[2] to eat their bread made of acornes.

'God hath to recken with us for many matters, but suerly amongst them all ther is none that will hasten his iudgmentes soner or drawe his iudgmentes the

---

1. See D'Ewes, p.366 for 'abuse of corn and grain', and Cromwell, f.90.

2. The words 'and frye' are written below here.

more hevely apon us then our unthankfullnes and the abuse of thes benefittes which he hath so mercifully and in so larg a mesure bestowed apon us.

'And if it should please him to deale more favourably with us then we either deserve or can look for, yet let us call to mynde I pray you that we are not owners but stewardes of the thinges of this world, that we must be called to render an account of this, in the world to come, how we have bestowed the thinges of this world. In the which we may offend 2 wayes, either in wretched keping or in wastfull spending; whereof we may fynd an example to serve for both in on man in the scripture and that is the rich glotton, of whom it is sayd, [he] was clothed in fyn lynen and purple, and fared deliciously every daye, but would not bestowe a lof of bread upon poore Lazarus.[3] /

[ii.] f.177   'I like very well of the matter conteynd in this bill, for it tendes to the taking away of a very foule and manifest abuse of one of the good creatures of God geven us for the necessary sustentation of our life, ffor the encrease and mayntenance wherof many good and holsome lawes have bene made in diverse parlymentes hertofore, and it hath bene very carefully thought of and provided for even in this present parlyment.

'But to what purpose serves it to take care of tillage, if we suffer the fruites of tillage to be consumed in this sort?

'Ther ar 2 sortes of persons very pernicious to the comonwealth in this behalf. The on is that covetouse wreche who, for his owne private lucre and gayne, doth carye over greate quantities of corne into other countries, leving his owne unserved. The other is that miserab[le] and cruell caytif that doth ingrosse and hord it up for a deare yeare, suffring it rather to be eaten with myse and corrupted with mustynes then that his poore honest neighbour should have it at a reasonable prise.

'But in my conscience both these albeit, they do [harm], do not so much offend against the lawe of charite and the dutie they owe to their country and comonweal (I meane the proportion of the corne being equall), as these do that do convert and imploye it apon so vile and bad uses as this is. "*Simulata sanctitas est duplex iniquitas*", saith a doctor of the Church. Counterfett holynes is a double iniquitie, iniquitie in it self and hipocrisie to bote.

'So I am of opynion that it is not so yll that good thinges be utterly loste and spoyld as when they be yll spent and imployd apon yll purposes. For the non user of any good thing is not half so yll as the misuser, althought[4] both be blamewoorthy.

'Is yt not a very lamentable thing that we should bestowe that apon our neckes to the setting fourth of vanitie and pride, which would stanch the hunger of many that starve in the stretes for wante of breade?

'And do we imagyne, that because God of his great goodnes, under her Majestie's moost gracious goverment hath blest this land with peace and all the fruites of peace even almoste for 27 yeares together, that ther can not come 7 leane yeares, as in the tyme of Pharroh, which shall eate up all the fatt which hath bene gathered in the 27 before?

'Looke but back I pray yow into those 7 yeares which went next before these 27 and yow shall finde within the compas of those 7 that the oken branche bare the bread for allmost all the poore people of England.

'Such tymes have byne many tymes, and such tymes may come agayne to sone. For I am persuaded though God have to recken with us for many matters, yet ther is none that will draw downe his plages either more hastely or heavely upon us then our greate unthankfullnes and grevous abuse of his benefittes.

'And if peraventure it should please him in mercy to spare us in this world, yet let us be well assured we shall render a straight accompt in the world to come, for we ar not owners but stewardes of the thinges of this leife which are lent unto us neither to hide in the grounde nor yet to make havock of at our plesure.

'On man may serve for an ensample in both cases. The riche glotton, who was *prodigus avarus*, a monster in nature: *prodigus* in that he bestowed apon his owne back and belly, and that every daye, most delicious meate and fyne lynen apparell; *avarus*, in that he would not vouchsafe poore Lazarus the cromes that fell from his table. This covetouse prodigall wretche is now where? As saith St Austen, he who denyed to a pore begger a bytt of bread to slak his hunger is now in hell, crying for a drop of water to quench his thirst and can not gett it.

'By this that I have spoken, yow percyve my meaning that I like very well of the matter offred in this bill. But when I do consider that the skillfull phisition in the cure of diseases doth know the cause is rather to be loked into then the disease it self, *quia cessante causa cessat et effectus*. Then me thinkes we might leave this course and take a nearer waye to the woode, and gather on bushe that may stopp 2 gappes, that is provide on remedy both for this mischeif and for a nother as yll as this, the which in very dede is the only cause of this. / And that is: to sett downe some reasonable sise apon our ruffes, which are   v. growne to such an outrageous and, as I may say, unconcionable lenght at this daye.

'The substance wherof as yow knowe is fyne holland, cambrick and lawne, all which as they be foreyne comodities and bought at greate and excessive prise, so, they say that knowe it and use it, that they are corrupted and worne out a great dele soner by reason of this starche then otherwise they would be being worne in their owne nature.

'And therfore in this respect, the waste of corne is in a sort more tolerable th[an] the other, because it is a commodite of our owne countrie and settes our owne nation a wor[k]. If then this which yow call starche, was first devised and is only used to stiffen our long ruffes, and that the mean and myddell sise neither nede to use it nor do use it, appoynt as I have sayd a convenient and reasonable lenght to our ruffes, and this starch will sone growe out of request and use. Gett it ageyn into those countrys from whenc it first cam.

'And here I have good occasion to remember what I have hard was sayd both plesantly and yet to good purpose by one in a parlyment, I think about

---

3. See Luke 16, esp. 19–24.   4. The final 't' is characteristic of this scribe.

8 of her Majestie's raigne, in the statute for caching of crowes and rookes,[5] at which tyme great complynt being made that these crowes did destroy mucche good corne and great care also being taken by the Howse for the destroying of them, one as I have hard stood up and sayd: "True it is that these crowes do devoure a great dele of corne and yow do very well to tak this care to se it reformed, but I will tell yow if yow will but hold yow contented but a while and men hold on to fell their woodes as they have begone, yow shall not nede to mak this lawe against these crowes, for they must gett them beyond the sea to brede ther for ther wilbe no dwelling for them here."

'I shall not nede to apply it to our present case for it is apparant.

'But me thinkes I hear on saye, "Yea but sir I pray yow consider that these longes[6] ruffes have lasted now of long tyme, and that they are but a fashon and that as fancye is the begetter of fashions, so as our fancyes chang our fashions will fall awaye. Tyme and experience will mak [them] laye that awaye, wherunto at the first yow shall neither drawe them by reason nor dryve them by lawe. Let them alone yet a litle longer, and yow shall see that some will leave them of because the fashion is taken up of every comen person, other som of necessitie as wearyed with the charge, and peraventure some of conscience [because] they see what inconvenienc growes by them." And truly he that saith so me thinkes he seeth somwhat what an altera[tion] we hav had in hattes, dublett[s] bu[7], and to this purpose will peraventure byd me call to my remembrance what a rule we had about a dosen years past for great hose and double ruffes,[8] the which differs from our case in hand only for that on is double the other long but both wastfull: what watching and warding at every gate for such as did weare them, and yet all to litle purpose, till tyme and experience made them fynd out the incumbrance of the one and the inconvenience of the other.

'So; as tyme and fancy hath begotten our long ruffes and our long heare, which is as unholsome wearing as the other is wastfull, so it may be they will bothe grow out of fashion agayne er it be longe.

'The which albeit it be lykely yet because it is uncertayn I could wishe ther were some consideranc had of it.

'For as towching this bill, the good mening may be frustrated dyverse wayes, by the devise of suche as seke to pervert all good and profitable lawes.'

5. *SR* iv.498–9 for 8 Eliz., c.15 (1566), 'An act for preservation of grain'.
6. *Sic.*
7. *Sic.*

8. See proclamation of 6 May 1562 in P. L. Hughes, J. F. Larkin, *Tudor Royal Proclamations* (3 vols., 1964, 1969), ii.190.

1. Recorder Fleetwood's diary, 23–28 November 1584

Text from BL Lansdowne 41, original, in Fleetwood's hand.
Printed. Wright, *Queen Elizabeth and her Times*, ii.243–5.

Lansdowne 41, f.45

[Addressed 'To my especiall good Lord, my Lord Treasowrer of England'.
Endorsed '29 Novemb[er] 1584
Mr Recorder to my Lord'.]

Dyarium a 22 Novembris usque ad 29.

23 [November].

First there appered in the Parliament Howse the knightes and burgeses, owt of all order, in troops, standing upon the fflowre making strange noises, there being not past vij or viij of the old parliamentes.[1] After this we were all called in to the Whit Hall and there called by name before my Lord Stuerd[2] and the rest of the Counsell, and after that we were sworne where by we loost the oration made by my Lord Chauncellor.[3] And after that Mr Treasourer[4] moved the Howse to make an elleccion of a Speaker, whereuppon he hym selff named my brother Puckeringe who sate next me, and there was not one word spoken. And then I said to my companions abowt me, 'Crie Puckering'; and then they and I begynnynge, the rest did the same. And then Mr Speaker made his excuse standing still in his place, and that done, Mr Treasourer and Mr Controller,[5] being by me called uppon, sitting nere, they rose and sett hym to his place, where indead they shuld have sett hym eyther before his speache or els at the begynynge, and his speache shuld have ben before the cheare. And that done we all departed untill Thursday that the Speaker was presented.

[Thursday, 26 November.]

And after his allowauns and retorne into the Court a bill was redd for order sake, towching the dew observacion the Sonndaies *etc.*

[Friday, 27 November.]

The next daye being Fridaie the said bill was ones agayne redd and committed. The comittees amownted in nosmber to lx at the least, all yonge gentlemen,

---

1. Cf. *Commons*, pp.81–2: 28% of 468 had sat in previous parliaments.
2. The earl of Leicester.
3. Sir Thomas Bromley.
4. Sir Francis Knollys.
5. Sir James Croft.

and at our metyng in the after none xx^{ti} at ones did speake and there wee sate talking and dyd nothing untill night, so that Mr Chauncellor was werie, and then wee departed home.

[Saturday, 28 November.]

Upon Satterday there were twoo or thre bills redd which were devised by my Lord Chieft Baron,[6] one for trialls, an other for demurrers, and a third as towching recusauntes. After this Mr Chauncellor / used a speache for the space of one howre and more. Mr Chauncellor's speache tended to a generalite, concluding upon the safetie of her Majestie. Mr Vizchamberlain[7] followed and his speache was above twoo howrs. His speache tended to particularites and speciall accions and concluded upon the Quene's Highnes' savetie. Befor this tyme I never herd in Parliament the lyke matters uttered and especially the thinges conteyned in the latter speache. They were *magnalia regni*. After this done comittees for this cause were appoynted.

But see what chaunced. A lewd fellowe called Robenson, free of the Skynners and borne in Stawnforth, satt in the Parliament Howse all the wholl daie and herd what was said. He was searched, and nothing found abowt hym. Mr Wylckes, Mr Topclyff, Mr Beale and I were sent to search his lodging but we found nothing. He is in the Seriaunte's custodie. We have made as yet no report.[8]

This mornyng I have examined Coffen of the gard and he haith made confession, the which I do leave with Mr Cofferer.[9]

6. Roger Manwood.
7. Sir Christopher Hatton.
8. D'Ewes, p.334.

9. Apparently John Abington (*CSPD 1547–80*, esp. p.668; *CSPD 1581–90*, p.668).

2. *Thomas Cromwell's journal,* 1 December 1584–29 March 1585

Text from Trinity College, Dublin, MS 1045

Trinity College, Dublin, MS 1045, fos.73–94.[1]

At the parliament begon the xxiij[th] of November in the xxvij[th] yere of the reygne of owr sovereyn ladye Qweene Elizabeth.

Yt was tolde that the Lord Stewerd[2] called the Howse in the Whyte Hall, not befor so used.[3]

Mye firste coominge to the Howse thys parliament was the firste deye of December.

A byll reqwyringe that yt myght be lawfwll for anye person havinge state of inheritance in anye parsonadge impropriat to present to the same and therbye that yt sholde for ever be disapropriat and that yt might also be lawfwll to assigne parte of the profyttes of the parsonadge to the increase of the livinge of the vicar or to the meyntenance of soome schoole or relief of any hospitall, withowt licence to alien[ate] in mortmeyne and withowt dawngier of anye *ad quod damnum*; the ij[d] tyme red and commytted.

A byll reqwyringe that Bocksted in Essex meye make, weave and row cloth aswell as Bockinge and other market townes, ij° red, agreed to be engrossed.

A byll reqwyringe that prediall tythes myght be peyed in suche sorte as theye have beene peyed within xl yeres laste paste, and that ther shalbe but ij libels exhibited for tithes dewe in one yere, the suite to be proseqwuted withowt deley or else costes to be awarded; composytions made with lessees for yeres

Preston in Holdernesse in the cowntye of Lankaster.

e.[4] pp.

c.

---

1. The MS is in poor condition in some places: there is some damage to the edges of pages, and some words/letters are unclear and faint to the point of illegibility. Missing words/letters have been supplied and indicated with the usual square brackets, and uncertain readings are also enclosed in square brackets.
2. The Earl of Leicester.
3. See D'Ewes, p.78 for 1563 where Whitehall is given, though the 'Lower House' appears for 1571 and 1572 (D'Ewes, pp.155, 205).
4. Marginal abbreviations are used throughout in the MS to indicate the progress of bills, and from 10 March, when they came from the Lords. In some cases they do not correspond with the stage reached in the text: so the tithes bill marked with a 'c' for 1 December was in fact committed on 3 December, as is also indicated at that point. These marginal notations may well, therefore, be later additions. ('e' denotes engrossment, and 'p' passing of bills.)

not to be anye cawse to bynde the parsons or vicares; no fine befor open demawnde in the church; no tythe recoverable not demawnded within v yeres: first red.

c.   A byll reqwyringe that parte of an acte made *viij° Elizabethae* restreygninge the caryadge over of Suffolke and Kentish clothes unwrowght meye in respect of Suffolke cowrse clothes under the valewe of v^{li} x^s the cloth be repealed; first red.[5]

c.   A byll reqwiringe that wher the plaintiff or defendant causeth theyse woordes to be entered uppon anye yssewe ioygned ('exeqwted *secundum formam statuti*'), that the sherive shall set downe xlviij names and that eche partye mey withdrawe xij names viij deyes befor the dey [of] returne and for assises xv deyes befor; none to be returned in reall actions except of iiij^{li} freeholde; in everye *tales* eche partye to stryke owt a iiijth part; no chalendge for the hundred but in reall actions: first red.

Commyttees were apoyncted to consider what statutes shall growe owt of force bye th'ende of thys sessyon of Parlyament, of the which my selfe was
nota   one. /

v.   *ij° Decembris.*

ordo Mr Lee, nowe sherive electe, desirethe that his atendance in the Howse meye be borne with, in respect that he ys to atende uppon his office, which was grawnted and that notwithstandinge he sholde continewe a burgesse.[6]

A byll preferred to ratifie conveyances to and from corporations notwith-standing the misnomer of the same, with a proviso not to extende to anye lease already avoyded; firste red.

e.c.   A byll reqwyringe perpetuitye in an acte formerlye made ageynste abuses of informers,[7] reqwyringe also that the defendant meye recover costes recoverable as other costes for the plaintiff, with further corporall punishement restreygninge the promoter to compownd; ij° red and commytted to me and others, Mondeye apoyncted in the Temple church.

A byll reqwyringe that in actions of the case det and contracte the shyer whe[re] the venwe ys leyed meye be alowed as parte of th'issewe, first red.

iij° Decembris.

c.   A byll that staple fishe and linge sholde be browght in Englishe botoms x yeres as bye *xxiij° Elizabethae* was befor enacted, first red.[8]

A byll reqwyringe that towneshyppes sholde not be chardged with the children borne owt of wedlocke, that the mother of suche bastarde as soone as yt was manifest that she was with childe sholde be had to the howse of correction, whypped, and hardly used in diet and otherwyse, the reputed father uppon dewe examination commytted to the ieyle withowt beyle for a yere, whypped ones everye monthe and bownde no more to commyt anye such facte and also to his good behaviowr; yf departed owt of the cowntreye me[y] be fetched owt of any other cowntye; the takinge of a seconde wyfe, living the former and no lawfwll divorce had, to be felonye: first red.

e.   A byll to make perpetuall a clawse of an acte in *v°* and *xiij° Elizabethae*

bye which was made lawfwll for Englishe men to carye heringes and   pp.
sea fishe beyonde the sea in shyppes which be crosse seyled and dischardged of subsydye, custom or poun[dage]; the ij^d tyme red, agreed to be
engrossed.[9]

A byll that wher defawt groweth in not aprehendinge persons in another   c.
hundred adioygninge to the hundred wher the robbery ys commytted, that
they meye be chardged with the moytye of the forfyture; no person to be
chardged which maketh freshe suite for v myles; he that refuseth / to make   f.74
freshe suite to be xx deyes imprisoned; yf anye of th'offendors be taken and the
reste disclosed, no penaltye to the cowntrey: ij° red and commytted.

A byll that no market or feyre sholde be kept, ware shewed, or stall buylte   c.
uppon the Sondeye, and where feyres were befor on the Sondeye the same to
be kept within iij deyes befor or after; an exception for heringes bye English   p.
mariners; no unlawfwll games, pleyes, bearebeytinges, wakes, kingegames and
suchelyke, hawkinge, huntinge, or rowinge with bardges uppon the Sondeye,
nor any . . . [illegible] for common cawses duringe the tyme of the service or
sermons: firste red after that yt was browght in bye the commyttees.

A byll entitle[d] 'A banke of generall charytye to relieve common neces-   r.
sytye' by which was reqwyred every man's beste garment at the tyme of his
death to be given to the erection of vij bankes at London, Yorke, Norwiche,
Coventry, Westchester, Bristowe and Exceter, and certeyn shyers alotted to
every of them, the stocke as yt myght be spared lente after the rate of v^li *per*
hundred to the Qweene and such as had neede, with diverse other lyke
circumstances: firste red, greatlye mislyked, put to the qwestion and reiected.

The byll concerninge tythes, ij° red and commytted.   c.

iiij° Decembris.

A byll that no shoomake[10] sholde be used in dyinge of sylck and lyke stuffes
uppon peyne that the stuffe so dwyed, or valewe therof shalbe forfeyted, the
moytye to the Qweene, the other moytye to suche person as wyll seaze the
same; first red.

A byll reqwyringe to revive a statute made in v Elizabeth[11] to have
continewance for x yeres that no hoye or plate sholde crosse the seas except to
Cane[12] and Norweye and farther that for everye tonne weyght caryed over sea
in any vessell ther sholde be [MS torn] mariner, that everye mariner myght
carye so muche in the shyppe as [? his][13] wages for that voyadge amownteth to,
and wheras [MS torn] flattes, shelves and chanels have beene used as common
to mariners and fyshermen, that the same may so continewe; firste red.

A motion was made on the behalfe of Mr Marmaduke Wivalde[14] beinge   *ordo*

5. 8 Eliz, c.6 (1566) in *SR*, iv.489.
6. D'Ewes, pp.335–6; *Commons sub* Lee, Edward.
7. 18 Eliz, c.5 (1575–6) in *SR*, iv.615–16.
8. 23 Eliz, c.7 (1580–81) in *SR*, iv.668–9.
9. 5 Eliz, c.5 (1562–3), 13 Eliz, c.11 (1571) in *SR*, iv.422–8 (clause i, 422–3), 545–6.

10. i.e. sumac.
11. 5 Eliz, c.5 (1562–3) in *SR*, iv.422–8 (clause vi, 423).
12. i.e. Caen.
13. MS torn.
14. Wivell.

visyted with sicknesse, that in respect therof he myght have leave [of]¹⁵ absence for a tyme. /

v. p. A byll concerninge heringe and sea fishe transported, iij° red and passed.

p. A byll concerninge Bocksted, iij° red and passed.

p.e. A byll concerninge the better usinge of the Sabothe deye, ij° red, agreed to be engrossed.

v° Decembris.

A byll prescribinge an othe to be taken bye th'undersherive and forme therof for the dewe returne of wry[t]es, first red.

c. A byll, everye man demurringe uppon any byll shall set downe the cawses of his demurrer that after iudgement execution shall not be steyed by wryt of error notwithstandinge that the defendant shall put in bonde to repeye the moneye yf the wryt of error passe ageynst him, no wryt of error after tryall bye verdict, and that wryttes of error meye be served of iudgementes in the Kinge's Benche, befor the iudges of the Common Place and barons of the Exchequer: commytted to me and others, but no deye prefixed; firste red and commytted to me and others.

p. The byll for better observation of the Sabothe deye, iij° red and passed.

vij° Decembris.

A byll recytinge a statute made *v° Elizabethae* concerninge tanned lether, that none but tanners meye sell or put awey any tanned lether unwrought and th'executers of such tanners, first red.¹⁶

r. A byll that none on the north of Trent sholde knitt hose and peticotes and suche lyke except th'inhabitantes of the towne of Richemond and other corporat townes, first red and reiected.

c. A byll to asswre certeyn landes bargeyned bye Edward Fisher to Mr Christopher Puckeringe, nowe Speaker, George Chune and Giles Flud; first red, commytted to commyttees to go to the seyed Fisher and examin the cawse and make reporte, his owne presence in the Howse not reqwyred in respect that he ys in execution.

p.p. The byll of Boxsted returned from the Lords with an addition extending the same to the towne of Langh[a]m, the additions thrise red and passed.

e. The byll of promoters brought in bye the commyttees, twyse red, to be engrossed.

c. The byll concerning Suffolk clothes, ij° red and commytted. /

f.75 *viij° Decembris.*

c. A byll that from hensforth no oke, ashe, or elme in Sussex sholde be felled, shied, topped, or lopped, or imployed abowt yron milles, and that for every vj lode of cole and iij tonne of yron, one lode of cinder sholde be bestowed in amending the highe weyes, and reqwyring the repeale of a proviso made in the statute *xxiij° Elizabethae* concerning woode expended in yron milles, bye which ther was an exemption of the wylde of Kent and Sussex within the compasse limited bye the statute; ij° red and commytted, in which commytment yt was thowght reosonable that those which had iron mills sholde be spared.[17]

The Speaker made a motion to the Howse concerninge certeyn knyghtes returned, not beinge chosen at the first cownty accordinge to the statute, whyther theye ought to continewe burgesses. Agreed that yf anye suche matter appered in the record, the Howse myght take notice therof; otherwyse not. The examination wherof was referred to certeyn commyttees.

The Lievetenawnt of the Tower[18] made a motion to the Howse that th'armor of the papistes myght be commytted to the custody of soome others leste yt myght be imployed ageynst her Majestye uppon any exployte. Agreed that commyttees sholde be apoyncted to drawe a byll, which was don.

ix° Decembris.

A byll reqwyringe that no strawngiers sholde be suffered to make glasse (or theyr children) and that no glasse howses sholde be kept within xxx myles of London, firste red.

A byll that no moore, hades or heathe sholde be burnte in Yorkshyer, Northumberland, Comberland or Westmerlande by anye person betweene the laste of Marche and firste of October uppon peyne of xl[s]; yf th'offendor be not fownd the towneshyp in which th'offense ys commytted to leese xl[s] except they put yt owt within an hower; a proviso, not to extende to suche as burne the same to mende the grownde for corne: first red.

The byll of tanners, ij° red and commytted to commyttees of the which I am one: Saterdeye the deye of meetinge.   c.

The byll of informers, beinge engrossed, iij° red, and longe disputed of, in fine agreed to be commytted anewe in respect that th'inforcing of th'informer to persewe was thowght very perilowse, which was after don and the same browght in ageyn, all being cut of but the continewance of th'olde law.

The byll of th'undersherives' othe, ij° red and commytted. /   c.

[x° Decembris][19]   v.

The byll for punishement of the mothers and reputed fathers of bastardes, ij° red and commytted.   c.

The byll ageynst the usinge of shoemake in dwyinge, ij° red and.[20]

A byll for reformation of errors in fines, firste red.

A byll for meyntenance of Plimowthe haven, first red.

Mr Recorder[21] made reporte that he and other the commyttees had accordinge to the truste reposed in them examined the decrees and other circumstances concerninge the byll exhibited for assurance of certeyn landes in Warwykshyer from Mr Edward Fisher to Christopher Puckering and others and that he had also conferred with the seyed Edward Fisher and hys wyfe,   e.

15. MS torn.
16. 5 Eliz, c.8 (1562–3) in *SR*, iv.429–36.
17. 23 Eliz, c.5 (1580–1) in *SR*, iv.667.
18. Sir Owen Hopton.
19. See D'Ewes, p.337.
20. *Sic.*
21. William Fleetwood.

who colde not denye the reosonablenesse of that which ys reqwyred, and had also warned him to have his cownsell there. Wheruppon yt was enqwyred whyther he had any cownsell there, and none being fownde, and Mr Heale besides declaringe that he was hertofor of cownsell with him and had sent woorde to him that he meante not to geynseye the byll, the same had a ij^d readinge and agreed to be engrossed.

xj Decembris.

A byll reqwyringe that xij wardes in Westmi[n]ster meye have xij burgesses to be named and chosen bye the deane or his steTerd, they to remeyne for one yere and so from yere to yere duringe lyfe, except bye soome offense they deserve to be removed; those xij to name xxiiij asistanstes;[22] yf the party chosen as burgesse refuse the place, he shall leese x^{li}, the asistant in lyke case to forfeyt xl^s; ij chief burgesses to be also chosen, they with the deane or his steTerd to have the punishement of incontinencye, breache of peace, inmates' anoyances, and such lyke within the lyberty, and to make orders not repugnant to the Qweene's prerogative or the lawes of the realme, as London dothe, with a proviso for the deanes and all other officers' former libertyes: firste red.

r.   A byll that in cityes, market townes, and other corporat townes the chief officers there maye have lyke awctorytye and meanes to take order for peyment of tythes as the cytye of London hathe by the statute of *xxxvij Henrici viij*;[23] where ther be no meyres, there iiij iustices of peace and vj of the substanciallest inhabitantes of the towne to have the direction: first red. /

f.76 p.   The byll for th'asswrance to Mr Puckeringe and others, iiij° red and passed.[24]

A byll reqwyringe that after Michelmasse next no persons be suffered to transport anye brode clothes or carzeys beyonde sea befor the same wrowght, rowed and dyed here in Englonde otherwyse than herafter foloweth, *viz*, from Michelmasse 1585 for every nine clothes unwrowght one wrowght, from Michelmasse 1586 for every viij unwrowght ij wrowght, from Michelmasse 1587 for every vij unwrowght iij wrowght, from Michelmasse 1588 for every vj unwrowght iiij wrowght, from Michelmasse 1589 for everye v unwrowght other v wrowght; none to dwye or worke any clothes but in cities, borowghes, or market townes; the clothes so wrowght or dwyed to be alowed bye the wardens of the clothe workers of London or chyef officers of townes corporat; no dyer to use any gall, tassell,[25] logwood, vitriall, slyx,[26] or other thinges hurtefull in theyr dwyinge; every cloth anealed to be viewed by the chyef officers befor the same be dwyed and suche market townes as have no suche officers yf yt be false to be marked with the lettre F; that yt maye be lawfwll to make and dwye cloths in suche sorte as the merchawnt shall reqwyre, notwithstandinge any statute made to the contrary; a proviso that yt shalbe lawfwll to worke clothes in all places wher yt ys nowe used, so as they observe the orders which others be subiect unto: first red.

A byll that no sherive shall levye anye yssewes but of hym by whom yt ys dewe, and that in all iuryes herafter to be returned an addition be added to the iuror returned as well in the *venire facias* and as[27] every processe subseqwent, and like sorte in the processe yssewinge owt of th'Exchequer.

A byll that no beyle for felony be taken of lesse summe than xl^{li} the principall and xx^{li} apiece the suretyes; for the peace and good behavior xx^l the principall and x^{li} apiece the suretyes; eche surety to be worth xx^{li} in goodes or xl^s in lande; no beyles in London or Westmister but bye ij iustices of peace wherof one to be of the quorum: first red.

A byll for the helpe of grawntes made to and from corporations notwith-   c.
standing the misnomer, ij° red and commytted.

xij° Decembris.

Mr Sans[28] chosen sherive of Kent desireth liberty of the Howse to departe, which was grawnted. /

Yt beinge declared that Mr Hall returned burgesse for Grawntham absenteth   v.
him self, yt was answered that the cawse therof was in respect soome orders   c.
hertofor passed ageynst him in the Howse, which were theruppon called upon to be red, and theruppon one order made beinge wantinge, th'examination of the orders was referred to me and others and order taken that Mr Arthur Hall sholde be browght to the Howse uppon Mondey and then the Howse to resolve theyr determinations concerning him.

Mr Bevell[29] compleygned that uppon speache uttered bye him in the Howse, another member of the same had chalendged him and used diverse unseemly speaches to him and tolde him that he had made manye lyes, and desired reformation. Agreed that the wryt of his returne sholde be firste dewlye considered, in that uppon his speaches, yf the wryt sholde warrawnt so muche, yt remeyned dowbtfull whyther he were a lawfull member of the Howse or no; and therfor the dealinge in the motion steyed untill reporte made by the commyttees in that behalfe.

The Lords, having delivered certeyn notes in wrytinge to owr commyttees conteygning soome alterations in the byll which we sent to them for the better observation of the Sabooth deye, the same were declared and severally con-sidered of bye the Howse and theruppon owr commyttees sent to them to make answer.

A byll sent to us from the Lords for remedyes uppon frawdulent conveyances.

A byll that notwithstandinge the imbezillinge aweye of the wryt and diverse other partes of a recovery, or notwithstandinge any razure, that the same sholde remeyne good and the recovery not to be reversed and that the wryttes of *sommoneas ad warrantizandum* sholde be *a quindena ad quindenum* and that no frawdulent devise sholde hinder the purchasor; first red.

A byll reqwyringe that Edward Fisher myght have libertye to sell parte of his landes for the peyment of his creditors, to bwinde him and his wyf and th'eyres

---

22. *Sic.*
23. 37 Hen VIII, c.12 (1545) in *SR*, iii.998–1000.
24. i.e. Fisher's bill.
25. i.e. 'teasel'?
26. i.e. 'slick'?
27. *Sic.* 'as in'?
28. Sondes, Michael (*Commons*).
29. Bevill, Robert (*Commons*).

of theyr bodyes and such as have anye estate to theyr or anye of theyr use; first red.

A byll browght from the Lordes concerning Sir Thomas Lucy.

c.   A byll that additions be made to the names of iurors herafter to be returned, ij° red and commytted.

A byll that everye Jesuit, seminarye prieste made in any place, and everye other prieste made within this realme accordinge to the Roomishe order, or by any pretending anye iurisdiction from the Pope nowe being within the realme, f.77   made since the Qweene's reygne, shall depart the same / within xl deyes after th'ende of this session of Parliament or els adiudged to be a treytor; yf anye of them after returne or abide here, lykewyse a treytor; theyr eyders and comforters, knowinge them to be suche, lykewyse treytors; all such being beyonde seas, not returninge uppon warning and submytting them selves, yf theye returne after, lykewyse treytors; yf anye releeve them or any of theyr colledges by any devise whatsoever, then in the praemunire; yf anye sende over sea anye of his chyldren or other person, except merchawntes sendinge over for merchawndize, or mariners, withowt licence of iiij°ʳ of the Cownsell, lykewyse in the praemunire; a proviso not to[30] extende to any person which shall carye over anye such person as befor ys mencioned so he set downe his name in wrytinge, declare where and when he tooke orders and howe longe he hathe beene in the realme: first red.

xiiij° Decembris.

A byll reqwyringe confirmation of the Qweene's letters patentes to Mr Water Rawley bye which the Qweene hathe grawnted unto him all suche lande beinge beyonde sea owt of the iurisdiction of any Christian kinge which he shall at his costes discover and get, and to take suche subiectes with him to dwell there, and they meye passe, anye statute to the contrarye notwithstandinge; the same to be helde of the Qweene by homadg and a vᵗʰ parte of the profyttes of the mineralls of golde and silver ore to be to her Majestye; they all to be the Qweene's homadgers; none to dwell or coome there but suche as he shall licence; the Englishe men's children borne there to be denizens; he also to have auctorytye to establishe lawes there not repugnant to the doctrine established in Englond or lawes of the same; the Lord Treasurer and iiij°ʳ of the Cownsell to have auctorytye to give licence to him to transporte anye thinge which he shall think necessary; recytinge also that he hathe already discovered a place called Windagancoza, desiringe the confirmation therof to him accordinge to the same letters patentes: first red.

Diverse bylls of compleyncte were exhibited to the Howse bye Sir Thomas Lucy and others conteygning grief conceaved bye the subiectes of the restreygning of so manye good preachers, of th'insufficiencye and wante of preachers, for theyr non-residence; and reqwyred that a petition myght be made to the Qweene for reformation. In fine the motion steyed in respect the Qweene had promysed to have a care therof.

ij bylls browght from the Lordes, the one concerninge the Saboth which we
sent up, the other concerning the assises and sessions to be helde at Carnarvan
in Wales. /

A byll that yf the Qweene or anye other be defrawded or incombred by
anye frawdulent conveyances made to anye person eyther in landes or leases
hertofor purchased *bona fide* not beinge copihold, by meanes of any secret and
frawdulent conveyance or encombrance made since the Qweene's reygne, that
he meye compleygne in the Starrechamber eyther of the partye using the
frawde or of anye other cleyming under them, and that the iudges there
apoyncted to the number of xij shall have power to heare and determin the
cawse, and that such order shalbe as effectuall as anye acte of Parliament in that
behalfe; a proviso that conveyances not being known to be made *bona fide*, in
consideration of mariadge or for th'advawncement of wyfe or childe or money
peyed or other recompense given, which shall not be inroled within a yere,
shalbe deemed fraudulent; a ij^d proviso not to extende to assurances made from
the purchasor bye fraudulent conveyance, the same being made *bona fide* by any
mattier of recorde or other lawfull or manifest meanes uppon good consideration, so as such ij^d purchasor were not privye or consentinge to the frawde; the
lyke for frawde of landes herafter to be purchased; provided alwayes that
notwithstandinge the conveyances hertofor made be fraudulent, yf the same be
inroled in the Chauncery, Kinge's Benche, or Common Place befor the
purchase hereafter to be made, that then the same shall not be impeached;
another proviso that yf the secret conveyance exceede not or concern more
then C akers of grownd, then the same beinge inroled in the role of the
sessions of the cowntye and openly procleymed there at the sessions nexte after
the date of the conveyance, that then the same shall not be impeached;
reqwyringe also that a brief transcript be made of all statutes merchawnt and
staple herafter to be knowledged, within vj monthes after the knowledginge
therof, and to be certefied to the clerke of the statutes at Westmister, who for
vj^d shall inrole the same, which yf yt be not don, then the same shall in respect
of such as shall herafter purchase any landes be deemed a secret conveyance;
that the partyes aforseyed shall also have power to inflict anye punishement to
the parties usinge fraude or beinge privye or assenting therto other then losse
of lyfe or member; yf anye person assentinge to such fraudulent conveyance do
not disclose the same to the party grieved within vj monthes or to the Lord
Chawncelor, then he shalbe punished di;[31] a provision made for revivinge of
suites abated by mariadg or death; ther ys also a proviso for all proceeding with
the ordinary number in such cases untill the tyme of the iudgement; the clerkes
of the inrolementes shall take but ij^d for a yeres search; the clerkes which ar to
inrole the assurances shall accordingely inrole the same and dewly keepe the
recordes and a kalendar therof uppon peyne of losse of theyr office and
punishement by fine and imprisonment; the clerk shall take but iij^s iiij^d for a
role; no clerkes for copyes of English byll or other mattier shall take but vj^d the

---

30. *Sic.*   31. *Sic.* 'demi'.

sheete, which sheete shalbe xv inches long and xj brode, the margent to be but ij inches brode; the acte to continewe for x yeres and to th'ende of the parliament folowing. /

f.78   In the afternoone.

A byll reqwyring that yf anye person pretendinge titell to the Crowne do make any invasion into the realme with ij^m persons or more, not having anye invasion made uppon them befor, or cawse any rebellion to be made, or yf anye rebellion be made for any person or anye hurte intended to the Qweene's person bye or for any person making such pretence, that such person and persons convinced therof by xxiiij^ty prescribed by lawe beyng warned to coome, and the same subscribed bye them inroled in the Chauncery and procleymed in London and York, then such person and theyr yssewe shalbe disabled to cleyme the crowne herafter; the eyders and assisters of such offendor, or affirmer of anye ryght in any person disabled, to be treytors; made lawfull to pursewe to the death all persons bye whom or for whom any suche acte shalbe attempted; a proviso that the Qweene uppon better lyking of the heyre of any suche person meye restore the seyed heyre and theyr heyres to suche ryght as they befor had, and not otherwyse, and as yf the partye offending were dead: first red.

r.   The byll for the livinges of the ministery in corporat and merket townes according to London disputed of, the Howse divided uppon the commytting or not commytting of the byll, and the no preveyled and so the byll reiected.

c.   Mr Rawleye's byll ij° red, argewed uppon and in fine commytted.

xv° Decembris.

c.   A byll for the sale of Edwarde Fisher's landes, ij° red and commytted to me and others.

A byll for assurance of certeyn landes to Sir Water Lucye, first red; *viz*, of Haversham and in Buckinghamshyer generall and Byshoppes Hatton in Warwykeshyer to Mr Astley.[32]

A byll reqwyringe that th'assises and sessions for the cowntye of Carnarvan in Wales meye alweyes be kepte there except in tyme of soome plage, first red.

c.   The byll for observation of orders in Westmister, ij° red and commytted.

e.   The byll for the Qweene's safetye, ij° red, to be engrossed.

e.   The byll ageynst Jeswytes, ij° red, to be engrossed.

xvj° Decembris.

The byll from the Lords for the assises and sessions to be kept at Carnarvan, ij° red. /

v.   The byll for hwe and crye, reformed bye the commyssioners, first red.

A byll reqwyringe that the delegates myght be persons certeyn, theye to have a fee and not to be advocates in other ecclesiasticall cowrtes, the regester there not to deale else where, firste red.

c.   The byll of recoveryes, ij° red and commytted having manye faultes fownde in yt.

The byll of the Saboth deye, th'amendimentes therin considered and additions made to one of the amendimentes, and so agreed to be sent to the Lords for a conference.

The byll for continewance of certeyn estatutes, firste red.

xvij° Decembris.

The byll for asswrance of certeyn landes to Sir Thomas Lucye, ij° red.

Mr Rawleye's byll browght in, excepted ageynst for ij cawses, specyally one in respect of lybertye gyven to him to take anye person with him which ys wyllinge to goe; the other in that yt was made lawful to carye anye thinge over bye licence: agreed to be engrossed.

ij bylls from the Lords, the one for restoringe in bloode of the Lord Thomas Heyward, the other for pavinge of Newerke uppon Trent.

The byll ageynst Jeswytes, iij° red and passed.

Uppon readinge of this byll, not longe befor yt was put to the qwestion, Doctor Parrey stept up and used woordes to thys effect, that he favored not the Jeswytes or seminaryes but was to speake for Englishe subiectes. He meante to saye no to the byll. He added that the byll was very peryllowse; nothinge therin but bloode, nothing but confiscation of owr goodes, not to the Qweene but to others; nothinge but dispeyer and terror to us all. He sayed he thowght the byll wolde passe thys Howse and the Lordes. He wolde reserve hys reosons to showe to the Qweene.

Uppon this speache, greatly mislyked, yt cam to the qwestion what sholde be don with him. Yt was argewed whyther he myght be commytted or not. Wheruppon the example of the commyttinge of Doctor Storye to the Tower for seyinge *ve regno cuius rex est puer* in the tyme of Kinge Edward the vj^th, the commytting of Mr Copley in Queene Marye's, the commytting of Mr Wentworth, a good member of the Howse, and of Mr Hall was vowched. In fine he was commytted to the serieant and after sent for in and interrogated whyther he wolde acknowledge hys fawlte and shewe hys reosons. He confessed the speach; he seyed [he] was still of the same opinion and meant / still   f.79 to reserve to him selfe the disclosinge therof to the Qweene or one grave lorde of the Cownsell, and hoped to be delivered; and theruppon returned to the Serieante's custody to be farther considered of.³³

xviij° Decembris.

The byll of delegates ij° red and commytted, of the which I was one.³⁴   c.

Mr Rawleye's byll iij° red and a proviso added and the byll passed.   p.

Mr Vicechamberleyn³⁵ declared from her Majestye that wheras she had desired t'understande the poynctes of the byll which wee had in hande for her Majestye's safetye, that he, havinge declared to her Majestye the summe therof, that her Highnesse did verye thankefullye accepte the great care we had of her

---

32. *Sic.*
33. For Story and Copley see *Commons*, ed. S.T. Bindoff, *sub*, Story, John and Copley, Thomas.
34. i.e. the bill on appeals from ecclesiastical courts (D'Ewes, p.341).
35. Sir Christopher Hatton.

preservacion, which he seyed that her Majestye seyed (but he myght not so seye) was more then her merite; notwithstanding she depended uppon the providence of God and was contented, in respecte of soome scruple, conceaved in soome, howe the alowance of the proviso myght be anye weyes contrariant to theyre othe formerly taken, that the proviso myght be lefte owt, and also that the acte sholde not extende to th'yssewe of th'offendor excepte th'issewe were also fownd fawltye; which was verye thankefwllye accepted.

He also declared that soome of the Privye Cownsell had also had conference with Doctor Parreye, who had declared hys reosons to the satisfaction of her Highnesse wherfor he refused to give his consent to the byll and whye he refused to declare his reosons in the Howse, and that [her] Majestye was satisfyed to accept his answer in good parte, notwithstanding commended and alowed verye well of th'order of owr proceedinge ageynst him; notwith-standinge, yf he submytted him humblye to the Howse and acknowledged his offense, wyshed us to pardon the same. Wheruppon he was sent for in, who beinge coome in, kneeled downe uppon hys [knees] a convenyent tyme and then, beynge wylled to ryse, he did ther first excuse him selfe in that he was never of the Howse befor, secondlye, publiqwelye confesse[d] that his speache was rashe, undiscreete and inconsiderate, and that he had therin commytted a fawlte and given iuste occasion of offense, wherof he asked forgivenesse of the hole Howse; and theruppon was dischardged. /

v.   *xix° Decembris.*

An[36] byll from the Lordes that all immediat tenawntes in Newerk uppon Trent meye bye[37] chardged with the paving of the streetes befor theyr houses and to continewe the same bye the order of the meyor and other officers of the towne; first red.

p.p.   A byll from the Lordes for the restoringe in bloode of the Lord Thomas Hawarde, ij° red and iij° red and passed.

A byll for additions to be made to iurors to be returned, reformed by the commyttees, first red.

c.   A byll for hue and crye ij° red and ageyn commytted.

c.   A byll for continewance of certeyn estatutes, of the which the byll for killinge of crowes was reiected, others offered to consideration, *viz.*, the acte of vagabondes, the acte of polityqwe constitutions concerning the navye, the acte concerninge foreygne wares *etc.*; first red.

xxj° Decembris.

c.   A byll for sale of Edward Fisher's landes for peyment of hys debtes, ij red after the commyttinge and ageyn commytted to the former commyttes of the which I was one.

e.   The byll of hue and crye ij° red after the ij[d] commytment, to be engrossed.

c.   The byll concerninge the othe of undersherives browght in bye the commyttees and anewe commytted to them.

Mr Vicechamberleyn returned thankes from the Qweene's Majestye for the great thankes we had sent her, which she wolde not confesse to have deserved *etc.*

The mattiers of compleynct exhibited from diverse cowntreyes concerninge the unlearnednesse of the ministery, griefs in respect of deprivations and suspensions of preachers refusing to make subscriptions and to answer to othe for small cawses, and the abuse of excommunication and suche lyke, being reduced into wryting, were bye the commyttees, of the which I was one, delivered to the Lords with reqwest to them for conference of meanes for redresse. Theye after sent for us ageyn, declaringe that they had red the same in theyr Howse, thowght not convenient to use conference untill the Qweene's consent had, in respect the Qweene's Majestye had undertaken therof; notwithstandinge, that they had agreed that the lords of the Privye Cownsell of theyr Howse sholde acqueynct her Majestye therwith, and theruppon that at the next session we sholde have answer. /

The byll for the pavinge of Newerke uppon Trent ij° and iij° red and passed.   f.80 p.

Mr Sollicitor[38] made report to the Howse that the commyttees had hard the cownsell of bothe partes concerninge the knyghtes returned for Huntington shyer, that they had agreed not to deale with examination of any matter in facte betweene Mr Crumwell and Mr Dorrington, but fownde soome imperfection in the forme of the returne, *vz.*, soome variance betweene th'indentures and th'indorsement, but desired a farther tyme to consider of presidentes in that behalfe.

A byll for the bringinge of the river of Mewe by agreement with the owners   c. to Plimowth, ij° red and commytted.

The byll for disapropriatinge of parsonadges browght in by the commyttees, first red.

The byll ageynst glasse howses ij° red and commytted.   c.

Mr Sollicitor made a motion that commyttees myght be apoyncted bye the Howse to consider of soome lawes nowe [out?] of use or unnecessarye, betweene this and the next session, that the same myght be revoked, which was very well lyked of and commyttees apoyncted for that purpose.

The Lord Chyef Justice of England, the Master of the Roles, the Lord Chyef Justice of the Common Pleas and the Lord Chyef Baron[39] cam to the Howse, browght with them the Qweene's letters patentes bye which theye declared that her Majestye had auctoryzed certeyn of the Higher Howse to adiorne the Parliament untill the iiij[th] of Februarye next, wheruppon owr Howse brake up.

iiij° Februarij.

A byll that the ij wardens and xij assistantes in Rochester meye taxe all persons   c. possessed of anye the contributorye landes hertofor chardged with the meyntenance of Rochester bridge towardes the meyntenance therof, that ij of

---

36. *Sic.*
37. *Sic.*
38. Sir Thomas Egerton.

39. Sir Christopher Wray, Sir Gilbert Gerard, Sir Edmund Anderson, Sir Roger Manwood.

everye parish sholde be present at everye election uppon peyne of xx[s]; ij° red and commytted.

e.   The byll towching the othe of undersherives, firste red.

c.   The byll concerninge Westmister browght in bye the commyttees and ageyn commytted.

The byll concerninge hue and crye iiij° red and ageyn commytted.

v° Februarij. /

v. c.   A byll from the Lords recytinge that the Qweene bye letters patentes hath encorporated a colledge in Oxford bye the name of provoste and schollers of Qweene's Colledge in Oxford and warden of the hospitall of God's House in Sowthampton and assured all theyr lands to them, desiring the confirmation of the letters patentes and that yt meye be enacted that theye shall enioye the landes and that the state of the lessees not exceeding xxj yeres shalbe renewed, yf above xxj yeres then made good for xxj yeres uppon reoosnable covenawntes; twise red and commytted.

e.   The bill that bye presentation to a parsonadge impropriat the same meye be disapropriat, that for x yeres men meye conveye or devise of landes for meyntenance of preachers, curates, poore people and schooles of learning, a proviso that none be presented to suche churche but preachers and that bye non residency or takinge a ij[d] benefice the person presented shall leese this presentation; ij° red, to be engrossed.

e.   The byll towchinge the othe of undersherives, ij° red, to be engrossed.

vj° Februarij.

p.   The byll concerninge the undersherives othe, iiij° red and passed.

The byll concerninge hue and crye beynge browght in bye the commyttees, agreed that an addition browght in bye them shold be added to yt.

p.   The byll concerninge impropriations iiij° red and passed.[40]

viij° Februarij.

p.   The byll of hue and crye iiij° red and passed.

p.-p.   The byll concerninge Qweene's Colledge in Oxforde iiij° red and passed.

r.   The byll from the Lords for remedye ageynst frawdulent conveyances ij° red, longe debated and greatlye impugned. In fine yt grewe to the question whyther yt sholde be commytted or no, and the Howse theruppon divided and the no preveyled.

ix° Februarij.

e.   The byll for dewe levyinge of yssewes after the commytment ij° red, to be engrossed.

iij bylls sent up to the Lords *vz.* concerninge hue and crye, the byll concerning disapropryinge of impropriations, and the byll concerninge an othe to be ministred to undersherives and other ministers. /

f.81   A byll for confirmation of the hospitall of St Jhon Baptiste in Elye to Clare Hall in Cambridge accordinge to the Qweene's letters patentes, first red.

The byll that wher iurors bye lawe were to be of xl^s freeholde, that nowe theye sholde [be] of iiij^li freeholde; uppon everye *habeas corpora* uppon the first returne x^s yssewes shalbe returned, uppon the ij^d xx^s, uppon the iij^d xxx^s, and after alweyes dobled; and lastlye that ij hundreders shall suffise: browght in bye the commyttees, first red.

x° Februarij.

A byll that no strawngier or strawngier's childe sholde use any glasse howse[41] except, for everye ij straungers that he employe for making therof, he employe one Englishe man and instruct hym to make the same; no glasse howse from hence forthe to be kept within xxij myles of London, vij myles of Guylford, or iiij^or myles of the downes: first red after yt was browght yn by the committes.

A byll that white and red clothes made in Glocester shire and Worster shire, and other shires of like makinge, which heretofore by lawe owght to be vij quarters broad, shall from hencfor[th]e be allowed if theie were vj quarters and a half broad; firste red.

A bill requyring that from hencforthe none showld be allowed to prynt any booke, other then such as be nowe stationers or have beene vij yeares prentyce to some prynter, nor to print any booke except the same be first examined and allowed of by suche as have aucthorytie; that such orders as have bene hertofore made by the Companye of the Statyoners and suche as shall be made hereafter by the allowaunce of the Lord Chauncelor or Lord Treasurer[42] shall be observed by all men; none to prynt any bookes untell he have certefied what number he will prynt; a proviso for such as be lycenced for the Queene, another proviso made not to preiudice the grauntes made unto the uneversities, another proviso for the Queene's printer: first red, and very much misliked. /

The bill towching Rochester brydge, *tertio* red and passed.   v. p.

A bill requyring that such as be put from the spirituall promotions, and such others as be admitted into the ministry and have no spirituale promotions, maie, during such tyme only as thie[43] shall not have any spirituall promocion, take leases and buy and sell as other men doe, the statute of *xxj° Henrici viij* notwithstanding; first red.[44]

A bill concerning the leiving[45] of issews, *tertio* red and passed.   p.

The bill for the better sufficiency of jurors, *secundo* red.[46]

This deye diverse disclosed that theye were served with subpenas and desired priviledge, wheruppon Mr Recorder, Mr Sans, and mye selfe, atended bye the Serieant, were sent to mye Lord Chawncelor to dischardge the partyes, which he refused to do except we colde shew soome recorde in theyr cowrt

---

40. The sentence is crossed through in the MS, though D'Ewes, p.346 records the reading on this day.
41. The MS' handwriting changes at the word 'except'.
42. Sir Thomas Bromley, and Lord Burghley.
43. *Sic.*
44. 21 Hen VIII, c.13 (1529) in *SR*, iii.292–6.
45. i.e. 'levying'.
46. The handwriting reverts to the first hand here.

to prove lyke alowance at other tyme befor, consideringe theyr bodyes ar not atached.

xj° Februarij.

The byll of Clare Hall ij° red.

    A byll for streyght whytes firste red.

p.   The byll for more sufficiency of iurors, iij° red and passed.

    Thys deye we sent up v bylls to the Lords, one concerning Rochester bridge, a ij^d concerninge the levying of yssewes uppon iurors, a iij^d more sufficiencie of iurors, a iiijth concerninge the pavinge of Newerk, a vth concerninge the sessions to be kept at Carnarvan; of the which the ij laste cam befor from the Lords.

    A byll that the water beyly uppon the Thamis from Stanes to Cicester shall look to the observation of the lawes made concerninge fish uppon peyne of x^{li}, not to let anye parte of his office uppon peyne of x^l, to keepe a cowrt in everye shyer of his beylywyk uppon peyne of x^{li}; first red.[47]

    Yeasterdaie one Mr Stepney, a member of this Howse, havinge made complaint that one Mr Kerle during the session had taken forth a subpena agaynst him out of the Starre Chamber, and that afterwards had also procured an attachement agaynst him, whereuppon order was taken that he shoulde be brought to the Howse by the Serieante; which this daie was performed

f.82 accordingly, and uppon examinacion of the cause / yt fell out that the *teste* of the subpena was after the parliament begonne. It fell out also that th'attachement was taken forth and the said Mr Steppney compelled to compounde for the sparyng of th'execucion of the same. Hereuppon yt grewe to the question of the Howse whether the said Mr Kerle had comitted two contemptes, one, or none; and uppon deliberate consideracion therof, in fyne yt grewe to resolucion that he had committed ij contemptes, the first in taking out the subpena, the second in taking out th'attachement; and theruppon ordered that he shoulde be comitted to the custodie of the Serieant for sixe daies, that he should paie to Mr Stepney the chardges he had been at for the Serieante's fees for his arreste, and also all such other chardges he had been at aswell for the coppie of the bill, the chardges of his owne answer, and all other chardges which had growen therby, or els not to be delivered out of custodie; the taxacion of which chardges was committed to Mr Sandes and Mr Morris:[48] which was after taxed to v markes.

Note that I was sicke from the xith of Februarye untill the xxijth of the same.

xxij° Februarij.

A byll for th'assurance of the ioyncture of the Cowntesse of Huntington in landes befor covenawnted to be conveyed unto her and in ij partes of the manor of Cantford; first red.

    A byll reqwyring that the penaltyes ageynst making of hattes *viij° Elizabethae,* the moytye to be forfeyted to the Qweene and the other moytye to th'informer, that no hatter sholde set up making of hattes but in townes corporat or within ij myles of London, nor to keepe anye more prentizes then one untill he have beene ij yeres a howseholder; first red.[49]

A byll that everye archebishop and bishop do in the Chawncery take an othe for his dewe obedience to the Qweene and for eqwall and dewe administration of such thinges as aperteygne to his office; that no bishoppe shall sweare anye canonicall obedience to anye archebishop: first red.

A byll ageynste takinge excessive fees in ecclesiasticall cowrtes, setting downe what fees meye be taken in everye case, that the byshop make no visitations but in person and that not but uppon iust cawses compleynd of; first red.

The Lords sent to us ij bylls, one concerninge impropriations wherin they made an addition, beyng befor sent from us; the other a byll for preservation of greyne and game. /

The byll for the sale of Mr Fisher's landes for the peyment of his debtes, iij° red and passed.   v. p.

The byll for moore burninge was returned from the Lords with an amendment.

The Lord Daker's byll iij° red and passed.   p.

This day we reqwyred conference with the Lords concerning the byll of the Saboathe dey and offered to them ij presidentes to consider of, bye which we tooke yt to be lawfull to make additions to additions.

This deye also the Lords delivered theyr answer concerninge owr petition bye the mowthe of the Lord Treasurer. Th'effect wherof was that certeyn of the Pryvye Cownsell of theyr Howse had communicated the same to her Majestye; that theruppon her Majestye had dealte with the archebishopp and bishoppes and that uppon conference theruppon had yt fell owt that soome of th'articles reqwyred were alreadye considered of to be reformed, soome other her Highnesse by her supreme auctorytye meante to reforme, and soome were not fit to be reformed as reqwyring innovation and impugning the Book of Common Prayer. Yf offenses were given in diocesses bye th'inferior, her Highnesse wyshed compleynct to be made to the bishoppes; yf the bishoppes offended, first to be privatlye admonished; yf that wolde not serve, further compleynct myght be made and redresse sholde be had. After that, th'Archebishop made particuler answer to every article, which was after set downe in wryting. Bye meanes I was a commyttee in theyse cases, other thinges were don in mye absence.

xxiij° Februarij.

A byll reqwyringe explanation of a brawnch of the statute of laborers made v Elizabeth, bye which ther was an exception for the cityes of London and

47. The handwriting changes back to the second hand from 'Yeasterdaie'.

48. The handwriting reverts to the first hand here.

49. 8 Eliz, c.11 (1566), in *SR*, iv.494–5.

Norwiche to take prentizes in such sorte as they myght lawfwllye have don before and that such as be free of the cytye of London of anye occupation meye use anye other occupation as they have hertofor used and accustomed; first red.[50]

f.83   A byll reqwyring that the prescription for peyment of tythes shalbe limited / from xl yeres now last paste, no more libels but ij for tythes dewe in one yere, the prohybytion to be extended no further then for such thinges as ar precyselye named in the prohybytion, and that for the rest yt mey be lawfull to proceede; first red after the bringinge in bye the commyttees.

p.   The byll from the Lords for th'asswrance of the ioyncture of the Cowntesse of Huntington, ij° and iiij° red and passed.

xxiiij° Februarij.

A byll that wher anye offices of the Kinge's Benche, Common Place or Excheqwer at anye tyme herafter shall becoome voyde, that the Lord Chawncelor, Lord Treasurer and others may have auctorytye to assigne soome competent portion out of the severall offices for increase of the livinge of the iudges, firste red.

A byll from the Lords reqwiringe ratification of such grawntes as have beene made to the Savoye and to make frustrate all grawntes made bye one Thomas Thurlonde, soometymes Master of the Savoye, being made for more than xxj yeres or wheruppon th'auncient rent ys not reserved or not being befor usually letten; that, notwithstanding, certeyn persons shall have auctoryty to examin the case of the lessees and to awarde such recompense to them as they shall thinke convenient; th'Archebishop to have auctorytye to visit and make such orders as he shall thinke convenient, not beynge contrary to the lawes of the realme; no lease herafter to be made above xxj yeres.

A byll reqwyring that wheras landes *etc* have beene hertofor given to the meyntenawnce of bridges, higheweyes, or relief of the poore, and the same are sythence conveyed to other uses, that such conveyances shalbe voyde; a proviso not [to] empeach any estate hertofor altered by Parliament, that leases herafter meye be made for xxj yeres, that iij iustices of peace meye take accomptes howe the rentes be employed; a proviso notwithstandinge that suche persons whose estates bye this meanes ar to be undon meye compleygne and have theyr griefes h[e]arde in the Chawncery and have suche relief as the cowrt shall thinke convenient: ij° red and commytted.

Mr Chawncelor of the Excheqwer[51] moved the Howse to offer a subsedye to the Qweene's Majestye and shewed diverse occasions bye which her Majestye had beene greatly chardged sythence the laste subsedy grawnted, wheruppon commyttees were apoyncted, *viz*, the Privy Cownsell and one of the knyghtes of every shyer. /

v.   Mr Vicechamberleyn declared that he had notefyed to her Highnesse the request of the House for soome more severe punishement then ordinary to be executed uppon Doctor Parrey,[52] that her Majestye took yt very thankefullye, notwithstanding wolde not agree to other dealing with him then th'ordinarye cowrse of lawe. And theruppon, for soome satisfaction to the Howse, entered to a discowrse of the life and treosons of Parreye. First he disclosed that Parrey duringe the Qweene's reygne had not receaved the communion, nor had coome to church but seldom, and that but for a fashion and company; that in the yere 1580 Parreye grewe firste discontented, the cawse a controversye between him and Mr Hewgh Hare. Upon which Parreye entered into suche action as at the sessions at Newgate he was condemned to dye. Afterwardes, notwithstandinge, obteygned a pardon and so had his lyfe from her whose recompense was sclender – to seek the Qweene's lyfe for the same. After which he had diverse tymes accesse to the Qweene. Notwithstandinge, he after transported him selfe beyonde the seas to Paris. There he gave him selfe to take delyght in veyne pastimes. There having continewed for a tyme he considered with him selfe that, his trade of lyfe formerly passed considered, he colde in reoson have no hope of advawncement at home and theruppon grewe to resolution with him selfe that the beste cowrse he colde take to obteygne favor and lyking abrode was to enter into publique profession of papystrye; and for signification herof resortethe to Benedicto Palmero,[53] a Jesuite in Paris towards the Scottish Qweene as yt was seyed, desyreth to be accepted of him and to be receaved to confession, to have absolution of his sinnes, and to be lykewyse receaved to reconcilyation to the Pope; all which was grawnted and performed accordingly. This was in the yere of owr Lorde 1582. All this notwithstanding, his former lyfe had beene such as he remeyned mistrusted, and as he yet got no great credit from Parys he tooke his iowrney to Venice. There he entered to discowrse with him self to leye a newe plot for increase of his credit, and that in ij cowrses; the first bye takinge uppon him to use all the meanes he colde for restoringe the Catholiqwe religion in England; the ij[d] that the beste meanes to bringe this to passe sholde be the destruction of the Qweene's Majestye. Mr. Vicechamberleyn seyed he trembled to speak of such a horror and preyed God longe to preserve her Highnesse. The better to pursewe this peryllowse plot he entered to acqweyntance with another Jesuite in Venice, more perillowse / than the firste. To this Jeswite he disclosethe his intention, notwithstanding sheweth that he was dowbtefull howe the destruction of the Qweene myght be adventured with safetye of conscience. He desireth th'advise of the Jesuite therin. Parreye set forth to the Jeswyt his petigree at lardg, sheweth that he was borne in Wales, that he was of kinred to nobles and others of good worshypp. He shewethe farther to the Jeswyte in what great slavery hys cowntrey was. The Jeswit, greatlye delitinge to heare of this purpose, gave him great incoradgement herin, asswred him that th'enterpryse was honorable, acceptable to the Pope, warrawnted bye the woorde of God, and sholde be merytoryowse to him in Heaven, advised him to go to Roome, that he wolde undertake he sholde there receave both asswrance and furtherance in the action. Herewith

f.84

---

50. 5 Eliz, c.4 (1562–3), clause xxxiii in *SR*, iv.421.
51. Sir Walter Mildmay.
52. For Parry and further action, see

D'Ewes, pp.355, 356 for 23, 24 February; *State Trials*, i.1095–112.
53. *Sic*; cf. D'Ewes, p.356: 'Palmes', *State Trials*, i.1100: 'Palmio'.

Mr Vicechamberlein bye the weye made protestation that he neyther had nor wolde deliver anye thinge but Parreye's owne woordes voluntarylye withowt coertion, withowt torture or threates of torture uttered and the most set downe in wrytinge, not onlye subscribed but holye of hys owne hande. And then proceeded and shewed that this Jesuite, for his farther asswrance in the mattier, undertook to acqweynct him with ij persons in Venice, the one embassador to the Kinge of Speyne, commonly there called the King of Speyne's secretary, the other the Pope's nuncio, called Campegio. The Jesuite acqweyncted Campegio with the mattier and then browght Parreye to Campegio who gave the alowance and encoradgement to the action. Parreye accuseth not the kinge of Speyne's secretarye as deal[er] in the cawse, thowgh named for that purpose. Pasporte was grawnted to Parreye which he tooke to Roome, an indulgencye was reqwyred for his sinnes, letters of great commendacion of Parreye and the mattier sent from Campegio to Cardinall C[omo], with which he goeth from Venice to Lyons to Cardinall Como, but because that pas[port?] was but to Como he seemed unsatisfyed and reqwyreth a newe l[icence] and that *sub verbo pontificis* from the Pope him self, which he obtey[ned]; notwithstandinge, afterwardes returned to Paris. There when he cam he fownde his credit greatly increased. Emongest other places he resorted to the lodginge of one Morgan, agent for the Qweene of Skots. This Morgan giveth him great interteygment,

v. caryeth him up to a higher chamber from the reste of the companie, / taketh uppon him knowledge of Parreye's good lyking to further the Roomysh religion and of the reste of his enterprise, giveth great commendacion to Parreye therin, sheweth that his doyng therin sholde be honorable and meritoryowse. Parreye seyed that in furtherance therof he wolde not feare to kill the best subiect in Englonde. Morgan replyed, that in no wyse wolde serve the turne and that therbye the Church sholde receave small benefit. Then seyed Parreye that he wolde kill the Qweene. Wherto Morgan seyed, '*Hoc fac et vives.*' Morgan took uppon him to acqweyncte noble and great personadges with the mattier, whom he named, but becawse that yt appeereth not bye the confession of Parrey that he dealte with them in the action, he thinketh yt convenient to spare theyr names. Yet ys yt trewe that Parreye hath had resorte to those personadges, but whyther onlye for pastime and such lyke, since none of them be accused he wyll not accuse them nor name them. He adviseth Parreye to mak present returne home for execution of his purpose, giving him assurance that the breath sholde be no sooner owt of the Qweene's bodye but that Barney Hurste[54] sholde be readye to invade Ingland with xx or xxx thowsande and that the Scottish Qweene sholde be set up. For his present eyde and advawncement Parrey heruppon returneth into Englond. He seeketh accesse to the Qweene, he creepeth in favor. The Qweene receavethe him into a gallerye, hath conference with him there alone. Parrey, to th'intent from thenseforth to be owt of suspicion, declareth to the Qweene that he hath mattier to reveale unto her which concerneth her owne safetye and delivering of her from great peryll. Nowe Parrey, areyed onlye in a gowne lyke a doctor, he kneeleth downe and craveth pardon of the Qweene. The Qweene demawndeth the cause. He discloseth that he had taken uppon him to kill her, that he had taken an oth and also the sacrament for performance of yt; but, seyeth he, 'all this shalbe for your Majestye's safetye, for,' seyeth he, 'bye this meanes I shalbe made privye to all conspiracyes ageynst your Highnesse, wherwith I wyll from tyme to tyme acqweyncte yowe.' The Qweene pardoneth him; besides, from tyme giveth him privat accesse unto her. This the Qweene imparteth not to anye of her Cownsell. Parreye notwithstanding still continewynge hys former purpose, entereth to consultation with him self where, when and howe the Qweene sholde be sleyne. Heruppon he resorteth to Mr Nevell, who had befor longe served the King of Speyne, a person discontented. Him he thowght a fit instrument. / This Nevill, Mr   f.85 Vicechamberlein seyed he colde not excuse for the[n] he sholde do wrong, as on the other syde he wolde not to grievowsly accuse in respect he had disclosed the mattier to an honorable person of thys Howse. Parrey, to th' intent to drawe Nevill to better lyking of him, calleth him Lord. He seeketh to bringe Nevill to the mislyke of diverse of the Cownsell, telleth him that such and such of the Cownsell were his enemyes in hys suite, that ther was not hope for him to preveyle there, setteth owt Nevill with great commendacion, entereth to the search of his petigree, emongst others greatlye dispreysed him selfe. On the contrarye parte, Parreye coometh to him and telleth him that Nevill[55] called him knave and seyed that he was an underminer of the sute and that he had nowe good accesse to the Qween and wolde do his errante. Yet on the contrarye part Parreye dealeth with him in disprayse of Nevill. After having drawen Nevill to misly[ke] of the state bye all the meanes he colde, he reqwyreth Nevell to his house. He perswadeth him that they myght do soome notable thing. First he tryed him with smaller mattiers, *viz.*, that Nevill sholde carye a brute down into the north that the Qweene was dead, that theruppon yt wolde fall owt that the Qweene of Skots sholde be set up; another tyme that they sholde take soome ylande in Kente; another tyme that Berwyke sholde be solde. Theyse synked not in Nevell's eares. He made small reckoninge of them: theye colde carye no credit. Lastely he tolde Nevell that he had a devise which wolde towch the mattier to the qwicke, but befor he wolde disclose the same he wolde have Nevell to take an oth and also to receave the sacrament, firste that he sholde not disclose the mattier, secondly that he wolde persewe the devise. Nevell rested uppon firste to knowe the mattier befor he made answer. In fine he tooke an oth but not the sacrament, bye meanes they had no convenient weye to get a priest to minister the sacrament. Heruppon Parreye disclosed to Nevell his purpose of destruction of the Qweene. Nevill deswaded him from that purpose. He colde not be satisfyed bye what warrawnt yt myght be performed. Parreye shewed unto him that his conscience was satisfyed in the mattier, that the action tended to the advawncement of the Catholiqwe religion; shewed unto him howe he was warrawnted therin by the Jesuytes,

---

54. *Sic*; 'Farnyhurst'?

55. The sentence is crossed through to this point.

that he had besides the Pope's dispensation for the same. He wyshed Nevell to
deale with soome Catholique / for hys farther satisfaction. Nevell met with a
seminarye, dealte with him therin. This seminarye disalowed yt. Herof Nevill
informeth Parrey. Parreye for his farther satisfaction offered him Allen's booke
to reade.[56] Th'execution of this horrible acte was firste meant to be executed at
Otlandes, but there, havinge in haste lefte his girdle and dagger behinde him in
a tente, he was dawnted at the very syght of the Qweene. Another tyme he
purposed to pursewe the same at St James bye one of theyse ij meanes. The
Qweene used diverse tymes a privat walk in her gardens with small or no
company. There the slawghter to be commytted, bardges to be prepared for
the conveying of them awey when the facte was don. Parrey to commytt the
facte, Nevill to be readye with the bardges. Or else, when the Qweene tooke
her coche privatly on the sodeyn with small company, he and Nevill eche of
them to be readye with v or vj men furnished with pistolls and then, the facte
being commytted, presently to have horses or bardges in readinesse, to use the
one or the other at theyr choyse. Parreye confessed further that twyse when he
meant to execute the facte he was driven to turne abowt and weepe. In fine
Nevill findeth him self trobled in conscience, perswadeth Parrey to desiste from
th'enterprise, giveth his resolution that he wolde no farther proseqwute yt, and
that except Parreye wolde do so also, he wolde disclose yt. When Parrey colde
bye no means continewe Nevill in the pursuite therof, he maketh semblance as
thowghe he wolde also desiste and give yt over. Heruppon shortly after Nevill
goeth into the north. At his returne back, beyng nowe very latelye, Parreye
giveth a newe onset uppon Nevill to perswade him to ioygne in the action.
Wheruppon Nevell discloseth the mattier to an honorable gentelman of this
Howse, and heruppon Parrey aprehended. Beinge chardged with the mattier,
denyethe yt not absolutely but answereth at his pleasure: seyeth yt ys not
lykly that he wolde enter into anye such enterprise, that he had disclosed
diverse thinges to the Qweene, that he had tasted of her favor, desired to
knowe who colde or wolde accuse him. Nevill heruppon browght to his face,
chardged him with the hole mattier, iustifyed yt befor his face, made offer bye
the sworde to adventure his lyfe in the iustification of the truth. Parrey at the
firste not denying the mattier, only chardged Nevell with recrimination as
consentinge with him; but in fine after confessed the hole matter as befor.
Parreye was asked what cawse of discontentment he had. Mr Vicechamberleyn
declared that ones the Qweene offered Parrey a pension of a hundred
powndes by yere which / Parrey refwsed. Parrey answered that befor he
cam into the howse where he then was – meaninge the Tower – that
yf the Qweene wolde have given him thowsandes, except she wolde withall
have beene browght to favor the Catholiqwes, he wolde not have given over
hys enterprise. Lastly, Mr Vicechamberlein shewed forth and red a lettre
wrytten from Cardinall Como dated the xxx[th] of Janwary 1584 bye which the
enterprise was leyed manifeste and the Pope's furtherance therof, which
originall lettre Mr Vicechamberlein shewed to be in Italian, sealed with the
cardinall hat and of Cardinall Como's owne hande, and so confessed bye
Parrey.

xxv° Februarij.

A byll to explane a statute formerly made for the mendinge of the weye betweene Midelton and the Kinge's Ferrye to chardge such as occupye lande there thowgh they dwell not there, first red.

A byll reqwyringe execution of a statute made *ij° Ricardi ij^i* restreygninge aliens to sell linnen clothe by reteyle and reqwyring further punishement of them for the same, a proviso that they make yt up in woorke; first red.[57]

A byll that persons dwellinge within iij myles of the sea in Norfolk meye be e. chardged with suche deye woorkes as meye be spared abowt mendinge of highe weyes, in amending of the sea bankes; ij° red, to be engrossed.

This deye Mr Chawncelor opened to the Howse the contentes of the c. Archebyshoppe's answers to owr petitions, wherwith the Howse were nothinge satisfyed, and agreed that commyttees sholde be apoyncted to set downe th'insufficiency of the same, of the which I was one.

This deye also he browght in the articles agreed uppon by the commyttees concerning the subsedy, which beinge red, yt was agreed the same sholde be delivered over to the Qweene's Atorneye to drawe upp accordingely.[58]

xxvj° Februarij.

The byll of vagabondes ij° red and commytted. c.

A byll that maryadges meye be at all tymes of the yere and inflicting c. punishement to such as shall grawnt anye licences in that behalf, first red and commytted to commyttees wherof I was one.

A byll that the takinge of a ij^d wyfe lyvinge a former wyfe, no lawfwll c. divorce beinge befor had, and in lyke sorte for the woman, to be felonye; ij° red and ageyn commytted. /

The byll of tanners being browght in bye the commyttees withowt v. e. amendiment, agreed to be engrossed.

The byll for swearinge of archebishoppes and bishoppes, ij° red, to be e. ingrossed.

xxvij° Februarij.

A byll that yt might be lawfull for the lords of fennes in the Yle of Elye to grawnte bye copye to such as be commoners anye parte of the same fennes not exceedinge x akers to a man, reserving j^d rente bye the yere, and ij^d for everye aker to be the fine uppon everye alienation; theyse x akers never to be severed from the howse; this to be ratified as awncient copiholde subiect to suche customes as other copiholdes; there the lord not to improve any parte to his owne use; the copiholders to meynteygne the diches and to plante wyllowes uppon the same; certeyn woode to be also planted uppon soome parte therof;

56. *Defence of English Catholics.* There are two lines crossed through here, apparently anticipating the later reference, on f.85v, to Parry and Nevill's face-to-face recriminations.

57. 2 Rich II, stat.1, c.1 (1378) in *SR*, ii.6–8.

58. John Popham.

the commyssioners of sewers to have the oversyght that they meynteygne theyr diches and bankes: first red.

A byll that nòne but gentelmen whose fathers have armes or such as meye dispende xx^li lande or spirituall persons of xxx^li promotions shall keepe anye hownde, greyhownde, hawke, ferret or net, none to hawke or hunte but uppon his owne grownd befor the corne be in shocke;[59] first red.

c.   A byll that in pleyne whyte streyghtes and pinned whyte streyghtes made in Devonshyer and Cornweyle yt meye be lawfwll to use heare flockes and yarne made of lammes' woll notwithstanding the statutes of v and vij Edward vj;[60] none of the seyed clothes to conteygne above xiiij yardes in length, to weye above xij^li in weyght, and one yarde in bredth; ij° red and commytted.

c.   A byll reqwyring that for the meyntenance of the pier at Lime such merchawnt[s] as lande there with theyr merchawndise meye be chardged with doble so much as they have hertofor used to peye to the cobbe viz[?] the pier, ij° red and commytted.

c.   A byll reqwyring that staple fish, heringe and linge meye be browght from beyonde the seas to anye port in the northe partes, they not to transport the same after into the sowth; ij° red and commytted.

p.   A byll, the conveyinge of a river to the haven of Plimowth bye composytion with the owner of the growndes, iij° red and passed.

p.   The byll for mey[n]tenance of the sea bankes in Norfolk, iij° red and passed.

c.   A byll for the better usinge of the hospitall of Eastbridge in Kent and relief of more persons then befor hath been used, iij° red and commytted to consideration whyther a rent which the Qweene had therowt be sufficiently provided.

Primo Martij.[61]

Bye meanes the Speaker was sick, the Howse sat not. /

f.87   *ij° Martij.*

A byll that no yron milles sholde be erected within vj miles of Cranborou[gh] in Kent, none herafter to purchase or ferme those which be erected, nor anye woode felled for to be employed in the milles but the owners' owne woodes; first red.

c.   The byll for augmentation of the iudges' livinges owt of the officers' fees, ij° red and commytted, the commyttees agreed to bringe yt in no more.[62]

e.   A byll to extende the lawe made *xviij° Elizabethae* for mendinge of the weye betweene Midelton and Kinge's Ferrye in Kent to such as occupye lande thowghe they dwell not there, ij° red, to be ingrossed.[63]

c.   A byll to enlarge the statute made ageynst accomptantes *xiij° Elizabethae*, to give libertye to sell the landes of such accomptantes beinge indebted to the Qweene, notwithstandinge the death of th'accomptantes; ij° red and commytted.[64]

Mr Speaker declared that beinge yesterdey sent for bye the Qweene, that [her] Highnesse was greatlye agrieved that we still proceeded in such cawses as we understood her pleaswre to be that we sholde not deale, namely owr petitions, the byll for swearinge of archebishoppes and bishoppes, and the bill concerninge bishoppes' visitations; declared that we therbye shewed a diffidence in her reformation which she meant to see reformed bye her supreme power; that she lyked not this publiqwe treatye, but eyther bye admonityon to the bishoppes, compleynct to her Privye Cownsell or her self. Lykewyse that the Qweene thowghte that the continewance of the Wedensdey to be fishe deye was verye necessary and commended yt to the Howse.

A byll recytynge that Jonas Skot was by frawde deceaved of his debte bye Brunswyke and Robert Wrythsley. Robert Wrythsley havinge the lande, a decree was made in the Starrechamber that Robert Wrythsley sholde reasswre the lande to Jonas Skot, Jonas Skot to make such amendes to Robert Wrythsley as the ij chief iudges sholde thinke good. Robert Wrythsley wolde not obeye the order; was dead in the Fleet. Reqwyred that this lande myght be bye Parliament asswred to Jonas Skot, suche amendes yelded to Richard Wrythsley, soone to Robert, as the ij chief iudges sholde thynke convenient. iij° red and passed.

The byll ageynst frawdulent conveyances *viz*, that all conveyances made to th'intent to defrawde a purchaser sholde be voyde ageynst the purchaser; the knowers of such frawdulent conveyances and iustifyng the same to leese a yere's valewe of the lande; estates made with a clawse of revocation, yf the / maker of suche estate after sell the same, to be voyde ageynst the vendor; no morgadge made uppon good consideration to be empeached; copyes of all statutes to be entered into a book; yf the conizer bringe yt not to be entered and after sell the lande, the lande to be dischardged ageynst the vendor; yf the clerke of the statutes enter yt not he to leese xx^{li}: ij° red and commytted.

The byll concerninge prentizes in London and Norwiche, ij° red and commytted.

iij° Martij.[65]

A byll for the denization of the children of Doctor Humfreye, Mr Sampson, and others, borne beyonde sea of Englishe parentes, first red.

A byll reqwyring that yf a divorce be had in respect of adulterye of the woman she sholde he debarred of dower and of all advaunciment grawnted uppon consideration of the mariadge, and that the husbonde meye lawfwllye marrye ageyn and the children to be legitimate; and in lyke sorte, yf divorce be bye the adu[l]terye of the husband, he to leese the benefit of his tenawncye bye the curtesye, her maryadg to another lawfwll and her children legitimate, first red.

e. pp.

v.
c.

c.

---

59. i.e. a group of sheaves.
60. 5 & 6 Ed VI, c.6, clause v (1551–2), 7 Ed VI, c.9 (1552–3) in *SR*, iv.138, 172–3.
61. 'Aprilis' first written, and then crossed through (and below).

62. *Sic.*
63. 18 Eliz, c.10, clause v (1575–6) in *SR*, iv.621.
64. 13 Eliz, c.4 (1571), in *SR*, iv.535–7.
65. 'Februarij' and then 'Aprilis' both written first and then crossed through.

A byll to revive a statute made *ij° Edwardi vj*[66] for the makinge of malte, altering, notwithstandinge, the peynes in the same limited, and restreygninge the makinge therof in June and Julye; no otes to be mingled with barleye eyther in the sowinge or malting; no wyvell or other evill malte to be mingled with the good; no evil malte to be offered to sale: first red.

A byll reqwyring that none meye wynde ende woll, *vz.* staple woll, but such as be sworne befor the wolmen of London not to suffer anye corrupt thinge to make it weyghty to be mingled therwith, and to have a certificat therof abowt him; first red.

A byll reqwyring that for the Qweene's safetye that yf anye make anye invasion into the realme or stirr anye rebellion or attempt anye thing to the hurte of the Qweene for anye pretending title to the Crowne, that then xxiiij of the Cownsell and other nobles, calling to them certeyn of the iudges, meye hear and examin the cawse and theruppon all such persons for whom such offence shalbe commytted and all other privies[67] shall after proclamation be disabled to have or pretende to have any title to the Crowne, and that theruppon yt shalbe lawfull to all persons to pursewe suche offendors, theyr eydors and comforters to the death; yf the Queene be sleyne, they and theyr yssewes privye to be lykewyse disabled and that yn such case yt shalbe lawfwll to the former commyssioners to proceed to th'examination and givinge of sentence and punishement of suche offendors and to use force for performance herof; none to be trobled for execution of this lawe; the othe of Association to be expownded accordinge to this lawe: first red. /

f.88   c.   The byll of tithes ij° red and ageyn commytted.

The byll of tanners iij° red, and uppon soome fawltes fownde therwith and declaration made of another byll drawen for better reformation of the offense, agreed to steye the qwestion untill the readinge of that byll.

The Lords sent ij bylls to us th'one wherof cam befor from us, *vz.*, the byll of Jeswytes, wherin they made soome alterations and annexed a schedule; the other for assurance of certeyn landes to the Deane of Excyter.

The byll of subsedye firste red.

This deye we sent up ij bylls to the Lords, th'one cam from them, *vz.*, for assurance of certeyn landes to Jonas Skot; the other for amendment of the sea bankes in Norfolk.

iiij° Martij.

This deye I, beinge apoyncted to atende the Lords with other committees concerninge the additions offered bye us to theyr additions to the byll for the better observation of the Saboath deye, was absent from the readinge of diverse bylls. Concerning the qwestion theruppon moved, the Lords agreed that we myght adde to theyr addicions, and for an order to be observed in tyme to coome, yt was agreed that aswell theye as wee sholde set downe what cowrse were to be alowed of in tyme to coome in the passinge of bylls and theruppon an order bye consent to be set downe. We after delivered owrs but receaved none from them.

Certeyn amendimentes in the byll of Somersetshyer clothes beinge red, yt   e.
was agreed that the byll sholde be engrossed.

A byll that no *latitat* for the byndinge of anye to the peace or good
behavyowr sholde herafter be grawnted out of the Kinge's Benche except the
partye which requyreth yt do first take an oth that he colde not have the same
grawnted in the cowntrey; first red.

ij bylls were sent to us from the Lords, the one for asswrance of certeyn
landes to the Lord Willowghbye, the other for the bringinge of a water to
Chichester.

The amendiments of the byll of frawdulent conveyances beinge red, yt was   e.
agreed that the byll sholde be engrossed.

The byll of vagabondes, wherin first such brawnches in the statute of *xiiij°*
Elizabethae,[68] / all such bye which roges ar to be commytted to the ieyle and   v.
such as impose felonye uppon anye offense and others. All vagabondes in every
cowntye ar to be viewed and theyr names and surnames entered into a book.
Such as were born or dwelte in the cowntrey bye the space of iij yeres ar to
be set on work; suche as were not ar to be conveyed to the place wher they
shall affirme theyr byrthe or dwelling bye the space of iij yeres to have beene;
yf they wyll name no such place, then to be sent to the howse of correction;
yf yt fall owt they name a place falsely, then to be whypped and sent to such
place as they shall then name. Yf the constable suffer anye roge to go abrode,
to forfeyt a peyne; yf anye be browght to a iustice of peace and he do not take
order for him, then the iustice of peace to incurre a peyne. Yf the roge placed
wyll not be ordered, then to be punished bye stockinge or whyppinge by
discretion; yf beinge so whypped or stocked he wyll not be reformed, then to
be punished in the howse of correction. Yf anye departe leaving his children
behinde him or his wyfe, the wyfe and chyldren to be placed with the
husbond. Howses of correction to be made in all shyers within a yere. Yf anye
unmarried woman be gotten with childe, the iustice of peace to examin the
mattier and to bynde the partye offendinge to be forthcooming; yf the reputed
father be gon to anye other cowntrey, he meye be sent for and browght into
the cowntye and there punished. Corporat townes that have iustices, theye to
have lyke auctorytye as iustices in shyers; yf theye wyll set up howses of
correction, theye meye; yf they use the howse of correction of the cowntreye,
theye shalbe contributorye to the cowntrey; yf they be overchardged, theye
meye be eyded bye the cowntrey. First red.[69]

v° Martij.

A byll of the Lords for assurance of certeyn landes to the Lord Wyllowghbye
from Edmond Herondon, heyre to Water Herondon, put in truste therwith at
the goynge over of the Duchesse of Suffolke beyonde sea in Qweene Marye's
tyme; first red.

---

66. 2 Ed VI, c.10 (1548) in *SR*, iv.51–2.   68. 14 Eliz, c.5 (1572) in *SR*, iv.590–8.
67. *Sic.*   69. Cf. D'Ewes, pp.360, 363.

A byll that such actions in which the title of lande or charters of lande ar called in qwestion meye be leyed in the cowntye where the lande lyeth, or else the cowntye meye be made parte of the yssewe; first red.

c. A byll ageynst grawntinge of *supplicavits* or *latitats* of the peace except the partye which preyeth yt take an othe that he colde not have yt uppon hys othe in the cowntreye; ij° red and commytted.

c. A byll that uppon iudgementes given execution meye be awarded notwith-standing anye wryt of error served, yf the partye wyll enter in bonde to repeye the moneye yf the iudgement be reversed, or else the moneye to be put in cowrt; ij° red and commytted to me and others.

c. A byll for the Qweene's safetye, ij° red and commytted.

The byll of vagabondes was this deye further argewed and ageyn commytted.[70]

c. The byll ageynst frawdulent conveyances, iij° red and passed.

In the afternoone the same deye was the byll of subsedye ij° red, to be engrossed. /

f.89 *vj° Martij*

A byll that no newe yron milles be erected in Sussex, Surreye or Kent; no bodyes of timber trees to be employed in makinge of coles for the yron milles or abowt the yron milles, no woode to be employed abowt the yron milles but bye owner of the woodes in fee simple; such as use caradges abowt the milles to be chardged with bringinge of cinder or other thinges necessarye for the mendinge of the hygh weyes, or else for everye lode of cinder and suche which he ys to bringe, to give ij^s vj^d: first red after yt cam from the commyttees.

e. The byll of tythes ij° red, to be engrossed.

p. The byll for mendinge of the hygh weye betweene Midelton and Kinge's Ferrye in Kente, iij° red and passed.

p. A byll ageynst small botes and ageynst using of nets not beinge ij ynches and a halfe betweene knots in Orford haven in Suffolk, iij° red and passed.

e. The byll for the Qweene's safetye with amendimentes, being ageyn red was agreed to be engrossed.

p. The byll for alowinge the decrease of the bredthe of whytes made in Glostershyer, Somersetshyer and Wylteshyer from vij qwarters to vj qwarters and a half; iij° red and passed.

This deye also beinge sent up to the Lords I was absent parte of the deye and therfor knowe not what was don in mye absence.

viij° Martij

The byll of Excyter from the Lords, ij° red.

c. The byll of the Savoye ij° red and commytted to me and others.

e. The byll for tryall of actions in the cowntyes wher the lande lyeth in certeyn cases, ij° red, to be engrossed.

e. The byll for streyght whytes in Devonshyer to be engrossed.

e. The byll of Lime Regis to be engrossed.

The byll ageynst processe of the peace to be grawnted above, to be　e.
engrossed.

The byll of yron milles ij° red, to be ingrossed.　e.

Margerye Dyke apoyncted to be sent for bye the Serieant for servinge Mr Richard Cooke, one of the Howse, with a subpena.

Mr Morgan and [MS blank] his man apoyncted to be sent for in respect hys servawnt did lye in weyte to assawlte [MS blank], one of the Howse.[71]

A byll of errors in fines in Wales ij° red and uppon a proviso reqwyred　c. to be added bye Mr Vernon, his cownsell and Mr Greye's admitted to the barre; in fine agreed a proviso to be added and drawen indifferently bye commyttees. /

In the afternoone.　v.

A byll from the Lords for bringinge the water of Chichester to the suburbes, ij° red.

The byll for landes given to the poore and highe weyes, first red.

The Lord Wylloughbye's byll ij° red.

The byll concerning Devonshyer carzeyes called dozens to leye the peyne uppon the weaver and for the better makinge therof; first red.

The byll of continewance of statutes, first red.

The byll of tanners, curriers, shoemakers *etc.*, first red.

ix° Martij.

A byll to restreygne the making of walles on eyther syde of the water called Dert coominge to Totneyes brydge, firste red.

The byll concerning landes given to the meyntenance of highe weyes, ij° red　c. after the commytment and ageyn commytted.

The byll ageynst sellinge bye reteyle bye strawngiers, ij° red and reiected.　r.

The byll for reformation of yron milles, iiij° red and passed.　p.

The byll of the Qweene's safetye, iiij° red and passed.　p.

The additions to the byll of Jesuites and schedule annexed bye the Lords,　c. first red and commytted.

The byll for actions of the case to be leyed in theyr proper cowntyes in　p. soome cases, iiij° red and passed.

The byll for executions to be had of iudgementes notwithstandinge anye　e. wryt of error swed, ij° red, to be engrossed.

x° Martij.

The byll of hattes and cappes *etc.*, ij° red and reiected.　r.

The byll concerninge the waterbeyly of the Tems, ij° red and commytted to　c. me and others.

The byll of shoemakers, iiij° red and passed.　p.

The byll of accomptantes with a proviso added, iiij° red and ageyn　c. commytted.

---

70. Cf. D'Ewes, p.363.　　　　　　71. D'Ewes, p.364 does not mention this.

p.   The byll for executions to be had notwithstandinge a wryt of error swed, iij° red and passed.

A byll concerninge th'armor of recusantes, first red.

r.   A byll for reformation of disorders in inholders and tavernes in London, first red and reiected.

l.   pp.   The Lord Wyllowghbye's byll, iij° red and passed.

p.   The byll for Lime Regis, iij° red and passed.

c.   The byll ageynst processe of the peace directed into the cowntrey, iij° red and ageyn commytted. /

f.90   *xj° Martij.*

p.   The byll for salte fishe, linge and heringes to be browght into the northe, iij° red and passed.

c.   The byll for continewance of statutes ij° red and ageyn commytted.

The amendimentes of the byll of Jeswytes red and assented to with newe addicions added bye us to the Lords' amendimentes and alterations in a schedule by them annexed. After the readinge of the same, the case beinge this. The same beginning with us, the Lords made alterations in the byll and besides annexed a schedule. We made one addition to theyr amendimentes and alterations in the schedule. The qwestion was whyther we were to enter the Lords' amendimentes to owr byll befor the Lords had reformed suche thinges as we desired amendiment of. Agreed, becawse the byll had his first passadge with us, that the Lords were first to amende theyr paper and schedule and then we to put in all the Lords' amendimentes and passe all together.

l.   pp.   The byll for amendment of the title of the bishop and deane and chapter of Exciter, from the Lords, iij° red and passed.

xij° Martij.

pp.   The byll of the subsedye iij° red and passed.

p.   The byll of fines with Mr Vernon's proviso annexed, iij° red and passed.

p.[?]   The byll of Eastbridge with a proviso annexed for the Qweene's rent. The proviso beinge red, the constitutions made bye th'Archebishop of Canterburye, reqwyred to be confirmed bye the byll, were red, uppon readinge wherof yt appeared that he which sholde be master of the howse was to be a minister; yt appeared that one of the constitutions conteygned that everye one which sholde have relief bye the howse sholde take an othe to obeye all constitutions which the Archebishop of Canterburye for the tyme beinge sholde make, and also that yt sholde be lawfwll for the Archebishopp to make constitutions, not beinge contrarye to the lawes of the realme; wheruppon the Howse, thinkinge yt convenient that such as sholde be masters of the howse herafter sholde be preachers, and mislyking to ratefye those constitutions, agreed that a proviso sholde be drawen for remedye herin.

e.   The byll of continewance of statutes, the amendimentes beinge red, was agreed to be engrossed.

xiij° Martij.

A byll ageynst makinge of starch of anye greyne, firste and ij^d [read], to be engrossed. /   e.

A byll from the Lords for the keepinge of the cowntye cowrt at Morpet in Northumberland, first red.   v. l.

A byll from the Lords ageynst sellinge of phesantes and partriches, first red.

Jhon Blande a currier was browght in bye the Serieant for seying that he and the curriers colde not have iustice in the Howse, who humblye submitted him selfe and asked forgivenesse of the hole Howse and was theruppon pardoned, peyinge his fees and taking the othe of obedience to the Qweene.

The byll of continewance of statutes, iij° red and passed.   p.

The amendimentes of the byll concerning landes given to the amendiment   e. of high weyes, beinge red yt was agreed that the byll sholde be engrossed.

A byll reqwyringe that yt myghte be lawfwll to all persons to take apprentizes as they myght befor the statute made 7 Henry 4, first red.[72]

The amendimentes of the byll of the waterbeylye, iij° red and passed.   p.

xv° Martij.

A newe byll concerninge the makinge of malte, first red.

A byll declaringe mariadge to be lawfwll at all tymes of the yere, being browght in bye the commyttees, first and ij^d red, agreed to be engrossed.

A byll for the makinge of neyles in certeyn cowntyes, first red and reiected.   r.

The byll for the better makinge of dozens in Devonshyer and other   c. cownties, ij° red and commytted, wherof I was one.

The Lords sent downe iij bylls *vz.*, the byll of Jeswites which befor cam from us, reformed accordinge to owr amendimentes, a byll for ratification of an award betweene the Lord Riche and Mr Barington, and a byll concerninge Plumsted marsh.

A byll from the Lords that th'assises and countye cowrtes for Northumber-   c. land myght be transferred from Anwyke to Morpet, ij° red and commytted.

The proviso and amendimentes of the byll of Eastebridge, iij° red and passed.   pp.

Th'amendimentes in the byll of vagabondes beinge red, yt was agreed that   e. the byll sholde be ingrossed and a proviso offered for Sowthwark to be considered of.

xvj° Martij.

A byll reqwyringe a farther tyme for the inninge of Plumsted marsh, first red.   l.

A byll from the Lords for confirmation of an awarde concerninge an   l. exchawng of certeyn landes betweene the Lord Rich and Sir Thomas Barrington, first red.

A byll for incorporation of curriers, first red.

72. 7 Hen IV, c.17 (1405–6), in *SR*,
    ii.157–8.

c.   A byll requiring that a statute made *ij° Edwardi vjⁱ* for the makinge of malte myght be revived, ij° red and commytted, of which commyttees I was one.[73] /

f.91 c.   The byll concerninge apprentizes, ij° red and commytted, of the which I was one.

p.   The byll concerninge pleyne whytes and pinned whytes in Devonshyer, iij° red and passed.

p.   A byll ageynst the usinge of starche, iij° red and passed.

p.   A byll declaringe that maryadges ar lawfwll all tymes of the yere, iij° red and passed.

p.   The byll for the waterbeyly uppon the Temmes, iij° red and passed.

l. pp.   Th'amendimentes and proviso to the byll of accomptantes, iij° red and passed.

The Lords sent downe ij bylls, one of the subsydye of the clergye with the confirmation therof bye the Archebishopp under seale, another for the incorporation of the hospitall of Christe in Sherborne.

r.   A byll that certeyn kindes of wares myght only be unladen at Sowthampton, ij° red and rejected.

c.   A byll concerninge the commyttinge of the armor of the recusantes to custodye, ij° red and commytted.

Ther were diverse bylls red in the afternoone, but I being then uppe in a commyttee uppon the byll of the Savoye was absent. The bylls red, as I am enformed, were theyse: the byll of the subsedye of the clergye, the byll of the incorporation of the hospitall in Sherburne, the bill concerninge the awarde betweene the Lord Riche and Sir Thomas Barrington, and a byll for the denization of [MS blank].

xvij° Martij.

r.   A byll ageynst sclawnderowse bookes of the state, libels ageynste cownselers; first red and reiected.

Th'amendimentes of the Lords in the byll of Westmister beinge red, the same were commytted [to the which we mad].[74]

pp.   The byll of the Saboth deye beynge newlye feyre wrytten was put to the qwestion and passed.

p.   The byll of vagabondes iij° red and passed.

c.   The byll for preservation of fesantes and partriches, ij° red and commytted.

c.   The byll for preservation of greyne and game was ageyn commytted.

pp.   Th'amendimentes of the byll concerninge impropriations were red and the byll passed.

Ther were bylls red in th'afternoone but I was not present therat, beinge uppon a commyttee; *vz.*, the subsedye of the clergye, the byll for the paving of Newe Wyndsor twyse red, the byll for the cornmeaters of London first red, and the byll for th'incorporation of Chester.

xviij° Martij.

A byll concerninge peltes and sheepes skins, first red.

v. p.   The byll of Chichester haven iij° red and passed. /

A byll that frawdes used to the preiudice of recoverors in common   e.
recoveryes shalbe voide ageynst the recoverors, ij° red, to be engrossed.

The byll for the inninge of Plumsted marshe ij° red and commytted.   c.   l.

A byll of tythes browght in bye the commyttees ij° red, to be engrossed.   e.

The byll confirminge the awarde betweene the Lord Riche and Sir Thomas   ll   pp.
Barrington, iij° red and passed.

A byll for punishment of such as desire to be admitted to anye benefice not
beinge qwalified accordinge to *xiij° Elizabethae*, first red.[75]

The byll of accomptantes iij° red and passed.   ll   pp.

A byll concerninge yron milles neere Crambrooke in Kent, ij° red and   c.
commytted.

A byll that yf leases be made for more then a hundred yeres not havinge the   l.
accustomed rent reserved, that the lessees shalbe chardgeable in case of
wardshyppe as persons havinge inheritance in landes; first red.

A byll for assurance of certeyn landes in Hackney to the Lord of Hunsden,   l.
first red.

A byll restreygninge anye to occupye currying of lether in London or within
iij myles therof not havinge alowance by the companye and the wardens of the
curriors of London, ij° red and commytted and greatlye mislyked by the
commyttees.

xix° Martij.

A byll for asswrance of certeyn landes in Hackneye to the Lord of Hunsdon,   l.
ij° red.

The byll of malte beinge corrected was brought in bye the commyttees,   e.
agreed to be engrossed.

The byll of Jeswytes, th'amendimentes of the Lords and owr additions and   pp.
amendimentes beinge entered into the parchement bye the clerke, the byll was
put to the qwestion and passed.

The byll for punishement of such as offer them selves to be made ministers   c.
or admitted contrarye to *xiij° Elizabethae*, ij° red and commytted.

A byll chardging lessees of landes for longer terme then a hundred yeres as   l.   c.
tenawntes of inheritance in respect of warrdeshyppe *etc.*, ij° red and commytted
to commyttees of the which I was one.

The Lords reqwyred a conference concerninge the Wedensdeye abrogated
in the statute of continewances, which theye greatlye impugned uppon the
conference, and we on the contrarye stoode to the mey[n]tenawnce of that we
had passed; and neyther parte seemed satisfyed.

The byll of recoveryes iij° red and uppon soome conference the qwestion
steyed until the next deye.

---

73. 2 & 3 Ed VI, c.10 (1548) in *SR*, iv.51–
   2. The next entry is followed by a
   repeated note of the previous day's
   reading and rejection of the nailmaking
   bill: it is crossed through.

74. The words 'to the which we mad' have
   been crossed through.

75. 13 Eliz, c.12 (1571) in *SR*, iv.546–7.

p.　　　The byll for pavinge of Newe Wyndsor, iij° red and passed. /

xx° Martij.

f.92 l.　pp.　The subsedye of the clergye, iij° red and passed.

　　　pp.　The additions made bye the Lords to the byll of moore burninge in the north, thrise red and passed.

　　　r.　The byll concerning landes given for high weyes, iij° red and reiected.

　　　e.　A byll for punishement of suche as enter into the ministerye not qualified accordinge to *xiij° Elizabethae*, browght in bye the commyttees, j° and ij° red, agreed to be engrossed.

　l.　pp.　The Lord of Hunsdon's byll, iij° red and passed.

　　　pp.　Th'additions and amendimentes of the byll of frawdulent conveyances made bye the Lords thrise red and the byll passed.

　　　l.　Th'amendimentes of the byll concerninge Sherburne hospitall twyse red and alowed of.

　　　　Th'amendimentes of the byll for th'inninge of Plumsted marshe being [read], ther was one desired to be h[e]arde, which had beene at great chardges of the work, wherin he reqwyred recompense, and uppon a bonde shewed forth, taken uppon passinge of the byll *xxiij° Elizabethae*, that those which were to have the lande sholde abide the order of certeyn arbitrators, yt was agreed that the lyke bonde sholde nowe to be taken and arbitrators apoyncted bye the Howse.[76]

xxij° Martij.

　　　c.　The byll reqwiringe auctorytye to grawnt certeyn commons in Elye bye copye of cowrt role, ij° red and commytted to commyttees wherof I was one.

　　　c.　A byll ageynst exactions of fees bye ecclesiasticall persons, ij° red and commytted.

　　　　The Lords returned to us ij bylls with amendimentes, the one concerninge fines, the other the byll of shoemakers, and a iij^d byll of theyr owne concerninge wardes.

　　　p.　The byll for punishement of such as enter unlawfwllye into the ministerye, iij° red and passed.

　　　c.　The byll concerninge recoveryes ageyn red and farther commytted.

xxiij° Martij.

　　　l.　Another byll from the Lords concerninge to chardge the landes of states in remeynder and ioynct estates to wardeshyppe, first red.

　　　e.　A newe byll beinge browght in bye the commyttees for avoydinge of frawdes to defeate recoveryes, the same was twyse red and agreed to be engrossed.

　l.　pp.　The byll concerninge the hospitall of Sherburne, iij° red and passed. /

v. l.　pp.　The byll for the holdinge of the cowntye cowrtes for Northumberland at Morpet, with the addition made bye us, that yt myght be there or Anwyk; iij° red and passed.

Th'amendimentes of the byll concerninge the armor of the recusantes,   e.
beinge red, yt was agreed the byll sholde be engrossed.

A byll for the sale of certeyn of the landes of Philipp Basset for the peyment
of his debtes, first red.

xxiiij° Martij.

The byll for the sale of certeyn landes of Mr Philip Basset for the peyment of   c.
his debtes, ij° red and commytted to commyttees wherof I was one.

A byll concerninge pirattes, ij° red and commytted.   c.

The byll of malte iij° red and passed.   p.

Th'amendimentes of the Lords in the byll of woodes, thrise red and agreed   l.   pp.
to be entered into the byll.

Th'amendimentes of the Lords in the byll of fines of Wales in which theye   l.   pp.
put owt the clawse of exemplifications and added a proviso; beinge thrise red
yt was agreed the same sholde be reformed accordingely.

The byll for the disarminge of recusantes, iij° red and passed.   p.

The byll of tythes iij° red and overthrowen uppon the qwestion.   r.

The newe byll concerninge leases of landes helde bye knyghtes service
drawen bye us in place of the Lords' byll, first red and commytted.

The byll of Plumsted marshe with soome amendimentes bye us, iij° red and   l.   pp.
passed.

A byll that preachers readinge th'Articles apoyncted to be red bye *xiij°*
Elizabethae, shall not be expulsed thowghe theye red them not befor; first red.[77]

xxv° Martij.

Margerye Dyke's sonne who served Mr Richard Cooke with a subpena owt of
the Chawncery was browght in bye the Serieant and submitted him selfe;
ordered by give a copye of the byll to Mr Cooke and to give him xxˢ for the
chardges of his answer, and was so dischardged peyinge the Serieante's fees.

Jhon Stokes was browght in for procuringe the areste of one Linge, servawnt
[to] Mr Carye Rawleye, uppon an action of trespasse, who submitted him self
and theruppon consentinge to the dischardge of Linge was dischardged,
payinge the fees dewe. /

A servawnt of Mr Pole's, beinge arested uppon a *capias utlagatum*, was   f.93
browght in. Uppon examination of the cawse, yt fell owt that he entered into
service since the parliament began and used fraude therin for th'onlye cause;
and yt was taken bye the Howse bye meanes of a lettre shewed forth, wrytten
bye the prisoner to his debtor, in which was a[78] conteygned a reqweste to helpe
him into service to one of the Howse, dated the vᵗʰ of December, which he
seyed he did wryte but for a colour. Yt was also suspected that Mr Pole him
selfe enterteygned the man but for that purpose, bye meanes priviledge had
beene befor demawnded for ij other of hys servawntes commytted to Bridwell

---

76. 23 Eliz, c.13 (1580–1), in *SR*,
   iv.676–7.

77. 13 Eliz, c.12 (1571) in *SR*, iv.546–7.
78. *Sic.*

for his[79] dealinge. Th'opinion of the Howse uppon the circumstances of the cawse seemed to be as foloweth. First, that priviledge was grawntable uppon a *capias utlagatum*; secondly, that thowghe the servawnt had entered uppon frawde into the service, yf the master were not privye therto that the master sholde have the priviledge for his servawnt; lastlye, that yf the master were privye, that then no priviledge was to be grawnted. Yt was also noted that Mr Pole had given small atendance during the session. Mr Pole him self also confessed that he gave his servawnt leave to go into the cowntreye and that he had not since his returne atended uppon him. Uppon the hole mattier yt was put to the qwestion whyther the priviledge sholde be alowed, and beinge dowbtefull whyther the yea or the no were the more, the House was divided and the no preveyled.

The newe byll for the chardginge of the interest of lessees above a C yeres to wardshypp, the ij[d] tyme red with the amendimentes and agreed to be engrossed.

xxvj° Martij.

The byll ageynst yron milles neere Cranborowgh in Kent was ageyn committed.

A byll for denization of the children of Doctor Humfreye and others, iij° red and passed.

A newe byll made bye us ageynst leases above lxxxxix yeres of landes helde *in capite*, iij° red and the Howse divided uppon the question and the no preveyled.

The byll of Westmister was ageyn browght downe from the Lords with newe additions bye them and a proviso annexed; the byll beginninge with us, theye havinge made additions, and so uppon the mattier, we having befor made additions to theyr additions, theye added a newe to owrs; which we allowed of the same and passed the byll. /

v.   *xxvij° Martij.*

This deye the Qweene was expected to have coome to the Howse but cam not, wheruppon Mr Speaker coominge to owr Howse, after preyer ended, only notefied the same and nothinge else don.

xxix° Martij.

p.   The byll for preservation of phesantes and partriches, being alter[ed] in soome poynctes bye us, iij° red and passed; notwithstandinge afterwardes the Lords mislykinge our alterations, the byll had noe passadge.

The byll of Lime Regis with soome alterations and additions was returned from the Lords and the alterations beinge thrise red the byll passed.

Th'amendimentes of the Lords in the byll of recusantes were red and agreed to.

The Qweene's generall pardon, ones red and passed.

In the afternoone.

The Qweene cam to the Howse and the Speaker made his oration and presented the subsedye; which accordinge to her Majestye's direction was answered bye mye Lord Chawncelor. Emongest other thinges he declared that her Majestye mislyked greatly that a byll passed the Lords for remedye ageynst frawdulent conveyances, advisedlye considered of bye them and the iudges, that the more parte of the Howse sholde dissent to have the byll commytted and to reiect the same withowt a consultation had with the Lords. That she lykewyse mislyked that we had dealte in cawses of religion, notwithstandinge her commawndiment given to the contrary in the beginning of the parliament.

Afterwardes the bylls were red and her Majestye gave her consent to all the bylls which passed bothe the Howses, except theyse nine bylls:[80]

1.   For the more reverent observinge of the Sabaoth deye.
2.   For the safe kepinge of the armor of the recusantes.
3.   For disaproppriatinge of parsonadges impropriat.
4.   For meyntenance of the navigacion.
5.   Ageynst makinge of glasse bye aliens.
6.   For keepinge the sessions at Carnarvan.
7.   For keepinge the cowntye courts at Morpet and Anwyke in the cowntye of Northumberland.
8.   Ageynst moore burninge in certeyn cowntyes in the north.
[9]. For naturalizinge the children of certeyn Englishe men borne beyonde the seas. /

After this the Qweene's Majestye her selfe made an [oration].[81] I colde not   f.94
well heare the contentes therof. After [which she] called mye Lord Chawncelor unto her, who shortly [declared] that her Highnesse' pleaswre was to adiorne the parl[iament to] the xxth of Meye next.

Yn this session of Parliament theyse bylls also passed owr Howse, which had no passadge with the Lords.

A byll of confirmation of the Qweene's letters patentes to Sir Walter Rawley concerninge Wingandicoza.

A byll that actions in which title of lande ys called in qwestion sholde be tryed in the cowntye wher the lande ys. Thys byll uppon the qwestion was overthrowen.

A byll that execution meye be awarded after iudgement notwithstanding anye wryt of error swed.

A byll concerninge the water beylye of the Temes.

A byll ageynst the use of starche.

A byll declaringe mariadges to be lawfwll at all tymes of the yere.

A byll for alteration of the statute of vagabondes in certeyn poynctes.

---

79. *Sic.*
80. See *EP*, ii.98, n.2.

81. MS torn here, and below.

A byll for punishement of suche as enter unlawfwlly into the ministery.

A byll ageynst unnecessary processe of the peace.

[The following two entries are written on the back sheet of this journal in the

v.   same hand as text:

'Mye bookes of the proceedinges in all the sessions [of] parliament in which I had anye entermedlinge.

I can not finde my booke of the xxiijth yere of the Qweene.']

3. *Anonymous Journal*

Text from BL Lansdowne 43, original, in the same hand as draft speeches in this volume.

Lansdowne 43, fos.164–75.

[Endorsed '27 Eliz.
   The report of diverse speaches uttered in the parliament by sundry persons uppon sundry bills exhibited there.']

In the bill of showmakers[1] a corryer complayned apon that he said he had no justice; that ther was but 50 at the passing of the bill; that their freindes wer awaye.

Demanded by the Speaker what punishment for sclandering the Howse.

Good reason losers should have their woordes. He is a poore man and many children. — Mr Threas[urer][2]

So base a fellow rather to be contemed then revenged; he can not sclander this Howse being of so great a state as it is. — Alford

We see noble men receve smale damages for sclanderous woordes against such men.

When he sayd his freindes were away he ment such as favord their bill and spake against this.

In the bill of mynesters to be 24 of age *etc.*[3]

'I remember about i of this Quene I was in comission for to visit the Englishe clargy, *tam in capite quam in membris*, and ther we had 4 sortes: — Recorder[4]

graduati, and all they were written in 2 lynes;

pii et docti, and they in six lynes;

penitus indocti, 2 skyns of parchment, dizardes and ideottes;

criminosi, that is dronkardes, whormongers.

And at that tyme we putt out on bishop, the Bishop of Peterborowe.

'Pius the 4, lying extreame sick, sayd, "I will tell yow within these 3 houres, wither ther be a God or ño, wither ther be a soule or no, wither ther be a hell and a heaven or no." This was on of their cheif bishoppes.

'I pray yow, Mr Speaker, let us have a new comission; at least let us passe this bill. If they stay it above, let them. *In magnis voluisse sat est.*'

'We speake much of dutie, but we do none. In other countries the shepe be so well taught and ar so dutyfull they will follow their sheppard thorough a markett towne, but our shepe will teach their sheppard, he can not dryve them — Alford

---

1. See D'Ewes, pp.365, 366–7: 13 March.
2. Sir Francis Knollys.
3. Possibly 22 March, third reading debate *EP*, ii.79.
4. William Fleetwood.

before him, but if on fall a leaping a dich or hedg, all the rest will followe though they breake their neckes for it.

'I lik not of these verball sermondes. I dare boldly affirme it, on homely doth more edefy then C of theis verball sermondes.'

Dalton   'I am not of that faction. It tends indirectly to thrust out 2000 mynesters; then what becomes of the sacramentes, baptysm, buryall?'

Alford   'It wilbe come of buryall as on did that threw him in to the earth and sayd "Farwell Anthony."'

That place, he that settes his hand to the plough, is ment that none can be putt out of the mynestery.[5]

Mr Chancelor[6]   'He is woorthy to be disabled for ever that will presume to entend him self into so high a calling being unfitt.' /

v. Dalton   'Wher will yow have sufficient number to supply?'

Strickland   'Yow may have a good many out of the inns of courte.'

Alford   'The lyvinges of 2000 parishes in England ar but 8^{li} by year. How can yow place a learned man ther?'

Chancelor   'Ther is none of 8^{li} in the Quene's bookes but is woorth 20^{li}; besides, who will not contribute to a learned mynester?

'The lawe would not be suffred to look back and putt out suche as were in.'

In a bill wither it might be comytted after the 3 reading.

Leukner   '*Deliberamus diu quod sat cito si sat bene*. Before the lawe is past, we ar iudges of it, after it is past, it is iudge of us.'

Agreed, may presently be amended, yf nede be, but not comytted for so it might be infinite.

Mr Carry Rawley's man arrested, his master came not at the Parlyment House all the latter session but was in the countrey. His man arrested lay in London, kept the place called the Revelation and there shewed pupittes and playes, yet priveleged.[7]

The Sergeant fees, xx^{s} for arrest and x^{s} a day as long as they be under arrest the party that arrested pay charges to the party arrested.

On Wurrall, servaunt to Poole of the Parlyment Howse, arrested by a Fleming, and appeared by his owne lettre that he wrote to one, in Parlyment tyme, to procure him to serve some honorable or woorshipfull man of the Parlyment Howse and therby he might come and talke with him towching the money he ought him: his clayme of priveleg not allowed, for the fraude. The [House] was devyded about it and ther was 69 that would have had him priveleged and 86 to the contrary. It was testified that the same Pole had 2 other servauntes that claymd priveleg the same parlyment also, which were in Bridwell about bawdye.[8]

The Recorder told to the Howse that he had sent for the Fleminge, who when he came to him he sayd he did speake him so fayr that he suspected and would come no more at him.

Fisher made compleynt to the Lords that he was fayne to eat or els starve, that his wife was fayne to mak fuell of crowes' nestes. Against which fals reportes proved by Sergeant Pukring, Speaker, that his wife feld the great trees, that he sent to Fisher being then in the Flete 4 marke and he bestowed it all apon a bankett on night wher he had musick and hores.

Fisher's father, a leud fellow, sayd he was persecuted of the papistes. Fisher the sone as leud, sayd he was persecuted of the protestantes.[9] /

In the bill of fraudulent conveyances.[10]

f.165
Recorder

'He that speaks of the sodaine to a bill of waight may be graveled, as I am like to be.

'The Starr Chamber is so called of a serpent called *Stellio*, so *Camera Stellionis* and not of *Stella*, starres. For as that serpent byting the finger it must be cutt of, so ther must be spedy redresse in causes.'

'I se this bill is of greate waight and therfor we had nede to advise and advise **Dalton** agayne of it and therfor, neither let us comytt it nor cast it waye but let it slepe till the next parlyment.

'I confesse fraud is to be detected, detested and punished. But as that is an yll medecyn, which cureth on disease and breades ten wurse in the body, so this bill.

'A man would be content to tak a litle poyson, to expell a greate deal, but not the contrary.

'Here we go about to remedy a mischeif with an inconvenience.'

In a bill to have certaine sceales of record in Wales as it is in England for exemplification of fynes *etc.*[11]

Ther is but 4 sceales of record in England: Chester, Durham, Lancaster, Great **Recorder** Sceal. None of all theise ever towched for mysusing, yow can not pled against any of these *Nul tiel record*, they be of that credytt.

'But against the sceal of the King's Bench or other courtes I may, for the clarke that hath the keping of them may be a knave, for the jugges do not see the sceal in a yeare.

'Our sceal of London of great credytt I tell yow, for I will feche C thowsand pound apon it at Anwarp, but yow can not borrow v grotes ther apon all your sceales in Wales.

'Mr Speaker, this bill hath bene 4 tymes in this Howse and throwne out, and now it is crept in agayne I can not tell how. I pray yow Mr Speaker look to it. For myne own part I care not for I have nera foote of lande in Wales, nor

5. Luke 9:62.
6. Sir Walter Mildmay.
7. 25 March (Cromwell's journal, f.92v).
8. D'Ewes, p.373 (25 March) has the voting figures as 69 to 85. See also Cromwell's journal, f.93.
9. Fleetwood reported on the committee's work on Fisher's bill on 10 December, and the bill was passed on 11 December (D'Ewes, p.338; Cromwell's journal, f.75v.
10. Second reading debate of 8 February (D'Ewes, p.346).
11. Cromwell (f.89) has the second reading on 8 March, though D'Ewes gives 22 February, the third reading being on 8 March. The bill was first committed on 19 December, and re-appeared as a new bill on 18 February (D'Ewes, pp.343, 353, 354, 364).

never entend to have'. And so he went out of the Howse presently to the enditment of Parry in the King's Bench. /

v.   Sir Edward Dymock found him self agreved by certaine speaches spoken of hym at a table of good credytt, concerning his speach in the Parlyment Howse for the want of mynesters in Lycoln shire.[12] Dymock will pike shame of his speach in the Howse.

In the end he sayd, 'I do not require his punishment, and I think him to base to contend withall.'

Alford   'I perceyve the gentleman that spak last ment me for he hath repeated much of the speach I made.

'Though his memory be freshe, yet he hath forgotten somwhat. I have bene of this Howse this 22 yeare,[13] and I have often tymes offended by my speach, but I was never reproched in speach befor now.

'To count me so base a person he hath no cawse, for I am a gentleman as well as he, of many discentes, though but a poor gentleman many gentlemen of my name.

'Inded I am weak and old, yet will I put up[14] no iniurye.

'I am no villayne nor slave, to give such termes; my education hath bene otherwise in travayl and study, and I never sarved any man.

'We do not assemble in charity, we do not consult so. We use bitter tauntes and termes, it ought not to be so.

'If I have offended I referr my self to the Howse.'

In the bill of Jesuites.[15]

Digges   'I am against the body of the bill.'

'Yow speake to late; it is past already'.[16]

'Then I speak to the addicion by the Lordes.

'They would make it felony wher we have made it treason, the punishment is to litle already.

'For these ar only the people that do endanger the Quene, who calling them selves Jesuites of Jesus who spilt his bloude for to save us, they under coulor[?] therof spill bloud.

'Ther is not so mucch feare of an ambitious fellow, for he doth it to the entent to lyve afterwardes, which he can not do, for ther is no hope to escape. But he that doth it to wynne heaven, he cares not for death, for that he accountes of. Mark those poore wretches that undertook to kill the Prynce of Orenge.

'I lik not that they may submytt them selves to a bishop or justice of peace and take the othe; who sees not, they have dispensations to lose them. Parry took the othe, yet dyed a catholik as he cald him self.[17]

'This bill is a moost dangerous bill. I pray God I be no prophett', *etc.* /

f.166   In the bill for mynesters to be 24 yeares of age and not to present them selves apon payne of 20[li] *etc.*, imprisonment *per annum*, disabled for ever.[18]

The venerable fathers moved that patrons that present unable might be included, as very necessary reson. But he did it not apon no other entent but to overthrow the bill.

In the bill of wardshippes come from the Lordes where men sued leases for C years or more.[19]

Williams[20] against it, wherupon cryde away with it.

Kingsmill [21] with it, saying it was but an explanation of the comon lawe before, and other reasons.

'I could neither[22] like these billes that looke bakewarde. He that spake last, Recordor spake good reason, but it was not lawe, for then what nede this bill be offred: none of your old statutes looke back. *Quia Emptores terarum* it was *Nemo imposterum*. The statut of Marleburg[23] that forbiddes feoff to his sonne to defraud wardshipp lookes forward onlye. Yow would think I had studied this year I am so ready and perfitt in it, but I promise yow I never hard this bill before but I could kepe yow here till 2 a clok with lik cases, for I had a collection of them till my book was pickt from me. But I have sayd thus much of old statutes that young men may note it in their tables.

'And I remember ther was a statut once made to look back. The Bishop of Winchester's cooke had spurge comffites geven him, do yow laught[24] at it, I tell yow it is no laughing matter when yow hear the end. He in reveng herof made certaine porege which an old woman dyed after she had eaten of them and so I think she would though she had not eaten of them for she was very old. But then was a statut for poysoners that they should be boyld to death in hott lead lett downe by litle and litle. I remember I saw on once when I was a litle boye sitting behind m[y] grandfather apon a horse and was taken away when I cryde for feare, for I tell yow it was a terrible matter to behold.[25]

'I could tell yow of others, and I think yow would be content to hear me these 2 houres *etc*. Many do not make leases so muche to avoyd wardshippes as fynes for alienation, for apon yeares they paye none. Leases for yeares forfettes in utlarye, which is more danger then the other advantag, then sett the hares hed against the gese giblettes.[26]

Spake for the comytting of it, considered of, digested by the lordes judges. Sollicitor[27] We must consider what is iustice and equite in the case.

Wardship befor William the Conqueror. 'But I can shew a record in King Stephen tyme of it. The service the moost honorable; the plowe next; then ther was orison, by colour wherof as they entred into wydoes' howses, so they gott all the land into their handes. Then the statut of mortmayn wherin the preamble declares they tooke away wardshippes because they dye in succession and have no heir. The same reason of leases.

12. 14 December (D'Ewes, p.339).
13. Alford was first returned in 1563.
14. ? '[with]'.
15. ? 9 March (D'Ewes, p.364–5).
16. 17 December (D'Ewes, p.340).
17. Parry was executed on 2 March 1585.
18. Perhaps 19 March (*EP*, ii.79).
19. Second reading debate on 19 March (D'Ewes, p.370)
20. Perhaps the lawyer David, though *Commons* suggests Richard.

21. Richard Kingsmill, Attorney of the Court of Wards.
22. *Sic.*
23. 52 Hen III, Stat. Marlb. c.6 (1267) in *SR*, i.20.
24. *Sic.* this is characteristic of this scribe.
25. See *SR*, iii.326 for 22 Hen VIII, c.9. (1530–1), and the case of the cook, though the Bishop is Rochester.
26. This sentence is written in the margin.
27. Sir Thomas Egerton.

'The barons' warres caused estates tayles to be devised, wherby their issue was not disherited by the treason of the father.[28]

'Men did devise a fraud in [MS blank] tyme, to defet wardshipp by enfeoffing their sonne and heire fraudulently. Wherapon a statut made. If they apon a fraud rising then did provid remedy, why should not we likwise when a new kynd of fraud ariseth? And for the tyme I se no reason why a statut might not look back if ther be reason why it should look back. /

v. 'If a man will stay a bill, good pollecy to say it towcheth corpora[tions] very nere, therfor looke well to it, they will cry "Away with it", when they understand it not.

'So in billes for justices of peace, penalty apon them, a good pollecy to bid them look to it to bring that penalty apon them selves.

'So in a matter of comoditie, as in the bill of wardes. It concerns yow all that have mannors holden of yow to be thus defeated of them.

So St Paul. It gott favour of the Saduces when he sayd "I am accused of the hope of our fathers."[29]

In the subsedy bill a proviso offred that papistes should paye double, as strangers did.[30]

In the bill of usury, that strangers should lett for 8 in the C.

Mr Chauncelor 'I like well of their zeal, but let us not put them in degre with strangers as thought we had no hope of them. Let it be a bage and note of our profession to deale myldly and of theirs to deale extreamly.

'If the other lawes were executed duly it wer well'.

The Recorder did aske leave of the Howse to go to the assises but was denyed of the Howse; he did aske of glory, knowing they would not spare him.

Afterwardes when he would have gone out a dores, they cryd 'No, No,' about xij a clock and would not suffer him.

Hare[31] This bill[32] is lyke Reynard the fox that putt on a fryar's wede and a payr of bedes at his girdle, that under coulour of relligion he might decyve the better. So this bill, title good *etc.*, bill of mending of hight[33] wayes, that those men that had of land geven to that use, should be called to acompt for 50 yeares past, and their estat made voyd that had imployed it otherwise.

This bill overthrown[34] being engrost and putt to the question and agreed by all many good matters in it, but because it was generall and looked back so farr not lyked.

Recorder 'I did advise him to make a privat bill, but he would not and therfor he shall see what will come of it.

'It is a very long bill: surely, Mr Speaker, all our billes ar long billes, full of *tautologia* and *cakaphonia*, pend in barbarous English.

'I remember once a bill of the subsedy had like to have bene overthrown it was so longe.

'Mr Temple,[35] who was as noble a Parliament man[36] as ever was in this Howse, would crye out of longe billes. I remember him, he was a very honest gentleman and he was buryed in the churchyard at [MS blank] very honorably.

'Lawes may looke back in particular cases somtymes as in Jonas Scott[37] which past this Parlyment to help him to his right, but no damages nor punyshment to the party. So Sir Henry Nevill had a lawe for him loking back and divers others.[38] For when men did the thinges and thought them no faultes, no reason to punishe them now for the fault, albeit reform the fault.' /

The bill of subsedy being read, which held almost 2 houres, the Speaker sayd,   f.167 'If I should recite particularly the taking of bondes and certificat, the collectors, *etc.* it would [take too long], therfor I refere yow [to] the bill of subsedy[39] of the last parlyment, for it is verbatim taken out of that. 20^d in the li and 12^d in the li; all strangers, double; and for every poll, 4^d.'[40]

In the bill for exemplification for the 12 shires in Wales, and the county palentyn of Chester.[41]
Mr Vernon[42] offred a proviso by his counsell.
Yelverton, a counsell on the other side, was againste it.
Mr Frogmorton[43] did ad to the record 200 and 50 woordes, after the writt of error delyvered to him. He did it of affection to his nephew Gray, not of corruption, and so he did certifye it and I thinke if he had done it in the courte iudicially and not in his chamber privatly, it had bene good enoughte.[44]

  The recorde was perished with rayne and eaten with myse.

In the bill of roges.[45]
That a great dele of money layd out to no purpose, no good came of it, of howses of correction.

  Outred Outrage[46]

28. This sentence is written in the margin.
29. Acts 26: 6.
30. *EP*, ii.56–7 suggests 12 March. See D'Ewes, p.366.
31. John or Nicholas (*Commons*).
32. It is not clear what is being debated here, and whether the subsequent mention of the bill for mending highways is by way of comparison. Cromwell describes a highways bill on 24 February, and D'Ewes records a new bill of highways on 6 March, and another (for lands for the poor and highways) on 8 March (Cromwell, f.83; D'Ewes, pp.355, 364, 367; Cromwell, fos.89v, 90v.) See also Cromwell, fos.86, 87, 89 for a particular highways bill.
33. *Sic.*
34. Perhaps the wardships bill (Cromwell, fos.91v, 93; D'Ewes, pp.370, 373).
35. Possibly John Temple who sat, as did Fleetwood, in 1558 (*Commons*, ed. Bindoff).
36. MS reads as noble 'a speaker', i.e. 'speaker' not deleted.
37. The bill passed the Commons on 2 March, and the Lords on 22 March (D'Ewes, p.362; *LJ* ii.104).
38. *SR*, iv.657 lists Nevill's 1581 act.
39. Repeated in MS. The words 'bill of subsedy' are a superscript insertion without a mark indicating the point of insertion. The meaning is clear, however.
40. First reading on 3 March (D'Ewes, p.362).
41. Second reading of 22 February? (D'Ewes, p.354).
42. D'Ewes, pp.364–5 (8, 10 March). The bill is the Welsh shires bill.
43. Not a member.
44. *Sic.*
45. The bill appears to have begun its progress through the Commons in December, having a second reading on 10 December, but becoming a new bill having a reading on 26 February and being passed on 17 March (D'Ewes, pp.338, 360, 369; see also Cromwell, fos.73v, 75v, 86, 90v, 91).
46. *Sic. Commons sub* Ughtred, Thomas.

The subsedy, reparation of brigges, hye wayes and musters, all these fall apon the subiect at ones, ar to burdensom. Now add to this, the relief and recyving of rogges. 'I have hard them seye they will rather heale[47] their howses: they speak it in a rebellous manner.

'I take it no reason, to punishe a man for idelnes and let him have no way to avoyd idelnes, that is, to provide no waye to sett him a woork.

'In many poore villages and hamlettes they have already more of ther owne then they have woork for. Then if yow will have him sent thither what shall he do ther? If yow have no howse, yow must buyld him on. Wher? Apon the comon. When he is in it how shall he lyve? Putt his head out at a hole and lyve like a cameleon of the ayre or burne him and the howse together or els starve.

'The rote herof is the decaye of towns, wher have bene xx or xxx ploughtes going and now nera on.

'I would wishe our wast grounds that beare nothing but brakes and bukes might be plowed up, to sett men [to] woork. Ther is in one county in England more wast land then in all Ger[many,] Fraunc and Italy.

'It is better the Quene to be a quene of people then of buckes.

'This carying by the justices from constable to constable till he come to the place of his birth or last abode troblesom and chargeable.'

Alford   'This bill hath 2 ennemise, *ocium* and *avaritia* or *parsimonia*. Justices of peace will tak no payne to se this executed.

'Let them not seke rule and goverment if they will not tak care.

'Better to be trobled and charged for a tyme then allwyes; after that these roges be thuse[?] setled, ease must nedes follow to the justices, and the comon wealth disburdened.

'In Flanders, wher there is in the quantity of ground of on of our countyes 8 persons for on, ther is no roges. They have trade to sett them [to] woork.[48]

'These idell roges ar the canker and vermyn that eat up the fruit of the lande.

'They that have puld downe townes, lett them be more charged then other.'

Digges   No difference betwixt valyantes beggers and gypsyes, but in face, and a litle legerdemayne. Otherwise all one. Gipsys were not hanged for stealing by the statut of gipsys, but for roges.[49] Idell education of youth is the rote of roges. /

v. Ireland   'We were very hott a whil but now ky[50] cold ageyne. Our peticions ar not loked to, we do nothing. As Dhemostenes did not beleve on that told him he[51] was beaten and wronged because he did not speak earnestly enought, so we.

'I would have her hoples to raigne and hedles to lyve.'[52]

In a bill for staple fishe, the burgesses of London speaking in it.[53]

Digges   'I can not so[?] mak a better reason then by a comparison.

'As if in a naturall bodye on lyme should drawe all the norishment unto it, that should serve all, the rest would decaye, as putt case the belly drawe to it, it would become a monstrous belly, or if it wer the head, how shall the handes and legges defend the head?

'London is the belly, or if yow will, the head of England, yet I pray yow lett the legges and handes lyve by it. Yow se by termes and prynces residences. I envy not this bignes nor wealth: I would it were bigger, but [MS blank].'

'In Flanders, in Holland, Gauntes, Brusselles, they do not seke to uphold on alone, it is not their pollecye.

A great advantag to the passing of a bill or comytting or engrossing to make the question when the Howse is desirous to rise, as at 11 or 12 a clock. /

'Mr Speaker I tell yow pleyne I did never lyke of statutes that do look backward.

f.168

'My Lord Dyer and I talke[d] once and he would be sone angry but he would be sone pleased againe.

'If this m[a]y go forward yow shall have many leases come creping out that sawe no light many yeares.

'The king offred to the Howse a bill to make his proclamacions of force of a lawe, which was denyed, then he to save his honour desired to have it passe and to qualify it, proviso, that it touch no man in lyfe, landes, liberty, body nor goodes.'[54]

In the House the order, first question wither comytted, or no, then, if wonne by voyces not to be comytted, then, wither to be engrost as it is.

bill of tithes in corporacions[55]

If any byll be at question with[er] it shalbe comytted or no, and can not be tryde by distinction of voyces, then some must go out, but they must sitt still that hold the old law still, that as they would kepe the possession of the law, so, their places.

'The Romynes counted it a villany to be whypped.[56]

Lancaster

'She that will lyve incontinently will lye impudently.

'If a man shalbe accused of such now, so any man in this Howse may be whipped.

'He that preferd this did lik Alcibiades who cutt his doge's tayle, so to put out more seryous matter.'[57]

'Mr Speaker, I pray yow hear me, I speak but seldome.

Berry

'Me thinkes, we go about to correct *Magnificat*.

'Me thinkes if this bill should pass yow bring our selves out of God's blessing into the warnesome.

'Besyde, we should take the iurisdiction of this cause from the venerable fathers.

'Further, I pray yow consider that we have many infirmitys and frailtys of the fleshe.'

'We come not hither to make lawes after the Laced[aemonians] or Romyns, but to make Christian lawes.'

Rawly

---

47. i.e. 'cover'.
48. These two sentences are written in the margin.
49. 1 & 2 Ph. & Mary, c.4 (1554–5), confirmed by 5 Eliz, c.20 (1562–3) in *SR*, iv. 242–3, 448–9).
50. *Sic.*
51. Repeated in MS.
52. *EP*, ii.65 suggests this is the presentation of petitions on 15 February.

53. The first bill's second reading was on 7 December, a new bill having a second reading on 27 February (D'Ewes, pp.337, 361).
54. These four paragraphs seem to refer to the wardships bill.
55. 17 December (D'Ewes, p.339).
56. See p.iii, n.45 for the progress of the rogues bill.
57. The MS divides the sentence after 'tayle'.

for burgesses
not to be
[a]lwyes of the
[bor]ough
townes.[58]

Recorder. Some so beggerly, nor a good gowne to their backes, 'and so few I have putt the hole town in the Counter at ones.' /

v.   Recorder

The king [caryes a scepter][59] *weares a crowne*[60], with a ball and a crosse, signifying that he hath none above him but God and Christe.

No more anoynted kinges but of England, France and Emperor.[61]

Leiut[enant of the Tower][62]

Wither it be lawfull to dispossesse a Christian magistrate. 'Now it is ment by Christian such as profess Christianity, but I do think none more unchristian.

'When I opened the matter Master Threasorer spide me wher I went about.

'Yow know Sir William more.'[63]

One in Quens Marye's tyme for saying, here be many provisoes but none for the lady Elizabeth: Tower.

Another, Story, sayd nothing, but, *ve terre ille cui [rex] puer est etc.* Hall. Peter Wentworth.

Liberty to speak to the bill, but not impertinent.

Habet parem auhtoritatem,[64] but, we have auhtority not one against another, but all against one.

Thre iudges Comon Place against one.

Dal[ton]

It were better the bill[65] toke no effect at this tyme and hope to have some better tyme, then that it should passe as it is, cominge and goinge from churche.

Let us not rune a head to passe it. *Ergo* the Lordes had rune a head already who past it so.

Alford

'I would have them convicted by ij wyttnesses, as it is in your lawes for newe treasons.'

Irlaund

'I[t] makes my hart leap for ioye to thinke we have such a jewell, it makes all my ioyntes to tremble for feare, when I considder the losse of such a jewell.'

Mr Ha[tton]

'Her Majestie takes it in most gratious and kynd part your great care for her that yow esteme her to be such a jewell: she sayth her self, though I may not nor will not say it, that your care is farr abov her woorthynes.

'Yow that be lawyers, forgett your selves and think apon your country,' *etc.*[66] /

f.169

In the bill for generall demmurers[67] Dalton sayd it would overthrow all learning and the lawe. 'Our forefathers so many reverend iudges, her Majestie's predecessors so many kinges, shall it be abolished in her Majestie's tyme?'

'And least yow thinke I speake for my self, I will tell yow how it towcheth yow, for therin I thinke yow will harken. It towcheth all your inheritaunces.'

Saunders[68]

'I have spent the better part of 20 yeares in the study of the lawe and therfor I do or should understand somwhat in this matter.

'I know that good pleading is the moost honorable and, praiseworthy in the lawe and I myslike of barbarisme,' *etc.*, 'but I would not have the clyente's purse pay for the counseller's cunninge.'

'It may seme strange that I will tell yow but yet it is not so strange as requesite. If the cause of the clyent be loost by the negligence or unlearnd pleading of the lawyer, let him answer him it agayne and I am content to let it passe, as the poore taylor that mulls clothe for a garandie.'

'I can say litle to the matter, for it is neither my profession nor studye, but I have some litle experience that I have bought and payd truly for. And therfor I speak with a feling spirite.

Digges

'I would not have lawyers stryve for woordes but for matter. This bill hath bene here in a former parlyment and I knowe and hard a grave old Parlyment man like well of this bill, and so do all the elder lawyers; but the younger do not. I would not have the sole[?] sounde of woordes and not substance, formes and fashions and not matter.

'Ther be ij mischeifs holpen by this bill: the delaye of iustice, the insupportable charge of the clyent.

'I had my self a cause which after long sute I lost by non suit by reason my counsell had pleaded amysse. I told and complynd to the iudge; he answered I had right but he could not help me, wherby I was fayne to go about agayne and so I was 3 yeares er I could bring it to that state it was in befor.' /

'Our Mr Littelton sayes that *beaupleder* is the moost honorable *etc.* It is true. But it is not this tryffling pleding and vayne pleading that is now used. Loocke in to the old bookes. Vayne exceptions: *iudgment si encentr gawdly*[?], *uncer iudgment*, and agayne *uncor iudgment*.[69] It is but bad French but yet such as is in my booke, *res ipsa*.

v. Recorder

'I remember, this bill was here when Memorance[70] was here in the Howse and certeyn appoynted, Yelverton on, and he satt ther where yow do Sir More,[71] and here satt by me.[72]

58. It is not clear if this marginal entry reflects Fleetwood's argument – perhaps on the poor law – or if it is someone else's (the journalist's?) comment.

59. Deleted.

60. Inserted.

61. *Sic.*

62. Sir Owen Hopton.

63. *Sic.* Is Sir William More meant? (On 23 February he spoke of Parry's punishment.) Cromwell's journal records that these precedents were cited on 17 December, and Fitzwilliam (f.18v) identifies Copley as the Marian case. (See also *Procs*, i.360 for Fleetwood in 1572).

64. *Sic.*

65. Presumably the discussion recorded here concerns the Queen's safety, and D'Ewes (p.355) alludes to consideration of 'dangers' to the kingdom the day before Mildmay raised the matter of the subsidy

formally. The bill to which Dalton was apparently speaking may be the safety bill, though the newly drawn measure was not introduced until 3 March, and 'cominge and goinge from Churche' is odd. Alford's comments could refer, however, to the means of dealing with alleged offenders in the safety bill(s).

66. These two speeches belong perhaps to 24 February (*EP*, ii.49–50).

67. 5 March? D'Ewes records second readings on 5 December and 5 March (pp.336, 363); cf. Cromwell, fos.74v, 88v).

68. Edmund Sanders? *Commons* identifies the speaker here as Miles Sandys.

69. The rendering of this law French and its punctuation is uncertain because of the MS's difficult hand.

70. i.e. Montmorency (See *Procs*, i.334, 364).

71. i.e. presumably Sir William More.

72. See *Procs*, i.410 (bill of jeofails).

'And that which was spoken then against the bill was spoken agayne now, almost woord for worde, and I told the Speaker so in his eare. And he is to be commended that could cary a tale away so well to recyte almost every woord of it.

'But I remember it past this House then, but I knowe how chaunce it past not the Upper Howse. The clark of the writtes of error sawe what a detryment he should take by it, and he overthrewe it. I will not name him, nor tell how he did it.

'Therfor, Mr Speaker, I tell yow of my soule and conscience this is on of the best billes of the Howse and I have bene of that mynd this 30 yeare.

'The lawe is not made to gett us money, but to help men to their right.

'I knewe a C[li] land once lost by cunninge pleading of 2 lawyers. I will not name them, they wer northen men. I sawe it and sight at it when I sawe it and could not help it. I knewe on for fals pleading banished the barr and practise.'

Sandes[73]   Being a comitte of the bill answered all the obiections made, and declared that it was a very necessary bill and would not overthrow pleading as was supposed.

Digges commonly doth speak last and therfor saith, 'Every matter must have an end and therfor to drawe this to a conclusion.'

Ireland   One moved wither private billes should be reade. Privat billes may be preferd to the Howse, but publick billes to be preferred in consideracion.

Digges[74]   Moved that Parry might be disburgessed and another chosen in his place.
Speaker   'It is your plesures he shalbe dismembred?' 'Yea yea yea.' /

f.170   Alford   Men to be favored that offend in penal statutes because they ar not faultes in their owne nature and against the lawe of God, but in pollecy.

In the bill of fraudulent conveyances after it came downe from the Lordes and spoken to *pro et contra*, and cryd away with it by some, the question grew wither it should be comytted, or no; some saye, or reiected. And by division of the Howse by 16 voyces, not to be comytted.[75]

Recorder   As the parlyment is but on daye in law and so in courtes of justice all the terme but on daye, and therfor any error may be reformed the same terme by the same iudgges.

So we heare. 'I remember in a bill agaynst vyntners, which was dasht here, afterwardes I and a company were had to a tavern by the vyntners and had good chere and came in the after none and revued it and it paste. I remember Mr Horsey said it was a good bill.'[76]

Alford   'I am dryven to considder what hath bene done and what is fitt to be donne.

'If poyson have bene offred us in glasse and we have refused it let us not recyve it agayne in gold, albeit it be clad in better attyre.

'We ar not to follow presidentes made in an after none, when comonly men ar more mery than[77] wise.'

Digges   'We ar not to followe presidentes made in taverns and tipling howses.'

Apon the first reading.[78]

Would have clarkes of the Starr Chamber excepted to take fees for writing as in tymes past, for he sayd it was fitt they should not be beggerly but meynteyned because they ar about the Counsell and great persons honorable.   Grafton

Did appeale that many that spake to the bill understood it not, but much more they that cryd away with it. Therfor it was in them levity and rashnes and let us therfor comytt it. 'It standes not with the gravity of this Howse and wisdomes.'   Mr Sollicitor

'I will not speak to the body, it is neither within my profession nor reache. I reverence as becomes me the lord[s?] and so withall let us hold our lyberties left us by our fathers and when a number do crye away with the bill as they may well: for any particular member to say this is levity and rashnes in them I say this is levity and rashnes in him to say so, therfor putt it to the question.' /   Digges

In the bill of idellnes and vicious lyving.[79]   v.

At the first reading of this bill fault founde with it that ther was so sever punishment for yll lyfe and nothing for idelnes.   Aldred

Now after the comitting, all is against idelnes and nothing against vicious lyfe.

'At that tyme it was spoken by on whose reasons I was sory ther was nera Phyneas here to stop up.

'He alleaged that Paul sayd is it lawfull for yow to whyp a Romayne. I wishe that he that reads scriptur but seldom would deale better with it and alleag it truly. Paul says is it lawfull to whyp a Romayn uncondemed. The Romaynes therfor [it] appeares did whyp.[80]

'This defence of vicious lyf savors of the anabaptistes or libertynes.'

'I delyvered my reasons in the fall of the leafe and he answers me agayne in the springe, but yet it hath no fruite at all.   Lancaster

'Ther have bene better bastardes, are and wilbe, then ever he was.'

The Speaker was sent for by the Quene, and declared the next day[81] how the Quene blamed him greatly for forgetfullnes that he suffred any such billes to be read as were by her forbydden and restrayned by the mouth of the Lord Chancelor.

That she rebuked her Counsell of the Lower Howse sharply.

She alleaged her commandment and our promise. She sayd she was and[82] the supream governor and so we tooke her and therfor to take order for reformation, [otherwise we did].[83]

73. Miles Sandys (*Commons*).
74. 18 February (D'Ewes, p.352).
75. 8 February (D'Ewes, p.346).
76. Edward Horsey was a committee on wine in 1576 (*Commons*; cf. *Procs*, i.383 for Fleetwood in 1572).
77. MS: 'and'.
78. *EP*, ii.84: 'nothing was said' on the first reading on 14 December. Neale placed Egerton's and Digges' speeches which follow on 8 February.

79. The new bill was committed on 5 March, and engrossed on 15 March. The earlier bill had been committed on 10 December (D'Ewes, pp.338, 351, 363, 368; Cromwell, fos.75v, 88v, 90v).
80. Acts 22: 25; cf. f.168 where Lancaster mentions the Romans.
81. The incident occurred on 1 and 2 March.
82. *Sic.*
83. Deleted.

Therfor herin we did derogat to her aughtority, we did mystrust her care and blame her of negligence.

And therfor shee sent us admonition the second tyme and did resolutly comande us to meddell no farther and to call in the bill of swearing of bishoppes.[84]

He told us also how she found fault, both in our negligence in cominge to the Parlyment Howse and departing before the rising of the Howse, and also, that she hard how Parlyment matters was the common table talk at ordinaryes, which was a thing against the dignitie of the Howse.

In a bill that the Lord Threasurer, Lord Chancellor *etc.* should at ther discretion take out of the officers' fees in every court and encrease the wages of the justices.

Alford Good that justices[85] have sufficient lyvinges that they may not tak bribes and be corrupted.

Many commyttes named, one naminge Mr Fanshew, another cryed no reason, for he was an officer of a court, and the Recorder moved that none such should be as might lose by it els ther would be hard hold.

Fanshew[86] 'I come hither as a comon wealth man and not as an officer. If any man envy my gaynes I would he had it. I see not why I may not be a comytte that am a clark to lose by it as Mr Recorder to be one who is shortly to be a judg and to gayne by it.' /

f.171   Sollici[tor][87] 'I would move yf yow so thinke good that in this interim and meane tyme, yow would cause a vieu to be made of all the statutes, and such as be *obsoleta* or unprofitable or overburdensom to the subiect may be taken awaye.'

Alf[ord] 'The bishopes ar not in that blame that is layd apon them for it is the gentlemen that ar patrons; for if they refuse, a *quare impedit* lyes against them.'

Chance[llor] 'The fault is not altogether in the gentlemen. The originall is in the bishops, for the gentlemen can present none but mynesters; all the mynesters ar of their orme making.'[88]

'Here be the showmakers crying and following ready to pull their bill out of my hande. I pray yow Mr Speaker let the Sergant call them in, he knowes them, they be his clyentes.'[89]

So bishops ar All knowe we have yll shoes one that is sure, but wither the fault be in the
yll tanners, yll shomaker or the tanner, that is the question.
coryed. Mr Colson[90] and Mr Mackwilliam had a graunt, but Mr Mackwilliam used us very honorably els we had bene undone.

Edward 3 had 2 jubiles, the 50 yeare of his raigne pardon all arrestes *etc.*

utas x octobris, that is eight dayes.

He that was freholder 40^s then may be 6^{li} now. Therfor, one 40^s frehold now is not of the account of sufficiency as he was to be thought than.[91]

In the bill of subsedyes. Comyttes be the knight of every shire, and towne corporat.

Northumberland, Comberland *etc.* pay no subsedy.[92] /

name
misspelt.

In the bill for the subsedy, Mr Chauncelor.

He entred in to it by a declaration of it.

'I nede not to remember unto yow, although it can not be remembred to often, to se so good loving and zelous subiectes.' So on the other side the ennemyse, which may be devided into 2 sortes: secret and open.

Wherof som potentates and prynces.

'Yow ar to wise to think that intermission of tyme makes any intermission of their malyce or changeth their affections that they lose any yeare, houre or moment to bring their desyre to passe.'

Secret ennemyse ar Jesuites and seminary preistes who instill in to the eares of her subiectes yll opynions of her Majestie.

That position sett downe in the Counsel of Constanc hath contynued hitherto and will contynew, as long as they contynew.

'Joyne to these those whom yow call papistes, who albeit they flatter them selves with the title of obedyence, yet I tell my conscience they that absolutly and thoroughly do acknowleg the Romishe aughtority, for he cares for no half papistes.

'Thuse yow see who be the parties, what be their fruites and scope.'

Now to contynew, this goverment amongest us to thinges requisit, lawe and force.

By lawe to provid for her Majestie's preservation.

By force, when law can not do it.

Nowe forces, as in 2 sortes $\begin{cases} \text{by land} \\ \text{by sea.} \end{cases}$

The which hath not bene mantayned without mervylous charge. 'I nede not to tell yow, yow know that dwell apon the haven townes, what charge in repayring went[?].'

Ireland.

'I assure yow as I am an honest man I speake of myn owne knowleg, for I have loked into it; it hath cost her Majestie of her owne revenue almoost as mucthe[93] agayne as she had at the last subsedy synce the last subsedy.

'I would be sory at my hart she should be constrayned to borrow apon interest, the right name is usurye.

84. 22 and 26 February (*EP*, ii.77; Cromwell, fos.82, 86; D'Ewes, p.361).

85. Committed on 2 March (D'Ewes, p.361).

86. Thomas Fanshaw, Queen's Remembrancer (*Commons*).

87. Egerton made this suggestion on 21 December (D'Ewes, p.345).

88. *EP*, ii.79 places these two speeches (on the bill for the better execution of the 1571 act) on 19 March, though they might have been heard at any time down to, and including, 22 March.

89. It is impossible to place these entries

with any certainty: the proceedings in the shoemakers bill began in early December and carried over to mid-March, but this section may be part of the business of 13 March reported at the beginning of this journal.

90. Colshill, Robert (*Commons*; see also *CSPD 1547–80*, p.569).

91. *Sic.*

92. Committees were appointed on 24 February, the day Mildmay made his speech.

93. *Sic.*

'She doth not bestow vayne expences apon vayne delightes nor buylding which other prynces do, but she is very temperat in this behalf.

'Th'effect of your subsedy Ireland saved from losing England, a noble iland, inhabited by a noble people.'

The losse of Calays dishonorable and shamfull.

'If therfor yow meane to avoyd thes mischeif[s] and to enioye the fruites of peace, which what they ar I ned not repeat, then ayd her.' /

f.172
Recorder apon the act for shomakers[94]

'I hard this matter comytted in this Howse befor, and ther wer 3 to 4 very learned phisitions, who did affirme that their dyed more of yll soules then by the plag and battaile.

'For the water putrifyes the nerves and causeth these rewmes and spitting and sputling.

'Yow have a kynd of high shoes, I can not tel what name yow give them, pantophes.

'Then 3 soules, one of them naught[?], they putt in frying pans.

'This blacking was not hard of till of late, that ther lether weares so redd.[95]

'Dr Gyfford[96] cald on for a commytte, but no fitt one for they care not how many get sicknes by yll shoes.

'My masters ther yow call apon men to have them comytte, yow think to please them but they come yow no thank[s] for your labor for they ar unwilling.

'This men[?] be called promoters, but they have gotten a fyner name, informer.[97]

'We mak lawes against them but the burden lightes apon the backes of the people of the kyndom.

'They wer wont to take an othe in the eschekker, but the King's Bench did recyve it without an oth, which made them to resort so fast thither as the Eschekker was fayne to do so to.

'They have poulten ahong at their girdell like a portas[98] and ar as perfight in it as I am in my pater noster.

'When I speak against penal lawes I speak not against her Majestie's profit, for she gettes litle by them.

'If the Quene were not our gracious lady, no man able to answer that which he forfettes to her apon penal lawes, in some cases C^l a daye.

'Promoter he that gives knowleg to an enformer.'

Eger[ton]   Promoter, caterpillers and bloud succker of the comon wealth.

'This is a prevy byll made of malyce to us of London. I tell them we will do iustice as uprightly or els let us have our skynnes puld and nayld.

'It requires, not to tak b[a]yl but befor ij justices, on of the quorum. Ther is no more but my Lord Mayor and my self,[99] and the Recorder of London must be made a dogbolt to run to Justice Young at Estcheip and Justice Harrys at St John's, M[r] Lyvetenant at the Tower.' /

v.   'We have such a company of asses can not so be a battilldore, in the parishe I dwell.

'Do yow laugh at it, no laughing matter, it is *res dolenda*.

'Here is Sir Nicholas Woodros[100] will[?] tell, yet I nere told him but now he shall heare it.

'I should knowe it perfyttly for I have ben the[se] 25 yeares and that I trow would make an asse perfytt.

'The gentlemen call it the Court of Facultyes. I can not tell but a leud faculty is it to make us spend so muche money in their court some tyme 70^{li}[?],[101] 20^{li} damages, we end it without any costes.'

'It is reason that if the byshop make any mynesters he should fynde them of his   Mr Rawley owne till they be in places.'[102]

In a bill for woode destroyd by iron mylles, no reason to comytt it to any that hath an iron myll, but it was.[103]

Mr Rawley's commyttes,[104] many that were to go in that iorny [to] Waingandacow.

Some knight[s] retorned the 2 county day after the wrytt. Question wither lawfull knightes, wither the Howse to examyne that or no, or recyve and the party greved to punishe the shreive.

Not the lettre of the lawe to be observed, for then all burgesses must be of the burrough townes.[105]

It is no reason to say the same bill hath bene reiected in former parlimentes, for   Sandes[106] we repeal many billes that we have made in former parlymentes.

Marcus Crassus would never speak after Hortensius: but I after many Crassi and   Pottes Hortensii.

'I had not thought to have spoken; I se so many apt and able men to speak.'   Sandes Sabboth internall, external ceremoniall.[107]

A bill entytuled, 'An act for restryning[108] of showmakers, tanners and corryers.' Ther was nera woord towching showmakers.

To thinges to be holpen, lether better, and shoes better therapon.

---

94. Fleetwood had been one of the committees for the first bill (D'Ewes, p.337: 9 December).
95. Dialect word for 'rubbish'?
96. Dr Roger Gifford, President of the College of Physicians, 1581–4 (*Commons*).
97. A bill against informers had a second reading on 2 December (D'Ewes, pp.334–5) but this may be Fleetwood still discussing the shoemakers bill. See *SR*, iv.717 for 27 Eliz, c.10 (1584–5) for confirmation of 18 Eliz, c.5 (1575–6).
98. A portable breviary.
99. The London members (apart from Fleetwood) were Sir Nicholas Woodrofe, Thomas Aldersey and Walter Fish.
100. i.e. Woodrofe.

101. MS blotched here: ? '30'.
102. These entries seem to relate to the bills on religion discussed towards the end of the session (*EP*, ii.77–83).
103. Committed 8 December. According to Cromwell (f.89) it re-emerged on 6 March (see also D'Ewes, p.337).
104. Raleigh's bill was committed on 14 December (D'Ewes, p.339).
105. See D'Ewes, pp.337, 338, 344–5; Cromwell fos.75, 76v, 80 for 8, 12, 21 December.
106. Miles Sandys (*Commons*).
107. Progress on this bill was drawn out and complicated (*EP*, ii.58–60; D'Ewes, pp.335–69 passim, esp. 335).
108. *Sic.* for shoemakers, see above, f.171.

Water Herenden, being enfeoffed in trust of certyn landes by Mr Bartie and the duches of Suffolk his wife who fled for relligion in Quenes[109] Marye's dayes, besides that he would not send them the revenue over sea, at their retorne claymed the land to his owne use.

They sued Water Herenden[110] in the Chancery but he would not. After his deathe Edward Herenden, his sonne, was content to have the same land assured by act of parlyment to the Lord Willoughby, which bill passed the Higher Howse by Edward['s] consent and declared his consent also in the Lower Howse, wherby the act passed. /

f.173   In a bill for Ortford[111] haven in Suffolke to take awaye certayn nettes that destroyd young frye they were so narrowe.

Fox[112]   'I have noted it often tymes that the country people have come in when the fishing tyme is with dungcartes and have caryed them full away with young frye, to fede their swyne, and dong their grounde. It hath greved my hart to see it.'

Recorder   'Ther is a water law called *Hippodromia*. It is no mervyl if yow that be towardes the lawe have no knowlege in it, for yow have no bookes of it, but we have a great many bookes therof in London.

'We have very good order for the ryver of Thames, it costes us a great deal of money and ther is a tyme that it is not lawfull to take certyne kyndes of fishe, as barbelles, and they be called fence monethes.

'I mervayl that any man will speak to maintyn such a nett as this is.

'Did ever any man see such a shamfull on as it is?

'Ther was in [MS blank] wher men did speake and ther was a halter and a cheyn of gold sett before him and if any man did speak against the common wealth he did weare a halter all that daye, if with the common wealth he ware the cheyn but he had it not for his labour.'

In the bill for grayne and game that came from the Lordes.[113]

Alford   'We must not consider our owne selves in this bill and our owne privat plesure because I think fewe of us contyned in it, but our poor neighbours in the country. We have taken away already moost of their pastymes, if we procede yet further we shall cause them to gruge. The welldoing of the prynce consistes greatly in the love and amitye of the subiectes,' *etc.*

Recorder   'Mr Speaker, in the like bill hertofore one Mr Browne[114] did demand a question of the Speaker, which was this. "And please yow, Mr Speaker, if a man do supp of my porege, is it lawfull for me to have a lick at his ladell?"'

Alford   At another tyme[115]: 'I am not so meane but I have x[li] by yeare and therfore without the compass, but I speak for the common subiectes, I see their libertyes be still dayly enchrocht apon. Our neighbours ar together by the eares for their libertyes. In tymes past prynces have departed with their owne rightes to glad their people and make them the willingler to obey them. Hunters be not greatly commended in scripture. Good for young gentlemen for exercise.'

Recorder   'King Egbert took all England for his forest. If I should speake in the Saxon tong yow would laught at me. The Great Charter, confermed with bloud, redemed with 5000 mark, confermed by generall counsell, no parlyment ever broke it. I was shent,[116] all, all hunkers in Sir John Spence's case.

'The king to please Londoners did disaforest round about London. Then yow will aske me why did he not Enfeild. Mary it was none of his, but afterwardes when he erected Marybon and Hyde he did write to the citie of London and had an act of Parlyment.[117] Mr Speaker, make a law against me if yow take me a hunting, but suerly it is a comfort to me when my Lord Russell and my good neighbours round about me and Sir William Pellam come to me, to ryde with them and shew them sport in my groundes and I have good store I tell yow. Therfor Mr Speaker let the old bill stand. I sayd *warrenam meam* but not *cuniculos meos*.'

Hunters in scriptures mystaken, for it is by a metaphore meaning oppressors, as Peter a fisher. And if some were as profitable to their country as they would seme popular, they would not so impugn this bill.   **Sir William Harbert**

'Men of x^{li} [lands] and C^{li} goods ar made in like degre which is not equall. CC will bu[t] by x^{li}, being at xx yeares' purchase. I can have no like advantag of his bagges as he may have of my grounde. On of x^{li} lande, bound to many services men of a thowsand pound goodes are not, therfore hauk in my ground to daye, hunt in his to morrowe.' /   **Wroth**

In the bill for the Quene's safetie.[118]   **v. Leukner**

'I meane not to speak against the bill,' *etc.*

'But if it might prolong her Majestie's life but for on yeare I protest I would be content to suffer death with the moost exquisite tormentes that might be devised.

'The bill is that the entent and meaning is and was of such as have taken the othe of Association; now we knowe that papistes have taken it,' *etc.*

'Ther is great contrariete in the oth for we have already taken an oth to be true to her Majeste and her lawfull successors. Now we may be[120] in a dangerous dilemma by this statute.'   **Harrys[119]** Name

Spake for a proviso that the Quene at her discretion by proclamation and enrolle[ment] in the 3 courtes of record might repeale it all or any parte.   **Gadock**

---

109. *Sic.*
110. Herendon's bill came down from the Lords on 4 March and had passed the House by 10 March (D'Ewes, p.363; Cromwell, fos.88v, 89v).
111. *Sic.* passed on 6 March (D'Ewes, p.364; Cromwell, f.89).
112. John Foxe (*Commons*).
113. D'Ewes, pp.343, 363, 364, 366, 368, 369 for 19 December and 4, 7, 13, 16, 17 March.
114. Edward, or Richard (*Commons*). It is impossible to identify the occasion.
115. This speech, and the three following, are in a different coloured ink from the rest of the page, filling the space originally left at the bottom of the page and then continuing in the margin.
116. Put to shame.
117. 28 Hen VIII, c.49 (1536), in *SR*, iii.709–12; see also *LP*, 11. 84–5.
118. The revised bill came to the House on 3 March and was dealt with again on 5, 6, 13 March (D'Ewes, pp.362, 363, 364, 367).
119. Perhaps Thomas Harris, though both Christopher and Robert (II) seem to be possible too (*Commons*).
120. 'May be' is an alteration from 'shal be'.

That wer a dangerous president.[121]

Chancelor In the bill for contynuance of the statute for killing of calves betwixt Easter and Whitsontide.[122]

Heale[123] Very inconvenient for our countrye for if he may not kill in that tyme the calf will eat up that which should relyve his children and howse and, therfor, I have knowne to avoyd the penalte of the promoter we have had xl kild in diches.

Recorder He reading of a booke whilst a bill was past sayd, 'Mr Speaker, we here at this end of the Howse crye "I" and "No", and in dede heare nera woorde'. Then being repeated againe sayd nothing at all to it.

'Mr Speaker, I have bene this xxx yeare of this parlyment; I never saw billes so illiterately drawne, and therfor we have such hacking and hewing at them and spend muche tyme.'

He moved for priveleg for Mr Rawly's man[124] and was ofte interrupted. 'By the faith I[125] yow shall all lye by the heles before I will speak for any of yow.'

When 2 replied on to the other. 'It is against the order, yow ought not to colloquye so.'

The first question will yow have it comytted or no.
The 2 will yow have it ingroste or no.

The scealers of clothes in the drapers' howse will sceale any clothe never so yll, for his fee.

Thought the cloth be not so broad yet if it hold his waight, yow shall fynd it in the wearing. The draper saith so because he may the better stretche it in lenghte.[126] /

f.174 In the bill that clothiers might make their clothes but 6 quarters and a half broad when it was engrost and going to the question.[127]

Alford 'I pray yow let us not be so hasty, this is a very dangerous bill neither gratfull nor profitable to the subiect.

'They have bene laboring this xx yeare to bring this to passe. It bredes discredit to our cloth in foreyn countryes the narrownes. It will make yow weare a whol pece in the shoulder of your lyveries.

'If it were impossible to make it so broad it wer another matter,' *etc.*

Recorder 'When I was named a committe in this bill it was cryde "No No." I trust I shall have your allowance to speak to it now'. 'Yea yea.'

'This bill hath bene thrown out many tymes already in this Quene's raigne.

'In the 27 of Henry 8[128] ther past a bill for the clothiers that they might make them but 7 quarters broad and now in the 27 of Elizabeth they attempt to bring it to 6 and a half. I beleve they be seen in astronomy and think to have good luck allwyes in the 27 yeare.

'At the first by *Magna Charta*,[129] order taken to make clothe 8 quarters broade.

'And afterward a statut made that all actes that should be therafter made against the great chartre should be voyd.

'Our *Magna Charta* confirmed in Fraunce.

'After that in Richard 2[130] a statut made for the breadth of our cloth.

'After that also in King John's tyme.

'They have gotten from 8 quarters to 7 and a half, from 7 and a half to 7, and now they would have from 7 to 6 and a half and the next parlyment I warrant yow they will require to have it but 6.

'I wilbe bold to looke in my tables, I see other men do it. It will speake substantially and truly for now it standes apon wyninge or losing.

'Ther was an alderman of London and a draper at the dore the last daye and spake to me to further the bill for, quoth he, "It is a good bill, and yow shall have cloth as good as ever it was and a yard as good cheap", and I do beleve him but yow shall have a yard of cloth narrower by half a quarter.

'And yow my masters that bye a C or CC yards for lyveryes recken what yow lose by that half quarter onlye.

'If a yard be at 16^s then the quarter is 2^s. Do yow laughte? Laught not at me no more then I do at yow. Yow dele uncivilly with me, it is yow allwayes ther in that corner of the Howse. /

'Ther be 3 sortes of woll, flese, fell, morkyn.   v.

'Ther be dyverse sort of the flese. Ther is on kynd of the back, a nother of the buttok, a nother of the neck, a nother of the sides; now, they mingle all these together and so make the cloth naught, but if they would do as Mr Wynchcombe[131] was wont to do, that is make severall clothes, of ech by him self, it would fall out otherwise.

'If it do not fall out so, hang me up at the parlyment dore.

'Mr Speaker, I am not feed, I speak my conscience and I thinke so of every man here. But let me tell yow withall *munus* hath more significations then on, and that will Mr Bracton tell yow to as well as I. Ther is *odium*, and *amicitia*, our countrey and[132]

Therfor good Mr Speaker.'[133]

121. It is not clear in the MS to which speech this sentence belongs.
122. 24 Hen VIII, c.7 (1532–3) prohibited killing between 1 January and 1 May, but c.9 prohibited killing calves under 2 years old, and this was repeatedly continued, as here in 1584–5 (*SR*, iii.423; iv.718; D'Ewes, pp.340, 343, 353, 363, 366–7, 16 December–13 March).
123. John Hele (I) (*Commons*).
124. Cromwell (f.92v) notes proceedings in the case on 25 March.
125. *Sic.*
126. The entries on this side (f.173v) are miscellaneous and it is not clear if the section beginning 'Mr Speaker, I have bene . . .' belongs to Fleetwood's speech, though it is not unlikely, or whether 'He moved for . . .' is also Fleetwood.
127. The bill was committed on 13 February and dealt with again on 4, 6 March (D'Ewes, pp.349, 363, 364).
128. 27 Hen VIII, c.12 (1535–6) in *SR*, iii.544–5.
129. 25 Ed I, *Magna Carta*, c.25 (1297) in *SR*, iii.117.
130. 3 Rich II, c.2 and 7 Rich II, c.9 (1379–80, 1383) in *SR*, ii.13–14, 33–4.
131. This probably refers to John, son of the famous Jack of Newbury (*Commons*, ed. Bindoff).
132. *Sic.*
133. *Sic.*

Umpton[134]   'Mr Speaker I am not feed.

'This bill hath bene spoken against more probably then apon profe.

'He that spake first his tale deserves the less credytt because I can shew it him in writing for he hath it from the searchers. That which I speak I speak apon knowlege: I preferr the clothier befor the sercher, and the truth befor them both. And yet I meane not to laye any such wager as hath bene offred, for I will not offer to be hanged if it be not true I saye, but I will gage my credytt apon it.

'The lawe makers hertofore, apon the reason that moved them then, brought the breadth of cloath from 8 quarters to 7; so reason moving us now why may not we bringe it from 7 to 6 and a half.

'The termes which have bene rehersed of our clothes which the strangers use, as bands, okyn [?] *etc.*, I care not of them and I thinke he understandes them not that spak them. But of this I am sure, what fault so ever is in our clothe, by what name soever yow terme it either in lenght or breadth, the marchaunt dothe answer it to the byer beyound the sea, and apon certificat the marchant is answered it of the clothier agayne,' *etc.*

Bronkard[135]   'I may wurst speake of a great many, yet that will I speak as truly as any that have spoken. I will not alleag auctority that cannot be seen, but here is the booke, and I will read yow the lettre of the law by which it appeares that in the tyme of *Magna Charta*, King John and Richard 2, in which tymes it was alleaged that order was taken for the breadth of English clothes, that then ther was no cloth made in England.

'This fault is not voluntary in the clothiers for they lose 40^s and can not gett by it 40^d, they answer the marchaunt. It falles out so, by a certeyn secrett mystery, cloth all of on waight, bredth and lenght comes from the myll some longer, some narrower then they were delyvered out.

'If ther should be 3^{li} added to every cloth as was requyred by him that spake first, in 5 thowsand clothes is loste a thowsand, so recken the custome that is lost to the Quene that way. So I conclud ther is neither truthe nor reason in that which hath bene sayd.'[136] /

f.175   A bill for the payment of Bassette's debtes.[137] Alleaged he had made two severall deputyes of an office he had of a receyvorshipp.

That he had sold it to two for mony and secrettly surrenderd it to a third. This Basset is a recusant.

In the bill of wardes[138] that none shall make lease above a C yeares.

Grafton, against it. That men that have leases of a M yeares can not mak out of this for a C. Beneficiall to officers of the courte.

Kyngsmill   'I trust I shalbe accounted an honest poore man. For any profitt I gett in my office more then the dignite of serving her Majeste I would a nother had it. I have gotten no lease synce I was officer, the wardes as well used and apon comleynt the committe dryven to compound reasonably, if they have exacted.'

Bacon[139]   'Many rather myslike of jelousy and are tymerous of that they conceyve not.

'I will open playnly to yow that this bill is harder in some poynt.' If he had as substantially answered that as he confessed it plainly. Speaking of the Quene woorthy to be respected, for his father had recyved by her ability to leave a 5 sonn, to lyve apon, but that is nothing to the matter. 'Then yow should have let it alone.'

'This bill hath ben spoken to of many very learnedly, ever as I have hard used hertofore.   Recorder

'I may be thought indifferent, for this I know, the Court of Wardes hath taken away almost all the wardes of our duchy.[140]

'All your courtes have their names of on thing or a nother: *Scacarium, Camera Stellata*. But now yow will say I am out of the matter: but yet the best is I will come in agayne, but some ther be that never come nere the matter at all, and if they be once out never come in agayne.

'Ther be 10 pipes, *vicecomitum, escaetrie*.

The Court of Wardes very honorable for iustice, 'I would all the rest of the courtes were so, they that have to dele ther shalbe very discretly and mercifully delt withall. I have found it so in myn own case or els I might have had that layd on my back would have made it crack.

'The pipe of the Court of Wardes dryed up 1000 markes a yeare. We must learne of them of London that are now searching the pipes because the water runnes not as it was wont to do.

'We have a terme in the law called *beaupleder*, that is yll pleding, *ironice*, for I tell yow we have figures in the law now and than as well as other.

'Richard 2 made blankes to dyverse with the great sceale and then they wrat what they listed, this slyftes the revenue. Let us give her Majeste her due revenue or els she must have subsedies and 15[s].

'I could putt yow a thowsand cases apon this poynt for I was a mote man 30 year together but I'l let it go and I tell yow plainly Mr Speaker the bill is a very good bill.' /

'I was a comitte in thys bill, and ther was ioyned with me such as I desire to have, that is men both learned and wise; and for my self I added my poor endevour also.   v. Sollicitor

'If I did think it would wrong or preiudice the subiect any way I would not allow of it or give my consent.

'For, thought I am an officer of her Majeste, yet I have children and may have land to leave them.'

'I will not speak against the bill, but I see many doubt of it. It is of great waight, it toucheth every man's landes. The greatest part towardes the lawe ar absent, therfor it were well it [were] better advised apon, and that we did signify unto the Lords so muche.'   Saunders

---

134. *Commons* identifies this speaker as Henry Unton, though Edward Unton is a possibility, as, perhaps, is George Upton.

135. Henry or William Brouncker (*Commons*).

136. This paragraph is written in the margin. Hereafter, a different ink is used, perhaps the same one employed for the speeches beginning on f.173.

137. See D'Ewes, pp.372, 373 for 24, 26

March: the bill was held over for the next parliament.

138. *EP*, ii.92 suggests this is from the final reading debate of 25 March, but 24 March cannot be ruled out (D'Ewes, pp.372, 373).

139. *EP*, ii.93 identifies this as Francis Bacon's first recorded parliamentary speech: Edward and Nathaniel were also sitting however (*Commons*).

140. *Sic.*

4. Sir William Fitzwilliam's journal, 23 November 1584–29 March 1585

Text from Northamptonshire County Record Office, Fitzwilliam of Milton Papers 2, fair copy of original.
Other MSS of:
Mildmay's speech, 28 November:
London: BL Sloane 326, Harley 6265. Oxford: Bodley, Rawlinson C.838 ('Rawl' in the footnotes here). California, USA: Huntington Library, Ellesmere 2584.
Mildmay's speech, 24 February:
London: BL Sloane 326, Harley 6265. Oxford: Bodley, Rawlinson C.838.
Commons Petition to Lords:
London: BL Lansd. 42 (two copies, one in the hand of a secretary, probably Whitgift's, the other in the hand of a secretary of Burghley's and endorsed by him ('Lansd. i' and 'Lansd. ii' in the footnotes here), Add. 38492, Harley 158, Lansd. 396. Inner Temple, Petyt 538/52. Oxford: Bodley, Tanner 78. Cambridge: Gonville and Caius 53 (incomplete; 'Gon' in the footnotes here). Petition printed in D'Ewes, pp.357–9; Strype, *Whitgift*, iii.118–24.
Whitgift's answer to the petition.
London: BL Add. 40629 (text and heading as in Fitzwilliam), Add. 38492 (text as that from which the marginal variations in Fitzwilliam are apparently taken; no heading, and ascribed in catalogue to Sandys). Oxford: Bodley, Tanner 78.
Answer printed in D'Ewes, pp.359–60, 'a little altered and enlarged', following neither of the Add. MSS exactly, and ascribed to Sandys on the evidence of the Commons Journal. See also Strype, *Whitgift*, i.350–4 (from D'Ewes).

Fitzwilliam of Milton Papers, 2, fos.1–39v.

Anno 1584 Moondaie the 23th of November the Queene came to the Parliament House.

Unto whose Majestie after the Speaker (which was Mr Seriant Puckkering) according to the usuall order amonge other thinges had made the petition in the name of the Nether House, that thei might have libertie and freedome of speache, it was aunswered him by the Lord Chauncellor that hir Highnes willinglie condescended therunto, onely shee restrained the cause of religion to be spoken of amonge them.

It was thought verye straunge that the Nether House should be restrayned in anie matter, but especiallie to speake or move that which [for the most parte][1] heretofore had his beginninge *vearie often*[2] from that place; which was the cause of religion; for by searchinge of the recordes it appearethe that from xxi^{mo} Henry 8 and a yeare or two after when the Pope first begann to stagger in England, [all or the more parte][3] *vearie manie*[4] of *the*[5] Church matters tooke theire beginninge from the Nether House.

vidz.
Kinge Henry the 8.

23 Henry 8 cap.4. Citations[6]	Segneurs:	The proviso for the Archbishop of Yorke added by the Commons	Gathered out of the Parliament roles:
24 Henry 8 cap.12. That no appeales	Commons		
25 Henry 8 cap.14 for punishment of heresie	Signeurs		
Submission of the Clergie cap.19			
	Commons:	here is mencyon that such Canons onelie shalbe executed as be not agaynst the kinge's prerogative or the lawes and statutes of the realme.[7]	
Annates cap.20	Signeurs		
Exoneration cap.21	Commons:	as in the first lyne.[8]	
Deprivation of Lawrence Campeigns Bishop of Salisbury and one Hyerom[9] Bishop of Worster			
straungers not printed	Commons:	with an addition by the Lordes that if within 4 monethes thei would come into Englande and submitt them selves to the kinge to be received to favour. /	

1. Deleted.
2. Inserted in a second contemporary hand.
3. Deleted.
4. Inserted in a second contemporary hand.
5. Inserted in a second contemporary hand.
6. Correctly 23 Hen VIII, c.9 in *SR*, iii. 377–8.
7. See *SR*, iii.461 for the proviso.
8. Refers to note above for c.19. See *SR*, iii.470 for the proviso in this act.
9. Jerome de Ghinucci was Bishop of Worcester. See 25 Hen. VIII, c.27 (1533–4) in *SR*, iii.483–4 ('Hierome').

v.	26	Henry 8 cap.1 the kinge's supremacie	Signeurs	
		The othe cap.2	Commons	
		First fruites cap.3	Signeurs	
		Suffragauns cap.14	Commons	
Henry 8	27	Not printed[10] dissolution of certaine religious houses	Signeurs	
	27	Henry 8 an acte wherby cap.15[11]	Signeurs	
	28	Henry 8 an act extinguishinge cap.10	Signeurs	
		An act compellinge spirituall persons to keepe residence cap.13	Commons	
		Release of pretended licenses[12]	Signeurs	
	31	Henry 8 an act abolishinge cap.14[13]	Signeurs:	*avec un billa per letr commurra*[14]
		Dissolution of Monasteries[15]	Signeurs	
	32	Concerninge trewe opinions cap.26	*non invenitur*	
Henry 8 et	34	ffor advauncement of religion *cap. primo*	Signeurs	
	35	Examination of Common lawes cap.16	Signeurs	

EDWARD 6

Edward 6	I.	Speakinge of the sacramentes[16]	Signeurs	
		Elexion of Bishops[17] cap.2	Signeurs	
Edward 6	I*mo*.	Suppression of Chauntries cap.14	Commons	
Edward 6	2° *et* 3°.	Uniformytie of service cap.2 *et* 3[18]	Signeurs	
		Eodem for preistes' mariages cap.21	Signeurs	
Edward 6	3° *et* 4°.	Abolishinge of Divers bookes and Images cap.10	Commons:	In the preface mencyon is that nothinge ought to be redd in the Churche but the holy scriptures and that which is taken out of the scriptures.

Eodem naminge 32 to peruse ecclesiasticall lawes cap.11	Signeurs	
Orderinge of Ecclesiasticall ministers cap.12	Commons	
5° et 6°. ffor uniformytie of prayer *cap. primo*	Signirs	Edward 6
ffightinge in Churches and the yardes[19]	Commons	
Eodem kepinge of holy Dayes and fastinge dayes cap.*3ᵉ*	Signeurs	
Marriages of Preistes cap.12[20]	Signeurs	

QUEEN MARYE

		f.2
1. Repele of statutes *tempore Edwardi sexti* cap.12	[MS blank]	*Mariae*
1. *Sessione secunda*: offenders against preachers and ministers in the churches cap.3	Commons	*Mariae*
1. ffor punishment of heresie cap.6	Commons	*Philippi et Mariae*
and 2. Repelinge the statutes against the sea of Rome cap.8	Signeurs	

QUEEN ELIZABETH

1. Restoringe the Crowne to the auncyent Jurisdicion *cap.1ᵐᵒ*	Commons

10. 27 Hen VIII, c.28 (1535–6) in *SR*, iii. 575–6.
11. The act enabling the king to nominate 32 persons for making ecclesiastical laws (*SR*, iii.548–9).
12. 28 Hen VIII, c.16 (1535–6) in *SR*, iii.672–3.
13. 31 Hen VIII, c.14 (1539) in *SR*, iii.739–43, for abolishing diversity of opinions.
14. *Sic.*
15. 31 Hen VIII, c.13 (1539) in *SR*, iii. 733–9.
16. 1 Ed VI, c.1 (1547) in *SR*, iv.2–3.
17. 1 Ed VI, c.2 (1547) in *SR*, iv.3–4.
18. Correctly 2 & 3 Ed VI, c.1 (1548) in *SR*, iv.37–9.
19. 5 & 6 Ed VI, c.4 (1551–2) in *SR*, iv. 133–34.
20. *Sic.* 1 Mary, c.2 (1553) in *SR*, iv.202.

	Uniformytie of Common prayer cap.2	Commons	
ELIZABETH	5. Assueraunce of hir Majestie's power *cap.1mo*	Commons	
	8. Makinge of Bishops and mynisters *cap.1mo*	Commons:	The proviso added by the Lordes.
ELIZABETH	13. Bringinge in of Bulls cap.2	Signeurs	
	Leases of Benefices cap.20	Commons	
	Reformation of the ministerye cap.12	Commons	
ELIZABETH	23. Reteyninge of subiectes in obedience *cap.1mo*	Commons	
Richard 2[21]	16. provision and *premunire* cap.5	Commons /	

v.   The Saturdaye followinge beinge the 28 of November all the common house with their Speaker mett together in their usuall place beinge the first daye of their sittinges; where Sir Water Mildemay knight, Chauncellor of th'Exchecor and one of the Privie Counsell used this speach followinge:

Sir Walter   'I doubte not but as you be all wise, and men of understandinge,[22] so yow
Mildmaye's   can easilie thinke that the parliament called at this tyme doth grow uppon some
speache in the   great and urgent occasion. To the ende therfore that yow may the better fall
Lower House: into the consideration of such matters as for the weight and necessytie of them
are meete to be treated one in this assembly, I wilby your favours remember
yow of these thinges followinge:

1. First of the present state and condytion of this tyme:

Capita praecipua: 2. Next what enemyes we have that doe envye the felicytie thereof:[23]
3. Thirdlye what they desire and looke after:
4. And lastly what it behooveth us to doe.

'Of everye one of these somewhat, to geive wiser men occasion to saye more.

'Touchinge the first yow see that we enioye freely the preachinge of the ghospell delivered from the superstitions and tyranny of Rome, benefitt without comparison,[24] farr beyonde all other, and powred uppon us by the mightie and[25] mercifull hande of God: yow see allso that it hathe pleased him to sett over us a most gracious Queen by whose mynistery this pure religion of God is restored unto us, for the doeinge wherof you knowe that shee adventured the malice of divers potent princes hir neighbours, mortall enemyes to our profession.

Primi capitis   'What is in hir besides needeth not much to be spoken of, shee is knowne
explicatio.   not onelie to us, but to all the worlde, to be a princesse of virtue of wisdome, provident in goverment, in worde and deede constant. In all actions iust and trewe, lovinge to hir subiectes and beloved of them. Temperinge mercye with iustice to the comfort of all those that live under hir.[26]

'Moreover through the goodnes of all myghtie God by the ministerye of this our gracious Queen we have enioyed peace now full xxvi yeares the like wherof so longe together hath not bene seene in any age before. The commodyties wherof maye appeare suffyciently by comparinge the blessednes of this our happie peace with the miserable state of our neighbours longe[27] afflicted with crwell warrs. We posses in all freedome and libertie our religion which is the cheife: our lands, lives and goodes, our wifes and children. They one the other side through civill and intestine troubles are bereaved of all those good thinges that we enioye, in daunger to fall at the lengthe into the greivous yooke of perpetuall servitude. /

'For the continuance of this our peace hir Majestie hath and doth mayntaine amytie[28] betweene hir and all the princes hir neighbours, and speciallie with the King and realme of Scotlande, a nation most worthie in this poynte to be regarded: for that dwellinge with us uppon one continent or firme lande[29] they maye most easelie with[30] litle charge[31] offende us. To tye them therfore more suerlie in frendship to this Crowne, yow knowe how that at hir great charges hir Majestie hath delivered them from the tyrannye of straungers that sought utterlie to oppresse them; and by puttinge out also the fire of civill warrs emongst them selves hath brought peace to that contrye, and preserved their yonge kinge from his cradell, more carfully then any mother doth hir owne childe: a great cause of gratuitie one their side never to be forgotten, and a note of perpetuall infamie if ever they should be unthankfull or breed this realme trouble. And if they doe, then worthie of no favour here.[32]

'By this peace it hath pleased God to blesse this realme with great plenty and with great wealth: maugre those execrable curses which the Pope hath thondered out agaynst us, but our gracious God shall make them all retourne backe uppon his owne heade.

'Touchinge the iustice of the lawe, who can saye but that the same is indifferently ministred to all the people of the lande? A thinge of great necessitie in goverment, for like as iustice is the verye stronge bonde of the common wealthe that keepeth the subiectes in peace and order, even so the negligent handlinge therof setteth all thinges loose and opens a gapp to all outrages, both in civill and criminall causes; whereof proceede ryotes, oppressions, theftes, murders, and all other disorders. How little they are borne with in this realme, let it be free for enemyes to say the worst: so they saye trewlye. And let it be iudged by comparison of that which is and hath bene done in other contryes.

'This beinge the present state and condytion of this tyme yet ther wauntes

f.3

Fraunce:

Vinculum reipublici.[33]

2ⁱ Capitis explicatio.

---

21. *Sic.*
22. Harl. 6265: '. . . all wise men so yow'.
23. Harl. 6265 omits (+ Rawl).
24. Harl. 6265 omits 'without comparison'.
25. Harl. 6265 omits 'mightie and'.
26. Harl. 6265: 'them'.
27. Harl. 6265: 'beinge' (+ Sloane, Rawl).
28. Harl. 6265 omits (+ Rawl).
29. Harl. 6265 omits 'or firme lande' (+ Rawl).
30. Sloane: 'and' (+ Rawl).
31. Harl. 6265 omits 'with litle charge' (+ Rawl).
32. Harl. 6265 omits this sentence.
33. Harl. 6265 omits this marginal entry.

not enemyes that doe not onelie envie our felycytie but seeke to overtourne it[34] utterlie if they coulde.

'Emongst which the most mortall and[35] capitall enemye is the Pope that both hateth us and the verye soile that we treade[36] one, if his power were aunswerable to his will.

Bulla Pii 5 1569.[37]

'To shewe this to be so it maye suffice to remember as the first of his open accions: that impudent and most blasphemous Bull which he pronounced against our most gracyous Queen, wherby his meaninge was to have deposed hir and to have ruined us all at one blowe. For to note a litle some of the poyntes therof: the Pope dreaminge that he is the monarche of the whole worlde and that the kingdoms of the earthe are in his disposition to be geiven and translated at his will, he[38] saith that our rightfull Queen hath invaded this[39] Crowne by wronge, that shee is an heriticke and a schismatike: and thereuppon commaundeth that none obey hir, nor hir lawes; he dischargeth all hir subiectes from their othes and naturall allegieaunce, and geiveth hir kingdome for a praye to anie other that cann gett it. And all this in *plenitudine potestatis* which he takethe[40] to him selfe without warrant, either of the lawe of God or the lawe of man. And that theise thinges might take their full exequution[41] he sent

1569

into the northe Moreton, an olde runnagate preist, to publishe the Bull, which he did and therby raised a daungerous rebellion conducted by the Erles of Northumberlande and Westmorlande to the perill of hir Majestie and hir whole state. /

v.

'But this throughe the goodnes of God not takinge place and her Majestie overthroinge this whole conspiracye: yet no ende for all that of the Pope's malicious practises, ffor not longe after other attemptes weare in Ireland by James

1578 The Lorde Graye then Deputie of Ireland 1580.[42]

Fitzmorris, the Erle of Desmond, Jhon of Desmond and the Vicount Baltinglas stirred and nowrished by Saunders, an other lewde preiste. And these also failinge: a flatt invasion at lengthe into Ireland by men of warr sent from the Pope with banner displayed seazinge a place uppon the sea called Smirwicke; and fortifyinge the same as an entrye to subdue all the rest. To these may be added the aydinge and intertayninge of the rebells and fugitives, which beinge unworthie to be named Englishe, are neverthelesse mayntayned and cherished by him to worke all the mischeife they can agaynst their owne naturall contrye.

'And for a full confirmation of his malicious purposes towardes us, that notable conspiracye is not to be passed over termed by the name of[43] *sacrum foedus* sett downe in the counsell of Trentt: knittinge together all popishe princes and states to the overthrow of the ghospell in all places, but especiallie in this kingdome. For that the Pope fyndeth that this noble realme of all the monarchies in the worlde doth most abase the dignitie of his chaire. So as there is in him against us *odium implacabile* for we can never make our peace with him. Uppon this capitall and princypall enemye depend divers other malicyous and secrett practizers and of them the most pernitious those that are called Jesuites and seminarie preistes: a rable of vagraunt runnagates that creepe beinge sent hither by him closely into sundry partes of the realme; and are occupied to stirr sedition and to nourishe the corrupt affection of evill subiectes, and all this under pretence of reforminge men's consciences and, as they terme it, to save soules. And that this is so there nedethe no other example but the late publicke arraynement of Campion and his fellowes detected not for the superstitious ceremonyes of Rome, but for most highe and capitall offences and conspiracyes: as the deposinge of our gracious Queen, advauncinge of an other in hir place, alteration and subversion of this whole state and goverment wherof thei were iustly condemned *foro publico* by orderly and lawfull proceedinge accordinge to the lawe of this lande, notwithstandinge any slaunderous and false libell that hath or may be[44] geiven out to the contrarie.

'And to prove evidently theire inwarde and setled hatred to the Queen and hir state, will you heare what thei saide beinge asked openly whether the Peope had authorytie to depose the Queen and whether hir Majestie was a lawfull and rightfull Queen, notwithstandinge any thinge that the Pope hath or might doe? They aunswered, "It is a question of divinytie, we praye you demaunde no such thinge of us." By which doubtfull speach it is apparant what iudgment thei were of in a matter of so great importance. But now to put that question out of doubt, and to stablish the Pope's authorytie therin, they have in a pamphlet[45] lately wrytten agaynst the justice of England both maynteyned the Bull and brought many examples to prove that the Pope may depose princes as he did Henry the 4, Fredericke Barbarossa and other emperors, and amongst all our kinge Jhon. By which now they are certaynely resolved, and would have all men knowe that there is no doubt to be made of the Pope's power in that case. And so we may rest perswaded of theire iudgmentes and desires if theire habylities were therafter. But will you heare further of an other notable libell intytuled *De persecutione Anglicana* wherin thei sett forthe the great and extreame persequutions used towardes the Catholickes as thei call them: amplifying the same with a number of false and impudent lyes as though we lived here in Englande under Nero, Domytian, Caligula, and such other tyrauntes, and not under a most gracious and mercyfull Queen,[46] /[47] forgettinge in the meane f.4
tyme the great favoure and clemency showed to all papistes even to those that be most obstinate;[48] and forgettinge also the cruell persequutions used in the dayes of Queen Marye by preistes against a great number of good subiectes that with their bloud sealed the profession of their faith, which cannot without manifest untruthe be reported of this tyme. Nevertheless, they spare not to publishe the same most falslye to the worlde in sundry bookes, and passinge

34. Sloane omits (+ Rawl).
35. Harl. 6265 omits 'mortall and'.
36. Harl. 6265: 'breed'.
37. Harl. 6265 omits this marginal note.
38. Harl. 6265 omits 'and that . . . will he'.
39. Sloane adds 'land and' (+ Rawl).
40. Harl. 6265: 'arrogateth'.
41. Harl. 6265: 'effect'.
42. Harl. 6265 omits marginal note (+ Sloane); Ellesmere has only '1580'.
43. Harl. 6265: 'them' (+ Rawl, Sloane, Ellesmere) rather than 'the name of'.
44. Sloane omits 'that hath or may be' (+ Rawl).
45. Allen's *Defence of English Catholics*.
46. Harl. 6265: 'princesse' rather than 'mercyfull Queen'.
47. The word 'they' has not been carried over from the foot of the previous page here.
48. Harl. 6265 omits 'even to those that be most obstinate'.

over in silence those most horrible massacres and murders of many inocentes

Fraunce: that for the profession of the ghospell have lost their lives in other contryes even in their veue: never called, never harde, never iudged accordinge to lawe.

'This may suffice to shew yow the dispositions of theis men and the fruites of their learninge, which they get in their two principall schools: the one at

Petrarcha:[49] Rome, the sinke of all evill and the nest of all treasons, as a poet of their owne calleth it; the other at Rheymes begonne by the Cardinall of Lorayne,[50] a deadly enemye to religion and this realme, where amonge other are maynteyned Alen and Persons, two notable and false traytors to this contrye as by their actes appearethe.

'By which yow may see how diligent thei be to provide schooles for the advauncment of papacy[51] now declyninge: and how negligent we be to sett up and cherishe schooles, for the suppressinge of popery and the mayntenaunce of the ghospell which we professe and make so great a shewe to love. Next unto these lewde hipocrites, you are to thinke uppon our home papistes their schollers that bare inwarde malice to this present state as maye appeare:

by their stubborne recusancie to resort to our prayers and sermons and specially sithen the publishinge of the Bull;
their secrett receyvinge and harboringe of Jesuites and preistes;
their contributions to them and other like here and byionde the sease;
their education of their children and kinsemen in poperie;
and by their violent and contynuall speaches and threates[52] against this tyme.

'To these yow may ioyne such rebells and fugitives as be runn out of this contry and busie themselves to worke all the harme thei can to us that[53] remayne behinde. Enemyes also they are to be accompted which pretend or favour pretensed titles. And such ambycyous foraine princes as be devoted to Rome and redye at the Pope's becke to trouble the state, of whose might and force our adversaryes make great vauntes.[54]

3[i] *Capitis explicatio.* 'What theise so many and malicious enemies desire and looke after it is[55] easie to understande: the deposinge of our most gracyous Queen or violence to hir most royall persone, to advaunce an other in hir place, that may bringe their purposes to effecte. By which onelie meanes they looke for alteration of religion, that is to bannishe the ghospell and to restore poperye with all the tyrannye of Rome and therby to subverte the whole state and goverment of this realme.

'And here I beseech you consider what a[56] chaunge there would be, if in the place of the present rulers, thos preistes, rebells, fugitives and papistes knowne to be cruell and dissolute and vayne were sett at the helme of the Church and common wealth. And if any doubt what a miserable chaunge this would be, let him but remember the late dayes of Queen Marye, when not longe after the deathe of that vertuous king Edward, the Pope's authorytie was wholye

Spayne:[57] restored; and for contynuance thereof a straunge nation, prowd and insolent, brought into this land to be lordes over us. Which no doubt would have followed, yf God in his mercye had not delivered us and preserved as the apple of his eye this precyous iewell our most gracyous Queen. Looke, I beseeche you, a litle backe into that tyme and see what terrible feare all the subiectes of this realme, yea the most forwarde in poperye, were overwhelmed with, both for the doubt they had to live under the yooke of straungers, and for the feare they had to loose their abbye landes. For albeit great care was had by the acte of restitucion of the Romishe authorytie that all men should[58] saulfly enioye such landes as thei had of that nature, yet it is certayne that imediately after the Pope sent out a bull to cursse all such as possessed goodes or landes of the Churche. Nether doth the Pope thinke that he cann be bounde by any actes of our / Parliament, for his power is so large and high above all kingdoms of the worlde as Storye, a devoute servaunt of his, saide once in this House,[59] that for us here to bynde the Pope was as much as if London woulde make an acte to bynde all Englande. And if any of his ministers shoulde geive their faithe, promise, yea or their othe, for men's securitie, yet that auncyent decree sett downe in the Counsell of Constance, that freeth them from holdinge faithe with such as they call hereticke, is in their opinion suffycient to discharge them, as it did the husbande of Queen Marye that contrary to the articles of mariage[60] which yow may reade in the acte made therof brought the realme into warrs to sett forth his owne quarrell, the ende wherof was the losse of Calys to the perpetuall shame and damage of this lande. Thus you may see the fruites of poperye, the like wherof or worse you are suer to looke for yf ever the Pope have a suer footing here. And that all these fearefull thinges may come to passe and[62] light uppon us they lett not to practize a playne invasion into this realme. As by the confession of Francis Throckmorton openly read at his arraignment, at large appeareth: wherin is discovered[63] the names of the forayne captaynes that should invade, the places where thei should lande, and the names of suche here as should ioyne in ayde with their Catholicke armye, as thei call it. By which meanes they thinke to bringe into this realme bothe forayne and civill warrs and to raise the like fire amonge us as hath bene through the Pope's fyerye tormentes[64] kinled in our neighbour contryes. And therof thei looke should followe devastation of whole contryes, sackinge, spoylinge and burninge of cytties and[65] townes and villages; murderinge of all

v.

Philipp Kinge
of Spayne[61]

49. Harl. 6265 omits this marginal note, as well as the one above.
50. i.e. Charles Guise.
51. Sloane: 'popery' (+ Rawl, Ellesmere).
52. Sloane: '... speeches and continuall threates' (+ Rawl).
53. Harl. 6265: 'and'.
54. Harl. 6265: '... adversaries both abroade and at home do usually make great vauntes' (+ Sloane, Rawl, Ellesmere).
55. Harl. 6265 adds 'evident and' (+ Sloane, Rawl, Ellesmere).
56. Sloane adds 'state and' (+ Rawl).
57. Harl. 6265 omits.
58. Harl. 6265: 'such'.
59. Harl. 6265 omits 'once in this Howse'.
60. 1 Mary, stat.3, c.2 (1554) in *SR*, iv.222–6.
61. Harl. 6265 omits this marginal note (+ Sloane, Ellesmere).
62. Harl. 6265 omits 'come to passe and'.
63. Harl. 6265 has 'were described' rather than 'discovered'; Sloane has 'is described' (+ Rawl, Ellesmere).
64. Harl. 6265 has 'fier brandes' rather than 'fyerye tormentes' (+ Ellesmere).
65. Harl. 6265 omits 'sackinge ... cytties and'.

kinde of people without respect of persons, age or sexe: and so the ruine, subversion and conquest of this noble realme, the utter rootinge out of the whole nobilitie and people of this land and the placinge[66] in of straungers.

Explicatio 4[i] Capitis.   'Uppon all which thinges thus remembred it remayneth to consider what behoveth us to doe; wherein I shall have neede to spende fewe wordes speakinge to yow that I am suer doe take the same to harte, and be of iudgment to thinke uppon remedyes.

'Yet a litle to shew yow my owne opinionn I say that, like as in a naturall bodye the head is the princypall member, by which the rest are directed, even so in a pollyticall bodye of a commonwealth the prince is the heade and cheife director of all thinges done in the same. And like as for the preservation of the heade in a naturall bodye, all the members are readie to adventure any daunger to save that without which they cannot contynewe: even so al the subiectes of a realme ought bothe to be carefull and shonne noe hazarde to preserve the prince their heade without whom all they must needes perishe.

'And therfore the first and princypall matter that we ought to thinke uppon here in this great counsell is to provide by the strongest lawe we can make, a suffycient suertye for the preservation of the[67] Queene's most royall persone agaynst all malicious enemyes as have bene and are knowne to be practizers[68] to hir perill and our confusion: as was lately seene in Somervile's treason, for the which he had his iust rewarde. Addinge therunto straight lawes also against troublers[69] of this state under pretense of titles either present or future, therby to cut of their expectation if thei or any for them[70] shall dare to lift up their handes or hartes to endaunger the persone or state of our gracious queene. And bycause that like as raginge waters would destroy whole contryes, except thei were kept in with stronge banckes, even so least these malycious roging[71] runnagates, these Jesuites and preistes, should overflowe and over runne all the corners of this realme to the distruction of us all,[72] lett us provide stronge and straight lawes to keepe them under from troublinge of this peaceable state, lettinge them finde how daungerous it shalbe for them to come here or once to put their foote one lande within any her Majesti's dominions. Straight lawes also if neede require would be made against the usurped authorytie of Rome that it never rise up againe in Englande like as it hathe be[en] done by[73] hir Majestie's noble progenitors, which provoked by the insolencye of the Romishe[74] prelates, have bene driven to provide very penall lawes to bridle them and their favourers.

Conclusio: 'And thus to conclude, seeinge the present state and condycion of this tyme is suche and so blessed as we all desire the contynuance therof, and seeing our daungers[75] be so many, so mightie and so malicious; and seeinge that which they seeke and looke after is no lesse then the overthrow of hir Majestie and this whole state, I leave it to your considerations to thinke uppon these matters as of thinges of the greatest weight that can be spoken of: and therewith to provide suche remydyes in tyme as may be hable to prevent and withstand so many and so present daungers.'

Finis[76]

After which oration finished Sir Christofer Hatton, Knighte hir Majestie's   f.5
Vicechamberlaine and of the Privie Counsell, in a longe course of speache
amonge other matters delivered these poyntes concerninge the Kinge of
Spaine's dishonorable dealinge with her Majestei, her Majestie most sincerely seekinge amytie and peace with him:

At hir first entrance shee sought league with him, the Lord Cobham and Sir   Notes taken out
Thomas Chamberlayne embassadors: he utterly refused it. They intreated with   of Mr Vice-
him about the restitution of Callys which in honour he was bound to have   Chamberlaine's
consideration of, consideringe that his late wife Queen Marye, Queene of   speache.
England, to winne him the towne of St Quintan's lost both it and the peace
of France, but he prosequuted that with Fraunce[77] and concluded it nothinge
respectinge Callis, neither concludinge her Majestie and hir realme therin.

He ioyned in frendship with the Crowne of Scotland against the Crowne of
England as appeareth by his decrees, wherin he commaunded that no ordi-
nance, or any kynde of artillerie, should be shipped from out of any his
domynions into England but into Scotland so muche as they listed. The second
tyme shee sought a league with him by the Lord Vicount Mountague, the Lord
Cobham, Sir Thomas Chamberlain: but they could receave no good and
directe aunswere, neither was any leauge concluded.

Hir Majestie after this sent an embassador resident, Mr Man,[78] who was most
iniuriously handled, for at his first arrivall his carriages weare searched and
ransackt and after taken from him: as though he had bene a spye or an open
enemye. At his cominge to the Court where he had thought to have found
redresse, there was he most coldlye used, no audience geiven him: but uppon
longe taryaunce and in conclusion him selfe a man verye well addicted to
Christe's truthe, and thereafter brininge up his children and famylie,
constrayned (mauger his heade) his sonne to assist the preist at masse. Besides
all this the king of Spayne cooppleth him selfe in leauge with the Pope against
the Queen our mistres, geivinge his worde to ioyne with him in any action
against England, as well appeared by the doeinges of his embassadoure the
Bishop of Aquila[79] who by all meanes he might sought to stirr rebellion in
Englande.

La Mott, governour of Gravelyn, cam over at that tyme disguised to consult
with Guerres[80] about rebellion and to sounde our havens and to see our

66. Harl. 6265: 'planting' (+ Sloane, Rawl, Ellesmere).
67. Sloane omits 'preservation of the' (+ Rawl).
68. Harl. 6265: 'practised' (+ Sloane, Rawl, Ellesmere).
69. Harl. 6265: 'troubles' (+ Rawl).
70. Harl. 6265 omits 'or any for them'; Rawl has 'of' rather than 'for' them.
71. *Sic*; Harl. 6265 omits.
72. Harl. 6265 omits 'of us all'.
73. Rawl: 'to'.
74. Sloane: 'popish'.
75. Harl. 6265: 'enemies' (+ Sloane, Rawl, Ellesmere).
76. Harl. 6265 omits (+ Sloane, Ellesmere).
77. The words 'but he prosequted that with Fraunce' have been added.
78. 1566.
79. i.e. De Quadra.
80. i.e. De Guaras.

strength. After, Choppin Vitelley came over to further the same rebellion which was the rebellion of the Northe.

Besides all this to shewe their malice towardes hir Majestie the Pope saincted all our rebelles beinge executed: the king of Spayne wrot to Roda his governor in the Lowe Contryes for the tyme, after the death of the Commendadore to releeve all the Northren rebelles with pencyons.

Notwithstandinge all this, hir Majestie still seekinge peace and amytie with the saide king was content to receive his embassador Don Barnardie De Mendosa as a resident, using him most honorablie, who for all that and besides his faithfull and most assuered promis that he would deale in no matter, wherunto hir Majestie should not be made privie, sought presently to have intelligence with the ministers of the Queene of Scotes, geivinge thereby intelligence to all hir frendes abrode, wherby both foraine and civill warr might arise. In which conspiracye this was the drifte, that the papistes at home should ayde the frendes and so purchase the Scottishe Queen libertie. He also intruded him selfe into Charles Paggete's[81] doeinges that was a great practiser with the forayne force and cam over hither under the name of Moke, brinninge worde what force was readie abroad and devised what waye was best to beginn at home. Besides all this: Francis Throckmorton a practizer for the Queen of Scotes and Morgaine[82] a dealer betwene Throckmorton and hir; bothe they had recourse to the said embassador shewinge him how thei had practized to have force from Rome, Spayne and Fraunce and that their intent was to sett the Queen of Scottes at libertie and to have a tolleration of religion in Englande wherunto he gave his likinge, sayinge that the matter was feceible.

About this Throckmorton was divers papers founde shewinge what noble gentlemen was in a redines to geive aide to this enterprise and also what privat gentlemen, and that Chesshire was a good contrye for them first to land in.

Mendosa uppon these reportes thinkinge all thinges to be in a readynes solycites his Master and the Pope to beginn. The Pope findinge him self unhable to attempt such a matter craveth ayde of the Spanish King, whose aunswere was that his Lowe Contry causes so soked / awaye his treasour that he was not in case to enterprise the matter bu[t] wisheth a stay untill he were more fitt for the matter: whereby their purpose was put off.

v.

But here the matter stayed not, for besides Don Johac[83] uncurteous usinge of divers of hir Majestie's ministers imployed in those affaires: as Mr Secratary Walsingham, Sir Edward Horsey, and afterwardes his owne uncurteous usinge of Sir Jhon Smithe at one tyme and Mr Wilkes[84] at an other tyme purposely sent unto him into Spayne. Newe practizes were devised against her as appeared by certayne papers found about a Jesuite lately taken, wherein was conteyned a contribution of divers for this action, an invasion of straungers, a rebellion of subiectes, overthrowe of the present state, the declaration of oportunyties and such others, and also how the Kinge of Spain hath geiven him a taxacion of the clergie of Spain to further him in this action; how he hathe appoynted his cheiftaynes, Lennox for Scotland, Guise for Fraunce; to send 8000 men readye furnished and 8000 men here besides of his owne charge, armor also for 300 men to come out of Scotland and with theis a great partei remayninge at home to receive them all which was disapoynted by the deathe of Linnoxe.

Hir Majestie used Mendosa curteiously for all this, but he most iniuriouslye chalenged hir for theise thinges followinge: aydinge the Lowe Contrye men; th'arest of the Gennases[85] moneye; assistinge Marques Hoverig[86] with money; hir favour towarde Mounsire and Donn Anthonio; Egramount Ratclife's[87] conspiracye against Donn Jhon.

Finis

Uppon the endinge of these speache[88] before the House rose, they all argeed to meete together the same after noone in the Checor chamber appoynting committies to the number of [MS blank] that mighte consider of some poyntes and forme of lawe for the preservation of hir Maiestie's saiftie wher meetinge at the tyme lymyted, Sir Walter Mildmaye, Chauncellor of the Exchecor and one of hir Majestie's Privie Councell, breakinge as it were the yse for the better entrance into the matter summarilye delivered this speache as followethe.

Videlicet /

What greate enemyes hir Maiestie had that did envie this State, which were   f.6

       1. Pope
       2. Jesuites
the   3. Papistes at home
       4. Rebells ffledd
       5. Fugitives

All which did shoote at one marke: namely subversion of the present state of this governementt.

The cause whie they did it was to displace our Queen to sett up an other.

The consultation followed:

How to meete with their future expectacion; that such as did make open

       1. Invasion into the realme
       2. Rebellion within the realme
       3. Or did practize to use violence against hir royall person

might feele a penaltie and that in the highest degree. /

After the matter thus opened, some gave their opinion that no waye could   v.
be invented so perfecte for hir Majestie's safetie as to take awaye that person in respecte of whom all the mischeifes had bene heretofore wrought towardes hir

---

81. Acting as one of Walsingham's agents, assuming the name of Mope according to *DNB*.
82. i.e. Thomas Morgan.
83. *Sic.*
84. Thomas Wilkes.

85. *Sic.* The Genoese bankers' money seized in November 1568.
86. *Sic.* Marquis de Havrech.
87. Brother of the earl of Sussex: see *CSP Spanish 1568–79*, pp.583–4.
88. *Sic.*

Majestie: which was the Queen of Scotes; and that unles some such order were provided as noe mischeife might proceede from hir who is the fountayne of all mischeife, they thought their proceedinges would be but in vayne.

It was aunswered that the mesninge was in this provision to touche noe particuler personn by name but thearbye so to provide for hir Maiestie's saiftie as if any one were to be suspected, from whom daunger might growe, that one thereby might be prevented, yf it fell out to be more then one, in like manner to foresee for all their doeinges, and so in generall be it but for one, or be their many that are to be misdoubted, that they all within the compass of the lawe may be comprehended, which wilbe as suffycient as if anie personne particularlye were named.

Uppon this by a generall consent of the comitties the drawinge of the matter into a forme of a bill was committed unto Mr Edgerton, hir Maiestie's Solyciter, Mr Kingsmeale,[89] hir Maiestie's Attornye of the Wardes, Mr Sannes,[90] Clarke of the Crowne in the Kinge's Benche, Mr Morrise[91] and Mr Owinge,[92] Councellors at the Lawe, who uppon the first of December in the same place exhibted a bill devided into six partes as followethe: /

f.7

The first parte.
If anie personne that doth shall
or maye pretend title to the Crowne
of this realme make anie open
invasion with the power of men to
the number of 2000, so as the invasione
bee not made by reason of anie former
warre to be heareafter made or
denounced againste the invador, or
stirr rebellion or geive aide to
rebellionn or shall devise or doe anie
thinge to the perill of hir Maiestie's
royall parsonne.
    Conteyneth in it
    1. Invasion
    2. Rebellion
    3. Perill to hir person.

In doubtinge what the number
shoulde bee it was holden moste
necessarie that a number certayne
should bee sett downe, for
avoydinge of confusion betweene
invasion and incursione,
especyallie for that the Scottishe
roades from whence invasion (if
anie bee) must needes come

might bee taken for invasions,
which are some tymes made
withe 1000 men and so perill
might growe to them that deserve
it not.

Wheruppon it was agreed that the
leauges betwene England and
Scotland shoulde be searched and
accordinge to the presidentes in
them conteyned the number
shoulde be sett downe.

In the leauges betweene England
and Scotlande no number was sett
downe.
In the leauges betwene Englande
and Burgundie an 100 was the
number. In the leauge betwene
Englande and Fraunc wherin
Scotland was concluded 300 was the
number.

It was thought necessarye that
albeit the number of 2000 shoulde
come into the realme in open
warre, yet it shoulde not be
accounpted no invasion if anie
occasion of warre were on our
parte first geiven to such frome
whom those men did come.

Some thought good to have
added herewithe the advouri[93] of
the prince from whence the
invadors should come, or by
whom the rebells should be
stirred upp.

But this was utterly reiected for that
many tymes invadors and rebells doe
not acknowledge by whose
procurement they take their
enterprises in hande. /

The seconde parte.   v.
The privie counsell, 5 Earles,
2 Bishopps, 6 Barones, the
Cheife Justices, the Master of
the Roles, the cheife Barone
and in default of them other
Justices of the Benches or
anie 24 of them, wherof 12 to
be of the Privie Counsell and sixe
of them to be Lordes of the
Parliament, shall examine and geive
iudgment and sentence uppon the

89. Richard Kingsmill.
90. Miles Sandys.
91. James Morice.

92. Thomas Owen.
93. *Sic*: avowry.

offences aforesaide in writinge,
mentioninge the names of the
Judges aforesaide and inrole itt
and proclayme it in London and
Yorke under the Greate Seale of
Englande.

The persone so adiudged to be
an offendore and his heires shall
loose his title to the Crowne
and be disabled.

Uppon this clause grewe some
speache that the lawe woulde
seeme uniust for that in all
criminall causes ther oughte to be
an accuser, the partie accused and
the iudge, which coulde not be
in this if the iudges, shoulde
proceede to iudgment before
sommounce geiven to the partie   Wheruppon this
accused to aunswere for him selfe.   proviso was added.

'Provided that notice shalbe
geiven to the offendor to
aunsweare to the matter and
shew his defence either in
persone or, by some lawfull
attournye.'

Conteineth in it
1. Commission
A 2. iudgement
3. Proviso. /

f.8   The thirde parte.
Yf anie acte or attempte be
to take awaye hir Majestie's
life wherby anie pretended
successor maye be advaunced,
that then everye person
attemptinge and the persone
for whom such offence shalbe
committed and all those that
maye clayme from by or under
him shalbe disabled to clayme
the Crowne.

The fourthe parte.
Yf anie persone shall advisedlie
and willinglie houlde and mayntayne
anie right or title in the person
offendinge [he] shalbe a traytor.

The fift parte.
Yf anie suche wicked acte or attempte
shalbe practised, taken in hande or
executed, wherby anie shoulde by the
untimelye death of hir Majestie bee
advaunced, that then it shalbe lawfull
for every persone to pursue, assaile
and prosecute to the deathe every
such persone offendinge and pretended
successor by whom, or for whom, anie
such wicked acte shalbe committed, and
their abettors, aydors and comforters
in that behalfe.

To this was opposed that iustice woulde faile if this acte were once committed, and therfore unless a heade were apoynted afore hande that shall geive iustice at that time and the courtes of lawe established by act to remayne in force in the intermeane tyme untill the Soveraine were knowne (for their debylytie groweth in that thei grounde uppon commission and not called by writte as the office of choroner is which ever endureth) it wilbe to smale purpose to proceede in this order, for hir Majesti beinge deade no place wilbe left for any commission which hathe noe force, but by her beinge, to sitt and determine uppon the punishing of the offendor. Wherunto was replyed that the latter pointe to make every man an officer woulde not be avayleable for the executinge of

This was reiected as a thinge that verye hardelie might be done. But the strengthe and life of the article was sayde to consist in that by the lawe nowe to be made, whosoever woulde prosecute the revenge was of him selfe an officer.

Againe that the same poynte also woulde worke great confusion and perill amonge the subiectes, it might be doubted in this respect, least that iustice, if that wicked acte should be committed, for be it, saide he, that a lewde persone committeth the villany in the behalfe of G, a pretended successor, and that G. is privilie consentinge therunto: the frendes of G. followinge that example of Cesare Borgio in Machavil, will execute that partie as an ill doer, and committinge the offence against the knowledge and will of G., wherby both the facte maye be salved, and the title saved to G. for the horrible facte beinge once donne and past remedye, and beinge knowne abroade that the persone offendinge is as an ill doer executed, and that by the appointment of G. the successor, who would suspect or at least what private man dare take uppon him to accuse G. as giltie of that crime, G.['s] estate beinge at that time as it wilbe

if hir Majestie should be once deade such question might growe amonge the competitors' frendes, eache faction strivinge to laye the fault from suche as they liked of, as greate slaughter might therby arise among them selves and no execution of iustice had for the princypall facte committed. /

v.

The sixt parte.
Provided that the Queene may
enable the heire of suche
person offendinge by proclamation
att London and Yorke and that
such heire so enabled by her
Majestie shalbe enabled onelye
by vertue of this acte and not
by anie other title to the
Crowne.
Conteyneth in it
an enablement.

Uppon this proviso grew great argument wh[e]ther men might saifelie in conscience yeeld that hir Majestie should restore them to abilitie of receavinge the Crowne whom thei by othe of Assocyation were bounde to persecute to the deathe: alledginge

It was aunswered that the entente of the othe and not the letter of the othe was to bee considered. The intent was hir Majestie's saifetie, her saifetie preserved, which remayned in hir owne construction and to be foreseene in hir owne pollycie how it should be, which might happelie that the othe taken advisedlye as it was coulde not bee dispensed with [by] hir Majestie.

fall out by restoringe of the offendor's heire (a great poynte of pollicye in deede for by persecutinge all the issue wherof the most parte, if not all, may be innocent of the crime a desperation might be thrust into them and so a greatter perill followe) our othe in allowinge thereof is not broken.

Besides this intendinge by lawe to preserve hir safetie, we must not unlawfullie preserve it, as we should doe by killinge the innocent for then our actions will not prosper as he saith that willeth *non facies malum ut inde veniat bonum.*[94] But seinge in this lawe some wordes maye be taken more strictly and other some may be taken other wise (as the partie offendinge by the letter of the lawe is severely to be punished) and the issue not offendinge by the equitie of the lawe to be untouched, let us take hold of thos that beste serve the intent, which is hir Majestie's saiftie, and thes comprehende the punishinge of the offendor and not of the yssue which never offended. For if we should doe other wise we should punishe the just as well as the uniust contrarye to that which is sett downe: *Absit ut puniatur iustus pro iniusto.* And that ill parentes have manye tymes good children we see by daylie proofe.

Againe it was saide that in lawe hir Majestie might restore the heire of the offendor and the subiect not breake his othe. For, saithe he, by th'othe of the Assocyation we are bounde to persequute to the deathe their

To this latter and seconde poynte it was aunswered that albeit in the subiecte it helde of necessitye as the case was sett downe, yet in the title of the Crowne it fell out other wise. As for example John a Stile attayntted of treason and exequuted,

94. This maxim has been attributed to Coke (H. T. Riley's *Dictionary of Classical Quotations* (1856)).

heires that may anie waye from, by, or under, them claime the Crowne; the father offendinge attaynted, attaintes all the bloode of the issue which beinge attainted by the father's acte are in lawe as deade and not capable of anie thinge. For the bridge beinge broken, how can thei pass over? So as the issue corrupted are not comprehended within the compasse of the othe, for that thei may not cleame from, by, or under, him attainted but remayne

f.9   to receive life and capacytie onely at hir pleasure, which toucheth not the subiectes' othe at all.

corruptes the bloode of William his sonne, wherby William is not to posses anie thinge of his father's. George the brother of John and uncle to William leaveth behinde him a great possession to discende to his nexte heire, which in lawe is the saide William. But that William is not capable of his uncle's lande by reason that his blood is corrupted by the attainder of his father. But standeth to them bothe and to all other as a deade man as touchinge the receivinge of any possession. / In the case of the Crowne it is otherwise. The Queen of Pyemount beinge next heire to the kingdome of Naples, after the death of Johne, the present Queene, upon some treason committed against the said Johne is attainted and executed, corruptinge thearby Ferdinando hir sonn's blood who was linially after hir deathe and the death of Johne the present Queen to enioye the saide kingdome of Naples and makes him therbye not capable therof. Still it must be supposed that Johne the rightfull Queene liveth. But Johne dieinge and the kingedome remaininge to faule of necessitie uppon the next heire, fauleth uppon Ferdinando the Queen of Pyemounte's sonne (for the Crowne faulinge lookes uppon no attayndor but takes the next in blood as though no attayndor weare) the verye faulinge therof cleares all disabilities and restores him to a capacytie by the right of his mother as if he had never beene touched in blood by hir attayndor. Thes sheweth that though the parentt be attaynted, and therby the blood of the sonne disabled, yet it

remayneth so but for a season, untill
the present inheritor against whom
the treason was intended (wherby
the attayndor grewe) shall decease.
After whom as unto the next heire
the kingdome presentlie descendes
unto the sonne as in right of
succession from the mother though
attaynted.

This beinge so, it is contrarye to our
othe that hir Majestie in hir life
time by our consentes should restore
the heire of the offendor. For albeit
the heire standeth disabled for the
present by the attayndor of the
parent, yet after hir death the saide
heire maye cleame the Crowne as
from, by, or under, the parentt
attainted. And our othe goeth that
we shall prosecute to deathe such
heires as may any waye cleame
from, by, or under, the parent
offendinge.

The daye after this longe argument and small satisfaction one of the committies
in the same place offered a proviso wrytten to be added to the same bill which
conteyned in effecte as ffollowethe.

The proviso offered
to be annexed to
the bill.

That if anie successor should combine
him selfe in leauge with the Pope,
alowinge and receivinge his religion,
[he] shoulde for that facte be disabled
for ever to cleame the Crowne. /

This proviso coulde in noe sort be allowed for three respectes.   v.

1. The first in that itt medled with succession and in effecte lymited it which
   waye it should goe, a thinge most dislikinge to hir Majestie and utterlye
   forbidden us to deale with.
2. The seconde for that it pointed at a specyall successor made manifest to all
   the worlde by a booke lately published by the Bishopp of Rosse and
   knowne to be of a contrarye religion to ours, so as *ipso facto* that successor
   weare to be disabled, whereby might followe presentt warre, to the
   endaungeringe of our present estate.[95]

95. See *DNB sub* Leslie, John for Ross's
    book, *A Defence of* . . . (1569) and the
    various editions.

3. The third the hasard that might growe by the example theareof to the generall cause of religion thorowe this parte of the worlde, ffor if this shoulde proceede and come to effecte amonge us, no doubt but the Pope and the Duke of Guise would take hold uppon this to worke the like withe the kinge of Fraunce for the disablinge of the kinge of Navarre, uppon whose good successe (so farr as worldlie witt can stretche) the eye of the whole Church is at this daye fixed.

Besides this it was saide that in comparinge of tymes we shall fynde what great mischeife had fallen uppon our selves had this bene put in practise by our predicessors. For had Queen Marye done the like, what had become of our soveraine by whom we nowe at this daye enioye the ghospell?

So as, in respecte it was a thinge forbydden by hir Majestie, it was to drawe present warr uppon our selves, the example was most daungerous to the Church at this daye, and that to our successors it might breede no small inconvenience; the proviso written was delivered to the partie that brought it in and no more speache had of it.

Uppon the Thursdaye before the cession ended beinge the xviith of December it was delivered to the House by Sir Christofer Hatton, Knight, hir Majestie'[s] Vicechamberlayne that hir Highnes findinge the proviso conteyned in the bill to breed suche argument and to make such devision, uppon hir gracious goodnes would have it cleane dashed out. Wheruppon the committies the same after noone mett in the accustomed place for the finishinge of the bill as it should be preferred to the Parliament house the daye followinge. /

f.10   In which assemble, after the proviso was strucken out, all other thinges, as it was thought, fullie perfited, a member of the House findinge him selfe as yet not satisfied, saide:

That to the bill as it was then penned he coulde in noe wise geive his consent, and that for two considerations.

Which were

the respect of his   1. Duetye towardes God
                      2. Creditte in the worlde.

1. The cause whie in duetie he was urged not to allowe of the bill was, that in th'Assocyation and the bill he founde a playne contrarietie: beinge by othe of the Assocyation, which he had taken, bounde to doe more then the bill nowe in penninge he was warraunted to doe by lawe; ffor proofe wherof saide he:

The private parsone offendinge.

'The othe willethe me with all manner of revenge to withstande, offende, and pursue all manner of persons whatsoever with theire abettors that shall attempt by acte, counsell or consentt to anie thinge that shall tende to the hurt of hir Majestie's royall persone, and by all my force to seeke their utter extirpation.

The pretended successor and his heires offendinge.

And also not onelie never to allowe, accepte, or favour anie that maye, or shall, pretende title to the Crowne, or anie that maye clayme from, by, or under such pretended successor as unworthie of the goverment of this realme, that by the death of hir Majestie wickedlie attempted by anie other person shall seeke to be advaunced to the same, but also to prosecute unto deathe all suche persone and persons and seeke revenge uppon them to their utter extirpation. /

'But this bill nowe in penning warrantethe me to pursue, assaile, and prosecute unto the death everie persone practisinge, takinge in hande, or exequutinge anie wicked acte or attempte therbie to haisten the untimelie deathe of hir Majestie.

'And also suche pretended successor with his aidors, abettors and counsellors in that behalfe, for whom suche wicked acte shoulde be practised, taken in hande, or exequuted.'

Thes two in his conceipte so farr differed as th'one encluded the pretended successor with his heires,[96] the other the successor alone with his aydors,[97] which unles he might see well reconcyled he durst not for his parte geive consent to the bill.

2. The cause whie for his creditte's sake he was moved not to allowe of the bill was, that the worlde might iustlie condemne him and all others of greate wantt in iudgement, who so rashlie woulde enter into the othe of Assocyation for doeinge of a thinge which afterwarde uppon better advisement thei could not warrantt them selves to doe by lawe, which the rather, as he saide, woulde be noted for that in common opinion the Parliament was called immediatelye to fortifie the Assocyation and in proofe fell out cleane otherwise.

1. The aunsweare to the first consideration conteininge matter of conscience and dewtie towardes God, was, that for the satisfaction therof, he must compare the equitie of th'othe of the Association, which he hadd taken, with the intente of the bill nowe in penninge; wherby hee should finde that though the expresse wordes in th'Assocyation seemed strictlye to comprehende more then thos in the bill, yet implicative the bill importeth noe lesse then the Assocyation, albeit in the punishment it seemed to fall much shorter. So as in due consideration they could not be called *contraria*: but were *diversa*.

To prove which, and that th'Assocyation and the bill nowe in penninge as they were bothe most lawfull, and concurred together in one sence, so they maye stande in equitie by them selves th'one without th'other, he proceeded in this manner of proofe: /

By the Assotiation we are bounde to prosecute him to the deathe that will undertake anie villanous fact against hir Majestie's royall persone, and anie that have maye or shall pretende title and their heires which shall procure the same therby to be advaunced to the Crowne, which othe as it is of it selfe most honorable and lawfull (for who will not prosecute suche as shall laye violent handes uppon our lawfull soverayne, the Lord's annoynted) so the ende therof is to be considered for the which it was taken: namelye hir Majestie's saifetye, and that consists as well in the punishment of suche as goe about to use violence against hir persone, as of those also with their heires that procure the

v.
The private persone offending.

The pretendinge successor with his aydors abettors and counsellors offendinge.

The aunswere to these two doubtes.

f.11

---

96. Underlined in MS.   97. Underlined in MS.

same, for theire advauncement to the Crowne. Which sheweth that the punishment extendes no farther then to suche onelie as worke and procure the mischeife, for the othe weare most unlawfull before God, and not sufferable amonge men if therby we were bounde to punishe as well the innocent as nocent. As for example, the parent offendor by this othe is punished and so is the sonne.[98] But how? The sonne beinge partaker with the parent in offence. But the parent offendor punished havinge a sonne not privie to the facte, or intent, most penitent for his father's offences, workinge all good offices in duetie and service, hopinge therby to purge him selfe, from his parente's crime: to punishe that sonne by reason of the saide othe were most uniust and horrible. So as not so muche the strictnes of the letter in the othe is to be considered, as the equitie of th'othe, which is to punishe the offendor onelie. And that othes unlawfull and rashlie taken are before God no othes, but severely to be punished if they be to be performed, by divers examples in Scripture is most manifeste.

By the bill nowe in penninge the partie committinge that odious acte and the pretended successor for whose advauncement such horrible facte is entended or committed shalbe persequuted to the deathe with their abettors, aidors and comfortors in that behalfe: a thinge of it selfe most alowable of all trewe subiectes to be performed. But by reason that the wordes in the bill faull shorte of the wordes in th'Assocyation, for the punishment, the ambiguitie riseth: which in my owne conceipte and to the satisfieinge of my owne conscience is thus to be reconciled.

The bill punisheth the pretended successor with his abettors, aydors and comfortors in that behalfe.

The othe punisheth the pretended successor with his heires.

Then be it the pretended successor haith an heire, an aydor, abettor, and comfortor, in that behalfe, the saide heire is punished by the entent of the bill and strictnes of the othe.

But if the saide heire be not privie to the parente's intent or facte then, as well by the equitie of the othe, as by the intent of the bill, he is to be freed from punishment of deathe.

2. For aunswere touchinge his creditt to the seconde consideration, he called to wytness the Counsell there present whether the Assocyation were not in execution before the parliament was thought of: which they all confessed to be most true. And that noe such meaninge was as that the parliament should presently follow for the confirmation therof.

> And this was the last conference had about this cause, beinge not att all preferred to the House, by the commaundement from hir Majestie to hir Councell that were members of the Lower House. /

[fos.11v, 12 & v, 13 all blank.]

f.13v[99]   This matter thus digested, thei entred into consideration which waye to barr the comminge in of Jesuites and seminarie preistes the onelie disturbers of the peace of the realme and the verye instrumentes to worke hir Majestie's distruction, accountinge the prevention of their arrivall heare a princypall poynte for the preservation of hir Highnes' safetie. Which matter was breiflie drawne into thes heddes followinge.

I.

Those that remayned in prison order was taken that thei should be sett at libertie to goe their waye whose names were thes:
Jeames Bosgreave
John Harte
Edward Rushton
Henrye Orton
Jasper Haywoode
Willam Tedder
Sammuell Connyers
Arthure Pitties
William Warrington
Richarde Clarke
William Hartlie
Richarde Morrice
William Deane
William Bushop
Robert Nutter
Thomas Stevenson
Jhon Collington
Christofer Thomp
Thomas Worthington
Jhon Barnes
Willyam Smythe
21.

All Jesuites and seminarie preistes and other preistes made beyonde the sea, or in anie of hir dominions, by anie authoritie or iurisdiction from Rome since the feast of St John Baptist in *primo* of hir Majestie's rainge[100] shall departe within 40 dayes after this cession out of England and all other hir dominions if anie passage serve uppon paine of highe treason.

They first beganne 1542.
Ignatius Lullo was the firste. It was thought good that if winde and weather should drive backe a gaine beinge inbarquid so as thei coulde not within 40 dayes be out of the realme, or if anie master of a shipp would purposeli refuse to transport them, that in suche cases theye should be equallie considered. /

I[101]
All other preistes made after this cession shall not come into the realme uppon payne of high treason.

f.14

98. This sentence is a marginal addition.
99. At this point the following appears: 'These two were bynotes not appertayninge to the matter. Phocas the Emperor gave Boniface the Pope 600 yeares after Christ the first supremacye that the Popes cleame.

Anno 30th of Edward the First, it appeareth that the people of this realme found themselves greived with the Pope's usurpation.'
100. *Sic.*
101. *Sic.*

It was moved that whosoever should teache the Romishe religion should be as a traitor, because betwene the Queene and the Pope theire can be no communion.

This was not allowed because theirby treason and heresie should be confounded: wherbye the adversarye should have a great advauntage to saye that nowe seinge we could not convince theire doctrine by doctrine we sought to quenche it by makinge it treason. And the[re]fore unles it were distinguished what treason were and what heresie is, it coulde not be well to have them thus coupled together.

Some would have the preistes of what nation soever included withe in this braunche, made by the Pope's authoritie. But that was saide woulde be construed as a dishonorable lawe, wherbye other princes' preistes should be indighted of treason comminge amonge us. And most fitt it was sayde to bee to applie the lawe to the obiecte which was our home Jesuites, who did all the hurt amonge us. For Englishe men would not be ledd with straunge preistes.

Finallie it was saide that it might seeme a verye harde case to make it treason for a man to come into the realme without doeinge of anie other thinge: yet for that it was most apparaunt that those persons onelye have done the most harme therfore it was verye necessarye to have it so enacted. /

v.

2.

If anie man wittinglie or willinglie receive the Jesuites into his house or releeve them [he] shalbe a traitor.

It was thought that this clause was over harde as it stoode and therfore wished that by a proviso no man should be condemned without accusation of two wyttnesses: the reason was that thorowe out all places of the worlde by the civill lawe governed it was so used.

It was aunswered that the order and lawes of this realme were repugnant to it, for if in such cases none shoulde be condemned but those that were by two wytnesses to be accused, men ill disposed would so provide as never to be condemned, and therfore circumstances often tymes, as fullie prove as wittnesses, which by our lawe is effectual. As for the civill lawe, we that be Englishe men have nothinge to doe with it but must looke to our owne lawe.

It was also uppon this pointe remembred that by a statute of 25^t of Edwarde the Thirde,[102] it was enacted that whosoever ayded or assisted anye that was an enemye to the Crowne of Englande should be a traytor: and in all the lawes that ever were made against traytors no proviso was used, and therfore in this case not to be alowed. /

3.

If anie of hir Majestie's subiectes
not beinge a religious persone
brought up in anie of the
seminaries retourne not by
a certayne tyme lymited by
proclamation [he] shalbe a
traytor though he retourne
afterwarde.

This clause at the first beinge penned that they shoulde retourne within 40 dayes after the proclamation was thought verie harde for that the place might be so farr of as that they shoulde not within 40 dayes bothe have notice of the proclamation and also retourne. Againe scholers, for they are the personnes now touched, be not ever more so well provided for ioyrninge as that they cann within so short space be provided for a iourneye: and therfore it was wished the tyme should be 6 monethes accordinge to the statutes of fugitives.[103]

Though the reason weare alowed that the time of 40 dayes might prove to shorte so againe it was saide that 6 monethes might prove to longe if the parties were nearer that should retourne, and therefore was it thought most requisite the distance of the place beinge uncertayne to referr it to the proclamacion and the time therin lymited. /

4.

v.

If anie persone shall sende
anie releefe to the Jesuites
after the 40 dayes by way of
exchaunge or other wise
wittinglie [or] willinglie
directlie or indirectlye,
the same persone to faule
into a premunire accordinge
to the statute of 16to Ricardi 2^{di}.

It was offered to have the first offence premunire and the second highe treason.

But this was not alowed because *pena* should not be *maior quam culpa.* /

102. 25 Ed III, c.2 (1351–2) in *SR*,
    i.319–20.
103. 13 Eliz, c.3 (1571) in *SR*, iv.531–4,
    explained by 14 Eliz, c.6 (1572) in *SR*,
    iv.598–9.

f.16

This braunche
is to remayne
but duringe hir
Majestie's tyme.

5.

No bodye to sende his childe
after the 40 dayes beyonde the
sease without licence obtayned
of hir Majestie and certayne of
the Privie Councell unles
cytizens or burgesses of townes
corporate or marchauntes to
learne languages for the followinge
of their trades or as marriners,
uppon paine to forfaite an 100^{ll}.

This braunche was thought harde in these two respectes

1. The first that men beinge in generall restrayned to sende over their children without licens inhibitethe the well disposed to sende over theire children alike with the ill.

2. The seconde that the licens is to bee gotten from hir Majestie, which would often prove a shute verye longe and difficult especiallie for the meaner sorte. And therfor was it wished rather to be from the Queene or 4 of the Privie Counsell.

It was confessed to be somewhat harde, but proofe shewinge that many tymes the children of suche as were them selves well disposed by sendinge over became moste wicked, and that the present mischeife also increasinge by others, was intollerable inforced the lawe one this sort. Besides this to shewe that this lawe is not so rigorous as in tymes past lawes to that effecte have bene, by a statute in Richard the 2^{di} tyme, it appeareth that none might goe at all.[104] /

v.

6.

Everie faulte committed against
this acte to be enquirable at the
Kinge's Benche or in anie other
courte within anie countie and
thorowe out all hir dominions.

7.

Anie master of a shipp maye transporte
anie Jesuite within 40 dayes so he
deliver theire names in wrytinge and
where theie tooke theire orders.

8.

This acte not to stretche to anie that
will within 40 dayes or 3 dayes after
this cession come in and submitt him
selfe to the Archbishop or other Bishop

or officer where he shall lande, settinge
downe under his hand within 6 dayes
after his arrivall his submission:
which officer shall conduct him to the
Bishopp or his Chauncellor to be
examined.

9.

If anie peare of the realme faull
into this offence, he to bee tried
by his peares, as in anie other cases
of treason.

Finis.

While this matter was a doeinge certaine complaintes were exhibited to the
Lower House the 13 daye of December from out of divers counties of the
realme, amonge which the counties of Warwicke and Essex were two, havinge
vearie manye of the handes of the gentlemen of the greatest woorship in the
same shires subscribed thereunto declaringe therin the wantt of suffycient
ministers for the instructinge of the people, wheruppon the / members of the   f.17
same House appointed a certayne number of them selves to meete in the
Checor chamber to consider of the matter and to devise some waye to be
offred to the Lordes of the Higher House in a conference with them for the
redressinge of the same and like abuses in the Church. Which daye of meetinge
fell out to be the 16 of December, where a member of the House, thought[105]
none of the committies for that purpose, tooke uppon him (in the defence of
the Bishops who bare the most blame for that matter) to shewe wheruppon the
grounde of the insuffyciencye of the ministrie grewe:

1. The barrennes of the universities to furnishe such
places with learned men after Queene Marie's dayes
which was popishe.

which
as he
saide was

2. The smalenes of the livinges to mayntayne lerned
men.
3. The fewenes in number of suche as retourned from
banishement after Queene Marie's tyme to furnishe the
cures with.
4. The Bishopps subiect to *quare impedit.*
5. The lawe made in king Henry 8 tyme for alowinge
non-residentes.
6. The sufferinge of so manye Bachellors and Doctors of
Divinytie to take degree in the universities who by
theire degree are capable of manye livinges.

But hereunto was aunswered:
That the universities, if it were once seene that learned men might have

104. 5 Rich II, c.3 (1381) in *SR*, ii.18.   105. *Sic.*

preferme[n]t, would soone furnishe outt suffycient ministers to serve the cures, and though it mighte seeme verye straunge to displace all suche of a suddayne as be insuffycient, because therby a great number of cures should be unserved, yet better it were to suffer an inconvenience for a tyme then to endure a contynuall mischeife.

That wher the livinge is but smale the people as by proofe is seen will willinglie supplie the wantt so thei may have a suffycient man.

That the Bishops beinge subiect to *quare impedit*, dare not but alowe of such as are presented thoughe insufficyent, is but a coolor because *13mo* of the Queen a statute was made that none shoulde be admitted to the mynisterye, but such as can aunsweare to the articles in Latine or have a specyall gifte.[106] /

v.   After which aunsweare made upon further conference amonge them selves thei digested their consultacion into certaine articles under this title,

videlicet;

'The humble petition of the Commons of the Lower House of the Parliament, to be offered to the consideration of the right honorable the Lorrdes spirituall and temporall of the Higher House.'

But thei were not presented to the Lordes before the xxi^{th} of the same moneth followinge:[107] in which meane tyme uppon the Tuisdaye,[108] the xvii of the same.

Uppon which daye the bill of Jesuites beinge ingrossed received his last readinge in the Nether House, one burgesse amonge the rest named Parrie, a Doctor of the civill lawe, stoode up and inveyed agaynste it, not in anie orderlie sort consideringe the partes by them selves but *ex abrupto*, sainge that it caried no thinge with it but bloud, daunger, terror, dispaire, confiscation and that not to the Queene's commodytie, but to other men's. And that he doubted not though it past this House and the Lordes, yet it shoulde come to suche a blessed hande as would use it therafter, naminge hir Majestie to whome onelye and to no bodie els he saide that he would geive the reasons of his speache.

Doctor Parrie his case.

The House with this founde them selves greatlie greived and that for too respectes: /

f.18   1. The first for that one onelie member theareof shoulde charge the whole bodie of that grave assemble with so horrible matters as the seekinge of bloude, daunger, terror, dispaire, and confiscation[109] of the subiect and that not so muche for the Queene's saiftie, which they woulde seeme to pretende, as for the satisfyeinge of theire owne greedie desires after suche matters.

2. The seconde that he woulde geive no reason to the House whie he used those wordes against the bill, a thinge contrarie to the orders of the House, but as it were in contempte of the whole Counsell, which had geiven theire consentes to so odious a matter as that was, he disdayned to yeelde to them as men unworthie the reasons which he conceived against it.

Wheruppon it was moved that, to the ende he shoulde nether see the particular men that invaide against him nor heare theire propper invectives, he mighte accordinge to the auncyent custome of the House in suche cases bee delivered to the Seriauntt to be conveyed forthe untill the House's pleasure were further knowne.

But this was gainesaide by one that thought it not agreable to the liberties and ffreedome of the House that anie member therof for shewinge his opinion in a bill redd amonge them selves should be taken from his seate and sequestred from the socyetie; ffor bothe as he saide it would touche the majestie of the House if men should not therin have *libera suffragia*, and also it woulde be moste perrilous to suche matters as shoulde be propounded amonge them: ffor that the onelie waye to have matters perfectlie understoode and rightlie disgested was to suffer men freelie to utter their conseites of both sides. Besides he thought, it was iniustice that seeinge all men in that place had like authoritie one as muche as an other anie member there should be punished by his fellowe member. His reason was: *par in parem non habet imperium.* /

For all this Parrie was delivered to the Seriantt by a generall consentt to be conveyed out. Which donne, one of the House in aunswere to the former speache, saide that the libertie and ffreedome of the House suffered everye man freelie to deliver his opinion of the bill redd, either with it or against it, for therein consisted bothe the majestie of the House, and the perfection of such matters as passed from them. But if anie man woulde speake impertinentlie to the cause neither fortifieinge nor confutinge the partes thereof, but abruptlie would utter a speach to the offence of the whole companie (for he that speakes must speake to the matter of the bill either with it or against it) that was by auncyent presidentes severelie to be punished: as appearethe in Edward the 6 tyme when Storye after a bill redd, criinge out, 'Veh regno cui Rex est puer' and makinge an invective theruppon was sent to the Tower for his laboure.

Likewise, when Coplie after an other bill redd in Q[u]eene Marie's time, for hir saiftie, saide 'But here is no provision for the Ladye Elyzabeth', [he] was also committed to the Tower.[110] This man's case nothinge differinge from the other deserveth no les punishment then thes unles he will at the bar either recant his speaches uttered, or yeeld to the House some reason whie he used them. And, wheras it was saide that iniustice was offred him to be taken from his seate by his fellowes not havinge more authoritie in that place then him selfe, trewe it is that *par in parem non habet imperium* comparinge them singelie together, yet in a number where albe equalls unles the more parte might over rule the lesser, it would prove preposterous and breede confusion; and that manie maye commaund one, all havinge like authoritie as of late dayes in this House by some examples, it hath bene seene, so it is daylie put in proofe in the courtes, bothe of the Queene's Benche and Common Please where, though everye justice hath equall authorytie, the Cheife Justice noe more then the punie, yeat maye three of them over rule the fourth.

v.

106. 13 Eliz, c.12 (1571) in *SR*, iv.546–7.
107. The Lansd. 42/94 copy of the petitions was endorsed '19 December 1584' by Burghley.
108. *Sic.*
109. The words 'bloude . . . confiscation' are underlined in the MS.
110. For Story and Copley see *Commons*, ed. Bindoff *sub* Story, John and Copley, Thomas.

Presentlie uppon this Parrie was by the Seriantt brought to the barr within the House where kneelinge, beinge demanded by the Speaker, first whether he would stande to the wordes which he had before uttered, and secondlie if he woulde, then whether he would geive anie reason whie he used the same, he aunswered that the wordes which he had spoken, he would avowe, and theruppon repeated them over as before. And the reasons whie he spake them, he would reserve to shewe to hir Majestie and none other.

Hereuppon as a prisoner was he delivered to the Seriantt, to remayne with him, untill order were taken for his further committinge. /

f.19   The next daye followinge, the Seriantt was commaunded to bringe him againe to the barr, where after the Speaker had admonished him to beware that he did not persist in the error whiche he had the daye before committed, but rather by an explanation of his wordes or by his submission to satisfye the companye, verie humblie uppon his kneese he declared that beinge ignorant of the orders of the House (for this was the first tyme as he saide that ever he was of the same) he hadd rashelye, untemperatelie, and unadvisedlie behaved him selfe in his speache, and most humblye craved pardon of the whole House for the same.

Whereuppon the Seriantt was commaunded to carrie him forthe againe, and after some speaches used, amonge the which it was saide that hir Majestie recommended his cause to the House to be used with clemencye, as well because he had uppon ignorance misused himselfe, as also uppon a zeale to hir service he brake forthe into those intemperate speaches; beinge brought agayne to the barr was certifyed by the Speaker that uppon his humble submission and hir Majestie's most gracious message in his behalfe, the House was contente to remitt the offence and to accepte of him agayne as a member of the societie.

Which with all humblenes he accepted: ffirst humblie thankinge hir Majestie, secondlie the House, and thirdlye beseechinge the companie to accepte of him as a member under thes condytions, that if ever he committed the like offence agayne, to reiecte him, as a persone unfitt to be of the socyetie. /

v.

The humble peticions of the Commons of the Lower House of the Parliamentt, to be offered to the consideration of the right honorable the Lordes Spirituall and Temporall of the Higher House.[111]

1.[112]   First, where by a statute made the xiii[th][113] of hir Majestie's raigne, it was enacted that none shoulde be made minister unlesse he be able to aunswere and render to the ordynarie an accompte of his faithe in Latine, according to certayne[114] articles sett forthe in a sinode holden in the yeare 1562 and mencyoned in the saide statute, or have specyall gift and abilitie to be a preacher: it may please your honorable lordshipes to consider whether it were meete to be ordered, that so many as have bene taken into the ministery since the makinge of that statute and be not qualified, according to the trewe meaninge and intent of the same, be within a competent[115] tyme suspended from the ministrye, and exequution of any function therto appertayninge, untill he shalbe founde of that abylitie which the statute required.

That wherin a sinode holden in the yeare 1575[116] it was[117] provided that 2. unlearned ministers heretofore made by anie Bishopp shoulde not from thence forthe be admytted to any cure or severall[118] function, it may allso like their lordshipes to advise, whether so manye as have bene since that tyme admitted, contrary to the forme of that article, should be within a competent tyme removed; and that for better explanation of that article, such be taken for unlearned as be not qualifyed accordinge to the statute before recyted, and provision be made for the dewe execution of that article so declared for ever hereafter.

Where also in that grave and weightie charge which, in the booke conteyninge 3. the forme of orderinge of preistes[119] established by the statutes of this realme, is prescribed to be delivered to all suche as shalbe receyved into the ministery they are admonished that they be the messengers, the watchmen, the pastors, and stewardes of the Lord to teache, to premonishe, to feede and provide for the Lord's famylie, to seeke for Christe's sheepe that be dispersed abroade and for his children in the middest of the noughtie worlde, to be saved through Christe for ever: with other remembrances of sundry weightie partes of their duetye. It may please their honors to consider of some good order to be geiven, that none hereafter be admitted to the ministery, but suche as shalbe suffyciently furnished with giftes to performe so high and earnest a charge. And that none be superfyciallie allowed as persons qualified accordinge to the statute of the xiii[120] of hir Majestie's raigne before recyted but with deliberate examination of their knowledge and exercise in the holye Scriptures aunswerable to the trwe meaninge of that statute.

Further, for as much as it is prescribed by the saide forme of orderinge ministers 4. that the Bishopps with the preistes present shall laye their handes severally uppon the heade of everye one that receiveth orders without mencyon of any certayne number of preistes that shalbe present; and that in a statute made in the xxi[th] yeare of the raigne of kinge Henry the viii it is affirmed that a Bishopp must occupie vi chapplinges at geiveinge of orders,[121] it / may be considered f.20 whether it be meete to provide that noe Bishopp shall ordeyne any minister of the worde and sacramentes but with assistaunce of vi other ministers at the leaste. And therto such onely [to] be chosen as be of good reporte for their life, learned,[122] contynually resiaunt uppon their benefices with cure, and which doe

111. Gon has 'December 1584' before this title; Harl. 158 adds (in another hand) 'in *anno* 27 Elizabeth' at the end.
112. Lansd. 42(i) has 'ministery' in the margin here; Lansd. 42(ii) has 'ministers' (+ Lansd. 396, Petyt).
113. Lansd. 396: '14th'; Petyt: 'xiiij[th]'.
114. Gon omits, and has a blank.
115. Gon: 'compleate'.
116. Tanner: '1572'.
117. Gon adds 'enacted and'.
118. Lansd. 42(i, ii): 'spirituall'; Harl. 158: 'speciall'.
119. Tanner: 'ministers'.
120. Tanner: 'xii[th]'.
121. 21 Hen VIII, c.13 (1529) in *SR*, iii. 294 (sect.xiii).
122. Gon: 'and learninge' rather than 'learned'; MS has apparently been corrected from 'learninge'.

geive testimonye of their cure[123] for the Churche[124] of God by their diligence in teachinge and preachinge in their charges.[125] And that the saide ministers doe testifie their presence at the admission of such ministers by subscription of their handes to some acte importinge the same. And further that this admission be had and done publickly and not in private house or chappell.

5. And where the admission of unnecessary multitudes to the ministery at one tyme hath bene occasion that the Church at this daye is burthened with so great a number of unable ministers, it may like their Lordshipes to advise whether some provision mighte be made that none be admitted to be a minister of the worde and sacramentes but in a benefice havinge cure of soules then vacant in the diocesse of such a Bishopp as is to admitt him, or to some place certayne where such minister to be made is offered to be interteyned for a preacher, or such graduates as shalbe at that tyme of their admission into the ministerye placed in some fellowshipp or schollershipp within the universities, [or] at the least that tryalbe made of their[126] order for suche tyme, as to their honorable wisdoms shalbe thought convenient.

6. That it be likewise considered whether for the better assuraunce, that[127] that none creepe into charges and cures beinge men of corrupt life, or not of knowen diligence, it might be provided that none be instituted, or by collacion preferred to any benefice with cure of soules, or received to be curate in any charge, without some competent notice before geiven to the parishes wher they shall take charge, and some reasonable tyme allowed wherin it may be lawfull to such as can discover any defect[128] in conversation of life in the person who is to be placed as is afore saide, to come and obiect the same.

7. That for the encouragement of many desireous[129] to enter into the ministery which are kepte backe by some condycions of othes and subscriptions wherof they make scruple, it would be considered whether this favour may be shewed them, that hereafter no othe or subscription be tendered to any that is to enter into the ministerye, or to any benefice with cure or to any place of preachinge but such onely as be expresslie prescribed by the statutes of this realme, savinge that it shalbe lawfull for everye ordynarie to trye any minister presented to any benefice within his diocesse by his othe whether he is to enter corruptly or incorruptlie into the same.

8. Whereas sundrye ministers in this realme, diligent in their callinge and of godlie[130] conversation and life, have of late yeres bene greeved with inditementes in temporall courtes, and molested by some exercisinge ecclesiasticall iurisdiction for omyttinge small porcions of[131] some ceremonies prescribed in the Booke of Common Prayer to the greate disgrace of their ministerye and emboldeninge of men eyther hardly affected in religion, or voyde of all zeale to the same, which also hath ministred no small occasions of

v. discouragement to the forwardnes of such as would / otherwise enter into the ministerie: some good and charitable meanes may be by theire honorable discretions devised that such ministers as in the publique service of the Church and in the administration of the sacramentes doe use the Booke of Common Prayer allowed by the statutes of this realme and none other be not from henceforthe called in question for omissions or changes[132] of some porcion or rite as afore saide, so their doeinges therin be voyde of contempt.

That for as much as it is noe small discouragement to many that they see such   9. as be alreadye in the ministerye openly disgraced by offycyalles and comissaries, who daylie call them to their courtes to answere complayntes of their doctrine and life, or breach of orders prescribed by the ecclesiasticall lawes and statutes of this realme:[133] it may please the reverend fathers or Archbishoppes and Bishops to take to their owne hearinges, with suche grave assistaunce as shalbe thought meete, the causes of complaynt made agaynst any knowne preacher within their diocesse and to proceede in th'examinacion and order thereof, with as litle discredite of the persone so complayned of (without great cause) and in as charitable sort as maye be, restrayninge their saide officialles and commissaryes to deale in any sorte[134] in those causes.

It may also please the saide reverend fathers to extend their charitable favours   10. to such knowne godlie and learned preachers as have bene suspended or deprived for no publique offence of life, but onelie for the refusall to subscribe to such articles as lately have bene tendered in divers partes of the realme, or for such like thinges. And that they may be restored to their former[135] places of preachinge, or at the least sett at libertie to preache where they maye be hereafter called.

Further that it may please the reverend fathers aforesaide to forbeare their   11. examinacions *ex officio mero* of godly and learned preachers, not detected unto them of open offence of life, or for publique maynteininge of apparaunt error in doctrine, and onely to deale with them in such matters, as shalbe [MS blank][136] in them. And that her Majestie's commissioners for causes ecclesiasticall be required (if it so shall seeme good) to forbeare the like proceedinges agaynst suche preachers, and not to call any of them out of the diocesse wher he dwealleth, except for some notable offence, for reformacion wherof their aide shalbe required by the ordynary of the saide preachers.

Item, that [for][137] the better increase of knowledge of such as shalbe imployed   12. in the ministerye, it may please their lordshipes to advise whether it may be permitted to the ministers of every archdeaconry within every diocess to have some common exercise and conference amongst them selves to be lymited and

123. Lansd. 42(i): 'cure' (+ (ii), Harl. 158, Lansd. 396).
124. Gon: 'their charge and church'.
125. Gon: churches'.
126. Lansd. 42(i): 'this (+ (ii), Harl. 158, Lansd. 398, ?Tanner).
127. Lansd. 42(i) omits (+ (ii), Harl. 158, Lansd. 396, Add. 38492).
128. Lansd. 42(i): 'defalt' (+ (ii)); Lansd. 396: 'fault' (+ Petyt).
129. Harl. 158 omits.
130. Lansd. 42(i): 'good' (+ (ii), Lansd. 396, Petyt).

131. Lansd. 42(i): 'or' (+ (ii), Add. 38492, Harl. 158, Lansd. 396, Tanner, Gon).
132. Petyt: 'charges'.
133. Gon ends here.
134. Lansd. 42(i) omits 'in any sorte' (+ (ii), Add. 38492, Petyt, Lansd. 396).
135. Lansd. 42(i) adds 'charges or' (+ (ii), Add. 38492, Harl. 158, Lansd. 396, Petyt, Tanner).
136. Lansd. 42(i): 'detected' (+ (ii), Harl. 158, Lansd. 396, Petyt, Tanner).
137. As in Lansd. 42(i) (+ (ii), Harl. 158, Lansd. 396).

prescribed by their ordinaries, both touchinge the moderations and also the tymes, places and manner of the same: so as the moderate[r]s of those exercises be preachers resiant uppon their benefices, havinge cure of soules, and knowne to beare good affection to the furtheraunce of suche profuite as maye growe by the same exercises.

13.[138]   Where complayntes [are] made of the abuse of excommunication, which is the highest censure that Christ hath lefte unto his Churche and many are greeved, aswell in regarde of the causes and matters wherin it is at this day[139] used, as of

f.21   the persons which have the common exequution / therof, and no redresse can be had therin, but by acte of Parliament: that some remedye may be thought off in that behalfe, before the ende of this session. And for reformation to be had herein, it may please their Lordshipes to consider whether some bill might not conveniently be framed to this effect, viz. that havinge ecclesiasticall jurisdiction shall not in any matter hereafter or to be moved in their courtes[140] (other then in the causes hereafter mencioned) geive or pronounce any sentence of excommunication: and that for the contynuaunce[141] of any person in causes dependinge before them, it shalbe lawfull to pronounce [him] onely contumax, and so to denounce him publickly. And yf uppon such denunciation as in excommunications hath bene used, the partie shall not submitt him selfe, nor stand to, nor abide, such order as is to him assigned within fortye dayes, then it shalbe lawfull to signifie his contumacie in such manner and sorte, and to such courte as heretofore hath bene used for persons so longe standinge excommunicate. And that uppon such certificate a writt *de contumaci*[142] *capiendo* shalbe awarded of like force to all effectes and purposes and with the like execution as the writt *de excommunicato capiendo* is.

14.   Nevertheles for so much as it seemeth [not] meete that the Churche should be left without this censure of excommunication, it may be provided that for erronious[143] crymes, as incest, adulterie, and such like the same be executed by the reverend ffathers the Bishops them selves with the assistaunce of grave persones [or else by other persons][144] of callinge in the Church with like assistaunce, and with such other considerations as uppon deliberation shalbe herein advised of. And not by chauncellors, commissaries or officialles as hath bene used.

15.[145]   Where licences for non-residence are offensive in the Churche, and be occasion that a greate multitude[146] of this realme doe want instructions, and it semethe that cases certayne, wherin the same may be hardly[147] allowed, can hardly be devised such as shalbe voyde of great inconvenience and daunger: it may be therfore considered by their honorable Lordshipes whether it were not convenient or necessary that the use of them were utterlye removed out of the Churche and so likewise of pluralities.

16.   But howsoever it maye be thought convenient to order those faculties, yet forasmuch as, besides the knowne duetie of a minister prescribed by the worde of God: her Majestie's iniunctions doe require in every curate a further qualytie of learninge then abilitie to reade onely, as may be gathered by the Bishops' articles[148] and by other charges imposed upon him to teache the principles of

religion as is sett downe in the 44th article.[149] And sithe also no facultie of pluralytie or non-residence eyther is, or can be, graunted,[150] but with condition to see the cure from which he is absent suffyciently served: it may please their honorable Lordshipes to consider whether it were expedient to provide[151] that as none now havinge licence of non-residence, eyther by law or faculty, or which herafter shall have, be permitted to enioye the benefitt of such licence except he depute an able and sufficyent preacher to serve the cure. And that no curate by him placed be suffered to contynewe in his service of that cure, except he be of suffycient habylitie,[152] and dothe weekely teache that congregation and performe the other duetyes of instructinge the youthe in the Catachisme prescribed[153] in her Majestie's iniunctions. /

xxi^{mo} Decembris   Spoken to the commytees of the Higher Hous by Sir   v.
1584   Water Mildmay at what tyme as the committees appoynted
               by the Commons of the Lower Hous delivered the
               peticions unto their Lordshipes.

'We are sente hither by the commons of the Nether Hous to exhibite unto your honorable Lordshipes an humble petition which they have to make unto you. The cause wherof groweth thus. The last session of Parliament, uppon occasion moved in the Nether Hous that session and the session then next before, the Commons at that tyme made their most humble petition to her Majestie by the mouthe of theire Speaker, that it might please her accordinge to that supreme authoritye which she hath over all causes and persons ecclesiasticall, to geive ordre for reformation to be had in some thinges then complayned of, which were: ffirst, the admittinge and allowinge of insufficyent mynisters in the Churche; next, the abuse of excommunication; and thirdly, the abuse in non-residentes and pluralities. In which matters by her Majestie's good favoure and licence three of the Common Hous had at the same last

138. Lansd. 42(i) adds 'excommunication' next to this number (+ (ii), Lansd. 396, Petyt (plural)).
139. Harl. 158 omits.
140. Lansd. 42(i): '. . . that none having ecclesiasticall jurisdiction shall in any other matter allreadie moved, or hereafter to bee moved, in their courtes' (+ other MSS, though Harl. 158 omits 'hereafter . . . causes').
141. Lansd. 42(i): 'contumacy' (+ other MSS, except Harl. 158).
142. Lansd. 42(i): 'contumace' (+ (ii), Harl. 158).
143. Lansd. 42(i): 'enormous' (+ (ii), Harl. 158, Lansd. 396).
144. From Lansd. 42(i) (+ (ii), Harl. 158, Lansd. 396, Tanner).
145. Lansd. 42(i) has 'facultees' next to number (+ (ii)).

146. Harl. 158: 'nomber' (+ Add. 38492).
147. Other MSS omit.
148. Lansd. 42(i): '43 article' (+ other MSS, though Lansd. 396, Petyt: '44 article'). For the articles see H. Gee and W. J. Hardy, *Documents Illustrative of English Church History* (1896), pp.481–4.
149. Lansd. 396 omits 'and by other . . . article' (+ Petyt).
150. Harl. 158 has 'residency', and omits 'eyther is, or can be, graunted'.
151. Lansd. 42(i) has 'it might be provided' rather than 'it may please . . . to provide'; Lansd. 42(ii): 'it maye bee provided' (+ Lansd. 396, Petyt).
152. Lansd. 42(i): 'of sufficient habilitie to preach' (+ other MSS).
153. Lansd. 42(i): 'required' (+ (ii), Lansd. 396, Petyt).

session some conference with my Lord Archbishop of Yorke and two other of my Lordes the Bishoppes. But that conference takinge not the successe [that] was looked for, the Commons addressed their humble petition to her Majestie, in the presence of all th'estates of the parliament. Unto which petition, it pleased her Majestie by the mouthe of the Lord Chauncellor to geive a most gracious aunswere.

'That as thees thinges did belonge most properlye to her superiorytie in rule over those causes, so she would be sory that any of them should remayne in that sorte, as her people should have iust cause and occasion of complaynt. And therfore her Majestie would geive order and commaundement to suche as were meetest to deale in them, for redresse of that which was amisse, so farre as there should be founde good and necessary cause.

'With which aunswere the Commons then rested satisfyed, most humblye thanking her Majestie for the same, assureinge them selves that her Majestie did accordinge to her most gracious aunswere commaunde the same to be done accordinglie, wherof we can have no doubt, knowinge her Majestie's most princely and Christian zeale towardes the advauncement of the religion of the Ghospell wherof she is of all the monarchies[154] in the worlde the cheife patrone, and which we have so many yeares freely enioyed under hir most gracious protection.

'Notwithstandinge, by complayntes receyved this parliament, brought from sondry partes of the realme, and uttered in the Nether Hous, it is found that nothinge is done for reformacion to suche purpose as in that honorable petition to her Majestie was desired, but that the former greifes doe continewe, and in some parte are muche increased.

'By which we meane not to charge my Lordes of the clergie, as though the faulte were in them. But rather thinke, that eyther lacke of convenyent tyme, or lacke of suffycient authoritie by lawe, was the occasion whie redresse is not had, as we veryli trust they were and are willinge to see doen.

'The matters thus beinge opened emongest us, we thought it not our partes to trouble her Majestie agayne with any new petition, havinge before received so gracious an aunswere: but rather to resort to your Lordshipes for your honorable helpe in the same.

'And to th'ende your Lordshipes should not be combred with tediousnes in speache, and least any thinge therby might be eyther mistaken, or misremembred, we have thought it fyttest to put our petition in wrytinge which with all humblenes we doe present to your honorable Lordshipes,
f.22   prayinge that it may please / you to receive it. And at your convenient leasure to peruse yt. So as there uppon we maye receive a favourable aunswere accordinge to the necessitie of the matters therin conteyned, humbly beeseechinge your Lordshipes further to accepte in good parte all that is wrytten in this our petition, and to interprett the same in the best sense, accordinge to our trewe and dutifull meaninge. And to geive us leave to attend uppon your Lordshipes agayne, when tyme may convenyently serve.'

The Lordes that were committees.

Spirituall   Archbishop of Canterbury

<pre>
                    Bishop of Winchester
                    Bishop of London
                    Bishop of Sarisburye[155]
                    Bishop of Chester
Temporall   Lord Treasorer
                    Lord Steward, Erle of Leicester
                    Erle of Kent
                    Erle of Sussex
                    Erle of Bedford
                    Erle of Pembrook
                    Lord Chamberlayne[156]
                    Lord of Hunsdon
                    Lord Grey
                    Lord Northe
                    Lord of Buckhurst
                    Lord Norrys
                Committees from the Nether Hous.
</pre>

The Treasorer of her Majestie's Hous	Sir John Higham
Comptroller of her Majestie's Hous	Sir William Mallory
Vicechambelayne	Mr Water Rawly
Chauncellor of th'Eschequire	The Queen's Sollycitor
Sir George Carye	Mr Thomas Crumwell
Sir Thomas Hennage	Mr Doctor Hammond
Sir Richard Knightly	Mr Barker[157]
Sir Robert Jermyn	Mr Francis Hastinges. /

The full and true aunswere of the Archbishop of Canterbury to the severall *petitions exhibited to her Majestie so neare as our remembraunces can supply.[158]

v.

*alias to the pet[it]ions of the Common House. March 1584.[159]

1. & 2. The first and seconde articles tende to one purpose savinge that the seconde reatcheth further to deprivation: misliked for 3 causes.

    1. Thinges shoulde be brought in question done by them as †mariage[s], sacramentes ministred.[160]

    2. It woulde be agaynst the rule of charitie to thrust out men that, havinge no meanes to live, their wife and children should be overthrowen.

†alias solemnization of mariages and administration of sacramentes.

---

154. *Sic.*

155. *Sic.*

156. Howard.

157. Perhaps Edward, though John and Richard are possibilities (*Commons*).

158. Tanner has 'The effect of the answear of the Archbishop of Canterbury to the petitions of the Comons' rather than this title.

159. These marginal readings are explained on f.23. They are all omitted in Add. 40629.

160. Add. 38492: '. . . soleminization of marriages and administration of the sacramentes' (+ Tanner): these two MSS omit the marginal note here, as they do at no.3 below.

*alias many
churches shalbe
left utterly
destitute and so
be deprived of
the etc.

3. Many* churches left utterly destitute, and so they deprived of the
benefitt of readinge service,[161] and godly homelyes, wheras it is better
to have that, then to want bothe it and preachinge.

That that may be done shalbe done in exercises to make them
more hable to exercise their ministerye.

3. It shalbe performed and hereafter he woulde take such care as they should[162]
rather complayne of want of ministers, then of insuffycient ministers.

4. Misliked, for causes not fitt to be revealed.

5. Graunted. It seamed to provide against the vagarant ministers,[163] the same
is all readye provided for by lawe, though not statute lawe, that none
should be ordeyned *sine titulo*, but he thought that it might reache to farre
to deanes, archdeacons, prebendes, masters of colledges, and such other as

†*alias* great
creddytt[164]

‡*alias* and
controversies
arise betweene
parishes and
them, and in
parishes amonge
them selves.

carry †greattest credytt and countenaunce in the Churche, which he
thought was not our meaninge.

6. He misliked the manner of this article: this testimoniall from the parishe
smelleth of popular election and might be preiudiciall to patrones, and
controversies arise betwene‡ the parishes and them, yea and amongest them
selfes. Some other kinde§ of testimonye he liked, as those that lived in
universities, a testymonie from the colledge, and for other from justices,
and some other, from the parishes[165] wher they had lived, it may fall out
that learned men might be sent to places farre of where they can not be
knowne. Therfore he misliked the manner of this article.

§*alias* some
other testimonie
he liked, as for
them that lived
in thuniversities,
a testymonye
from the
Colledge where
they were
brought up.

To the 5 articles** in[167] generall he saide
they did tende to bringe an immunitie
ymediatly,[168] especially of the ministers: that
it was not tollerable in a setled state of the
Churche: that it tended to the maintenance
of controversies alredie stirred up in the
Churche[169] against the statute of uniformytie
in use of common prayer.

**alias* 5 articles
followinge[166]

7. The first freeth them from othe of canonicall obedyence, wherein we
privilege them[170] more then Bishops them selves are priviliged,[171] who
sweare canonicall obedience to their metropolitan and from subscription
which though it be not warranted by statute yet doth it stand by lawe in
force as he hath learned by the best lawyers. That it was contrary to the use
of all reformed churches in Christendome, as farre as he knewe, and to the

††*alias* addicion,
in and to the
Booke of
Common
Prayer.[173]

f.23

use of this[172] ever since it was reformed, in kinge Edwarde's dayes offred
in streight tearmes and practized in this Queen's tyme hitherto.

8. This freeth them from all iurisdiction both temporall and ecclesiasticall, and
the heigh commission too, ffor matter of omission, alteracion, subtraction,
addicion††, it might[174] be occasion of scisme. *Quot altaria tot scismata.* /

9. It freethe them from chauncellors and comissaries and in effecte from the
jurisdictions of the Bishops them selves, for that the chauncellors doe[175]
nothinge but by their appoyntment.[176]

10. They that are deprived are iustly deprived, that which is done is iustlye

done, and so wilbe avowed; but if they will retourne and submitt them selves, he will shew them all favour and frendshipp.

11. The *dealinge (*ex officio*) is necessarie used[177] in all courtes, in the Starre Chamber, Chauncery and other courtes, misliked first by Jesuites, and seminaries, and from them derived to other that mislike goverment, and would bringe the Church to an anarchie.

12. For exercises aunswered before, that they would provide for it[179] in †suche sort as they thought good. But he ment[180] not to renewe prophesies, which did breed contentions and that they should not be publique.

13 & 14. He‡ liked not to bringe newe orders into the Churche; thoughe contumacyes are often uppon small matters as of xii^d, yet contumacye it selfe ys a great offence and the lesse the cause is wherupon it arisethe the greatter is the offence.[181] That it was not more severe then in the court of comon lawe, wher upon occasion of not appearinge to aunswere to lawe they did §proceede to impresement[182] and outlawrye which was puttinge

161. Add. 38492: '. . . ministring the sacramentes reading of service' (+ Tanner, Add. 40629).

162. Add. 38492: 'as men shall', rather than 'they should' (+ Tanner).

163. Add. 38492: 'ministry' (+ Add. 40629, Tanner).

164. Add. 38492 omits this and the two following notes.

165. Add. 38492 has 'colleges where they were brought up and for others from justyces of peace and of other men, and from the parishes' rather than 'colledge . . . parishes' (+ Tanner).

166. As in Doc.6.

167. Add. 38492: 'following in'.

168. Add. 38492 omits (+ Add. 40629, Tanner). The word is underlined in the MS.

169. Add. 38492 adds 'that they never were' as does Tanner, though omitting 'never'.

170. Add. 38492 has 'they should be priviledged' rather than 'we privilege them' (+ Tanner).

171. Add. 38492 omits 'are priviliged' (+ Tanner).

172. Add. 38492 adds 'our churche' and 'first' before the subsequent 'reformed' (+ Tanner).

173. Add. 38492 omits this note.

174. Add. 38492: '. . . in and to the Booke of Common Prayer. It wolde' (+ Tanner).

175. Add. 38492 has 'because they do' rather than 'for that . . . doe' (+ Tanner).

176. Add. 38492: '. . . by the appointement of the Bishops'; Tanner: 'by the Bishops' appointemente'.

177. Add. 38492: '. . . necessary for exercyse of Bishops and commyssioners' iurysdiction used' (+ Tanner); Add. 40629: '. . . necessary for usinge of Bishopps' commissioners' iurisdiction used'.

178. Add. 38492 omits this note, as well as those for 12, 13, 14 (+ Tanner).

179. Add. 38492 omits 'for it' (+ Tanner).

180. Add. 40629: '. . . good he and his brethren he meant'; Add. 38492: '. . . should be thought good by him and his brethren he' (+ Tanner).

181. Add. 38492: '13, 14. Where it is required that to pronounce contumacy should serve for pronouncing excommunication, it seemed to bring new censures into the Church, thoughe contumacy aryse often upon small maters, as of 12^d, yett contumacy itself is a great offence and the lesse the cause is wherbye it aryseth, the greater is the offence' (+ Tanner).

182. *Sic.*

183. Add. 38492 reads as marginal note (which it omits) from 'proclamation' to 'goodes' (+ Tanner), as does Add. 40629, though starting 'imprisonment, proclamation . . .' rather than 'impressment . . . goodes'.

*alias the dealinge *ex officio* necessarie for exercise of Bishops and commissioners jurisdiction used etc.[178]

†[*alias*] sort as should be thought good by him and his br[e]thern, but he ment etc.

‡*alias* Where it is required that to pronounce contumacye should serve for pronouncinge excommunication it seemed to bringe in newe censures into the Churche. *Tum ut in textu* thoughe contumacies etc.

§*alias* proceede to proclamation of rebellion and outlawrye which was puttinge them out of protection, imprisoment and losse of goodes.[183]

them out of protection and losse of goodes. That laye persones doe not excommunicate, they doe onely pronounce the sentence according to lawe. The minister that *denounceth, he excommunicateth.[184]

That it shoulde be provided for, and that some minister a preacher shoulde be joyned in comission with the chauncellor, and so to pronounce the sentence. That in enormyties, matters of cryme[185] as adulterye, Byshops[186] them selves though it were to their great travell and trouble would deale.

15 & 16. These tende to[187] pluralities and non-residencie, faculties for non-residence, necessarye: as in case of sicknes, wher it might fall out that absence for longer tyme then is lymyted by statute,† for chaunge of aire, may be thought necessary,[188] in sutes of lawe, and other necessarye causes, him selfe had graunted but one and that to a man of 80 years for one yeare now ended he never had graunted any for perpetuall non-residency nor never woulde.

For‡ the grauntinge of facultyes is her Majestie's doinge,[190] who hath co-mmitted it to his discretion: *I am*§ the onely[191] officer.

For pluralyties he thought it not convenient it should be taken awaye. Him selfe had enioyed the benefitt of facultie. That it would be a great discouraginge to learned men, yet that they had purposed nowe, to restrayne it to Masters of Arte and preachers, and not Masters of Arte or preachers, which distinction was often cause of inconveniencye *and that*★★ their should not be above a daye's ioyrney a sunder.

That their should be a suffycient *curat*‡‡ *in a preacher's benefice*, where they are[192] not resident, so the lyvinge be suffycient to fynde a compentent[194] minister and preacher. That he knewe two benefices, bothe of them not able to fynde a preacher.[195] Desireinge all men to thinke well of them if not in respect of the places which they beare, yet to yeelde them charitable judgment, as preachers and their brethren. That some of them had bene preachers before *some*†† *of us* were borne, at the least when we were in our[196] swadlinge clowtes.

Memorandum that this *alias* written in the margent signifieth that wheareas theare weare too coppies of the awnsweare made by the Archbishop to the petitions th'one did differ from the other as the lines drawne differ in woordes. /

Reasons whie the Commons are not satisfied with the aunswere of the right reverend father the Lord Archbishop of Canterbury to the petitions lately exhibited by them to the consideration of the right honorable lordshipes of the Higher House.

The aunswere delivered from the most reverend father in God, the Lord Archbishop of Canterbury to the first and second articles of the peticions was conceyved to this effecte.

Marginal notes:

*alias denouncethe the sentence etc.

†alias statute. When health can not be recovered but by chaunge of ayre may be thought necessarye.

‡alias That the etc.[189]

§alias I am, saide he, onely her officer.

★★alias and that the benefices should not be etc.

‡‡alias a suffycient preacher a curate in the benefice where etc.[193]
v.
††alias some were borne

That the saide first and seconde articles tende to one purpose savinge that the seconde reacheth further to deprivation: misliked by his Lordship for 3 causes:

1. For that thinges shoulde be brought in question done by the unlerned ministers as solemnization of mariages and administration of the sacramentes.

2. That it would be agaynst the rule of charytie to thrust out men that havinge no meanes to lyve, their wyves and children should be overthrowne.

3. That many churches shall be left utterly destitute and so be deprived of the benefitt of ministringe the sacramentes, readinge service, and godly homelyes, wheras it were better to have that, then to want bothe it and preaching.

Which aunswere and reasons under his Lordshipp's favour we take to be insufficyent for theis causes.

First, for that in the first article there is required a suspension onely from the ministery and execution of any function therto apertayninge untill they shalbe founde of the habylitie which the statute made in the 13 yeare of her Majestie's raigne requireth.

And in the 2 article a removinge of such insuffycient ministers within a competent tyme is onely desired.

Neverthelesse, we are very sorye that the Lordes spirituall have so muche forgotten themselves in makinge so many insuffycient mynisters, beinge so well admonished to the contrary both by the said statute and by their owne canon.

We doe not fynde that the suspendinge or removinge of suche insuffycient ministers will bringe in question thinges done by them in the Churche no

184. Add. 38492 has 'the sentence he excommunicateth' rather than 'he excommunicateth', and omits the marginal note (+ Tanner).
185. Add. 38492: '. . . enormous matters of crime (+ Add. 40692, Tanner).
186. Add. 38492: '. . . and such lyke Bishops'.
187. Add. 38492: 'touche' (+ Tanner).
188. Add. 38492 omits marginal note and has 'is by statute lymyted when healthe be recovered but by change of ayr may be thought necessary' (+ Tanner) rather than 'is lymyted . . . necessary'.
189. Add. 38492 omits and has 'that the' rather than 'for' in text (+ Add. 40692, Tanner).
190. Add. 38492: 'authoryty'.
191. Add. 38492: '. . . (sayd he) onely her . . .' and omits marginal note

(+ Tanner); Add. 40692: '. . . onelie her . . .'.
192. Add. 38492 has 'the benefyces should not be above one daye's iorney a sunder, that ther should be a sufficient preacher curate in the benefyce where any was' rather than 'their should . . . they are' (+ Tanner); Add. 40629 has 'a preacher in benefice' rather than 'in a preacher's benefice'.
193. Add. 38492 omits both parts of this note.
194. *Sic.*
195. Add. 38492 has '*conclusio*' before this closing paragraph (+ Tanner, Add. 40629); Add. 38492 starts the paragraph with 'He desired that', Tanner with 'He desired'.
196. Add. 38492 had 'their cradles and' rather than 'our' (+ Tanner).

more then the contynuinge of them in their places will doe, snys [197] if there be anie question in lawe whether they be ministers, the same is not taken awaye by their remayninge in the mynistrye.

But concerninge this scruple, althoughe such mynisters are made other wise then the said statute lawe and canon requireth, yet are the thinges by them done in the Churche, as maryages and administracion of the sacramentes, not to be brought in question.

Concerninge the rule of charytie we thinke more consideration ought to be had of the sowles of Gode's people which are like to perishe, for want of spirituall foode, then of the feedinge of suche as agaynst lawe and unworthely have bene admytted into the mynisterye.

Touchinge the 3 reason that churches would be lefte destitute, theire places might be supplyed by suffycient mynisters, and partly for a tyme by readers no ministers as is all readye used.

3. The aunswere to the 3 article was conceived to be that the petition in that article should be performed, and that his Lorshipp[198] herafter will use suche care, as men shall rather complayne of want of mynisters then of insuffycient mynisters, which aunswere is well liked so there maye be some good assurerance[199] of that promise by some penall lawe to be made. /

f.24   4. His Lordship's aunswere (as was conceived) to the 4 article was that he misliked the petition, the causes whie no fitt to be reveiled.

Oour desire is to understande thos causes wherby we maye receive a full and direct aunswere, for in our opinions nothinge is required in that article but that which is meete and convenient to be graunted, and we thinke the Bishops have noe cause to mislike therof sins by that meane they should have a good testimonye of their upright proceedinges, and for that by lawe there must be sixe ministers at the gevinge of orders and the same to be done publickly as we take it.

5. His Lordship graunted the 5 petition, which we well accept nevertheles desireinge some good assuraunce and provision by lawe for the same, syns we fynde in the articles agreed upon by the clergie of the province of Canterbury *anno* 1575 the like thinge ordered, and yet the same syns that tyme not performed.

6. His Lordship's aunswere to the 6 article was conceyved to this effecte: that his Lordship misliked the manner of this article; this testimoniall from the parishe smelleth of populer election, and might be preiudiciall to patrones, and controversyes arise betweene them and parishes and in parishes amonge them selves.

This aunswere we take under his Lordship's favour to be impertinent to the petition, for that there is noe testimoniall required in this sixt article from the parishe, neither concerneth it any populer election to our understandinge sins nothinge is desired but a competent notice before to be geiven to the parishes of the persone that shalbe their minister, and some reasonable tyme allowed wherin it may be lawfull to discover and obiect any defecte in conversation of life in the persone to be placed. And this petition varieth not muche from the order alreadye prescribed in the bookes of orderinge of mynisters.

7. The aunswere to the 7 article was conceived to this effecte. That it freed the ministers from the othe of canonicall obedience wherin they should be priviledged more then Bishops them selves, who sware canonicall obedience to their metropolitan, and likewise freeth them from subscription, which though it be not warranted by statute, yet dothe it stand by lawe in force as he hath learned of the best laweyers. That it was contrary to the use of all reformed Churches in Christendom as farre as he knewe, and to the use of this our Churche ever syns it was first reformed, in King Edward's dayes offered in more straight termes and practized in this Queen's tyme hithertoo.

Wherunto we saye that noe suche othe of canonicall obedience is required by the lawes of this realme either common lawe or statute lawe.

Yf any such othe be appoynted by lawe the same as we take it is by the canon lawe, which is not to be allowed.

Concerninge subscription, sins it is confessed that the same is not warranted by the statutes of this realme we desire to knowe by what lawe the same should be warranted.

To urge such a subscription, we thinke it not convenient, sythens no statute lawe requirethe it. If the mynisters offend agaynste the statute made in the first yeare of her Majestie's reigne or any other, they be subiect to be punished by the same lawe.

And sythens by the statute made in the 13 yeare of the Quene's raigne a certayne subscription is prescribed, we thinke it not convenient to have the ministers urged to any other kynde of subscription, for no doubt the parliament then would have bounde them to more, if more had bene requisite. /

8. The aunswere to the 8 article was conceived to this effect that it freed the   v. ministers from all jurisdiction bothe temporall and ecclesiasticall, and the Highe Comission too, for matters of omission, alteracion, subtraction, addition in and to the Booke of Common Prayer. It would be occasion of schisme. *Quot altaria tot schismata.*

We see not how these inconveniences mencioned in this aunswere will followe yf this petition were graunted, sithen the petition requirethe that onely suche ministers as in the publicke service of the Churche and in the administration of sacramentes doe us[e] the Booke of Common Prayer allowed by the statutes of this realme and none other, be not from hencforthe called in question for omissions or chaunges of some portion or rite, so their doeinges therin be voyde of contempt. And with all we fynde in the Booke of Common Prayer established in King Edward's tyme that touchinge kneelinge, crossinge, they may be used, or left, as every man's devotion serveth without blame.

9. The aunswere to the 9 was conceived to this effect. that it freeth the ministers from chauncellors and comissaryes and, in effect, from the jurisdictions of the Bishops them selves, because they doe nothinge but by the Bishops' appoyntement.

The petition is that it may please the reverende fathers our Archbishops and

197. *Sic.*   199. *Sic.*
198. *Sic.*

Byshoppes to take to their owne hearinge with such grave assistance as shalbe thought meete the causes of complaynt, made agaynst any knowne preacher within their dioces, and to proceede in th'examinacion and order therof with as litle discredyt of the persone so complayned of without great cause and in as charitable sorte as may be, restrayninge their offycialles and comissaries to deale in any sorte in those cawses: which petition freeth not the ministers or preachers in effect from jurisdiction of the Bishops sins the hearinge and orderinge of complayntes in that behalfe is desired to be done by the Bishops themselves.

10. The aunswere to the 10 article was conceyved thus, that suche of the preachers as were deprived, are justly deprived; that which is done is iustly done, and so wilbe avowed. But if they will retourne and submitt them selves his lordship will shew them all favour and frendshipp.

Whether they are justly deprived or not we stand in doubt. We would be gladd to knowe by what lawe. For as we take it they are not deprived by any common lawe, or statute lawe of this realme. And we would be very gladd to fynd his Lordship as charitable to theise godly and learned ministers who faithfully and diligently have fedd the flocke of Christe as he sheweth him selfe towardes the unlearned, insuffycient and unlawfull ministers.

And we further desire of his Lordship an aunswere to the latter parte of this petition, that is, whether the Bishops wilbe content at the leastwise to sett at lybertye to preache those godly and learned ministers heretofore deprived or suspended for not subscribinge.

11. The aunswere to the 11 article was conceived to this effect, that the dealinge *ex officio* was necessarye for exercise of Bishops' and comissioners' jurisdiction used in all courtes, in the Starr Chamber, Chauncerye and other courtes, misliked first by Jesuites and seminarye preistes, and from them deryved to others that mislike goverment and would bringe the Churche to an anarchie. /

f.25   Which aunswere we thinke all together insuffycient sythens the examples shewed agree not with the matter wherunto they are applyed, for neither in the highe Court of Starre Chamber nor in the Chauncery is there any such examinacion used *ex officio mero*. But such agaynst whome bills of complayntes are exhibited are onely examined concerninge the matters obiected in the bill examinable in the court and circumstances therof and no further. Neither doe we fynd any such manner of proceedinges in examinacion *ex officio mero* to be warranted by the common lawe of this realme, but one the contrary we fynde it agaynst the lawe of the realme for a Bishop to cite or call men before him to take an othe at his commaundement or pleasure agaynst the will of the partye cyted.

Yf the Jesuites and seminary preistes have misliked that kynde of examinacion the same hath bene for other causes then the petition meanethe. Which petition tendeth not to the mislike of goverment or to bringe the Churche to an anarchie, but this examinacion *ex officio mero* semeth to savour of the Spanishe inquisition and devised in the Romishe hierarchie.

12. There was noe publicke prophecyinge desired by this article and so we would have his Lordship to conceyve.

13. His Lordship's aunswere (as it was conceyved) touchinge the 13 article was to this effect, where is required that to pronounce contumacye should serve for pronouncinge excommunication, it seemeth to bringe new censures into the Churche.

Though contumacye arise often uppon small matters as of xii^d, yet contumacye it selfe is a great offence and the lesse the cause is wheruppon it risethe the greatter is the offence.

That it was not more severe then in the course[200] of the common lawe, wher uppon occasion of not appearinge to aunswere to lawe they did proceede to proclamation of rebellion, or utlagarie, which was puttinge them out of protection, imprisonment and losse of goodes.

That laye persons doe not excommunicate, they doe onely pronounce the sentence accordinge to the lawe. The minister that denounceth the sentence he excommunicateth.

That it should be provided for and that some minister a preacher should be joyned in commission with the chauncellor and to pronounce the sentence.

Wherunto we say we seeke to bringe no new censure into the Churche but a convenient remedy to be used in smaller matters, as of instance etc, in steade of excommunication, which we thinke not fitt beinge the greatest censure in the Churche to be drawne into these small actions. And their lordships in our opinions may as well allowe of this peticion of pronouncinge contumacye as to admitt this new forme of proceedinge to excommunication mentioned in the aunswere of this article.

Further, we doe not fynde that excommunication for small matters as for xii^d is no more severe then the course of the common lawe. The common lawe allowethe no utlagarye in any sute for any less somm or dammage then x^s, neither is their any man utlawed but after many proces and proclamations. Proces of rebellion is not used for trifles, nether yet otherwise then after divers former writtes and proces awarded and retourned, neither ought an utlagarye by the common lawe to be accompted so servere as excommunication, siyns therby the offender is caste out of the Churche of God and delyvered unto Sathan.

We doe understand, by suche as are learned in the cyvill and ecclesiasticall lawes, that the minister of the Churche notefyinge th'excommunication dothe not therby excommunicate, and therfore the aunswere in that behalfe we take to be insuffycient and desire a better. /

That his Lordship useth this moderation in facultyes for non-residencie we like it verie well, and desire some assureraunce by the lawe that the same may be always contynued by his lordship and the rest of the reverend fathers his brethern.

v. 15.16.[201]

---

200. *Sic.*   201. *Sic.*

In that his Lordship will not have pluralities taken awaye we see[202] not how we can stande with his former promise because a pluralitie implyeth a libertie of non-residencye.

Wher his Lordship saithe that the takinge awaye of pluralyties would be a great discouraginge to learned men, we thinke it rather a discouraginge to learned men, when they see livinges suffycient for many engrossed by one.

The canon allredy alloweth but xxvi myles distance, we would be lothe the daye's joyrneye should extend any further: for we thinke it to farre.

Wheras it pleaseth his Lordship in the behalfe of him selfe and the residewe of the reverend fathers the Bishops to desire a good opinion to be had of them with a charitable iudgement: we beseeche their lordshipes to thinke that we esteeme of them accordinge to the greatnes of their place duetifully, and of many of them for their good giftes of learninge and preachinge reverently. And we further beseeche their lordshipes to conceive fovorabli[203] of this our proceedinge, not esteeminge us accordinge to our particuler persons agaynst whom they may except for yeares, but as a parte of the great counsell of the realme assembled in the name of all the comynaltie, and to consider thise our requestes not as proceedinge from any of us in particuler, but from all the comons of the realme in generall.

f.26

The order of adioyrninge this cession of parliament to the 4th of Februarye.

The one and twentie daye of December beinge commonly cauled St Thomas' daye this cession of Parliament was adioyrned to the fourth of Februarye[204] by letters pattentes first sentt from hir Majestie to the lordes of the Upper House, and after brought downe to the Nether House by the Lorde Cheife Justice of Englande,[205] the Master of the Roles,[206] the Lord Cheife Justice of the Common Please,[207] and the Lorde Cheefe Barron,[208] as sent unto them frome the Lordes.

This was thought straunge, for as it had bene used heartofore that the too Howses by consentt for a weeke in Christmas, or at Shraftide, have adioyrned the parliamentt: so was it never seene that so longe a vacation as six weekes was had without the presence of the Prince's persone.

[rest of f.26 left blank]

f.27

The 15th of Februarie 1584.

In the Checor Chamber.

The daye and in the place abovesaide the committies that were appoynted before the adiourninge of this cession to consider of a bill for the Queene's saiftie mett together for the same pourpose where Sir Walter Mildemaie, one of the number, declared that whereas there was a bill digested into forme for the preservation of hir Highnes' saiftie readie to be presented to the House the last sittinge, and by reason of the adiournement staid, it was thought necessarie to consider againe of the same that if anie thinge were therin mistaken it might be amended, if anie thinge were wantinge it might be thereunto added, or if neede were to frame a newe bill accordinglie as this late horrible facte intended towardes hir Majestie by Parrie should move them.

Where uppon, beinge remembred that the othe of Assocyation did so creatlye disagree withe the bill alreadie drawne, one of the committies wished that if there weare a newe course to be taken for hir saifetie there mighte be an explanation of the othe of Assocyation inserted to the same, suche as everye bodie shoulde stande unto for the exequuting thearof.

But that was not allowed by reason that men absolutelye havinge sworne to the stricte wordes thereof coulde not satisfie them selves by an other man's exposition, and therefore was it wished that either the othe it selfe shoulde be made a lawe, or els should worde for worde be annexed to the lawe with this addition, that whosoever shoulde exequute it shoulde not be in daunger to loose either land life or goods; for unles it were so provided for the othe taken coulde not free th'executor theareof from the punishement of the successor if he list to call the matter in question. And beinge the onelye waye to terrifie ill-disposed men from executinge theire purposes to sett before them their certayne punishment / without hope of pardoninge, it was desired further to be   v. sett downe that neither hir Maiestie nor hir successor shoulde pardone anie suche personne detected of anye suche horrible offence towardes hir Highnes, for if shee or they whosoever should, then bothe the ill-disposed might uppon hope to escape the boldier enterprise his facte, and all those that had taken the othe to prosequute suche should breake the same.

It was saide that this latter demaunde coulde not be yeelded unto, or at leaste were to smalle purpose, for too respectes, the one because we went aboute theareby to conclude the successor which would not be unles the successor wears present to geive consent theareunto.

Beinge many competitors and some straungers, the straungers can not be present with us.[209]

The other was we shoulde thereby overthrowe the prerogative which weare a matter that woulde never take place; for albeit saide he, it maye be alledged that a lawe made naminge the prerogative concludethe the prerogative and that the prince hath no iniurye thereby: *quia volenti non fit iniuria*. Yet by daylie experience we see that wheras by the lawe no man shalbe shrife twise within three yeares; no judge shall have his owne contrye in circute; no murderer shalbe pardoned; all which conclud the prerogative, the prince dispenceth with them all by hir prerogative. And so in like sorte although it may be saide if the successor will come in by discentt, and not by conquest, he must be agreeable to the lawes he findeth readye made, and that in hir Maiestie's tyme there is a lawe made that concludeth the successor, yet in the one and in the other, if prince and successor use theire prerogative to disable that which by their prerogative they have made, who dare controle it? No doubt but that it is a goode sayinge *hoc possumus quod iure possumus*: but so rarely hathe it beene used in matters of this nature as fewe examples can be produced theareof. /

To drawe this question to an ende it was saide that for as muche as it was   f.28 evident by the experience of the bill and Assocyation disagreeinge such

---

202. MS repeats 'we see'.
203. *Sic.*
204. The words 'to the fourth of Februarye' are inserted in the text's hand.
205. Sir Christopher Wray.

206. Sir Gilbert Gerard.
207. Sir Edmund Anderson.
208. Sir Roger Manwood.
209. Marginal note is added in the second hand.

diversitie of opinion arose as coulde not be reconsiled, the best course weare to make hir Maiestie privie to that was alreadie doone, and to aske hir advise in what order they shoulde further proceede, which beeinge yeelded unto there were appointed for that pourpose.

1. Sir Frauncis Knowles, Treasorour of the Housholde
2. Sir Jeames Croft, Controler of the Housholde
3. Sir Christofer Hatton, Vicechamberlayne
4. Sir Walter Mildemaye, Chauncellor of the Exchecor
5. The Lorde Russell
6. Sir Thomas Hennage, Treasorer of the Chamber
7. Mr Egerton, Solycitor to hir Majestie

which the same night had accesse to hir Majestie then lyeinge at Somersett House. And so not longe after was presented unto the committies by them that had the managinge of the former bill for hir Highnes' saiftie this forme of a lawe conteyninge these heddes as followeth /

[ff.28v. and 29 left blank]

f.30   But before this matter was brought to a full perfection and ripenes, the xxiiii^th daye of Februarie next followinge Sir Walter Mildemay, knight, used this speache in the Common House for the procureinge of a subsidie to be graunted to hir Majestie.

'In the beginninge of this cession I troubled yow withe the remembraunc of some such thinges as I thought woorthie of consideration in this assemble of Parliament: emongest which I noted unto yow how many and how malicyous enemyes we have that doe envie this state and tyme; of whome some be open, as the Pope and all the princes and states that have ioyned in confederacie to execute the Holye League agreed uppon in the last Counsell of Trentt, some be seacrett, as Jesuites, seminerie preistes, our home Papistes, fugitives and rebelles.

'Howe their malice hath appeared is sufficyently seene, by rebellions stirred up in Irelande and Englande, and by the late invasion into Ireland: in which disposition you maye be sure thei remayne still, for as the waves of the seae doe one followe uppon an other, without intermission, see thes men have no ende of theire practises whensoever oportunitie maye serve them, nourished with hope, that att the lenght thei maye attayne that they seeke for, which is the deposinge of the Quene our most gracious soveraigne, the alteration of re- ligion, and the subversion of this whole state and governementt.²¹⁰

'But God hath disapointed²¹¹ them.

'Yet as men that see a daungerous tempest comminge doe not leave all to hope, but laye too their owne handes and industries how to avoyde it, so we beinge threatned and seeinge so darke a cloude of perill like to fall uppon us, ought not [to]²¹² bee negligente, but, with all the care and circumspection we can, provide afore hande suche thinges as shalbe hable to preventt or resist the same, that we be not to seeke when we shall have neede. /

v.   'This provision ought to bee in two degrees. One by lawes for the preser- vation of hir Majestie's most²¹³ royall personne, and for the punishment of those secrett enemyes that seeke to undermine this estate: bothe which you have put in suche forwardnes alreadie as their is no doubte of their good successe.

'The other is to prepare forces both by lande and by sea to defende the realme, and to withstande anie attempt that may be made either abroade or at home; the carefull provision wherof heretofore, and the puttinge of the same in order in tyme,[214] hath preserved us from daungers entended against us.

'But this not withoute greate charge, as Ireland which alone sithens the last cession of parliament hath consumed the hole subsidie and xv[ths] then graunted and more.[216]   Anno 1580[215]

'Next, the charges of fortification at Barwicke and uppon the sea cost in divers partes of the realme.

'Thirdlie, the greate provision of pouder and munition lately made, the masse whereof is more then in any former tyme; and is more to be accompted of then monie it selfe, for suche thinges cannot at all tymes be gotten for monie.

'And last, the newe buildinge and repairinge of the navie, put nowe in better strength and better readines then at anye tyme before this: a matter of greate importance, ffor the navie, beinge iustlie termed the wall of Englande, is a thinge of all other principally to be cared for.

'Besides, other extraordinarie charges abroade to maintaine peace at home.

By meanes of all which so great and so necessarie charges hir Majestie hath spent of hir owne revenwe, for the defence of the realme, allmost as muche more as the ayde graunted by the last parliament did amount unto: which I doe not speake unto yow, by gesse, or by coniecture, but by vewe of hir Majestie's recordes that conteine hir receiptes and paymentes, which shee hath done bothe for the necessitie of the service that could not be otherwise maintayned, and to avoyde borrowinge uppon interest beinge as yow knowe a most perrillous canker hable to eate upp even the states of princes.

'But this maye seeme straunge to yow, that two xv[ths] and a subsidie as great as anie ever before, so latelie graunted shoulde / not bee sufficient, not onelie   f.31 to aunswere and maynteine theise charges but also to leave in hir Majestie's cofers a good remaine besides. This I my selfe woulde likewise marvaile at, if two thinges did not move me, which I thinke will move yow also. One, the costlines of the warres and the greate increase of prices of all thinges in this age, farre surmountinge the tymes before. And the other, the easines of the taxation of the subsidies which how favorable thei be handled in all places no man here can be ignoraunte.[217]

'If I should tell yow how meanelie the great possessors[218] in the contrie and

210. Harl. 6526 omits 'and governementt'.
211. Harl. 6265: '. . . both hath and shall disappoint' (+ Sloane, Rawl).
212. From Harl. 6265 (+ Rawl).
213. Harl. 6265 omits.
214. Harl. 6265 omits 'and the puttinge . . . tyme'.

215. Harl. 6265 omits marginal note.
216. Harl. 6265 omits 'and more'.
217. Harl. 6265 omits 'which now . . . ignoraunte'.
218. Sloane: 'possessions' (+ Rawl); Harl. 6265: 'possessioners'.

the best aldermen and citizens of London, and the riche men of the realme are rated, yow woulde marvell at it. So as thereby a verye great deale lesse than is geiven to hir Majestie is paide into her cofers, so muche as I dare assure yow this last subsidie is farre lesse then that which went before. And this I saye not to inhaunce men's taxations, but to lett yow see that subsides thus favorablie rated, come shorte of that which yow maye thinke hir Majestie haith brought into hir receipt. But all that which hath come that way, and a greate deale more of hir owne, hir Majestie[219] hath spent uppon the publique affaires of the realme, and never awhitt uppon vaine expences for pleasure or delight[220] as other princes use. By reason wherof these effectes have followed:

'The realme of Irelande an auncient and precious juell of the crowne of Englande saved out of the handes of our enemyes that were readie to devoure it, which otherwise would have bredd to this realme most daungerous and evident perrilles.

'The towne of Callis beinge lost in the dayes of Queen Marye by the ill-government of a sorte of preistes that mynded nothinge so muche as the restitution and[221] establishinge of Poperie was a marvelous blowe to this realme, and so is like to prove when so ever warres shall happen betwene us and the Frenche. But if Irelande, a great kingdome, shoulde light into the handes of a potent prince our adversarie that were hable to kepe it, it will prove an other manner of matter, than the losse of Callis. For Ireland beinge an hole region furnished with so manye notable havens, so inhabited with manie stoute people, and so nere our maine lande, would no doubte shake this hole state and every parte therof, farr more daungerouslye then the meane of anie private towne[222] can doe.

'You see also how this our naturall contrye of Englande, the principall marke that our enemyes shoote at, hath bene defended from all their malicyous practizes. For though their hatred towardes us be implacable, and their desire to over-runne us insatiable, yet seing as they have done, that by hir Majestie's provident circumspection, thei coulde not finde hir unprepared, their enterprises have quailed, and we have lived in peace, free from those mischeifes that
v.   they extended, which peace if we meane to holde / and continewe it behoveth us in time to consider: bothe of hir Maiestie's greate charges alreadie bestowed, and of those which of necessitie she must bee at for the saufegarde of hir realmes and subiectes.

'And theruppon to offerr hir such an aide, as maye be aunswerable to the greatnes of the charges incydent to matters of this weight and importaunce.

'Wherin we shall show our selves deutifull to so gratious a Queen that governs us with iustice, and keeps us with peace: and carefull also of the preservation of hir Majestie and of this noble realme and of the maynteinance of Gode's trewe religion now taught amongst us which ought to be more deare to us then life, landes or goodes, or anie thinge that we have.'

Finis.[223]

It is to be remembred that from the beginninge of this seconde sittinge sondrie of the Lower House founde them selves at divers tymes greived that the cause of religion tooke no better succes. And uppon the motion of this matter of subsidie, one burges amonge the rest thinkinge the oportunitie verie fitt, the rather for that hir Majestie expectinge a benevolence from them woulde the sooner yealde to theire lawfull and necessarie petitions, declared in the House to this effecte ffollowinge:

'Our case', quoth he, 'is most lamentable that havinge the worde of God sincerelie preached amonge us and his sacramentes rightlie administred, and that, next under Gode's mercyfull goodnes, by the greate care and industrye of hir Majestie most vertuously and godlilye disposed, such ministers shoulde be about hir Highnes as, not onelie will not informe hir of those abuses and enormyties which are by corruption or in the better sence by great over sight of suche as hath the charge of / matters ecclesiasticall comitted unto them f.32 creapt into the Churche, but also doe keepe from hir gracious sight those humble peticions for the redress of the saide abuses lately exhibited from us of this House to their lordshipps of the Higher House: we hopinge that uppon some conference had betwene both Houses as touchinge them, a speedy redresse by hir Majestie's royall assent should have bene had therin. And to e[n]ter into a consideration what those peticions are, they seemed in the iudgment of all men of reason, bothe for the humylitie in penninge of them, as also for the substance of the matter conteined in them to be so alowable, as without all doubtes, if hir Majesty had once redd them she could not, consideringe hir zeale towardes the buildinge of the Lorde's house, but with all speed cutt off those abuses wherof they complaine beinge thinges so bourdenouse and intollerable to the consciences of the godlye, as nothinge can be more. For how can it be that she whose studie hath ever bene like a most naturall mother towardes hir tender children, for the preservation of hir subiectes' bodies in healthe and tranquilitie, can carelesslie or without any touch or feele of greife pas over the ruinatinge and everlastinge overthrowe of those hir subiectes' soules? Wherfore as a poore member of this House, well wishinge to the generall grounde of our salvation, I most hartelye desire that some number maye be chosen from amonge us which may in most humble manner crave of hir Highnes onely the vouchsaifinge to reade our petitions, wherunto if by their suete shee may be woone (for in my owne opinion as yet hir Majestie hathe never seene them), I am most assured, consideringe hir princely mynde so bent to the advauncment of all vertue and goodnes, that she will with speede geive redresse to the faultes that are in them complayned of.'

This speach made a deepe impression into the myndes of the whole assemblie in so muche that divers gave their opinions that the motion by him made was requisite and good, wishinge that the same might be prosecuted: yet it did not preceede to anye perfection, for by risinge of the House, the daye beinge then farr spent, it stayed for that tyme, and as it should appeare some

---

219. Harl. 6265 omits 'and a greate ... Majestie', and has 'been spent' rather than 'spent'.
220. Harl. 6265 omits 'or delight'.

221. Harl. 6265 has 'but the' rather than 'so muche as the restitution and'.
222. Sloane: 'man' (+ Rawl).
223. Sloane omits (+ Rawl).

faulse brother amonge the rest, resortinge unto the Courte, declared unto hir Majesty the whole course of the matter, who not well likinge therof commaunded that the Speaker, Mr Seriantt Puckeringe, should presentlie attende hir pleasure beinge then at Grenewich, which withe out the privitye of the House he did. /

v.

And the seconde daye of Marche followinge, when the Lower House were assembled together in theire usuall place, he declared that uppon hir Majestie's specyall commaundement beinge the daye before at the Coourte their to attend hir pleasure, he received from hir Highnes to deliver unto the House in forme followinge:

That at what time as by hir allowance he was made the mouthe to the Lower House, she gave this caution that in no wise such matters shoulde be medled withall, as at that tyme shee forbad: amonge which the matter of religion was one wherin contrarie to hir commaundement we had intermedled, a thinge which shee so muche misliked as well for the matter it selfe, as the order in handlinge therof as shee greatlie blamed hir counsell that there satt, be cause they woulde not staye and interrupt the course. And in generall condemned the whole House that would enter into the discourse of anie matter which shee had expresslie forbidden, and especyally of that wherin she onely, and none other, is to deale beinge the supreame heade of the Churche, and by the lawes of the lande onely appointed to provide for the same which shee had great good will to doe as by proofe should appeare.

To thinke that all thinges in the Churche stande in good and perfect estate she doth not, bycause by complaintes made she findeth that some thinges be amisse. But the manner that we used in seekinge the redres of them arguethe to hir, consideringe hir express commaundement to the contrarye, a mynde to breake hir commaundement, a full intent to abridge hir authoritie, or els a distrust that shee will not performe what shee hath promised: which is a great advauntage to the enemyes of the Churche, who besides that they maye vaunt of a disagreement amonge our selves, as setled in noe religion, maye condeme hir Highnes, either to be careles what proceedinges be in the Church, or negligent to redres matters most concerninge the Churche.

This hir Majestie saide was a verie harde matter to be laide uppon hir meaninge towards those matters as shee did: for as shee knewe the doctrine preached in this Church of Englande to be as sincere as might be possible, so shee knewe the discipline therof not so perfecte as might be, but blameable as we of the House had complayned. Yet to redres it in suche open manner as we f.33 sought, wherby the whole state ecclesiasticall / might be overtourned or at the least defaced, that shee most misliked; for as shee found it, at hir first comminge in, and so hath mayntayned it this xxvii yeares, shee ment in like state by God's grace to contynue it and leave it behinde hir, notwithstandinge to reforme certaine thinges amis, but in a more secrett order than this. Moreover shee

saide it was noe smalle g[r]eife unto hir Majestie that anie suche matter of
unkindenes should pass betweene hir and hir subiectes, findinge by manie and
soundrie proofes that noe prince in the world had more lovinge subiectes than
shee had, and in that respecte it gave hir the more greife, that about one and
the selfe same matter shee should be driven to sende to those hir most lovinge
subiectes a seconde restrainte, wherby either a mistrust might growe in hir of
thire disloyaltie towardes hir selfe, or some conceipte might enter into them of
hir carelesnes in a matter of so great moment. But most of all it greived hir that
we would so proceed, consideringe the restraynte shee had geiven to the lordes
of the Upper House, bothe spirituall and temporall, to deale in the same
matter, to them she saide, to whom it properly apperteyned, for unto us beinge
the lower and thirde House, and so the meanest, such matters did nothinge at
all belonge. And albeit the love she founde in hir subiectes towardes hir selfe,
so zealous and fervent as no prince could have more, and hir lovinge care
towardes us, suche as was beseeminge a naturall prince towardes the like
subiectes, wrought in her a marveilous strife, whether she should sende anie
message that might be sower or offensive to the House or not; yet as a carefull
mother over hir tender children, she could not but admonishe them of their
breache of duetie, with this commaundement that they should no more
intermeddle with those matter,[224] for shee woulde receive no motion from
them that should concerne the lawes of the Churche: willinge us hereby not
to consider of hir Majestie as that shee would dispossesse hir selfe of that
supreame authorytye, which shee hath over the Churche, but that shee will
uppon complainte geive eare to suche matters, marrie in a more privie sorte
then now was used. And withall shee did wishe, that suche as did finde them
selves greived in that nature, should first resorte to the Bishop of the dioces,
from whome, uppon complainte made, if they shall receaive no suffycient
aunswere or redres, then hir Majesty moved theirin, will see redres had;
always provided that those matters which they complained of be no trifles, but
matters of substance.

Finis.

  With this message the House found them selves so greatlie moved and so v.
deeplye wounded as they could not devise which waye to cure themselves
agayne, for so theire case stoode, as either theie must offende their gracious
soveraigne towardes whom, in respecte of their singuler benefittes that they
received by hir most blessed and happie govermente, theie durst not so
muche as to lifte up one evill thought or imagination, or els to suffer the
liberties of their House to be infringed, wherby theie shoulde leave their
children and posteritie in thraldome and bondage they themselves by their
forefathers beinge delivered into freedom and libertie. By this conceipte a
greate amasement fell amonge them and sondrie tymes manie of them mett in
privat sorte to devise howe they might salve this sore so greevously inflicted

224. *Sic.*

uppon them. Manie wayes were invented. Some thought best to have the Speaker displaced, for that he durst enterprise to goe to the Queen without the privitie of the House. Other thought better to have some one stande upp and openlie to refuse the acceptinge of anie suche commaundement from hir Majestie, because it touched the libertie and freedom of the House: but one other mislikinge bothe these coorses, for that therby an open devision woulde growe betweene hir Majesty and the subiecte, wherby great mischeife might followe to the generall state of the realme, wished rather that some waye might be wrought underhande that shoulde as forceibli restore the libertie of the House as anie violent action openlie used: and therfore thought best that some bill conteyninge matter for the reformation of th'abuses of the Churche which were the thinges principallie forbydden, and wherby the liberties of the House were touched, might be drawne and presented, and that, there redd would sufficientlie restore the auncyent liberties againe to the House. This opinion was allowed, and theruppon was drawne a bill under this title 'An acte for the better execution of a statute made in the xiii[th] yeare of thee Queen's Majestie's raigne, for reformation of certaine disorders touchinge ministers of the Churche', which was delivered to the Speaker with a full conclusion amonge them selves that if the Speaker should refuse the acceptinge therof, then that partie who first devised this course should with a speache which he had prepared have maynteined the liberties of the House to the uttermost. But the bill was received, though not redd untill the xvii[th] daye ffollowinge the reporte of the Speaker's message delivered by him to the Lower House from hir Majestie.[225] /

f.34   In which meane time uppon the xi[th] daye of Marche the bill of subsidie, ingressed, beinge brought into the Lower House, and receivinge the third readinge, before it was put by the Speaker to the question a member of the same House made this motion:[226]

That all such papistes as were recusantes might be ceased in the subsidie accordinglie as the straungers which paide double to the Englishe: his reason was, that seinge they refused to live accordinge to the lawes of the realme, theye were not to be accounted as subiectes, but as fforriners and thereafter to bee taxed.

It was aunswered by an other member of the same House in this sorte:

That the selfe same matter was by the selfe same partie motioned the parliament last goeinge before this, but by a generall consentt reiected: what reason then ledd the House he well remembred not, but for his owne parte still remayninge in that opinion was thereunto ledd by these reasons as followethe.

That whereas it was moved nowe, the bill beinge ingrossed and receivinge his third readinge, it was farr out of season, especiallie consideringe that before the saide bill for the subsidie was drawne in paper, the House had concluded that it should conteyne the same articles in everye pointe and none other that the former acte for the subsidie did: which could not be if this motion tooke place, because it would alter the bodie of the bill.

That to laye a punishment uppon the recusantes in respect of their obstinacye as he thought it verye necessarye, so would he have provided that the same punishment so inflicted should bee convenient: which this in noe wise coulde be, bothe for that the paine therof is but lite and of noe validitie, beinge but double to that which the subiect payethe; and also because a greatter paine than that, namely xx^ll a moneth, is alreadie imposed uppon them, which is burdensum and maketh them to stoope.

Besides, two great inconveniences hee saide woulde hearbie followe.

The first, by shewinge our selves forward in uringe so smalle a greife uppon them as this we shoulde (consideringe what hath bene layde uppon them hearetofore and still contynuid) be noted to leave the badge of the ghospell now preached which is clemensie and gentlenes, and shewe the fruites of the contrarie religion, which is sowernes and crueltie, a thinge utterlie to be shunned of us, and to be lefte wholie to them as the cognisaunce of their profession. /

The seconde, in cooupllinge them with the straungers we should geive them   v. cause to thinke that we had wholy secluded them frome oure societie, not accountinge them as naturall borne Englishe men, and thereby drive a desperation into them: which is contrarie to the course taken in our former lawes, as namelie in the bill for the Queen's saifetie and the bill of Jesuites, wherin a libertie is geiven that such as will conforme them selves to the due obedience that subiectes ought to use maye willinglie be received, shewinge therbye that we doe not reiecte and refuse them as men unworthie of our companye and fellowshipp, but be they never so ill, yet that we live still in hope to winn and reconcile them.

This opinion prevaled in
overthrowinge the other.

Uppon the xvii^th daye of Marche, beinge the Wednesdaye, the bill for the better execution of the statute made xiii of the Queen for the reformation of the unlearned ministrie was cauled for, and desired to bee redd in the Lower House, at which motion a bourges of the same House standinge upp declared that, wheras it appeared by the title of the bill that the matter therin conteyned was such as was comprehended within the commaundement from hir Majestie, it was not requisite the same shoulde bee redd, for the thinge beinge forbidden by hir Highnes the House coulde not avoue the doeinge therof.

Which speache of his, though not one man particularlie confuted, yet with a generall voyce thorowe the House the bill was cauled on to the readinge, which it then received: and on the Tusedaye followinge beinge the xxiii^th 227 of the moneth it passed the same House beinge the same daye amonge other billes sent to the Lordes where the daye followinge it received a reedinge, and was

225. The bill had its first and second readings on 18, 19 March (D'Ewes, p.370).
226. The anonymous journal records the episode (f.166v) and the speech recorded there and attributed to

Mildmay seems to be a briefer version of what appears here. The subsidy bill had its third reading on 12 March, according to D'Ewes (p.366).
227. D'Ewes, p.371: 22 March.

greatlye inveaied against by the Archbishop of Canterbury, Doctor Whitegifte, in the selfe same course that the bourges which withstoode it att the first in the Lower House used. But therunto the Erle of Leicester replied seeminge muche

f.35   to mislike the Bishops' order of dealinge / in that nature, which rather tended to move hir Majestie to offence towardes the Commons, than yealded anie good reason whie the same shoulde not proceede for, saide he, evermore hath it beene accompted a thinge most necessarie that when a statute standinge in force hath anie ambiguitie in it or wanteth force for the better executinge it selfe, the same shoulde be explaned or strengthned by an other statute, other-wise the doubtes that maye therby growe or the want of power to performe the intent will rather breede offence to the common wealthe than good, contrarie to the mynde and intent of them that first invented the lawe. And that this bill nowe in hande importethe noe other thinge is most playne and evident.

This was the last speache that was harde touchinge that bill, wherwith the Lower House held them selves satisfyed, who nothinge so much regarded the consummatinge therof to the perfection of a lawe, as they ioyed in the passage thereof from theire House to the Lordes, wherby theire wounded libertie had nowe recoived healthe and saifetie.

I shoulde have shewed you how, in the meane tyme betweene the xvii and the xxiii of Marche in which space the bill for the better execution of an acte maide the xiii of the Queene laye a pawsinge, there was a bill presented to the House cauled the bill of recoveryes,[228] wherin was a clause lookinge backe to meete with suche faulshoodes as had beene within a space used for the defetinge of recoveryes orderlie passed, which bill receivinge his third readinge the xx[th] of Marche, and uppon that third readinge beinge founde fault with, and wished to be committed, bredd muche argument uppon these two pointes:

ffirst, whether it were good that anie lawe shoulde looke backe or not;
secondlie, whether a bill havinge receyved his thirde readinge may after the thirdd readinge be committed or not?

As touchinge the first:
It was saide by one that lawes ought to looke backe of necessitye. The reason was that seeinge in makinge of lawes noe such perfection coulde bee sett downe, but beinge made man's witt could finde some waye or other to shunne the daunger of them, wherby the offendor might escape unpunished: the onelie meane to staye the ill-disposed were for them certainely to knowe that a succeedinge lawe should come, which in lookinge backwarde should remedye that which the precedent lawe coulde not take hould off. /

v.   An other saide as it was most perillous generallye to have lawes looke backe, so was it most necessarye in some causes to have them to looke backe: which he prosecuted thus. To make a lawe looke backe whereby anie privatt man shalbe punished might prove manifeste iniustice, because the offendor might be noe offendor at what tyme he committed the offence, by an after lawe made punishable. For how can it be saide, a man to committ fault in doeinge of a matter when noe laws was extant at the doeinge therof to make it faultie? But when a great abuse is founde out towardes the common wealthe wherby daunger both hath growne to it, and dalye dothe growe by the same, to make a lawe retchinge backwarde to redres that is most necessarie and iust.

The third man saide that the generall grounde to stand uppon in this case was to make noe lawe looke backe, but when an open fraude knowne generallie were to be redressed, or els when the parties might be cauled to aunsweare who theareby weare to be touched: which opinion stood for the best.

As touchinge the seconde:

Uppon the diversities of opinions in that pointe, for some saide they never sawe a bill ingrossed committed, and so grounded uppon the president not to be lawfull. It was by one saide that as presidentes were necessarie to instruct the House, what had bene done, and thereby did geive the better lighte howe to proceede in matters a doeinge, so weare they in noe sorte to bynde the House, what should be done: for beinge a free counsell it can not be concluded, but hath still a power remayninge in it, so longe as matters continue there in debatinge, accordinge to the necessitie of the causes in handlinge, either to alter, make newe, or continewe anie president; otherwise they had not the freedome they claymed, in the respecte they were in subiection to their predeccessors' orders. Besides great inconvenience was saide might otherwise followe, for manye times at the last readinge imperfections be found in bills that were not before seene, which if thei should so pass from them, might overthrowe the same in the Upper House, whereby many good matters should finde evill success. And this speach prevayled. /

Uppon the Monedaye beinge the xxix[th] of Marche hir Majestie cam to the Parliament House for the prorogation of the cession untill a further tyme, unto whom after the Speaker, which was Mr Seriant Puckeringe, had recyted howe graciouslie hir Majestie for her parte, and how favourablie the Lower House for their partes, had inabled his disabilities, he devided his oration before hir into fowre cheife heddes: f.36

The Speaker's oration to hir Majestie at the prorogation of the Parliament.

1. What great benefittes we received by the parliamentt.
2. Our humble thankes for hir free pardon geven at this time.
3. An humble suite to remitt all suche offences as by ignorance were committed in the consultacion.

228. The bill, and also a new bill, had readings on 18, 19 and 23 March (Cromwell, fos.91v, 92). The concern about retrospective legislation had also appeared in the debates on the wardships bill (Anonymous journal, f.166).

4. An humble request that hir Majestie
would vouchsaife to geive life to the
woorkes, not onelie of our handes, but
also of our duetifull and loyall myndes.

Which fowre poyntes he prosecuted in mannor ffollowinge.

The firste.   That by hir gracious assentinge to have a Parliament cauled and by hir favourable permittinge the longe continuance of the same we had full scope and libertie first to consider how to advaunce Gode's true service and religion, which consisteth in continuinge such good and holsome lawes as hath bene heretofore made for the same purpose, or els in alteringe or abrogatinge them if neede so required. Secondlie, to cast for and provide wayes and meanes how to conserve hir Majesty in saiftie, the onelie soule and breathe (as he termed it) of our common wealthe, and with[out] whom it were unpossible to reape those blessinges which now we doe. And lastly to provide suche thinges for our selves as might be altogether profitable and nowise hurtfull; concludinge this parte with an humble prayer to God that hir Maiestie mighte live many dayes after us, wherby our posteryties might taste of the like prosperitie which we by hir happie and blessed raigne have so manye yeares enioyed. /

v. The seconde.   Amonge which unspeakeable benefittes received from hir Majestie's blessed raigne and governement, she beinge the pillar of our wellfare and felycitie, he saide it was not to be accounted the least that hir Majestie in her wisdome, knowinge it to be most necessarye to have lawes for the refourminge and bridlinge of our corrupt nature (which otherwise, accordinge to the lustes therof, would wander to farr beyonde all compas, yet seeing the frailtie thereof to be suche as noe penaltie appoynted for the restrayninge of the same can staye us from the breakinge of thos lawes and incurringe the daunger therof), uppon hir greate love towardes hir subiectes and meare mercie have geiven a free pardon, wherby we stande released from these punishmentes which otherwayes the lawes would have inflictt uppon us. A most highe and princely vertue he termed it, and for the same as well in the name of [the] lordes of the Upper House, as in the behalfe of the commons of the Lower House, he yealded hir Majestie most humble and duetifull thankes.

The thirde.   Theise hir motherlye and naturall affections towardes hir subiectes ioyned with hir gracious and princelie mynde, gave him, he saide, encoragement with all humblenes to crave of hir Majestie a favorable construction of the whole proceedinges in this cession, as well of those that particularly touched himselfe, as also the rest concerninge the assembli of the Lower House: in the which all in generall from the first to the last (one onelie wretched caitife excepted uppon whom due punishement had lighted, nether yet such as they wished, accountinge that which he had, rather too favorable in respect of his offence, then other wise) bare towardes hir Maiestie suche faithefull duetifull and reverende hartes, that if anye thinge had passed from them wherin hir Highnes might finde hir selfe discontented, as haveinge thereby hir intentes or purposes crossed and overthwarted, he durst in all their names protest and avowe that it was never so ment amonge them. But as men covetinge uppon ferventt zeale, to surmount as it were the boundes of duetie and affection, might doe in that sorte ignorantly rather to offence then otherwise, which thinge most apparantlye was seene in them by the handlinge of the bill for hir Majestie's saiftie, wherin though they intended a course farr beyonde that which was nowe sett downe, yet findinge the same to dislike hir clement and pitifull nature held them selves contented with that which was delivered to them as best likinge to hir Highnes; so likewise in the matter of petitions beinge a thinge most concerninge the service of allmightie God and consequentlie the prosperous contynuance of hir Majestie: the two onelie thinges which they thought them selves bound in conscience and duetie to have greatest care and consideration / of, they straight surceased from medlinge with them after hir commaundement was once delivered, geivinge such reverende regarde thereunto, that receivinge from hir mouthe an absolute commaundement no further to proceede in them, not one man stoode up to impunge[229] the same. Ledd therunto with this reason: that hir Majestie havinge supreame authoritie over all such causes bothe had geiven order to the cleargie for the well lookinge unto them, and also woulde see the same duely and sincerely executed.

    Untill that time, this he saide was theire course: if anie fault was sithens by them committed, he humblie in their names craved pardon for the same, wishinge most vehementlie that such abilitie of speache weare in him as theerby he might make knowne to hir Majestie their carefull indevour towardes hir service, accordinge to the measure he saw them entende it. Which he saide was unpossible for him to doe.

    Lastlie, he most humblie besought hir Majestie, both in the name of the lordes of the Upper House and also of the commons of the Lower House, that wheras bothe Houses with great diligence and traville had digested divers thinges into forme readie to be made lawes; wherof some concerned hir Majestie's owne saiftie, other the generall state of the realme, some were bills appertayninge to privatt persons, which thoughe in hir sighte mighte seeme but small, yet to those whom they did touch were matters of great valeiue: it would please hir of hir gratious goodnes to vouchesafe to geive the same life, imytatinge therby our heavenlie God, whose persone uppon earthe shee represented. For otherwise were they never so well composed and reduced into good order and frame, the[y] should remayne but as thinges senceles, and all their paines theruppon imployed should be but frustrate, and their workes prove fruitles. Neither was it sufficient as he thought for hir Majestie onelie to geive life to those thinges which they presented, because that with bare life they coulde not longe endure, but must unto that life proceedinge from hir Majestie's mouth, have also added a nutriment, which he termed to be hir straight and earnest commaundement to all hir iudges and other officers to see these lawes duelie excouted. For, saide he, lawes havinge never so righte a course in makinge, unles they have the like course in executinge, can nothinge

    f.37

    The 4.

---

229. *Sic.*

at all availe. And as hir Majestie maye for the great providence she hath in guidinge this state in quiett and peaceable goverment, and the conservinge the people in theire due obedience towardes God and her selfe, commaunde to be imployed att her direction their landes, lives and goodes, so in token therof withall humblenes of mynde, they presented unto hir Highnes amonge manye other two lawes: one touchinge the preservation of hir Majestie's person in saiftie wherby she mayy perceive what litle regarde they have to them selves for the future in respect to contynue the present still amonge them, which is hir Majestie; the other conteyninge a smale gifte of sume part of their substance, /

v. led therunto by seinge the unnaturall disposition of some home borne subiectes, and the daungerous intentes of foraine enemyes againstes whose attemptes as it is most requisite for hir Majestie to have treasor in store, either to imploye in open warrs, or frugallie after hir accustomed order to bestowe other wayes for the avoydinge of further charges, so with all duetifull alleigance they offred this as an earnes-pennie to shewe, that all the rest is att hir commaundement to be employed whensoever: concludinge with a prayer to the God of godes and Lorde of lordes for ever to preserve hir in peaceable state and felycitie.

Finis. /

[rest of f.37v. left blank]

f.38

The Lorde Chauncellor's aunswere to the Speaker's oration.

    The Lorde Chauncellor, by hir Majestie's commaundement makinge awnswere to the speache used by Mr Speaker, declared that the humble disablinge of him selfe showed his great habilitie, notinge thereby the difference betwene one that is merelie ignoraunt, and a man indued with wisdome: wherof the former assuminge more unto him selfe than in truth is in him, in his doeinge sheweth nothinge but pride, arrogancie and ostentation, th'other still mistrustinge a wantt, where as there is none in deede, with meekenes, humilitie and fearefullnes entrethe into all his actions, professinge as that wise and grave philosopher did, *hoc unum scio, quod nihil scio.*[230] Which vertue when he had applied to the Speaker, with this encouragementt that his humble demeanure before hir Majestie in his speache had greatly added to hir gracious opinion before conceived of him, he passed from that matter to the 4 principall divisions of his oration, which he severally handled as ffolloweth:

Firste.   The first wherof he saide conteyned in it two poyntes

summonce

which were   and

continuance.

Wheruppon after he had greatlye commended the Speaker's wisdome in managing the same parte, shewinge what benefittes the subiectes thereby received, his Lordshipp also noted hir Majestie's great care to have the matters of hir kingdome carryed in a due and right course; who after shee had cauled hir estates to gether to consult uppon suche causes as were needefull for the same, would not in short tyme or uppon anie light occasion dismiss them, but held them still together till matters were digested to a full perfection and ripenes, which he concluded to be shuch[231] a vertue in hir, as for the same we were most bound to thanke allmightie God.

By two reasons his Lordshipp saide she was induced to doe that which in his seconde division he noted, namelie to geive a free pardone.   Seconde.

1. The first, her princelie duetie which necessarily required it.
2. The second, the good affection of hir lovinge subiectes towardes hir, which verie truelie deserved it.

Takinge heruppon occation to saye that justice and mercye as they be the onelye princlye vertues that adorne such as exercise the goverment of an imperiall state and crowne, so eache of them have their due places and seasons to be executed and used in. For, saide he, as the rigor of the lawe is to be put in ure where stubborne and headdie breache of the same by anie persone is committed, so requisitely must mercye and remission be exercysed when, more uppon frailtie than anie selfe will, men chaunche to offende: in which case hir Majestie / conceives hir loving subiectes nowe to stande, towardes whome   v. longer then she should well deserve, either in this sorte or in anie other that is within hir reache and power to doe, she would not desire to live.

As touchinge the humble petition in the thirde poynt remembred,   The third. comprehendinge a remittall of ignorantt offences committed as welby him selfe as by the whole bodye of the Lower House, his Lordship saide that hir Majestie's pleasure was he shoulde declare unto him that she easelye might pardone him of anie offence, beinge a man that had nothinge at all offended. And so likewise such contemptes as by the bodye of the Lower House in generall hath bene committed, she may easelye remitt, because she knowes none by them to be committed. But yet he saide that some perticular persons there were amonge them, whom hir Majestie coulde not suffer to escape but would see them punished as the case requirethe. For they in a heddye and violent course forgettinge the boundes of modestie and good manners most audaciouslie and arrogantlye did forroone[232] theire elders beinge wise and discreete men, to the derogation of hir Majestie's authorytie to the contempt of the honorable assemblie of the Upper House, and to the breache of the orders of their owne House: all which manifestly appeared by two severall matters happeninge in this cession. The one in that they would meddle with causes concerninge the Church and religion, a thinge by reason of the perfection of the same (for noe church in the worlde is better governed than ours) altogether needles, and also at the beginninge of the cession by hir Majestie expressly forbydden; yet was that commaundement of hirs so lightlye esteemed, and as itt weare in despite of the clergie that knewe not which waye to governe theire office, they so proceeded, as hir Majestie was forced by his mouthe, (naminge the Speaker of the Lower House) in the middle course of theire matters to forbidd the same agayne. A straunge example his Lordshipp saide this was; and, but with so element a prince as hir Maiestie is not so quietly

230. Socrates (Diogenes Laertius, II, 5.16).   232. *Sic.*
231. *Sic.*

to be endured. The other, in that they contemteously and disdaynfullye reiectid such matters as cam from their betters, the lordes of the Higher House, whose proceedinges they ought withall reverente and duetifull manner to have received and accounted of. And amonge manye other, the arrogant usinge of the bill of fraudulent conveiances, a cause first deepely considered of by hir Majestie's owne persone, with th'advice of hir iudges the greatest learnt men of the realme, digested afterwarde by the wisedom of her nobylitie of the Higher House and learned counsaile there. And lastly, beinge by their lordships with hir Highnes' commendacion sent downe was so scornefully and dispitefullye receyved by the Commons of the Lower House as uppon the first readinge they spurnde it out of dores, not vouchsaifinge it so muche as a committall, the usuall course in all matters by they never so base of condition. /

f.39   This waywarde and perverse dealinge his Lordship saide was so farr unlike to be committed by anye wise men, as in regarde of the state of the place and gravitie of the counsell of the Lower House, where the same was committed, hir Majestie could not impute the offence to the generaltie of the same, but to some number amonge them, and yet such a number as, *maior pars vicit meliorem.* Wherfore, beinge apparantt by th'example of this disorder that noe grave consultation could ever followe in Parliament unles good remedye weare provided for the eschewinge of the like hereafter, his Lordshipp's conclusion of this part was that hir Majestie entended severelie to punishe the authors of these misdemeanners for th'example of others.

The fforthe.   The forth and last part conteyninge in it a dooble petition to have not onely life, but also nourishmentt, geiven to such thinges as shoulde nowe be presented to hir Majestie, his Lordshipp saide hir Highnes did willinglie condescende to the same, and for the former would use the ordynarie course, which was to geive hir royall assent by the mouthe of the Clarke unto suche bills as she thought necessarye to be made lawes.

And for the seconde, as hir Majestie knewe it impossible for hir selfe alone to performe all partes in the execution of justice through out hir realme though shee be supreame justicer, and that it woulde bee inconvenient in divers respectes if she should in hir owne persone take uppon hir the administracion theareof: so sheo mentt to committ the execution of hir lawes now to be made to inferiour ministers suche as had the administracion of other lawes heretofore made, to whom she woulde geive most straight commaundement and charge to see these new to be made with the rest duelye and sincerelye executed. Among which his Lordshipp saide, that hir Majestie made especyall note of two,

which were   1. the bill for hir saiftie,
            2. the bill of subsidie;

v.   and conceived by the framinge of the former how muche we entended hir good, carelesslye regardinge ourselves, yet so / farr, as that we hadd passed hir commaundementt therein.

Likewise by the offeringe of the latter she found that with our lives, our goodes were also readie to be imployed at hir will and pleasure.

Two such tokens of trewe and loveinge subiectes as greatter coulde not be, trustinge in almightie God that the ffirst shoulde never bee put in proofe, and for the seconde as shee did most graciously accepte of it, regardinge the myn[d]es of them that did present it, so would shee retourne it frome whence it came if it onelie concerned hir selfe. But everye man geiveing to him selfe, by geiveinge unto hir she woulde retayne it, as a storer untill such tyme as occasion shoulde be offered to laye out bothe that and hir owne for the publicke commoditye.

This beinge in substance delivered by the Lorde Chauncellor in aunsweare to the Speaker's oration his Lordshipp after hir Majestie had used some speache hir selfe, much tendinge to the fore sayde poyntes, dismissed the companye, proroginge the Parliament to the xx^th daye of Maye nexte followinge.

THE SIXTH PARLIAMENT:
29 OCTOBER 1586–
23 MARCH 1587

Documents

JOURNALS

HOUSE OF LORDS

Parliament roll of proceedings relating to Mary Queen of Scots, 15 October–2 December

HOUSE OF COMMONS

1. Proceedings relating to Mary Queen of Scots, 15 October–2 December
2. Anonymous journal, 23 February–8 March

The reason for calling this parliament was, Lord Chancellor Bromley said, the extraordinary circumstance of Mary's supposed involvement in the Babington Plot and her consequent guilt according to the act of 1584–5. The parliament roll (Lords Journals) for the first session ending on 2 December 1586 is a formal record of proceedings relating to Mary Stuart, and includes the opening ceremonies and Speaker Puckering's request for privileges: the three-man commission (Burghley, Whitgift and Derby) acted on Elizabeth's behalf in the Lords in her absence. It opens with a number of prorogations preceding the eventual opening on 29 October. The events of that day are also covered in Lords 1 which includes the explanation – hardly sufficient – for Elizabeth's absence. The Lords roll also refers to Commons' discussions, and the drafting and approval of the joint petition (Doc.7) to Elizabeth, and includes reports of Elizabeth's speeches on 12 and 24 November. The account of proceedings in the Commons (Commons Journals 1) on the same matters devotes much more time to full accounts of these speeches (Docs. 8iv, 10ii). Both journals show the enormous emphasis on demonstrating that all men were of one mind in this case; that Mary had been given the chance to defend herself; and that the English Queen was reluctant to act against one 'of that estate and quallity soe nere of her bloud and of her owne sexe'. Despite considering the possibility of other ways of dealing with her as requested by Elizabeth 'for two severall dayes' all agreed there was no other way because Mary could not be trusted to behave.[1]

Much of this is repeated almost *ad nauseam* in accounts of various speeches made in the Commons. Sir Christopher Hatton was the first to speak against Mary on 3 November. He was followed by Mildmay (Chancellor of the Exchequer), Sadler (Chancellor of the Duchy of Lancaster), and Secretary John Wolley. Doc.1 is apparently a summary of their speeches demonstrating Mary's 'filthy and detestable' crimes and calling for her death: Sadler commented that failure to execute her would reflect badly on Elizabeth. Hatton in particular set out the familiar catalogue of her crimes and those of her associates. Her complicity with Babington made her guilty under the act of 1584–5. The death of Elizabeth had been planned, and as Mildmay said, England had been threatened with the 'heavy yoke of Rome'. Wolley proposed that the day's speeches be summarized into a 'bill' and presented to the

1. Commons Journal 1, p.309.

Lords and Elizabeth so that the matter might be 'orderly dealt in'. Doc.2 is an undated set of notes which Hatton may have used on this occasion. Folios 39–42 of BL Egerton 2124 contain his own notes on Mary Stuart. They were folded in half, and then half again, across their width; and the notes which are printed here are written in the four columns which have been formed as a result.[2] These notes – as their first line suggests – were probably drawn up as the basis of a speech intended for Parliament, and in fact they used the material in the preceeding folios.[3] It is hard to say how far Hatton followed them in detail: the 'etc' at the end of the first sentence in Doc.1 may suggest a drastically abbreviated introductory section more fully represented in this Egerton MS. Both accounts, however, show a thoroughly prepared set of charges against Mary.

Doc.3 is a fuller version of Mildmay's speech, though it is set out almost in note form. The benefits of living in Elizabeth's Protestant England are explored, and Mary's failings repeated, including her ingratitude to Elizabeth. Mildmay also noted Elizabeth's rejection in 1572 of the safety bill as an example of her graciousness, and he stressed Mary's unwillingness to accept the opportunity which had been given her to defend herself. The Jesuits and seminary priests also had their role to play: they would not cease their efforts to expel the English from their own lands and redistribute them to foreigners. The House must therefore concentrate on providing speedy means by which this could be prevented.

The speech (Doc.4) attributed by Neale to Job Throckmorton probably belongs to the debate of 4 November, though the MS is a copy, undated, and carries no attribution itself. (This applies to the other speeches included here, since they all come from the same MS.) The speech was full of eloquent, ironic venom against Mary and 'our Romish crewe', yet its main purpose was to stress that mercy towards Mary was now inappropriate. Elizabeth's rejection of the 1572 bill had produced 'a heape of treasons and conspyracies'. Now the law must, and could, be allowed to take its course. It is not certain that another speech included at this point (Doc.5) belongs to 4 November, or even to Parliament. The origins of the MS are unknown; and it was not used by Neale. However, it looks as though it was written for Parliament because its first sentence refers to Bromley's opening brief when it talks of the 'mayne matter that we ought most to looke unto', that is the safety of Elizabeth. It may have been delivered in the debate or the meeting of the committee of 4 November, but it is possible that it was part of the discussion in the Lords on this matter. Whoever was responsible for this speech clearly intended to demolish any objection to the argument that Mary be executed. Though Mary and James are not mentioned by name, the targets are clear: the speech confronts the argument that if 'the Scottishe ladie' were to die, the 'first boughe' of the tree would become troublesome. The suggestion is treated as 'some odd astronomicall prediction': God would surely protect England, having showed so much care for so long. James' own religious upbringing would isolate him, it was said, from other Catholics. In a speech which was less brilliant than

Throckmorton's, yet which had its own telling phrases, the author moved inexorably to the conclusion that Mary must die.

The agreement of the Houses to petition Elizabeth for Mary's execution also involved the Speaker's gathering of arguments to reinforce it when it was presented on 12 November (Doc.6).[4] Here the message emerged again: allowing Mary to live would be dangerous to Queen, realm and religion. The freedom of Englishmen, and their property, were at stake. It would be cruelty to Elizabeth's subjects if Mary were spared again, as in 1572. The links between the Queen and subjects – 'sonnes and children of this land' – meant far more than the blood ties between Elizabeth and Mary; and Puckering pleaded that Elizabeth no longer be careless with her own life and the safety of the Church and realm. The draft of the petition itself, amended by Burghley and Egerton (Doc.7), also stressed Mary's treachery, as well as the fairness of proceedings against her and the unanimity of those involved. It stated that Elizabeth's mercy was contrary to the wishes of many of her subjects. Solicitor General Egerton's amendment to the draft version to the petition is significant at this point, for it spoke of Babington's active role and Mary's own privity. A passage on the Bond and the oath taken by its signatories was deleted, however, Burghley and Egerton apparently preferring to rely on the argument that Mary's death was permissible, even required, in justice. In a passage towards the end Egerton spoke of the lack of any solution other than Mary's execution.

Elizabeth's reply survives in several versions, and we cannot tell which most accurately reflects what may have been an extempore speech (Doc.8). A copy bearing her own amendments was approved for publication and may therefore represent some rethinking after the event. She deleted the 'by her' which had affirmed Mary's direct role in the plots against her life, though Mary was still said to have 'fallen into so great a crime'. Elizabeth boasted that she had recently written to Mary after the discovery of treasons ('her' deleted) to offer safety in return for confession. She also deleted 'her that was' before 'the contriver of them' (treasons) and would not admit that the act of 1584–5 was framed particularly against her. For various practical reasons, however, it was appropriate that the case be submitted to a commission as provided for by the act. After all this she said she would delay until she knew for sure what to do for the sake of the Church and the commonwealth.[5]

The second version purports to be an account based on notes taken at the delivery of the speech itself. It follows the Lansdowne version fairly closely,

2. On f.42v.

3. See C. Read, *The Bardon Papers . . .*, p.83.

4. See *EP*, ii.114–15 for the suggestion that Elizabeth had seen the petition before presentation.

5. Since the unamended copy of this version among the Petyt MSS is (perhaps) in Alford's hand, Neale concluded that he may have been the original 'reporter' of this speech (*EP*, ii.129–31, esp. 130, n.2). However, the omission in the Petyt MS of Landsowne's final paragraph – where Elizabeth said she needed divine guidance – could just as easily indicate Alford's incomplete copying of his source.

though the sentiments are sometimes more fulsome, perhaps reflecting the more spontaneous atmosphere of the occasion.[6] We also learn from this version that her explanation of her absence from Parliament – fully interwoven into the Lansdowne MS – came after the speech itself had been completed. In the Stowe MS account (Doc.8iii) Elizabeth's absence is referred to in the second sentence of what is a short and pithy version. The attribution of blame to Mary is most bluntly stated here, for the Scottish Queen is described unambiguously as 'the roote from whence all thes practizes spronge'. This version also has the strongest statement of the obligations placed on Elizabeth's subjects by virtue of signing the Bond. The fourth version provides an introductory paragraph summarizing the preliminary speeches by the Lord Chancellor and Speaker supporting the presentation of the joint petition: the speech itself appears in the account of Commons proceedings (Commons Journal, 1). This account is similar in broad outline to Doc.8ii, though it is perhaps more starkly condemning of Mary's role when it speaks of 'that person whyche wythe so foule treasons hath steyned her estate and bloud', rather than her being 'drawen . . . to shorten the daies of her Highnes'.[7] Both versions contain the famous and important notion that consideration of her subjects made it impossible to overlook Mary's enmity towards her: had they both been milkmaids with pails on their arms, this might have been feasible. But generally Doc.8iv does not match the elegance of Doc.8ii, especially in the passage about the visibility of princes and their doings: this also comes nearer the end of the speech in the journal account and therefore corresponds with Elizabeth's own amended copy.

Doc.9 is a discussion of problems surrounding the prospective execution, and Elizabeth's safety. It was not used by Neale. This very important MS appears to be a contribution to parliamentary discussion, though its origin is unknown. It is constructed in speech form, and closes having discharged 'my particuler duetye in this general consultacion of manye'. On Monday 14 November the Speaker had reported the meeting of 12 November with Elizabeth, the House had been adjourned until Friday, and Hatton had also said that Elizabeth wished to avoid executing Mary, if this were possible. He also said that members in the meantime could 'exhibit their conceits in that case', either to any of the Privy Councillors in the House, or to Mr Speaker.[8] This document was perhaps the result of this injunction, and it may have been intended for delivery after the adjournment. It identifies the central problem: whether 'one absolute prynce may have power over an other of the same sorte'. Even if there were no legal doubt that Elizabeth could proceed, would it be expedient to do so? Would Mary's death end the dangers to England, or would it be better to keep her alive and a prisoner? The author of this document recalled that Roman emperors named their successors and brought them into government, and urged that this be done now: 'for want of a knowen head, al thinges shalbe in tumult'. It was conceded that Elizabeth might be worried about the dangers of 'two sonnes in one fyrmament', but the solution was to bind her declared successor so closely 'as that he may rather be a moone to take his light of the sonne'. There could be no clearer demonstration of the topicality of the unsettled succession after nearly thirty years of Elizabeth's reign.

There are two versions of Elizabeth's second speech (Doc.10) to a delegation from both Houses on 24 November, one of which again shows her own corrections to a copy whose precise relationship to what she said that day is unknown, yet which she wished to adopt as the basis of a published account. Many of the corrections are merely stylistic, yet others dilute some harsher anti-Marian tones. A particularly self-deprecating passage was deleted in favour of a more formal admission of her faults. A reference to a wish to *'establish'* God's Church and religion 'wherein I was borne and bread and wherein I hope to die' gave way to recalling how she *began* her reign with 'suche religion . . .'. In the course of dealing with princely virtues, especially justice, a passage which denied that Elizabeth had respected the 'person to the alteration of my censure' was excised and replaced with something more densely 'Elizabethan'. All this was a prelude to the famous 'answer answerless', a section apparently causing Elizabeth considerable difficulty. Finally, she claimed that acceding to the Lords' and Commons' petition might actually 'breed perill of that youe labor to preserve'. The ideas that Elizabeth apparently wanted to convey on this occasion flow more freely in the second version than they do in her own amended copy.[9] Some of the sense of the phrases she deleted concerning the Church of God and her own circumstances remain here. Similarly, the passage devoted to the 'scole of experience' and the princely virtues is more clearly developed. The idea, finally dismissed by Elizabeth, that she had made a show of clemency also appears closer to the end of the speech than in the Lansdowne account.

On 22 February, soon after Parliament reassembled, Hatton told the Commons of the dangers Elizabeth believed were confronting England.[10] Mildmay's speech on the need to provide financial aid followed (Doc.11), and spoke, *inter alia*, of the need to remember 'Holland and Zeland and other provinces united, tyed unto us both by ancient amity and by religion'. 'Favorable taxation' meant that the Queen did not receive the full amount of subsidy grants, and only if further help were given would Englishmen be able to continue to enjoy 'liberty of consciences' among other things.

Job Throckmorton's speech (Doc.12) is probably the one referred to in the anonymous journal, and which caused him to be reprimanded later.[11] He lamented the plottings of Catholic princes in Europe, rejoiced at the fall of 'the Scottish dame' and that threats to the realm had been defeated with God's help. Nevertheless, it was necessary to be vigilant and perhaps, he said, we should

6. The 'direct speech' version in CUL Ee, ii.12 omits some important phrases and has none of the 'commentary' which is integrated into the Exeter College account.

7. Commons Journals 1, p.305; Doc.8ii, f.52.
8. D'Ewes, p.402.
9. See Commons Journals 1.
10. *EP*, ii.166–8.
11. *EP*, ii.169–73.

pray for 'some competente and moderate scourge'. Throckmorton's imagination also led him to see that the offer of the Low Countries' sovereignty (to which, he said, we had a legal right) was a further sign of God's goodness when we could not rely implicitly on anyone else: even James of Scotland could be a snake in the grass. This remarkable and colourful speech is, however, striking not least for its closing passages. When all was said and done, our own wretchedness remained a major problem: 'our bodyes are in Englande, our harts are at Rome', and we therefore must hope that God induce Elizabeth to ensure that her subjects might be 'throughly instructed and trew Christian discipline established'.[12]

The need to consider the Low Countries followed naturally from what Hatton had said, and from the appointment of a committee to consider the subsidy.[13] Even without Throckmorton's call for acceptance of the sovereignty it is hard to see how the issue could have been avoided, and easy to see why support for the notion continued to be expressed. Speaker Puckering's account of the committee's deliberations on 24 February was written in law French, perhaps because it was more suited to rapid note-taking (Doc.13).[14] Its length is enough to make it difficult to believe it was compiled after the event from memory, unless aided by rough notes which do not appear to have survived. Occasionally Puckering's hand and his use of abbreviations make for some uncertainty, as does his note-taking itself: the meaning of Bainbridge's contribution is not, perhaps, wholly clear. The underlying meaning of the MS is, however, not in doubt: the emergence of a proposal for a benevolence, some preliminary points for a petition involving the hitherto unconsulted Lords, and a formalized request to Elizabeth to consider acceptance of the sovereignty are the main ingredients. The points which underpinned this were just as important too. The MS is eloquent about concern for fellow Protestants, of the need to protect trading interests in Europe, and of the major strategic considerations involved in the shifting political balance. The section headed 'Mete and nedefull' constitutes a catalogue of England's essential interests in the Low Countries.

Two further documents, from Puckering's papers (Docs. 14, 15) appear to have been prepared as part of the committee's work, though they were not apparently delivered to the Queen.[15] The first summarized the contents of the petition which might be made to Elizabeth urging acceptance of the sovereignty of Holland and Zealand, and offered a benevolence to fund the enterprise. Puckering's notes show that he was keen to assure Elizabeth that money would be available, advising her to appoint commissions to investigate what the yield would be. Folio 31 seems to be another attempt to provide a sequence of argument which kept the subsidy and the benevolence separate. The former would prevent the enemy moving against England, but it was suggested that the problem would be properly solved only if sovereignty was accepted, because without it the Low Countries might 'fayle to perfourme ther assistans and servyce'. He also emphasized the strategic and commercial reasons for England's involvement which appeared in Doc.13, and claimed that 'our people would murmure' if unemployment grew too much as a result of the disruption of trade. The other paper (Doc.15) is a draft of a speech, probably for delivery by the Speaker, and again strongly urging acceptance of the sovereignty on the basis of bonds of common religion and economic interests.[16] Though the decision in this matter was 'wholly' referred to the Queen herself, Neale considered this to be insincere, since the Queen could not receive the benevolence unless she took the sovereignty. But Puckering was surely correct to stress the conditions under which an offer of an annual, non-parliamentary, benevolence by the wealthier men of the realm was being made. It is also by no means clear that some of the marginal notes in this MS reflect Puckering's cultural limitations: perhaps they were explanations and apposite illustrations intended to emphasize Puckering's point in delivering the speech itself.[17]

The discussions concerning Mary before Christmas, and foreign matters since the resumption of business, both necessarily emphasized Catholic threats to England and its Church, as well as the danger of an enhanced Spanish presence in the Low Countries. By the beginning of March, however, Cope's radical proposals for a Presbyterian church had been presented to the Speaker and impounded; several members were imprisoned; and Elizabeth (presumably) had ensured that Peter Wentworth's questions concerning liberties were not even formally put to the House. In another speech attributed to Job Throckmorton and probably delivered on 27 February (Doc.16) we have a further example of outstanding oratory which illustrates the way contemporaries could see necessary connections between the great issues of the day.[18] Throckmorton complained about the 'show of freedome' in the House, which was nevertheless told that religion and the succession were not to be discussed. He argued that Elizabeth's safety was the main reason for Parliament's meeting, and said that reform of the Church was necessary to achieve this. Referring to Mary's execution in approving terms, he said that to 'reforme the house of God and to settell the Crowne . . . shall be 10 tymes better don'. He appears to have referred to the rejection of Cope's bill and book, though if this is the speech made on 27 February, Throckmorton must have assumed that the Speaker's intervention, and that of Dalton, would deal it a mortal blow. Much of this speech was directed towards arguing for a reformation of the 'dumb ministry', which, Throckmorton said, bred treason. He also argued that Parliament could reform religion, and that experience showed that leaving it to 'grave fathers' meant that nothing was achieved.

Wentworth's questions (Doc.17) – printed here in the two versions which have survived – were most obviously framed so as to elicit information about how freely members might speak in matters that 'concerne the glory of God and our true and loyal service to our prince and state', though this is a general,

12. Pp.50–1
13. *EP*, ii.166–8.
14. See *EP*, ii.176–9 for treatment of this document.
15. *EP*, ii.179.
16. F.40.
17. Cf. *EP*, ii.180.
18. See Commons Journals 2 (Anonymous), f.92v.

rather than a specific statement.[19] All available manuscripts are copies, and there is nothing to suggest that any of them was Wentworth's own, or indeed what had specifically prompted them. The two lists are not identical, and Lansdowne has more questions than the Cotton version. It must also be said that some of the questions appear to relate to the standing and functions of Parliament rather than focusing more narrowly on the speaking rights of individual members. While some questions, especially the first in the Cotton list, can be interpreted as embodying a concept of unlimited freedom to speak in the House (and may be a good example of the deceptively innocent question) others touch on connected issues such as the secrecy of debate. The following document (Doc.18) is the speech which Neale believed was written, though not delivered, in favour of putting Wentworth's questions.[20] The MS is not dated, and there is no obvious clue to the identity of its author. It is reminiscent of Wentworth's speech of 1576, and its main purpose appears to be to establish the need for free speech. The significance of the denial that 'this' is innovation, and of the questions why 'may we not innovate' and 'Are we not bound to innovate good orders as well as good laws?' is by no means clear in this MS. The writer objects to the breach of secrecy in Commons' proceedings, and produces alleged precedents showing that it had been upheld in the past.[21] What strengthens the argument that this document was intended to support Wentworth's drive for procedural enlightenment this session comes in the plea that the House answer 'these questions by question', presumably a reference to Wentworth's questions: in this way Elizabeth's displeasure could be avoided.

Sergeant Puckering's prominent role in attempting to suppress the debate on religion can be seen in Document 19: though the manuscript is undated, it may be suggested that it records part of the speech made by him on 2 March.[22] It claimed that the 'Puritans' would upset the well-established *status quo* in the Church to the detriment of the subject. But it was left to Hatton, Mildmay and Egerton to explain the fuller ramifications of Cope's bill and book on 4 March (Docs. 20–22) after the question of the imprisoned members had been raised by Sir John Higham.[23] It is likely that Hatton owed substantial parts of his speech to Bancroft.[24] Claiming that the Queen had brought the Church to a 'perfection' never before seen in England, Hatton said that its rejection in favour of Presbyterianism would drive thousands to atheism and Catholicism: soon after he argued that the shortcomings of the Church could be reformed without structural change. Two versions of the speech are included, the second described by Whitgift's endorsement as a summary of Hatton's principal points, and the 'exordium' in this second account, repeating much of what has gone before, appears to mark the point at which the first version is most directly reflected.[25] A final section, again entitled 'exordium' also appears to be a summary of the speech.[26] Though speaking of Presbyterianism's threat to laymen and their rights and possessions within the Church, Hatton said the greatest danger was to Elizabeth's authority and revenues, the latter being especially important in the maintenance of peace for the benefit of the realm.

Mildmay (Doc.21) also stressed the practical consequences of implementing Presbyterianism: the loss of the Queen's revenues would redound to the subjects' cost, he said. The good work which had been done in the Church should not be swept aside, and popular election of ministers was no way to achieve reformation.[27] He argued that Parliament was not equipped to decide 'which reformed Churches we shall follow', and that the Commons should await the advice of learned divines and the Supreme Governor's own action.[28] Egerton reiterated much of what had already been said, adding that the Queen's loss of the clerical subsidy would amount to about a third of the lay subsidy (Doc.22).

What is especially interesting about Docs. 19, 20 and 22 is that they attempt to brand Protestants, albeit the more extreme kind, as men who would help England's Catholic enemies. Puckering's speech alleged that disruptive Presbyterians were worse than Jesuits and would help to open the door to a threatened Spanish invasion. Hatton seems to have wondered how far the Presbyterians would go against Elizabeth, and conjured up the spectre of *Vindiciae contra Tyrannos* (Doc.20). The subject, he said, would be freed of his oath of fidelity. His final insult was to draw a parallel between them and the Papists (a point developed further in Doc.20ii). Egerton's contribution was to point out that the Presbyterians' wish to abolish all existing legislation concerning the Church, including the anti-Catholic laws, would leave men free to 'maynteyne the Pope's pretensed jurisdiccion'.

The prohibitive tone of these messages is repeated in Doc.24. This bears no date, though references to 'your full consentes' (to the Supremacy Act), to the 'platforme which is desired', and to 'your petition' suggest that it was drafted on behalf of the Queen in response to the committee, established on 8 March, to discuss a 'motion to be made' about Church matters which still troubled members.[29] In this riposte it was alleged that the quest for reform would weaken rather than strengthen, and that it was harmful for men to become accustomed to change. More striking, however, was the insistence that the Crown's prerogative was offended, even by the submission of a petition. There is no certainty that the document was delivered to the committee, or, if it was, when this happened.

19. Cotton Titus FI, f.289v.
20. *EP*, ii.156; D'Ewes, p.410.
21. I have not been able to verify the references to Henry IV's and V's reigns. They appear again in Cromwell's gatherings on liberty which Neale assumed had been prepared for the committee, though there is nothing in the MS itself to confirm this. (*EP*, ii.164–5).
22. See Commons Journals 2 (Anonymous), f.94v; this document was not used by Neale.
23. *EP*, ii.158.
24. P. Collinson, *The Elizabethan Puritan Movement* (1967), pp.313–14; an endorsement on the document also appears to link it with Bancroft's discourse.
25. F.135v.
26. F.137v.
27. Fos.116v–17, 120.
28. Fos.119–v.
29. *EP*, ii.162–4.

The anonymous journal of Commons proceedings covering the days from 23 February to 8 March, is a small MS (about 15 cm × 20 cm) consisting of pages previously stitched together, and probably forming a pocket notebook. There is no obvious clue to its authorship. Its entries are mostly in note form, sometimes brief to the point of becoming almost cryptic, and in places the handwriting is not easily read. These circumstances suggest that it may have been written on the spot – in the House and at committee meetings – as a personal *aide-mémoire*, rather than for others' benefit. The journal notes Throckmorton's speeches on 23 and 27 February, but provides much more information about the discussions in committee on the Low Countries, their sovereignty and the mooted benevolence. There is an apparently incorrectly dated account of the meeting of 24 February,[30] and others for 27 February and 6 March. The speeches by Hatton, Mildmay and Egerton against Cope receive extensive coverage: they should be read with Docs. 20–22. If this journal was indeed written as proceedings unfolded we would expect these long speeches to be extensive summaries at best, and comparison with the separates lends weight to this. The elements of Hatton's speech in the journal are much the same as what appears in Doc.20, though the journal suggests that Hatton did not wholly follow the form as set out there: there is, for instance, no obvious reference to Carthage.[31]

The journal notes some other sensitive areas, namely the purveyors bill on 2, 3 and 6 March, and the unease over the members detained after the Cope incident, though much more space is immediately devoted thereafter to the second reading debate on a bill concerning fish. So despite the Queen's original intention that there should be no business other than that of Mary Stuart, members and other circumstances ensured that what Neale once called 'the normal, legislative business of Parliament' also appeared.[32] Doc.23 concerns a committee meeting on a bill 'against forestallers, ingrossers and regraters, providinge that all men may not buy barly to malt it', which apparently had its first reading on 2 March. A committee was appointed to meet on 6 March, according to D'Ewes, though this document is dated 7 March.[33] Mildmay's son-in-law William Fitzwilliam, who sat for Peterborough in this parliament, may have attended this meeting, though it is not certain that the handwriting of this heavily amended MS is his own. One of the aims was to limit the malting of barley so that some could be used for bread. The discussion of practical obstacles was thoroughgoing, and no easy solution could be seen. In a passage which was apparently intended for deletion, it was said that corruption might ensue from giving justices of the peace the power to issue licences for malting. In the end, though, it was felt that they they were, after all, the men 'to whome the carriage and guidinge of the coontrie in most matters was committid'. The committee also considered how to deal with those 'contractors' who engrossed certain kinds of merchandise and drove up prices, though others apparently argued that 'contractors' were not at work. There were instead 'good' merchants who bought up stocks for valid and beneficial reasons, and prices were brought *down* as a result. All this was in turn denied. It was further claimed that retailers who had arrived to present their case to the committee had there encountered contractors (also called to give evidence), and that they had withdrawn for fear of not being able to buy from them in the future 'if theie were knowne to complaine'. It is perhaps no wonder that the 'matter proceedid no further'.

Although Lords 2 is not dated and bears no title, there can be little doubt that it is the text of the Speaker's speech addressing the commissioners who represented Elizabeth at the ending of the session. It referred to bills passed by both Houses, including the subsidy bill, and gave thanks for the general pardon. Referring to the subsidy grant Puckering said that it would not cover Elizabeth's expenses to date or those to come: it was a pledge of devotion and readiness to 'employe whatsoever wee doe possesse besydes'. Neale agreed with Puckering's description of his speech as 'rude and unpolished'.[34] This may be too harsh, and it is unreasonable to look for gems of oratory at this point. Given the nature of the session, and that it was presumably incumbent upon him to be emollient in these last moments, his task was not an easy one. Puckering was surely correct to stress that what he called the 'preposterous zeale' of a few members was no sign of disobedience or a general wish to disrupt proceedings. But given Elizabeth's resistance to pressure on a number of fronts, other than Church matters, the Speaker's thanks that the Queen had allowed members to 'make meanes to her' sounds like limp politeness.

30. See also Doc.13.
31. Cf. Commons Journal 2, f.97.
32. *EP*, ii.162.
33. It was not used by Neale.
34. *EP*, ii.190–1.

1. [House of Lords] Herald's account of opening proceedings, 29 October 1586

Text from BL Add.5758, original.

Add.5758. fos.83–4.

[Endorsed '*de parliamento 1586*.']

The parliament begon by commission *29 Octobris 1586*
being Satterdaye at ix or x of the cloke

The Archebushope of Canterbury	The Lord Threasurer of England	Th'erle of Derby Lord Steward at this parliament.

Die Sabati 29 Octobris 1586   The Queen's most excellent Majesty beinge urged upon sundery causes, chefly ij viz, for the pretence of forreigne invasion and secret practize of the murther pretended of her royall person (whom the Almighte hathe and styll shall protect to the confusion of her secrett enemies) sommoned the parliament upon a purposed dissolution of the parliment presedent, as by proclamation apperethe, which after certeyne ij [y]eres of prorogations by ij comissions was by a nother comission begon in maner and forme followinge.

First the Lords assembled in theyr roobes at ix of the clok in *camera picta Sancti Edwardi dicta Westmonesterii*, which chamber was hanged and prepared by the industrie and direction of Mr Norrys, gentleman huisher for the parliament, and Mr Symon Boyar, gentleman huisher for the Queen, with stooles or formes covered with redd saye for the Lords only. And the formes for the Lord Chancellor and judgges and others were bare.

Nota that the Lord Stuard this daye, th'erle of Derby, went in to the Lower House to tak retorne of the wryttes and swere the burges[ses] at vij of the clok and cam to the Upper Howse agayne to his place.[1]

The Lords thus placed: the Deane of Westminster with iij assosiates and the Bishop of Salisbury assistant as deane of the Queen's Chappell in his robes. The deane kneling began the Letanie and ended with the prayer for the Queen's Majeste. Then the said Bishop of Salisbury went up into the pulpite and began a sermond out of the begining of the [MS blank] Psalme. Wherein he noted the practizes of invasion pretended to the realme, the conspiracies attempted

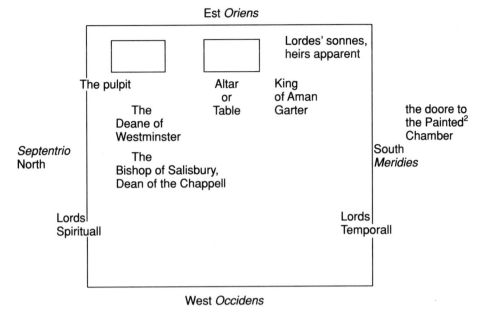

The gentlemen and knightes of the Lower House had place appoynted to staye here during the sermond.

agaynst her Majeste's person proceding from the pope of Rome and the Rheymistes, detectinge amongst other these abhominable Poopes[3] viz, conjourors, poysoners, negromanciers, idolators, these conspiracies to proceed. Concluding with David, the protection of her Majeste's[4] to be in God our refuge and deliverer.[5]

Which finished, the Lords went into the Parliament[6] Chamber and took theyr places first according to theyr degrees and dignites. Then cauling for the Nether Howse to enter viz, Mr Threasurer,[7] Mr / Comptrolor,[8] Sir   v. Christopher Hatton and other the knightes and burgesses. Then stood the Lord Chancellor[9] up at the woll sak and declared that her Majeste had deputed [? her authority] in her absence for sundery causes respected and by her Majeste's comission for the houldinge of this parlement, and delivering the same unto the Clerk was there redd openly unto those iij named. And they imediately arose and toke theyre place making obeysance to the seat royall. Then the Lord Chancellor cam with reverence to them and kneled downe to them three and received the forme of his oration, and so with obeysance passed by them and went to the usuall place at the barre behynd the seate on the right hand,

1. The following is a simplified form of the diagram in the MS.
2. MS: 'P'.
3. *Sic.*
4. *Sic.*
5. e.g. Ps 14: 6, 59: 16; 62: 7, 91: 2.
6. MS: 'P'.
7. Sir Francis Knollys.
8. Sir James Croft.
9. Sir Thomas Bromley.

and there began his oration for the especiall caulinge therof, viz, for her Majeste's savetie from perell of conspiracies for foreyne invasion was first and without demand of subsidie.[10] Lastly comanding theim to make choyse and ellection of theyr Speaker and to repayre to the same place agayne within[11] on Mondaye next after.[12]

10. See Commons Journal, 1, p.302.
11. *Sic.*
12. A further diagram follows showing the seating of the Lords with the three commissioners in front of the throne, and the Speakers and others at the Bar.

2. [House of Lords] Speaker's speech at close of Parliament, 23 March 1587

Text from BL Harley 6846, original draft in the hand of a secretary of John Puckering, Speaker.

Harley 6846, fos.17–18

'Right honourable, and my verie good lordes. Albeit the conscience of myne owne inhabilitie to performe this weightie service dothe so muche the more discourage me at this present, as I have often heartofore found my selfe foyled in wrastlyng with the same: yet, when I consyder that your good lordships doe represent unto me the person of her Majestie's selfe (my most gratious and benigne mystresse, by the hande of whose helpfull favour I have bene sundry tymes releaved from the grounde and sett on foote), I doe inwardly recomforte my selfe with assured hope, that as your good lordships doe participate her roial auctoritie, so you will also imitate her most gratious clemencie; and that as her Majesties[1] hath endewed you with ample power to bestowe her most generall and free pardone, so it will lyke you, not only to extende the same particularly unto me (in most liberalle measure) whylest I shall endevour to doe this office of thankes to her Majesties in the behalfe of all her most loving commons (represented in this present assemblie), but also by your honourable wisedomes to supplie in your reaport to her Majesties, whatsoever the imperfections of this my rude and unpolished action.

'And heare (first of all) wee humbly desyre that the unfayned and entier thanks of us all bee rendred to her most excellent Majesties for that (assembling us in this present session of parlement) she hath gyven unto us the opportunitie and advauntage, not only to conferre amongst ourselves, and to make meanes to her Majesties for remedie of suche domestical enormities as doe annoy and greive us within the realme, but also to be instructed of sundry great and imminent daungers intended against us by the forein enemies of our felicitie and wellfare; and withal to testifie by outward signes that duetie of thankfulnesse whearin wee stand inwardly obliged to her Majesties, for that her most intentive and continual care that she maynteyneth over us. And as touching this present assemblye of her Majestie's most liege and loving Commons, I cannot but avowe and testifie (in that duetie, which in the Lorde I owe

---

1. *Sic* (and throughout).

unto her sacred Majesties) that howsoever I my selfe have bewrayed myne owne insufficiencie to be the mouthe and interpretour of so grave and wise a bodie, and howsoever also some verie fewe of theim have fallen and offended, rather by infirmitie of iudgement and through a preposterous zeale, then of any eyther disobedience to her Majesties, or intention of distourbance to our better proceadings: yet generally, the whole numbre hath from tyme to tyme, no lesse readyly assembled, then quietly conferred, and painfully travailed, in this session, for the glory of God, the service of her Majesties, and the commune good of the realme. /

v.   'In which parte, that your good lordships rest not only in my reaporte, but may (by the fruites theim selves) bee induced to iudge of theire labour accordingly, I doe heare present unto yowe the formes of those lawes, which (for the shortness of the tyme) have been agreed upon by my Lordes heare, and us her Majestie's Commons. Of the which, some doe tende to the correction (if it be possible) of suche popishe, obstinate, and hard-harted recusantes, as hytherto will not bee suppled with any the oyles of her Majestie's lenitie; others are bent to the terrifyeng of all future dislioaltie,[2] by present dish[e]rison of the posteritie of suche as have trayterously offended against her Majestie, and by prevention of all subtile and fraudulent conveighance that they have made to save the forfeiture that theire faulte hath brought unto the Crowne; others are drawen for the advauncement of commune justice by taking away suche delayes therof as by preten[ce] of error have lately crepte into the courtes: and others are invented as fitt meane[s] to styrre up the labour of our nation and to revive that industrie, which by many late immunities hathe declined greatly amongst us. Touching all which, wee humblie beseeche your good lordships that if the same have bene (upon the touchestone of her Majestie's most excellent wysedome and approved iudgement) founde meete to passe abroade, then it may like your lordships for the full and perfect strengthening of theim, to inspire into theim the life of lawe by the breathe of her Majestie's roiall assent and auctoritie, according to that plenitude of power which her Highness hathe woorthyly committed unto yow; and that for the propagation of her Majestie's honour to our posteritie, they may be added to the volumes of her former most religious, politique, and profitable statutes.

'Further more, wee doe heare reknowledge her Majestie's great bountie and singular favour, and doe instantly beseeche your good lordships that our most humble and hartye thankes may be presented to her Majesties for this her most gratious, generall, and free pardon, as whearby some of us shall escape the stroake of lawe that iustly might have reached unto us for our remisse and secure cariage of our selves; others shall avoyde the deserved paynes of theire wilfull transgressions; some shalbe warned by her Majestie's indulgence not to offend so gratious a sovereigne; others shalbe feared to fall againe into the lyke faultes, least they fynd not the same (or the lyke) favour: and wee all, and every one, shalbe eyther quyted, eased, amended, or admonished by it.

'Finally, forasmuche as wee cannot but see that her most excellent Majesties hathe in great wysedome and highe magnanimitie taken the opportunitie of arming sundry bandes of her subiectes for protecting our afflicted neighboures, the Christians of the Lowe Countries, against the iniurious violence of the popishe and Spanishe ambition that seeketh us in theim, and shooteth at us thorowe theim; and that the same so heroicall an enterprise cannot be maynteyned without a greater masse of treasure / then the ordinarie revenues   f.18 of her Majestie's crowne may bring unto her, wee doe heare with the consenting hartes and handes of us all offer unto her Majestie's use, one usuall subsidie and two fifteenes, not as any sufficiencie for her Majestie's expence already defrayed, and muche lesse for the coste and burdeine that is to come, but only as an outwarde testification of that syncere and thankfull love and duetie that wee owe and beare unto her, and as an earnest peny and pledge of our hartye devotion any readynesse to employe whatsoever wee doe possesse besydes at her Majestie's [co]mmaundement and disposition: humbly praying your good lordships to assure her Majesties on our behalfe, that wee will not only direct our dayly prayers unto God for the preservation and long life of her Majesties, but shalbe founde from tyme to tyme most ready to dedicate and consecrate our goodes and landes, liberties and lyves to and for this, or any other, her Majestie's honourable service and employment.'

2. *Sic.*

1. Four speeches against Mary Queen of Scots, 3 November 1586

Text from Oxford: Bodley, MS Tanner 78, original account.

Tanner 78, fos.14–16v.

November 3° 1586.

Sir Christofer Hatton:

'The summary cause of the sommons of this parliament is to provyde for the safetie of our most gracyous sovereigne, whose goverment is the minister of Gode's goodnes to us and our felicetie, yet is it not without troble and principall malignors, etc. The Queene of Scottes, so called, beinge the hope of all idoletry and, in myne opynion, of a nomber of subiectes terming them selves Catholiques conceyved to be a present possessor of the crowne of England, a matter that concerneth us all most deepely and to be looked unto, is a principall maligner of this state and us all good subiectes. The maner of the Queene of Scottes' lyfe and her practises from the begininge most fylthy and detestable, yf you looke well into them you shall well fynd that her ambisious mynd, grounded in papistry, hath still thirsted after this crowne of England, and our overthrowe. As, first, being marryed into France she there tooke upon her the armes of Englande, sett them downe in her coynes and all other such matters. Secondlie, her husband in France dyinge, she disposed her self to marry a subiect of Englande, and of the nobiletie, namely the Erle of Lenox, in hope therby to enter partlie into the hartes of the people, and come nearer the crowne, of whose death the world thinketh her gyltie. Afterwardes, she being banyshed Scotland for the death of her said husband and cominge into this realme, wher she was protected by her Majestie (albeit the Scottes procecute her not with the sworde, for it cold not be, but in iustice bringing forth her owne lettres to accuse her for his death practized and comitted by her and th'erle Boddill, wherunto her Majestie harkened not), yet, notwithstanding that favour, aspyring still after this crowne, she practized to marry with the Duke of Norfock and therupon to styrre rebellyon to come to the crowne, her self and the Duke both dissembling this matter, wherupon ensued the Duke's destruccion together with the Erle of Northumberland, Westmorland, and many moe gentlemen. Yea, the same tyme where she dissembled this, greatly pretendinge one matter and intending an other, she imployed one Rudolphin her ministre to move Pius Quintus the Pope to excommunicate her Majestie, our sovereigne, and to discharge her subiectes of their allegeans towardes her; which Pius Quintus did by his bulles with the Queene of Scottes' privetie.

Wherupon this late spoken of rebellion by the erles followed etc. This ended, and the Duke deade, she practised with Thomas Throgmorton, Sir Francis Englefeld, Doctor Allen to move forren forces to invade this realme and sett her at libertie and this crowne upon her heade. This not fallinge out she moved then to stirre up the Kinge of Spayne and the Pope to the greate dessignement, wherunto Doctor Allen brought answer of good forwardnes, and from tyme to tyme writt her mynd to Charles Padget: all which matters were in / handlinge   v. in Anno Domine[1] 1583, '84, '85, '86, and imparted to Ballard the seminarye who by the direction of Charlls Pagett and the rest made the same knowne to Babinton, who willingely embraced the same disignment, which was to kill owr most our most[2] gracious soveraigne, wherin he shewed all forwardnes. This abhominable act was by Doctor Gefford and Gefford[3] a reader beyonde the seas perswaded unto them and comendid to be most meritorious to Ballard, Morgan and Pagett. This Ballard beinge a principall actor was the Queen of Scottes' intelligencer two yeres. But not longe before this time on Parry, lately executed, was delt with Morgan and Charles Pagett to kill owr soveraigne, but by Gode's goodnes was diservedly executed: for this peece of service in advysinge of this matter the Queen of Scottes gave them and giveth yett unto Morgan a pencion and comendid hir[4] hyghly to the King of Spaine. Now to proseed, on Babington undertoke this disignment to kill our Quene and that six shold performe it, whereof he writt accordingly to the Queen of Scottes, begoon thus, "Most dread Lady", etc. "to whom onely and to none other I owe obedience", etc.; and therby made knowne unto hir that the killinge of owr soveraigne was undertaken by six noble gentlemen, whose heroycall attempt he wished might he rewarded to them selves yf they lived and yf they died to ther posteritye. He desired to knowe what forraine forces upon this execcusion wold he readye; he saide portes for landinge places must be knowne; and with one hundreth undertooke her enlardgment. Note by the waie Babington and his complices entendid the death of our soveraigne; invasion; rebellion; settinge up the Queen of Scottes; spoilinge of the welthiest of the realme; killinge all the lordes in the Starr Chamber; takinge of Killingworth castell and with the armowre and munition ther to sett upon us, etc. To this letter of Babington the Queen of Scottes writt awnswer, *videlicett*: comendinge Babington highly for his zeale in religion, wherin she proffered to spend life, land and goodes, and promised that the gentlemen that undertoke the designement shold be throwghlye considered; advisinge him furth[er] that care must be taken what ayde was to be loked for in this lande, what forraine forces weare to be expected and for how longe the[y] weare provided, wher a ffitt place might / be fownde for landinge, whether and to what place they   f.15 shold asemble, what succour from Flaunders, Fraunce and Spaine would come; she liked well that six were apointed for the designement, and advysed further that fowre tall men well horsed shold be redy to bringe her knowledge of the

1. *Sic.*   3. *Sic.*
2. *Sic.*   4. *Sic.*

execcusion by severall waise and that the postes showld be intersepted. Thus
farr the lordes and commisioners have fownde her giltie so that in this place I
deliver nothinge but *rem gestam* and the trueth, for God forbid I should speake
otherwise or showld live to do it in so waightie a cawse. And that this is so it
is manifest by Babington and Ballarde's owne confesion subscribed with ther
owne handes, and by Curle and Nawe, the Queen of Scotes' secretaries,
voluntarie depotisiones[5] writen with ther owne handes, who both awnswer
that this former lettre the Queen ther mistres reseyved from Babington, that by
her direction Nawe made this foresaide awnswer therunto, then Curle put it
first into English, afterwardes into cipher, by her commandement and so sent
it to Babington in the Queen of Scotes' owne sipher wherin Babington wrott
to her, which cipher was fownde in the Quene's cascet and known by
Babington and Ballerd, which Tuchburne[6] disciphered the lettres which she
writt to Babington. And the more to satisfie you all of her Majestie's most
honorable and wise dealinge in thes matteres, when the Queen of Scottes'
papers were browght to the Cowrt by Sir Walter Aston, Mr Manners and Mr
Baggott,[7] she wold not peruse or vewe any of them before she had all her
Cownsell then attendaunt at the Cowrt present, viz. the Erle of Shrewsburye,
Lord Chamberlaine, Lord Cobham and Mr Seccrettarye Walsingham, whom
she cawsed to se them and subscribed[8] ther names so as nothinge cowld be or
was added or deminyshed. And for your better perswasion that the Queen of
Scotes was the rote of all thes matters the concurencye of her leters towchinge
this matter to Chareles Pagett, the Bishop of Glascoe, the Lord Pagett,
Barnarden de Mendoza and Docter Lewes may sufise, for they all import all on
matter, the killinge of owr soveraigne. She hath handled it in Flanders, Spaine,
v.   France and Italie. She writ to Docter Lewes to congratulate with / the new
Pope, and to wish him to confirme the bull of good Pius Quintus for the
excomunication of our soveraine. She alured by all menes possible the
Catholikes of Scottland to joine also in this accion, and wrote also to Mendoza
that yf the kinge her son wold not becom a Catholiqe[9] she wold worke that
the Lord Hameleton and Chareles Pagett shold deliver him into his handes and
further bequeath unto him all her interest of this crowne of Englande. She
practised that this sommer a stirr shold be raised in Ireland and Scottland when
this disigement was in hande, which was don in both places. Her advice
further in Babington's letter was that the Catholiques of this lande shold make
for ther cowler of rysinge that it was don onely to defend them selves from the
Puritans, which nowe especially by one of them in Flanders, by name the Erle
of Lecester, growne stronge, of whose mallice they were afraide, that this stirr
beinge in Irelande and our soveraigne goinge abowt to supose that a blowe
showld come sudainelie owt of Flanders unexspected, which dyvelishe
practyses if any shuld take place we shuld ether be forsed to forsake God or our
lyves. Yeat wee may comfort our selves in one poynt, that Rome by no
meanes[10] and the papistes beeing unhable to alure wyse and ould men to
execute ther abhominable desines because ther intentyons are looked into,
begine to practys with lusty yong youthes who, they assayling with the promis

of promosyon and preferment, perswade to take in hand ther wicked devises. And now, my masters, how neerly theis most abhomynable proceedinges of the Quene of Scottes the root and grond of all theis treasons, who in all her actyons pretendethe one thing and styll dothe intend another, viz. only the crowne of England, her Majestie's deathe, the alteracyon of relygion and the distructyon of us all, from whose cruelty the Lord delyver us, how neerly the[y] concerne you, judge your selves. And now to conclud with my opynyon, I speake as in the presens of almighty God, *Ne periat Israell periat Absolon.*' /

Sir Walter Mildmey: f.16
  'My masters, you have herde very wisely and plainely declared unto [you] a most rare and abhominable conspiracy intended against her Majesty, owr most gracious soveraigne, ye, even in the highest degree, for the takinge awaie of her life. Wherin, albeit I dowbt not but you ar satisfied that a mere truth hath bene delivered you, yet I have thowght it my duty to speake myne opinion of three speciall pointes which conserne the same, viz. against whom the treason was comitted, by whom it was concluded, and to what end it was entended. It was comited against our most gratious soveraigne in goinge abowt to take awaye her life; it was concluded upon by the Quene of Scotes, a principall actor and rote of that conspiracye; it was don of flatt purpose to kill owr soveraigne, sett the crowne of this realm one the Queen of Scotes' hed, alter religion, overthrow us all and lay upon us or our posteritie the hevey yoke of Rome knowne to a nomber of you. This Queen of Scottes hath bene the cawse of much blode, who remaininge, her Majestie, whose safty we all owght to provide for, canot be in saftie, etc. He agravated thes three last pointes towchinge the first part Mr Vicechamberlaine discorsed, and in the end gave flattly his oppinion that the rote of thes evells must of nesesitie be taken awaie yf her Majesty shold be in saftie, wherof he praied the Howse to have considerasion, thinkinge it allso expedient that all of them showld depely consider of the premises in ther consienses before tomorowe, when this so waightie a cause might againe be handled.'

Sir Raph Sadler:
  'You have herde by theis honorable and grave gentlemen the manor and circumstances of the late most rare and abhominable conspiracy declared, the rote and grownde of all which is the Queen of Scottes, as apereth most evedently, who livinge ther is no saftye for our most gratious soveraign, into whose hart God for his mercy put a willingnes (yea, even to the performance) to take awaye this most wicked and filthie woman by justis, who from the

5. *Sic.*
6. i.e. Tichborne (see *The Bardon Papers . . .*, p.87 and nn.1, 4 for his confessions).
7. These three men served as deputy lieutenants under the earl of Shrewsbury (*CSPD 1581–90*, p.440).

8. *Sic.*
9. *Sic.*
10. The words 'by no meanes' have been partly deleted.

v.   begininge / hath thirsted for this crowne, is a murderer of her husband (for I have sene by her owne letter and hand to the Erle Bodw[ell], with whom she wrowght his death, to that end), and is a most detestable traitor to our soveraigne and enemye to us all. Yf the Quene's Majesty do not justice upon hir, assuredly it wilbe thowght and saide that eyther her Majesty liveth in seccurety,[11] regardinge the welth nothinge[12] and quiet of this realme and subiectes, or elce plainely that she is afraide to do it', etc. He agravated all the former sircumstances, and concluded as Sir Walter Mildmey did, havinge made a longe and great discourse of the circumstances of this substance.

Mr Secretary Woolley:

He devided the maters before rehersed into fowre speciall pointes to be noted, sett down and considered of by the whole Howse, viz. crimes obiected, testimonye of the crimes, the censures of the Lordes beinge commisioners hereupon, and the consideration whatt to do towchinge the same. Thes and the summe of the speches delivered this day he desired might be drawne into a bill, considered of, preferred to the Lordes and her Majesty, to the end it might be orderly dealt in according to the opinion of thes honorable personages which had spoken. Which was assented unto.

---

11. The MS is not wholly clear: it could read 'loveth insecurety'.

12. *Sic*, i.e. ? 'nothinge the welthe'.

2. Notes for Sir Christopher Hatton's speech, 3 November 1586

Text from BL Egerton 2124, original, partly in Hatton's hand. *Printed. The Bardon Papers: Documents Relating to the Imprisonment and Trial of Mary Queen of Scots*, ed. C. Read (Cam. Soc, 3rd ser., xvii (1909), 90–3.

Egerton 2124, f.42v.

To acquainte the parlament with the brief summe of cawses. For a rarer cawse then ever heretofore, *etc.*

<u>so detestable crimes</u>[1]

God forbid that your ruine, and change of kinge's lief, sholde have ben before the chief argument of your assemblies.

Her misfortune and undeserved calamitie is suche, who never ment more harme to subiects' lief then to her owne.

Wonderfull and myraculus stay of the <u>holye hand</u>.[2]

That to her untollerable grief she hath seene stayned the noble English nacion with a fowle blotte of *etc.*, which is stayed by God's providence.

She chargeth yow to acknowledge his admirable benefites, from whose goodnes and no deserte, all this comethe.

She voweth to God that the daunger of her owne breath never did equall that mone.

She hath thowghte meete to use you as a counsell (for so yow be) to be made acquainted with suche things as may tuche neerely both her and your selves. And therefore *etc.*

Intollerable ambicion	The title and armes of England.
	Refusing to revoke *etc.*
	Several practises for advancement
	Privie to the bull.

Si ius violandum est, regnandi gratia violandum.[3]
Pro regno licet esse sceleratum.
Per fas et nefas ambit, quae cupit ambitio.

---

1. Words underlined here are Hatton's insertions.
2. Words underlined here are Hatton's insertions.
3. Cicero, *De Officiis*, III, 82; C. Read considered these Latin quotations to be scriptural. This cannot be wholly correct: they are drawn from a broader and sometimes elusive range of sources (*The Bardon Papers . . .*, p.90, n.1).

| Extreme malice | { | Content to betray her sonne.
Yeld her selfe and title to *etc.*
Affecteth this Pope for *etc.*
Wishethe to dye rather *etc.* |

Scelera non habent consilium.
Furori nec ratio, nec modus inest.

| Cruell and blodie dysposicion | { | Foraine invasion.
Civill rebellion.
Destruccion of her Majestie. |

Viri sanguinum non dimidiabunt dies suas.[4]
Magnis sceleribus iura naturae intereunt.

| Ungodlie sleights and subtelties | { | Her manifold practises in pretending one thing and intending an other. |

Non est prudentia, nec consilium adver[sus] Dominum.[5]
Sedet in insidiis, ut interficiat innocentem.[6]
Qui fodit foveam, incidet in eam.[7]

| Persistance from her yowthe | { | By consideracion of the whole course of her lief, and actions. |

Cuius initium sine providentia, eius finis cum poenitentia.
Errare humanum, in errore perseverare diabolicum.[8]

[from this point on the notes are in Hatton's hand]
1. Intention of the Chatho[lics].[9]
2. Larger advertisment.
3. Promise of lettres, Mendo[za], *etc, scilicet.*
4. The trustey messinger.
5. Escape cleryd.
6. The Catho[lics] not stir.
7. Scot[land] a partie: not stirr.
                    Pretend on thinge and intend an other[10]
      Reformacion of religion
1. But alteracion of the crown.
2. The boke of Remes.[11]
3. A treaty.
4. Signinge the assotiacion.[12]
5. Chatho[lics] agaynst the purytans.
6. Helpe of France.
7. Good shew to hir son.
8. Lord Hamleton[13] succession.
9. Hir Majestie's saftie.
10. Trust in Naw.
11. Stirr in Irland.

The first practize sortynge with this last accion
was handelyd by

Throckmorton ⎫
Englefeyld ⎪
Doctor Allen ⎪
Hir selffe too him ⎬ 6 persons
Doctor Lews ⎪
Charles Pagett ⎪
Mendoza ⎭

After hir intelligence with Babington
she did wright too

Charles Pagett
Mendoza
Englefeyld
Lord Pagett
Bishop of Glasco.

4. *Sic.* Ps 55: 23.
5. Pr 21: 30.
6. Cf. Ps 10: 8.
7. Eccl 10: 8.
8. Cf. Cicero, *Philippica*, XII, 2, 5.
9. This section (points 1–7) is based closely on an earlier section of the Egerton MS setting out the case against Mary (Cam. Soc, 3rd ser., xvii.88–9).
10. This section (points 1–11) is based closely on an earlier section of the Egerton MS setting out the case against Mary (Cam. Soc, 3rd ser., xvii.74–7).
11. Composed by Grately and Gifford at the English college at Rheims as an attack on the Jesuits.
12. i.e. the Bond of Association, according to f.46.
13. Lord Claud Hamilton.

3. Sir Walter Mildmay's speech against Mary Queen of Scots, 3 November 1586

Text from BL Sloane 326, copy.
Other MSS. London: BL Harley 6265; Lambeth Palace 250.
Oxford: Bodley, Rawlinson C 838.

Sloane 326, fos.95–104

Tertio Novembris 1586.   In the Comon Howse.

In this horrible conspiracy to take away the life of our most gracious Queen,

theis thinges are to be considered:
- first, against whom;
- next, by whom;
- thirdly, to what end

the same was intended.

[1.] Against whome

And first it was intended[1] against our most gracious Quene Elizabeth.

A quene annoynted.

The daughter of that most noble and famous king Henry the viij[th]. Against the lawfull and rightfull[2] inheritoure of this crowne. /

v.

That entred peaceably into her kingdome and was receyved with greate ioy and acclamacion of all her people.

To whom the nobility and clergy of the realme sware their homage and obedience.

Spayne

That hath del[i]vered us from the yoke of Rome, under which we were intollerably pressed; and from the tiranny of a prowd and cruell nation that was like to be master[3] over us.

That upon her first entry delivered the realme out of warr, wherein she found [it],[4] and shortly after, from a greate and weighty debt, wherewith yt had byn long charged.

That hath kept the realme almost xxviij yeres full in peace, notwithstanding malicious practices abrode and dangerous rebellions a[5] home, both here and in

f.96

Ireland, which shee hath / suppressed to her greate honour and our greate saufety.

What a singuler blessing of God peace is, and how happy a thing yt is to lyve in quietnes and to enioy freely our landes, lyves and libertyes is so apparant, as it need not to be amplifyed.

And if any man could not conceave this so greate a blessing except he felt the lack of it, lett him cast his eyes over the seas into our neighbours' countreys, and there behold the miseryes and calamityes which thos people are brought into by civill warrs stirred upp by thoes that seeke to bring the like trowbles here.

Moreover, against a most Christian princes, that hath restored and maynteyned the true religion of the Gospell amongst us, maugre the Pope and all his confederates: besides her indifferent administracion / of justice to her subiectes without respect of persons, which all men must confesse, yea her enemyes if they will say truely.

A noble quene, renowned through the world, and knowne to be religious, vertuous, faithfull, unspotted in word or deed, just in all her accions, mercifull, temperate, bountifull, beloved of her subiectes, good to all, hurtfull to none.

This is that royall and excellent person, against whom this most treasonable conspiracy hath byn devised.

Touching the second poynt, though there have byn many malicious enemyes and trayterous subiectes that have entred into this conspiracy, whereof some of late have iustly suffered, according to their desertes: yett the principall conspirator and the very roote, from whom all th'other / lewde weedes do spring, is that lady whom we do commonly call the Quene of Scottes.

A princesse sometymes placed in the seate of a kingdome; and now almost xx^tie yeres past deprived and deposed from her state, for horrible and odious crymes, wherewith she was charged, and specially for the murther of the Lord Darneley her late husband, and for her mariage afterwardes with the Earle Bothwell, the principall actor in exequcion of that hainous, and unnaturall murder.

This lady being for the same ymprisoned in Scotland, escaped out of prison, and thereupon adventured a battaile with her subiectes, and after the losse thereof, was driven to flye into England for safegard of her life. Here she was receyved and defended from such as did pursue her.

And here she hath byn ever sithence honorably enterteyned at the Queen's Majestie's charges with all curtesey / and humanity, notwithstanding that it was certeynely knowne to her Majestie that this lady imediately upon the death of Quene Mary claymed the crowne of this realme, seeking to dispossesse our rightfull quene, and never yeilding when shee was at liberty, to renownce that untrew clayme, butt upon condic[i]ons not fitt to be agreed unto.

Sithence her being here she hath conspired against her Majestie without intermission of her practices, the most notable whereof are the rebellion in the north, raised by the Earles of Northumberland and Westmerland; the next the mariage intended betweene her and the Duke of Norffolk, meant[8] to have byn

v.

2. By whom[6]

f.97

See an act of parliament made in Scotland, *anno Domini* 1567 capit. 79.[7]

v.

---

1. Harl.: 'attempted'.
2. Harl. omits 'and rightfull'.
3. Harl. omits.
4. From Harl. (+ Lambeth).
5. i.e. 'at'.

6. Lambeth omits this marginal note.
7. *Recte* 19: see *Acts of the Parliaments of Scotland* (12 vols, 1844 etc.), iii.27–8; Harl. omits this marginal note (+ Rawl).
8. Harl.: 'meaning'.

strengthened with an invasion by forreyne forces, to the overthrow of our Quene and this state; and lastly this most cruell and[9] heynous conspiracy, to take away the life of / our sovereigne Quene, that should have byn exequted by Babington and others, all encouraged and directed by her how to proceed, as hath byn most apparantly proved before such lordes and others as were appoynted by her Majestie's commission to heare and examyne the same, and thereupon to give sentence and judgment which they have done accordingly.

And though she were heard at large, both patiently and favorably, to say for herself any thing shee could, in answere, of the matters alledged against her, yett the force of[10] the proofes, and the force of the trueth was such as she could by no meanes avoyd them except her single negation without any other ground, should have byn taken, against the direct confessions of Ballard the preist, and Babington, the principall dealers for her in this cause, and the voluntary confessions and depositions of / James Maw,[11] a Frenchman, one of her secretaryes, and Gilbert Curle, a Scotch man, an other of her secretaryes, both most inward and privy[12] with her in[13] all her secrete affayres, who have testifyed by their hande wrytinges shewed to her, and against which shee tooke none exceptions, neyther against the persons; and which they likewise affirmed before the lordes and other the commissioners, that Babington's lettre to this lady, which conteyned the platt for this horrible treason, came to her owne handes, and the answere made by her, declaring her privity and assent, and her owne devise besides how the same should be done, was made and wrytten by them, by her expresse commandement and direccion, and this they affirme to confesse for declaracion of the trueth without imprisonment, never offered torture, never putt in feare, never promysed reward or ympunity.[14] /

And whether it be reasonable to beleive her bare denyall in her owne case being *pars delinquens* against thoes direct and manifest proofes, lett all men that are indifferent judge.

But such is the nature of ambition and desire of a kingdome, which knowes no kindred, as her eyes were blynded and shee not able to see the danger that shee was like to fall into, whereof also she was admonished by Curle as he saith.

Neither could shee remember the greate benefittes and favours which our gracious Quene hath many wayes and many tymes shewed unto her amongst the which theis may be noted: th'expelling of the French out of Scotland, by the jorney to Lythe,[16] whereby after the death of Frauncis the French king her first husband, she entred peaceably into her state and kingdome, which otherwise had byn brought under the servitude of / Fraunce and she never like to returne into her countrey, the French having so greate a footing there, and the lordes and people of that countrey so unable to resist them, had not our Quene at their humble sute releived them, and saved their kingdome for her.

Next the putting out of the fyre of the civill warrs in Scotland by the jorney to Edenburgh Castle, whereby the young king her sonne hath byn ever sithence preserved in his estate.

The restitucion also of Lythe[17] to her, and of Hume and Edenburgh castles

f.98

v.

f.99
*Nulla fides
regni nec sancta
societes*[15]

v.

to her sonne, our Quene not reteyning any thing in Scotland. And all this at her Majestie's greate charges, with losse of many of her subiectes both by sea and land.

One singuler favour amongst the rest is meete to be remembred, which is: / that after the Scottish Queen's flight out of her owne countrey, and her arryvall here in England, there came hither from thence a greate ambassage to follow the cause against her, and thoes were of the principall noble men and councellors of that realme, as the Earle of Murhay, then Regent of Scotland, the Earle Morton,[18] the Bishopp of Orkney, the Lord Lindsey,[19] Mr James Mackgill, Master of the Rolls, or as they terme him, Clerke of the Registre, and Sir William Matland called Lord of Lidington, the Cheif Secretary of that realme. Theis according to the commission which they had from all the states of that lande, made peticion to the Queen's Majestie to have justice against this lady, and that either she might be tryed here in England, or that she might be returned to receyve her tryall in Scotland, for the horrible murder of her husband, / which they offered to prove her guilty of by her owne hand wrytinges, and other evident testimonyes, which thing if it had bin granted to them then this woman in all apparance had not byn here now to trowble this kingdome. But our most gracious Queen taking compassion over her, and being of a most milde and mercifull nature, tooke such order betweene thoes lordes and her, as they returned home, and her life and honour were saved, a benefitt never to be forgotten on her part.

Neyther ought shee to forgett another very greate favour and grace shewed to her by the Quene's Majestie, that when after the rebellion in the north, wherewith she was deepely and manifestly charged, both the howses of Parliament, that is to say the Lordes and Comons, had passed a bill against her, touching thoes her offences: yett our gracious Queen continewing still her accustomed / and naturall clemency, stayed her royall assent from that bill, much to the greif of her good subiectes.

All theis and many other favours and graces her Majestie hath shewed to this lady, thinking thereby to reclayme her from the evill course she held, and to wynn her to love her Majestie unfaynedly[20] for ever, all which notwithstanding it appeareth, that neyther the feare of God, neyther respect to honour, neyther naturall affinity, nor infinite benefittes receyved, could stay her from continuall and malicious practices, and lastly from this most cruell and detestible conspiracy against our most gracious Queen's life and state.

Th'end whereunto theis practices tended, is evident enough:

To advaunce this Scotish lady to the present possession of this crowne, / and

f.100

v.

f.101

3. To what end[21]

v.

9. Harl. omits 'cruel and'.
10. Rawl omits 'the force of'.
11. *Sic*; Claude Nau, Mary's secretary (other MSS: 'Mawe').
12. Harl.: 'secret', and omits subsequent 'secret'.
13. Rawl omits 'her in'.
14. Lambeth omits 'or ympunity'.

15. Harl. omits this marginal note.
16. Harl.: 'Leigh'.
17. Harl.: 'Leighe'.
18. Harl.: 'Morley'.
19. Rawl: 'Lincely'.
20. Harl. omits.
21. Harl. omits this marginal entry.

thereby to overthrowe the Church of God, not only here but in all other countreys where the Gospell is professed.[22]

And so to restore popery and to bring us againe under the bondage of the Pope, upon whom this woman doth cheifely depend, and he being indeed the most capitall and mortall enemy of our Quene and her state. The cause whereof is, for that he feeleth that this realme of all other monarchies in the world doth most shake the dignity of his triple crowne.

And therefore by a most ympudent and blasphemeous bull, he hath not spared to pronounce our most gracious and rightful Queen to be an intruder into her kingdome, and an usurper of this state, saying that she is an excom-

f.102   municate heretique and thereupon absolveth all her subiectes from their / oath and fidelity, and giveth her kingdome for a pray to any that will seeke yt.

To strengthen and performe the same was made that wicked confederacy, which they call the Holy League, sett downe in the late Councell of Trent, and after confirmed by the popish princes, enemyes to our religion.

From hence hath sprung all the former mischeifes intended against this realme, and lastly, this most horrible enterprice against the sacred person of our Quene.

And this hath sett a worke and encouraged all theis lewd traytors being perswaded that it is not only lawfull, but also meritorious, to bring the same to

v.   effect, wherein many traiterous subiectes that are fledd out of the realme / have ymployed themselves most maliciously, as Allen, Parsons, Morgan, Charles Pagett, D.[23] Gifford, and other. Theis be the fruites of popery, and this divinity they learne at Reyhmes and at Rome.[24]

And herein may be seene the lewde doinges of thoes Jesuites, and semenary preistes, that of late yeres have swarmed in this realme, a rable of vagaraunt fryers, and false hipocrytes, who pretend as they say nothing here but the saving of soules, but indeed their errand is to destroy us both in body and soule, and by secrete practicing of this conspiracy to bereave us of our deare sovereigne and so to kill us all at one blowe; of which practices there is none ende, but as the waves of the sea, without stay, doe one rise and overtake another, so the Pope and his lewde ministers be never at rest, but as fast as one enterprice

f.103   faileth, they take / an other in hand without lett of tyme, hoping at the last to prevaile; and thereby also all our English evill subiectes both at home and abrode, hoping to be greately advanced in this realme. And yett if they looke back to Queen Marye's tyme, and see the feare that the greatest papistes were then in, they should have no such cause to promyse themselves great thinges here, specially if they remember what terror came then upon all men, and what danger they were in to lose landes and liberty by the tiranny of the Pope and cruelty of the Spaniard, for they are not assured to speed better then other, but may be assured of that which hath byn aunciently spoken, that ambitious princes do love the treason, but not the traytor. Together with this detestable conspiracy they ioyned an intention to raise rebellion within the realme, and to

v.   bring us into civill warrs / and such as will never ende without all the mischeife and confusion that can be ymagined.

Their meaning being also to invade the realme with forces out of forreyne countreys, to be sent by the King of Spayne, the Duke of Guise, and the Prince of Parma, with all which, this Scottish Queen hath had continuall practice and intelligence; thereby to bring upon all the good subiectes of this land, fyre, and sword, effusion of bloud, burning,[25] sacking, and spoyling of cittyes, and townes, wasting and depopulating of whole provinces and countreys, with all other insolencies and crueltyes, that necessarily follow eyther civill or forreyne warrs.

And finally to make a plaine conquest of this noble realme thereby to turne out all the subiectes / from their landes and goodes, and to distribute the same   f.104 to strangers, and so to establish here a perpetuall tiranny never to bee reformed.

This is the scope, and this is the end, unto which all theis execrable conspiracyes have byn devised and intended.

Seing therefore that the life of our most gracious and dreade[27] sovereigne is   *Conclusio*[26] sought to the destrucion of us all, and seing it is manifest by whom, and to what end the same was devised and entended:[28] it remayneth now to consider what is to be done, in so greate and weighty a case, wherein generally[29] yt is most requisite and[30] necessary that sure provision and care be had that we may be out of the like danger hereafter, what person soever the same do concerne, and that without delay; but particularly in the / manner and[31] order of the   v. proceeding herein, as the ymportance of the matter deserveth, there is necessary further consultacion by such committees as the Howse shall appoynt, which may bee done after the same be further spoken unto by any that are willing to declare their opinions in that which hath byn opened.

---

22. Harl.: 'preached', Lambeth: 'preached and professed'.
23. Presumably 'Dominus' here, and Gilbert rather than his cousin George. However, Harl. has 'Ed', and Lambeth omits 'D. Gifford . . . fruites'.
24. i.e. the colleges there.
25. Harl. omits 'effusion of bloud, burning',

and has a marginal note (in a hand not unlike Burghley's): 'effects of pp[?]'.
26. Harl. omits.
27. Harl.: 'deare' (+ Lambeth).
28. Harl. omits.
29. From Harl. (+ Lambeth).
30. Harl. omits 'requisite and'.
31. Harl. omits 'manner and'.

4. Job Throckmorton's speech against Mary Queen of Scots, 4 November 1586

Text from New York, Pierpont Morgan Library MA. 276, copy.

The Pierpont Morgan Library MA 276,
(Phillipps MS 13891) pp.3–9

Againste the Scottishe Queene, that shee ought not to live: that mercy in that case is both dreadeful and dawngerous.

'I thanke God with all my harte for thease good beginninges. No question but the cause is a very worthy cawse, and my hope is (though greate bee the corruption of our time and thoughe Sathan doe wounderously bestirre himselfe in this last age) yet that this Howse will not afoarde us a face to speake againste yt.

'Yet rather let Roome and Rhemes with that vyperous broode of our conspiringe Jesuites; let Fraunce and Spayne and those kingdomes that are allreaddy druncke with the lyes of that antichristian beast: let thease hardely with theyr confederates (for yt suteth best with their profession) have the prayse and pryviledge of this woorke.

'Why, hath not I pray you the very syncke of the stewes founde out her patrones amonge thease? A Harding, a Stapleton, a Parsons, and I knowe not who to defend yt?

'Nay, hath not the murder of her Majestie (whom the Lorde still preserve in despight of Sathan) founde out an Allen, a Campion, a Bristow, a Saunders, a Gyfforde, and I knowe not who?[1] Ye have heard the Devill himselfe, I trowe, or rather (yf ye will) the Devill herselfe to authorize yt.

'Was there ever, thinke you, a more pestilent or horrible slaughtor then that of the Admirall[2] of Fraunce, such a tragedy as I thinke former ages have not felte and I hope succeeding ages shall nevere see, a tragedye that / ffor treacherye and bloudde can not well be matched by any of those hellishe stratagemes of the Turke himselfe; and yet had it his patrons, and hath still I warrant you.

'For such is the good nature, yea, such is the kinde humour of our Romish crewe, that were the case ten tymes more desperate then yt is, yea, were the facte in that height and degree of iniquitye as the horror thereof might goe neere to darken the sonne, yet should yt not wante by theyr good willes an orator to smooth yt, an advocate to pleade for it, nor a champion to avowe yt in any courte whatsoever.

'And in deede I remember that not longe after that bluddy day at Paris there came out a booke forsoothe in Latine – in excuse? nay more, by your leave, then in excuse – in flatte commendation and allowance of that brutishe inhumanitye, puffing up with immeasurable commendations that bluddy and mercilesse kinge (who yet I beleeve had his fill of bloude before he dyed), tearming him with a feared forheade, "*mitissimum, clementissimum, pietatissimum, venerandae pietatis*", and I knowe not what, thinkinge belyke by his brazen pen to stay the bloude of Abel, that yt should not cry to the Lorde for vengeance from the earth.

'Neyther, to say the truth, ought this in any sorte to seeme strange unto us, that out of such fountaines of iniquitye should aryze (even by the just judgmente of God) a kinde of frothe of unshamefastnesse to the view of the worlde.

'Well, yf a salable tongue in a desperate cause bee one of the prides and ornamentes of there profession, let them hardly have the honor of yt: let not us goe on with them nor ons / come neere them in this vayne of   p.5 unshamefastnesse.

'In a kingdome of the gospell (where both prince and people thorough the mercye of God have longe felte the sweetenesse of a holy and religious peace) let yt never be sayed for shame that there was founde a man that durst ons stayne his mouth in defense of her whome I proteste unto yow I knowe not how to describe.

'Yf I should tearme her the daughter of sedition, the mother of rebellion, the nurce of impietie, the handmaide of iniquitie, the sister of unshamefastenesse; or yf I should tell you that which you know allreaddye, that she is Scottishe of nation, French of education, papist of profession, a Guysian of bloude, a Spaniarde in practize, a lybertyne in life: as all this were not to flatter her, so yet this were nothinge neere to dyscrybe her.

'Ye have seene her anatomy allreadye, ye have hearde her whole life and practises reasonablye layed fourthe unto you by an honourable personage, to whose worthye speache yet this one thinge may bee added, that were his guyftes and sufficiencye redoubled (as no question but the Lorde hath blessed him in great measure that way) yet would her wickednenesse[3] (say or doe what he can for his life) still surmounte his discription. In whose verie ymage one may lively see featured that which is written of olde: *serpens oculata, ambitiosa mulier, fedifraga horribili vigilantia, celeritate in conficiendis malificiis, etc.* Such a

1. Among these leading figures Richard Bristow had been prominent at Rheims, and Thomas Stapleton supported the notion that the Pope could urge Catholic subjects to rebel against non-Catholic princes. Nicholas Sander(s)' publications earned him a bad reputation among Protestants, but he had also been involved in the Fitzgerald mission to Ireland. Throckmorton may be referring to George Gifford, rather than his cousin Gilbert.

2. Coligny.

3. *Sic.*

creature whome no Christian eye can behoulde with patience, whose villanie hath stained the earth and infected the ayre, the breathe of whose malyce towarde the Church of God and the Lorde's annoynted, our dreade Soveraigne, hath in a lothsome kynde of savour fumed up to the heavenes.

'To finde a man, I say, amongst us, so farre spente in so abiecte a cause, what were yt? A grief to the godly, a wounde to our profession, a stayne and reproche to the whole lande? /

p.6   'Therefore my trust is, as I sayed in the begyninge, that the whole House will willingly without any farther questioninge or replye, yeald theire free assentes and allowance unto the cause and that *cum applausu*, even with joyninge of handes and joye of harte in respecte of her Majestie's safetye and of the good of Gode's Church, as one of the worthyest causes that ever this honorable assemblye dealte in, one of the happiest blowes that ever her Majestie gave, one of the greatest blessinges that ever fell to the lande, one of the fayrest ryddances that ever the Church of God hadde.

'O but mercye, you will say, is a commendable thinge and well beseemeing the seate of a prince. Very trew in deed: but how long? Tyll yt bringe justyce in contempte and the state of the Church and commen wealth in danger; and then I hope yt be time to take out a new lessonne.

'Sure, yf clemencie bee vertue in deede, her Majestye must have double iniurye. Yf shee have not her share in it above all the prynces and potentates of the earthe; nay, what will you say? Yf this wretched woman herself (heere now layed before us as a spectackle) have beyonde all expectation tasted of the sweetenesse of this lenitye even to the preservinge of her lyfe, then I am sure you will confesse that this her monsterous and unkinde requitall deserveth to be nayled on the postes and corners of our streetes as a hatefull recorde to all posteritie.

'*Anno 14°* of her Majestie (yf I bee not deceived) there was a notable bill passed against her from both the Howses sufficient in truth to have hampered her, yf her Majestie had gyven lyfe to yt by her allowance. And I am veryly perswaded that that one statute (yf it had been afoote) had freed us from a number of those miseries that have befallen us sens; but yt was not Godd's will. /

p.7   'For when yt came to the upshotte that her Majestie should ratifie the whole by her royall assent, then a man might easely see where mercy and lenitye hadde taken up theire seate. It was so contrarye to her nature to sheade bloude that (notwithstandinge the thinge were porposely devysed for her owne safety) shee woulde none of yt, and soe yt was dasshed (as yee knowe) to the greate greefe and hartesore of her best-affected subiectes.

'But what came of it? The dasshinge of yt you see had lyke senes to have dashed us all out of countenance, had not the God of Israell from heaven put in foote for us. And what gotte her Majestie, I pray you, by this her lenitye? Even as much as commenly one shall gett by saveing a thiefe from the gallowes: a heape of treasons and conspyracies huddleinge one in the necke of the other, sufficient to affright bothe prince and people.

'The good Regente of Scotlande, that worthy Earle of Murrey, felt himselfe the smarte of this lenitye by savinge from death that wretched Hamleton that was afterwarde the instrument of his bane.[4] And yf her Majestie have escaped the like dawnger no gramercye to the arme of fleashe: shee may trewly say, and we all with hartes and handes lyfted up to heaven may trewly saye, that her deliverer sleepeth not.

'Well, sythens there is a new agew now raigning amongst us, wee must needes seeke a new remedye. The oulde receipte will not serve; the disease is so festered and ranckled within that yf you applye nothinge unto yt but a lenytive the patient dieth for ytt.

'It is now highe time fore her Majestie I trow to bee ware of lenitives and to fall to coresyves an other while, and to launce an ynche deeper then ever shee did, yf shee meane to sitte quietly in her seate. /

'To which effecte Craterus'[5] counsell to Alexander the Greate ought not in   p.8
wisdome to be forgotten: "*sunt quaedam beneficia quae odimus*", certaine benefittes hatefull; namely, to be endebted to one asmuch as thy lyfe cometh to, this is a hatefull benefitte and a thinge that the ambitious heade is impatient of to the death.

'Therefore yf her Majestie of her wounted clemency should now bee drawen to pull backe her swoorde of justyce and to give this wretched woman her life, it were sure a verie dreadfull and perillous presidente; and what a sea of mischeifes her aspyringe minde might afterwarde undertake to cancell soe greate a recognysaunce my harte rueth to thinke, and I leave yt to your wisdomes to coniecture.

'For ambition (you knowe) ys like a quicke eele in a man's bowells that never giveth rest, and no julippe can queanch the thirst of a kingdome, but only bloudde.

'There is now then none other way of safetye left to her Majestie but only to let her bloudde *in cephalica* that would soe fayne have filled our lande with riveres of bloudde, to the lamentable outcryes of all posteritie, that yt may bee trewly sayed of her as Tomyris sayed of Cyrus: "*satio te sanguine quem sitiisti*".[6]

'Now if any should make scruple at the lawfullnesse of yt, why, shee is a murderer and a shamefulle murderer; nay, shee is a murderer of princes, the Lorde's annoynted. I would that were all to, for there bee princes (ye knowe) that doe but pester the earth, and though yt bee not lawfull to lay handes on them, yet the Church of God might verie well spare them; but she hath attempted the death and destruction of that prince of whom (because flatterie is an odious thinge, and farre unbeseeminge the wisedome and maiestie of this Howse) I will say nothinge – let the afflycted of forraine nations speake.

'Well, yt may bee yt will be yelded unto, the case beinge so manifest that shee ought in deed to dye the death. But who muste bee the judges, con-

4. In 1570.
5. Alexander's general.

6. For Tomyris and Cyrus see Herodotus, i.205–14.

demners and executioners of her? That is the poynte: wheare shall a man have an assemblye or parlement of princes to do the feate? /

p.9   'No, no, wee neede never sayle so farre nor reach so highe: thankes bee to God theire is redresse ynough at home. Why, I pray you let me aske you one question. May not one wryte uppon the doores of this Howse *Quid von?*[7] So the thinge bee warrantable by the law of God, I hope we may. Under the warrante of Gode's law, what may not this House doe? I meane the three estates of the lande. To deny the power of this Howse ye knowe is treason: therefore to say that this Howse is not able to cutte of tene such serpentes' heades as this is, not able to reforme religion and establishe succession, yt is treason; for why? To deny the power of this Howse is treason.

'No, I dare not say but that this House can doe all thease, and ought to doe all thease. And when the Lorde will (and our synnes leave provokinge his wrath) yt will sure doe all thease.

'Sythens then the thinge is lawfull to be don, and this House hath absolute power to doe yt, her Majestie may be well assured that infinite frightes and feares will possese the hartes of her best affected subiectes tyll yt bee don in deede: *wisdome crieth on celeritye, for dawnger is bredde by delaye.*

'The yssue then of the whole is that we be all ioynte suteres to her Majestie that Jezabel may lyve no longer to persecute the prophetes of God, nor to attempt still in this maner the vyneyarde of Naboth by bloudde; that so the land may be purged, the wrath of God pacified, and her Majestie's dayes prolongued in peace to the comforte of us and our posteritye, which the Lorde graunte for his Christe's sake.'

7. *Sic.*

5. Speech against Mary Queen of Scots, in committee(?) 4 November 1586

Text from Hertfordshire County Record Office 10548, ? original fair copy.

County Record Office, Herts, 10548, fos. 1–3

'Wheras it is obiected that if the Scottishe ladie were according to hir due desertes cut of, that yet that mayne matter that we ought most to looke unto, to witt, hir Majestie's safetie and preservation, were not provided for: becaus the first boughe that was cutt from that same unhappie tree may upon the same pretextes attempt the like treacheries, yea and more desperately perhaps pursue the same by howe much in wordlie fetches he is not inferior to the stocke from whence he was taken and in meanes to manage such mischiefes doth farre goe beyond hir, as who not onelie hath with hir common alies in forraine countreyes but the countenaunce of a kingdome and people at commaundement, and is altogether out of the handes of such amongest us as either by their wisedome or power, or both, might prevent such attemptes.

'To speake my mynd frelie, thoughe this be urged with all advantage possible, to terifie weak fleshe and bloud and to effect the sparinge of the moste heynous transgressor of the world, yet it carieth not with it any force to winne that for which it is alledged, namelie, either to delaie, or els quite and cleane to dashe, the execution of one so manie waies tainted and so iustlie condemned. For in this question, as in other important consultations, subsequent calamities (of which we have no better ground than humane coniecture, and than the which also the wind it self is not more waveringe and uncertaine) are not so much to be doubted as moste imminent and deadlie daungers, not feared onelie but in some measure felt also, would be by all meanes possible, and that with speed and expedition, avoided. Wherof, besides the present necessitie demaundinge this duetie, this reason also, verie pregnant and pithie, maie induce the same: becaus that whatsoever care of our heades or toile of our handes shalbe imploied for the preventinge of that which maie fall out (we, or any other lyvinge, not knowinge when, wher or howe) shall not onelie (that not cominge to passe which was feared) be labour lost and vexation of spirite, but we our selves forciblie hindered, by the distracted thoughtes and conceites of our owne hartes, from applyinge of a present plaister to our wound more than deadlie if it be not without delaie holpen.

'Our state in this action (if we yeld not to the execution of moste iust sentences but stand debatinge upon after clappes) maie not unfitlie be resembled, as me thincketh, unto a verie good shippe laden with aboundaunce of riches and infinite treasure, having also in it a mightie master, manlie mariners, wealthie merchauntes and others, who beinge in a sore storme and terrible tempest in the middest of the great ocean and readie to be swallowed up with everie surge of the same, cease to think of the present pinch and payne, and leave to laie their handes to labour for avoydinge the same, by enteringe into some deepe thoughtes and lardge discourses of certaine flyinge flawes that by reason of some odde astronomicall prediction (which whether it will hitt, yea or no, they knowe not) they feare shall assault or fall on them in the narrowe seas, or at the shoare side rather.

'I will not take upon me to prognosticate, for I have no skill in that facultie, neither lieth it in me to foretell, but stirre up my self rather hartilie to beseech the Lord mercifullie to preserve the life and raigne of our[1] / dread soveraigne Elizabeth and graciouslie to graunt peace and trueth in our daies, and the daies of our posterities. Onelie I speake nowe as a man indued with sound affection to my prince and countrey, and so farre as I can discerne by the eies of fleshe and bloud, that if we do not, as moste wise and skilfull phisitions, applie to this daungerous disease not onely a moste stronge but also a moste speedie medicine, in all humane iudgment we maie looke for nothinge els but that it wilbe the bane and playne soare, yea the death and destruction of us all.

'But to come more nighe to the matter and to remove that which seemeth most to hinder the accomplishment of this so blessed a worke. All that we are to looke for from that younge kinge must flowe of necessitie either from him self and his owne forces, or els from his frendes and favorites, for his foes surelie will not further him in that that maie growe to his greatnes and the better inable him to make his match good with them.

'For him self, thoughe we graunt he be sharpe in witt and in childish yeares hath the courage of a man, yet is ther not sufficiencie in him either to direct, or to manage and maynteyne, matters of such moment, which besides depth in iudgment and manlines of harte require manifold experiences and most costlie expenses, he havinge not atteyned the former, thorowe lacke of yeares and observation, and not beinge able to reach the latter for want of wealth, unwiselie brought upon that nation by the meanes of the warres of the French faction ther. Moreover, thoughe he had subteltie in his soule, mischief in his mynd, hatred in his harte, plottes in his head, power in his hand, money in his purse, or whatsoever els we can imagine for the fittinge of him to this foule feate, what reason is ther in us either to suppose or to suspect that he would deale so hardlie with hir as directlie or indirectlie to attempt hir ruine that must be his rysinge (if he have any), and who hath so manie waies for rare benefites bound him and all his issue after him (if they can see it and will confesse it) to all faithfulnes and fastnes for ever? That I maie saie nothinge of that common coard and bond of Christian profession which (as appeareth both by the trueth of God's word and the longe assured peace that thees two landes have enioyed and yet do thorowe the doctrine of the gospell) is the moste forcible of all other, and will sonest free men from such divelishe devises.

'But let us put the hardest (and yet neither reason will lead us or charitie will lett us so do, the premisses considered) that in mischief he ment such a matter as here is obiected, and that the matters alledged were without . . . [unintelligible word], yet shall we see that we have two mightie bulwarkes or butteresses, the weakest wherof can hardly be approched, much lesse battered, with such feble assaultes. For what? Shall disloiall practisers, either home-bread people or forraine foes, as Scottes, French, *etc.*, have more witt to devise and strength to performe mischief then faythfull frendes and duetifull subiectes shall have wisedome to foresee, power to prevent and waies more to defeate and brake back, yea to overthrowe, all their idle imaginations and lewd attemptes? Or thoughe that should faile us (which yet I hope shall never fall out), shall man in his malice agaynst the good be able to match with the Lord in his might and love towardes his sayntes? Or should we that have had so manifest and manifold proofes of God's great goodnes and infinite power, in the gracious preservation of hir Majestie, distrust that he will do the like still for hir and us? As thoughe God had bin pleased to bestowe that kindnes upon us to the end that we should yeld him for it so synnefull a service? Or as thoughe it had bin his will to free us from the stinge of a serpent that hath bin / revived by the   f.2 heate of our fire and lieth nowe lurking at home in the bowells and bosome of our land, to the end that we should dread the hissinge of a frosen snake in the north?

'Touchinge his frendes and favorites, as we need not much to feare them becaus they are accordinge to his owne constitution and state, who, sith he, the first mover of so weightie a matter, is weake and insufficient, must also of necessitie be feeble and infirme: so he him self hath lesse cause to flie unto them or to fawne upon them, becaus they be but as bruised reedes or broken staves, then readie most fowlie to faile him when he is prest moste to relie upon them. Which yet that it might more playnelie appeare, let us examine them in the particulors and as you would saie, one by one, that so the evidence of this trueth may more clearelie breake forth.

'If he should make account by papistes to uphold this practise and purpose, he is greatlie deceived, as whos devotion, thoughe it have bin much to his mischievous mother becaus of that little hope they had by hir to establishe the Romishe religion, yet will they not, either under pretext of title or otherwaies, stand soundlie affected to him, whos education they mislike and whos present profession they persecute even unto death; who also will never be perswaded to thincke that he myndeth to use them further, or to any other end, than by them, as by a steppinge stone, to leape over the water of his present troubles and to enter into the possession off a moste florishinge kingdome, which once atteyned, they shall find his faith so fowlie dissembled.

'And as for thos of the reformed religion, havinge him in ielousie for his

---

1. MS repeats 'of our'.

former slippes, and bearinge a watchfull eie and holding a hard hand over him that he plaie not the like prancke, ther is lesse likeliehood that they should be used as actors or authors in this tragedie. For besides that which hath bin before insinuated touchinge them, we have them lincked faste unto us by a double chaine, as first by thos speciall favours that they have found here and els wher at our handes when they were not able any manner of waie to helpe them selves, and secondlie by that holie and precious faith which both they and we playnelie professe: neither of which they can violate without a fault that never shalbe forgotten before God or man, if they be either his head to devise, or his hand to performe, so mischievous a plott of disloialtie and treason.

'If he would hope of helpe from his people at home for the performaunce of this practise, we aunsweare that that is a verie weake staffe to leane upon, not onelie becaus the multitude it self is naturally moveable and most commonlie inconstant (as manifold examples in that nation above the rest do playnelie prove), but also becaus that beinge divided by diversitie of opinions in religion he can not looke to have them fast to him self when they are not lincked one of them to an other, but disioyned rather by that which maketh the greatest rent off bodie and mynd that possiblie can be. Secoundlie we saie that thoughe they were as fast glued together in sound affection one of them to an other as ever were people, and all of them readie to serve their soveraigne in all thinges enioyned, yet could they not effect so notorious a transgression, as well becaus they them selves are weake and want wealth (two sore stoppes greatlie dauntinge the dispatch of such deseignes) as also becaus ther is an infinite number of true harted and faithfull Englishe subiectes of all sortes, both noble and unnoble, that would thorowe God's goodnes stand as a wall of brasse in that respect betweene their sinne and hir Majestie's person and state.

'If he expect and sue for favour from Spaine or would fayne have favour from Fraunce, and specially from the Guisian faction, his allies and kinsmen, he maie looke till his hearte ake, as we saie, and his eyes starte out of his head, and yet be frustrate of all aid to. For, for the Spaniard, he hath his handes full and f.2v   more than he / can well turne him unto, as everie man may playnelie perceave that hath but a . . . [unintelligible] of sound iudgment. And if we would but weighe the longe and chargeable warres of the Lowe Countreyes, the late revoltinge of the West Indians, as also the feare that he hath of the fallinge awaie of Naples, Sicile, Portugale and other places (which he and his auncestors have atchieved by most uniust and cruell conquest, and by tyrannie hold in bondage more hard than that of Egypte), we shall easilie yeld to this trueth. Besides ther is little or no likelyhood at all of this, that howsoever he would further him in the catholicke cause (as they call it) by men yf he had them, or money and munition if he could spare them, that yet he would aid him in the atteyninge of a most wealthie countrey and kingdome, as well becaus the Spaniard in a hautie harte that he hath would have none growe great but him self as also becaus he him self fayneth to be a competitor here, this beinge naturall to all men in all estates and degrees, even in meane matters to preserve them selves, and much more in the compassinge of crownes and atteyninge of scepters.

'As for Fraunce, it self in the state it nowe standeth can not either presentlie or for tyme to come aford him any helpe at all, as which for all furniture fitt for such a feate, both of men, money and munition, lieth utterlie wast by meanes of the former civill warres, and by reason of the present hurlie burlies about religion and succession is readie to yeld up the spirite. And if the state of that kingdome, that hath heretofore caried the countenaunce of the greatest glorie in Christendome, can not further him, though perhaps it would favour him, what shall any particulare member of that languishing bodie be able to accomplish for his cause in this behalf? For if in a bodie beadreaden[2] as we saie, and see by experience, neither the whole can helpe any part, nor any part performe office and duetie to the whole, much lesse yeld service to others without, then what hope can be had of relief from that realme, in whom, if ever in any people, that sayinge of the prophet[3] is found most true, the whole head is sicke, the whole harte is heavie, from the sole of the foote to the toppe of the head ther is nothinge whole therin, but woundes and swellinges and soares full of corruption; they have not bin wrapped, nor bound up, nor mollified with oyle: their land is wast, their cities are burnt with fire, strangers devoure their land in their presence, and it is like the overthrowe of strangers.

'Of all wordlie[4] helpes (for heavenlie he must looke for none in so mischievous a matter) ther remayneth nowe none but the Guise, who of all others, thoughe he make greatest bragges, is the least able to annoy us or to aid him; as who in his boastes is much like to an old lion, who thoughe he roare and yell much, is yet notwithstandinge nothinge at all terrible, whos clawes are coped, whos fanges are broken, and whos . . . [unintelligible] bones are burst in sunder; who also for his owne offences and the synnes of his forefathers (wherunto he is a more iust inheritor than to all the liveliehood that ever they lefte him) is odious to God and man, and for his crueltie hated at home, and for his crafte and pestilent practises abhorred abroad, yea no where, no not amongest his owne favorites well thought of, but esteemed rather as a furie of hell or a firebrand of stuffe[?], not onelie to kindle a flame in that distressed French nation but to cast the coales of contention, as the Pope's boutefeu,[5] into all the partes of the world; whos malice thoughe it be much for the managinge of such matters, yet is his abilitie verie meane, or none at all, to further such develishe devises, as who thorow an infinite number of mos[t] heynous and horrible transgressions hath so wasted his wordlie[6] wealth and desperatelie consumed a great deale of the demaynes of the crowne of that cruell kingdome wherin he liveth and eateth the aire[?], and is so deeplie indebted / to princes   f.3 and potentates abroad that he is neither able to maynteyne his causes conceaved in Fraunce, and amongest the rest his pretended title, nor to recover such

2. i.e. bedridden.
3. Isa 1: 5–7.
4. *Sic.*

5. i.e. firebrand.
6. *Sic.*

territories as he supposeth (and it maie be in trueth) the Spaniard with-holdeth from him, nor longe to uphold his private porte and state that he beareth, all which and everie one of them, sith they touch him more nighe in honour and credit than this crased cause, he would more he[ar]telie pursue than presentlie he doth, both at home and abroad, if he could tell howe.

'To conclude in a word out of the premisses. Sith now the younge prince is left post alone, as we saie, and sith of him self we hope that he is not willing, and that as in respect of his power we knowe he is not able, to performe the mischief rather imagined on our parte than ment from him and his, either we must confesse our selves to be afraid of our owne conceites, as it were skarrecrowes and imagined bugges, or els the fantasie of feare fallinge to the ground, we must go roundlie forward to the removeinge of hir that by hir life can not but worke us all much wo.'

6. Reasons against Mary Queen of Scots delivered to Elizabeth, 12 November 1586

Text from BL Cotton Titus F.i, original draft in the hand of John Puckering, Speaker.
Other MS. Stowe 358 (copy of Cotton).
Printed. D'Ewes 400–2 (from Cotton).

Cotton Titus F.i, fos.282–6.

[Headed in a later hand 'The somme of the reasons delivered by the Speaker of the Nether Hows at ther first audienc in November 1586. The Speaker was Mr Sergeant Puckeringe and this memoriall is all his owne hand'.]

Onles execucyon of the iust sentens be doone,

1586
29 Elizabeth

1. [her][1] your[2] Majestie's person cannot any while be safe
2. The religyon cannot long contynew amonges us
3. The most florishing present estate of this realme must shortlye receive a wofull fall.
4. And consequentlye in sparing her, [the Queen's Majestie's person] your Majesty shall not onlye gyve corage and hardynes to th'enemyes of God, of [her] your Majestie's selfe, and of [her] your kingdome; but shall discomfort and daunt with dispayre, the hartes of [her] your loving people, and deservydlye provoke the heavye hand and wrathe of God, etc.

And that sumarilye for these reasons ensuyng.

Fyrst, touching the danger of your Majesty.

Bothe she and her ffavorers think that she hathe right, not to succede, but to enioye your crowne yn possessyon. And therfore as she ys a most impacyent competytor (acquaynted with bloode) so wyll she not spare anye meanes that may take you from us, being th'onlye let that she enioyeth not her desyer.

She ys hardyned in malyce against your royall person, notwithstanding that you have done her all ffavor mercye and kindnes, aswell in preserving her kingdome, as saving her lyef, and salving her honor. / And therfore ther ys no place for mercy wher ther ys no hope of amendment, [and syns] or that she wyll [not] desyst ffrom most wicked attemptes: the rather for that her malyce

v.

1. Words in square brackets have been deleted in the MS.

2. Words underlined have been inserted by Puckering.

apperyth suche that she makethe as yt were her testament of the same to be executed after her deathe and appoynteth her executors to performe the same.

She affyrmeth yt lawfull to move invasyon. Therfore as of invasyon vyctorye may ensue and of victorye the death of the vanquished, so dothe she not obscurelye [hold] professe yt lawfull to distroye you.

She holdes yt not onlye lawfull but honorable also and merytoryous to take your liffe etc, as being depryved of your crowne by her holye father. And therfore she will (as she hath contynewallye doone) seeke yt by all meanes whatsoever.

She is gredy of your deathe and preferrythe yt before her owne lyef, for in her late dyrectyon to some of her complyces she willed what soever became of her the tragicall execucyon should be perfourmed on you. /

f.283   Ther ys by so much the more danger to your person syns the sentens then was before, by how muche yt behovethe them that wold preserve or advance her to hasten your deathe now (or never) before execucion done upon her, as knowing that you and none els can gyve dyreccyon for her deathe (and that by your deathe the sentens hathe lost the force of execucyon) and otherwise they shold come to late, yf they toke not the present oportunitye to help her.

Her ffrendes hold invasyon unprofytable while you lyve, and therfore in ther opynion your deathe ys fyrst and principallye to be sought as the most compendyous waye to wynne the realme by invasyon.

Some of th'eldest and wisest papistes [think] set yt downe for a speciall good dryft to occupy you with conceyt that the preservacion of her lyef ys the safetye of your owne, and therfore you may be assured that they verilye think that her lyef will be your deathe and distruccion. /

v.   For so muche as concerns the religyon etc.

It is most perillous to spare her that hathe contynuallye breathed the overthrow and suppressyon of the same, being poysoned with poperye from her tender youthe, and at her age joyning in that falslye termed holye league and ever syns and now a professyd enemy of the truthe.

She restyth whollye upon popish hopes to be delyvered and advanced, and ys so devotyd and dotyd in that professyon, that she will (aswell for satisfaccion of others as feeding her owne humor) supplant the gospell wher and whensoever she may: which evill ys so muche the greater, and the more to be avoyded, as that yt slayeth the soule, and will spread yt selfe, not onlye over England and Scotland, but also ynto all partes beyond the seaes wher the gospell of God ys maynteyned, the which can not but be excedingly weakened, yf defectyon shold happen in these ij most valyant kingdomes.

Touching the happye estate of this realme.

The Lydians saye, '*unum Regem agnoscunt Lidi: duos autem tollerare non possunt*'. So we say, '*unicam Reginam Elizabetham agnoscunt Angli: duas autem tollerare non possunt*'. And therfore, syns she / sayethe that she is Queen here and we neyther can nor will acknowledge any other but you to be our Queen, it will folow yf she prevayle she wyll rather make us slaves then take us for children.

f. 284

And therfore the realme sighethe and gronethe under feare of suche a stepmother.

She hathe alredye provyded us a foster father and a nource, the Pope and King of spayne, ynto whose handes yf yt shold mishappen us to fall what can we els looke for: but ruyne, distruccion and utter extirpacion of goodes, landes, lyves, honors and all.

Whilest she shall lyve th'enemyes of [God] th'estate will hope and gape after your deathe; by your deathe they trust to make invasyon profytable for them, which cannot be but the same shold be most lamentable for us. And therfore yt ys meete to cut of the head of that hope.

As she hathe alredye by her poysoned bates brought to distruccion more noble [houses] men and ther houses and greater multitude of subiectes during her being here, then she shold have bene hable to have doone yf she had bene in possessyon of her owne crowne and armyd[3] in the fyeld against us: so will she still be contynuall cause of the like spoile to the great losse and perill of this estate. And therfore this realme neyther can nor maye endure her. /

Her sectaryes[4] do wryte and prynt that we be at our wytes' and worlde's end   v. yf she overlyve your Majestie, meaning therby that th'end of our world ys the begynnyng of theirs. And therfore take her awaye and ther world wilbe at an end before yt begyn.

Syns the sparing of her in the xiiij[th] yere of your raigne,[5] popish traytors and recusantes have multiplyed excedinglye. If you spare her now agayne they will grow bothe inumerable and invyncible also.

Mercye now in this case wold in th'end prove creweltye against us all. *Nam est quedam crudelis misericordia.* And therfore to spare her, ys to spill us.

She is onlye a cosen to you, in a remote degree. But we be sonnes and children of this land, wherof you be not onlye the naturall mother but also, the weddyd spouse. And therfore muche more ys dew from you to us all then to her alone.

It wold excedinglye greve and wound the hartes of your loving subiectes if they shold see so horryble vyce not condignelye punyshed. If any be wavering yt will wyn them to the worse parte, and many wyll seke to make ther owne peace, wherfore aswell for comfort of the one, as staye of the other, and retayning of all, it ys most needfull that justice be doone upon her.

Thousandes of your most loving subiectes of all degrees which have for speciall zeale of your safetye made othe before God to pursew to deathe by all fforcible and possible / meanes, suche as she ys by iust sentens now found to   f.285 be, can not save ther othes yf you kepe her alyve. For then eyther we must take her lyef from her without your dyrectyon, which wilbe to our extreame daunger by th'offens of your lawe, or els we must suffer her to lyve against our expresse othe, which wilbe to the uttermost perill of our owne soule wherwith no act of Parliament or power of man whatsoever can yn any wise dispence.

3. Stowe: 'army'.
4. Stowe: 'secretaries'.

5. i.e. in 1572, by refusing to assent to the bill agreed by the Lords and Commons.

And therfore seing yt restythe whollye in you by a most worthie and iust execucyon of this sentence to kepe us upright and ffree us in bothe, we most humblye and ernestlye beseche you etc. that spedye justice be doone upon her. Wherby, your selfe may be safe, th'estate of your realme preservyd, and we not onlye delyvered from this troble of conscyens, but also recomforted to endevor our selves and all ours into whatsoever other perill for the preservacion and safetye of you.

Lastlye.   Gode's vengeance against Saule for sparing Agag [and][6] against Achab for sparing the life of Benedad[7]: both which were <u>by the iust iudgement of God</u> depryved of ther kingdomes for sparing those wicked princes whom God had delyvered ynto ther handes of purpose to be slayne to deathe by them as by the mynisters of hys eternall and devyne justice.

How muche those magistrates wer comended that put to deathe those mischevous and wicked Quenes Jesabell and Athalia.[8]

How wiselye Salomon proceded to punishement in putting to deathe his owne naturall and elder brother Adonias,[9] for the onlye intencyon of a mariage, which gave suspycion of treason. /

v.   Wherin ys no more desyred of your Majestie then the very
1.2. pope (now your sworne enemye), some of these late conspyrators,
3. and this wicked ladye her selfe have thought fytte to fall on
1. her. He in like case gave sentens, '*vita Conradini mors Charoli: mors Conradini vita Charoli.*'[10]
2. They in ther best myndes and remorse of conscyens setting downe the best meanes of your safetye, sayd, he that hathe no armes can not fight, and he that hathe no legges cannot runne awaye, but he that hathe no head canne do no harme. *Pisces primum a capite foetet.*
3. She by her voluntarye subscribyng to the late Associacion etc, gave this sentens against her selfe. And after in her lettres of these treasons to Babington wrote that if she were dyscovered yt wold gyve sufficyent cause to you to kepe her in perpetuall close prison, by which last woordes she cold meane nothing els but paynes of deathe.

Therfore, we seing on th'one syde how you have to th'offens of mightie princes advanced religion; with what tender care and more the[n] motherlye pietye you have alwayes cherished us the children of this land; with what honor and renowme you have restored th'auncyent rightes of the Crowne; with with[11] what peace and justice you have governed; with what store and plentye you have raygned over us.

On the other syde seing that this enemye of our felicitye seeks to undermyne the religyon etc; to supplant us and plant strangers in the place; to transferre the rightes of the Crowne to that Italyan priest and the Crowne to her selfe or some other from you; and therfore lyethe in continuall awayte to take your life, etc. /

f.286   Therfore we pray [her] <u>you</u> etc, for the cause of God; his Churche; this realme; our selfes; and your selfe. That you will no longer be careles of your lyf our soverayne safetye; nor longer suffer religyon to be threatenyd, the realme to stand in danger, nor us to dwell in feare. But eaven as justice hathe gyven rightfull sentens etc, so you wyll grant execucyon, that as her lief thretnythe your deathe, so h[er][12] deathe may (by Gode's favor) prolong your li[fe.] And that this evill being taken from the ear[th] we may prayse God for your deliverans and pray him for your contynuans and with the psalmist saye, *Dominus fecit judicium*[13], the ungodlye is trapped in the woorkes of her owne handes.

And so pray God to enclyne her hart to our iust desyers etc.

6. Stowe also omits.

7. 1 Sam 15: 9–10; 1 Kgs 20: 34, 42.

8. Cf. 2 Kgs 9: 33–7; 2 Kgs 11: 20.

9. 1 Kgs 2: 22–4.

10. Pope Clement IV of Conradin of Hohenstaufen and Charles of Anjou, cited in S. Runciman, *The Sicilian Vespers* (1958), p.115.

11. *Sic.*

12. Edge of MS apparently cut here, and below in two places.

13. Ps 103: 6.

7. Petition of Lords and Commons for the execution of Mary Queen of Scots, presented 12 November 1586

Text from California: Huntington Library, Ellesemere 1191, original draft in a clerk's hand, amended by Thomas Egerton and Lord Burghley; formerly among Bridgwater MSS (HMC xi, 7, 130).
Other MSS London: BL Add. 48027 (Yelverton 31), copy of Ellesmere, bearing on f.653 at the end 'Memorandum: that the enterlining[s] in the Roman letter were of the hand of the Lord Thresorer'. Thus it registers Burghley's insertions, though not those which were subsequently deleted. Egerton's changes are incorporated into the text, though there is nothing to show that this has happened; Add. 38823 (as amended Ellesmere); Cotton Caligula C ix (as amended Ellesmere).
Printed D'Ewes, pp.380–82

Ellesmere 1191

May yt please your moost excellent Maiestie, our moost gracyous soveraigne. We your humble lovinge and faythfull subiectes, the Lordes and Commens in this present parliament assembled, having of longe tyme, to our intollerable griefe, seene by howe manyfoulde moost daungerous and execrable practyses Marye the daughter and heyre of James the Fyveth, late Kinge of Scottes, dowager of Fraunce and commenlie called the Quene of Scottes, hath [sought to][1] compassed the destruccion of your Majestie's sacred and moost royall person (in whose saffetie next under God our chiefe and onlye felycytie doth [whollie] consiste), and therby not onlye to bereave us of the syncere and true religion of allmyghtie God, bringinge us **and this noble crown**[2] back agayne into the thraldome of the Romishe tyrranye, but also utterlie to ruynate and overthrowe the happye state and commen weale of this moost noble realme; which, beinge from tyme to tyme by the great mercye and provydence of God and your Highnes' singuler wysdome foreseene and prevented, your Majestie of your excedinge great clemencye and princelie magnanymytie, hath [not onlye,] eyther [by connyvencie] moost gracyouslie passed over [the same], or with singuler favour [remytted] *tollerated*[3] (although often and instantlie moved [to the contrarye] by your moost lovinge and faythfull subiectes *to the contrary in tymes of your parlementes and at many other tymes*) [but] *and* hath also protected and defended the [sayd Marye] *said Scottysh Quene* from those great daungers, which her owne people [by the justice of the lawes of [her owne] *that* realme], for [sundry her] *certeyn* detestable crymes and offences **to hir imputed**, had determyned against her. [And fyndinge that] *All which notwithstandinge*, the same [Marye] *Quene* [hath bene] *was* nothinge moved with [all] these and many other your Majestie's moost gracious favoures towardes her, but rather obdurate in malyce, and by hope of contynuall impunytie imbouldened to prosecute her . . . [word illegible] *cruell* and myschevous determynacion by some speedie and vyolent course. And now latelie . . . [word illegible] *a* verie daungerous plott beinge conceyved and sett downe by Anthony Babington **and others** that sixe desperate and wycked persons shoulde undertake the execucion of that moost horryble enterpryse, to take awaye your Majestie's lyefe (whome God of his infynite mercye longe preserve), she [the saide Marye][4] did not onlye gyve her advyce and dyrection uppon everye pointe and all cyrcumstaunces concerninge the same, makinge ernest request to have it performed with all dylygence, but dyd also promyse assuraunce of lardge rewarde and recompence to the doers therof: which beinge informed to your Majestie, yt pleased your Highnes upon the earnest sute of such as tendred the saftye of your royall person, and the good and quyet estate of this realme, to dyrect your commission under the greate seale of England to the lords and other of your Highnes' Privie Counsell, and certen other lordes of Parliament **of the gretest and most auncient degree**, with some of your **principall** judges, to **examyn**, heare, and determyne the same cause, and thereupon to gyve sentence or judgement accordinge to [the] *a* statute in that behaulfe made in the 27th yeare of your moost gracious raigne. By vertue wherof the more parte of the same commissioners, **being in nombre xxxvj**[th], havinge [with longe and grave delyberacion] **at sondry tymes** fullye hearde what was alledged and proved against the saide [Marye][5] *Scottish Queen* **in her own presence** touchinge the saide crymes and offences, and what she coulde saye for her defence and excuse therein, dyd **after long deliberation** gyve theire sentence and judgment **with one consent**, [That she the saide Mary had] *That the deathe and destruccion of your royall person was imagyned and compassed by the said Anthony Babington, with the privyty of the same Scottish Queen and that she her selfe dyd also* compasse[d] and imagyne[d] the death and destruccion of your moost royall person.

   Nowe forasmuche as wee your moost humble loyall and duetyfull subiectes [doe], **representyng to your most excellent Majesty** [*being the head,*][6] **the unyversall state of your whole people of all degrees in this your realm, doe** well perceyve and are fullie satisfyed [that] **that** the same sentence and judgement [to

---

1. Words in square brackets are deletions.
2. Words in heavy italics are Burghley's insertions.
3. Words in light italics are Egerton's insertions.
4. Add. 48027 has these words, though they are underlined.

5. Add. 48027 has this word, though it is underlined.
6. Words in heavy italics and square brackets are deleted insertions by Burghley.

be in] *is in* all thinges moost honorable, iust, and laufull, and havinge carefullie [depelie] and effectuallie (accordinge to our moost bounden dueties) wayed [and consydered upon] [*upon and consydered upon*][7] *and consydered upon* what grounde and cause so many trayterous complottes and daungerous practyses againste your Maiestie's royall person and estate, *and for the invadinge of this realme*, have for the space of many yeares past growne and proceded, doe **certenly** fynde **and undowtedly ar perswaded** that all the same have bene from tyme to tyme attempted and practysed by, and for, the sayd [Marye] *Scottysh Quene*, and by her confederates, mynisters, and favourers, who conceyve an assured hope to atchieve speedelie, by your Majestie's untymelie death, that which they have longe expected, and wherof duringe your Majestie's lyffe (which God longe preserve to our inestymable comforte) they despayre: to wytte, to place *her* the sayd [Marye] *Scottysh Quene* in the imperiall and kingelie seat of this realme, and by her to banyshe [hence] *and dystroy* the professors and professinge of the true religion of Jesus Christe, [to replant heresie and papistrie, to destroy] *and* the auncyent nobylytie of this lande, and to bringe this whoale state and commen weale [to] **to forrayn subiection and** utter ruyne and confusion. Which theyr malycious and trayterous purposse they will never ceasse to prosecute by all possyble meanes they can, so longe as they may have their eyes and imaginacions fyxed upon that ladye, the onlie grounde of their treasonable hope and conceiptes, and the onlye sede plotte of all daungerous and trayterous devyses and practyses against your sacred person. And seinge also what insolent bouldenes ys growne in the harte of the same [Marye] *Quene* throughe your Maiestie's former excedinge favour*s* and clemencie*s* towardes her, and therupon wayghinge, with heavye and sorowfull hartes, in what contynuall perill of suche lyke desperate conspyracies and practyses your Majestie's moost royall person and sacred lyffe (more dere to us then our owne) ys and shall be styll, without any possyble meanes to prevent yt, so longe as the sayd [Marye] *Scottysh Quene* shall be suffred to contynue, and shall not receyve **that due** punyshment [of death] [*for hir desertes*] which by justyce and the lawes of this your realme she hath so often, and so many wayes, for her moost wicked and detestable offences deserved [and which the moost parte of us your lovinge subiectes have in the name of God and with the testymonye of good conscyences by our severall oathes voluntarylie taken, and by one unyforme maner of wrytinge of Associacion under our handes and seales, vowed, and bounde our selves to prosecute to the uttermoste]: therfore, and for that we fynde that if the sayd ladye shall nowe escape the due **and deserved** punishment of death for these her moost execrable treasons and offences, your Highnes' royall person shall be exposed to many more and those more secrette and daungerous conspyracies then before, **and such as shall not or can not be forseene and discovered, as these hir late attemptes hath bene**, and shall not hereafter be so well hable [in course of justice] to remove and take awaye the grounde and occasion of the same **as now by justyce may and ought to be doon**, we doe moost humblye and instantlie beseche your moost excellent Majestie, that aswell in respecte *of the contynuaunce of the true Christyan religyon now* *professed amongest us, and* of the saffetie of your moost royall person and estate, as in regarde of the preservacion and defence of us your moost lovinge, duetyfull and faythfull subiectes, and the whoalle commen weale of this realme, yt maye please your Highnes to take speedie order that declaracion of the sayd sentence and judgement be made and publyshed by proclamacion. And that therupon dyreccion be gyven for further proceadinge against the sayd [Marye] *Scottysh Quene* according to the effecte and true meaninge of the sayd statute. *Because upon advysed and great consultacion wee can not fynd that there is any possible meanes to provyde for your Majestie's saffetye [but by this, (which wee houlde to be the beste) or by some lyke course to be devysed for]* but by the iust and spedye executyon of the said Quene. The neglectinge wherof maye procure the heavy[8] displeasure and punyshment of allmightie God as by sundry severe examples of his great justice in that behalfe lefte us in the sacred scriptures doeth appere. And if the same be not putt in present execucion wee, your moost humble and duetyfull subiectes, shall therby (so farre as man's reason can reache) be brought in utter despayre of the contynuance amongest us of the true religion of allmightie God, and of your Majestie's lyfe, and the saffetie of all your faythfull subiectes, and the good estate of this moost florishinge commen weale.

7. Words in light italics and square brackets are deleted insertions by Egerton.

8. The passage beginning 'Because . . .' is not an insertion, but Egerton's own direct contribution to the draft.

8. *Separate texts of Queen's reply to petition, 12 November 1586*

i. Text from BL Lansdowne 94, copy amended by the Queen.
Other MSS. Inner Temple, Petyt 538 / 10 (copy in the hand of Francis Alford(?) of the text as in Lansdowne before amendment, with some verbal differences and omitting the last paragraph); BL Add. 38823 as in Lansdowne after amendment, probably a copy taken from the printed tract).
ii. Text from Exeter College, Oxford, 127, copy.
Other MS. Cambridge University Library Ee. ii. 12 (as Exeter College, but in direct speech and with some variant readings).
iii. Text from BL Stowe 361, copy.
iv. Text from BL Harley 158, copy (as in the journal, Cambridge University Library Gg. iii. 34, except for introduction).
Printed. R. C[ecil], *The copie of a letter to the right honourable the Earle of Leycester* (1586), the official account of the events of 12 and 24 November, giving the text of the Queen's speech of 12 November as in Lansdowne after amendment; tract reprinted, Holinshed iv.929–40, *Somer's Tracts*, i.225–36.
Printed: W. Camden, *Annales . . .*, (with some variations), e.g. (1625), Bk 3, pp.168–72; (1635), pp.324–6. Camden's *The History of the Most Renowned and Victorious Princess Elizabeth . . .* (1688), pp. 363–5 has a version based on the printed tract.

i: Lansdowne 94, fos.84–5[1]

[Endorsed '1586. The former copy of her Majesty's first speach the 12th of November'.]

f.84v.   [A copy][2] of her Majestie's most gracious answer delivered by <u>hir self</u> [personally] <u>verbally</u> to the petitions of the Lords and Commons <u>being the estates</u>[3] of [hir][4] Parliament [the 12th of Novembre 1586.]

'The[5] bottomles graces and immeasurable[6] benefitts bestowed upon mee by <u>the</u>[7] Almightie [God] are[8] and have bin such, as I must not only acknowledg them but [also] admire them, [accomp][9]ting them as well miracles, as benefitts, not so much in respect of his divine Majestie with whome nothing is more common then to do thinges rare and singuler, as in regard of oure weaknes, who cannot sufficiently set forth his wonderfull woorkes and [graces] [benefitz][10] <u>graces</u> which to mee [ward] have bene so many, so diverslie folded and imbrodered one [within] <u>upon</u> another, as in no sort [I] am <u>I</u> able to expresse them.

'And although there liveth not any that may more iustly acknowledg themselves infinitely bounde unto God, then I [may], whose life he hath [wonderfully] <u>miraculously</u> preserved at sondrie tymes (beyond my merit) frome a multitude of perills and daungers, yet is not that the [thing] <u>cawse</u> for which I [ac]count my self <u>the</u> deepliest bound to give him [the most hartie] <u>my humblest</u> thanckes, or to yeld him [the] greatest recognition, but this which I shall tell[11] you hereafter, which will deserve the name of wonder. If rare things and seeldom[12] seene be worthie [so to be accounted] <u>of account even this it is</u> [namely] that as I came to the crowne with the willing hartes [of my] <u>of</u> subiects so do I now after (xxviij yeres' raigne) perceave in you [all] no deminution of [youre] goodwilles, which if happelie I should wante, well mowght I breath, but [not] <u>never</u> thincke I lived, [if that were diminished].

'And now [notwithstanding] <u>albeit</u> [if] I finde [apparantlie] my life hath bin [most] <u>ful</u> daungerouslie sought, and [my] death [by her] contrived <u>by suche as no desurt procured</u> it yet am I [in respect] thereof so cleare frome malice, which hath the propertie to make menne gladde, [and reioycefull] at the falls and faultes of theire [enemies] <u>foes</u> and make them seeme to do [things] for other cawses when [as with] rancor [they are stirred to pursue theire intentions] <u>is the ground</u> [as I protest it is to mee, and hath bene a thing most greivous to thincke], <u>yet</u> I[13] <u>protest it is and hath bin my grevous thoght</u> that one not different in sex, of like estate and my neare kinne, shold be [so voide of grace, or false in faith as now to seeke my death, by whome so long her life hath bene preserved, with th'intollerable perill of my owne] <u>fallen into so great a crime</u>. Yea I had so litle purpose to pursue her with any coloure of malice, that as it is not unknowne to some of my Lords here (for now I will play the blabb) I secretlie wrote her a lettre upon the discoverie of [her] <u>sondry</u> treasons, that if she [wolde repent her thoroughlie of her evill course,] <u>wold</u> confesse [it] <u>them</u> and privatlie acknowledge [it] <u>them</u> by her lettres unto [mee] <u>my self</u>, shee never should <u>nede</u> be called for [it] <u>them</u> into <u>so</u> publike question. Neither did I it of [any] minde to circumvent her, for then I knew as much as she cold confesse, and so did I write.

'And if [at this present] <u>even yet</u>, now the matter is made <u>but</u> to apparant, I thought shee trulie [were] <u>wold</u> repent[ant] (as perhapps she wolde easely

1. The MS is damaged in parts.
2. Words in square brackets are deletions.
3. The words underlined in this heading are Burghley's insertions.
4. Inserted and deleted.
5. Words missing because of mutilation of the MS have been supplied from the printed text.
6. Petyt: 'innumerable'.
7. The words underlined in the text are Elizabeth's insertions.
8. From printed text.
9. From printed text.
10. Inserted and deleted.
11. From printed text.
12. From printed text.
13. From printed text (Petyt omits).

appeare in outward sheowe <u>to do</u>) and that for her none other wolde take the matter uppon them, or that we were but as two milke maides, with pailes [under] <u>upon</u> oure armes, or that there were no more dependency upon us, but myne owne life were onlie in [perill] <u>danger</u>, and not the whole estate of youre religion and well doings, I protest (wherein you may beleeve mee, for [al]though I may have many vices, I hope I have not accustomed my tongue to be an instrument of untruthe[s]) I wolde most willinglie pardon and remitt [her] <u>this</u> offence. /

f.84   'Or if by my death other nations and kingdomes might truely say, that this realme had[14] attained a <u>ever</u> prosperouse and florishing estate, I would (I assure you) not desire to[15] live, but gladlie give my life to th'end my death might procure you a better prince.[16] And for youre sakes it is that I desire [most] to live, to keepe you from a worse. For[17] as for mee, I assure you, I finde no great cause I sholde be fonde to live: I take[18] no such pleasure in it, that I sholde much wishe it, nor conceave such terror[19] in death, that I shold greatlie feare it, and yet I say not, but if the stroke were[20] comming <u>perchance</u> fleshe and blood wolde be moved with it, and seeke to shunne it.[21]

'I have had good experience and triall of this [life] <u>world</u>, I know what it is to be a subiect,[22] what [it is] to be a soveraigne, what [it is] to have good neighbors, and sometime meete evill willers.[23] I have found treason in trust, seene great benefitts litle regarded, and in stead of[24] gratefulness, [contrary] courses of purpose to crosse. These former remembrances,[25] present feeling, and future expectacion of evills, I say, have made me thinke[26] [them] <u>an ivel is muche the bettar the les while hit dureth</u> [as][27] <u>and so them</u> happiest that are soonest[28] hence, and taught mee to beare with a better minde these[29] treasons, then is common to my sexe, yea with a better hart perhaps then is in some menn. Which I hope you will not merely impute to my simplicitie, or want of understanding, but rather that I thus conceived, that had theire purposes taken effect, I sholde not have founde the blow, before I had felt it, nor though my perill shold have bene great, my paine shold have bene but small and shorte, wherein as I wold be loth to dye, so bloodie a death, so dowbt I not but God [will] <u>wold have</u> geve<u>n</u> me grace to be prepared for such an event, <u>chance whan hit shal</u>, which I referre to his good pleasure.

'And now as towching theire treasons and conspiracies together with [her that was] the contriver of them. I will not so preiudicate my selfe, and this my realme, as to say or thincke that I might not without the last statute by th'auncient lawes of this land, have proceeded against her, which was not made particulerly to preiudice her, though perhaps [she and her practises] <u>hit</u> might then be suspected in [respect of ther inclination, and the] <u>respect of the</u> disposition of [those, that depended on her] <u>suche as depend that way</u>.

'It was [also] so farre frome being intended to intrapp her, that it was rather, an admonition, [a] <u>to</u> warn[ing], [and diswasion unto her, frome incurring] the daunger thereof, but sith it is made, and in the force of a lawe, I thought good, in that which might concerne her, to proceede according therunto, rather then by course of common lawe, wherein if yow the judges have not deceaved mee, or that the bookes you brought mee were not false, which God forbidd, I mowght as justly have tried her by th' auncient lawes of the lande.

'But yow lawiers are so nice and so precise in sifting and scanning every word and letter, that many times yow stand more upon forme then matter, uppon syllabs then the sense of the lawe. For in this strictnes and exact following of common forme she must have bene indited in Staffordshire, [have] <u>and</u> bene arraigned at the barre, holden up her hand, [and] have bene tried by a jurye, a proper course forsoth to deale in that maner with one of her estate. I thought it better therefore (for avoiding of [all] <u>thes and more</u> absurdities), [and more honorable]³⁰ to comit the cause to the inquisicion of a good nomber of the greatest and most noble personages / of this realme, of the judges and others of good accownt, whose sentence I must approve.

'And all litle inowgh for wee princes I tell you are set on stages, in the sight and veiw of al the worlde duly observed. Th'eyes of many behold our actions, a spott is sone spied in our garments, a blemish quickly noted in our doinges. It behoveth us therefore to be carefull that our proceedings be just and honorable.

'But I must tell you one thing [further] <u>more</u> that in this late acte of Parliament you have laied an hard hand on mee that I must give direction for her death, which cannot be [to mee] but most greivous [and displeasaunt] <u>and an yrksom burdon to me</u>. And [to th'intent you do not] <u>lest you might</u> mistake mine absence frome this parliament (which I had almost forgotten), although there be no cawse why I should willinglie come amongst multitudes, for that amongest many, some may be evill; yet hath it not bene the doubt of any³¹

14. The words 'might ... had' are from printed text.
15. The words 'would ... to' are from printed text.
16. The words 'might ... prince' are from printed text.
17. The words 'keepe ... For' are from printed text.
18. The words 'fonde ... take' are from printed text.
19. The words 'conceave such terror' are from printed text.
20. The words 'not, but ... were' are from printed text.
21. The words 'to shunne it' are from printed text.
22. The words 'what ... subiect' are from printed text.

23. The words 'neighbors ... evill willers' are from printed text.
24. The words 'litle ... of' are from printed text.
25. The words 'These former remembrances' are from printed text.
26. The words 'say ... thinke' are from printed text.
27. Inserted and deleted.
28. From printed text.
29. The words 'beare ... these' are from printed text.
30. Petyt: 'honorablie'.
31. The words 'not ... any' are from printed text.

suche daunger or[32] occasion that kept[33] mee [away] <u>from thence</u>, but only the great greif to heare this cawse spoken of, especiallie that [this] <u>such one of state and kin shold nide so open a declaration and that this</u> nation sholde be so spotted with blotts of disloyaltie, wherein the lesse is my greife for that I hope the better part is myne, and those of the worse not much to be accounted of, for that in seeking my destruction, they <u>might have</u> spoiled theire owne sowles.

Her Majestie referred the further knoledg hereof to some of the Lords there present, wherof the Lord Threasurer seemed to be one for that he stood upp to verefy it.[34]

'And even now cold I tell you that which wold make you sorie. It is a secrett, and <u>yet</u> I will tell it you (although it be knowen I have the propertie to keepe counsaile but to well, of [ten] <u>times</u> to mine owne perill). It is not long since mine eyes did see it written that an othe was taken within [14] <u>few</u> daies, either to kill mee or to be hanged themselves, and that to be performed ere one moneth were ended.

'Hereby I see youre daunger in mee, and neither can or will be so unthanckfull or carelesse of your consciences, as to take no care for youre safetie.

'I am not unmindfull of youre othe [of] <u>made in the</u> Association manifesting [to mee] your great[35] goodwilles and affections taken and entered into <u>upon good conscience and true knowledge of the guilt</u>[36] for safegard of my person, donn (I protest to God) before I ever heard [of] it, or [litle] <u>ever</u> thought of such a matter, till [3][37] <u>a</u> thowsand [of] <u>handes</u> with many[38] obligacions were shewed mee at Hampton Court, signed and subscribed with [th'andes] <u>the names</u> and seales of the [best] greatest of [my realme] <u>this land</u>. Which [nevertheless] <u>as</u> I <u>do</u> acknowledge [as an] <u>the greatest</u> argument of youre [loyall] <u>true</u> hartes, and [trew] <u>great</u> zeale to my safetie, [for which I thincke my self bounde carefully to consider of it, and respect you therein][39] <u>so shal my bonde be strongar tied to gretar care for all</u> your[40] <u>good</u>.

'But for [asmuch as] <u>that</u> this matter [is verie] <u>is</u> rare, weightie, and of great consequence, and [that I have not yet perused youre petition,] I thincke you do not looke for any present resolution, the rather for that as it is not my maner in matters of farre lesse moment to give speedie awnswere without due consideration, so in this of such importaunce, I thincke it verie requisite with earnest praier to beseech his divine Majestie, so to illuminate myne understanding and inspire mee with his grace, as I may do and determine that which shall serve to the establishment of his Church, preservacion of youre estates and prosperitie of this common wealth under my charge. Wherein for that I know delay is daungerous, you shall have with all conveniency our resolution delivered by our message [to yow all]. And what ever any prince may meritt of theire subiects, for theire approved testimony of theire unfained synceritie, either by governing iustly, voide of all partiality, or suffrance of any iniuries donn even to the poorest, that do I assuredly promis inviolablie to performe for requitall of youre [good] <u>so many</u> desertes.'[41]

32. Petyt adds 'other'.
33. The words 'daunger . . . kept' are from printed text.
34. Marginal note in same hand as heading: Petyt omits.
35. The words 'your great' are from printed text.
36. The words 'knowledge of the guilt' are from the printed text.
37. Petyt omits.
38. The words 'with many' are from the printed text, perhaps left out in error by Elizabeth, though Petyt omits.
39. Petyt ends here.
40. From printed text, perhaps left out in error by Elizabeth.
41. BL Lansd. 103, f.64 is endorsed 'Extractions taken by the Queen's order in reformation of somme errours in report of her speeche, the 12¹² of November 1586 in her withdrawing chamber.' In fact the document also relates to Elizabeth's later speech on 24 November (Doc.10i), and it assembles passages and phrases which are closely related to what appeared in the Queen's amendments to the copies, or version, of her speeches as printed here (Docs. 8i, 10i). In particular, a paragraph on the association oath and Elizabeth's acknowledgement of her subjects' loyalty appears in much the form given it by her amendments in Doc.8i, and it includes the words 'with many and your' which she appears to have left out of her amendments. Towards the end of the Lansd. 103 document there is also the passage, as rendered in Doc.10i after amendment, about the need to weigh information carefully 'for we princes may not heave all to our selves'. However, by no means all the amendments to Docs. 8i and 10i appear in Lansd. 103; and some of its own phrases do not form part of the Queen's approved and amended text (indeed, a few are much as the unaltered parts of the texts in any case. So, Lansd. 103 has (for the 12 November speech) the phrase 'I must needs my self with my owne hand writing', probably referring to that part of the speech where Elizabeth discussed her anguish of having to implement the law against Mary: it does not appear in Doc.8i, before or after amendment. For the second speech, the phrase 'I will not bost, my sex doth not permit it' appears in connection with her discussion of the four princely virtues: again, this is not in the speech for 24 November as drafted or amended. (Neither is it part of the version which is part of Commons journals 1.)

    The sequence of events in the production of Lansd. 103, f.64 and Docs. 8i, 10i is by no means clear, and Neale's speculation (*EP*, ii.130, n.2) seems to be based on questionable assumptions about who was likely to be at meetings with the Queen.

ii: Exeter College, Oxford, 127, fos.51v.–3

Notes of the Queene's speeche to the Lords and Commons of the Parliament in answere of their peticion exhibited the xij of November 1586 by the Lord Chancellor unto her Majestie for the speedie execucion of the Scotish Queene, as neere as my capacity without tables could serve to note them, and my memory next morning might avayle to set them downe.[1]

First, her highnes told them that when shee considered the profownde and bottomles depth of Gode's wonderfull and miraculous workes and fownde them soe infinite and marvelous that whosoever would take in hand to set them forth (though hee were of the ripest witt and most perfect iudgment) could but disgrace and[2] deface the admirable greatnes of the same, she, though it would wonderfully amaze the minde of any body to speake truely but of the least of them, yet she would presume to tell them of one wounder which seemed to her to be the greatest that ever shee could thinke of; ffor if that were a wonder the like therof[3] was never hard before, or for the strangenes or greatnes thereof could never bee ymagined nor increased, then that which shee would tell them could not be taken but for an exceedinge marvaile. And that was not the miraculous benifits which God most abundantly[4] had bestowed upon her, espetially since shee was a queene soe multiplied in hopes[5] and curiousitie[6] imbrodered one upon an other, and[7] intricate and many-fowlde wrapped up togeather, that shee might not well unfowld then;[8] neither was it his longe and oft most gratious protectinge of her life which even of late hee defended from the fury of many most rigorous and pestelent conspirators in such strange and wonderful mannor as, if therein hee hand[9] not extended he[10] divine powre to the uttermost, she had not beene there to speake to them at that time, ffor the which shee could not in speech utter how depely shee held her selfe bownde unto him, and yet without the continuance of his singuler goodnes her deat[h] might still be easily wrought; but that which shee accompted soe miraculous a wonder was that in the time of her 28 yeares' raigne she evidently sawe that the love and goodwill of her people was noe one respect diminished: of whome, though there were a fewe of the worst sort lost,[11] which shee could not but lament (in that shee feared they had therewith lost their owne), yet shee hoped the best parte was hers, which was noe small comfort unto her. This shee thought to bee as rare and strange a thinge as shee could thinke one.[12] And as shee knowledgeth her selfe highly / bownd unto

f.52

God for preservinge her from soe many daungers and bestowinge upone her soe many singuler benifits, for the which with all humility shee yealdeth him most grate thankes,[13] yet shee protested before the face of the Almighty that she gave him far more exceedinge thankes for that in 28 yeares' raigne the love of her people were noe whit diminished then shee did for her[14] straung and oft preservinge of her life; for without that shee desired not to live, assuredly thinkinge that a princesse' life deprived of this[15] subiects' love well might be called a breathing, but suer it could not be accounted life. And the affectionate love she sawe in her subiects towardes her was th'onely ioy of her life, the which (notwithstandinge) she said was not voide of sorrowe and greife. Thereuppon protestinge before the face of God that since she was borne shee was never soe oppressed therewith, nor ever soe pensive nor heavie in hart, and that not for feare of death, for she thought them most happie who, dyinge in the grace of God, were soe well at rest; and yet perhaps if she sawe the stroke cuminge shee might as sone shrinke as an other, howbeit she conceved therein small cause of greife for, as they well knewe, if the conspiracie against her person had taken effect her life would have beene soe short as her death could not longe have beene greivous; but now that one of her owne sect[16] and state, of her owne blod and soe neere her kinswoman, could be drawen to hazard her owne life to shorten the daies of her Highnes, that she vowed before the liveinge God was far more grevious unto her then if by any other meanes her owne life were presently to be taken from her, the which she vehemently protested, if she might be suer to leave her subiect[s] in religious and peasable felicitie after her, shee would not desier to have prolonged one hower. And yet for all this shee did not any whit the more malice her, but from the bottom of her hart beseeched God to send her grace inwardly to repent as shee migh[t] have good cause to forgive her; the which shee could with all her hart be contented to doe if there did depende noe more thereon then the perrill of the[17] life, wherin she sought them to beleve her, in that she trusted it could not be sayed that shee had at any time defiled her mouth with lies, protestinge that malice wrought not in her princly hart as generally it did in mindes of meaner

1. Cam is headed 'An answer by owr Quene to the peticion of the Parliament Howse for the speedye execution of the Scottyshe queene'. The speech is reported directly, rather than indirectly as here: the resultant verbal changes are not noted below.
2. Cam omits 'disgrace and'.
3. Cam: 'whereof'.
4. Cam has 'of his goodnes' rather than 'most abundantly'.
5. Cam: 'heapes'.
6. Cam: 'curiouslye'.
7. Cam adds 'so'.

8. *Sic*; Cam: 'them'.
9. *Sic*; Cam: 'had'.
10. *Sic*; Cam: 'his'.
11. Cam: '. . . sort which have lost theire owne soules' and then omits 'which shee . . . owne'.
12. Cam: 'of'.
13. Cam has 'immortall prayse' rather than 'most grate thankes'.
14. *Sic*; Cam omits 'then shee did . . . life'.
15. Cam: '. . . prince's lyffe depryved of the love of his subiectes'.
16. *Sic*; Cam: 'sex'.
17. *Sic*.

persons. And soe making a fine definition of malices, she said that[18] malice commonly urged the least occation that might happen to the uttermost extreamitie, but in her it moved all the pittie that might bee imagined: ffor besides that shee had beene[19] with many great iniuries past, now in this last

v.   point of her / conspiracy, wherein shee could not but tell them that in regard of her selfe shee had played the foole, before shee revealed her knowledge to any of her Councell (for shee could but too well keepe councell in the perill of her owne estate) shee privily sent to her, not by any cawtell to intrap her, for well shee knewe her guilte before, but freindly to perswade her to confesse her offence, truely promisinge upon her honour that if shee would soe doe shee should never bee brought to any[20] shame. Whereby they might see how free her Highnes was from the lest sparke of malice, yea soe free as shee vowed before the face of God that if yet shee might see any hope of her sownde repentance and amendment and that shee would cease to pursue the practise of her Highnes' death and that shee might bee suer that noe oath[21] would attemt the same in her behalfe, shee would surely pardon her. But her longe preservinge[22] in the same did argue an imposibility of performance of[23] any better disposition of minde, wherein she thought large promises might be made, but therein small could be th'assurance. Howbeit she protested that if they two were but milkemaides with pailes upon their armes, and that there depended noe more upon the matter then the perill of her owne life, shee would clerely forgive and pardon her: such was the force of her malice. And soe protested that the greife which shee tooke for the Scotishe Quene's desperate estate exceeded far th'account shee made of her owne life, the which, but in respect shee desired to leave her people in like florishinge estate after her as under God shee had these 28 yeares maynteyned them, shee vowed before God shee carred not a pinne if it were ended tomorow next. Wherein she desired them to beare with her, hopinge they would not thinke shee was altogeather voide of iudgment or feelinge of her owne estate, but that she did see that everie small delay of iustice in this case was a great perrill to her person; or that wanted reasonable feare, though shee were not soe ferfull as comonly woemen are, perhaps not soe ferefull as some men. And well shee knewe what it was to be a subiect, and had tried what it was to bee a prince, wherefore she required them to thinke that princes ought to bee more presise in their dealings then common persones, and that their accions were like the starrs in the skie whereon the eyes of all the wourld were fixed and a small blott in princes' doings was a marvilous foile in the sight of all men, and that a meane man might committ tenn faultes without note where a prince could not escape the least fault without a great infamie. And that was the cause that moved her to proceede in th'examinacion of these waightie matters by the greatest and noblest of the realme, authorised thereunto by her commission under her Great Seale. And therein to make more hast then good speede she thought it [not][24]

f.53   convenient, thought[25] the perill of her life required it. / And yet if shee would bee hastily moved shee never had more cause then at that instant, for, to tell them a matter whereof they never hard before, shee did assuer them that two strange felowes were come newly over and set aworke to deprive her of her life, and that they had promised to doe the same within one fortnight or one month at the farthest or otherwise they yeald themselves to bee tormentted to death; wherein shee called a great man[26] to witnes, sayinge that that would make some startle which little moved her. Besides shee sayed that well she knewe shee might call her in question and trie her by the common lawes of the realme if shee had not thought it more fitt to hold a more calme and quiet course therein. And soe presentinge her selfe neerer the Speaker, shee towld him that they[27] lawyers were soe fine that they would not followe the meaning of the lawes but strictly iudge accordinge to the lettre of the same; and if shee should put them to that, then they should see how the case stoode.[28] First, shee should bee endited in Stafford sheire forsooth, with twelve simple men of that countrie; then shee should hold up her hand at the bar and bee tried by other such twelve[29] men, and soe condemned and iudged shee should be accordingely executed: a fitt manner noe doubt for a prisoner of her estate. But now for want of better forme in the comon lawe shee must be a director of her execution, wherein they had done her a great pleasure, noe dout: for the last Parliament beginninge[30] a law which her Highnes disliked, they had proceeded in an other whereunto shee gave her consent, and therein shee was exceedingly behouldinge unto them for they had left th'execucion thereof onlie unto her. Marrie, for matter of Associacion shee held her selfe deeply behowldinge unto them, and to all such as were therein sworen, for that it was frankely done of all her subiects without contradiccion of any, wherof she had noe knowledge untill at the least three thowsand bonndes were presented unto her in his[31] house at Hampton Court, and who demised[32] the same shee knewe not, but she was fully perswaded that for her saftie it was the most honest and faithfull act that ever subiects performed, and soe shee tooke it, and for the same yealded them great thankes; as alsoe for the great care of her saftie, to which end they had this session most grave[ly] and wisely consulted and proceeded, wherein shee would endevoure her selfe to content them as for whome she cared more then for her life. And soe concludinge that by their leaves shee would / take some time to consider of their peticion in that it concerned a   v. person of great estate and matter rare, whereof the like was never heared before, and a cause of the greatest waight that might bee, wherein shee would consulte with God and the wisest of her Councell. She promised that after

18. Cam naturally omits the comment 'And soe . . . said that'.
19. Cam: 'borne'.
20. Cam adds 'open'.
21. *Sic*; Cam: 'other'.
22. Cam: 'perseveringe'.
23. Cam omits 'performance of'.
24. Cam has 'not'.
25. Cam: 'though'.
26. Cam: 'you my lordes'.

27. Cam omits the comment 'And soe . . . that they' and continues 'As for you lawyers, ye are so fine . . .'.
28. Cam renders the phrase 'and if shee . . . case stoode' as 'And yf I would lett you alone with that, then should we see howe the case stood'.
29. Cam adds 'ignorant'.
30. Cam: 'you wold have made'.
31. *Sic.*
32. *Sic.* Cam: 'devised'.

resolucion therein taken they should shortly here from her. And soe shee arose and went downe from the cloath of estate (where shee sat) to retire her selfe, but presently returned sayinge that shee had almost forgot one thing shee ment to tell them, namely that least any doubt should bee conceaved of her not cominge to the beginning of the Parliament shee did assuer them that though there were good cause for her to know how comitted[33] her person into the presence of the multitude, yet in truth there was in her noe such feare; but being loth to here soe many fowle and grevious matters revealed and ript upp shee had small pleasure to be there present. And soe they most affectionatly prayinge unto god for her longe and happie raigne over them, shee for the same yeeldinge great thankes departed.

33. *Sic*; Cam: 'howe I do comite'.

'My lordes and gentlemen, I can not but accept with much kyndnes this your peticion, wherin I perceyve the greate love you beare towardes me and the provydent care you have taken for my person. Yt was not the ffeare of perille that made me abstayne from cominge to the parlyment, but that in trewth yt should not a lyttell greve me to heare a prynce anoynted as my selfe and of my owne blude to have byn talked of for hir unnaturall and desperate attemptes agaynst my person. I protest before God that althoughe yt hathe pleased him in his manyfoulde mercyes, bothe when I was a subiecte and sence I cam to the crowne, to protecte me from so manye dangerus and creuell practizes tendinge to the distruckcion of my person, fare beyonde the pollice of anye humayne creture to prevente, yet it is not that that makes me accnowledge my selfe most heighly bound unto him; but this I esteme to be his most exelente and devyne benyfyte, that yt hathe pleassed him to establishe his gospell now almost xxviij[th] yeares in this my kingdome (beinge so often and so dangeruslye interupted by the attemptes of fforrayne and domesticall papystes and enymyes) and that in this my longe tyme of government I fynde no dyminucion of your good wylls, but rather increase therof. This is that, that makes me more bounde unto his goodnes then anye other worldly gyfte whatsoever. I must confesse that the perillus enterprises of thes late traytors did greatly perplex me in regarde some of them weer soo neare unto me, and consederinge the roote from whence all thes practizes spronge was from one of my owne sexe, bothe noblly borne and of our owne blude. God is my iudge, I have not sought hir mallisiusly (as you all that weer of the Parlyment in the 14 yeare of our raynge[1] can testyfye), ffor whan you had concluded agaynst her, I onlye was hir ffrynde and spared her; I received hir into my proteccion and defended hir from the fury of the Scottes whan she resorted hether for refuge, and am yet so ffare from mallinging[2] hir (as God knoweth) yf yt weer not more for ffeare of the rootinge oute of the gospell and in respecte of the motherly love and care I beare to you (my lovinge subiectes) and the contrys that be governed by me, yt is not yet any danger or perile that could betyde my selfe should macke me yeld to your peticion. But such hath your affeccion and zeale byn towardes us, never beinge moved by me or any other by my privitie, that many thoussandes of you

---

1. *Sic.*   2. *Sic.*

received the Othe of Assosiacion and so fare bownde your consyences to doe me good as no lawe can ffree you thereof. And I wyll nowe playe the blabbe and delivere that unto you which I never ment to have disclossed, as heer

Lord Treseror

standeth one by us can beare us wyttnes, that yf of late whan I wrytte unto the Scottich Queene to confesse those treasons practized betwyxt hir and Babbington for the spedy dispach of me, she would have relented and semed penytent for so ffowle a conspyracie in confessing the treuthe, I promised hir of myn honour she should never be called in publicke question or dishonored for the same. And I doute not but this wyll ffre me from all susspicion of mallice. I sent to be hir peeres and tryers the most noble persons of our statte and the wyssest and larndeste iudges of our land to avoyd the slanderus reportes of our forrayne enemye, wheras I might have tryed hir by a iurye of xij men by the comen laues of our land, yet I thought yt a³ unsemlye thinge a person so nobly borne and of our owne lynage should be indeighted, areyned and hould up hir hande at the barr wher peradventure some carpinge attornye or cavelinge lawyer that have studyed on the back syde of his boocke, rather then loocked into the depthe of the lawe, might have sett downe some falce notes to have advertized our fforrayne enemyes contrary to our laufull procedinges, as hertofore some malissius person have done. We princes stand alwayes as upon a stage for all the world to behould, and those smale offensis that pryvate men pase over withoute speech or mislicke ar accownted very heighnus in princis. And therfore yt behoveth us very circomspectlye to loocke and advice

v.

our selves both of our accions and procedinges. / This shalbe our conclusion and therunto truste I have more care of you and my contryes then my owne selfety;⁴ but yf my lyfe have breed your happines and ffelicetye I must humblye thancke God he hath preserved me for your saftyes, and yf my death might perpetuallye establishe the gospell amongst you and breed that contenewall securyte to you and yors that I wyshe, I would most wyllinglye gyve my lyfe for you. And for this your peticion I accepte yt in most kinde and lovinge maner, and wyll, after some deliberation taken of so weighty a matter as concerneth the dathe of a prynce, send you my resolucion, althoughe you have fforwarned me that *mora trahit periculum.*'

3. *Sic.*   4. *Sic.*

iv: Harley 158, fos.156–7

After that my Lord Chauncellor in the name of the Lords, and Mr Speker for the Comons, had delivered her Majesty a peticion for the present executinge of Mary, late Queene of Scottes, and eyther of them proved by many and greate reasons that hir Majestie's life could nott be in safitye, relligion contignewe, nor the comon wealth stand except hir life were take[n] awaye, and that without delaye, which neither seased to seake the deathe of the Queen, the advauncement of Popery and the corrupcion of the state. And therefore most humbly and instauntly besought hir Highenes to showe justice to that woman which had deserved yt, and mercy to the whole realme which nowe craved yt att hir handes. Ytt plesed hir Highenes to call nere unto hir the Lords and Comons sent as comissioners from the parlement there assembled and in her owne person most gratiouslye and wisely to give aunswere as followeth.

'Whem[1] I remember the bottomles depth of Gode's greate goodnes towardes me [*etc.* as in Cambridge University Library Gg. iii 34, the journal of proceedings relating to Mary Queen of Scots, 15 Oct.–2 Dec. 1586].

On saturdaye the 12 of November 1586 in the Chamber of presence att Richmond.

---

1. *Sic.*

9. *Considerations for the Queen's safety, 17 November 1586*

Text from BL Add. 48027 (Yelverton 31), probably a copy.

Add. 48027 (Yelverton 31), fos.222–3

[Endorsed '17 November 1586.

Considerations for the parliament touchinge provision to be made for her
Majestie's safetie.']

Considerac[i]ons of the horrible actions in these perilous tymes, uppon counsel
in Parlement demaunded, for her Majestye's preservation.

Twoe thinges fawle in this considerac[i]on, the fact and the person.

For the fact, it is subversion of religion established, invasion of the realme by
forreyn enemyes, inward rebellion and cyvyl warres, and the murthereng of her
Majestye's most royall person: every which particuler act, as it deserveth most
crewel deathe, so altogeather any thing that may be invented to exceede the
same accordeng to the numbre and qwalitye of the crymes.

Uppon the person lyethe the whole weight of this consideracion. She is a
qweene, of absolute power, and here deteyned a prisoner. It may by lawe be
disputable whether one absolute prynce may have power over an other of the
same sorte, and whether a prynce imprisoned within the realm of an other
[may]¹ by any means procure his libertye with the destruction of hym by
[whom]² he is deteyned. And whether by reason of the offense he becummeth
subiect to the lord of territorye where he hathe offended. It is in lawe disputed
bothe *pro et contra*, if a bushop offendeng in the diocesse of an other bushop
may be punished or deprived, if the offence reqwire it, by the diocesan there.

But let it be withowt all controversye lawful to execute the offender, yet
wold it be considered whether it be expedient or not, and what wer most
convenient to be done in this case; and therwithal consyder lykewise whether
she be the chiefe and onlye cawse of these attemptes, and whether if she be
taken awaye the daunger wyl cease, or els be more or lesse, wheruppon wyl
appere what is lyke to be the safest way for her Majestye's preservacion.

These attemptes thus desperatlye enterprised ar begon eyther for causes
spiritual or temporal, or bothe.

Those that be spirituallye moved and pretend a zeal to the religion that they
have embraced doe preferre the same before their lyves, for the advauncement
wherof they have vowed theyr deathes, and present theyr bodyes withowt
regard to the same, which mynd wyl not cease in them by the ceaseng of her
lyfe, haveng a perswasion emongest them selfes that by the effusion of their

blood (wherbye they imagyn that they becum martyrs) the subversion, or as they terme it the conversion, of this realm wylbe wrought.

Suche as for temporal respectes have enterteyned the practize, doe hope by turneng the streame and fisheng in a trobled water to get gayns, wherof som fewe and of smal power may relye on her, but al theyr myndes and intencions ar set uppon chaunge of state, which wyl contynewe in them so long as the same standethe in uncertentye.

They that myxe religion with polycye, and ar sturred up eyther by malice to her Majestye, or for revenge, or els for love they beare, and desyre they have to advaunce the other, it wold be considered whether the end of that miserable wooman wold be the end of their attemptes.

At this present she is the instrument wheruppon the most parte of them al have playde, as wel for the opinion they have conceaved of her tytle, as for the religion she maketh shewe to professe. /

But althowghe she hathe often stolen intelligence bothe from and to them,   v. yet hathe not the same bene so freelye, nor theyr workinges have bene with suche securitye, as wold have bene done, if free accesse might have bene had unto her. Neyther durst ever anye, eyther forreyn enemyes, or inward rebells, attemp[t] any armes, untyl they had som head abrode. And althowghe many practizes have bene devised for her escape, yet wer they neyther of great multitudes nor of great forces; and as their enterprises wer daungerous to them selfes, so wer they lykelye to be discovered, and her self in that action to be most in daunger. But if she be taken away, and they have turned their myndes to som other to whom they may have better accesse, and have their devises more free, withowt fear of apprehension in the practizeng therof, it is to be feared what end their work may have in an ambitious mynde, desirous to raigne, styl gapeng for this realme. Let it therfore be wel considered whether it be not the greatest securitye for her Majestye to hold her styl in her handes as a condempned person, to be executed alwayes at her pleasure, uppon whom at this tyme they relye wholye, and whose lyfe is a stoppe to others, and her person for many her abomynable factes odious to al good men, that may so safely be kept as theyr hope of intelligence may fayl them, and the fear of the looseng of theyr head, at al tymes that they shal make any attempt, may staye them; which being once cut of, their cawse ceasethe not ever a whyt the more therbye, but revenge wyl the more kendle and set them on, and their devises ar lyke to take more daungerous effect when they shalbe owt of doubt of imminent and apparent danger bothe of the person for whom they imploy them selfes and of the practizers therof, whom your honors shal not be able so wel to discover abroad as yow may doe at home.

Now it is a thing worthye of great consideracion whye so clement and merciful a prynce as her Majestye is, under whom al maner of subiectes lyve in great peace and tranqwillitye, is thus maligned, that her deathe is sought; the which can not be for any personal cawse, but that extendeth beyond her

1. MS obscured by sealing wax.   2. MS obscured by sealing wax.

person, as offended with her goverment, or religion, or bothe. Wherin it may be concluded that it is bothe for religion and goverment that they seeke her overthrowe, but chiefely relegeon. And herein as it is not meete eyther to alter her peaceable goverment, or to enclyne to any other false religion, so wold it be deeply considered how she may contynew them bothe and her safetye withal.

It is to be thought whoe wold enter into the secret iudgementes of God that he hathe used bothe mercye and vigour, and hathe to som mayme that[3] she hathe applyed bothe oyle and vinegre. The discloseng of these treasons by his onlye means hath bene bothe merciful and wonderful; his sufferance of these attemptes, and the feare that this good ladye may be tormented withal, is sharper then to our considerac[i]ons might fawle uppon so good a prynce, in whom wee can not conceave any other offence, but that the same sawce is ministred to her which she suffereth her subiectes to tast of, whoe stand bothe in the lyke fear and / daunger after her decease as her Majestye presentlye feelethe, and it is not to be doubted but that the assurance of the one wyl assure the other.

f.223

When ther was cawse at any tyme whye the old Romayn emperors dyd suspect any treason or trechery to be wrought against them, for their better safetye in their empire *designabant successorem*, whom they ioyned in goverment with them. I may remembre that the late Duke of Florence, whoe governeng that state by force, stode alwayes in feare by partialityes to be bereaved of his lyfe, dyd for the establishement of his dominion and his owne safetye take his sonne into goverment with hym.[4] What greater securitye and ease of hart can cum to her Majestye then to establishe suche a one as may manage the most difficult affayres? Oppose hym self against the enemyes? Passe throwghe the daungers? And be alwayes a back and ayde to her Majestye? Whoe whylest the forces of this land may be united and applyed by her direction and commaundement, maye more fyrmelye, and with lesse daunger of the subiectes, be placed then, when for want of a knowen head al thinges shalbe in tumult, and the forces called and devided into many partes to the utter destruction, as is lykelye, bothe of the realme and subiectes, of whom her Majestye hathe professed to take suche care as it is to be hoped for that she wyl not leave them in suche daunger.

Moreover, her Majestye may be wel asseured that these meschevous devyses ar imagined against her uppon hope that by her fawle suche dissention wyl followe as they may escape unpunished and expect reward, which attemptes they wyl leave when theyr hope therof shalbe cut of, and suche a one here placed under her as shalhe able to resist theyr attemptes and be redye at al instantes to pursewe and persecute al offenders, which in my symple conceyt wylbe the onlye waye of her Majestye's securitye and stoppe the wycked enterprises of al her enemyes.

The fear that is conceaved of twoe sonnes in one fyrmament, and of the one riseng and the other setteng, which is so deepely impressed in her Majestye's mynde, may be with good consideracion so qwalifyed, and he that shalbe set up so tyed, as that he may rather be a moone to take his light of the sonne, then to yeld it of his owne power; which discourse becawse it is long and weightye I wyl not enter into but leave the same to graver consyderac[i]ons, thinkeng it a lesse inconvenience to hazard the daunger which may be doubt-ful, in this case, then to leave it apparent and open to the other.

Thus myche in discharge of my particuler duetye in this general consultacion of manye.

3. Repeated in MS.
4. The reference may be to Cosimo de' Medici who had died in 1574 at 55, but had given a large role in government to Francesco for about ten years before.

10. *Separate texts of Queen's speech, 24 November 1586*

i. Text from BL Lansdowne 94, copy amended by the Queen. *Other MS.* BL Add. 38823 (as in Lansdowne after amendment, probably a copy taken from the printed tract).
ii. Text from BL Harley 158, copy (as in the journal, Cambridge University Library Gg. iii. 34, except for introduction).
Printed. R. C[ecil], *The copie of a letter to the right honourable the Earle of Leycester* (1586), the official account of the events of 12 and 24 November, giving the text of the Queen's speech of 24 November as in Lansdowne after amendment, with some variations; tract reprinted, Holinshed iv.929–40, *Somer's Tracts* i.225–36.
Printed: W. Camden, *Annales* . . ., (with some variations) e.g. (1625), Bk 3, pp.173–7; (1635), pp.326–8. Camden's *The History of the Most Renowned and Victorious Princess Elizabeth* . . . (1688), pp.366–8 has a version based on the printed tract.

Lansdowne 94, fos.86–8[1]

[Endorsed 'The 2 copy of her Majesty's second speach 24 Novembre. Before her Majestie corrected it'.]
'Full grevous is the way whose goeing [in][2] on[3] and [out] ende [findes] bredes comber for the hier of a laborious journey.

  'I have strived more this day then ever in my life whither I shold speake or [hold my peace] use silence. If I speake and not complaine I shall dissemble. If [contrariewise] I hold my peace your labor taken weare [in] ful vaine.

  'For me to make my mone weare strange and rare, for I suppose youe shall find few that for theire owne perticuler will comber youe with such a care. Yet such I [doe] protest hath bene my greedie desire and hungry will, that of your consultation might have falne out some other meanes to work my saftie ioyned with youre assurance (then that for which youe are become so ernest suitors), as I protest I must needes use complaint, though not of youe but unto youe, and of the cause; for that I doe perceave by youre advises, praiers, and desires, there falleth out this accident, that onelie [the bane of my iniurer] my iniurar's bane must be [the suretie of my life] my life's suretie.

'But [if there liveth anie creature so vile or wicked of concept, as once to carrie that thought of me,] if any ther live so wicked of nature to suppose that I prolonged this tyme only, pro forma, to the intent to make a shewe of clemencie, thereby to set my praises to the wyerdrawers <u>to lenken them the more</u>, they doe me so great a wrong as they can [never] <u>hardly</u> recompence. Or if anie [perverse] person [doe] <u>ther be that</u> thinke or imagine that the least vaineglorious thought hath drawne me furder herein, [thereby to be glorified,] they doe me as open iniurie as ever was done to anie liveinge <u>creatur</u>, as he that is the maker of <u>all</u> thoughts knoweth best [to be true] <u>to be tru</u>. Or if there be anie that think that the lordes appointed in comission durst doe no other as fearinge therebie to displease, or to be suspected to be of a contrarie opinion to my safety, they doe but heape upon me iniurious conceipts. For either those put in trust bie me [for this action] to supplie my / place, have not performed theire dutie towards me [in that I gave them in chardg], or els they have signified unto youe all, that my desire was that everie one shold doe accordinge to his conscience, and in [that] <u>the</u> course of theise proceedings shold enioy both freedome of voice, and libertie of opinion <u>and what they wold not openly, the⁴ might privatly to my self, declare</u>. It was of a[n honorable] <u>willing</u> minde and greate desire I had, that some other meanes might be found out wherin I shold have taken more comfort then in anie <u>other</u> thinge under the sonne. And [seeinge] <u>sins</u> now it is resolved, that my suretie cannot be established, without a princess' head, I have iust cause to complaine that I, who have in my tyme pardoned so manie rebells, winked at so manie treasons, and either not produced them, or altogether slipt them over with silence, shold now be forced to this proceeding against such a person. I have besids during my reigne seene and hard manie opprobrious bookes and pamphlets against me, my realme, and state, accusinge me to be a tyrant. I thank them for theire almes; I believe therein theire meaninge was to tell me newes, and newes [to me] it is <u>to me</u> in deede, I wold it weare as [great news] <u>strange</u> to heare of theire impietie. What will theie not now say, when it shall be spread, that for the safetie of her life a maiden Quene could be content to spill the blood even of her owne kinswoman? I maie therefore full well complaine, that anie man shold thinke me given to creweltie, whereof I am so guiltless and innocent, as I shold slander God, if I shold saie he gave me [such] <u>so vile</u> a mynd. Yea I protest [unto youe] I am so farre from it, that for myne owne life I wold not touche her, neither hath my care bene so much bent how to prolong myne, as how to preserve both, which I am right sorie is made so hard, yea so impossible.

'I am not so void of iudgment as not to see myne owne perill, nor yet so ignorant as not to know it weare in nature a foolishe course, to cherish a sword to cut myne owne throat, nor so careless as not to waigh that my life daiely is in hazard, but this I do consider / that manie a man wold put his life in danger,

v.

f.87

1. There are some words at the top of the MS, probably Elizabeth's, which have been made illegible by overwriting (itself illegible) in black ink.

2. Words in square brackets have been deleted.

3. Words underlined have been inserted by the Queen.

4. *Sic.*

for the safegard of a kinge, I do not say that [I meane to doe so] <u>so wil I</u>, but I praie youe thinke that I have thought upon it. But sith so manie hath both writen and spoken against me I praie youe give me leave to say somewhat for my self, and before youe retorne to your contries lett youe knowe [youe have travayled for me] <u>for what a one yow have passed so carefull thoghts</u> that will never be forgetfull of youre exceding cares for my safetie. And as I thinke my selfe [greatelie] <u>infinitely</u> beholdinge unto youe <u>all</u>, that [youe] seeke to pre- serve my life by all <u>the</u> meanes youe [cann] <u>may</u>, so I protest that there [is no living] <u>liveth no</u> prince [that ever hath bin or can be more thankfull unto youe for it] <u>nor ever shalbe more mindful to requite so good desarts</u>: wherein as I perceave youe have kept your old wont in a generall seeking [of] the [safetie of] <u>lengtning of</u> my [life] <u>dayes</u>, so [doe I conceave that I am] <u>am I sure that</u> never [hable to] <u>shal I</u> requite it, unles I had as many lives as youe all; but for ever I will acknowledge it while there is [in me anie life] <u>any my brethe left me</u>.

[‘Next I will make <u>you</u> my confession [to him that made me,] and say before youe all, that I am a synner, full of faults, a wretch that have bene much forgetfull of my dutie towards God, for if I shold say otherwise I shold offend both God and youe, and most of all forget my self. And seeing so manie pennes have ben used to discourse the actions of youer governoure, I wil say some- what for my self.] <u>Althogh I may not iustefie but may iustly condemne my [selfe] sondry faultes and sins to God, yet for my care in this gouverment let me acquaint you with my intents</u>.

‘When [I] first I tooke the [crowne] <u>sceptar</u>, [I not somuch remembred the cepter, as him that gave it, and therefore sought to establish in this kingdome, his Church and that religion, wherein] <u>my titel made me not forget the givar and therfore began as hit became me with suche religion as bothe</u> I was borne in [and], bread <u>in</u>, and [wherein I hope to] <u>I trust shall</u> die <u>in</u>, [then entered I into the schole of experience what fitted a king to do and theare I sawe he skant was well-furnished if either he lacked iustice, temper, magnanimitie or iudgement][5] although I was not so simple as not to know what danger and perill so great an alteration might procure me, how manie great princes of the contrarie[6] [that terme themselves Catholique] <u>opinion</u>, wold attempt all they

v.   might[7] / against me, and generallie what enimitie I shold therebie breede unto my self; which all I regarded not, knowing that he for whose sake I did it [wold safelie] <u>might and wold</u> defend me, for which it is that ever since, I have bene so dangerouslie prosecuted, as I[8] rather marvell that I am, then [that I am not] <u>muse that I shuld not be</u>, if it weare not God’s hollie hand that contynueth me beyond all <u>other</u> expectation.

‘I was not simplie trained up, nor in my yewth spent my tyme altogether idly, and yet when I came to the crowne, then entred I first into the scole of experience; bethinking my self of those things that best fitted a kinge, justice, temper, magnanimitie, judgment; [for I found it most requisite that a prince shold be endued with justice, that he shold be adorned with temperance, I conceaved magnanimitie to beseeme a royall estate possessed by whatsoever sex, and that it was necessarie that such a person shold be of judgment.[9] Of which last two I will not speake, for that I am not greatlie trobled with them; and yet I remember well that Salamon saith, that nothinge is more requisite for a king then judgment: for the first, this maie I truely saye, that I was never led to consent to anie thinge that I thought uniust, I never preferred anie in respect of the preferrer, if I thought him not my self worthie of the preferment, nor ever in matter of justice respected the person to the alteration of my censure; I never lent my eare to corrupt my iudgment, or changed my opinion of any, but by the iust motion of those, that weare by me put in trust, to examyne the cause, wherein as in a thing comon to all Princes I must of force use some for theire advice, yet will I this take upon me that to my knowledg]. <u>For the two latter I will not boast. But for the two first this may I truely say: among my subiectes I never knew a difference of person wheare right was one, nor never to my knowledge preferrd for favour what I thought not fitt for worth, nor bent myne eares to credit a tale that first was told me, nor was so rashe to corrupt my iudgement with my censure er I heard the cause. I will not say but many reportes might fortune be brought me by suche as must heare the matter whose partiality might marre the right, for we princes cannot heare all causes our selves. But this dare I boldly affirme</u> my verdict want [ever] with the truth of my knowledg.[10] /

['As it was] <u>but ful wel</u> wished [by] Alcibiades [to] his frend that he shold not   f.88 give anie aunswere till he had recited the letters of the alphabet, so have I not used <u>over</u> sodaine resolutions in matters [of anie weight nor determyned oft without deliberation] <u>that have touched me ful nere. You wyl say that with me I think</u>. And therefore as touching youre counsels and consultations, I conceave them to be wise, honest, and conscionable: so provident, and carefull for the saftie of my life, (which I wish no longer then may be for youre good) that though I [can] never <u>can</u> yeld youe [due] <u>of</u> recompence <u>your due</u>, yet shall I indevoure my self to give youe cause to think your good will not ill bestowed, <u>and strive to make my self worthy for such subiectes</u>. And as for your petition [I shall praie you for this present to content your selves with an aunswer [without aunswere] <u>answerles</u>, [which it,] <u>for</u> if I shold say it shold not be done, (by my faith) weare more then I ment <u>to tel you</u>. If I shold say it shall be done, it weare more then I cold now assure or were convenient here to be declared:

5. The insertions from 'with suche religion' to 'or iudgement' do not seem to be in Elizabeth's hand.

6. The words 'although I was . . . contrarie' have been underlined, though not deleted. They occur in the printed text.

7. The words 'wold attempt all they might' have been underlined, though not deleted. They appear in the printed text.

8. The words 'for which . . . as I' are deleted, though they occur in the

printed text, and they seem to be necessary to retain the sense of the text.

9. The words 'for I found . . . of judgment' are underlined in the MS (and omitted in the printed text) rather than being clearly crossed through.

10. The insertion 'For the two . . . knowledg' does not seem to be in Elizabeth's hand (same as on f.87).

I therefore protest as there was never anie Prince more beholding unto her subiectes then[11] I [am un] to youe, so was there never prince, more willing to do youe good then I in my mynd, though I may fayle in the means.]

'Your judgment I condemne not, neither do I mistake your reasons, but praie youe to accept my thankfullnes, excuse my doubtfullnes, and take in good part my aunswer aunswerles: wherein I attribute not so much to my owne judgment, but that I think many perticuler persons may go before me, though by my degree I go before them; therefore if I shold say I wold not doe what youe request, it might peradventure be more then I thought: and to say I wold do it, might perhaps breed perill of that youe labor to preserve, being more then in youer owne wisdoms and discretions wold seeme convenient, circumstances of place and tyme being duely considered.'

11. The word is (? wrongly) deleted.

[Endorsed 'Queene Elizabethe's speeche and aunswer to the Lordes and Comones of Parlemente concerninge the proceedynge agaynste the Queen of Skottes'.]

The Lordes and Commons of the parliament throughe their humble suite and hir Majestie's gratious favor havinge accesse to hir royall person, my Lord Chauncellor for the Lords, and for the Commons Mr Speaker, made answere to a comaundement sent the Mondaie before from hir Maiestie to the parliament that they should advise and consulte together, whether possiblie the relme, religion and hir Majestie's person might be in safetie by anie other waie or meanes found but then by the death of the Scottishe Queen, which if they should doe, hir Majestye should be most glad and thinck hir self right happie for the same. The aunswere of my Lord Chauncellor and Mr Speaker was that both the Lords and the Commons had carefullie considered of hir Majestie's comaundement, and the matter beinge longe debated amonges them, and the opinion of everie one demanded, not one amonges them all did thinck that there was or could anie other waie be found for the suretie of hir Majestie and the realme then that conteined in their former peticion for the execucion of justice uppon the Queen of Scottes. And therefore they insisted thereuppon and humblie desyred hir Majesty to have consideracion thereof as the necessitie of the cause did require. To whome hir Maiestie then spake as foloweth.

'I perceave you have well considered of my last message [*etc.* as in Cambridge University Library Gg.iii.34, the journal of proceedings relating to Mary Queen of Scots, 15 Oct.–2 Dec. 1586.]

On Thursdaie the 24 of November

11. *Sir Walter Mildmay's speech for supply, 22 February 1587*

Text from BL Sloane 326, copy.
Other MSS. London: Harley 6265. Oxford: Bodley, Rawlinson C. 838.

Sloane 326, fos.105–11

xxiiij[to] *Februarii*[1] *1586.*   In the Common Hous.

The former speech was by Sir Christopher Hatton.[2]

'That which hath byn spoken may sufficiently informe us both of the perills hanging over this realme by malice of enemyes, and what in duety, and for necessity, we ought to do. And that is:

'To be ready with life, landes, and goodes[3] to serve and defend our most gracious Quene and her state against all dangers that may be attaempted, from the Pope, from Spayne, from the Guises, or from evill subiectes.

'And because as you heare greate thinges are threatned, against her Majestie and state,[4] from Spayne: we ought in tyme in this greate Councell of the realme, to provide a sufficient resistance against so mighty a storme that is
v.   comyng upon us, and is likely to fall upon / England, or Irelande, or both.

'England our native countrey one of the most renowned monarchies in the world, against which the Pope beareth a specially eye of envy and malice; envy for the wealth and peace that we enioy through the goodnes of Almighty God, powred upon our most noble Queen and her realmes, malice for the religion of the gospell which we professe; whereby the dignity of his triple crowne is almost shaken in peeces.

'This malice together with his desire of revenge, even to the subverting of this state, the Pope hath shewed both by open and secrete attempts. Open, as the rebellion in the north, the rebellions in Ireland, and the invasion into that realme by strangers; secrete by the practices of thoes false hipocrites, the Jesuites
f.106   and seminary preistes sent hither to / corrupt her Majestie's subiectes, and to stirr them up to rebellion, treason, and conspiracy, so farr as to take away the life of our Quene, so deare and precious unto us, and upon whom the saufegard of us all doth so much depende.

'All which, together with his practices and provocations of forreyne princes, do[5] overrunne this realme, are grounded upon that most ympudent and[6] blasphemous bull, published from Rome against the sacred person and estate of our gracious Queen, whereby is thundred out so proud a sentence of excommunicacion and deprivation, as it is now holden by the Pope and his favorers to be a thing not only lawfull but also meritorious, to destroy our Queen, to invade our countrey, and to destroy us all, as we should be no more a nation in the world.

'And though peradventure they will not be hasty to invade this / realme,   v. knowing how well we love our Queen and our countrey, and what a hard reckoning they shall fynde here if they offer us any wronge; yett it is not unlike that some of theis great prepayracions, so much bruted, will light upon the realme of Ireland, whereof we oughte to be no lesse carefull then of our owne countrey.

'For Ireland being a great kingdome and a principall flower of this crowne, having so continued above 400 yeres, we may not suffer any part thereof to be touched, except we will bring our owne into perill; for as Ireland is a large and fertile soyle, so is it furnished by nature with many notable havens, such as no land in this part of the world hath the like, so as if a mighty enemy should settle himself there, it is easy to see how dangerous such a neighboure would prove to the whole state of this realme. /

'Att both theis kingdomes our enemyes do shoote; and their scope is by   f.107 invasion and rebellion to subdue and conquere all, with purpose as yt seemeth to roote out from them the English nation for ever. And if it fall not out according to their desires, as with Godde's hellpe yt never shall, yet at the least they will do their best to trowble the Queen and her state, to burne, to spoyle, to kyll, to robb, and all other wayes to annoy us.

'The calamityes like to ensue thereby may be seene by the terrible flames raised by them in our neighbours' countreys, where you may behold fyre and sword, depopulating, and[7] wasting of cittyes, townes, and countreys, with all other miseryes that warre doth bring with yt.

'And as we ought to be carefull for our owne countrey, so we may not forgett[8] the countreys of Holland, and Zeland, and other provinces / united,   v. tyed[9] unto us both by ancient amity and by religion, which of all other is the strongest bonde that can be amongst people.[10]

'Theis her Majestie hath taken into her proteccion upon greate and necessary cawses, as you have heard. If shee should be driven to abandon and leave them now, then we are to looke for present danger to follow both to the Queen and all her domynions.

'For theis countreys being so nere as they be unto this, if the Spanyard

1. All MSS have 24 rather than (correctly) 22 February.
2. Harl. omits this note of Hatton's speech of 22 February (D'Ewes, pp.407–9).
3. Harl.: '. . . lief and godes (*sic*)'.
4. Harl. omits 'against her Majestie and state'.
5. Harl.: 'to'.
6. Harl. omits 'ympudent and'.
7. Harl. omits 'depopulating and'.
8. Harl.: 'neglect'.
9. Harl. omits.
10. Harl. omits 'that can be amongst people'.

possesse them agayne, and command[11] all at his will, then considering the great number of shipping that he shalbe able to make there, he may with little difficulty invade us when he list, and cutt of and ympeach the whole trade of our traffique, which is one of the greatest partes of our politie[12] and comon wealth, and will touch all the people of this land from the highest to the lowest. /

f.108   'Therefore to prevent all theis mischeifes and dangers[13] that be so evident and so yminent, if they be not foreseene: it is requisite that her Majestie do make a greater preparacion then at any tyme heretofore shee hath done.

'For seing our enemyes do advance themselves to the uttermost, and as it were do sett up their rest in their forces against us, it is necessary that we should be ready to answere them with the like.

'The rather for that their full intent now appeareth: for the exeqution of the Holy League, so much spoken of in the world, a plott longe agoe prepared by the Pope and his confederates to overthrowe the gospell in all places where the same is professed, as by their dealinges against her Majestie, against the King of Navaire, and against the protestant Princes, and states, of Germany hath byn lately made very manifest. /

v.   'So as greate and strong preparacion must of necessity be putt in readines by her Majestie both by sea and by lande.

'By sea is[14] one of the thinges we ought cheifely to regarde, being rightly termed the wall of England: for which her Majestie with her provident care is so furnished with great and good shipping for the warr, as in no age the like, and such and so many as no prince in Christendome may compare with.

'By lande God hath blessed her Majestie with nombers of good, valiaunt, and faithfull people, able and willing to adventure their lyves for the service of so gracious a Quene and defence of their countrey, so many indeed as none other prince is able to bring of his owne subiectes.

'Mercenary soldyers, what they are, how costly, how unsure, and how little
f.109   service done by them, other princes feele, and I trust we shall never / have cause to prove.

'To put all theis forces in order, and to maynteyne them by sea and by land with men, munycion, and other necessaryes, you can easely considre it wilbe requisite to prepare a greate masse of treasure, being as you know, termed of old, the synowes of the warre.

'The burden whereof you can easely see is and wilbe farr heavier then her Majestie of her owne shalbe able to beare without the helpe of the realme.

'And therefore yt behoveth us with franck and willing myndes to offer unto her Majestie such an aide as may sufficiently support her forces against thoes greate preparacions, entended to ruyne her and us all.

'This motion may seeme somewhat straunge to you, that not above two
v.   yeres past have granted a subsidy and two / ffifteenes as greate as any before that tyme. And in reason this might be thought somewhat to soone after th'other were yt not for two cawses that might leade you to thinke otherwise.

'One, the favorable taxacion used in all places for the subsidy being every tyme lesse then other, and by custome hard to be reformed: whereby not the sixth part of that which is given by the statute doth come to her Majestie's cofers.

'The other is the greate expence of treasure which her Majestie hath defrayed within that tyme for the defence of her state and her realmes; which hath byn so much as I dare assure you, all that was given the last parliament doth not amount much above th'one halfe of the whole charges, the rest being supplyed out of her Majestie's owne revennewes, a thing that princes / heretofore never used to doe; her Majestie thereby also avoyding borrowing upon interest, that did in tymes past so farr eate into the state of this crowne. f.110

'Her ordinary charges besides, as her houshold, the navy, the ordenance, the garrisons at Berwick and other places in England, and her standing garrison in Ireland are to be considered: for theis are to be verified by the recordes of her Majestie's treasure to be farr greater and larger then in the tyme of any forreyne[15] prince, which every man in his private expences can easely judge.

'All which being, as they are, most trew, lett us lifte upp our heartes and stretch out our handes to so greate and good a worke as this is; and spare for noe charge[16] to preserve the religion of the gospell amongst us, to save our most noble Quene, our countrey, our lives, landes and / libertyes, which our most malicious adversaryes seeke to deprive us of, if their powers were answerable to their willes. v.

'If yt be[17] thought that this present charge comyng so soone after the last wilbe over burdenous to the realme, lett yt be considered on the otherside, that except this provision be made in tyme, the burden wilbe greater hereafter: ffor if the enemye should take hold of any part of England or Ireland, or if he should be wholly master of the Lowe Countreys, as he seeketh,[18] then of necessity her Majestie shalbe forced to maynteyne greate and continuall armyes, both by sea and land, for the saufegard of her estate and of us all. The charge whereof must needes be so greate as yt will prove in th'end untollerable, and yett necessarily to be borne, / except we should suffer them to overrunne us at their pleasure. But if theis enterprizes now prepared against us be sufficiently resisted and disappoynted (as through the goodnes of almighty God there is no dowbt), then we shall fynde this present charge, if it were more, well bestowed, for we shall thereby discourage them for ever, and we shall still enioy all thoes good things which we have so long had: a liberty of consciences in the sincere profession of the gospell, and peace in freedome from civill and forreyne warres, which the Lord our God in his aboundant mercy by the ministry of our most gracious Queen hath largely powred upon us. f.111

11. Harl. omits 'them agayne and command'.
12. Harl.: 'pollicie'.
13. Harl. omits 'and dangers'.
14. Harl.: 'is'.

15. Harl.: 'former'.
16. Harl.: 'coste'.
17. Harl.: 'It is'.
18. Harl. omits: 'as he seeketh'.

Conclusio[19]
v.

'And therefore to conclude, seeing that we lyve under so gracious a Queen that hath don so many and so great / thinges for us,[20] and seing that the ymplacable malice[21] is such as we are to looke for at their handes all the mischeif they can bring upon us: itt behooveth us now presently to thinke upon theis matters, as the weight and necessity of them deserve; and so to shew ourselfes ready and willing towardes[22] our gracious Queen as she be not unfurnished of that which is needfull to answere so greate forces intended against her and us, that our enemyes fynding her Majestie in such a readines may either stay their malicious purposes, or if they do proceed, they may feele sufficient resistance to their owne confusion and the safety of us all.'

19. Rawl omits.
20. Harl. adds 'and seing that the preservacion of her lief and state is so deare unto us'.
21. Harl. adds 'of our enemies'.
22. MS repeats.

12. *Job Throckmorton's speech on the Low Countries, 23 February 1587*

Text from New York, Pierpont Morgan Library MA 276, copy.

The Pierpont Morgan Library MA 276,
(Phillipps MS 13891) pp.28–51.

'About some 20 yeares agoe and upwardes (as I take yt) there was a greate
meetinge and conferance at Bayun in the utmost confynes of all Fraunce
bordering upon Spayne, wheareunto were sente at that instante certayne
secrete messengers and agentes from sundrye quarters, as namely one from the
Emperor, one from the Holy Father, one from the Duke of Savaye, one from
the Scottishe Queene – I must not there leave out Queene Mother, for then
the pagente were not worth looking on. This vyage and metting had many
smoothe and goodly pretenses: one was for the French Kinge to visitte his
syster, then Queene of Spayne, whoe by appointment met him, attended upon
by the Duke of Alba and some othere nobles of that countrey; an other was to
heare the playntes and grievances of the distressed people of that quarter whoe
had byn strangely outraged by the Guysian faction, and this kinge wold needs
beare the worlde in hand forsooth that he would himselfe in person not only
be partaker of there griefes but redresse there miseries, to the terror of others
and the example to posteritye. But wee must marke what kinge yt was: yt was
the same king that wept to the Admirall over night, and gave him up to the   Charles the 9[1]
butcherye to bee cut in pieces in the morning. An other of his pretenses was
to viewe his navy which then was sayed to lye alonge that shoare. But what
soever the pretenses were (as in such cases, ye knowe, yt is noe harde matter
for prinnces to set on coulers) the worlde knowethe that the very
deseignemente of the whole consultation was nothinge els but a pestilente
conspiracye against the Churche of God and the professers of holy religion, as
by the prartyses[2] that did afterwarde bolte out might verye well appeare. /
    'Nowe yee must understand that the King of Spayne himselfe was not at this   p.29
meetinge, nor any of the greate ones afore mentioned, neyther the Duke of
Savoye nor any of the rest, no, the Cardinall of Lorayne himselfe was not there
(though I dare say for him, good man, hee would have beene lothe that such
an enterpriese shoulde have been taken in hand without his counsell), noe, nor
great man in ambassage from any of these: only certayne meane fellowes of
shrewde wytte, but of base accounpte and of no marke and name. And what
was the reasonn of that, a historiographer of theire owne dothe not let to tell

---

1. In another hand.   2. *Sic*; presumably 'practices'.

us: "*quo cautius et secretius sacrum hoc foedus sanciretur*", that all this bussynesse myghte bee contrived (as yt were) under a curteyne. He calles yt *sacrum foedus* because at this meeting there was a solemne othe and vowe taken on all sydes, with the sacrament received uppon yt at a holy Masse, to performe and put in execution such thinges as were then agreed uppon in cownsell.[3]

'And because ye shall not neede to doubte that so sacred an exercyse as the Masse is, dothe commenly bringe forthe fruites of the same sappe and nature that the tree is of; yee shall here (yf you please) see layed before you (as yt were) the *capitula* and sum of those thinges that were then agreed uppon in counsell very proportionable to the former conclusions of the Counsell of Trent, no doubte greately benefytiall to all Christendome yf they had taken

p.30   effecte: marke then[4] / (I pray you) well.

'The first was the rooting out of the house of Bourbon with all the Hugonots in France: one good fruit yet, and yf the rest be answerrable to this yt will make a man in love with the Masse, I trowe. The second was the sackinge of the cyttye of Geneva with the reducinge of those territoryes to the quyet obedience of the Duke of Savoye, who makes tytle to them. The third was the bringinge of the free estates in Germanye into an absolute subiection of the Empyre; a matter of greate difficultie and in a maner of impossibilitie, but yet the Masse woulde do yt, that is certayne: ffor yf yee will beeleeve theire legendes yt hath wrowghte as greate feates as that cometh to. The fourth was the pacifiinge of the troubles in the Lowe Countrey with the pruning out of suche as were suspected to bee of the religion (whereof there were not manye in that age) and the bringing all thinges there to the peaceable obedience of the Kinge of Spayne: to the effecting whereof the government of that countrey was within a whyle after (as ye knowe) allotted to the Duke of Alba. The fyfte and laste was not the least, I tell you, nay, it seemeth lyke wyse men they kept the best and weightiest for the last, as yt were to cloze up the mouth of all. And what was that? For sooth, the restoring of the pseudocatholyke relygion in Englande by deposing of Queene Elizabeth and settinge up the Scottishe Queene.

'How thinke yow? Would you wishe for any better fruites from suche a conferance? They say the Masse is an unblouddy sacryfice, but yet sure wee see yt hath the yll happe to end many times in verye shrewde and blouddie practises. Well, wee that have lived to see that wee have donne – the succese of all this conspiracie to fall owte noe better to there likeing, the house of Bourbon to bee on foote, and notwithstanding all those massacres as many or

p.31   rather more protestantes / in Fraunce then ever ther were; the cytye of Geneva and those terrytoryes (though yt may bee in some distresse) yet (thankes bee to God) nothinge neare that thralldome and miserye as was then levelled at; the free states in Germanye farre from any such absolute subiection as was dreamed of; the Lowe Countryes farther out of the obedience of the King of Spayne then at that tyme they were, and the number of those of the religion encreased; lastly, the Scottish dame by the good providence of God brought low to the dust, her Majestie florishing in the feare and favour of God: wee that have lived to see all this, what may wee say? May wee not trewly saye as was sayed of them of the tower of Babell?

> *"Edificat populus scansuram nubila turrim*
> *Confusis linguis dissipat hosce deus."*[5]

The kinges and princes of the earth assembled themselves and layed theire headds together against the Lorde and his annoynted; but he that sittes on high, even our Jehovah, hath laughed theire devises to scorne.

'About some foureteene yeare agoe there was a certeyne man taken in the northe, I have forgotten his name, but I well remember he was *valet de chambre du roy* – I might have sayed varlet *de chambre du roy* well enogh, for a wreched irreligious varlette hee was in deede – groome of the chamber to Charles the Ninth. This man was sent frome the Frenche King, for no good to Englande I warrante you, with certayne letters to the Scottishe Queen, certayne letters, tokens and an armour to the yonge Scottishe King. After he was taken, being conveyed up hither, he was by order from her Majestie and her honorable Councell sent downe agayne to deliver his message / and tokens to the Scottishe King. When hee came to Barwicke, hearing that thinges fell out crosse to his expectation, namely that Edingborow castle was then new taken[6] by that honorable gentleman of worthye memory, Sir William Drewry, he rappes mee out an othe and strykes his hand on his breaste: "I thinke", sayethe hee, "God be sworne Englishe, there is nothing will prosper agaynst the Queen of England." With what affection that wretched man spake yt, I knowe not. But sure, wee that have lyv[ed] in the eyes of all men so choked (as yt were) with blessinges of God beyond deserte, wee that have lyved to see her Majestie's lyfe, so deare unto us, pulled out (as yt were) even out of the lyon's jawes in despight of hell and Sathan, may trewly (not in any pryde of harte but in humblenesse of soule to our comfortes) confesse that in deede the Lorde hathe vowed himselfe to bee Englishe. p.32

'It is very trew in deede that the Holy Father hath cursed us to the verie depth of the grave, yf that would serve the turne. But what have wee lost by that? Sure it is worth marking, and mee thinkes yt is an argument unawnswerable to prove the Pope to bee that man described in the Apocalypse, I meane that man of sinne, that beast with the marke in his foreheadde,[7] to prove him, I say, to be Antichrist agaynst all writings and wreastinges to the contrarye, that look where he curseth, the Lorde continually blesseth, and on the contrary, where hee blesseth, the finger of Gode's wreath[8] is never from thence: marke yt I pray you well.

'Fraunce and Spayne hee hath stroked with his blessinges. Will yee a little in the eye of wisdome behould the judgement of God / upon those kinges and in the kinges uppon the kingdomes: for *quicquid delirant reges ple[c]tuntur* p.33

---

3. Cf. N. M. Sutherland, *The Massacre of St Bartholomew and the European Conflict, 1559–1572* (1973), pp.35–46.

4. *Sic.*

5. Cf. Gen 11:1–9.

6. i.e. May 1573 (by Sir William Drury).

7. Rev 14: 9.

8. *Sic.*

Achyvi.[9] The judgement of God can not lyghtly fall uppon a kinge but the whole state and body of the realme muste bleede for yt. For Fraunce, Katherin de Medices (I hope I neede not describe her) hath not many (thankes bee to God) lefte of her loynes to pester the earth with. And those that she hath yet lyving, trewly, to speake indifferently, she may have as much comforte of them as the adder hath of her broode; whether they sucked theyr mother's breastes I know not, but sure, yf they did not, it seemeth their nources were greately to blame in steede of milke to suckle them up with bloudde from their infancye. In which regarde Queen Mother may sure bragge above all women in Europe, that shee hath brought us into this worlde suche a litter (to her prayze bee yt spoken) as few women have don: *lupinos catulos jaucibus sanguinolentis natos in pernitiem ecclesiae*, whose principall delight (synce they came first out of the shell) hath bin in nothinge allmost but in hypochrisye, filthynesse of life, and persecuting of the Church of God.

'As to him that now holdeth the scepter there, doe ye not see him smiten [with] barreynesse? Is that all? Nay, doe yee not see him striken with a fearefull kynde of gyddynesse, as yt were a man in a traunce or extacye, not knowing amiddest all those garboyles which way to wynde himselfe to any certayne resolution for his life, sometimes to the Guisian faction, sometimes under hand to the King of Navarra, that a man may trewly say of him, *"umbras timet qui deum non timet"*, he is afrayed of shadowes that feareth not the Lorde. /

p.34   'For him of Spayne, whome yt lyketh some in this age to make so terrible unto us the rather to discorage us from this good motion of the Lowe Countryes, sure, as terrible as he is and though yt lyke the Pope never so much to blesse and to imbrace him as his oldest sonne, yet it seemeth hee is not exempted from the hand of God nether for all that. His profession we see superstitious, his religion idolatrous, his lyfe some thinke lycentious, his mariage wee all knowe incestuous, great uncle to his owne children, a sinne that must needes light full heavely uppon his soule without repentaunce; wherin allso, by the waye, is layed before us an other unavoydable marke of the antichristianisme of our Holy Father, that in the height of his pride hee dare doe that which no creature under the sunne, neyther saincte nor angell, no, not Lucifer himselfe, I thinke, durst ever presume to doe, that is, to dispense with the written revealed will of God: a pride of all prides. And yet hath the poore Spanish King in this case (such is his misery) non other shield to shadowe himselfe from the wrath of God but only a bare syly Romish dispensation, which, alas, in the day of his accoumpte will bee founde to weake a playster for so greevous a wounde. For a prince or a greate state to slyde, sometimes, to slyppe awrye or fall of frayeltie were an other matter, being a thinge incidente to fleash and bloudde; but to sticke or continue in sinne and in a knowen notorious sinne, to live and dye in the same, nay (that more ys) to leave behinde him the printe and impression of that his wretchednesse as a hatefull monument and recorde to posteritye – that is, his dominions to be

p.35   possessed by an incestuous race of bastardes – / that in his old age, when hee should have greatest comforte, hee may sitte him downe in his cheayre and behoulde the ruyne of his howse before his face: can there (thynke yow) come any greater plage to a prince then this?

'O, but yow will say, this is but his private faulte: hee is a mightye king for all that, many rich countreyes, populous nations, golden mines, and I know not what. It is trew in deed, we denye yt not, neyther ys his powere to bee contemned. But yet, as mightye as he is, it seemeth, by your leave, the Lorde hath put a snaffle in his mouth for all that. Yee knowe whate is sayed of the covetous man, "*avaro tam deest quod habet quam quod non habet*"; what use I pray you hath the covetous of all his goodes; what use, I would fayne knowe, hath the King of Spayne of all thease his dominions? Are they not all to him by a mightye hand of God an [MS blank], that is, rather a burden then a defense to the bearer? And yf yt be trew (as some thinke) that in the yeare's ende, when he cometh to some up his accowntes, his receites doe lyttle more then answeare his disbursementes, where is hee then? What miracles worketh hee amiddest all his wealth? Is he not forced mawgre his headde to make peace with the sworne enimye of all Christendome? A notable judgment of God.

'Nay, further, have we not lyved to see him stryken with a sottish kinde of madnesse and such an extraordinarye frenzye as I beleeve never prince nor father was smitten with all? That ys, to yealde to the drawing of the harte bloudde of his owne sonne, and to suffer his wife to bee in the house of Inquisition certayne dayes, / weekes, or monethes, and not to dare to mutter against yt: a strange case for a prince. And surely when I consyder how the poore gentleman ys in deede hampered with that wretched howse of Inquisition, that he dare doe nothing but by lyne and levell from their dyrection, let him seeme never so terrible to others, I must needes lyken him to a certeyne kinge in a Maygame, whom the constable sette by the heeles for his disorder.

'And thus yee see, a man with haulfe an eye may easely beholde the judgment of God uppon both thease kinges, notwithstanding the blessinge of the Holy Father. Whether any of them hath the leprosye of the body I know not, but wee are well assured both of them have the lethargye of the sowle, that ys the sleeping sycknes; yea, and I feare mee the sleeping sicknesse to deathe; stryken with blyndenesse, and the miserablest blyndnesse that ys, that ys the blyndnesse of holy religion, a pharoicall blyndnesse, a hardnesse of harte, that neyther the sound of the gospell nor the judgmentes of God can waken them out of theire drowsinesse and securitie: yf a man would wishe a plague to the deadlyest enemy hee hath, can his imagination conceyve a greater then this? And yet are they still shrouded under the blessing of the Holy Father. And there hardly lett them sticke for us; wee will never envy them that blissefull estate. This poore angle[10] of Englande his good fatherhoode (ye see) hath accursed: we thanke him for his kindenesse and wee thanke God for yt, and I beseeche the Lorde he may curse us still, that God infinitely may blesse us. /

9. Cicero, *De Divinatione ad M. Brutum*, I,   10. *Sic.*
    16 (and Horace, *Epistulae*, I, 2, 14).

p.37   'Yet, by the way, this is not spoken neyther to lull us in the cradle of securitie, thereby to glaver our selves with any pleasing conceyte, or false perswation of our betternesse or deserte above other nations. I hope both prince and people have long agoe imprinted this lesson in their harts, "*si peccatum est, si meritum, non sed Christi*". I hope wee have all learned to say with the prophet, 'To thee, o lord God belongeth mercy, to us shame and confusion of face,' *etc.*[11] For, yf all thease our forrayne enemys were by a wounderfull metamorphosis become so many sworne and assured frendes unto us, yet were it no hard matter (ye know) for the Lord to shyver us and shatter us in peaces for all that. Hee that can fill our land with flyes and greshoppers to our destruction and mak the verye sune (which shineth to our comfortes) to parch us to the verye death yf [it] please him, ys yt not good trembling under his hande, thinke yow?

'And therefore yf any man be so unwise to thinke that in this our peaceable estate serving us as a sheilde of securitie wee have not so greate neede to loke about us, nor so greate cause to bethink our selves as other nations where the fiery broyles are yet unextinguished, let him remember Phillip of Macedon whoe after he harde thease joyfull newes all at one instante, how his horse hade

p.38   woone the bell at the Olympian / games, his lifetenant Parmenio had overcome the Illyrians in batayle, his wife Olimpyias had brought him a sonne to succeede him in his kingdome, was so farre frome triumphinge and insulting uppon yt that hee fell fourthewith to lifte up his handes to the heavens, praying his fayned gods that after so greate good happe hee mighte bee scourged with some competent misfortune. Well knew the heathen kinge (thoughe the trew and living God were to him unknowen) that nothing continuethe long in one state on earth; that blessings and crosses come *in alternis vicibus*, by course; that after the comedye of good happe is ended, then looke for the tragedye of mishap to followe. Therefore sythens hee knew hee must bee plauged, his desyer was to bee plagued within a measure.

'And surly yf with a sengle eye wee doe weigh yt well there is other maner of good newes to be brought unto us then ever was to Phillip. For yf yt be trew that in the middest of forreyne broyles wee only have hitherto sate safe at home; yf yt be trew that for thease 28 or 29 yeares togeather wee have enioyed a rare and blessed peace, to the astonishment of our neighbours rounde about us; yf yt be trew that her Majestie's government, compared with her progenitors', bee in wisedome equall, in mildenesse and mercye superior to them all;

p.39   yf yt bee trew that no wretched / practise of all the rable of our conspirators cold never yet lay holde on her Majestie's person to the wounding of Gode's Church (such hath been the mighty and mercyfull hand of our God towardes us): yf all thease thinges, I say, bee trew, as with any face they can not well be denyed, what are wee then to doe but to pray with Phillip of Macedon and to desyre our immortall and everlyving God that after all thease good blesseinges it would please him to vissite us with some competente and moderate scourge, to lay no more uppon us then he gives us strength and patience to beare, and when he doeth strik us (as he ys all dead fleash that lookes not for it) it may be don with a fatherly hande or as the pitifull mother doeth, watering her stripes with teares.

'Wee are not sure so buzzardly blynd to thinke wee shall allwayes escape the rodde, allwayes enioy thease Alcion dayes of peace, allwayes have manna in our mouthes: yf nothinge els yet *rerum humanarum vicissitudo*,[12] the chawnge and whirling about of the affayres of the worlde will preache unto us the contrarye. Yf in safety to dreade dawnger, and in the highest seate of our felicitye to have an eye to afterclappes, bee thought wisdome even in common policye, what brutishe unsensiblenesse ys yt in us amiddest such bitter fruites as wee [see] dayly blossome forthe to feede our selves still with a wan hope of Gode's patience, yet more patience, and no repentance? Surely, to speake indifferently, our God hath forborne us even longe enough, neyther ys there any nation under the heaven that may more rightly and by good tryall say that Jehovah is the God of patience, long suffering, / slowe to wrath and of greate compassion,   p.40 then may the Englishe nation. Therefore (as I sayed before) this is not spoken to rocke us asleepe in the cradle of securitie or (as the prophete sayeth) to lay pillowes under our elbowes.[13] The drifte of this whole discourse hathe been to none other ende then this: only to lay before us that the cursing of theire unholy father and the blessinge of our hevenly Father doe comonly light in one subiecte, very proportionable to that which is written in the 109[th] Psalme,[14] which methinkes may right[l]y bee verefyed on her Majestie: Though the[y] curse, yet thow shalt blesse; confusion shall be upon all those that rise up against mee, but thy servant shall reioyce.

'And even now agayne as yf the Lorde had dealte sparingly with us heare to fore, or as yf the fountaynes of his mercy had ben restrayned to this day, beholde (as yt were) a new supplye and freashe charge of the blessinges of God uppon us, beyonde all expectation. Beholde, I say, an evidente signe that the Lorde hath yet once more vowed himselfe to bee Englishe, notwithstanding all our former unthankefullnesse and wret[c]hed desertes to the contrarye: that is, this offer of the Low Countreyes, a thing, no doubte, that our forfathers wold have benne gladde of, a thing that her Majestie's progenitors the kinges of the lande would willingly have redeemed with any price. Beholde, I say, this so rar[e] and extraordinarie and[15] blessing by the good providence of God fallen (as yt were) into our lappes unloked for, as / yf the Lord should say to us from   p.41 heaven: "Will[16] I see the complots and snares that are layed against you on every side; I see the driftes of Sathan and his suportes againste you[r] prince and countrey; I beholde the curssinges and banninges of tha[t] strumpette of Babylon; I see the rage of Spayne and the dissembled league of Fraunce; I see the distempered humors of yll affectted subiects within your owne bowells. All thease and everye of thease and whatsoever is els in the ymagination of man's harte to worke your mischiefe is cleare and manyfest before me. And though

---

11. Cf. Dan 9: 7.
12. Cf. Terence, *Eunuchus*, Act 2, scene 2, 44.
13. Ezek 13: 18.

14. Verse 28.
15. *Sic*.
16. *Sic*. presumably 'well'.

your sinnes do swarme in aboundance, yet I know yt is not for your synnes' sake, but for my name's sake, and the holy religion that you professe that this wretched generation doeth hate yow. And therefore, yf you will contynew still in my feare, yf yee will reverence me hencforthe, not in lippes only, but in soundnesse and syncearitye of harte, yf ye will refourme your Church and lyves in tyme, I will here offer yow a meanes wheareby ye shall bee able to stande alone, ye, and to withstande all the forayne invazions of your ungodly enemyes. Yee shall well perceyve and the world shall knowe that I can even in this age make Jonathan and his armour bearer alone able enough to daunte a whole hoste of the uncircomcysed Phillistynes", *etc.*

p.42   'Thus and thus it seemeth to mee that the Lorde doeth, as it were, sounde in our eares concerninge this cause / wee have in hande, being in deede a cause of that importaunce to us ward as in the reiectinge or the refusall thereof I can see nothinge but a fearefull beholding of some lamentable distresse in time to come. I know the Lorde in his infinite power can worke without meanes, as he can feede the bodye without breade; but yet willfully to reiecte the meanes when yt is offered, what is it els but to tempte the Lorde and provoke his wrathe? Yf yt be wisdome then to use meanes but not to trust in meanes, then let us a lyttle cast our eye rounde aboute us to see (yf we neglecte this offer of the Low Countreyes) where els there ys any other meanes, (for that ys a matter to be thought uppon), any other anchorholde of safetye, any other assured frinde or neighbour to relye uppon, so nigh us, so neere us and every way so importing us as this.

'Spayne ye knowe ys our sworne and professed enemye. And what better reckening, I pray you, can wee make of our deare brother of Fraunce? Wee have in deede a certeyne league with him, but alas ye know this cheyne will soone bee unriviled because yt hath not so muche as one lynck of Christianitye to holde by. And howsoever wee league yt or temporize yt with him wee may rest assured he ys in a farre deep[er] league with Spayne.

'They both, ye know, are *filii dilecti* of the Holy League, that ys, sworne to keepe no league nor faythe with heretikes (for so they repute us), and wee poore abiectes stande excommunicate. What trust then I pray yow in such a league fellowe? And will yee see the right portrayture and discription of this our league brother? Then looke uppon wretched Parrye's letter[17] to her
p.43   Majestie and there / yee shall see him notably featured out in his coulers that all the pensills of the best phisiugnomors in Fraunce are not able more lyvely to lay him fourth unto yow: the French King (sayeth hee) is Frenche, yow know him well enough; yow will finde him occupied when hee should doe yow good; hee will not loose a pillgrimage to save their[?] kingdome, *etc.* I promise yow for mine owne parte I beleeve yt. Therefore trust him they that liste and league yt with him as ye will, yee shall finde this to bee an undeceyveable rule while ye lyve: in whom there is no religion, in him there is no trust. Wee have hade to late and lamentable experience of yt in treacherye of som of our lewde countrey men beyonde the seas. But I doubte not the Lorde will fynde them and ferette them out well enough; I never knew yt

otherwise yet (marke yt when ye will) but he that sowed in treason did reape in vengeance. Well, in whom ther is no religion, in him there is no trust: a Frenchman unreformed is as vile a man as lyves, and no villeynye can make him blushe. Whether then shall wee cast our eye? Northewarde towardes the younge impe of Scotlande? Alas, it is a colde coast (ye knowe) and he that should sette up his rest uppon so younge and wavering a headde might happen finde colde comforte to, I tell yow. Yee knew his mother (I am sure) did ye not? Then I hope yee will all joyne with mee in this prayer, that whatsoever his father was, I beseech the Lorde he take not after his mother, for then woe and double woe [to the] church of God. And how hee may degenerate from the humour of his auncesters I know not. /

'I know not, but I have harde yt sayed of a boye that [1½ lines crossed out] as *accidens inseparabile*. But I will not so much [MS blank] this king as wholy to balance his disposition, eyther by disent or by the naturall infection of his countrey: for yt may bee religion and good education hath cleared from that corruption, as wee hope yt hath and wee judge the best. In which regarde, as yt shall not bee amisse for us to pray for him, so neyther can yt bee amisse for her Majestie to carye still a jealous and wakefull eye over him. What secrete intelligence Doctor Alen hath I know not, but this I wote well, that in his publyke *Apologye*[18] hee gives him a shamfull commendation. How thinke yow then? May yt not serve as a reasonable *caveat* for her Majestie to suspecte him, when a man of Alen's humour falles a praysing of him; when Lovayne and Doue and that rable of our English seminaryes beyonde the sea have such an inwarde lyking of him, can hee bee an yll–mynded subiecte amongste us that there uppon crieth "*Latet anguis herba*",[19] and feareth some mischief to bee abroche?

'Well, then, wee see no hope of Spayne, no trust in Fraunce, colde comforte in Scotlande: whether then shall wee directe our course? When all thease passages are estopped, is there any man amongst us so dimme sighted that doeth not heere playnlye behold the very finger of God directing / us (as yt were) by dyametre to the Low Countreys, as who should say, "There only is the meanes of your safetye, there only is the passage layed open unto yow, there only and no where els is the vent of your commodityes." And in deed I have harde yt credibly sayed that Holland and Zealand alone are able to make more shipping then hawlfe the realme of Englande, a matter of wisdome to bee consydered of to him that eyeth well our estate, ffor *omnis natura* (ye know) *querit conservationem sui*, even by the very instincte of nature everye thinge thirsteth yt selfe.[20] Therefore, yf wee should now bee so bewitched to sitte downe (as yt were) and to suffer the unbridled fury of the Spaniarde to overrune that poore distressed nation, where were wee then? Might wee not then happen to crye with rufull cheare, all to late: "*Tum tua res agitur paries dum proximus ardet*".[21]

p.44

p.45

---

17. i.e. of confession.
18. i.e. for the colleges at Rome and Rheims (1581).

19. Virgil, *Eclogues*, 3, 93.
20. *Sic.*
21. Horace, *Epistulae*, I, 18, 84.

And in such an ingratitude how iustly might the Lorde expostulate with us in the day of our visitation? Nay, ye that were nothing touched with the miseryes of our brethren, yee that had no bowelles of compassion to see your neighbours' conduytes runne bloudd, shall now crye your selves till yee bee comfortlesse and languishe in teares without hope. And what els might wee then looke for as the dewe hyre of our desertes but that some easterne winde showlde by Gode's just judgment arize to blow the remaynder of those sparckles hitherward, thereby to kindle an unqueanchable flame (which the Lord divert) even in our owne bowells? And yf the Lorde should so deale with

p.46   us, were yt not *eadem mensura*? / Were hee not still a righteous God? Therefore wisdome biddes have an eye to this geare in time and beware of *sero sapere* whyle yee lyve.

'Now for the lawfullnesse of the action I hope there bee no man heere that doubtes of yt, for yt is well enough knowen that those countreys are not, nor never were, as Spayne is, that is, any absolute governement without limitation eyther to the king himselfe or any of his predecessors. It is knowen that upon the infringement of their awntient priviliges, as the bringing in of strangers, or the enforcement of them to the bondage of any foreyne yoke, and such lyke, they are fourthwith discharged of theire feaultye and alleagaunce, and at their libertye make choyce of any other governor whatsoever. This, I say, is knowen, and I have hearde yt credibly sayed to bee of awncient recorde in the court of parleament at Paris at this day, where uppon Monsieur was enstalled (as yee know) Duke of Brabant, even by the assent and allowaunce of the Frenche King himselfe. And is not the Frenche King a Catholyke, I pray yow? I trow hee bee: hee deceiveth the worlde els. Then yt is a cleare case that the King of Spayne (howsoever hee holde there now by Stafforde law, as they say, that is by the swoorde)[22] hath in truth and equitie lost the right of his soveraignetye even by the judgment of the Catholykes themselves. And yf yee aske mee how hee hath lost yt, I answeare, by tyrany and bloudde, or rather, yf ye will, by the just judgement of God (who supplanteth the wicked and blouddethirstie in a moment): ffor as yt is trew on the one syde that *justitia et*

p.47   *charitas validae sunt principis / arces*, so yt is as trew on the other syde (marke yt when ye wille) that *nulla tyrannorum vis diuturna fuit*.

'For the people of that countrey themselves, I doubte not but they desyre even from the bottome of their hartes to lyve under the obeysance of her Majestie before any other prince or potentate of the earth. In deede yt may bee that heeretofore, when our people went stragling thither I know not how, without any grounde or warrant eyther of law of God or man, seeking rather their owne private gaine by spoyle then tendering the miseryes of their brethren; it may bee (I say) that then they hadde no such liking of our nation. But sence that time now they have once tasted of the sweetenesse and equallitye of her Majestie's government under an honorable Generall (why[23] by his wisdome hath emblazoned her name there and renowned her scepter to posteritye) I perswade my selfe that now they thyrst for nothing more then to lyve under the happie subiection of so Christian a governesse.

'Well, her Majestie hath allready published to the view of the worlde certeyne causes of her honorable deseignementes in that action, sufficient in truth to satisfye any man that will bee satisfyed with reason. In deede there are a certeyne fyre of good fellowes in this age who bleede still on the discontented vaine, whom nothing can satisfie but bloudde: thease her Majestie must never looke to satisfie with reason. It is sufficient therefore that she doeth therein satisfie her owne conscience and the children of God: ffor the rest, *macrescant invidia et pereat spes impiorum*. Amonge those causes alleaged / by her Majestie   p.48 there is one very notable, on, yf ye marke yt, most worthye of a Christian prynce and worthy to bee recorded to all posteritye: that shee there professeth to enter the action for Gode's cause, to procure them safety (sayeth she, for those are the very wordes) to the honour of God, that they may serve him syncearely as Christian people according to his holy woorde. That is in playne Englishe to succour the afflicted for the cause of religion, ffor as Tully sayth of *patria* so may wee more trewly say of *ecclesia, omnes omnium charitates ecclesia una complexa est.*[24] A cause that a prince may thanke God that ever he was borne to sette in foote in, yea, and yf the hazard of his kingedome should come in question for this cause, hee were to lyfte up his handes to heaven and to give God thankes for yt. Therefore as the Romans writte in theire enseignes (but for their owne glory) "*Parcere subiectis et debellare superbos*",[25] so her Majestie may thinke herselfe happye, yf the Lorde will vouchsafe her that honour, trewly to write in her enseignes (not for her owne glory, but for his glorye and the comforte of his Church) "*Sceptrum afflictae ecclesiae consecratum*": which may bee to her as a seale of her happynesse, a testimony of her election, a comforte to her even in the agonies of death, and an undoubted argument of Gode's greate mercie towardes her, in that he hath called her out (as yt were) from among the other wretched prynces of the earth to make her his good instrument to succour the afflicted members of his crucified sonne – a favour that the Lord hath not imparted to every prynce, I tell yow.

'Now, albeit this cause be never so worthy a cause, / the people of that   p.49 nation in all humblenesse desyring yt, the regarde of our own safetye (yf wee tender our posterytye) enforcing yt, the cause of God and religion exacting it at our handes, yet is yt to be feared that the crookednesse of our age will neverthelesse afforde us some to woorke in countermyne agaynste yt. But what bee they? They bee, I dare warrant yow, of the gallantes of the worlde that can discourse yt att will, that can shew yow *Terra Florida* in the mappe, that had rather bee skillfull in everye thing then sounde or well affected in any thing. Such bee they in whoses[26] mouthes nothing soundes well but loyaulty and peace, whose hartes yet, yf they were opened, I feare mee there would bee founde within the impression of some treacherous and blouddy swoorde. But cursed and twyce cursed bee hee (I hope yee will all joyne with mee in this

22. 'Stafford law' is club law, the pun being on 'staff'.

23. *Sic*; presumably 'who'.

24. Cicero, *De Officiis*, 1, 57.

25. Virgil, *Aeneid*, 6, 8, 53.

26. *Sic*.

extra[c]tion) cursed bee hee that waketh at his owne advauncement and sleepeth at her Majestie's safetye, that overtreadeth all thinges that may endawnger her person and starteleth at every thing that may come neare his owne.

'Well, but yf wee goe with this action wee shall sure pull Spayne on our headdes, yow will say. And so hadde wee better doe I take yt (yf there bee no remedye) then to pull the wrath of God on our heades. I have hearde yt by credible gentlemen reported of King Edwarde that in such a lyke case as this is, when some of his Councell had told him that yf hee tooke such a course, or yf hee did not temporize a little, hee woulde sure pull some of the kinges his neighbours on his heade, hee made them this answeare: "Why, (sayeth hee)
p.50   yee are deceyved in mee. I trust to lyve to have / them all uppon mee, yea, all the princes in Europe mine enemyes, only for this cause of religion": a notable resolution of a Christian prince who knew right well that he never stoode alone whom God and his angelles did assist. Elizaeus' servant, mentioned in the booke of Kinges[27], uppon the sight of so huge an army of the Assyrians as did environe them, grew (as yt should seeme) in a great feare and sayde, "Alas, mayster, what shall wee doe." Marke Elizaus' awnsweare: "Feare not, (sayeth hee) for those that are with us are more then they that are with them." With that his eyes beeing opened hee behelde the mountayne overspreade with horses and chariotes of fyre, that is with the host of heaven. Even so, yf yt would please the Lorde that in this honorable and Christian defence of the Low Countreyes wee might now take such course as wee might thereby bee assured with Elizaeus of the host of heaven on our syde, then were it not the armie of fleashe that wee should neede to feare. In deede, yf the Lorde once fight againste us, then no marvell yf every little noyze bee as the sounde of a pasinge bell, and every wynde as a blaste of dispayre unto us: for *horrendum est* (ye know) *incidere in manus dei viventis.*[28]

'No, no, yf wee examine yt aright it is some thing els. It is neyther Spayne nor Fraunce that wee have cause to feare. It is our owne synne and wretchednesse, yea, our contynuance and delight in synning, that doeth dayly breathe for vengeance, our uncercumcised hartes, our unreformed lives, our hipochrisye, our outward shew of religion without any inwarde touch o[f]
p.51   conscience: our / bodyes are in Englande, our harts are at Rome. And (yf ye marke yt) the reformation of our lyves is in many poyntes much after the reformation of our Church at this day: outwarde conformitie and obedience to the law of man is in a maner the whole some of our religion in this age. This is the very thinge that our spirituall governors seeme to desyre and this the only thing that our carnall gospellers seeme to practize.

'Therefore for the redresse of thease, yf yt would please the Lorde so to worke onc[e] in her Majestie's harte that her poore people of the lande might bee throughly instructed and trew Christian discipline[29] established, that thereby our lyves might bee reformed and the wrath of God pacified: then should she not fayle to heare the Lord sound in her eares as hee did some tyme to Josua, "As I was with Moyses, so will I bee with thee; I will not fayle thee nor forsake thee, neyther shall there bee a man able to withstande thee all the dayes of thy lyfe."[30] And then should wee not neede to feare eyther the fury of Spayne or the treacherye of Fraunce or the hoste of the Assirrians or all the power of hell and darkenesse; then might wee safely say, in confidence of Gode's favour, "*Irruat in nos universa papistarum cohors*"; then might wee rest assured with Paule that neyther heighth, nor depth, nor life, nor death, nor awngelles, nor principalityes, nor powers, nor[31] thinges present, nor thinges to com, should bee able to separate us from the love of God in Jesus Christ, whose kingdome the Lorde hasten for his electes' sake.'[32]

27. 2 Kgs 6: 15–7.
28. Heb 10: 31.
29. *Sic.*
30. Josh 1: 5.

31. The words 'nor principalities, nor powers, nor' are obscured or deleted.
32. Rom 8: 38–9.

13. *Committee's debate on the Low Countries, 24 February 1587*

Text from BL Harley 6845, original in the hand of John Puckering, Speaker.

Harley 6845 fos.34–9

[Endorsed by Puckering (f.35v.) 'Comittees debating about assistans for mayntenance of the Low Cuntryes' and 'Ne semble que la Royne veut emprendre le soverayntie sur cet offer de benevolens l'ou nous nyt tye a maynt et contynew ce benevolens'.]

f.36 *24 Februarii* 1586. *Apud comittee.*

[Mr Wrothe][1] 1. Pour nede: d'embracer ce effectualment les Low Cuntryes.

Sir Walter 2. Pour encorager luy d'offer de nous mesme (ove espe que le pays veut fayr
Myldmaye semble) [de][2] nostre[3] benevolens, comme voluntarie subsidye pour 2, 3 ou
plusieurs ans si le gwer cy long contynue,
a preserver people
tye par ancien amytie
par strayter bond, scilicet religion,
tyercement pour avoyder dangerous neighbour;
mes si par soverayntye, vel autrement [left a luy][4] pour[5] ayd al eux, a leave a
luy[6] a consyder.

Mr Wrothe Que son meanyng qu'el prendra soverayntie.

Sir Thomas That we come for consultacion and every consultacion must be iust, honorable
Cicyll and nedefull.

Mr Tresorer[7] Question sy l'offer de benevolens sur condycion qu'el prendra soverayntye:
vel qu'el maynt le cause, que le Low Cuntrye ne myttera lours testes subs
Spaynes pees,[8] vel qu'ils maynt lour privilleges.
Il ne semble bon a mover a prendre soverayntie, mes que nous assist eux de
lour (et nostre) enemyes.
Issent que lour et nostre defens etant perfourme cibien en l'un comme en
l'autre suffist,
quar el peut maynt lour forces, lour resistans, lour privilleges sans soverayntie;
mes a preferrer qu'en nostre opynion le soverayntie est le myelx,
mes nei d'offer nostre benevolens ove tyeng condycion que sy el ne accept le
soverayntye qu'el n'avera ryen.

Mr Bembrig[9] En religion ils sont devyde, si Spain peut par pact traher peace et d'avoir
monarchie over them, nous ne poymes estre en peace.
Ideo mielx a maynt gweres versus luy abrode,

et a prendre soverayntie si el voile.

Mes si el prest que proteccion par auncien league: donque d'avoir frank traffyk sans avoir corporacions, c'est cause de mover nous en amitye d'ayd eux.

Mes le matter que nous desyer est d'estre sure d'avoir ce que nous loke for, et nei estre disceyve de ce.

Nostre scope d'occupye King Spain la ove foren force plus tost qu'il occup nous icy.

A leave ce a sa Majestie, comme temps discryera, quid best.

Mes en nostre opinion nous plus desyer qu'el prendra soverayntie.

Mes si d'assister them ce serve nostre purpos, a fayr diversyon del Spanish forces that waye quel autrement peuvent estre employ versus nous (quar nous ne seke conquest).

Ne nous ne sache si le soverayntie offer al nous quar n'avomes l'enstruccions qu'autres ont.

Le bond, humanitie de distressed; de religion; de utilitye pour traffyk. /

Il entend le question sy soverayntie, nec ne.

Si l'accion estre undertake

soit answerable,

just,

vel [conscyonable][11] nedefull[12].

Le pais distres quia nobillitye distressed and put away.

Just quia [comerse et][13] pactes entre nous et lour subiectes (et nei soverayns). Nedefull pour comerse pour traffyk et trade.

Pour ce que charges la Royne par occasion grand en Irland, auxi en Scotland, a subdue faccion et force ayd la.

Et darrenment en le jades expenses en Flanders (quel ce subsidye ne contervayle).

Ideo nedefull d'ayder la Royne ove benevolens en quel le myelx sort et nei poore sort estre charge.

Le matter ad este[14] debate devant Royne mesme par counsellers, etant d'amb partes reasoning al darrein agre estre emprest pour honorable, just, et nedefull pour profyt.

Just devant Dew d'assister, uphold and maynt religion la encrease et advance la plus nostre aydes mys la:

null warre cy iust comme ce que garr[ant?] par God.

Just et garr[ant?] devant men est pour assistans

Mr Francis
Bacon

v.
7 Mr Edgecombe[10]
8 Mr Harbert,
Mr Requestes

9 Mr
Vicechamber-
layne[15]

---

1. Deleted.
2. Deleted.
3. Inserted.
4. Deleted.
5. *Sic.*
6. Inserted: 'pour . . . luy'.
7. Sir Francis Knollys.
8. *Sic*; i.e. 'feet'.
9. Robert Bainbridge.

10. Puckering(?) appears to be counting the individual speakers, though Mildmay is later designated '10', despite already having spoken (above).
11. Deleted.
12. Inserted.
13. Deleted.
14. i.e. '*a été*'.
15. Sir Christopher Hatton.

par quel el prest rien del King Spain ne a prommyser ascun a luy mesme.
El ne prest null profyt de luy.
El n'empech King Spain privelleges et profytes.
Son entent suscipere bellum ut unde pax oriatur.
Le comiseracion del afflycted d'eux
                de nostre sank[16]
                de nostre nomme par mar[riage] la.
Regie est succurrere lapsus.[17]
Est honorable a prendre tiell matter, cy garr[ant?], quia ne procede de malyce, ambycion, covetousnes, ne vaynglorye: mes
est de necessitye et profytable preserver proximes vicynes, tum tua res agitur, etc.
Neclect them. Lose domynion of narrow seaes and put ynto the mightie monarce's handes that all the world cannot now gyve him, scilicet, navygacion.
Donque ad argent del Indiaes.
Nous styfle en nostre traffykes et suffocate en nostre comodyties icy.
Vide comment mightie est en Germanye ore.
Whither shall we carye our comodyties s'il ad Low Cuntryes? /

f.37   Ad este pollicye de par[d] de la a stopper nostre vent de drape.
Veut vent ses wolles en Low Cuntryes l'ou nostre serve.
Il veut mytter en tielx lyew ou nostres vyendra a styfle nous, quar Spain plus riche en wooll qu'England est.
Ce prova ces payes estre nostre profyt,
quia a defendre eux gentes et pays
le market overt et bon et bref retorne.
Perder eux perder toutes.
Ceo nyt solement matter en nostre oyels.[18]
Le comissyoners de France pour maryage[19] brake out en parler that in no wise Spain peut avoir Low Countryes en monarch degre;
quar donque ce part Christendom ne peut ce endure.
Et move que nous et ils take part par partes, set out.
Le fyne que nous veut emprendre ove justice et equitye.
Et ils veulent avoir ce in droyt et en proprietie, scilicet soverayntye.
Sur ce nous grew cold et le treatye brake of.
Par quel appiert les Frences voy les Low Cuntryes cibien comme nous.
Le Gwyes crew ore cy potent par purse Spanish que overrule le roy de France.
Le purpos la League bien sache a overrunne nous toutes.
Consyder: sans nous ils ne peuvent stand
              grand charges darrein an, nous la expend
              et grand honor al nostre natyon pour ceo.
Il semble que crowne Anglais ne peut emprendre Low Cuntryes sans grand ayd del subiectes d'Angliter,
quar donque gwer versus Spain, et toutes ses confederates, autrement suffocate en nostre commodityes at home.

Avomes confydens en la Royne, qu'el ne veut [spend][20] save[21] halfpeny del subiect, mes qu'el ne veut saver farthing de sa soe.

Si estoymes del subsidye, el must expend solonque la rate, comme peut last par temps, et nei tout al un temps.

Ceo assistans ew, ne veut maynteyner les Low Cuntryes.

L'offer del Low Contryes:

1. de soverayntie.   Quel parta ove ce nomme a paier pour
                     ceo, en charge proper a defendre ce.
2. de proteccion.   Mesme le semble charge.
3. si null de eux accept, donque de assistans. /

En ceo regard les fertes et forces del [Holland and Zeland][22] enemye[23] [et la a   v.
repell eux][24] a voyer quel forces nostre amyes avoir a repell eux;

comment peuvent resister l'enemye,

et comment peuvent estre maynteyne.

Lour account ne sustayne mes par nostre charge and present expens;

et d'estre repaye sur la peace (pour quel avomes volles)

fait requyer que 5000 footemen et 1000[25] horsemen

al yceux ad et serra honorable paye,

quar null fault de ce en la Royne, quar el ad pay tant

comme el doyt payer.

Il pitye vous a voier nostre returned soldiours want,

ce fait par autres que doyt paier, quar Low Cuntryes nyt hable quant alomes al camp nyt pour men ne pour vytayle,

Et donque fait mys icy pour voluntaryes, et issent grant quant ils vyent la toutes ala en camp et bon successe, l'enemye retyre donque, quant nous hable avoir la campe.

Mes ceux voluntarye English del States paye, queux vyent [nyt] home nyt paye.

Poyes voier par ce que ceux gentes nyt hable a payer et s'ils want ayd perhaps veulent slyder de nous.

Que par humble peticion al Royne a move le cause d'emportans al Royne et   10 Sir
l'estate le roylme.   Walter
                                                                           Myldmaye
Ideo d'embrace more roundlye:

1. d'entend le dispocicion sa people;
2. d'encorage luy a proceder, d'offer benevolens de nous.

16. i.e. 'sang'.
17. i.e. 'lapsis'.
18. i.e. 'yeux'.
19. i.e. with Alençon: see e.g. W. T. MacCaffrey, *Queen Elizabeth and the Making of Policy, 1572–88* (1981), pp.271–9.
20. Deleted.
21. Inserted.
22. Inserted and deleted.
23. Inserted.
24. Deleted.
25. See C. Wilson, *Queen Elizabeth and the Revolt of the Netherlands* (1970), p.86 citing J. Du Mont, *Corps Universal Diplomatique* (The Hague 1725), v.454: article 2 said that the Queen should be repaid within five years of the signing of a peace.

Nous poimes mettre nostre wishing del un plus del autre.

Si vyendra en question si l'un plus fyt que l'autre, ce veut fayre question quel nei ore fist pour nous a disputer;

3. le maner del execucion del benevolens, quar mielx ne unque offer en pays, que ne bien performe.

Issent que ne serra conus al Roy Spain la want de bon volunt del pays.

Mr Alfourd   De offer nostre opynion. Depuis qu'est offer soverayntie al Royne que nous semble fyttest (sans preiudycer sa opynion et counsell) que prester subsidye (el trouvera subiectes redye largelye nyt pour iour ne pour an) pour assister de ce. Par soverayntie el ad comaundement et profyt, quel en temps peut easer nostre present burden.

Et men veulent aler willinglye al sa Majesties service, et nei a lours et hope de melyor pay, qu'ils fount. /

f.34   Le Low Cuntryes n'entend soverayntie autrement qu'a preserver lour privilliges
Mr Treasorer   comme ils avaient d'autre prynces, et nei pour nous a comaunder lour purses a nostre pleasure.

Distinguishe. Si emprest soverayntie ils entend s'ils dona weke assistans vel nei, que la Royne maynteynera le gwer, quel est le matter les States desyer.

Mes d'assistans, le Royne nyt tye al eux s'ils ne dona tyell mayntenans comme serve bien la Royne.

Mr Vyce-   Si nous enter fortement averomes le soverayntye quant nous pleist, vel d'avoir
chamberlayne   tiell peace comme nous mesme volomes.

Et ces iours opera bien conus et contynew,

veut further ceo woorke al grand purpose,

et est tyell consultacion comme ce royalme n'avait ce 100 ans.

12 Mr Attorney   Mova d'entrer en proporcion quel chescun payera, mes ce generalment denye;
Wardes[26]   mes d'estre voluntarye par cours de benevolens, scilicet comme chivaler un chivall et 2 foote men pour example. Et autre un chivall. Autre un foote man. Vel ii al footeman solonque lour bon volunt.

Vel argent en lyew de ce.

Mr Tresorer   Mova que serra par argent delyver.

Mes nei d'avoir tresorer enter nous quar c'est d'avoir homme de countenance et d'avoir gard d'assister luy.

Mes de payer l'argent al coffers la Royne est le voye; quar el ad sufficient tresor et bien gard.

Mr Pembridge   Qui veut set out footeman, et veut paier al purse la Royne tant comme ses gages vyendra par an.

Mr Wrothe   Semble que serra capten del chescun pays, quel avera amyes icy a mytter ce oustre le mere al capten a paier.

Et ne vyendra en le Quenes tresorers hand. (Quel Mr Vice-chamberlain mesme l'opinion).

13 Mr Salting-   King Spain maynt par son argent quel il ore want et apprompt de son clargie
stoke[27]   et subiectes. Et il ad ore 5 fletes venant de severall partes ove argent. Est wishe d'avoir niefs prepare de meete ove eux par la voye, quel veut faier fyne del gwer, et bon peace.

En temps Henry 8 furent benevolens. Par comissyon en le pays a sacher quid | 14 Sir William
veut de bon benevolens. | Moore

Doubta del dispocicion Low Cuntryes quant lour turne serve, ou quant want | 15 Sir Harry
de maynt les gweres. Ideo semble null assurance peut estre de eux si nous ne | Knevette
emprest soverayntie et estre la forter qu'eux.

King Spain ne veut ne peut estre plus versus nous qu'il est, quar ad iure al
Holly League et nostre distruccion.

Il mova a meddle ove King Spain nerer home, scilicet par ayd Don Anthony
usque al Portugall a mover revolt la. Et stop les havens et seas par ce.

Un peticion al Royne, qu'en regard que nous avons oye (par le declaracion | f.38
d'un honorable person)[28] de sa Majestie, le grand entencions del Pape et Roy
de Spayne enconter sa Majestie et sa domynions, quel accrew partim par le
practise del unholye League pour suppresser le religion etc, et partim pour ceo
que nous ayd le distressed vicynes del Low Cuntryes, quel sa Majestie ad
(cibien pour advancement de religion la, come pour garder eux del tyrannye
del Spanyardes) ayde, [a sa grand cha][29] le quel accion fuit just devant Dew de | Just: devant
uphold et maynteyne religion la, le quel est mult advance et encreas la plus | Dew
nostre aydes al eux dones, et null gwer est cy iust come ceo quell est garr[ant?]
par Dew.

Just auxi et garrant devant men d'eux assister, [quia el prest rien del Roy | Et devant homes
Spayne][30] d'avoir comiseracion dyceux, cy prochen vicynes ove queux nous
avons marye et sumes de sank et nosme et sumes d'auncyent league d'amitye,
et de commerse et traffyke.

Ove queux en toutes nostre treatyes pour traffyk avomes delt ove les gentes
cibien come ove lour magistrates et ne unque ove [le magistrate][31] lour
superiour et prynce,[32] sans les gentes.

Et regie est succurrere lapsus.

E sa entent suscipere bellum ut inde pax oriatur.

Est honorable d'emprendre matter cibien garrant quia ne procede de malyce, | Honorable
ne covetous[ness], ne vayneglorye, (de conquerer).

quia a preserver eux nostre prochen vicynes | Mete and
est de garder grand et fort enemyes plus furder from us. | nedefull:

Tum tua res agitur, etc.

Par eux avomus vent de nostre comodityes,

brefe et safe retorne de nostre traffyk.

Neclect ceo et donque

nous perda le domynion del narrow seaes,

nous myt a le mayne del mightiest monarche ceo que tout le mond ne poit luy
doner, scilicet navigacion. /

Il ad argent del Indeaes a server son purposes. | v.

---

26. Richard Kingsmill. | 29. Deleted.
27. Identified in *Commons* as Richard | 30. Deleted.
    Saltonstall (also in *EP*, ii.178–9). | 31. Deleted.
28. i.e. Hatton on 22 February. | 32. Inserted: 'lour . . . Prynce'.

Il est cy mightie en Germanye, qu'il ad espye en lour counsels.

Nous n'avomes donque null lyew a quel a caryer nostre comodityes,

quar ad este son pollicye de stopper nostre vent de drape la.

Issent qu'il mesme poit anoyer nous, et auxi utter ses woolles la (quar el est accrew riche en woolles);

et en quelcunque liew nous myttomes nostre lane la voit auxi estre son lane de hynder nostre market.

Issent que perdant le Low Cuntryes, nous perda nostre bon et redy market, et brefe et safe retorne.

Et issent serromes suffocate en nostre comodityes demesure.

Nous voiant le seriousnes del cause,

et qu'est just, honorable, et nedefull d'emprendre ut supra,

et que les revenewes del Crowne ne veut ceo sustayner,

avomes agree al ii fiftenes et subsidye: mes yceux ne veulent discharger le matter al affect.

De nostre bon volunt nous offer d'encorager la Royne d'emprendre ceo roundlye,

que nous et toutes les nobles, gentils, et homes d'abillitye volomes doner al mayntenance de sa soveryntie del Low Cuntryes, de chescun de eux un grand benevolens durant le gwerre.

Note[?] question si soveraintye vel ayd.

E a pryer sa Majestie (si el issent semble expedyent) d'emprendre le soverayntie quia autrement (sans prendre soverayntie) quant nous serve eux, et vyent al pinche de lour allowans d'ayde (ils nyent tenus al nous par bond de obedyens) ils voyent disceyve our expectacion, issent poyent revolt quant avomes serve lour turne. /

f.39   Et nostre Angloys ne voyle avoir tiell corage de server eux, comme quant ils serve la Roygne.

Ideo en nostre opinions (savant le dyrectyon al sa Majestie), nous teigne sa surest voye d'emprendre le soverayntie, et entent comme poymes ove dutye nous desyer ceo, et volomes adventure nostre biens, teres et vyes, en sa servyce dycell.

ii. Translation of Harley 6845, fos.34–9.[1]

[Endorsed (f.35v.) 'Comittees debating about assistans for mayntenance of the Low Cuntryes' and 'It does not seem that the Queen is willing to undertake the sovereignty on this offer of benevolence where we are not tied to continue and maintain this benevolence'[?].][2]

24 February 1586. In committee.   f.36

1. For the need: to deal effectively with the Low Countries.   Sir Walter
2. In order to encourage her, to offer of our selves (hoping that the country is   Mildmay
willing to do likewise) our benevolence, as a voluntary subsidy for 2, 3 or more
years, if the war continues so long, to preserve a people bound [to us] by a
long-established friendship and by a stronger bond, namely, religion, and
thirdly to avoid a dangerous neighbour; though whether by [accepting] sovereignty, or otherwise by giving them assistance, he left to her to consider.
That his meaning was that she should accept sovereignty.   Mr Wrothe
That we come for consultation and every consultation must be just, honourable   Sir Thomas
and necessary.   Cecil
The question is whether the offer of a benevolence [is] on condition that she   Mr Treasurer
will accept the sovereignty: either she supports the cause, that the Low
Countries will not put their heads under the feet of Spain, or they maintain
their privileges.
It does not seem good to move [her] to accept sovereignty, but rather that we
should assist them against their (and our) enemies. Thus their and our defence
is achieved, being safeguarded as effectively by the one way as by the other,
since she can maintain their forces, their resistance, their privileges, without
sovereignty.
[We may] put forward that in our opinion sovereignty is the better way, but
not offer our benevolence with a tying condition that if she does not accept the
sovereignty she shall have nothing.
They are divided in religion; if Spain can by a treaty make peace and have   Mr Baynbrigge
dominion over them, we cannot be at peace.

---

1. This translation is a very slightly   2. The word 'veut' appears sometimes to
   modified version of the one prepared for   mean 'can'.
   Neale. One or two uncertainties of
   meaning remain.

Therefore it is better to support wars against Spain abroad; and let her accept sovereignty if she wishes. But if she undertakes [their] protection through the ancient league: then to have free trade, without corporations, that is a cause to move us in friendship to assist them.

But what we want is to be sure of having what we look for, and not to be deceived in that.

Our need is to keep the King of Spain busy there with a foreign army more quickly than he can threaten us here.

Mr Francis Bacon
Left that to her Majesty, as time would show what is best. But in our opinion we prefer that she should accept sovereignty; nevertheless if she assists them, that serves our purpose, by diverting Spanish forces over there which otherwise could be employed against us (for we seek no conquest).

We do not know whether the sovereignty is offered to us, for we have not the instruction that others have [?].

The bonds of pity for the distressed; of religion; of [their] usefulness for trade. /

v.
Mr Edgecombe
He understands the question [to be] whether sovereignty [should be accepted] or not.

Mr Herbert, Master [of] Requests
If the action is to be undertaken it must be answerable, just, or necessary.

The country is distressed because the nobility is distressed and put away.

[Action is] just because of the treaties between us and their subjects (and not [their] sovereigns); and necessary for commerce, intercourse and trade.

By reason of the charges of the Queen in the great events in Ireland, and also in Scotland, to subdue faction and force assistance there, and lastly in the former expences in Flanders (which this subsidy does not countervail): it is necessary to aid the Queen with a benevolence in which the better sort and not the poor are to be charged.

Mr Vicechamberlain
The matter has been debated before the Queen herself by councillors arguing on both sides; and at last agreed to be undertaken as honourable, just and necessary for profit.

It is just before God to help to uphold and maintain religion there, where it increases and advances the more we help them there: no war is so just as the war which is acceptable to God.[3]

It is just before men and acceptable[4] to give aid by which she takes nothing from the King of Spain and expects no gain to herself. She takes no profit from him; she does not interfere with the privileges and profits of the King of Spain; her intention is to embark on war that from it peace may come. Pity of those afflicted peoples of our own blood and our own name, by marriages there, [reminds us] it is a royal action to aid the fallen.

It is honourable to undertake such a matter, thus acceptable, since it proceeds not from malice, nor ambition, nor greed, nor vainglory, but is necessary and profitable to save our near neighbours: then is your own property at stake [when your neighbour's house is on fire].

Neglect them and we lose dominion of the narrow seas and put into the mighty monarch's hands that which all the world cannot now give him, namely, navigation.

Then he can carry silver from the Indies and we shall be held up in our trading and be suffocated by our commodities here. See how mighty he is in Germany now; whither shall we carry our commodities if he has the Low Countries? / It has been his policy by the loss of them to stop our vent of cloth. He wants f.37 to sell his wools in the Low Countries, where ours are sent; he wants to stifle us by sending his into the same places that ours go to, for Spain is richer in wool than England is.

This proves that these countries are our profit, since to defend them, people and country, [is to maintain] the open market and a good and quick return: to lose them is to lose all.

This is not a matter in which we alone are concerned.

The commissioners of France for the marriage broke out and said that in no wise could Spain willingly have the Low Countries in monarchy, for then this part of Christendom could not endure; and moved that we and they should each do our part, set out.

The end was that we wanted to undertake [the Low Countries] with justice and equity and they wanted to have them in right and in propriety, namely, sovereignty.

On this we grew cold and the treaty broke off.

By which it appears that the French are as conscious of the Low Countries as we are.

The Guises are now grown so strong through Spanish money that they overrule the King of France.

The purpose of the league is well known: to overrun us all.

Consider: without us they cannot stand
            great charges last year, we spent there
            and great honour to our nation for that.

It seems that the English crown cannot undertake the Low Countries without great aid from the subjects of England, for it entails war against Spain and all her confederates, otherwise we shall suffocate in our commodities at home. We have confidence in the Queen, that she does not want to save a halfpenny of the subject, but that [no more] does she want to save a farthing of her own.

If we go no further than a subsidy, she must spend according to the rate, so that it can last the time, and not all at one go.

This assistance had, she is not willing to maintain the Low Countries.

The offer of the Low Countries:

1. of sovereignty: that they give up this name to pay for it,
                     as their own cost of defending it.
2. of protection: the same cost.
3. if neither of these is accepted, then, of assistance. /

For this, look at the fortresses and forces of the enemy, to see what forces our   v. friends have to repel them; how they can resist the enemy; and how they can be maintained.

3. Or 'warrantable by'?   4. Or 'warrantable'?

Their account is only sustained by our charge and present expense; and to be repaid on the peace (for which we have wished) by insisting on their true payment of 5000 footmen and 1000 horsemen [?], for there is no fault in this matter in the Queen, since she has paid as much as she ought to pay.

It would move you to pity to see our returned soldiers' needs; it is by others that they must be paid, for when we go into the field the Low Countries are not able to supply us either with men or with victual.

And so they sent over here for volunteers, and this being thus granted, when they see everyone there take the field and good success, then the enemy retires and we are able to hold the field; but these English volunteers paid by the States, they see neither home nor pay.

You can see by this that these people are not able to pay and if they are not given aid, they will want perhaps to slip away from us.

Sir Walter Mildmay   That by a humble petition to the Queen to move that the cause is of importance to the Queen and the estate of the Kingdom.

Therefore to embrace it more roundly:

1. to take note of the disposition of her people.

2. to encourage her to preceed, to offer her a benevolence from us. We can put forward our desire for the one way of proceeding, rather than the other, but if it comes to the question whether one way is more suitable than the other, that is a point which it is not fit for us to discuss at this time.

3. the manner of putting into effect this benevolence, for it is better never to make an offer for the country than not to implement it, thus making known to the King of Spain the want of good will of the country.

Mr Alford   To offer our opinion: that since sovereignty is offered to the Queen it seems best to us (without prejudicing her opinion and counsel) to provide subsidy (she will find subjects ready to gives generously for more than a day or a year) to assist this undertaking. [?]

By sovereignty she has command and profit, which in time can lighten our present burden; and men go willingly into her Majesty's service, and not into theirs; and hope for better pay, which they shall have.[?] /

f.34
Mr Treasurer   The Low Countries only offer sovereignty in order to preserve their privileges, as they have done to ther princes, and not that we should command their purses at our pleasure. Distinguish. If the Queen undertakes the sovereignty, they know that if they give little assistance or none, the Queen will maintain the war: which is what the States desire. But if she only helps them, the Queen is not tied to them if they do not give her sufficient support.

Mr Vicechamberlain   If we enter in strength we shall have the sovereignty when it pleases us, or make such a peace as we ourselves desire; and these days' doings well known and continued will further this work to great effect; and it is such a consultation as the kingdom had not had these hundred years.

Mr Attorney of the Wards   Moved to enter into the proportion which each person should pay, but this was generally denied. Rather to be voluntary in the form of benevolence, namely, for a knight one horse and two footmen, for example; for another, one horse; another one footman; or two to the footman, according to their good will; or money in lieu of this.

Moved that it should be given in money; but not to have a treasurer among us, for that is to have a man of standing and a guard to assist him, but to pay the money into the coffers of the Queen is the way, for she has the means of receiving and guarding it. Mr Treasurer

Whoever wishes to set out a footman, and wishes to pay his contribution into the Queen's purse, may give as much as his wages will come to by year. Mr Pembridge

It seems that there will be a captain of each county, that he will have friends here to send the contribution beyond the sea to the captain to pay out, and that it will not come into the hands of the Queen's treasurer. (Mr Vicechamberlain was of the same opinion). Mr Wrothe

The King of Spain was maintained by his silver,[5] which he now wants and borrows from his clergy and subjects. And he has now five fleets coming from different places with silver: it is his wish that ships should be prepared to intercept them by the way, which would mean the end of the war, and good peace. Mr Saltingstoke

In the time of Henry VIII there were benevolences. Commissions went through the country to find out who wanted to give a good benevolence. Sir William Moore

Doubted the disposition of the Low Countries when their turn had been served, or when they could no longer maintain the war. Therefore it seems that no assurance can be had of them unless we undertake the sovereignty and are there in greater strength than they are. Sir Harry Knevette

The King of Spain neither wishes nor is able to become more against us than he is, for he has sworn to the Holy League and our distruction.

He moved to interfere with the King of Spain nearer home, namely, by helping Don Anthony as far as Portugal, to raise a rebellion there; and thus to stop the havens and seas.

A petition to the Queen, that since we have heard from her Majesty (by the statement of an honourable person) of the great intentions of the Pope and King of Spain to oppose her Majesty and her dominions, which arise partly through the activities of the unholy league to suppress religion etc. and partly because of our aid given to the distressed neighbours of the Low Countries, whom her Majesty has assisted (as much for the advancement of religion there, as to protect them from the tyranny of the Spaniards), the which action was just before God, to uphold and maintain religion there, the which is more advanced and encreased there the more our assistance is given to them; and no war is so just as that which is acceptable to God. f.38

Just: before God

Just also before men and acceptable to aid them, to take pity on them, these near neighbours with whom we have married, who are of our blood and name, with whom we have an ancient league of friendship, of commerce and intercourse. and before men

5. Or 'money'?

With whom in all our commercial treaties we have dealt with the people as well as with their magistrates and never with their superior and prince without the people.

And it is a royal action to aid the fallen.

And her intention is to embark on war that from it peace may come.

honourable   It is honourable to undertake a matter so worthy since it does not proceed from malice, nor greed, nor vainglorious desire for conquest.

Meet and necessary: because to preserve them, our near neighbours, is to hold great and strong enemies further away from us.

Then is your own property at stake, etc.

By them we have vent for our commodities, quick and safe return for our trading.

Neglect this and then we lose the dominion of the narrow seas, we put into the hand of the mightiest monarch that which all the world cannot give him, namely, shipping. /

v.   He has silver from the Indies to serve his purposes.

He is so mighty in Germany that he has spied into their counsels.

We have then no place to which to carry our commodities, for it has been his pollicy to stop our vent of cloth there.

Thus he can at the same time annoy us, and sell his wools there (for he is grown rich in wools); and wherever we send our wool there also will be his wool to hinder our market.

Thus, losing the Low Countries, we lose our good and ready market, and quick and safe return.

And thus we will be suffocated in our commodities beyond all measurement.

Seeing the seriousness of the cause, and that it is just, honourable and necessary to undertake as above, and that the revenues of the crown will not sustain this, we have agreed to two fifteenths and one subsidy. But these will not discharge the matter effectively, and of our good will we offer, to encourage the Queen to undertake this roundly, that we and all the nobility, gentry, and men of

note: question whether sovereignty or aid.   ability wish to give, each one of them, for the maintenance of her sovereignty in the Low Countries, a large benevolence, while the war lasts.

And to beseech her Majesty (if she thinks it thus expedient) to undertake the sovereignty, since otherwise (not accepting sovereignty), when we help them, and they see their allowance of aid insufficient (they not being tied to us by the bond of obedience) they will want to deceive our expectation, and thus may revolt when we have served their turn. /

f.39   And our Englishmen will not have such heart to serve them, as when they serve the Queen.

Therefore in our opinion (saving the direction to her Majesty) we hold the surest way to be to accept[6] the sovereignty, and as much as we can with duty we desire this and wish to adventure our goods, lands and lives in her service in this cause.

6. Or 'undertake'?

14. *Points of a proposed petition on the* Low Countries, *February 1587*

Text from BL Harley 6845, original draft notes in the hand of John Puckering, Speaker.

[Endorsed by Puckering (on f.33v.) 'Poyntes of a petycion to have byne exhibyted to her Majestie about the Low Cuntryes. February 1586 in Parlyament'.]

To make petycion to her Majestie.

And therin ffyrst to gyve her Highenes thankes that·yt hathe pleasyd her to have suche care of our safetyes, as to imparte unto us suche dangers as may concerne us, that we may counsell how to prevent and avoyd the same.

And for that she hathe alredye bestowed great charges in defending and preventing occasyons of our danger, [and more ys like to bestow therin by occasion of preparacions entended against us.]¹

In regard therof, and that her Majestie ys like to bestow muche more charges for our safetye and defens, by occasyon that great preparacions are made beyond seaes tending to our danger, we offer ij fyftenes and one subsidye.

And sins it pleasyd her Majestie to let us understand the complottes of dangers pretended:

In which we find the same to grow partlye for our religion, partlye for that we have ayded the Low Cuntryes; the defens wherof we fynd comodyous [[(and that for many reasons particulerly to be set down)]² and also to be safetye to this realme (for particuler reasons to be set downe); and on the contrary yf Spayne shold enioy that cuntrye we shold fynd great discomodyties, yea and great dangers to our realme and state (for particuler reasons to be set downe); we humbly desyer her to deale throwlye with the defens of the Low Cuntryes.

In the consyderacion of which enterprise we, so far as our poore skyls do reache, [cannot fynd any]³ do fynd no⁴ way so avaylable (leaving nevertheles the same to her Majestie's higher wisdome) as to accept the soverayntie therof, the same being (as we understand) offryd to her Majestie.

(And that for these and these particuler reasons etc.) /

Which thing to [do, will]⁵ undertake we perceave will drawe with yt exceding charges, not fyt to be borne of the revenewes of the Crowne.   v.

---

1. Deleted.
2. Deleted.
3. Deleted.
4. Words underlined are Puckering's insertions (throughout).
5. Deleted.

We, to th'end her Majestie shall not [stik]⁶ <u>be discoraged</u> for the charge, do offer that yf now, or at any tyme after, yt shall please her Highnes to accept the soverayntie of the cuntries of Holland and Zeland, that we will most willinglye and largelye yeld a voluntarye yerlye contribucion, suche and so muche for our particuler partes, and so far furthe as shall well become all that be of the better sort of the realme, as ioyned unto her Majestie's treasure may well defray the burden and charge of the sayd warres.

And to th'entent that her Majestie may be assertenyd, and also assured, of the perfourmans of the same <u>before she shall accept the same great charge</u>, we <u>do</u> offer and desyer that whensoever yt shall please her Highnes to [take lyke]⁷ <u>think yt expedyent</u> to take the sayd soverayntye, and to be willing to understand the value of our contribucion, that she may and wyll dyrect her comissyons to understand what wilbe gyven, and upon returne and knowledge therof <u>finding the same answerable to the charge, then</u> to do therin as best shall seame good in her highe and princelye wisdome. /

f.31   Devyde the consyderacions of the subsidye and of the benevolens:
[subiectes looking ynto her]⁸
[the respect of the]⁹
We having received from her Majestie knowledge of th'emynent dangers entended
[ffor help agaynst the same and to prevent the same]¹⁰
by enemys great and strong
and preparacion against us very great
part in respect of religion
part in respect of our assistans to the Low Cuntryes our distressyd neighb[ours]
we, seing the charge so great to sustayne the meanes of prevencion as not <u>well</u> to be borne by her owne revenewes, have [not onlye]¹¹ gyven subsidye and ij fiftenes
[but also yn hope she will take soverayntie].¹²
<u>And finding how necessarye to deale throwlye with the Low Cuntryes, understanding that they offer her</u>
[And]¹³
[we offer a benevolens of contribucion of the better sorte (for it is found by experyens that the Low Cuntry people, not being tyed <u>by comandment</u>, have adventured the hole accion for lak of perfourmans of ther partes and dutyes) and also men will not so willinglye serve (as yf they whollye serve for the Quene)]¹⁴
In regard of mayntenance of religion.
as also that they, and we, be of auncyent leage
separatyd with a small sea
have had contynuall traffyk and commerse
have linked in mar[riage] together and so knyt in blood and name
very profytable for us the short way of transport
the readye market ther

the spedye and safe retorne.

On the contrarye

the losse of that cuntrye, losyth us th'use of the narrow sea, as by example may appere by that we are excedinglye hyndred by the poore towne of Dunkyrke barryd havenyd, but what might we feele yf we had Flushing and all the port townes of Seland and Holland against us?

We should therby have our ffrendes turned against us, the mightiest monarche placed hard over against us so furnished with shipping (to his monyes) as all the world besydes could not furnishe hym agayne, /

redye to shote over to us <u>all his forces</u> at all assayes with a short cutte.   v.

At least therbye our vent for our draperye [were stoppyd][15] and other our comodyties were therbye <u>so</u> stoppyd.

So as we shold be suffocatyd in our owne ffatte,

That our people shold not be set on worke, nor hable to sell ther wooll clothe and other comodityes, that they wold murmure within them selves. Redye to mutynye.

Therfore to th'end her Majestie wold have care to preserve those cuntryes from th'enemye, eyther by ayd or soverayntye. But, in our opynions and desyers by waye of soverayntye: wherin we will expend our goodes, landes and lyves, and which we think more safe, for that else they may (as by experyens we fynd they have done) when we have most nede at the pynche to wyn or lose all, for want of being tyed by dutye of obedyens and comaundement, fayle to perfourme ther assistans and servyce and so overthrow all our travayles and charges;

or els, when we have servyd ther turnes to our intollerable charges, they may at ther libertye revolt and turne to th'enemye.

And agayne our owne people and natyon will not serve with so good corage the stranger, as to serve her Majestie's selfe ther.

And therfore to desyer her Majestie to accept our dutifull and loving offers of our hartes, handes and helps; and to deale throwlye in the defens and preservacion of the Low Cuntryes (yf so we might eftsones repeat by taking the soverayntye) yf not, yet in suche other sorte as best might serve in her pryncelye wisdome, the glory of God and help of our neighbours and safe[ty] of this realme.

6. Deleted.
7. Deleted.
8. Deleted.
9. Deleted.
10. Deleted.

11. Deleted.
12. Deleted.
13. Deleted.
14. Deleted.
15. Deleted.

15. A *proposed speech to the* Queen *on the* Low Countries, *February 1587*

Text from BL Harley 6845, original draft in the hand of a secretary of John Puckering, Speaker.

Harley 6845, fos.40–2

[Endorsed by Puckering 'Speache to have bene used to her Majestie about the Low Cuntryes. February 1586'.]

'Suche, and so great (most excellent, and gratious Soverigne) hath bene the intentive care and provident wisedome of your Majesties[1] continually watchyng for the peace and prosperitie of us all your natural subiectes ever sythence that your Majestie's most ioyous and happie attaynement to the Crowne of this lande, that seldome wee needed to requyre any thing which your Majesties had not already forseene and provyded for us. Againe, suche and so exceeding tender hath alwayes bene your princely love and aboundant clemencie towarde us, that whensoever wee addressed any o[ur p]eticions unto you, wee have alwayes departed from your Majesties, eyther gratif[ied a]ccording to our owne hartes desyre, or (at the least) satisfied to the full, of your most roial resolutions, and sweetly seasoned aunsweares. And therfore, the whole estate of your Majestie's Commens (represented in this present assemblye) knowing that (amongst many other your princely circumspections) your Majesties hath (most wysely, and in good tyme) forseen the daunger threatened unto us by the warres in the Lowe Countries, and hath for prevention therof (in a sorte) receaved those afflicted regions into your kingly and Christian protection, they doe render by me to your most excellent Majesties theire most humble, entier, and unfayned thankes for the same. And, susteyned with the assurance of that your native and accustomed bountie (wherof they have many a tyme most comfortably tasted), they have also commaunded me to present (on theire behalfe) before the seate of your sacred Majesties this theire humble and earnest suite, the which whylest I shall endevour to disclose, I beseech your gratious Majesties to relieve me with the same your princely pardon that hytherto yow have vouchesafed unto me.

'Wee, your Majestie's most loial and bounden subiectes, cannot but greatly admire and magnifie that high wisedome and magnanimitie of harte whearwith it hath pleased the almightie Lorde to bless and adorne you: on the one parte, for that in the midst of a most ioyous and flourishing peace, your Majesties hath yet forseene the right opportunitie of enterprysing warre; and on the other parte, bycause your Majesties neyther entised by ambition, moved by covetice, nor drawen by revenge, but in the true feare of God and without any the vaine feare of men, hath (no less for the quarreil of true religion, then for the helpe of / others, safetie of your selfe, and commune good of us all) armed some bandes of your subiectes for protecting our distressed neighboures of the Lowe Countries against the bloodthyrstie violence of the Romanistes and Spaniardes that labour to devoure theim. A most charitable, Christian, and honourable enterpryse, carying justice with it in regarde of the cause it selfe, and mere necessitie in respect of us and theim whome it doth concerne.

v.

'For the cause is cheifly God's, whose eternal trueth is oppugned by theim, in defence wherof your Majesties need not feare to adventure your treasure, crowne, life, or dignitie, synce of him you have receaved theim all for his owne service, honour, and glorie. It is secondarily the cause of your neare neighbours and [al]lyes, and (in theim) the cause of us all your owne liege, homeborne, and na[tura]l subiectes, whome by office you have hytherto, and may for ever by justice preserve and defende. God and nature hath sundered theim and us by a small sea only, to the ende that wee might afoarde our mutual aydes eche to other in whatsoever storme of necessitie. They and wee have bene auncient freindes, fast-souldered togeather, not only by the bond of commune trafficque and dailye entercourse, but also by sundrie instrumentes of alliance, and most apparant offices of singular love, favour, and freindship. Theire persons have bene (now many yeares togeather) most iniuriously tormented, slayne, and slaughtered; theire goodes taken and spoyled; theire beautiful and riche cities beaten and sacked; and theire countrie (for a great parte therof) miserably layed waste an dispeopled. Yea, wee feare (most noble Sovereigne), wee feare that the flame of this fyer (if it be not the more speedyly quenched) wille spread it selfe over the sea, and consume us to the like ashes. For, the Spanyshe enemie (that continually aspyreth by ambition, and creepeth still on *plus ultra*) seeketh us by theim, shooteth at us thorow theim, wysheth and voweth that the ende of theire warre may bee the begynnyng of ours, and meaneth by a bridge, layed (as it weare) over the backes of theim, to transporte the warre into Inglande, and to putt in execution heare that heavie and horrible crueltie whiche many miserable nations have long felte and endured by him.

The cause

Their persons

Our persons

That is the Spanishe poesie yet further.

'To this feare, the observation of his conquestes (atcheived by blood) in the Indies, at Naples, and in other places, dothe move us; his kyndelyng and blowyng of that fyer in Fraunce which yet presently burneth theare, doth leade us; and the continual despites offered by him to your Majestie's subiectes and servantes in his owne countrye, ioyned with his actual attempt upon your realme of Ireland, and his undermynyng practizes heare at home in the midst and bowels of your realme of Ingland, / doe drawe and enforce us.

f.41

'But, be it (most noble Soveregne) that our feare is but vayne, that his ambition may be bounded by the sea, and that he shal never dare to invade or come aboord us. Yet is it certeine (most excellent Queene) that if your Majesties shall eyther forsake the afflicted estate of theise countries, (as all other

1. *Sic.* and throughout.

kings and princes hytherto seeme to have done) or shal not roundly and readyly reache unto theim that comfortable ayde of your sovereigne hande (which none other prince or potentate may so sufficiently and seasonably perfourme), it is certaine I saye, that the enemie will speedily surprise and grype theise Low Countries (that were never so lowe, as nowe) and thearby at once bothe possesse him selfe of the mouthes and gates of all the great ryvers that flowe out of Germanie, and withal become maister and commaunder of all the riche and wealthy navigation, trafficque, and shipping that is in the worlde.

Pluto, the god of riches. [Eo]lus, the god [of wi]ndes. [Nep]tune, the god [of] the seas.

'Then shall it come to passe, that even as his Indies have already made him Pluto of all the sylver and golde, so the Lowe countries shal crowne him Eolus and Neptune of the wyndes and the narrowe seas. Then shall it lye in his owne power, eyther to sterve the Germanes with cold and nakedness for want of that cloathe which they have nowe from us, or els to putt theim into his owne cloath and liverie; and thearby to cloye and glutte us with the overflowing stoare and plentie of that for which wee shall fynd no vent at all. Then shall our stately shippes (that nowe bee the wooden walles, and wyngs of the realme) become unserviceable to us. Then shall our treasure riches (that be mainteyned, not by mynes, but by merchandize aloane) continually fade, diminishe and decay. Yea, then shall the auncient gloarie and renowme[2] of this your Majestie's kyngdome be eclipsed, the bright candle of the woord of God shalbe extinguished, the hartes of the Inglishe nation shalbe appalled, and they and theire lande togeather thus enfeabled shalbe an open bootie and unbloodye conquest; eyther to him selfe, or to any other, that will demaund it.

'The fearfull contemplation of which horrour and calamitie (most deere and gratious Sovereigne) hath so deeply pearced the inwarde thoughtes of us all your Majestie's most liege and loving Commons, that wee have resolved heare to prostrate our selves togeather at the feete of your most excellent Majesties; and for the religion of God (which you have ever loved), for the welfare of your people (that he hath gyven to your charge), for the honour of the realme (which hytherto you have most gloriously maintayned), for the safetie of your selfe, (then which (after God) nothing in this worlde can be more deare unto us), most humbly, hartilye, and instantly to obteste and beseeche your most excellent Majesties that as it hath / already lyked you (in great wisedome and godly courage) to putt your foote into the protection of theise Lowe Coun- tries, so it may also please you resolutely, firmely, and constantly to proceade and goe forward in the same, readily to embrace this great opportunitie offered for the enlargement of your roial honour, and to receave into the bosome of your princely pitie theise distressed estates, that have layed downe theire greavous moane, and powred foorth their wooful complaintes before you.

v.

'The whiche thing, wheather it shal please your Majesties to perfourme it by acceptation of a sovereigne power and absolute auctoritie over theim, or by any other capitulation and agreament, wee wholy referre to your owne highe, princely, and most excellent wysedome; as knowing and acknowledging, that the affaires of your roial estate are not to be directed by us, but to be managed by your selfe. For, "*Tuum (O Regina) iubere, nobis iussa capessere fas est.*"[3] Howbeit (if with your Majestie's free pardone, wee may open our whole desyre) wee rather wyshe (if at the least it may so be found good in the ballance of your owne tryed iudgement) that they should of olde assured freindes become adopted chyldren to your Majesties, and felloe subiectes with our selves. By which meane (as under the correction of your roial wysedome wee do yet thinke) they on the one syde shalbe twyce tyed to your Majesties, once by theire allegeance, and againe by your benefite, and on the other syde the alacritie and courage of your owne souldiors and servitors shalbe redoubled, when they shal perceave that they adventure not theire lyves for pay only (as mercenarie men) but for theire owne Prince, estate, and felloe subiectes, which wyl bee as ready to hazarde their lyves and al, for theim againe.

'And now (most noble and deere Sovereigne) forasmuche as wee our selves cannot but knowe and understand, first that so haughtye and heroical an enterpris is not to be atcheived without a greater masse of treasure then the usual revennews of your highness' Crowne may yeeld unto you; and then, that the price of warre may not (as of other things) bee aforehand sett downe and esteamed, but must from tyme to tyme be furnished and supplied, as the extraordinarie charge of the affaire it selfe will aske and requyre: therfore wee doe heare first (with the consenting hartes and myndes of us all) offer unto your most excellent Majesties one general subsidie and 2 fifteenes, not as any sufficiencye for your Majestie's charge already borne (and muche lesse for the burdeine that is to come), but only in testification of that entier love and thankfull duetie that wee doe owe and beare unto you, and / for an earnest penye and pledge of our unfayned devotion and readynesse to employe whatsoever wee possesse at your Majestie's disposition and commaundement.

'And furthermore, for that wee have lately understoode (by the declaration of an honourable person,[4] therto directed by your Majestie's commaundement) that your highnesse' inveterate enemies (the Pope and his eldest son, the king of Spaine) have presently in hande some daungerous intention against your Majesties and your dominions, partly for the putting in ure of that cankred conspiracie which they falsly call the Holy League, and partly for revenge to be taken upon you for yeelding your aide to those poore afflicted Christians of the Lowe Countries, whearby it may come to passe that this warre shalbe drawen along both to a more continual and farre greater expence then wee may yet forsee: wee doe heare likewyse promise and vowe to your roiall Majesties (in that duetie which in the Lorde wee beare unto you) that if it shall lyke your Majesties to take upon you the sovereigntie of theise oppressed countries, wee will continually followe and feede this your most honourable and holy warre with a yearly benevolence and contribution of money, to be levyed amongst the knightes, esquiers, gentlemen, marchantes, burgesses, and other the wealthier persons of your realme, during so long tyme of that warre as your

Virgil's verse to the Quene Juno: which you may omitt, if you will.

f.42

Theis underlined wordes may be omitted.

---

2. *Sic.*
3. Virgil, *Aeneid*, I, 7, 7.
4. The reference is probably to Sir Christopher Hatton's speech of 22 February.

Majestie's selfe shall fynde cause to commaund and use it. Finally, as wee will not faile to direct our dayly prayers to God for the preservation and long life of your Majesties, so will wee dedicate all the rest of our goodes and landes, togeather with our liberties and lives to be spent and spylte in the same, or any other your Majestie's honourable service and employment.'

16. Job Throckmorton's speech on the Bill and Book, 27 February 1587

Text from New York, Pierpont Morgan Library, MA 276 (copy).

The Pierpont Morgan Library MA 276
(Phillipps MS 13891)
pp.13–27

'The cause being so waighty as yt is, and worthy indeede the deliberation of the gravest heades under the sun, I willingly confesse unto you that in the inwarde feelinge of mine owne insufficiency I am haulfe appalled to deale in yt; yet I wishe for Syon's sake, and for Queene Elizabethe's sake, and for England's sake, and for our posteritye's sake, that I coulde in any sorte lay it open unto you according to the waight and worthynes of the matter, wherein thoughe fleashe and bloudde bidde me be sylent, yet the stearne of my shippe (which is my conscience) windeth me quite an other waye. Therefore carryinge before me none other olyve branche of intercession then the bare testimonie of my loyall harte in the presence of God, I humbly crave your patience for a while.

'I am sory I must begine by the way of complainte unto this honorable assembly that such poore unworthy members of this House as I are strangly (I knowe not how) quite frustrate of our hope: ffor when wee come first into this House there is layed before us a shew of freedome in our entrye, and yet we fynde by the sequell we are threatened with bondage before we goe fourth. This freedome of ours, as yt is now handeled heere amongst us, I can very well lyken to a certeine lycense graunted to a preachere to preache the gospell freely, provided allwayes that he medle neyther with the doctryne of the prophetes nor the apostles. Pardon mee (right honorable) is not this, I praye you, the very image of our freedom in this House at this day? Ye shall speake in the Parleamente House freely, provided all wayes that ye medle neyther with the reformation of religion, nor the establishment of succession, the verie pillers and grounde workes of all our blisse and happines, and without the which (let us solace our selves never soe muche with songs of peace and all peace) dreadefull despayre will bee the end of our foolishe hope.

'In thease causes of soe great waighte that reach so highe and pearce so neere the marowe and bones of Church and common wealthe, yf any of the infferior sorte heare amongst us doe happen in some zeale to overstrayne him selfe, surely, ye that are honorable, ye that are wyse, ye that are grave and grayheadded ought in equytye to beare with them, bycause the faulte is in your

p.14   selves. / I have harde it often sayed that the next way to put the foole to
sylence is fore the wise man to speake in the cause him sellfe. Such as are
nearer then wee by calling, ought of right to bee warier then wee in watching;
who beinge in place, and having dayly oportunity offered them to take this
holy cause in hande, oughte (in reason) to be the first that shoulde cry out and
sett the beacon on fyre them selves. But alas, ye see when gray heares grow
sylent then younge headdes grow venterous, when greate babes[1] will not then
meane men shrincke not, when they that shoulde speake bee muette then burst
out they that should bee stille. It is wondered at above, that symple men of the
countrey shoulde be so forwarde, and it doeth amate[2] us in the countrey that
wise men of the courte should be so backeward: if yt bee more then nede in
us to feare every thinge, it is lesse then dew in them to sytte downe with *omnia
bene*, and feare nothinge. Is it a faulte in a pryvate man to be to busye, and can
it be excused in a counceller to be to sleepye? To charge any man in particuler
is more I knowe then I have warrant for: but my hope is those that are
religiously wyse will yet be so farre from justifying them selves in this regard
as in the examination of there owne hartes betwixt God and them they will
crye out from the depth of theire soules, "*Peccavimus cum patribus nostris*",[3] it is
to trew, o Lord, we have not heerein answered the duty of our callinge.

'Yf a question were now propounded to the whole House, what is the
cheife cause of all our meetinges and consultationes in this honorable
assemblye, answere I am sure would readely and roundely be made, "The
safetie of her most excellent Majestie"; which beinge in deed a matter of so
greate consequente, I muse trewly it doeth not rouze us in some other sorte
then yt seemeth yt doeth, ffor as in the safetye of her person is included (ye
know) all the blisse that our hartes can desyre, so on the contrary, in the losse
p.15   of her person (shall I neede to lay before / you so dreadefull a spectacle?) all
blyndenesse light uppon him that seeth not our miserye. Sythens then the
whole levell of all our deseignements is (as I take yt) the safetye of that
inestimable treasure of her royall person (whom the Lord still preserve) I could
wishe that every one of us would now in thease last unrulye dayes lay the
matter so neere his harte as yt should sounde a fathome deeper with him then
ever yt did. Therfore, let yt be farre from us once to dreame of any plotte for
her Majestie's safety only for this day, for this weecke, for this yeare; for that
were to foule a bleamishe to the loyaultye that we make shewe of. But such
a plotte whereon might bee buylte her Majesty's safetye in continewance, this
were in deed a consultation worthy of this honorable assemblye, worthy of the
wisdome and majestie of this House, for the which all posterity should have
cause to prayse God, yea and to honour your memorialls with this good
reporte, that the holy ghoste him selfe was sure Lord Presydente of this
assemblye.

'Nowe when the wisdome of man hath beaten his brayne to the botome and
devised what he can for his lyfe, this will bee found in the ende the surest and
safeste way for her Majestie (as hath beene notablye towlde you): to beginne at
the house of God, and to prefere the reformation of Jerusalem before all the
fleetinge felicities of this mortall lyfe. For this is indeede *recto incedere pede* when

the magistrate taketh the cause of God in hande to the harte, so prefixing before his eyes the bewty of Syon as he sayeth to him selfe with a Christian resolution, "*Potius quam aliquid detrahatur de gloria Christi. Ruat non modo pax, sed et caelum et terra.*"

'As to that man as shall continually smoothe up all our breaches with a blast of good wordes, tellinge us that all thinges are well allreadye, neyther Church nor / commen wealth needes any betteringe or reformation, let him uppon better advisement refute him selfe, I will never stande now to shape him an answere. Only this I will say, that the same spirite that deceived wretched Kinge Ahab may also (yf the grace of God bee not the greater) deceive godly Kinge Jehosophat, neyther can there bee a more perillous and pestelent receipte for her sacred Majestie then to bee a lying spirit in the mouth of her prophetes.[4]

'It is some thinge, I confesse, that the husbandman hath donne when he hathe cleared his ground of weedes and thistles: but yf he sitte downe there and doe nothing els, neglectinge the care of tillage and seede, his labour is lost and he and his poore famylie may perishe for all his toyle. In lyke sorte it was (out of all questian) a very worthy acte that was lately done at Fothringhey – the cuttinge of from the earth of that wreatched Athalia. But what, shall wee there uppon sett up all our sayles and sing peace upon Israell? Is all done, thinke you, now that is don? Is there nothinge left undon to moove the Lorde to impatience? Ye are to wyse (I am sure) to thinke yt. And ye knowe the Lord hath plagues enoughe in store for the contemners of his worde: he that is authour of all meanes, can he wante meanes, thinke you, to bee avenged on our unthankefullnes? No; let us assure our selfes that the same God that can rayze up stones unto Abraham for the defence of his Church, can also rayne downe haylestones upon Pharao for the overthrowe of the wicked.[5] Therfore, as the phisitians are wonte to say that after a man is new let bloudde hee must take heede he sleepe not uppon yt, least the vaine brust[6] out agayne, even soe, yf I were to give her Majestie advise upon my alleageance, I would humbly desire her that after / so many and mightie delyverances shee woulde beware shee sleepe not uppon them in perill of her life, least the vaine of those mischiefes burst out agayne afreashe thorough her securitye.

'It was sure well done of Abiah to pursue the wycked by the edge of the swoorde, but, by your leave, yt was better don of Jehosophat to worshipe God from his harte.[7] It was well don of Jehu to leave not one of the line of Ahab to looke ageynst a walle, but yt was better done of Josiah to reforme the house of God thoroughly.[8] It was well don of Kinge Henry the 8th, her Majestie['s] most noble father, to raze frome the earth those dennes and cloysters of iniquitye, but yt was better don of Kinge Edwarde to plante trew relygion and the gospell heere amongst us. Even so, no doubte, it was well and worthylie

1. *Sic.*
2. i.e. dismay.
3. Ps 106: 6.
4. 1 Kgs 21 and 22.

5. Exod 9: 18.
6. *Sic.*
7. ? 1 Sam 8; 2 Chr 17: 3–4, 20: 3.
8. 2 Kgs 10: 11, 17; 2 Chr 35, esp. 18.

p.16

p.17

don of her Majestie to execute justice uppon that Guysian impe, one of the principall shute anchors of all our discontented heades, but yet, by your favour, to reforme the house of God and to settell the crowne to the blisse of posterity shall bee 10 tymes better don, and the glorioust woorke that ever princesse dide.

'In which regarde have they not harde measure, thinke you, to be tearmed mislykers of the state that wishe a betteringe and a reformation of the state? Is it a condemninge of the religyon to wishe all corruptions purdged from the religion? Can they trewly be sayed to dislyke the good beginninges that wishe them blessed with a happie increase, yea, (and yf yt were possible) crowned up with joyfull endinges to the blisse of posterity? O mercifull God, into what lamentable dayes and times are we now fallen into? To bewayle the distresses of God's children, it is puritanisme. To finde faulte with corruptions of our Church, it is puritanisme. To reprove a man for swearing, it is puritanisme. To

p.18   / banishe an adulterer out of the house, it is puritanisme. To make humble sute to her Majestie and the High Courte of Parleament for a learned ministerie, it is puritanisme. Yea, and thease are of the cunning sleightes of Sathan and his instrumentes in this age and I feare me we shall come shortly to this, that to doe God and her Majestie good service shalbe coumpted puritanisme:[9] ye knowe on whom it pleased good Mr Babington to bestowe this name and tytle

my lord of   – on twoe verie honorable personages and as worthy councellers as any her
Lecester and Sir   Majestie hath, of whose service and fidelytie shee hathe had good tryall. But let
Amias Pawlet   all such wretched atheistes say and mutter what they liste; the Lorde send her Majestie stoare of such puritanes.

'Touching those thinges that have beene heere thus propounded unto us (I meane the booke and the bill), mee thinkes it were good before wee did reiecte them in this sorte wee did harken a little to the counsell of Gamaliel (for the same reason is of discipline as of doctryne) yf yt bee of God, folly to thinke by bitternesse, discountenance or harde handeling to suppresse yt;[10] for if truth bee (as some wryte) of the nature of camemell, then the more ye tread on yt the better yt groweth, or yf yt bee of the nature of the paulmetree, the more ye presse yt the faster yt ryseth. And in deed I never reade that the cause of God received any foyle by bitternesse or persecution: ffor that which the wisdome of the world thinkes to bee the dashinge and overthrow of all, the Lord by a contrary wind (as yt were) turns to the mayntenance and uphoulding of all, even to the shame and confusion of man. And therefore thease ordinary invectyves of our dayes, with thease unchristian outcryes of innovators, en-

p.19   emies to the state, / and I know not what, as they may well wounde and disgrace the persons, so they can never weaken nor discredyte the cause whyle the world standeth. And let us take heede, for yf yt be trew that this plotte heere layed before us bee indeede warrantable by the law of God, justifyable by the power of the worde, and allready unanswerably prooved to the viewe of the worlde, let us take heed, I say, that this our willfull reiecting of yt in this hatefull maner (clozing our eyes (as yt were) to the beames of Gode's truth) bee not fearefully punnished upon us and our posteritye.

'In a letter of King Edwarde's to the Devonshiere men who were up in armies and would need forsooth have the 6 articles revived among other things, it is recorded thus: "Was your servyce good in Latine? Then it is good in Englishe, for it is nothinge alltered, but translated; unlesse ye mislyke to speake with knowledge that which before ye speake with ignorance, *etc.*" And I pray you, is not this the very image of a greate parte of our reformation at this day? May not a man yet trewly say to this day, "Was your service good in Latine? Then it is good in Englishe, for it is lyttle or nothinge alltered, but translated?" So that poperye (the mor is the pytie) hath not yet received soe full a banishment out of the lande but that shee may trewly write to her freindes beyonde sea (as busshopes doe when they bee removed) "*Anno translationis nostrae.*"

'For the other particuler deformityes of our Church I knowe your wisdomes see into them well enough, beinge such as in truth may better bee coulored with wordes then defended with conscience. But above all other the foulest, the most shamefull, and unworthyest of all is (as hath bene / often and notablye told you) our dombe, ignorante and unlearned ministerye – a thinge growen in a maner desperate of all honest defense. Therefore, as aunciente father Augustine, being asked what was the chiefe poynt of Christianitie, made answere, "Humility. Humility. Yea", sayeth hee, "yf I were asked a thowsande times I would say, humility". Even soe must I, yf I were asked what is the bane of the Church and commen wealth, awnswere make, "The dombe ministerie, the dombe ministerye"; yea, yf I were asked a thowsande times, I must say, "The dombe ministerye." — p.20

'I meane our bare reading ministery, when the lofe is cast whole and unbroken to the people of God. Yee knowe what the eunuch sayed to Phillip in the Actes: Phillip, finding him readinge the prophete Esay, "Un[der]standest thou (sayeth hee) what thow readest?" Marke his answere: "How can I (sayeth hee) without an interpretor, without a guyde or a teacher? – εαν μη τις οδηγηση με, unlesse one goe before me."[11] A very foolishe answere in the eunuch, yf our principle at this day bee trewe; and twentye to one that Phillip the evangelist was some puritane, who did not barely content him selfe to bidde him reade on for God would blesse yt, but he beganne at the same text and preached unto him Jesus. Lykewyse the Levytes in Nehemiah were sure some puritanes, who did not only reade the texte, but they delyvered the sense unto the people.[12] Well, I hope there bee no man heare of this minde, that ignorance is the mother of devotion: that wretched and ragged opynion is hissed oute of the schoole of our hartes long eare this, I hope. Nay, rather, is yt not the mothere of error, the mother of treason and / sedition? Yf yt bee, — p.21
then woe bee to the dombe ministerye, which by this meanes must needes bee

9. The words 'that to do ... puritanisme' are written in the margin as an insertion.

10. See Acts 5: 34–40.

11. Cf. Acts 8: 30, 31.

12. Neh 8: 7.

eyther mother or grandemother of treason, ffor *quicquid est causa causae est causa causati*. Ignorance of the holy wil of God is the cause of treason, it will bee graunted (I am sure); but the dombe ministery is the cause of such ignorance: *ergo* the dombe ministery is the cause of treasonn.

'This the Jesuits, our seede men of sedition, doe see into well enough I warrante you, and that makes them thus bolde, as they bee, with their poyzoned assaultes to invade the flocke, which alas, ye know, they may easely doe when the shepehearde that should bee our gardien of defence hathe never an eye to see on. And will yee see the mischiefe of yt, ffinding us thus rawe and unarmed as they doe? Marke, I pray you, where they beginne to make their breach, at the conscience of man, I warrante you, where, when they have florished a while with the powerfull excommunication of Impius Quintus – that coulde never erre, for soothe! – they fall in the ende to buzze into theire poore clyentes' heades this perillous and pestilent aphorysme. Marke yt I pray you well, and ye may happen light on the conducte heade whens all our treasons are deryved: if a man have a conscience (say they) to doe any thing – they never stande to aske whether yt be a good conscience or no – but yf he have a conscience to doe any thing, though it be a naughty conscience, an erronius conscience, yet yf he doe it not, he synnes mortally. And why? For sooth because he had a conscience. As, for exaumple, yf a man bee perswaded in his conscience that hee ought to abuse an other man's wyfe, that he ought to murder and lay handes on the Lorde's annoynted, or doe any other vellenous or beastely acte (the very mention whearof would make your eares to glowe), / yet if hee doe yt not or doe not his best to doe yt, hee synnes grievously. And why? Forsooth because of the tendernesse of his conscience. Is not this good dyvinnity, thinke yee? And so by this fyne receipte of theirs they have brought yt miraculously to passe that that forlorne wretch that slewe the Prince of Orenge and thease late traytors of ours that have soe horribly and unnaturally attempted the death of her sacred Majestie (execute as many of them as ye list), they all suffer for their conscience, that is out of questian, the resolution is sette downe at Rhemes; but yf to lyve wretchedly and die unpenitently bee a badge of their catholyke conscience, let them keepe yt to them selves. This conscience, I tell you, is the *noli me tangere*: "Lette mee alone (say some) with the secrecye of my conscience." And what is that? That is asmuch to say, let mee alone with the overthrowe both of Church and commen wealthe: ffor under the wynges of this serpentyne conscience is hatched the broode of all thease pestilent conspiracyes.

'Now yf the cause of all this bee the domme ministerye, why then, *a contrario*, the redresse of all this must needes bee a learned ministery. But it is strange, when we come to complayne of this, why every man in a maner ioynethe with us: "I would to God it were redressed for me", sayeth eche one. Nay, there is one good fellow (but I can not light on his name) tells us in a certaine printed pamphlet that the grave fathers them selves doe wishe there were a learned and able ministerye. Sure, yf yt bee so, wee are gladde of yt with all our hartes. But yet (right honorable) because the distresses of / Gode's

p.22

p.23

chilldren are smally releived by thease shales of wordes, wee are humble suters unto your honours, and by your honours unto her Majestie, that, for his sake that dyed for us, our thyrste may bee no more queanched in this maner with an emptye cuppe. A strange jeast indeede to tell us a tale of men's secrete wishes and desyres of their hartes, when the soules of Gode's children lye bleeding and panting for reliefe, when whole countyes and countreyes within the lande (as so many lyving witnesses agaynste all such unsavorye pleadinges) doe perishe in theire ignorance for want of sustenance and instruction.

'Amiddest thease our distresses (right honorable) whyther shoulde wee flye but to this high courte? Yf wee may not bee harde heere, wee are at an outlarye; wee knowe not which way to turne us. To leave yt to the grave fathers (as some woulde have yt) alas lamentable experience hath made us in a maner dispayre of any good successe from that coast: what wee may find of yt heereafter I know not, but hitherto wee may trewly say it hath been as a northen wynde that seldome bloweth good to the Church of God. And albeit the gyfts and graces of Gode's spirit were redoubled upon the grave fathers, yet to balance their credites and wisdomes with the 3 estates of the lande were (as I thinke) rather to abuse them then to reverence them; neyther may it well bee don without greate iniury and preiudyce to this honorable courte. For is the cause honest, godly, profitable, and of greate weight? Who should deale in it, or who should have the honour of yt, but this high courte? And though this parleament were not sommoned / to make any new lawes, yet mee thinkes it p.24 were a very honorable course to reforme some olde lawes, or (at least-wyse) to open your eares and admitte into your presence the lamentable outcryes of the poore distressed soules of the lande, whose humble sute and grievances shall bee layed before you when you please. And yt may bee some of them stande now at your dore, thirsting for releife. Alas, is there law to expell out of the ministery a learned man, of lyfe unteynted, and is there no law to banishe thens an adulterer, an incestuous person, a drunckarde, a dombe hyrelinge, a swearer, a blasphemer, or such lyke? Wherof yf yt come to examination, I feare mee yee will blushe at the number. Surely, yf there were such a bracke or lamenesse in the law, can there come any greater honour to this High Courte of Parleamente then to reforme yt with speede, that thereby the Lord mighte have cause to bleasse us still in the mighty preservation of our Theodosia?

'Well, for conclusion of all I will only putte you in minde of that which one of the learnedest men in the lande boldely wryteth to one of the worthyest councellers of the lande. It were no matter yf I did name him, and yf I doe name him, I protest unto you it is with reverence that I name him, as one of the starres and lightes of Gode's church in this age, Mr Whytaker, the dyvinity Reader in Camebridge, to no meaner a man then my Lord Treasorer: "*Parum aut libris, aut legibus profici, quousque firmum et idoneum ministerium in ecclesiis constitutum fuerit* – Lyttle good to bee don with all your bookes and lawes (marke yt well) tille there bee a learned and able ministery established in your churches." A / very worthy speache and a trew speach; for, till that day come p.25 (right honorable), lay your heades togeathere, make what lawes yee will, cutte of as many serpentes' heades as yee list, assure your selves (which way soever ye turne) there will still bee a clowde before your eyes threatening misery and desolation in the hazarde of her Majestie's person. Till this monster of our unworthy ministery bee banished the lande there is no remedy, the prophetes of God have threatened it, it is a case unavoydable: the Church muste needes looke for heresyes, the prince for treasons, the land for hurleburleyes, the people for destruction.

'But yf none of all thease things should come to passe now; yf yt should please the Lorde to blesse us still beyonde measure as the hath don (as the commen maner of the worlde (ye knowe) is to beleeve inclusive of mercy and exclusive of justice, that the Lorde is made all of mercy), yf none of thease threatened and deserved miseryes should befall us (as our only hope and refuge is in the mercy of God), what then? Shall Cassandra bee punished for fearing the distruction of Troye? Shall Calphurnia bee plagued for dreaming she saw her husbande all blouddy in the Senate? Shall wee bee sommoned to appeare and our alleageunce bee called in question for shrincking at the swoorde that hangueth shaking over our heades? Alas (right honorable) how harde a thinge and allmost impossible it were for a harte fraight with dysloyaulty to budde out any such frute, let wisdome weighe.

'Well, Caesar before hee came to the senate house of Rome had warnings a man would [have] thought sufficiente to have keepte him frome that his bane and blouddy ende, yf the providence of the highest had not determined yt should bee soe. The Lorde Hastinges[13] lykewise (mentioned / in the chronicles) had some forwarninges of that which befell to him in the Tower, but he, good gentleman, thinking every man to meane good fayeth (as he did himselfe) came even to[14] trust to the place where he was treacherously and tyrannously murdered. Chastillon, that worthy Admyrall of Fraunce, had they say som intelligence aforhande of that brutishe Parisian slaughter, but what the sequell was wee see: it was not Gode's will they should escape that bitter cuppe. Such are his secrete judgementes, that those that did so constanctly professe his name should bee *tanquam oves ad lanicuam*,[15] and glorify him by their death. The Prince of Orenge lykewyse, after many woonderfull warninges, mighty escapes and delyverances, could not yet avoyed the balefull blow in the ende. Thease and such other may (yf yt please God) bee warninges to pull her Majestie by the slieve, and me thinkes the remembrance of them should sometymes awaken her out of her sleepe, and crye to her "*Cave, Caesar*". But yf the lease of our blisse and happynesse bee nowe expyred and the tyme bee come that God will pay the multitude of our synnes with the longe deserved rodde of revenge, then surely shall thease bee but dombe shewes woorking no effecte. For who doubtes but there is a scourge dew to us? Longe peace, rare quietnesse, unwoonted blisse, happye governement, caulmenesse at home, broyles abroade, gospell preached, wealth abounding, no awaking out of wickednesse, no amendement of maners, religion boldely professed in mouth and badly prac-tised in lyfe, an open resistance of the holy disciplyne of God: surely he is wourse then blinde that lookes not for a scourge.

p.26

'Let this then bee the yssue of the whole, that wee cease not every one of us (without delay) to flye to the Lorde in humble prayer and repentance that it would please him in mercy to cancell the recorde of our unthankefullnesse and to waken her Majestie's harte / before the day of her accoumpte, that shee   p.27 may remember the greate weighte of her calling, therby to reforme with speede such thinges as are amisse, especyally her ignorant and unlearned ministerye. That, as shee hath ben the beginner, so she may bee the finisher of the woorke; as she hathe hade the prayze to bee the planter of the Gospell, so shee may have the honour to bee the reformer of her Church to the redoubling of her happynesse in Christ Jesu. That her governement over us, and our obedience towardes her, may bee seasoned in his feare unto the ende, that so the Lorde may bee mooved to blesse us still with her, and her with peace, and peace with plentye; that her days may bee aged, her raigne prosperous, her blisse endelesse; that the last day of her lyfe may (yf soe please him) bee the last day of this earth, that when shee sleeteth[16] hens to our earthly discomforte, we may then beeholde his sonne Jesus sitting in his throne of judgement to our endelesse and everlasting comforte for ever.'

13. The story is from More's *History of Richard III*: see *The Complete Works of Sir Thomas More*, ii (ed. Richard S. Sylvester, Yale 1963), 48–51.

14. *Sic.*

15. *Sic.*

16. *Sic*; 'fleeteth'.

17. Peter Wentworth's speech and questions on the liberties of Parliament, 1 March 1587

i. Text from BL Cotton Titus F.i. copy.
Other MSS. London: BL Stowe 358 (copy of Cotton), Add. 32092 (questions only).
Cambridge: Cambridge University Library Gg.iii.34 (questions only).
Printed. D'Ewes 410–11.
ii. Text from BL Lansdowne 105, copy: another version of the questions only.
Printed. E.H.R. xxxix.48 (from Lansdowne).

Cotton Titus F.i, fos.289–90

A speech of Mr Peter Wintworth[1] to the Speaker of the Commons House of Parliament concerning the liberties of the knights and burgesses of the same House.

Anno 29 Regni Regine Elizabethe.

'Mr Speaker, forasmuch as such lawes as God is to be honnored by, and that alsoe such lawes as our noble soveraigne and this worthye realme of England are to be enriched, strengthened and preserved by from all forraigne and domesticall enemies and traytors, are to be made by this honnourable councell: I as one beinge moved and stirred upp by all dutifull love and desirous (even for conscience sake) and of a minde to sett forwardes Gode's glorie, the wealth, strenght and safetye of our naturall Queene and common weale, doe earnestlie desire by question to be satisfied of a fewe questions to be moved by yow, Mr Speaker, concerninge the liberties of this honnourable councell. For I doe assure yow (I praise my good God for it) that I doe finde in my selfe a willinge mynde to deliver unto this honnourable assemblie some litle taste and accompt of that simple talent which it hath pleased my keind God, of his singuler favor and goodnes, to bestowe uppon me to gaine to his highnes' honnour and glorie, and in him, and for him, to shewe unto my noble prince and common wealth true faithfull and dutiefull service. Of the which minde I am sure (Mr Speaker) heare are manie godlie, faithfull, and true-harted gentlemen in this honnourable assemblie, howbeit the want of knowledge and experience of the liberties of this honnourable councell doth staye and hold us backe, for as wee have a hartye desire to serve God, her Majestie, and this noble realme even soe

are wee / fearefull and lothe to give or offer anie offence to her Majestie or   v.
unto her lawes, the which wee presume wee shall not doe if wee keepe
ourselves within the circell of them. And noe man can observe that whereof he
is ignorant. Wherefore I praye yow (Mr Speaker) eftsones to move theis fewe
questions by question whereby everie one of this Howse maye knowe howe
farre he may proceede in this honnourable councell in matteres that concerne
the glorie of God, and our true and loyall service to our prince and state; for
I am fullie perswaded that God cannot be honnoured, neither yett our noble
prince or common weale preserved or mayntayned, without free speech and
consultacion of this honnourable councell; both which consist uppon the
libertyes of this honnorable councell, and the knowledge of them alsoe. And
soe here are the questions (Mr Speaker). I humblie and hartylie beseech yow
to give them readinge, and God graunt us true and faithfull hartes in
aunsweringe of them, for the true, faithfull, and hartie service of our mercifull
God, our lawfull prince, and this wholl and worthie realme of England will
much consist hereafter uppon the aunsweres unto theis questions; wherfore it
behoveth us to use wise, grave, and godlie consideracion in aunsweringe of
them.

'Therfore the Lord direct our tongues that we maie aunswere them even
with his spirit, the spiritt of wisdome, without the which our wisdome is
nothinge els but ffoolishnes. The questions followe.[2]

'Whether this councell be not a place for anie Member of the same here
assembled ffreelie and without controllment of anie person,[3] or dainger of
lawe, by bill or speeche to utter anie the greiffes of this common wealth
whatsoever touchinge the service of God, the safetie of the prince and this
noble realme.

'Whether that great honnour may be done unto God and benefitt and
service unto the / prince and state without free speech in this counsell which   f.290
maye be done without it.[4]

'Whether there be anie councell which cann make, adde to, or diminishe
from, the lawes of this realme but onelie this councell of Parliament.

'Whether it be not against the orders of this councell to make anie secreate
or matter of waight which is here in hand[5] knowne to the prince, or anie
other, concerninge the high service of God, prince, or state without the
consent of the House.

'Whether the Speaker or anie other maye interrupt anie Member of this
councell in his speeche used in this House tendinge to anie of the forenamed
high services.

'Whether the Speaker maye rise when he will, anie matter beinge propounded without consent of the House or nott.

---

1. *Sic.* and in Stowe.
2. Cam reverses the order of the second and
   third question here.
3. Add. omits (+ Cam).
4. Stowe corrects this to 'with it' (+ Add.,
   Cam).
5. Add. omits 'which is here in hand'
   (+ Cam).

'Whether the Speaker maye overrule the House if[6] anie matter or cause there in question; or whether he is to be ruled or overruled[7] in anie matter or nott.

'Whether the prince and state can continewe, stand, and be maintayned without this councell of Parliament, not alteringe the governement of the state.'

Theis questions Mr Puckering pocketted up and showeth Sir Thomas Hennage whoe soe handled the matter that Mr Wentworth was sent to the Tower.[8]

6. Stowe: '. . .' if any matter or cause be there in'; Add. has 'in' rather than 'if' (+ Cam).

7. Add. adds 'by the House' (+ Cam).
8. Add. omits this paragraph.

[Endorsed 'P. Wentworthe. Questions, towching the libertie of the Parleament Howse'.]

Questions to be resolved of by the Howse of Parliament.

1. First, whether the prince and state cann be mainteyned without this court of Parliament.
2. Item, whether there be any counsell that cann make or abrogate lawes, but only this court of Parliament.
3. Item, whether free speache and free doinges or dealinges be not graunted to everye on of the Parliament Howse by lawe.
4. Item, whether that greate honor to God, and those greate benefits, may be doon unto the prince and state without free speache and doyngs in this place, that may be donn with them.
5. Item, whether it be not an iniurye to the whole state, and against the law, that the prince or Privie Councell should send for any membre of this Howse in the parliament tyme, or aftre the end of the parliament, and to checke, blame, or punishe them for any speache used in this place, except it be for trayterous wourds.
6. Item, whether this be a place to receyve supplications of the greves and sores of the common wealth, and ether that we should be humble suters unto the Quene her Maiestye for releffe, or els to releve them here as the case requireth.
7. Item, whether yt be not against the orders and liberties of this Howse to receyve messages, either of commaundinge or prohibiting, and whether the messenger be not to be reputed as an enemye to God, the prince, and state. /
8. Item, whether it be not against the orders and liberties of this Howse to make any thinge known unto the prince that is here in hand to the hurte of the Howse, and whether the tale carriar be not to be punisshed by the Howse and reputed as an enymye unto God, the prince and state.
9. Item, whether we doo shewe our selves faithfull unto God, the prince, and state, in receyving suche messages, and in takinge suche tales in good parte, without punisshinge of the messenger and tale carriar by the order and discretion of this Howse.
10. Item, whether he or they be not to be estemed, reputed, and used as enimyes unto God, the prince, and state, that shall doo any thing to infringe the liberties of this honourable councell.

v.

18. *Speech on freedom of speech in support of Peter Wentworth, prepared for 1 March*

Text from BL Harley 1877, copy.

Harley 1877, fos.55–7

'Mr Speaker [sweet] (indeed) is the name of libertie but libertie yt selfe is (indeed) and (indeed) a value beyond all inestimable treasure, and the greatest value and most inestimable treasure that can possibl[ie] be, or grow to any natyon or people by this sweet libertie is when they may frankly and freely use it to the service of God, their prince and universall[1] of ther countrie, and common weale. And for that this high and honourable counsell is the only ordinary place for these high services, I am hartely to intreat you all to doe your best indevours to quicken, revive, and reedefie the sore ruined walles, and sweet value of this free libertie, and the inestimable treasure therof, to witt freedome of speech, and consultacion in this honourable counsell. For to yt it is due. And to further these high services I am to put you in remembrance, that this honourable House and assembly is termed a counsell, yea (Mr Speaker) the great counsell of England, and highest court of this realme. Sufficient reasons to prove it ar these. First all courts ar here to be controlled. Here may and ought to be made such lawes, as God is honored by; heare ought to be revoked and frustrated, all such lawes as God is dishonoured by. Here we ought to counsell with the wise men of this realme for the maintenance of the Queen's Majestie's estate. Here lawes ar to be devised for the preservacion of her Majestie's person and this noble comon wheale, and punishment of any traytors or treason therunto. And if it may be knowne that any persons, within the realme, or without, intend any perill either to her Majestie's estate or person, or to this noble common wealth, here must be devised how to cutt of such ill weedes, and how to withstand their traiterous purposes. Here must be studied and foreseene, that if any charge do come upon her Majestie, and this her realme, how it may be honourably sustained and supported. Here ought to be devised how her Majestie may be inriched and made strong, wherby she may withstand the malice of her enemies and th'enimyes of this her noble realme. Here lawes ar to be made for the common weale, to be frustrated, to be added unto, to be deminished or taken from, even such and in such manner as ar for the wealth, strength, benefitt, good ordering and preservacion of this whole and worthy realme, and of every part and degree therof. Here that offence and person which law cannot punish: this honourable counsell and high court may. Yea, this honourable and high court may iudge of all titles, even the highest, and may also take away liffe, lyme[2] and inheritaunce, and he is a traytor that saieth it wanteth power. So that it may be rightly said of this honourable counsell and high court, what [can it] not [do] in matters that concerne the goverment of this honourable common weale. And to conclude, no other counsell or court hath authoritie to doe all those waightie bussinesses, but only this high court. The reason is the prince and common weale have no other place to complaine unto of ther greifes, or to receave releife of them; but only this honourable counsell and high court.

'Out of infinite members[3] of wonderfull benefittes and furtherances that do grow unto the cause of God, unto our ledge prince, and unto this noble realme, [from] this high counsell and court I have thought good to present unto your wisdomes and veiwes these few instantes, to th'end that wee may all resort unto our kind God with due heartie and fervent thankfullnes for his inestimable providence and goodnes, in erecting this honourable counsell and high court; the which may iustly and truely [be] termed and have these epethites given unto it: the very holsome nurse and nursery, the only true cureing surgeon and phisicion of the cause of God, our prince, and common weale. For by that they all ar nursed, cherished, and releived, and also all woundes, sicknesses, and sores therof may be cured and healed, if God do blesse it with knowledg and wisdome; for in God and in Christ ar hide[n] all the treasure of wisdome, and knowledg, saieth St Paul.[4] So that God graunt us grace earnestly to seeke both wisdome and knowledg of his Majestie sithence he is the only giver of them and that it is to be obtained only at his Majestie's handes.

'Now somewhat I do iudge it good to say of the[5] benefitt of taking of counsell generally, and the rather to stirr us upp and to humble our mindes to a reverence therof, lett us heare what high comendacions the holy ghost giveth of it. Then what praises the weake wisdome of man (the which is foolishnes before God) doth say therof. Solomon a king, and the wisest king that ever was, or ever shalbe, or rather wisdome it selfe, even the spirit of God in him, said: "He that heareth counsell, is wyse; wher no good counsell is, ther the people decay, but wher ther be many that can give counsell, ther is wealth."[6] "Through counsell the thinges that men devise go forward, without counsell thoughtes come to naugh[t], but in the multitude of counsellors ther is stedfastnes."[7] And for a resolucion therof / Salomon saieth: "Establish thy   v. thoughtes by counsell."[8] And that counsell is to be taken cheifly of God. He saieth: "Ther is no wisdome, neither understanding, nor counsell against the Lord."[9] David a man according to Gode's one harte also said: "Thy testimonies

1. *Sic.*
2. *Sic.*
3. *Sic.*
4. Col 2:3.
5. MS repeats.

6. Cf. Pr 12: 15; 11: 14.
7. Cf. Pr 15: 22.
8. ? Pr 16: 3.
9. Pr 21: 30.

ar my delight and my counsellors, and giveth these sound reasons to prove it, for the Lord breaketh the counsells of the heathen, and bringeth the devises of the people to naught."[10] Saying farther: "The councell of the Lord shall stand for ever."[11] The childred of David said: "Aske counsell now of God, that we may know whether the way which we goe shalbe prosperous." The answere was: "Goe in peace, for the Lord guideth the way which ye goe" (Judges 18. 5, 6). The Lord graunt us grace to aske counsell cheifely of this counsellor, who is only able to guide our way in peace and to make it prosperous. Now to the opinion of sondry philosophers. Aristotle saieth counsell is an holy thing. Counsell is the key of certeintie, sayth Socrates. Ther cannot be a more devine thing then to aske counsell, saieth Plato; good counsell is the begining and ending of every good thing, saieth Zenophan; and Socrates saieth in another place, a wise man ought to take counsell for feare of mixing his will with his witt. Now I will rent[12] the saying of [the] Roman emperior, who said, though a few might determine a matter, yet aske counsell of many; his reasons ar these, for one will shew thee the proffitt, another the inconveniences, another the perills, another the damage and another the remedye. Thus you have heard what passing benefittes come by takeing of councell. To all thinges and to every purpose under the heaven ther is an appoynted time, saieth Salomon, a time to keepe sylence, and a time to speake; a time to leave, and a time to take and give loveing and faythfull counsell.[13] And so my earnest suite unto you all is, (sithence this is the only time for tounge service) that you will hartely serve our good God, our noble prince and this whole and worthy realme by your free speech uttered from true hartes: for a certaine thing it is that unto every counsell free speech is due. Then (*a maiore*) it must (of necessetie) be due to this high and great court, the which is not only termed, but is (indeed and in truth), the highest court of this realme and greatest counsell of our noble England.

'Now to the duties of those which be put in trust to give counsell. Jesus the sonne of Syrach saieth, "Keepe not back counsell when it may do good, neither hide thy wisdome when it may be famous."[14] But Jesus Christ the high counsellor delivered his talentes to his servantes, saying "Occupie untell I come". And unto him which imployed his talentes to his gaine Christ said it is well donne: "Good servant and faithfull thou hast bin in a little, I will make the[e] ruler over much, enter into thy master's ioy".[15] But unto those which do conceale counsell, when it may do good, the wisdome of Jesus the sonne of Syrach saith, "Wisdome that is hidd and treasure that is hoar[d]ed, what proffitt is in them both?"[16] Lastly, the inconveniences and perills that do grow unto every of us by concealing of counsell in this high counsell ar two. The first is treason, and disobedience to God. Treason to God in betraying his service with sylence; disobedient to God thus, for we disobey his commaundement in that wee do not lay out and imploye his talentes bestowed upon us to his gaine. And thus it is recompenced even by Christ his owne sentence, who said: "Take the talent from that unprofitable servant and cast him into utter darknes: ther shalbe weeping and gnashing of teeth."[17] Mr Speaker, this is the due reward we all must looke for at the Lorde's hand if we hide our talentes and do not lye them out (in this counsell) to the Lord his gaine, and to the gaine of our noble prince, and common weale. The second inconvenience that ariseth hereof is treason to the prince and realme. The reason is the prince and common weale ought aswell, and as much, to repute and iudg him a ranke traitor unto them both that keepeth silence when he heareth them betrayed, and will not speake against it, to th'end it may be stayed or prevented, as he which betrayeth them both. It agreeth with the opinion of the heathen philosipher Tullie, who said ther be two kind of iniuries, th'one in him that offereth wronge, th'other in him that resisteth it not with all his powre; and Christ said, "He that is not with mee, is against mee."[18] So that whosoever doth bring in doubt or question whether free speech be due to this honourable councell or not, doth bring this high councell and court and the authoritie therof in doubt and question, the which (as I take it) is the highest treason to God, our prince and common weale, that can possiblly be devised, as our goverment standeth. The reason is, certaine it is, that God, our prince and state / cannot be honored by any law made or revoked, neither yet our noble prince, and worthy realme, be ither preserved or maintained without it, for in this high court all equitie and iustice ought to shine, even as the sonn when it is at the highest wherof both poore and riche may take refreshing; wher (also) must be reformed all the oppresseons, extorcions, wronges, and enormities within the realme. Wherfore as the iniury is great to God, our prince, and common weale to stopp and stay free speech, so is it wonderfully perillous and intollerable, and he unworthy to be a member of this high councell, but to be throwne out of it with all shame, violence, and hatred of every true English heart as an ennemie unto the service of God, prince, and state, that shall offer but the lest preiudice or hinderance therunto. That may be now (Mr Speaker) the cheifest meane to serve God, our prince, and realme faithfully and hartely to love them all, truely and unfeinedly. The which is my espetiall, dutifull and only suyte unto every one of this honourable assemblie. "Above all thinges put on love, which is the bond of perfectnes", saieth St Paul.[19] The note is it bindeth and kniteth togeather all the duties that passe from man to man. And St Paule setteth forth a true paterne of love (to this House) in these wordes, "Let no man seeke his owne but every man another's wealth."[20] Now love is dutifull, for Christ saieth, "This is my commaundement that ye love one another."[21] Christ leaveth not there but prescribeth with what an earnest love wee ought to love on another: "as I have loved you," saieth he.[22] And St John saieth that Christ laied downe his liffe for

f.56

10. Neh 4: 15.
11. Ps 33: 11.
12. *Sic.*
13. Cf. Eccl 3: 1, 7.
14. *Sic.* the reference is elusive: cf. ? 1 Kgs 10: 7.
15. Mat 25: 21.
16. Cf. ? Eccl 7: 12.

17. Mat 25: 28, 30.
18. Cf. ? Cicero, *De Officiis* 1, 13; Mat 12: 30.
19. Cf. Col 3: 14.
20. 1 Cor 10: 24.
21. John 15: 12.
22. John 15: 12.

us. Therfore ought wee to lay downe our lives for our brethren, saieth he.[23] This is our dutie and herein would true love appeare.

'Now I have heard of the learned, that the defunction[24] of love is a fervent, a fierie affeccion of the heart settled and caried with an exceeding delight to serve God, our noble prince, and every degree of this noble realme. This were a ioye of ioyes, such hartes were to be ioyed in, yea heaven and earth would ioye in them. And this were but our duties, then here would be no curtesie made, but striveing who should rise up first in the defence of the libertie of this high and honourable councell when any preiudice is offred unto it, for by it (as our goverment standeth and as I said before) God is cheifly honored and our noble prince and common weale ar only preserved and maintained. And (it semeth in my simple iudgment) greatly weakenned and preiudiced by the last speech.[25] First in that it is obiected that the Queen's Majestie liketh not of innovacions. I answere (Mr Speaker) this is no innovacion, but rather a renovacion, or rather the seeking of a continuacion of the decayed castile, and only ordinary strength of the true and faithfull service of God, prince and common weale. And who dare tell her Majestie what we ar in hand withall in this high counsell without the consent of the House if it be in matters of importance, for the[26] warr a betraying of the secretes of this high and great counsell, and who dare bewray it, for that warr an intollerable fault.

'To prove it so I do thinke it good to recite a few presidentes (therby) to shew you how ill the wisdome of this House could (in former ages) beare with this iniurye offred to this honourable counsell, and how severely they have punished it. In King Henry 4 his time, a knight named Terrill did bewray the secreetes of the House to his Majestie. The wisdome and true hartes of the House tooke it so offensively that they committed him to the Towre during that sesseon, and further order by Act of Parlament made for that only purpose, that he should never be of the House againe, nor any of his posteritie. And in King Henry 5 his time the Speaker of the House named Fuller did likewise bewray the secrettes of the House to the Bishop of Norwitch, then Lord Chancellor; the House for a censure did put him out of his Speakershipp, and committed him to the Towre during that sesseon and made choyce of a new Speaker.[27] And I have divers times heard of auntient Parlament men that the wise and famous prince King Henry 8 would never seeme to punish, nay, that which is much lesse, not once to shew him selfe agrieved or offended with any Parlament man for any speeche used in that Parlament House. And surely (Mr Speaker) his wisdome saw a great reason therfore, for he providently forsaw that the iniurie is great that is offred to the service of God, to himselfe, and to v.   all kinges that should succeed him, and to the whole / realme both for the present and future time, when any member of this House is either blamed or punished for any speech used here, or any bill preferred into this House, by any other authoritie, then by the authoritie therof. The profound reason that moved his Majestie to be of that mind (no doubt) was for that he did wisely waye that the true and faythfull service of God, himselfe, and realme would be greatly hindred and stayed therby, iudging that the House would be then much more terrefied to speake for, or to preferr, that which was good, but that which was pleasing, yea albeit yt were perillous to the service of God, himselfe or state. And his wisdome did iudge the one a very poysone to the service of God, himself, and state, and the other a sweet, holsome, and comfortable restorative to further the high services of them all. Thus much concerning the wisdome and foresight of that prudent prince.

'And now I say that the holly ghost commaundeth us to eschew evill and to do that which is good, and to abhorr that which is evill and cleave to that which is good; yea he threateneth us in this manner, saying, "if ye do wickedly, yee shall perish both yee and your king".[28] And surely (Mr Speaker), in my simple iudgment these sentences of the holy ghost ar most aptly to be applyed to this high and great counsell, for here ar the highest and greatest services to be donne to God, our prince, and state. The neglect wherof will iustly deserve that we should all perish as we ar threatened in the last sentence, or at the least as many as do neglect ther duties in this counsell. And the case is very hard with us poore Parlament men (Mr Speaker) when we deserve to hang in hell (by the iustice of God) if we neglect his service, or the service of our prince or state, in this counsell: and may neither serve God, our prince, or state truely nor faithfully heare, but ar sure of displeasure, and punishment therfore. It is a smale comfort for an honest and true-harted man to be of this counsell. And yet the law of this realme and the writt wherby they ar elected and authorised doth commaund such to be elected and chosen. And the true dutie of a counsell and counsellors consisteth in thes poyntes cheifly; as namely, to deliberate, to conferr, to consult, to speake freely, to cast doubtes and to lay forth falshood sometimes ignorantly, sometimes wisely, that is to say even of purpose, to the end to make truth to shine, and shew it selfe in his[29] excellencie, wherby it may florish and tryumph in victorie, and that the illfavored face of falshood may be discovered and it overthrowne, wherby it may blush and be ashamed of it selfe, and that occupacion.

'And now (Mr Speaker) I ask these questions why may we not innovate. Nay, ar we not bounden in honour to the House, duty, honestie and good consciences to innovate good orders, as well as good lawes; have not former parlamentes left us many presidentes therof to ther great and ay induring honor as examples of the power of the parlament for us to immitate, yes doubtles? And have we lesse powers then former ages or parlamentes have had?. If we say we have lesse power, then wee wee[30] all traytors to the service of God and of

23. 1 John 3: 16.
24. *Sic.*
25. Assuming the speech *was* written in advance, it may be that no one in particular was intended here; or perhaps it was easy to predict that men like James Dalton would oppose Cope's proposals, which may be what is in mind here.
26. *Sic.* ? 'that'.
27. These references to the reigns of Henry IV and V are elusive, and perhaps wrong: the see of Norwich did not provide a Lord Chancellor during Henry V's reign (or Henry IV's or VI's).
28. Rom 12: 9; 1 Sam 12: 25.
29. *Sic.*
30. *Sic.*

our noble prince and common wealth, both for the time present and for the time to come also. The reason is given before, which is we betray this counsell, the which maintaineth the service of them all, if we do affirme our power not to be as large as it was at any time in former ages (as yet is in truth), then ar we (likewise) traytors if we do not use our power and put it in dayly experience and practise when it may do good, and cause of service if offred. And (Mr Speaker), sithence that thinge cometh now in question that will both clense and scoure this sweet and comfortable fountaine from whence issueth all ordinary liffe, defence, and furtherance to God his causes, and to the welth, strength, and preservacion of our noble prince and worthy realme; if any do goe about to stopp the course therof, and do it wittingly or willingly I do affirme that he plainely uttereth and sheweth his hart to be malicious, fixed, and bent unto them all. "Charitie is not suspicious", saieth St Paul.[31] / And therfore let us make the best of [that] which is said, and use all good and lawfull means to cause a brother to see his fault, wherby he may correct and amend it. And also that the residue may feare to give the like offence. "Loveing admonition is both godly and dutifull", saieth David, "let the righteous smite me for that is a benefitt, and let him rebuke me, and it shalbe a precious oyle that shall not breake my head".[32] Therfore if offences be committed unwittingly I beseech you, let us forbeare to important[33] on another, for if ye bite on another, saieth St Paul, take heed least ye be consumed on of another.[34] But if any shall offend herein after admonition, he doth then plainely utter a malicious harte to the service of God, prince, and common weale, and deserveth the iust reward of an enemy to them all; and we cannot shew true hartes, if forciblly we withstand him not, and reward him according to his demerittes. For if any be voyd of feare to offer such an intollerable iniurye as to indevour to stopp and stay the clensing and scouring of this sweet fountaine, to witt the fredome of speech and consultacion in this high and honourable counsell, from whence all the aforsaid great and wonderfull benefittes do insue, namely, all ordinary defence and furtherance to God, his causes, or the princes or states, it will plainely shew want both of love and courage in us all if we should not sett forward the clensing and scouring therof, as yea more earnestly and hartely then any adversarie doth hold it back; for what shame and dishonestye were it to us all if we did not love God, our prince and state generally, neither yet our ffrendes, kindred, wives, nor children particulerly, but should want of hart and courage (in this high counsell) to benefitt and serve them all. I cannot but condeme him as unworthy to be a member of this high and sacred counsell that will either be afraid, or shew want of love hartely, to serve in any of these high services.

f.57

'To stirr up the dull and unfeeling sentences of all and every of us (therfore) to serve God, our noble prince, and state truely, hartely and earnestly, and all by clensing and scouring this sweet, holsome, and comfortable fountaine, from whence (as I sayd before) yssueth all ordinary liffe and defence unto them all and furtherance to ther causes, I have thought it needfull to give yee the simple tastes of the wonderfull benefittes that do grow unto the cause of God, our prince, and state by this high court [and] great and sacred counsell. Albeit not in such plentifull measure as a man of wisdome and knowledge can yeld in matters concerning the high service of God, prince, and state, for I acknowledg my vessell to be feeble, emptie, and of smale abilitie for such high services, and do therfore earnestly desyer those whome the Lord hath blessed and furnished with able giftes, wherof here ar many (praised to[35] his name for it) to supply my want.

'And so to conclude (Mr Speaker), I am in humble, harty, and fervent manner to require every one of this honourable counsell to stick earnestly to the former motion, to witt, that the House may answere these questions by question, to th'end that we may be all incouraged truely and dutifully to performe these great and high services, being assured through knowledg that we shall not only know then how to avoyd her Majestie's displeasure, but also be out of daunger of lawes. And (in truth) herein (Mr Speaker), we shall procure the great favour of God, iustly deserve the love both of her Majestie, and the whole state also, and I do verely perswade my selfe that her Majestie is both so godly wise and loveingly disposed to the cause of God, her selfe and to her true subiectes, that she wilbe highly offended if but the least preiudice that may be shalbe offred to this high and honourable counsell, being the greatest counsell of her noble England, sithence her Majestie's wisdome seeth and hath felt (by many late experiences) the great good and benefitt that cometh therof to the cause of God, to her owne safety and to the preservacion of her noble realme and faythfull subiectes therof. I protest unto the liveing God that I do stand for the liberties of this honourable counsell / ffor thes three respectes and endes, chefly and only. First, of true love that I do beare to the preservacion of this worthy realme, and all the people therof, for a perfect knowledg doth assure me that this high counsell and court is the cheifest nurse and nursery, phisition, and surgeon, to heale all the woundes, sores and sicknesses of the prince and comon weale. Next, unto that providence and favour of our mercifull God whose infinite wisdome and goodnes did (of his great favour and love towardes this noble realme) ordaine this high counsell and court for the aforesaid most happie, blessed, and godly respectes and endes only. Therfore I hartely beseech you eftsoones (Mr Speaker) to aske those questions, to th'end that the House may answere them, by question; for I hope that our kind God, our loveing and lawfull prince, and this worthy realme shall find no enemyes here to hinder them, but true and faithfull counsellors to further them.'

v.

---

31. 1 Cor 13: 4.
32. Ps 141: 5.
33. *Sic*; ? 'importune'.

34. Gal 5: 15.
35. *Sic*.

19. *Part of Speaker's speech,*
2 March 1587 (?)

Text from Queen's College, Oxford, 284, copy.

Queen's College, Oxford, 284, f.35

A copie of part of Sergeant Puckring's speech to the House of Commons, when he was Speaker of the Parliament in [blank] *Reginae Elizabethae.*

'And specially you are commanded by her Majestie to take heed, that none care be given or time afforded to the werysome sollicitations of those that commonly be called Puritans, wherewithall the late Parliaments have been exceedingly importuned: which sort of men, whilest (in the gyddinesse of their spirits) they labour and strive to advance a new eldership, they do nothing else but disturbe the good people of the Church and common wealth; which is as well-grounded for the body of religion it selfe, and as well guided for the discipline as any realme that professeth the truth. And the same thing is allready made good to the world by many the writings of godly and learned men, neither answered, nor answerable, by any of these new-fangled refiners. And as the present case standeth it may be doubted whether they or the Jesuites do offer more danger, or be more speedily to be repressed: for albeit the Jesuits do empoysen the hearts of her Majestie's subjects under a pretext of conscience to withdraw them from their obedience due to her Majestie, yet do they the same closely and only in privy corners. But these men do both publish in their printed books, and teach in all their conventicles, sundry opinions, not only dangerous to the well-setled estate and politie of this realme by putting a pyke between the clergy and the laitye, but also much derogatorie to her sacred Majestie and to her Crowne, aswell by the diminution of her antient and lawfull revenues and by denying her Highness' prerogative and supremacy, as by offring perill to her Majestie's safety in her own kingdome. In all which things, howsoever in many other points they pretend to be at warr with the popish Jesuites, yet by this seperation of themselves from the unity of their fellow subjects, and by abasing the sacred authority and Majesty of their prince, they do both joyne and concur with the Jesuits in opening the dore and preparing the way to the Spanish invasion that is threatned against the realme.

'And thus, having according to the weaknesse of my best understanding, deliverd her Majestie's most royall pleasure and wise direction, I rest there, with humble suit for her Majestie's most gracious pardon in supply of my defects, and recommend you to the author of all good councell.'

20. *Sir Christopher Hatton's speech on the Bill and Book, 4 March 1587*

i. Text from PRO SP Dom Eliz. 199/1, original draft in the hand of Dr Richard Bancroft, chaplain to Hatton.
Other MS. Lambeth Palace 178.
Printed. Strype, *Whitgift* iii.186–94 (from Lambeth).
ii. Text from Oxford: Bodley, MS Tanner 79, copy in the hand of Whitgift's secretary.
Other MS. London: Lambeth Palace 178 (first section only).
Printed. Strype, *Whitgift*, i.491–3 (first section only, from Lambeth, omitting the last four Latin tags).

SP Dom.Eliz.199/1

[Endorsed by Bancroft 'Towchinge the bill and the booke exhibited in the parlament 1586 for a further reformation of the Churche.' and in a second contemporary hand 'Dr Bancroftes discourse uppon the bill and booke exhibited by the puritanes in Parlament. 2 *Martii*[1] 1586.']

Exordium. 'That wheare the booke and bill hath beene greatly comended,' *etc.* 'And althowgh in respecte of manifold busynes,' *etc.* 'I have taken no further paynes in[2] worde of God then concerneth the due information of a true Christian man as well in matters of faithe as of manners,[3] by the one to be instructed in the sinceritie of true religion, how to beleeve, and by the other, how to directe my actions to Gode's glorye and the profett of my contrye; and besides, thowghe I have deemed it ever more an especiall parte of Christian sobrietye for everye man to conteyne him selfe within the bowndes of his owne vocation, and not to presume too much upon his owne knowledge to dispute, decide, and determayne ecclesiasticall matters, appertayninge proper[l]ye to the lerned doctors and grave fathers of the Churche: yet, for as muche as a greate parte of this desired reformation cometh within the compasse of my profession, towchinge matters of state, I have thowght good to crave your heedfull regard' *etc.* 'whilest I shall open unto yow sundrye pointes of verye great consequence towchinge the same.

---

1. *Sic*; Hatton spoke on the subject on 4 March.
2. Lambeth adds 'the'.
3. Bancroft has substituted this for 'conversation'.

'The whole reformation
begone in King Edward's
tyme and undertaken
by her Majestie
consisteth cheefly
in the establishment:

{
Of a true goverment of the Churche
greatly corrupted and falsely usurped by
the Bishop of Rome.
Of the pure doctryne of Christ by a
sownd reformation and repurgation therof
from poperye.
Of a goodly order for publike prayer and
adminstration of sacramentes with other
holly rites and ceremonies: insteed of
the popish Masse, barbarous service and
many other corruptions.
}

'This reformation was made, upon most grave consideration, by the cheef lerned doctors and fathers of this Churche. It hath beene eftesones fyned and refyned and by her Majestie at lengthe browght to suche perfection as the profession of this reformed religion in England hath beene ever synce the cheefe keye and stay therof in all the reformed churches of Christendome. What ioye was once in England for this reformation? Howe manye letters have beene written hither by strangers to congratulate the sinceritie and happines therof? And how many chalendges have beene made and bookes written in defence of the same? Our adversaries abrode have been mightilye refuted. "*Sed inimici hominis, domestici eius*".[4] For amongest all the assaultes made hitherto by sundrye sectaries against this our reformation ther was never any to my knowledge comparable to this late bill and booke, exhibited here amongest us.

'My purpose is to deale onlye with that parte which towcheth the goverment: how be it as by the waye I can not but remember unto you how not withstandinge the lawe made *anno 1°* of her Majestie that who so ever shalbe[5] eyther by worde or writinge, deprave *etc.* the Booke of Common Prayer *etc.*, this bill tearmeth the same to conteyne diverse imperfections, grosse corruptions and so manye repugnances with the word of God, as that scarse any parte therof remayneth sownd. In respecte wherof it earnestly desireth to have the same wholy abrogated, and doth offer an other newlye made unto us, to be established.

'Wherin, first my masters, (I will speake but like a politike man) will you alter the whole forme and order of your service; will yow take that booke from us, which wee have beene persuaded to thinke both good and godly, and give us a new, accomptinge the other corrupt *etc.*? Might it not have suffised, to have reformed the errors? If yow aunswer that there weare so many, it cold not be otherwise done, will any man beleeve yow? What will the people saye? Assuredly, wheare as yow pretende hereby to worke wonders, yow shall drive them by thowsandes either to become atheistes or papistes. I tell yow ther is an olde note of schismatikes or heretikes which is verye riffe amongest us, and I

2 Tim. 2,[6] 7   think it is in the scriptures: "*Semper discentes, et nu[n]quam ad scientiam veritatis pervenientes*". Assuredly all good men doe begin herby to suspecte yow.

'Secondly, if I be not deceyved, I finde a shamefull sleyghte and cuninge pointe, smothlye passed over in this booke[7] exhibited. It is well knowne that some ringe leaders in this schisme have tawght that it was unlawfull to have a prescript forme of service in the Churche: but now theire fellowes have framed us one. Belike they ment every such kind of service to be unlawfull except it weare of theire owne makinge. But in good earnest: doe yee meane indeed as yee wold seme? Shall wee have a Booke of Common Prayer, to be usuallye red and observed in our churches, so as the common people who can not read by often hearinge one forme of prayer may learne the same, to theire great comfortes els whear? What meanethe the booke then, when in the rubricke before your chapiter of publike exercises such an order is theare prescribed as doth never permitt the cheefe parte therof, that is the confession in the first chapiter, to be red in the Churche? Besides, what menethe this? Ther is a forme of service sett downe to be used before and after the sermon, which is indeed the whole service, and yet in the rubricke after the same it is thus written: "It shall not be necessarye for the minister daylye" *etc.*; and in the c[h]apter of baptisme: "He prayeth in this maner", or such like; and in the chapter of the Lorde's supper: "The minister geveth thankes, either in these wordes following or the like in effecte". So as for any thing I see, althowghe to please us withall ther be in shew a booke pretended, yet in truth ther is no such matter but all or the most parte is left to the ministers spirite. These men do therfore verifye the proverbe: "*Aurum subaeratum, tussis pro crepitu*".[8]

'Towchinge the 2 parte of our reformation, that is true doctrine repurged: I take it the whole summe therof is conteyned in 39 articles of religion sett owt by lawe *anno* 1562. Wherof I find by this bill and booke 3 of them wholy condemned or abrogated: the 34, of the traditions of the Churche; the 35, of homelies; the 36, of the makinge of bishops and ministers. Besides it semeth unto me that one of[9] articles of our beleefe is in effecte abrogated: *descendit ad inferos*. But this is a question it semeth amongest devines; I will not medle with it. How be it I remember that abowt 7 yeares synce there was written a booke to the like purpose by one Carlile, which her Majestie by the advise of the best lerned of her clargye forbad as a verye dangerous booke and assertion.[10]

'But all this while I am almost besydes my purpose. Leaving therfore in this sorte matters of divinitie I will come to speake of our goverment, which in some pointes is quit overthrowne, in some greatly shaken, and by some very muche dangered. That which I doe therfore mislike in this bill and booke towching our goverment is 1° verye iniurious to us of[11] laitie, to the cheefe of the clergie, but especially unto her Majestie.

'First for our selves. It appearethe in the 6 chapiter of this booke that when any ecclesiasticall man shuld dye or be remooved, *jus patronatus* shuld be in everye presbyterye, and the elders, I knowe not how, shuld present to the

---

4. Mi 7: 6.
5. Lambeth: 'shoulde' (correctly).
6. *Sic* (+ Lambeth); *recte* '3'.
7. Lambeth: 'bill'.
8. The notion of *aurum subaeratum* appears in Persius, *The Satires*, V.106, though the latter, less delicate part of this tag does

not: see R. Taverner's edition of Erasmus' *Adages* (1577).
9. Lambeth adds 'the'.
10. Christopher Carlile's *Discourse . . .* (1582) had been interdicted soon after it appeared.
11. *Sic*; Lambeth: 'the'.

lyvinge. Which towcheth us all in our inheritances, and besides torneth to our no smale reproofe, in that of auncient tyme havinge receyved such credite and authoritie, wee onelye shuld be thowght unworthye to contynew our right *etc.* Nay surelye I can not see but that if we weare all as wee pretende, there cold not be many presbyteries errected in this land more able to present fitt men to any of our lyvinges then wee our selves, if wee wold use but those helpes appointed by law alreadye. For my owne parte *etc.* But yet in this matter wee are further towched. Here are orders sett downe for the burdoninge of everye parishe with one pastor at the least, a doctor, ij deacons at the least, besides I knowe not how many elders to be found in equitye, if they be poere and do labor in the causes of the Churche, by the releefe of the parishe as well as any of the rest: but neither bill nor booke doe speake one word, with what lyvinges or howe these officers shalbe maynteyned. Wherin there is a peece of cuninge used: supposing that playne dealing wold have hindered theire purpose. For indeed theire meaning is to drawe from us, maugre our heades, our impropriations; and if the spoyle of the bishops and cathedrall churches will not serve theire turnes (as certaynly they can not, theire number beinge so great), then doe they sett it downe that wee are bounde to surrender owt of our handes our abbay landes and such other possessions as have at any tyme belonged to the Churche. It is wonderfull to see how dispitefully they write of this matter. They calle us church robbers, devourers of holly thinges, cormorantes, *etc.*, affirminge that by the lawe of God thinges once consecrated to God for the service of his Churche belonge unto him for ever, and that wee keepe suche goodes and livings contrarye to our owne consciences: as appeareth in the booke *Of Ecclesiasticall Goverment* and an other which came to my handes the last parlament, entituled *A Complaynt of the Commonaltye*.[12] Wherby wee may see what is intended against us: how for the enritchinge of them selves they labor by our owne consentes to impoverishe us; and withe what reprochefull speaches they handle us. For my own parte I have some impropriations *etc.*, and I thanke God I keepe them with a good conscience *etc.* Many wold be undone. The law approveth us *etc.* The rule (*cui bono*) maketh me to thinke that these whott, busye reformers do rather seeke ours then us *etc.*

'For the overthrowe of the present estate of the clergye by this presbyterye, especiallye archbishops and bishops *etc*, as beinges[13] calinges not agreeable to the worde of God (as the bill saieth), I will leave it to the divines, being a matter withowt my reache: althowghe in my conscience in[14] doe see the necessitye of those dignityes and authorities for avoydinges of contention and the better reputation of theire calinges, as to the same purpose wee have in the civill state noblemen and gentilmen; and doe veryely hold that parte of the bill as a lewde untruthe. This onelye I do iudge that hereby a greate indignitie is offred to the honour of this realme, in seekinge to spoile the same of one essentiall parte of the second estate, to alter the honor of our parlamentes, and to bringe into it a barbarous aequalitie, which hathe usually hitherto beene *noverca regnorum et mater confusionis.* And as thowghe it weare unlawfull for her Majestie to conferre honor wheare indeed oftentymes it is best deserved.

'But to come to that which most of all shuld towche us, her Majestie's estate: I finde this platforme iniuriouse to her supremacye, to her strength and to her person.

'For her Highnes' supremacye, it consisteth principallye as I gather owt of the statute to that purpose *1°* of her Majestie, *1°* upon her title of supreme head or governor; 2. her authoritie in making ecclesiasticall lawes; 3. upon the right that the last appellations in such causes shuld be made to her Majestie's Chauncrye: all which pointes are in a maner wholy abrogated by this bill and booke. For althowghe it be said therin, that the soverainge[15] majestie is placed by God in highest authoritie under him within theire dominions over all persones and causes as well ecclesiasticall as civil, yet marke how the booke interpreteth it selfe: for soth theire dominion they speake of is this, that the soverainge[16] must see and commaunde the orderinge of them, as God hath appointed by his worde. He must not make any him selfe by his ordynarye authoritie, but see others make them: whiche is not a soverainge[17] authoritie *in causas,* but *in personas;* and is caled *potestas facti, non iuris.*

'Secondlye, wheare this bill affirmethe that the guidance of the Churche is comitted to the pastors, doctors and elders, that they by common consent might directe all the affayres and busynes of the same, *qui dicit omne nihil excipit;* wheare it saieth that the presbyterye hath authoritye to chuse, electe, ordayne, and upon occacion, to remove and displace all ecclesiasticall officers, and (as the In the end booke saieth) to visit, decide causes, appointe theire owne meetinges, conferences and synodes: what is lefte to her Majestie? Or wheare is the fulfillinge of that lawe which saieth that all authoritie to visite, reforme, redresse, order, electe, correcte, make lawes, abrogate lawes, call synodes *etc.* is annexed unto her royall dignitie and doth not appertayne to any other (in a Christian Crowne kindome[18]) but as deryved thence?

'Thirdlye, it appeareth both in the bill and booke that if any difficulties or In the end aggrevanses doe arise in these presbyteries, ther lyeth no appeale but from the presbyterye to the conference, from that to a provinciall synode, and thence to a nationall: wheare as when her Majestie's father did first abandon poperye, this was his cheefest endevoure, that the appeales which weare made to Rome might be[19] degrees come unto his Chauncerye. So as hereby it is manifest (as I thinke) that this newe devise is verye iniurious to her Majestie's supremacye.

'Now of the second point, how it diminishethe her Majestie's strength and abilitye. In my conceyt her Majestie's strength standeth verye much upon her

---

12. See Anonymous Journal, f.99v for these works.
13. *Sic.* Lambeth: 'beinge'.
14. *Sic.* Lambeth: 'I'.
15. *Sic.*
16. *Sic.*
17. *Sic.*
18. *Sic.*
19. *Sic* (+ Lambeth).

revenues: large tributes and great ritches are indeed *nervi reipublicae, ornamenta pacis, subsidia belli.*[20] Now what a losse shuld her Highnes[21] if (as hath beene said) all her impropriations shuld be taken from her? But what if they deale with her Majestie in her tents[22] and first frutes as with her impropriations? Surelye the booke of Ecclesiastical Discipline[23] nameth the exactinge of the same *nundinationum et*[24] *spoliationum direptiones, etc.*

pag.88

'Lastelye towchinge her Majeste's[25] person or saftie, I accompte it hereby greatlye endangered, in that her Highnes is made subiecte to the presbuteries' censures, reprehensions, suspentions and excommunications: which thowgh it be not preciselye there named, yet I am sure none will denye it, sith it is so largelye sett owt in the Ecclesiasticall Disciplyne. For who knoweth how farre they will proceede, if her Majestie doe neglecte theire excommunications? Is it not, thinke yow, verye well knowne what owtragious assertions are made hereof in your cheefe presbyterie men's bookes? Doth not her Majestie understand what is sett downe hereof in thes bookes, *De iure regni apud Scotos,*[26] *De iure magistratuum in subditos,*[27] *Vinditiae*[28] *contra tyrannos,* and others? Yes indeed.

'So as to conclude I assure yow, so farre forthe as I am able to looke into these matters, I thinke, all circumstances considered, there was never moved in any parlament to my remembrance, and urged with suche importunitie by those who wold be reakoned her Majestie's best-affected, most faithfull and most dutifull subiectes, a matter of greater inconvenience and meescheefe.

'For I praye yow wherin differ these men in this cause from the papistes? The Pope denieth the supremacye of princes: so doe in effecte these. The Pope yeeldeth unto them onlye *potestatem facti, non iuris; in personas, non causas:* no more doe our reformers in this point. The Pope wheare he entreathe doth abrogate all such lawes as any prince hath made in Church matters to his dislike: and so wold these men doe with all the lawes, cannons, constitutions and orders heretofore made in the Churche, as is expressed in the last sentence of the bill *etc. Ita fiat repetitio reliquorum.*'

Saunders[29]

---

20. Cf. Cicero, *Pro Lege Manilia,* 7, 17 or *Orationes Philippicae,* V, 5.
21. Lambeth adds 'sustaine'.
22. *Sic.* Lambeth: 'tenths'.
23. Walter Travers' *Ecclesiasticae Disciplinae. . .*
24. Repeated in MS.
25. *Sic.*

26. By Buchanan.
27. By Beza.
28. *Sic.* Lambeth: '*Vindicta*'; the tract is attributed to Stephanus Junius Brutus, though cf. Doc.20ii, f.135.
29. i.e. Nicholas Sander(s).

ii: Tanner 79, fos.134–8

[Endorsed by Whitgift 'The some of Sir Christopher Hatton speaches in Parlament against the bill and boke of the Puritaines 15 February 1586'.][1]

Certayn mischeifes ensuing the Puritans' demaundes and platforme.

1. It overthroweth her Majestie's supremacie, which consisting[2] cheifly in these 3 heades: her title of supreme government[3] over all persons and causes ecclesiasticall; that no lawe be made and put in practise without her particuler assent; that the last appellation in causes ecclesiasticall be made to her Highnes' Chauncery, as it was before to the Pope. All three in effect must be abolisshed.

For the first: they say the prince, being no elder, is in the number of those *qui facile debent pati se regi et gubernari*, and not the supreme governor.

For the second: the making of all ecclesiasticall lawes they ascribe to their senate wholly, and doe give to the prince authoritie only to punish such as offend their orders, which in deed is to give her Highnes' government *in personas tantum, non in causas, ad potestatem facti, non iuris*.

For the third: their appellations lye from the eldership to a conference; from that to a provinciall; and from this to a nationall Synode, which must definitively end all.

2. It taketh from her Majestie that part of her praerogative royall wherby she is patrone paramont of all the benefices in England accruing to her by lapse or otherwise.

3. It taketh from her Majestie, and all other of the laity, that part of their inheritance wherby they present unto ecclesiasticall livinges: *ius patronatus*.

4. They hold it unlawfull to pay to her Majestie the first fruites and tenths of their livinges, or that ether her Majestie or any lay man should have in their possession any impropriations. /

5. They require to have moe colledges built for the encreasing of that number v. which is to furnish their presbyteries; and that all the Bisshops' livinges and such landes as appertayned heretofore unto abbeies may partly be ymploied that way, and partly to the better maintenance of their presbyteries.

6. It overthroweth both archbisshops and bisshops and so consequently one of

---

1. This attribution does not appear in Lambeth; the date (also Whitgift's hand?) reflects what appears on f.137v.

2. *Sic* (+ Lambeth).

3. *Sic*. Lambeth: '. . . title and supreme government'.

the cheefe degrees of the estate of this realme, desiring as of necessity an aequalitie of ministers.

7. It overthroweth all the ecclesiasticall constitutions, lawes and ordynances which have bene made ever synce the Apostles' tymes, that so they may make such other as shalbe thought meet in every congregation.

8. It overthroweth a great part of the common lawe and statutes, as (besides those which depende upon her Majestie's supraemacie) the Statute of Mortemayne, *etc.* If this platforme should goe forwarde it may boldly be averred that one whole man's life of parlementes would not be sufficient to make lawes which might bring it to any tolerable state of government.

9. It overthroweth the present division of this land into parisshes and requireth a newe to be made answerable to their fancies.

10. It maketh her Highnes subiect to their excommunications, and so consequently is not unlike to prove a matter of great danger. For if her Majestie should be excommunicated and not yeeld therunto, the cheif authors of this platforme doe affirme that then, *lege seniorum*,[4] which they say holdeth in kingdomes, her Majestie's subiectes, or any others, are freed from their oathes of fidelitie. /

f.135   What dangerous propositions the cheif patrones of this newe devised government have publisshed of late yeares – how naturall borne subiectes may rebell ageinst their prince, depose him and execute him – every man knoweth who have redd the booke entituled *De Jure Magistratuum in Subditos*, Bucchanan *De Jure Regni apud Scotos*, and Junius Celta intituled *Vindictae*[5] *contra Tyrannos*.

11. It condemneth the government of the Church ever synce the Apostles' tymes, and conteyneth many moe straunge assertions, and some impossibilities, *etc.*

> *Ne sutor ultra crepidam.*[6]
> *Malum bene positum ne moveas.*[7]
> *Omnis mutatio periculosa.*
> *Mutatio quae adiuvet utilitate, novitate perturbet.*
> *Veteribus legibus novas surrogare, est vim et robur legibus adimere.*
> *Cui bono.*[8] /

v.   *Exordium.*
In divinitie I am no further seene then for the information of my Christian conscience in faith and conversation.

By the one to be instructed with synceritie of true relligion.

In the other to direct my actions to God's glorie.

I thought it Christian sobrietie for every man to contayne himself within his owne vocation, not praesuming of himself to dispute, decide or determine Church matters, but to leave it to whom it appertayned.

And therfore in those high misteries I will wholly referr you to them that can better satisfy you in the matters I speake of.

But as touching the reformation, the booke and bill offred, I will open unto you some fewe poyntes, etc.

That hath bene done by Henry 8, Edward 6 and her Majestie hath consisted upon these poyntes:

1. To establish a true and faithfull government of the Church corrupted and usurped *etc.*
2. To deliver the pure doctrine of Christe by a sound repurgation from poperie.
3. A godly order of publique prayer and administration of sacramentes: in steed of Masse and other idolatrous services.
   Inimici hominis domestici eius.

This reformation consydered by the cheifest learned of the Church, by her praedecessors, and herself, hath bene fyned and refyned with gladnes at home and congratulation from abroad. /

But, contrary to the lawe, this labour is depraved and suffreth imputation of imperfections, grosse corruptions, and repugnancies with the word of God.

But will you take away the whole Booke and give us wholly a newe f.136 reformation, with a forme of common prayer, without shewing the errors of the old, or the assured perfections of the newe?

This course will either drive us back to Papisme, or meerely corrupt us with atheisme.

I pray God you offer us not *aurum subaeratum, aut tussim*[9] *pro crepitu.*

But touching civill government, very iniurious to us, the whole clergie, and principally to her royall Maiestie.

The presbyterie taketh from us *jus patronatus.*

It toucheth us with singuler reproch, that in our Christian consciences we should not as syncerely proceede herein as the elders.

That they put upon our parisshes and lordshipps so many ecclesiasticall ministers as in no wise we shalbe able to maynteine: for therof in their bill and booke nothing is spoken.

Playne dealing herein would hinder the cause.

For they have designed the spoyle of the bisshops, of calling and living, of cathedrall churches, *etc.*

They will pull from us chauntries, impropriations, and all abbey landes.

And so you may see *cui bono* the matter tendeth of these busy reformers.

But touching her Majestie's estate.

They drawe from her the supremacie.

Her authoritie to make ecclesiasticall lawes. /

Her jurisdiction touching appellations to be made in the Chauncerie.   v.

Hereby the revenue of the Crowne shalbe decayed.

The subiect shall fynde a heavie burden in the supplie of the same.

---

4. *Sic.* Lambeth: '*lege feudorum*'.
5. *Sic* (+ Lambeth).
6. Pliny the Elder, *Natural History*, xxxv, 36 (10).
7. Cf. the proverbial '*malum bene conditum ne moveris*'.
8. Cicero, *Pro Milone*, xii.32; the rest of this folio is blank.
9. *Sic* (*tussis*).

The tenths and first fruites cleerly gone.

The subsidies of the clergie cleerely wiped away.

The proffitt of temporalties *sede vacante* also gone.

Her Majestie loseth her jurisdiction in calling assemblies and synodes, a parte of her praerogative royall.

She loseth the recognition of her subiectes in her supremacie ecclesiasticall.

All lawes and statutes ageinst the Pope for maintenance of the same are cleerely taken away.

All other lawes for the obedience for the obedience[10] of the subiect are cleerly abolisshed.

They leave to the Quene.

To see and commaund the ordering of them, but not to choose, appoinct, elect or order any of them or any thing amonges them pertayning to themselves, or the Church.

And so it followeth that the sovereign authoritie should be *in personas* but not *in causas*; and so you knowe she should have *potestatem facti non iuris*.

All our appeales must now be to the presbyterie, which being taken from the Pope by Henry 8 must now be made their holy office.

And so must we first seeke out their conference.

And thence to their provinciall synode.

And if there our cause take no end, then to a nationall Counsell.

But how to assemble the same I fynde not. /

f.137
It weakeneth greatly her Majestie.

In taking from her her treasure and revenues:

Which in a monarchicall estate be *nervi reipublicae, ornamenta pacis, et subsidia belli.*

It endaungereth her royall person.

She is made subiect to the presbyteries' censures and reprehensions:

To their suspensions and excommunications *etc.*

And in their violent course what this will bring forth, she hath not only perceived in their owne peevish pamphlettes, but in the libell entituled *De Iure Regni apud Scotos.*

In an other *De Iure Magistratuum in Subditos.*

In a third, called *Vindicatae contra Tyrranos, etc.*

So in conclusion.

I never did see or heare of bill or booke, petition or lawe, caryeng in it so many notable mischeifes and inconveniences as these here exhibited doe shewe forth unto us.

For my parte I doe conclude of it as of a factious practise to snare and entrapp honest and religious subiectes for their own glorie and wealth.

Let us therfore see how neere these sectaries drawe to the Pope in this their device.

The Pope denieth the supremacie of princes: soe doe they.

The Pope yeeldeth princes *potestatem facti non iuris*, and so *in personas* but not *in causas*; and so doe they.

The Pope doth abrogate all ecclesiasticall lawes as a jurisdiction meerly appertinent to his supreme authoritie; and so doe our reformers, for the more power and authoritie of their presbyterie. /

And so doe you heare my true and syncere reporte as touching my opinion of this booke and bill.   v.

The Pope taketh all appellations to himself, and so doe they.

The Pope taketh from princes anie interest of first fruites, tenthes, *etc.* And so doe they.

The Pope excommunicateth princes, and so would they.

Exordium.   *Februarii 15°*
1586[11]

The reformacion already, yeeldeth {
a lawfull government,
true doctrine,
a godly Booke.
}

The commendacion of the Booke and doctrine.
Of the abrogating of the Booke.

The government.

The bill and book is iniurious. *vz,* {
to the laitie,
to the clergie,
to her Maiestie.
}

Of the laitie.

It taketh from them their {
patronage,
impropriations,
abbey landes, *etc.*
}

Of the clergie.

It overthroweth {
the estate therof,
their livings. /
}

Of her Majestie   f.138

It is iniurious [to] {
her supremacie,
her praerogative,
her revenue,
her person,
her lawes.
}

Of supremacie.

It giveth her {
potestatem facti only,
no authoritie to make lawes ecclesiastical,
no appellations.
}

10. *Sic.*
11. The date is apparently in the same hand as the text. This section is a concentrated note-form summary of what has gone before. Parliament, adjourned on 2 December, resumed its session on this day.

Of her revenues.

It taketh from her
$$\begin{cases} \text{tenthes,} \\ \text{subsidies,} \\ \text{commodities } \textit{sede vacante,} \\ \text{first fruites,} \\ \text{impropriations, } \textit{etc.} \end{cases}$$

Of her person.

It maketh her subiect to their censures, *etc.*

Conclusio.

It standeth upon a comparison betwixt the Pope and the Puritanes.

21. Sir Walter Mildmay's speech on the Bill and Book, 4 March 1587

Text from BL Sloane 326, copy.
Other MSS. London: BL Harley 6265. Oxford: Bodley, Rawlinson C. 838.

Sloane 326, fos.112–21

Quarto Martii 1586 In the Common Howse.

Upon occasion of a bill with a booke annexed, offered in the Howse for reformacion of the Church.

'To enter into all the particularityes of this bill, and booke, offered for reformacion of the Church, wilbe very hard, neyther is the same necessary.[1] But so farr as my capacitie and memory will serve, I meane to note unto you such inconveniences as are like to follow if they should take place.

'The bill standeth upon a preamble and an act. The preamble long,[2] conteyning a repeticion of thinges done in the Church, in the tymes of King Henry the viij[th], King Edward the vj[th], and our sovereigne lady Queen Elizabeth. The act short, wrytten in fewe lynes. The booke / annexed very long, standing upon many and divers particuler poyntes and orders.   v.

'Both the bill and the booke do tend to the present[3] alteracion of this goverment and state of the Church established amongst us, and to the planting of an other forme.

'Whereupon doth follow a generall repeale of all lawes and statutes heretofore made or used for matters or cawses ecclesiasticall. To cancell and cutt *uno ictu*, so many lawes, made so many yeres past, even from the statute of Magna Carta, is a thing that hath never byn offered in this Hous, neyther is it convenient.

'Statutes are often, and so may be repealed as occasion doth serve, but to make voyd so many lawes, old and newe, in one generall short lawe / before every of them be considered, is utterly unmeete, and hath never byn seene in

In the tyme of King Henry the iij[d4]

f.113

---

1. Harl. omits 'neyther is the same necessary'.
2. Harl. omits.

3. Harl. omits, and places before 'state and goverment'.
4. Harl. omits this marginal note.

this counsell. It shall suffice that you be remembred of some late statutes made in her Majestie's tyme, as the statute made the first yere of her reigne for recognition of her supreme authority over all persons and cawses ecclesiasticall within her realmes and domynions, a little[5] due unto her by the law of God, and so acknowledged by all the states and people of the realme, and whereby also is banished the usurped authority of Rome. Whereunto all[6] the subiectes are bounde by oath, sett forth in that statute, specially all persons ecclesiasticall, all officers and ministers in any court or place of service, all graduates in the universityes and studentes of the law.[7]

'Next a statute made in the vth yere of the Queen whereby all knight[s] and burges[ses] of the parliament / are prohibited to enter into their places, or to give their voyces here, except they first take the same oath.[8]

'The penaltyes also conteyned in divers statutes made in her Majestie's tyme against such as should maynteyne the Pope's authority; and against the sayers or hearers of Masse; and against reconciliacions, and absolucions, and such other lewde thinges brought hither from Rome.[9]

'A statute in the xiij[th] yere of her Majestie for the ordering and[10] admitting of sufficient and learned ministers and curates to serve in the Church.[11]

'The statute in the xxiij[th] yere against recusantes, for not resorting to the Church. All theis and some other that might be spoken of should by this bill be cleirely made voyd.[12] /

'What loosenes would follow of that, and what scope should be left to all thoes evill-disposed persons bridled by thoes lawes is easy to considre. Besides the great iniury and indignity offered to our most gracious Queen that hath governed us so long, so christianly, who by this meanes should be iniustly depryved of all her lawfull authority in Church matters, due unto her by all lawes, divine and humane, and which the whole realme hath so duetifully recognized.

'By this repeale of all lawes and statutes touching ecclesiasticall cawses and offices, there followeth a cleire displacing out of the Church not only of the names, but also of the authorityes, and functions, of bishopps and all other ordinary ministers and officers now used in the Church.

'Whereby their jurisdiccions are gone, which now they use in cawses / matrimonyall, cawses testamentary, cawses of tythes, and other, for which neyther this bill nor this booke provideth any remedy.

'How necessary it is that theis cawses which are daylie in use, should not be without ordinary places[13] of judgment, it needeth no proof.

'For if there be not persons authorized to heare and determyne the matters and questions that daily do arrise touching lawfulnes and unlawfulnes of mariages, and touching the legitymacion and illigittimacion of children, which the law now requireth to be certifyed from the bishopp of the diocesse; or if testamentes be not orderly proved before judges, whereby the validity of them, together with the goodes and debtes of the testator and the legacyes given by him also may sufficiently appeare; or if there be not ordinary places of

v.

f.114

v.

judgment where all persons both ecclesiasticall / and civill may resort and   f.115. receyve justice for tythes deteyned uniustly: then it is easely seene, what mervelous confusion, disorder, and losse, will and must fall upon the subiectes of the realme. Of all which the devisors of this new plott (as it seemeth) had noe consideracion.

'Neyther did they see that by this their device there will fall to the ground all cathedrall churches, together with the members and officers of the same, as deanes and prebendaryes, places and rewardes for learned men, a thing that could hardly be spared.

'And herein it is fitt to remember what should become of the landes and possessions of bishopps and cathedrall churches, which by this plott should be displaced and discontinued. Her Majestie I am sure will not encrease her revennewe by any such meane, she favoreth the Church more then so;[14] and to dispose them abrode / otherwise, no man of judgment will thinke conven- v. ient, they were not so easely gotten together.

'In place of bishopps, deanes, prebendaryes, and all other ministers and officers[15] ecclesiasticall now in our Church, the booke establisheth in every church or congregation as it is there termed, a pastor, a doctor, elders and deacons, the pastor to preach and minister the sacramentes, the doctor to teach, the elders to governe, and the deacons to gather and distribute almes. All theis are to be chosen by the assent of the whole congregacion and to be disposed by them as cawse shalbe given.

'Upon which theis thinges are to be noted:

'First, no saving for the present incumbentes, now placed in the Church, so as what shalbecome of them neyther the bill nor the booke do make any provision. /

'Next, by this new forme of goverment there is taken away all patronages   f.116 that belong eyther to her Majestie or to noble men, gentlemen, or other possessioners, or to any colleage of learning in each of the universityes.

'There is no dowbt but many evill-disposed patrons, eyther by corrupcion or affeccion do present unworthy men to benefices, upon whom it is requisite some greate penaltie were layd, but it is not to be dowbted likewise, but that many, specially such as feare God and love the Gospell, do take greate and[16] singuler care to bestowe their guiftes upon thoes that are sufficient, both for

---

5. Harl: 'tytle'.
6. Harl: 'also'.
7. Cf. *SR*, iv.352–3 and 5 Eliz, c.1 in *SR*, iv.403.
8. 5 Eliz, c.1 (1562–3) in *SR*, iv.402–5.
9. 5 Eliz, c.1 (*ut supra*); 13 Eliz, c.2 (1571), 23 Eliz, c.1 (1580–1) in *SR*, iv.528–31, 657–8.
10. Harl. omits 'the ordering and'.
11. 13 Eliz, c.12 (1571) in *SR*, iv.546–7.
12. 23 Eliz, c.1 (1580–1) in *SR*, iv.657–8.
13. Harl: '. . . should be tried in ordinarie places'.
14. Harl. omits 'she favoreth the church more then so'.
15. Harl. omits 'and officers'.
16. Harl. omits 'greate and'.

sincerity in doctrine, and uprightnes in conversation. And amongst other there is no feare that colleages in universityes should err in such a matter, both for their ability to judge, and for the choyce they have of such as be meete within their owne howses. And yet in case of error or corrupcion there is left to the

v.   bishopp sufficient authority to reiect and refuse thoes that / shalbe found unmeete.

'Whether that election which the booke appoynteth, being meere populer,[17] will reforme this fault is greately to be dowbted. For besides that the same will bring with it contentions, factions and confusions amongst the vulgar people, it is also to be considered what may be done by lordes of townes, and ritch men ill-affected in religion, in placing of evill ministers, for there is little question but the lord or cheif of the towne being evill given, the common multitude, that depend upon them eyther for love or feare, will choose none other then he shall like of. And so if you looke into many partes of the realme, you shall fynde yt by that meanes more likely that the churches shalbe served rather with[18] ignorant or ill-affected preistes then with zealous and godly preachers. It followeth to be considered how theis ministers shalbe

f.117.   maynteyned. / Many parishes are so small as they be not able to fynde one, how then shall they maynteyne two or more? And yet in the booke there is utterly[19] no provision certeyne for them; ffor of tythes there is nothing spoken.[20] And if they shall live upon the devotion of the people, what a bare and uncerteyne releif will that be, is easely seene.

'If the meaning be they should lyve upon the tythes: there is, nor can be any payable or due but unto such ecclesiasticall persons an carry title eyther of rector or *vicarus*. Neyther can sute be made for recovery, or payment of tythes, by any other then such, whereof (as yt seemeth) the devisors of this plott had no remembrance, or rather lacked judgment to consider what in such a matter was convenient and necessary.

v.   'Somewhat also is to be said of the / elders. Theis the booke woulde have to be godly and wise men. How such meete and able persons wilbe found, specially in countrey townes, and small villages, is to be thought on. But such indeed they had neede to be, for their authoritie is very greate, not only in eleccions but also in excomunycacions and censures of the Church, which they only are to doe, with the assent of the whole congregation. And yet if the parties excomunicate doe disobey, there is noe order in the booke how to compell them, as now in our Church is used by a wrytt *de excomunicato capiendo*, and so ymprisonment till he made satisfaccion.

'One generall thing also is to be remembered that the pastors and doctors upon occasions rising amongst them may assemble themselves with the rest of the ministers in that countrey, or province, and so further as yt should seeme through the whole realme assemble all in a synode or nationall councell,

f.118.   and there / make orders without the lycence, knowledge, or authority of the Queen. How dangerous that wilbe, and what inconveniences are like to ensue upon such meetinges, all men of judgment may see very apparently.

'Besides yt is not to be forgotten what losse her Majestie were likely to susteyne, if this device should take place. And that in two thinges specially.[21] One in the first fruits and tenthes, now payable by all persons ecclesiasticall, amounting yerely to the some of xx$^{m \, li}$ at the least. And th'other in the subsidyes granted from tyme to tyme by the clergie, being at the least a third part of the whole granted by the laitie.

'And if theis two greate thinges should be thus taken from the Crowne you must looke that our burden shalbe the greater to supply thoes lackes, without which her Majestie shall not be able to maynteyne her estate. /

'There is also consideracion to be had of theis thinges following, as: v.

'The slaunder that may be cast upon us by Jesuites, semenaryes and papistes, that we be not yett agreed upon the service of our Church, where we meane to rest.

'And the recusantes may say that we have done them wrong, to force them to come to our common prayers, which our selves do mislike.

'And because the title of the booke pretendeth an ordering of our Church, according to the best reformed churches; it may be demanded which reformed churches we shall followe, in this so greate an alteracion, and how we may have sure knowledge of their orders, wherein we may not stay our selves upon printers that for gayne are ready to publish any thing, but upon autentique, and assured certificate from thoes churches. /

'And herein also whether we shall take our patterne from Germany   f.119 where the light of the Gospell was first opened in this latter age, or from Swyzarlande which was next, or Denmarke, or Fraunce, or Scotland, or from any other, for it is like that all theis differ in some poyntes of orders. And how they may stand with the quiett goverment of this realme is greatly to be weyed also.

'All theis have forsaken the Pope, as we have done, and every of them thinketh that their churches be well reformed.

'If yt be said we must follow that church which is best reformed according to the word of God:

'That is to be seene and examyned by men learned in the scriptures, and in the orders of the primitive church, which will require a good[22] tyme, being of so great weight, and tending to the alteracion of the whole goverment of the Church. /

'How we in the Nether Howse representing the commons of the realme,   v. shalbe able to discusse, and determyne upon so greate thinges, is also to be thought on, except the same be digested and prepared for us by learned divines as in former tymes hath byn used.

---

17. Harl: '. . . more popule[?]'.
18. MS repeats 'rather with'; Harl. omits 'rather'.
19. Harl. omits.
20. Harl. omits.
21. Harl. omits.
22. Harl. omits.

'And as yt was in the tyme of King Edward the vj[th] for reformacion of the Church in common prayers, and other thinges, brought into a forme by Bishopp Cranmer, Bishopp Ridley and other excellent clerkes, who did assemble by the Kinge's authority and spent long tyme in the same, and so brought their labours to the parliament.

'The like whereof was done in the Queen's Majestie's tyme that now is by Grindall, Juell, Pilkington, and other famous learned men, for restituc[i]on of our Church overthrowne in Quene Marye's tyme. Which forme they after good deliberacion / agreed on, and so was the same exhibited and authorized by Parliament.

f.120

'But what then, some will say, be there no faultes in our Church that need reformacion, and shall we have no remedy? Would to God there were no cawse to complayne of thinges amisse in the Church. No dowbt there be many thinges meete to be reformed. In all ages there have growne faultes,[23] and so will do, to th'end, so long as we lyve here in this worlde, under the Church that is rightly called militant, and so long as the same is governed by men, subiect to affections, and corrupc[i]ons. Neyther do we lack remedy for redresse thereof, if we will use the same as we ought. For by act of Parliament made in the first yere of the Queen there is left unto her Majestie sufficient authority, upon informacion of any thing amisse in the orders or goverment of the Church, to reforme, alter, add, or demynish, so much and in such sort as her Majestie by advice of / learned[24] and wise men shall thinke convenient. Now we that have lyved so long in the profession of the Gospell, under the proteccion of her Majestie's most Christian goverment, that in the begining did restore unto the realme the sincere religion of God, not respecting the dangers that might come to her estate by greate princes, her neighbours, adversaryes to our religion: we I say have no cawse to dowbt, but our most gracious and good Queen for the zeale that she beareth to the furtherance of the Church of God, and for the care shee hath over us, will upon any humble peticion to be made unto her, be most ready and willing both to here the greifes that may upon iust grounde be exhibited unto her Majestie, and with all sincerity and expedicion give such remedy therein, as the cawses shall necessarily require.

v.

f.121

'In the meane tyme, thankes be to God, we lyve here under a / Christian princesse, in a Church that professeth the trew religion of the Gospell, whereof we are assured by thoes thinges which are the trew notes of the Church of Christ. And thoes are not the externall showes of the Church, which the Romaynes stand upon, as universality, antiquitie, and succession of bishopps, being groundes false and uncerteyne, and such as the learned men on our side have sufficiently refuted. But the notes and markes[25] of the trew Church of Christ[26] are the sincere preaching of the word of God, and the right administration of the sacramentes. Thoes we have as purely, and cleirelie, tought and used, in our Church, as may be founde in the best reformed churches in Christendome, which is a greate blessing of God powred upon this realme, for the which we ought to be thankefull, first to him and then to her Majestie that hath and doth maynteyne the same amongst us. /

'And for other thinges touching the order and goverment of the Church so farr as there is cawse, lett us follow that course for redresse with all humility which is fitt for us, and is most like to prevayle.'   v.

23. Harl. omits.

24. Harl. adds 'councell'.

25. Harl. omits 'and makes'.

26. Harl. omits 'of Christ'.

22. Thomas Egerton's notes for his speech on the Bill and Book, 4 March 1587

Text from PRO SP Dom.Eliz. 199/2, original notes in Egerton's hand.

SP Dom.Eliz. 199/2

[Endorsed in the same hand as the second endorsement of S.P.Dom.Eliz. 199/1 'Mr Sollicitour's notes. Towching the bill <u>against pluralities</u> and booke of <u>common prayers put up</u> in parlament by the puritanes. 2 *Martii*[1] 1586.']

That it may be enacted by your Maiestye with the assent of the Lordes and Commens, that the booke hereunto annexed conteyninge the thinges aforesayd and intytuled 'A booke of the forme of commen prayers, administracion of the sacramentes *etc*', agreable to Godde's worde and the use of the best reformed churches, and every thing therin conteyned, may be from henceforthe authorysed, putt in ure and practysed throughout all your Majestie's domynions, any former lawe, statute or custome to the contrary notwithstandinge. And that asmuche of all former lawes, customes, statutes, ordynances and constitucions as lymitte, establishe or sett furthe to be used any other servyce, administracion of sacramentes, commen prayers, rytes, ceremonyes, orders or governement of the Churche, within this realme or any other your Majestie's domynions or cuntreyes, be from hence furthe utterlie voyde and of none effecte.[2]

By this bylle thes alteracions wyll folowe:

Archbysshoppes, byshoppes and all ordynarye mynysters are taken away.

Cathedrall churches overthrowne.

Personages and vycarages destroyed.

Advousons, patronages, and impropriacions undone and taken from the owners.

Paryshes and dyvysions of congregacions by dyocesses and provinces are confounded.

Payment of tythes and other lyke Churche duetyes dyscharged.

The forme of tryall of the valydytye of mariages, and of bastardye, which the commen lawe appoynteth to be by the certyfycate of the byshoppe, taken awaye, and none other provyded.

The forme which the lawe appoynteth for probate of testamentes and commyttinge of the admynistracion of the goodes of persons dyinge intestate, ys taken also awaye, and no provision for yt.

All ordynarye jurysdiccion and courtes ecclesiastycall taken awaye generallye. And in stede therof all authorytye commytted to the mynysters and the eldershippe. Wherin ys to be noted how harde a thinge yt is to have meete men for eldershippe, in moost of the contrey paryshes of Englande.

The elders are not lyke to provyde a more learned mynysterye, beinge theym selves unlearned, but rather the contrarye, and to breede contencion and confusion.

There is no provision of lyvinge for the pastors and doctors, and tythes beinge taken awaye, yf they lyve upon almes perhappes they wyll not lyke theyr interteynement longe.

Many paryshes are not hable to fynde one mynyster, much lesse to maynteyne a pastor and a doctor, and so to be charged with twoo.

The order for disciplyne ys insuffycyent and too weake. For excommunycacion is appoynted to be by the elders and the whoale congregacion, which must nedes breede contencion and confusion.

There is no order appoynted for punyshment of excommunycate persons, yf they contempne and disobeye.

The Quene's revenue of the Crowne shall be decayed and taken from her, and yt wyll be a heavye burden for the subiectes to supplye otherwayes.

The tenthes and fyrst frutes is taken awaye, which amounteth to xx m^{li} *per annum* at the leaste.

The subsydyes of the clergye amount at the least to a thyrde parte of the whoale subsydye of the laytye.

The proffette which her Majesty hath of the temporaltyes of byshoprycks *sede vacante* ys also taken awaye.

The Quene's supreme authorytye and governement ecclesiastycall ys quyte taken awaye.

Assemblyes and synods may be by the mynysters, without the Quene's authorytye, and her Majestye hath no power to calle any synods or convocacions, which is inconvenyent and agaynst her prerogatyve royall.

The oathe for recognycion of the Quene's Majestie's supreme authorytye in caus[e]s eccles[iast]ycall ys taken awaye.

All lawes and statutes agaynst the Pope's authorytye, and the penaltyes for maynteynynge of the same, are also made voyde, and so every one shall be lefte at libertye to maynteyne the Pope's pretensed jurisdiccion.

The lawes and statutes agaynst recusantes are taken awaye and so theye are lefte at libertye to doe as they lyste.

The penaltyes agaynst hearinge and sayinge of Masse are also taken awaye.

---

1. *Sic*: the speech was delivered on 4 March. The words underlined are insertions, perhaps in a different hand.

2. This paragraph is in a clerk's hand. The rest is in Egerton's hand.

By the statute made *anno 1°* of her Majestie's raigne she hath full power to reforme by her commyssion all herysyes, schysmes, errors and abuses in the Churche, and therefore there is no nede of any new statute to be made by Parlement in that behalfe.

23. Sir William Fitzwilliam's account of proceedings in the committee on barley, 7 March 1587

Text from Northants County Record Office, Fitzwilliam of Milton Papers 178 and 179, original in Fitzwilliam's hand(?).

Fitzwilliam of Milton Papers, 178(a), (b), 179

Anno 1586

By reason of the greate dearth of corne and especiallie of barleie, <u>which then bie the extreeme price of wheate and rie was</u>[2] the ordinarie breade corne that yeare <u>in such places</u> where it might bee had, [wheate beeinge so extreeme deare and scarce,][3] the proviso in the statute for maultinge,[4] that sundrie men might [beie] <u>buie</u> barleie and toorne it into mault was thought unnecessarie and inconvenientt, because thearebie the barlie in manie shires wheare it grewe plentifullie was convertid into mault for the servinge of other counties, [<u>which beeing destitute of that kinde of graine</u>][5] [wheare litell or no barleie groweth, but use to make theire mault of otes as the Northwest shires doo and leave] <u>that wantid that graine and</u> the ppeople of the same shires <u>wheare it grewe left</u> unprovided [of] theareof, almost to theire famishinge.

This cause was movid in the Parlament House and committid to certeine for the further consideringe theareof, which committie was houlden at the Guildehaule in London within the counsell house theare.

Att the first openinge of the matter in this committie it was thought good that the gennerall makinge of mault [shoulde be] licensid by that statute shoulde bee restrainid, <u>onelie for this yeare of scarsitie</u> into sum convenientt number of men's handes that shoulde bee thought most fitt [<u>onelie for this yeare of scarsetie</u>] for that poorpose, and the rather because it was provid

7ᵐᵒ Martii Die
Martis 1586[1]

---

1. D'Ewes, p.412 gives 6 March; see also the anonymous journal (f.94v) for the first reading.
2. Words underlined are insertions.
3. Words in square brackets are deletions.
4. The act against regrators of 1551–2

(5 & 6 Ed VI, c.14) in SR, iv.148–50 exempted the buying of barley for conversion to malt.
5. Words underlined in square brackets are deleted insertions.

that manie welthie men of other trades, as woollen drapes, mercers, [and grase] and grasiers in the coontrie, gave over theire owne trades and toornid theire stockes into maultinge, which as was alegid consumid all the barleie so as the people weare readie to famish for breade.

Heareuppon grewe the consideration uppon these three pointes:

who shoulde make mault,
howe much mault theie shoulde make,
and by whoose licence theie shoulde make it.

1. In that anie bacheler beeinge servinge man or other might by the statute buie barleie and convertt it into mault; and that other rich men finding the gaine theareof left theire owne trades and <u>venturing uppon the statute</u> gave them selves theareto, disfoornishinge thearebie not onelie those counties of [thei] theyre bred corne by convertinge moare theareof into mault then was necessarie for that place or shire, but also impoverishinge the ordinarie husbandman [<u>who takinge monie aforehande for his crop uppon bande to deliver moare quarters then hee is able</u>] by buinge his crop <u>at a meane rate</u> with moonie aforehand <u>by obligacion</u>, [and] <u>the</u> covenant[inge <u>therin</u> to have so manie quarters, either had the same for a vearie smaule price, or, missinge of the number and thearebie havinge the bonde forfitid into his handes, compellith the poore husbandman that is not able to repaie the forfature to furnish him at the next crop at such a price as shall bee to <u>much</u> under foote] <u>wheareof</u> [<u>a number of</u>] <u>theie most commonlie</u> [hath] <u>forfeitid, and weare driven to make the same good with theire crop the next yeare following upon the like meane rate of price</u>: it was thought good [<u>that the justices of the peax shoulde by the lawe nowe to bee made</u>[6]] <u>that</u> in everi towne <u>sum</u> certeine men that [shoulde] wentt with [tilthes] <u>a plowe land at the lest</u> [to] <u>shoulde</u> make mault and none other. [or els to discharge[7] whome theie thought best from makinge of mault wheare there weare moare of that trade then weare thought necessarie] Heareuppon [grewe] weare remembrid these inconveniences.

Those men, [<u>which shoulde bee so apointid in everie towne</u>] though theie [made] <u>might make</u> sufficientt for theire owne uses and <u>sum other fewe</u>, yeat coulde theie not <u>bee able to</u> satisfie theire neighboures <u>generallie</u> and gentilmen for the[ire] provisione of theire houses [<u>which for the most part spende vearie largelie</u>] for want

of

1. moonnie to by the graine with;
2. extraordinarie help <u>beside theire setlid houshoulde</u> to intende onelie the [same] <u>maultinge which lasteth but for a season;</u>
3. [and roome] sufficientt [for] <u>roome of</u> housinge fitt for the same trade.

The utter undooinge of such men as onelie from theire youth followid no other coorse, nor theire father's befoare them, but maultinge [which was iniustice].

The overthrowe of manie townes in the realme [that] which occupiinge[8] tillage have for manie yeares [have] stoode onelie by maultinge.

The greate hinderance to manie that latelie have left other trades and for maultinge have with there stockes [that of late have] built vearie faire and large houses [for maulting], which by this order ar to bee pluct downe, or els to stande without use.

[The corruption and extortion that woulde rise by makinge of those licenses, either by the justices or theire clearkes: and much greater if theie had authoritie onelie to discharge, for them everie man beeing left at libertie to mault if hee list, presuminge by his moonie to continue his trade still and theare by also to thrust his neighboure whome hee misliketh from the same trade, will not care what to geave either for the enrichinge of him self or damaginge of th'other whome hee misliketh.

The parccillitie and corruption that woulde appeare among the justices by that choice, and the injustice that might theareon followe.[9]

For the avoidinge of all which inconveniences it was wishid that the lawe [onelie] uppon good consideration shoulde determine what men and howe mani shoulde mault [and that it shoulde bee left to the discreation of no officer] in each shire, wheareone as well theie that had no other trade might bee thearein stil maintanid, and such as contrarie to the lawe had entrid into that science might bee abarrid.

But that was founde so difficult both for the quallitie of the persons and the number [so unpossible] as it was saide that by no meanes it coulde not bee, for [when the lawe had apointid] make it that the lawe did apointe a number [it woulde], yeat must it leave the[ire] sufficiencie of those so apointid to the discreation of the officers [which unles theie weare the justices of the peax must bee] otherwaise a greate gap woulde bee made to the promouter: which people [because theie bee] howe offensive theie bee to all sortes [weare in no case to bee alowid of] is apparantlie knowne. And thearefoare was it concludid as the best opinion theare, if all other doughtes to bee obiectid might reasonablie bee awnswerid and [this] a lawe for this matter take effect, that the justices of the peax to whome the carriage and guidinge of the coontrie in [all] most matters was committid might also have [a] the iudgment of this.][10]

It was saide that all these inconveniences might bee sufficientlie provided for if th'other too partes weare accordid on.

Wheareuppon the seconde part touchinge the quantitie to bee made cam in question which gave greate occasion of speach, for thearein everie man spake

6. There are further deleted insertions here, though they are illegible.
7. There are deleted insertions here, though they are illegible.
8. There is an inserted illegible word here.
9. *Sic.*
10. The passage from 'The corruption . . .' to this point has been crossed through with diagonal lines, though there are also insertions and deletions within it, as indicated.

as the nature of the shire whearein hee was plantid gave him cause. As for example sake, theie that dwelt in counties whearein much barleie grewe findinge the dearenes of the graine and scarcitie theareof by convertinge the same into mault to serve other shires wheare no quantitie of that graine [groeth] did growe, spake vehementlie to have a rate and stint sett properlie for the sarvinge of theire owne shire, and no moare in respect of theire bread. Others that dwelt in countries sarvid with mault not of theire owne growinge theie pleadid as harde to have the former ffreedoom in maultinge continuid, for other waise theie shoulde bee as greatelie distressid for drink as th'other weare for bred. So as thorowe the vearie impossibillitie to accorde these differences [these] this pointe remainid [undecidid] at large as befoare.

The thirde and last pointe conscerninge by woose[11] licens these maulsters shoulde woorke was marveluslie arguid on both sides: for [sum by theie that] sum there weare which wished [in the first pointe] that the lawe onelie might determine of the quallitie and number of those that shoulde exercise the trade of maultinge in each shire [coulde not], in no wise agreeing that the justices of the peax shoulde have the apointinge of anie to that trade, or the disablinge of anie from that trade. Theire reason was the corruption and extortion that might growe by either of those meanes as well by the justice him self as his clearke: for if theie have authoritie to [appointe] geave licence under theire handes and seales, said theie, who dougteth that the person [who] which desireth to bee [apointid] licensid will omitt the trade of his livinge for geving of moonie, or the justice, or at least his clearke, will not under hande make his markett as good as hee can in th'admittinge of the partie, consideringe the multitudes of that sort ar to bee drawen into a fewe, and everie one will push to gett the place for himself.

Contrariewise, if theire authoritie bee to discharge men from that occupiinge, the mischeefe in all shewe will bee greater, for then the lawe leavinge [it] at large that misterie of maultinge as it nowe standes [everie], gevinge onelie [the] an authoritie of restraininge [anie] sum [onelie] to the justices in theire discreation, all the occupiers of that trade must nedes stande subiecte to [their] theire affection and passions; whearebie, unles the gentilmen that bee in office bee of the better nature and disposition, what for envie and malice to the parties them selves [and] or pleasinge other theire owne frendes that mislike anie of those maulsters, the men of that trade shall ever bee in daunger to bee put from theire livinges. What briberie and extortion woulde heare uppon followe theie thought was apparant to all men. And thearefore remainid in [this pointe as theie did the first] opinion that the safest and best waie weare to [geave] leave the licensinge of such onelie to the lawe.

This was saide woulde derogate much from the authoritie and creditt of the justices, beeinge in theire kindes judges of recorde and havinge manie great and waightie matters committid in trust to their charge; but [because men made of flesh and blood ar subiect to affection] for the avoidinge of these mischeefes before namid, and maintenance of the creditt of the place theie houlde, [as] it was thought most requisite by the better opinion to committ this matter to theire discreations [so for the avoidinge of the foresaide mischeefes the better opinion would that theie shoulde geave] <u>with this proviso: that theie shoulde neither geave anie or</u> / [them but not] <u>or disalowe</u> [them] <u>anie</u> privatlie 178(b) in theire houses as too of them, wheareof one beeinge of the coram, in other cases maie doo; but openlie at theire quarter cessions sittinge uppon the bench, and that three at the least, wheareof too to bee of the coram, to geave theire consentt by hande and seale to the same.

Thus far foorth helde this cause, debatinge withoute anie conclusion, so difficult provid the matter. Wheareuppon an auncient gentilman, a member of the House <u>Mr Seriant Fleetewoode</u>, [beeinge theare presentt] <u>the Recorder of London</u> saide that hee had learnt in times past of wise common wealth men [in the Parlament House] that there weare [sum] mischeefes oft times happeninge in the kingdom which weare uncurable, of which sorte, consideringe the <u>present</u> time, hee thought this to bee: one shire so dependid uppon the help of an other as want <u>in this dearth</u> must needes go thorowe them all. Likewise hee learnt that it was an impossibillitie for one lawe to settell one direct order in a misterie usid in divers shires, for that everie shire hath his wantes and supplementes accordinge to the nature of the soile, or coostom of the coontrie; as for example the arte of clothinge hath for everie shire it is tradid in, severall statutes, and yeat not brought to that perfection, which men desire. The art of tanninge differeth almost in everi shire wheare it is usid. 'If then', said hee, '[if] in the clothing of the bodie theare is such hardnes to settell one order, howe is it possibill for the feedinge of the bodie whearewith everie shire of the realme is alike interessted, that wee shoulde make one lawe certeine, especiallie in this time of dearth when everie shire almost in that point differeth one from th'other. And thearefore for the remediing of this mischeefe, everie shire must have his particular lawe accordinge to the disposition of the coontrie, which as it is unpossible <u>nowe to be had</u>. So lett us cease to debate anie moare theareof and praie to God for the eande of this dearth which will easelie decide this controversie.'

> *Anno* 13: E. cap: 25[12] The mischeefe that groweth <u>to the realme</u> by those contracters that ingros these kindes of merchandies, namelie ffrutes, spice, oiles, <u>sugar</u>, and such [bee thease] <u>like from the merchant that bringeth them in bee thease</u>.

By takinge them all into theire handes thei bar the retailor from buinge at the first hande, and cause them to buie from them at greate and excessive prices according to theire owne pleasures.

The retailor <u>who taketh at excessive prices these merchandise from the contracter</u> must [bee a gainer and selleth theareafter] <u>in the sale of them</u> to the

11. *Sic.*
12. This refers to the continuation statute of 1571 (*SR*, iv.561–2) which extended the life of 5 & 6 Ed VI, c.14 against regrators, though stating that it was not to extend to wines, sugars, spices, currants and other foreign victuals.

ordinarie man that coometh to his shop for parcells of those wares [as hee <u>dailie</u> spendeth them <u>must</u>] needes bee <u>a</u> gainer towardes the maintenànce of his owne livinge, and thearefore hoisteth up the prices accordinglie.

The chapman that buieth quantities to serve sheeres with (that bee scituate far from London) and [use] <u>is</u> not of abilitie to laie downe readie moonie, forsaketh his trade because the retailor, paiinge so deare to the contractor, is not able to geave anie longe daies without hee take most excessive gaine for his wares, whearebie [the coontriman is disapointid] <u>both the</u> chapman of his occupation, and the contriman of his necessarie uses, ar clean disapointid.

The chapman, buinge these wares at those extreeme rates, <u>consideringe his daies of paiment</u> hath no les reason to utter them to his gaine [then the retailor had] to the common coontriman (that is onelie servid at his handes) then the retailor had in that respect of his prices to the contractor; whearebie the wares ar raisid to the most extreeme prices, haulf in haulf at the least: as peper, wheare it was woont to bee soulde for ij^s vj^d the pounde, is nowe woorth v^s iiij^d. Dates that weare at xij^d the pounde bee nowe at iiij^s, great reasons[13] and prunes that weare soulde for ij^d and ij^d ob. the pounde bee nowe iiij^d and v^d the pounde.

The coontriman by this meanes is driven to buie at the fift hande, and that at most extreeme prices; not onelie in regarde of the fift retoorne which is a cause sufficientt to raise the matter, but cheefelie in that these contracters havinge once ingrossid the whole mas into theire handes [foreseeinge] sett the prices accordinge to theire owne likinge.

These contracters beeinge ever moare great monied men, and seeinge the extreme gaine that riseth by this trade, desirus <u>each man</u> to encroch to [them selves] <u>him self</u> moare and moare, findeth the meanes to have an invoice in the coostom house wheareupon hee knoweth what quantitie of everie sorte coometh in; and theareupon providinge moonie sufficientt for the whole quantitie, practiseth with the merchant that first bringeth it in, <u>wheather hee bee forrener or home man</u>, to buie the whole from his fellowes [with the].

The merchantt foreseeinge this, pollitickelie enhaunseth his prices knowinge that these contractors havinge the whole trade in theire handes, and liinge in waight the one to preventt the other, will <u>geave</u> what so ever is demaundid <u>rather then theie will forsake the merchandiese</u>. Whearebie the price is [enhaunsid] <u>raisid</u> at the vearie first hande from that it was woontt to bee.

To avoide these mischeefes it was desirid that the[se] proviso in the same statute touchinge engrossinge the foresaide thinges might bee taken awaie, and that it might bee enactid that the merchant who bringeth in the commodities shoulde sell to no holesale man for the space of foreteene daies after his coominge into the river, but onelie to the retailor, and after that time to sell to whome and as much as hee list: presuminge heareuppon that the retailors, beeinge men of no great wealth but buinge onelie so much as maie furnish theire shopps till newe shall coom in againe, and enforcid to make as presentt sale theareof againe as convenientlie theie maie, must utter theire wares to the common subiect at reasonable prices.

To this was amnswerid that theare weare no such men as weare namid contractors, but that divers good merchanttes oft times bought up all the wares of those kindes for these considerations followinge.

First, that the merchantt <u>who brought them in bee not kept long liing on the river, but</u> by a spedie retoorne might bee alurid rather to coom hither then to go to anie other place, which hee shoulde not finde if hee bee left onelie to the retailer that manie times is not storid with moonie.

Secondlie, that there might bee a stoare continuallie in the Cittie to preventt the wantt that might coom, either by the ill-takinge of those thinges in the partes wheare theie growe, or els by the trobles of the sease whearebie the shippinge can not quietlie pas: the want wheareof appearid at that time in oiles, which weare xxxij^s or three and thirtie shillinges a pipe by reason of the scarcitie, wheareas theie weare ordinarilie befoare at xxv^s.

Thirdelie, bo bringe those commodities to a resonable rate, which those marchantes did by this meanes. Theire speedie retoorne to the retailor requirid no greate gaine and the retailor, buiinge at theire handes for reasonable prices, was to bee controlid <u>by theire reporte</u> if hee shoulde excessivelie sell to the subiect: which convenientlie coulde not bee if theie bought at the first hande from the merchant with whome theire bargaines weare secrett and unknowne <u>to anie</u> but to them selves. An example of this was the alluns[14] which while theire[15] weare onelie in Coostomer Smithe's handes helde the price of xxj and xxij^s and nowe coom into divers men's handes bee soulde for xxviij^l.[16]

179

Heareunto was replied

Contracters most certeine there weare, for divers merchantes weare knowne to have [soulde] left theire trades and toornde the merchandies into a stock of moonie awaytinge poorposelie those toornes.

That the merchant can not endure anie longe staie uppon the water lest the charge of vittailes and other inconveniences shoulde eate up theire gaine, and time shoulde bee lost which is most precious with them [it], was well knowne and alowid of; but that this obiection helde not it was manifestid that all the merchantes that tradid hither with those commodities (unles it weare the Arogonsies[?] that can not coom into oure river) have storehouses of theire owne to laie up theire wares in, and so use to doo so as no longer staie neede to bee made with those commodities uppon the water then them selves best like.

The time of xiiij daies is no longe delaie, after which time the contractor maie doo what he thinkes good in buiinge the remaine of the retailor.

The merchant that bringes in those commodities can not bee driven from

---

13. *Sic.*
14. *Sic.*

15. *Sic.*
16. *Sic.*

hence to anie place. The reason is theie can have no such utterance in anie place of those wares as theie have heare; for no other place spendes so much of those thinges as wee doo. And that theie must needes bringe them to us is as manifest, for wheare theie growe theare is such aboundance of them, especiallie of currantes, as unles theie sende them awaie to us theie must cast them awaie: there owne coontries ar not able or will not expende them.

The hinderance of a stoare can not by this order coom amonge us; ffor if the retailor by all that is brought the stoare remaineth with him of so much as coometh in that yeare.[17] If hee bee not able to deale with the whole, then the contractor taketh the rest with whome that stoare remaineth so as by this meanes the whole mas of that which is brought in betweene those too sortes of men is recevid and kept for the realme.

The thirde pointe [coulde] – that prices by them weare brought downe-coulde in no wise bee agreed unto for that common experience shewid otherwaise, howe so ever that matter of allam fell oute. And that the prices and theareuppon dearth of all those commodities grewe by the contracters, thirtie retailors of the grossers preferrid a bill that daie and in that place to the committies with theire names underwritten shewinge in articles the same effect. But when theie sawe certein of those contracters in presence (for of both sortes weare commaundid to bee theare that daie to instruct the committies) theie presentlie helde theare peax and woulde proceede no further, for feare lest theie shoulde never buie anie moare wares of them if theie wear knowne to complaine.

The matter proceedid no further, but was left as befoare; and in the departinge, such as favorid the retailors castinge with them selves that, though this coorse of xiiij daies or such like time had taken effect, yeat the merchant that brought it in to gett his moonie all at once woulde have compoundid <u>secretlie</u> with the contractor, and by drivinge of the retailor beyeonde his time have [defeatid him] brought the whole to his handes, theie agreed that it was not unlikelie so to faule out, but that in time woulde amonge them selves have beene brought to light and at the parlament followinge a remedie founde oute for the same.

---

17. *Sic.* the meaning is not clear here. The MS punctuates with a colon at this point.

24. Queen's answer to a petition for reform of the Church: reply to the committee appointed on 8 March 1587

Text from Lambeth Palace 178, copy in the hand of a secretary of Archbishop Whitgift.
Printed. Strype, *Whitgift,* i.494–5.

Lambeth 178, f.88

Why you ought not to deale with matters of religion.

Hir Majestie is fullie resolved by hir owne readinge and princelie iudgement upon the truth of the reformacion which we have alreadie; and myndeth not nowe to beginne to settle hirself in causes of religion.

Hir Majestie hath bene confirmed in hir said iudgement of the present reformacion by the letters and writings of the most famous men in Christendome, as well of hir owne dominions as of other countries.

Hir Majestie thinketh it verie inconvenient and daungerous, whilest our enemies are labouringe to overthrowe the religion established as false and erroneous, that we by newe disputacions shoulde seeme ourselves to doute thereof.

Hir Majestie hath fullie considered not onelie of the excepcions which are made against the present reformacion (and doth finde them frivolous), but also of the platforme which is desired: and accounteth it most preiudiciall to the religion established, to hir Croune, to hir government and to her subiectes.

Hir Majestie thinketh that though it were graunted that some things were amisse in the Church, yet seeinge she is fullie perswaded and knoweth it to be true that for the verie substance and grounds of true religion, no man livinge can iustlie controulle them; to make everie daie newe lawes in matters of circumstances and of lesse moment especiallie touchinge religion, were a meanes to brede great lightnes in hir subiectes, to nourish an unstaied humour in them of seekinge still for exchaunges. *Malum est et reipublica noxium assuefieri homines ad facilitatem mutandarum legum.*

If anie thinge were amisse it appertaineth to the clergie more properlie to see the same redressed. *Unicuique in sua arte credendum. Quam quisque norit artem in hac se exerceat. Navem agere ignarus navis timet.*[1]

Hir Majestie taketh your petition herein to be againste the prerogative of hir Croune. For by your full consentes it hath bene confirmed and enacted (as the truth therein requireth) that the full power, authoritie, iurisdiccion and supremacie in Church causes which heretofore the Popes usurped, and tooke to them selves, shoulde be united and annexed to the imperiall Croune of this realme.

1. Cicero, *Tusculanae Disputationes*, 1, 41;
   Horace, *Epistulae*, 2, 1, 114 for the second
   and third of these tags.

[Journals: House of Lords] Parliament roll of proceedings relating to Mary Queen of Scots, 15 October–2 December 1586

Text from Hatfield House, Herts, 216/14 (original).
Other MSS. London: BL Cotton Titus F i, Stowe 358 (copy of Cotton), Harl. 6803, Add. 48027 (Yelverton 31) Derbyshire: County Record Office, D 258m/65/11 (formerly of Chandos-Pope-Gill MSS)
Printed EHR, xxxv 106–13 (from Hatfield, with some abbreviations).

Hatfield 216/14

Memorandum. Where the Quene's Majestie by her writt summoned her parliament to be begonn and holden at Westminster the xv[th] of October in the xxviij[th] yeare of her Maiestie's raigne, as by the same writt more playnelye appeareth, her Highnes uppon certen greate and waightye causes and consideracions her Maiestie speciallye movinge, by the advise of her Privye Counsell and of her Justices of both her Benches and other of her counsell learned, dyd proroge and adiorne the saide parliament untill Thursdaye being the xxvij[th] daye of the saide moneth of October, by vertue of her writte patent sealed with the Greate Seale of England and bearing date the eight daye of the same moneth of October; whereuppon the saide xv[th] daye of October the Archbishopp of Canterbury with diverse lordes and others her Maiestie's counsellors repaired to the parliament chamber commonly called the Upper House, and there in the presence of diverse lordes spirituall and temporall dyd open and declare that her Highnes for dyverse good causes and consideracions her Majestie speciallye moving, had by her Highnes' saide writt proroged the saide parliament from the saide firste day of sommons thereof untill the xxvij[th] day of the saide moneth. All which matter being soe notified to the saide assemblie, the writt for the saide prorogacion in the presence of all that assemblie was there read by the Clarke of the Upper House publiquely and openly, the tenor whereof ensueth, *ad verbum*:[1]

---

1. Letters patent recited here. Harl. , Add.
   do not include letters patent.

Memorandum. Where the Quene's Maiestie by vertue of her writt patent sealed with the great seale of England bearing date at Hinchingbrooke the eight daye of this instant moneth of October in the saide xxviij[th] yeare of her Highnes' raigne did proroge and adiorne this present parliament unto the xxvij[th] day of the same moneth, as by the same writt more plainly appeareth, her Highnes uppon certeyne greate and weighty causes and consideracions her Majestie speciallye moving, by the advise of her Privye Counsell and of her Justices of both her Benches and other her counsell learned, dyd by vertue of her writt patent sealed with the Greate Seale of England bearing date at Westminster the xxvj[th] day of October in the saide xxviij[th] yeare further proroge and adiorne the said parliament from the saide xxvij[th] day untill Saterdaye being the xxix[th] of the saide moneth of October; whereuppon the saide seaven and twentith daye Sir Thomas Bromley knight, Lorde Chauncellor of England, with diverse lordes and others her Majestie's counsellors repaired to the parliament chamber commonlie called the Upper House and there in the presence of diverse lordes spirituall and temporall the said Lord Chauncellor dyd open and declare that her Highnes for the causes afore rehearsed had proroged the saide parliament from the saide xxvij[th] day untill Saterday being the xxix[th] day of the saide moneth. All which matter beinge soe notified to the saide assemblie, the writt for the same prorogacion in the presence of all that assemblie was there reade by the Clark of the Upper House publiquely and openly, the tenor whereof ensueth verbatim:[2]

After, on Saterday the nyne and twentith day of October in the saide xxviij[th] yeare of her Maiestie's raigne, when all the lordes had taken their places in their robes and the knightes, citizens and burgesses sommoned to this parliament were present, and that both Lordes and Commons expected her Maiestie's comyng, Thomas Bromley knighte, Lorde Chauncellor of England, dyd openlie declare unto them that her Maiestie for diverse greate and weightye causes could not be personallie present in the saide parliament as she had determined, and that therefore her Highnes had given full power and aucthoritie unto the moste reverend father in God, John, Archbishoppe of Canterbury, and to the righte honorable William Lorde Burghley, Lorde Thresorer of England, and Henrye, Earle of Darbie, Lorde Steward of her Maiestie's househould, to doe for her and in her name all those thinges tendyng to the glorie of God and the good governement of the common weale of this realme which were to be donn and performed in the same parliament, and alsoe to proroge, adiourne and contynew the saide parliament as occasion shoulde require. And thereuppon the saide Lorde Chauncellor delyvered the saide lettres patentes unto the Clarke of the Parliament to be publiquely read, which he did openlie reade accordingly, the tenor whereof ensueth in *hec verba*:[3]

The lettres patentes being read, the saide three lordes leavinge there owne places went to a seate prepared for them on the righte side of the chaire of estate beneth the steppes. Then the Lorde Chauncellor going firste to the saide lordes, and conferringe a while with them, went to his accustomed place and there in wise and grave manner made intimacion of the cause of the sommons of this parliament, which as he saide was not for ordinarie or usuall causes, as for makinge of lawes, whereof her Majestie thought there were more alreadie made then were ether duelie obeyed or dulie executed,[4] nor for requiring of fyftenes and subsidies, of which although there were some present cause, and the same when occasion soe served moste mete and convenient, yet her Maiestie would not chardge her lovinge subiectes soe farre at this tyme; but that the cause was rare and extraordinarie, of greate waighte, extreame perill and moste daungerous consequence. Then he declared what daungerous practizes had byn contrived of late, and howe miraculouslye the mercifull providence of God had by discovery thereof beyond all humayne pollicie preserved her Maiestie, the destruccion of whose sacred person and of the happie and quiet estate of the realme was moste traiterousely compassed and ymagined, wherewith her Maiestie's pleasure was that the Lordes and Commons in the same parliament assembled as the greatest counsell of the realme should be throughly acquainted. And here he shewed what myserye the losse of our moste gracious and noble soveraigne would have broughte generallie to all estates of the realme, and saide that althoughe some of the conspirators and traitors had suffered accordinge to their demerittes, yet it was nedefull that further consideracion should be had for the safetye of her Maiestie's moste royall person and the preservacion and continuance of the quiet state of the realme; and therfore moved the saide lordes, knightes, cytizens and burgesses that they would bend their cares and endevours to provide for the same, adding further that to th'ende that they mighte orderly procede therein, they of the Common House should make present choise of some one amongst them to be their Speaker, and to present hym to the lordes her Maiestie's commyssioners as sone as convenientlie they could. Then the Clarke of the parliament read the names of them that were appointed to receive and trye the peticions offered this parliament, *videlicet*,[5] And then the lordes the commissioners adiourned this parliament unto Mundaie next following.[6]

At which daye the Commons presented John Puckeringe, Serieaunte at the Lawe, who was their Speaker the laste parliament, as one chosen againe by them, who although he verie eloquently and modestly excused him self and humblie desired to be dischardged of that chardge, was to his greater[7] comendacion denyed that request, and soe with worthie praise of his former

---

2. Letters patent recited here. Harl. , Add. do not include letters patent.

3. Letters patent recited here. Harl. , Add. do not include letters patent.

4. Cott: '. . . Then were dulie obeyed, not . . .' (+ Stowe).

5. The names are listed. Harl. omits, and does not give the list (+ Add.).

6. The Chandos MS (folios unnumbered) is headed '1586. A true copie of the whole roll of the session of Parliament holden in the 28 yeare of the raigne of Queen Elizabeth concerninge the great cause of the Scottish Queene.' There is then a list of ten members of the Lords assigned as triers of petitions, and of a further ten members, peers and bishops. The second page of the MS begins 'And then the Lordes . . .' as here.

7. Harl. : 'great' (+ Add.).

service in that place was admitted their Speaker. Then the saide Speaker, protestinge his dutifull affeccion and devocion unto her Maiestie's service, shewing withall the readie good will and earnest zeale which he by former experience had found in every member of the saide House, made certeine peticions unto the saide lordes the commissioners, whereof the firste was that it would please her Maiestie to graunt unto them aswell free libertie of speche in the treatinge and debatinge of such matters as should fall in consultacion amongest them of the same House, as also all such immunities, priviledges and fredomes for them and their servantes as in former parliamentes heretofore in the tyme of her Maiestie and of her moste noble progenitors have byn used and enioyed. And touchinge hym self he humblie desired that he mighte from time to tyme have free accesse unto her Maiestie for the understanding of her Maiestie's good pleasure and resolucion in such causes of ymportaunce as should be thoughte requisite and convenient, and lastly, that if it shoulde happen that he should in any sorte mysconceave or mysreporte any message or charge delyvered or commytted unto hym by the saide House, that it should not be precisely taken or construed against them, but that he might have leave to reforme and alter the same according to the true intent and meanings of the saide House. Whereuppon the Lorde Chauncellor after conference firste had with the saide lordes her Maiestie's commissioners, made answere unto the saide peticions, *videlicet*, that her Maiestie's pleasure was that the Speaker and Commons should have and enioye all such liberties and priviledges as any other had and enioyed in the tyme of her Maiestie's moste noble progenitors. And then the Lorde Chauncellor by direccion of the saide lordes the commyssioners adiorned the parliament untill Fridaye then next following.

After, on Saterdaye the fifte day of November in the saide eight and twentith yeare, the Lorde Chauncellor declared at good length the greate and manifold favors which the Quene's Maiestie of her moste roiall disposicion had shewed to the Quene of Scottes, not only by the princely entertaynement which since her comynge into this realme she hath many yeares received at her Maiestie's handes to her Highnes' exceadinge greate charg, and in protectinge of her honor and lief from the violent pursuyte of her owne people for soundrie moste wicked and horrible offences by them ymputed unto her, but alsoe in tollerating and with moste princely magnanimity and gracious clemencie lightly passing over sondrie former daungerous practizes by which the saide Scottishe Quene had compassed and intended the distruccion of her Highnes' most royall person and overthrowe of the happy state of this realme, notwithstanding that her nobilitie and commons in sondrie parliamentes and at other tymes had often moste instantlie moved her Majestie to procede against that ladye according to her demerittes and the justice of her Maiestie's lawes. He declared further that the saide Scottishe Quene as a person obdurate in malice, not regardinge these and many other her Maiestie's most gracious favors towardes her, had continued still the course of her former practizes, and whereas latelie one Anthony Babington and diverse other desperate persons had moste traiterouslie combyned and confederate[d] them selves together by vowe and oath in a moste horrible enterprise by murther to take away the lief of her Majestie, the saide Scottish Quene was not onely privie and assenting to that conspiracy but was alsoe a principall actor therein, and did direct, comforte and abett the saide conspirators with perswacion, counsell, and promise of reward, and earnest obtestacion to procede and accomplishe the same. Whereuppon her Majestie at the earnest request of such as tendred the safetie of her royall person and the quiett of the realme, did direct a commyssion under the Greate Seale to sondrie lordes and others of her Maiestie's Privy Counsell and a greate nomber of lordes of Parliament of the greatest and moste auncient degree, assisted with some of the principall judges of the realme, to heare, examyne and determine the same according to a statute in that behalf made in the seaven and twentith yeare of her raigne; who to the number of sixe and thirtie havinge attended the execucion of the saide commyssion and diverse daies and tymes heard the allegacions against the saide Scottishe Quene in her owne presence and hearing (she being permitted to saie what she would in her owne excuse) did with one assent finde her culpable both in privitie and consent to the saide crymes obiected against her and alsoe in compassing the Quene's Majestie's deathe, and had thereupon geven their sentence and judgment accordinglye.

After, on Mondaye the seaventh[8] day of November, while the Lordes were in consultacion aboute the matter of the Quene of Scottes, certeine of the Common House came upp and desired conference with some of the lordes of this House, what nomber yt should please them to appoincte aboute the greate matter of the Quene of Scottes alreadie opened unto them. Whereuppon the Lordes chose out to the number of one and twentie, *videlicet*, the Archbisshopps of Canterburie and Yorke, the Lorde Treasorer,[9] the Lorde Steward, the Earles of Northumberland, Kent, Rutland and Sussex, the Bisshopps of London, Durham, Winchester and Worcestre, the Lorde Howard Lorde Admirall, the Lorde Hunsdon Lorde Chamberlaine, the Lorde Cobham, Graye, Lumley, Chandos, Buckhurste, DelaWare and Norris. The place of meetinge was in the owter parliament chamber that afternoone at two of the clocke. There was alsoe appoincted to attend the saide lordes the Lorde Cheife Justice of the Common Plees, the Lorde Cheif Baron of the Exchequire, and Justice Gawdie.

After, on Tweseday the eight of November, the sentence and judgement pronounced by the comyssioners againste the saide Sccottishe Quene was openly reade[10] and thereupon the principall evidences and prooffes whereupon the same sentence and judgment was grounded, and all the processe and proceading in the execucion of the saide commission, were alsoe shewed forth, read and declared; upon the hearing whereof all the saide Lordes dyd with one assente allowe the same sentence and judgement to be honorable, iuste and lawfull.

---

8. Chandos: '17th'.

9. Harl. omits names hereafter, continuing 'etc' (+ Add.).

10. Harl. continues: 'viz. That etc. And thereupon . . .' (+ Add.).

After on Wednesdaye the nynth of November, the Lordes the comittes made reporte unto the whole House that they had at severall tymes conferred with the comittes of the Common House touchinge the greate cause of the sommons of this parliament, by whome they did understand that the commons in the Lower House had not only with greate deliberacion openlie debated the same cause but had alsoe selected seventie learned, grave and discrete persons of that House to consulte together touching the same, who had likewise sondrie private metinges and conferences in that behalf; whose opynions and resolucions being after openlie declared in the same Common House, they all thought good and desired to heare at large the sentence and judgement geven and pronounced by the commissioners aforesaide and the princypall evidences and prooffes whereuppon the same was grounded. Which being openly read, declared and shewed in the saide Common House, the saide Commons, after longe and advised deliberacion and consultacion had thereupon, wayinge diligentlie aswell all the partes and circumstances of the same evidences and prooffes as the whole processe and proceading in the execution of the saide commission, did all with one full consent conclude and agree that the same sentence and judgement was in all thinges most honorable, iust and lawfull. Whereupon the comittes of both Houses after longe conference and deliberacion had in that behalf dyd conclude and resolve that in respect of the preservacion and safety of the Quene's Maiestie's most roiall person and the happie estate of this realme and the common weale yt was expedient and necessarie that the Lordes and Commons assembled in this present parliament shoulde all ioyne together in moste humble and instant peticion to her Majestie, that it would please her to cause declaracion of the same sentence and judgment to be made and published by proclamacion, and thereupon to give direccion for further spedie procedinge againste the saide Scottishe Quene according to the effecte of the saide statute.

Accordinge to which their resolucion they did forthwith cause a forme of peticion to be devised and sett downe in writing which being after advisedlie heard and considered by all the said comittes of both the saide Houses, the saide Lordes the comittes dyd the saide nynth of November presente the same in the saide Higher House, whereupon the Clarke of the saide Higher House did the same day openly reade the same peticion, the tenor whereof followeth in theis wordes:[11]

After the reading whereof all the Lordes did with one assent conclude and agre that the ymportaunce and necessitye of the cause was such as dyd enforce them to use all humble and instaunt meanes soe farre as might stande with their duties to move and presse her Majestie to proceade against the saide Scottishe Quene according to the said statute; and therefore resolved to preferre the saide peticion to her Maiestie soe soone as mighte please her Highnes to graunt them accesse to her presence.

After which, on the saide nynth daie of November, certeine of the Common House dyd eftsoones come and desire further conference with some of the lordes of this House what nomber yt should please them to appoint touching the said greate cause. Whereupon the Lordes appoincted theis lordes following, *videlicet*, the Archbishopps[12] of Canterburie and York, the Lorde Burghley Lorde Treasorer, th'Erle of Darbye Lorde Steward, the Earles of Northumberland, Kent, Rutland and Sussex, the Bisshopps of London, Durham, Winchester and Worcester, the Lorde Howard Lord Admirall, the Lorde Hunsdon Lord Chamberleine, the Lord Cobham, Graye, Lumley, Chandos, Buckhurst, DelaWare and Norris; and the place of meting was in the saide utter parliament chamber at three of the clock in the after none of the same daye.

After, on Thursdaie the tenth daye of November, the Lordes the comittees made reporte unto the whole House that upon further conference with certeine comittees of the saide Lower House they dyd understand that the saide peticion was alsoe openly read in the saide Lower House and that upon advised and due consideracion thereof all the saide Commons did with one full consent (none gainsaying) resolve and conclude that the ground and matter of the saide peticion was in all thinges most iust and true, and that fynding the daunger of her Majestie's person and of the whole realme to be soe great and ymminent the necessitye of the cause required that they should with all speede possible present that their most humble sute and peticion to her Maiestie, and that therefore they humblie desired that their Speaker and certeine of the said Lower House might be admitted to ioyne with certeine of the lordes of this House to preferre theire saide peticion to her Majestie in the name of all the Lordes and Commons in this parliament assembled. Whereupon all the Lordes dyd verie willinglye assent and thereupon made choise of theis lordes following, *videlicet*,[13] the Lorde Chauncellor, the Lorde Burghley Lord Treasorer, the Earle of Oxford Lorde Greate Chamberleine, the Earle of Darbie Lorde Steward, the Earles of Northumberland, Kent, Rutland, Sussex, Pembroke and Hartford, the Lorde Howard Lord Admirall, the Lorde Hunsdon Lorde Chamberleine, the Lordes Aburgavenney, Zouche, Morley, Cobham, Graye, Lumley, Chandos, Buckhurst, DelaWare and Norris.

Afterwardes, upon Twesdaye[14] the fiftenth daye of November, the Lorde Chauncellor declared unto the whole House that upon Saterdaie then last past being the twelveth of the same the saide Lordes the comittees and the Speaker and certeine of the Lower House had presented and delyvered in writing their saide peticion to her Majestie and had in moste humble and instante manner besought and moved her Highnes, in regard of the saffetye and preservacion of her Maiestie's moste royall person and the common weale and good estate of the whole realme, to graunt unto them the effect of that their most iust and humble sute. And that her Maiestie receaving their saide peticion in most gracious manner did thereupon use unto them a moste godlie, grave and

---

11. Petition recited here; Harl. continues 'Most etc' (+ Add.), thus omitting the petition.
12. Harl. continues 'etc, and the place ...'; Add includes the Archbishop of Canterbury and continues 'etc, and the place ...'.
13. Harl. : 'viz. The lord Thresorer etc ...' (+ Add.).
14. Add.: 'Thursday'.

princelye speche, which was uttered with such maiestye and conteyned matter of such rare and singuler wisdome that he coulde not nor would presume to reporte the same unto them, but for theire satisfaccion and comforte to touch summarilie some fewe partes thereof, which were theis. That her Majestie dyd yeald unto almightie God her most humble thanckes for his contynuall and infynitt goodnes and mercies towardes her, who had soe many tymes and soe myraculously preserved her, and in this most speciallie, that as she came to the crowne with the willing hartes of her subiectes soe now after eight and twentie yeares raigne she perceived in them noe dyminucion but rather increase of their good will, for which as she dyd acknowledge her self moste depelie bounden to his dyvine maiestye soe she did moste gratiously and thanckfullye accept the entyre love and most dutifull affeccion and good will of her moste loving subiectes. She declared her exceading greate care for the maintayning of the true relligion of almightie God and for the preservacion and happie estate of her people and the common weale committed to her chardg, desiring not to lyve longer then her lief might be ymployed therein, and wishing to give her lief to th'end her death might procure them a better prince. She protested unto them what exceading greife she conceaved that either they should have occacion to offer or she to receave any such peticion as this which was presented unto her. And fynallie her Highnes saide that for that the matter was rare, waighty and of greate consequence, and that her manner was not in matters of farre lesse moment to give spedye aunswere without due consideracion, soe in this, being of such ymportaunce, she would with moste earnest prayer (which she thought verie requisite) beseche almighty God to direct her with his grace that she might doe and determine that which shoulde tende to the establishment of his true religion and the prosperitie of her most loving subiectes and this common weale, and thereupon woulde with all conveniencye resolve of her answere unto them. He declared further that on Monday following, being the fourtenth of November, her Maiestye upon deliberacion had of their peticion aforesaide did give him in commaundment to signifye unto them that as she dyd take greate comfort and did give God most humble thanckes in that it pleased hym of his infynite mercy to give unto her soe loving and faithfull subiectes, soe she was greately greved that she should be occasioned for the saffety of her self and her realme to use soe severe and sharpe a course contrarie to her owne disposicion and nature as the saide Lordes and Commons assembled in the saide parliament did by their peticion move and urge her unto, and namelye against one of that estate and quallity, soe nere of her bloud and of her owne sexe. And that therefore her Majestie did will and require them to consult and devise[15] according to their wisdomes to the uttermost of their understanding and skill yf any other meanes could be provided for her Maiestie's safetye and the preservacion of the realme and common weale, which yf they coulde doe she woulde most gladlye followe and better like of.

Afterwardes on Saterdaye the nyntenth of November many wise and grave speeches being made touching the saide question propounded by the Lorde

Chauncellor by her Majestie's commaundment, all which in th'end tended to one effect, that their Lordshippes after longe consultacion and greate deliberacion thereupon had coulde not fynd any other waye then was alreadye sett downe in their peticion. Then the Lordes agreed that the matter shoulde be put to the question. And being particulerly asked every one his severall voice, they all aunswered (not one gainsaying) that they could fynde none other waye of saffetye for her Majestie and the realme.

Item: the same day certeine of the Common House desired the Lordes to appoincte some of the lordes of the Higher House to conferre with them upon some questions moved unto them by her Maiestie's commaundment touching the matter of their peticion aforesaide. Whereupon the Lordes made choise of theis following, *videlicet*, the Archbishoppes of Canterburie[16] and York, the Lorde Tresorer, the Lorde Steward, the Earles of Northumberland, Kent, Rutland and Sussex, the Bishopps of London, Durham, Winchester and Worcester, the Lorde Admirall, the Lorde Chamberlaine, the Lorde Zouche, Cobham, Graye, Stourton, Sandes, Chandos, DelaWare and Norris; and their meting was appointed to be in the saide utter parliament chamber the Mondaie following at two of the clock in the afternoone.

Afterwardes, on Twesdaye the two and twentith daye of November, the Lordes the comittees dyd make reporte to the whole House that upon further conference had betwene them and the committees of the Commons House they did understand that her Maiestye had sent her comaundement to her commons of the Lower House to such like effect as she had donne to the lordes of the Higher House, and that thereupon they the saide Commons dyd spende severall dayes and long tyme in debating of the saide question aswell by a chosen nomber of comittees speciallye assigned and appointed in that behalf as openly in the saide Common House, and that after long deliberacion and grave consultacion thereupon had, the matter in the end being publickly put to the question in the same House, they did all conclude and agree with one full consent (not one gainesayinge) that they coulde not fynd or devise any possible meanes to provide for the safetye of the common weale and state of the realme and the preservacion of her Maiestie's most royall person but by such course of proceading as ys conteyned in their saide peticion. And that therefore the saide comons in the saide Lower House did humblie desire their Lordshipps to appoint some of the saide lordes to ioyne with theire Speaker and some of the Lower House to delyver theire saide aunswer to her Maiestye, and moste instauntlye to beseeche her Highnes to proceade according to their former peticion. Whereupon the Lordes, understanding the opynions and resolucions of the saide Commons to be in all thinges consonant and agreable with their Lordshipps' determinacions aforesaid, dyd nominate and appoincte theis lordes following for delyvering of their saide aunswere to her Maiestye, *videlicet*, the Lord Chauncellor, the Archbishopps of Canterburie and Yorke,[17] the Lorde

15. Chandos: 'advise'.
16. Harl. continues 'etc, and their meeting . . .' (+ Add.).
17. Harl. continues 'etc' (+ Add.).

Burghley Lorde Treasorer, the Earle of Darbye Lorde Steward, the Earles of Northumberland, Kent, Rutland and Sussex, the Bishopps of London, Durham, Winchester and Worcester, the Lorde Howard Lorde Admirall, the Lorde Hunsdon Lorde Chamberlayne, the Lordes Zouche, Cobham, Graye, Stourton, Sandes, Chandos, Buckhurst, DelaWare and Norris.

Afterwardes, the fyve and twentith day of November, the Lorde Chauncellor declared to the whole House that on Thursdaye the foure and twentith of November the lordes laste before named, and the Speaker of the Lower House with certeine of the same House, had accesse to her Maiestye at Richmonde. And that he the saide Lorde Chauncellor for the lordes of the Higher House and the Speaker for the Commons did declare unto her Highnes their aunswere as is aforesaide, and dyd further in moste humble and instaunt manner beseech and move her Highnes that she woulde be pleased for the preservacion and saffety not only of her moste royall person but of the whole estate of the realme to graunte and take order that effectuall proceadinge might be spedilie had according to their saide peticion. And that thereupon her Majestie in moste princelye and gracious manner dyd thanckfullie accept those their consultacions and labors, protesting neverthelesse that yt was an exceading greif unto her to perceive that by theire advises, prayers and desires there did fall out this sorrowfull accident, that onlie her iniuror's bane must be her live's suertye and that her earnest desire was rather to have founde by their consultacions some other meanes for her owne safetye ioyned with theire assuraunce, and that therefore touching their peticion, the matter being of soe greate waight and ymportance, her Highnes thoughte good to take yet some further deliberacion before she would make direct aunswere unto them, willing them for the tyme to content them selves and to take it in good parte.

Afterwardes on the seconde day of December the Lordes taking their places in their robes, the lordes her Maiestie's commyssioners went to their place appoincted, and the Speaker and the commons of the Lower House there present. Then the Lorde Chauncellor, going firste to the lordes her Maiestie's commissioners and conferring a while with them, went to his accustomed place and there declared unto both the Houses in howe good parte her Maiestie did accepte theire labors and travells ymployed this parliament and that she rendred unto them all her moste heartie thanckes for the same, and that for the better satisfaccion of soe loving and faithfull subiectes her Highnes was contented to yeald soe farre unto their peticion, that the saide sentence should be divulged presentlye by proclamacion under the Greate Seale of Englande.

Then Master Speaker, yealding most humble thanckes to her Maiestye in the names of the knyghtes, cytizens and burgesses of the Common House that it pleased her Maiestye to condiscende soe farre unto their peticion that proclamacion shoulde presentlye be made, humblie desired the lordes the commyssioners and other the lordes of the Privie Counsell to be earnest mediators to her Maiestie to graunte alsoe unto them the effect of the residue of their saide peticion, and further that it woulde please them to graunte that aswell the saide peticion as theire whole actes and proceadinges in this present session of Parliament touching the saide greate cause might be entred of recorde in the rolles of the same parliament. Whereunto the Lorde Chauncellor aunswered that diverse of the Lordes had byn and woulde be humble and earnest suitors unto her Maiestie for the effectuall accomplishment of theire desires, and that theire Lordshipps were well pleased that theire saide peticion and all theire actes and proceadinges touching the saide cause should be entred of recorde in the rolle of the same parliament according as they desired. And thereupon the saide lordes the commissioners did in her Maiestie's name adiorne the saide parliament untill the fiftenth daye of Februarie next.

1. *Proceedings relating to Mary Queen of Scots, 15 October–2 December 1586*

Text from Cambridge University Library Gg. iii.34, copy.

Cambridge University Library Gg. iii.34, pp.302–17

The petycions aforsayd exhybeted to the Quen's Majestie by the Lordes and Comons ageynste the Quene of Scotes in the parlyament holden the xiiij[th] yere of her Hyghnes' reygne dyd not move here eyther to dyshable the sayd Scottyshe Quene or to execute here accordyng to theyre desyre.[1]

In the xxviij[th] yere of here Majestie's reygne the sayd Scottyshe Quene practysyng newe treasons ageynst her Hyghnes' person and realme, here Majestie sumonyd a parlyament to begynne the xv[th] of October followyng, whyche beyng adiornyd to the xxvij[th] therof and from thens to the xxix[th] of the same, John Whytgyfte Archebusshope of Caunterbury, Wylliam Burleghe Lord Threasorer of England and Henrye Erle of Darbye then Lorde Stewarde were specyall comyssyoners to supplye her Majestie's place at the sayd parlyament; at whyche daye Thomas Bromlye, then Lord Chauncelor of England, declared here Majestie's pleysure to the Lordes and Comons consernyng the cause whye the sayd parlyament was then summoned, as hereafter insuythe.

The sum of his speche was that the Quen's Majestie had cauld this her Great Counsell not to make anye lawes, because there were more lawes then were well executed, nor to have a subsydye althowghe subsydyes were verye convenyent as occacion shold requyere, but only for advyce consernynge the great treasons practysed by the late Quene of Scotes and here accomplyses for the dystruccion of here royall person, the abolyshyng of Gode's trewe relygion and the utter ruyn of the comon welthe of this realme by procurynge forren invacion and so to make a concueste thereof.

Afterwardes John Puckrynge esquiere, Seriea[n]t at Lawe, beyng electyd Speker presentyd and acceptyd to that place. The Comons dyd consult what was beste to be don therein, whereapon theye chose xl[ti] comyttees to consydere thereof; who after sondrye meetynges and long argumentes amongst theym tochyng the sayd waytye matter they drewe a petycion to be /

p.303 exhybetyd to her Majestie and afterwardes by the order of the Howse made motyon to the lordes of the Upper Howse that yt wold pleyse theym to joygne with theym in that accion.[2]

Whereapon xx[ti] of the lordes and busshopes were apoynted comyttyes to dele with xl[ti] the sayd comyttyes of the Lowere Howse tochyng the sayd matter; who aftere two meetynges and conference had agreed joyntlye to exhybet theyre petycion to here Majestie for the puttyng in execucion of the statute made in the xxvij[th] yere of here Hyghnes' raygne ageynst Marye Quene of Scotes for here treasons comytted, *etc.*[3]

But before the conclucyon thereof the treasons, *etc.* practysed by the sayd Quene were openlye redde in the Comon Howse and the whole proces of the lordes procedyng at Fotheyege ageynst her for the same. Whereapon all the whole Howse with one consent agreed to the sayd petycion.

Imedyatlye aftere two of the lordes of the Uppere Howse and two of the counsell of the Comon Howse *vz.* Mr Vycechamberleyne, Sir Chrystofer Hatton knyght, and Mr John Wolleye esquire, were sent to here Majestie to know here good pleysure when the sayd comytteyes myght wayte apon here Majestie to exhybet theyre sayd petycyon.[4]

At the daye apoynted[5] all the sayd comyssyoners cam to the Court at Rychemond, and there the Lord Chauncelor in the name of the Lordes and Comons of the parlyament exhybeted to here Majestie the sayd petycion ingrossed in parchement alegyng dyvers aucthoryetyes and other argumentes to move here Hyghnes to assent thereunto. And amongst other speches sayd that she was sworne at here coronacion to do justyce, so that yt were harde to denye justyce to anye one, but myche more to denye justyce to all here people humblye cravyng the same apon theyre knees at here Majestie's hande. /

Afterwardes the sayd Speker pursued the same with very great and waytye   p.304 resons to move here Majestie to assent to the sayd petycion; to bothe whyche speches here Hyghnes aunsweryd as hereafter insuythe.

'When I remember the bottomles depthe of Gode's great benefytes[6] towardes me I fynde theym to be so many, or rathere so infynyte in theymselfes, as that they exede the capasytye of all men, myche more of anye one to be comprehendyd.[7] And consyderynge the manyfold dangers intendyd and practysed[8] ageynste me whyche thorowe the goodnes of almyghtye God I have alwayes escaped, I muste needs saye yt ys admyrable and myraculus – yf that be a myracle which ys beyonde and above the reason of man – that nowe I lyve. Yet do I not thanke God for that, nor for all the reste, so myche as for this, that after 28 yers' reygne I do not perceave any dyminycion of mye subiectes' good love and affeccyon towardes me. This ys the thynge I moste joye in and that wherein I take my greatest comforte, and withowt whyche I wold not desyre to lyve: for then lyfe shold be a dethe unto me, who do not thynke yt lyfe to brethe but to lyve with that comfort and joye of lyfe whyche ys fytte for me to have. But together with this my greatyste joye I conceyve no smale greefe that there shold be sum wythein my realme of myne own subiectes found so wycked and dysloyall as that they shold seeke to take away

1. See *Procs*, i.274–90.
2. All this by 7 November.
3. 8 November.
4. Hatton reported to the House on 11 November.
5. 12 November.
6. Harl. 158: 'goodnes'.
7. Harl. 158: 'apprehended'.
8. Harl. 158: '. . . dangers and practizes'.

my lyfe, and most of all that one of myne owne sexe, state, and kynne shold be consentynge[9] thereunto and gyltye thereof; wherein notwythstandynge I muste needs saye they wold have done no worse to me then to theymselfes, for that in sekynge to dystroye my bodye they sowght the dystruccion of theyre own soules. I thanke God suche dysloyall subiectes are but fewe; I am sure I have the hartes and good wyls of the greter parte.

'For theys horryble treasons and practyses, to tell yow truly I muste protest that I am not greevyd in respect of my selfe or of myne own lyfe which for yt self I do not regarde, knowyng that the lesse lyfe the lesse synne. And I assure yow for myne own parte I am so farre from desyrynge to lyve as that I thynke

p.305   that that person to be moste happye which ys alredye ded. / Wherefore the regarde of lyfe whyche I have ys in respecte of yow and the reste of my good subiectes, knowyng that my blood could not have byn shed but yors and thers shold have byn spylte lykewyse, whose happye and good estate yf I were sure myght be redemyd and preservyd wythe my dethe, I proteste before almyghtye God I wold not desyre to lyve.

'And nowe as tochyng that person whyche wythe so foule treasons hathe steyned here estate and blood as that I cannot thynke of here but to mye greefe: I may seeme peradventure to bere here mallyce and to be desyrous of revenge, and mallyce I know bryngythe forthe rashe judgement and hastye procedynge often tymes; but I take God to wytnes (from whome no secretes of hartes can be hydden) I bere here no mallyce nor seeke other revenge but thys, that I wyshe wythe all mye harte that she maye be repentant for thys and all other here crymes. And that yow maye the better perceave howe malycyouslye I have procedyd ageynste here I wyll declare a matter unto yow wherein I shall becum a blabbe. After theyse laste conspyracies and treasons were dyscoveryd unto me, of myself I sent and wrote unto here, gevynge here to understand that, yf she wold confesse the truthe and by here lettres advertyse me for what cause, and by whose means, she was indusede to consente thereunto and wytheall dyscover the conspyrators in thys accyon, assurynge her that I delt not cautelouslye with here to drawe from here the knowlege of any thynge whereof I was already yngnorant,[10] I wold cover here shame and save here from reproche: whyche offre of myne she utterlye refusede and stedfastlye denyed her guyltynes therein. Notwythestandyng, I assure yow yf the case stode betweene here and my self onelye, yf yt had pleysed God to have made us bothe mylke maydes wythe payles on owr armes so that the matter shold have rested betwene us two, and that I knewe she dyd and wold seeke my dystruccion styll, yet could I not consent to here dethe. Naye to saye ferther,

p.306   the case standyng as yt dothe, yf / I were assured that she wold repent and desyste frome ferthere attemptes (whyche perhaps may be promysed, but yt were harde to truste wordes where suche deedes hathe gone before) yea, yf I could perceyve howe besydes the practyses of the Scottyshe Quene here self,[11] I myght be ffreed from the conspyracyes and treasons of here favorers in this actyon, bye your leaves she shold not dye. This ys the malyce I bere unto this woman and so shold I deale wythe here[12] yf the case were onlye myne own, and dyd conserne mye lyfe alone; whyche ageyn for yt self I must pleynlye tell yow I lyttle esteme, consyderynge that I have lyved many yers, that I have lyved as a subiecte[13] and in place of rule, and that I have tasted of those sorrowes and trobles whereunto eche kynde of lyfe ys subiecte, and have felt more greefes and fewere joyes then happelye to the world I maye seeme to have don; and yet must I needs confesse that the benefytes of God to me have byn and are so manyfold, so folded and ymbroderyd one apon an othere, so dubled and redubled towardes me as that no creature lyvynge hathe more cause to thanke God for all thynges then I have.

'But to retorne to the matter I wyll tell yow the cause of the maner of mye procedynges with the Scottyshe Quene and whye I dyd not deale by[14] the course of the comon lawe of the realme. I knewe verye well the same to be suffycyent, ffor God forbyd that the auntyent lawe shold be defectyve to ponyshe a person whyche shold offend in so hyghe a degree. But yow my masters of the lawe are so fyne, yow regard so myche the wordes, syllabels, and lettres thereof more then the trewe sence and menynge in deed, that often tymes yow make the same to seeme absurde. For yf I shold have followed that course of the comon lawe, ffor sothe she must have ben indyghtyd by a jurye of twelve men in Stafford shyre,[15] she muste have held up here hand, and openlye byn areygned at a barre, whyche had byn a propere maner of procedynge wythe a woman of her qualytye, I meane here qualytye by byrthe and not by condycion. Yet thys waye I myght have used, accordyng to the comon course of the lawe, as I was assured by the / judges of the realme who shewed it me wrytten in theyre bokes – I meane not the pettye ffoggers of the lawe who loke more on the owtsyde of theyre bokes then studdye theym wythein. But I thowght yt myche better and more fytte to have her tryede by the moste honorable and auntyent nobylytye of the realme, ageynst whom and whose procedynges no exepcyons myght or can be taken.

p.307

'And nowe to cum to the matter in hande. And fyrst to speke of your othe of Assotyacion: of all other thynges I take yt moste thankfullye at yowr handes and note therein your syngulere zeale and affeccion towardes me, in that yt was don and offred by yow not beyng requyred by me, nay, which ys more, I assure yow I never knewe of yt untyll three thowsand bandes with seales thereof were brought and shewed unto me at Hampton Court. And besydes I muste needs saye that yow shewyd great conscyence and consyderat delynge therein in that yow wold swere to pursue to dethe all and everye person whyche shold seeke mye lyfe and the place whyche I hold, and not eny one, thowghe sum of yow myght intende here above otheres whyche nowe ys in questyon. And further yet by lawe the partye offendynge ys fyrste to be tryede and convyctede, wherefore I muste thanke yow specyalye for thys above all the

9. Harl. 158 has 'consent as' rather than 'consentynge'.
10. *Sic.*
11. Harl. 158 omits 'here self'.
12. Harl. 158 omits.

13. Harl. 158 omits and has a blank space.
14. Harl. 158 has 'leave' rather than 'not deale by'.
15. i.e. because she was at Chartley Hall at the time of the alleged offences.

reste. And yet bye your leaves yow have leyd a harde and hevye burthone apon me in this case, for nowe all ys to be done by the dyreccion of the Quene, a course not comon in lyke cases.

'But for aunswere unto yow, yow shall understande the case ys rare and of great weyte, wherefore I muste take suche advyce as the gravetye thereof dothe requyre. And yet I knowe delayes are dangerous and I have smale reason to use myche deleye at thys tyme, ffor I wyll tell yow a secrete which ys moste trewe, there are yet sum lyvynge who wythein fortene dayes have undertaken to take awaye my lyfe and have offred to be hanged yf wythein a monethe yt be not performede. There are sum here present / whyche I am sure knowe thys to be trewe, yet trulye I am afreyd neyther of theym nor of dethe, thowghe perchaunce seynge dethe to all fleshe ys dredfull I myght be at the verye moment ferefull thereof. But I thynke they wold provyde my dethe shold be so soden and so vyolente that yf theyre purposes shold take place I shold have smale tyme or respyte to be afreyde.

p.308

'To your petycyon I muste pawse and take respyte[16] before I gyve aunswere. Prynces yow knowe stand apon stages so that theyre accyons are vewed and beheld of all men, and I am sure mye doynges wyll cum to the scannynge of manye fyne wytes, not onelye wythein the realme but in forren contreys, and wee must loke to persons as well abrode as at home. But this be yow assured of, I wylbe moste carefull to consyder and to do that whyche shalbe beste for the saftye of my people and moste for the good of the realme.'

Then here Majestie havyng ended here speche and beyng gone from here seate of estate a lyttle towardes here prevye chambere, she retorned ageyn and sayd:

'I wyll not leave yow in an error for that perchaunce yow maye thynke the cause of mye not comynge to the parlyament amongst yow to be the fere I have of myself, whyche ys not so, but the greef which I shold have contynualye to here of theyse causes.'

The sayd speches of here Majestie was delyveryd by the Speker unto the Lowre Howse the Monday followynge.[17]

The verye same daye Mr Vycechamb[er]leyne delyveryd from here Maiestye to the Howse that here Hyghnes had forgotten to to have spoken unto the comyttyes at theyre beyng with here, which was that yf there myght be anye meane or devyce found whereby the relygyon of God, the prosperous estate of this comon welthe, and the lyfe of here Majestye myght be preservyd without the takynge awaye of the lyfe of the Scottyshe Quene, the same wold be moste gladsum to here Hyghnes; and therefore wylled that they shold consyder therof and consult what myght be done therein. /

p.309

Whereapon the sayd comytties beyng apoynted by the sayd Howse to consulte and delyberat apon the sayd message, dyd two severall dayes traveyle therein, alegynge all suche argumentes and obiectyons as could be by theym devysed ageynst the executyng of the sayd Quene, and the preservacion of here

Majestie, the contynuance of trewe relygyon in thys realme, and the good estate of the same also conservyd.

In the sayd consultacion notwythestandynge all obiectyons on the behalf of the sayd Quene of Scottes theye could not devyse anye other meane for the saftye of here Majestie, the contynuance of relygyon and preservacion of the comon welthe then th'execucion of the sayd Quene of Scottes.

Whyche theyre resolucion was approvyd by the whole consent of the Lowere Howse, not one contradyctynge the same.

Then yt was agreed bye the whole Howse that the lordes of the Uppere Howse shold be moved that the sayd comyttyes myght have conference with the comyttyes of the Lordes tochyng the sayd mattere, whereunto the Lordes assentyd.

Twentye comyttyes for the Lordes and the sayd xl^{ti} for the Comons mette togethers and after grave debatynge of the matter theye all resolved that there was no other remedye tochyng the saftye of here Majestie, relygyon, and realme but th'execucyon of the Scottyshe Quene as aforsayd.

Whereapon were apoynted two lordes of the Privye Counsell for the Upper Howse and Mr Vicechamberleyn and Mr John Wolleye of the Lowere Howse to move here Majestie that the sayd comyttyes myght have accesse to here Hyghenes to gyve aunswere to the sayd message sent by here to bothe Howses.

Aunswere beyng retorned to bothe Howses that here Majestie was pleysed all the sayd comyttyes shold cum unto here the Thursdaye followynge about one of the clocke in the afternone, which was don accordynglye.[18] /

All the sayd comyttyes of bothe Howses beyng before here Majestie, the   p.310
Lord Chauncelor fyrste declared to here Hyghnes that after the Lordes had delyberatlye consyderyd of the sayd message but could devyce no waye for the saftye of here Hyghenes' lyffe, the contynuance of the trewe relygyon, and the preservacion of the comon welth but onelye bye the dethe of the sayd Scottyshe Quene, and also sayd that everye one of the lordes from the lowest to the hyeste was partycularlye asked his opynyon therein, all which gave theyre consentes and voyces accordynglye.

Afterwardes the Speker declared that all the Neyther Howse not one contradyctyng the same dyd assent with the Lordes in judgement as aforsayd, and also shewyd dyvers obieccions with the aunswers made in the Howse consernyng the same.

Fyrste, whether the Scottyshe Quene shewyng hereself repentaunt and takyng othe with promyses to desyste from further suche treyterous attemptes was to be credyted and therebye all danger avoyded.

Whereunto was aunswered that syns so manye treasons bye here comyttyd ageynst here Majestie, here faythe so often broken notwythestandyng the Quen's pardonyng the same in the xiiijth yere of here reygne, not delyveryng

16. Harl. 158: ? 'time'.   18. 24 November.
17. 14 November.

here to the Scottes who demaunded here that theye myght execute here for here great offences there comytted, neyther suffryng here to susteyne publyke shame for the same but used here wythe all kyndnes, that yet notwythestandyng she hathe perceveryd in here trayterous deylnges: she no more in anye wyse to be trustyd.

He also obiectyd whether yf she could put in hostages for the premysses[?], as the sonne of the Duke of Gwyse, here own sonne the Kyng of Scottes, and also bandes from the Kynge of Spayne and other great prynces myght be a suffycyent remedye, *etc.*

Whereunto aunswere was made that neythere hostages nor bandes of the whole world could countervayle the lyffe of owr Soveraygne, who beyng sleyne, / none cold deteyne the hostages or sue the bandes and so the same was to no purpose.

p.311

He also obiectyd whether yf she were kept streytlye in prysen that then here trayterous practyses myght be prevented.

Whereunto aunswere was made that that course had byn alredye taken and yet she hathe not byn steyd from here wyked and trayterous practyses; besydes, that here favorers wold the soner seeke the lyffe of here Majesties[19] thereby to delyver here owt of prison: and the Quene beyng sleyne, who then wold withhold here?

He also obiectyd yf the Pope wold withdrawe hys bull of excomynycacion and promesse hereaftere no more to deale ageynst here Majestie, whether that myght suffyce.

Whereunto aunswere was made that no truste nor confydence was to be geven unto hym that estemed here Majestie and subiectes as herytykes, with whom promesse and faythe was not to be observed accordyng to the Counsell of Constance, where yt was decreede *quod fides cum hereticis non est conservanda.*

After the Speker had made the sayd obiectyons and aunsweryd the same, and so concluded that ther was no waye whereby here Hyghenes' lyfe myght be preservyd, relygyon maynteynyd, and the floryshyng state of this comen welthe contynued, he moste humblye apon his knees in the name of all the Comons as so bye theym comaunded that yt wold pleyse here Hyghnes to do execucion according to the statute in that case provyded. And that here Hyghnes wold remember the othe of th'Assocyacyon which here faythfull subiectes had taken and the which shold be a great clog of conscyence unto them yf she shold lyve whose dethe that had vowed.

After whyche speches delyveryd here Majestie made answere to the same as hereafter ensuythe. /

p.312

Fyrste, here Majestie sayd to the Lord Chauncelor that the menest pryncees of Germanye had theyre Chancelors to speke for theym whom they used as theyre mowthes, and that he was here Chauncelor and shold speke for here also, but sayd she thowght yt not resonable that the same mowthe whyche had moved here in those causes shold nowe ageyne make aunswere to the same.

Then here Majestie turned to the lordes and sayd that she never had a greter stryfe wythein here self then she had that daye, whether she sholde speke or be

sylent, leste yf she sholde speke in shewyng here affeccion she myght seeme to
dyssemble, and yf she shold be sylent she myght do theym wronge in not
aunswerynge theyre expectacions. And then withe a lowe voyce she spoke
unto theym of the compleynte whyche afterwardes she spake unto the Commons as insuythe.

'I perceave yow have well consyderyd of my laste message sent unto yow
procedyng[20] from an erneste desyre and a hungrye wyll in me that sum waye
myght be by yow for mye saftye devysed wytheowt the execucion of that acte
whereunto by your petycion I was moved. But nothyng beynge found for mye
satysfaccion in that behalf, I muste needs make a great compleynte, not of yow
for I make yt unto yow, nor of myself, but of mye case, whyche at this present
ys suche, by reason of the manye practyses ageynste me and the greate
mysschyef intended towardes me, that nowe the bane of the iniurer must be
the onelye cure of mye dangere; whereof to thynke yt grevythe me not a lyttle,
consyderynge that there be sum whyche wyll not styck to shed[21] theyre owne
blood for the sake and defence of theyre kynne, and by me yt shold be sayd
hereafter a mayden quene hathe byn the dethe of a prynce here kynswoman,
a thyng in no sorte deservyd by me howe so ever by the dyspyte of malyce yt
may be reported of me. I have cause to thynk howe narowly myne actyons are
lyke to be syfted and fynely scanned by sum good fellowes abrode who spare
not to publyshe pamphletes, lybells and bokes ageynst / me wythe detestacyon   p.313
of me and mye governmente, gyvyng me for an almes (I thanke theym for yt)
to be a tyrant, that from whyche alwayes my nature above all thynges hathe
moste abhorde. But I thynke they ment to send yt me for newes, for that I
never knewe or harde that ever I was suspected thereof before. I wold theyre
wyckednes were lyke newes unto me and that the same were no more trewe
of theyme then this ys of me, but I truste bothe I and theye shall lye in owr
graves ere that yt shalbe provyd trewe by me. Suche rebels there are beyond
the seas. I hope there are no suche wythein the realme; I praye God there be
not, but I wyll not swere yt. But to clere mye self of that fault, thys I maye
justlye saye: I have pardoned manye traytors and rebels, and besydes I well
remembere half a score treasons whyche have byn eyther coveryd, or slytelye
examyned, or lette slyp and passed over, so that myne actyons have not byn
suche as shold procure me the name of a tyrante; yet this of my self must I
needes confesse, thowghe for that cryme I am not justlye to be towched I am
a wreched synnere and humblye desyre pardon at his handes ageynste whome
I have offendyd for the same.

'And nowe to saye more unto yow of mye self. When I fyrste came to the
coepter and crowne of thys realme I dyd thynke more of God who gave yt me
then of the tytle, and therefore my fyrste care was to sette in order those
thynges whyche dyd conserne the Churche of God and this relygyon in
whyche I was borne, in whyche I was bred, and in whyche I trust to dye, not

19. *Sic.*   21. Harl. 158: 'sheld'.
20. Harl. 158 omits.

beynge ygnorant how dangerous a thyng yt was to work in a kyngdome a sodene alteracion of relygyon, and that yt was lyke to be a foundacion and a ground for suche great kynges and prynces as were myne enymyes to buyld and worke theyre devyses uppon, yll intendyd ageynst me. But I commytted my cause unto hym for whose sake I dyd yt, knowyng he could defende me, as I

p.314   must confesse he hathe done unto thys / tyme and dowt not but he wyll do unto the ende.

'After that I dyd put myself to the scole of experyence, where I sowght to lerne what thynges were most fytte for a kynge to have, and I found theym to be fowre, namelye, justyce, tempre,[22] magnamynytye,[23] and judgement. Of the two laste I wyll saye lyttle because I wyll not challenge nor arrogate to my self more then I knowe there ys cause; yet thys may I saye and trulye, that as Salamon, so I above all thynges have desyred wysedome at the handes of God, and I thanke hym he hathe geven me so myche judgement and wytte as that I perceave myne own imperfeccions manye wayes, and myne ignorance in moste thynges. As for magnamynytye I wyll passe yt over; and for the course of justyce I proteste that I never knewe dyfference of persons, that I never set one before an other but uppon iuste cause, neyther have preferred anye to offyce or other place of caulynge for the preferrers' sake but that I knew, or was made beleve, he was worthye and fytte for yt. Neythere dyd I ever lende myne eare to anye person contrarye to order of lawe to pervert my[24] verdycte. And for tempere, I have had alwayes care to do as Augustus Caesar[25] who beyng moved to offence, before he attempted any thynge was wylled to saye over the alphebet; and I truste suche hath byn myne actyons and the caryage of my self as that mye subiectes have no cause in that respect to repente theymself for theyre prynce: and that I am slowe enowghe in myne actyons I am sure there are suffycyent wytnesses here present.

'And nowe as tochynge yow, I muste needs saye and confesse that there was never prynce more bound to his peple then I am to yow all. I can but acknowleg your great love and exedyng care of me to be suche as I shall never be hable to requyte havyng but one lyfe, except I had as manye lyves as yow all. But I wyll never forget yt whyle I shall brethe. And thowghe I maye want the means and the wytte, yet surelye I shall never want the wyll to requyte yt.

p.315   And so I praye yow tell theym / all, I do but acknowlege, I cannot requyte.

'And as for your procedynges in this cause, I assure yow I do not myslyke your judgement[26] for they are grounded apon sure groundes, uppon the worde of God and great reason; neyther do I misconter[27] your petycyon, I know yt dyd procede from erneste and dutyfull affectyon towardes me. But peradventure yt maye seeme strange unto yow that I shold cheryshe a sword in myne owne realme to shed myne own bloode. I do not saye, I wyll do so, and yet I knowe there are manye whyche ventre theyre lyves often tymes[28] for a lesse matter then the saftye of a kyngdome. And happelye in this case I myght adventure myche, were yt onelye wythe danger of myne own lyfe, whyche I proteste before God I chyeflye regarde in regard of yors. But yt seemythe moste strange unto me that everye one, bothe of yow mye lordes and the reste, shold all agree in one that yt shold be a thyng moste harde, or rathere ympossyble, for me to lyve in saftye wytheowt execucion of your demaunde. And here I muste saye unto yow, yf anye person be so wycked to thynke that the laste message which I sent unto yowe was a thynge don *pro forma tantum* and that I ment yt not in deed, or that yt procedyd from a vayne gloryous mynde, as that I sowght therebye the more to be commended for clemensye and gentlenes of nature, or that I ment to make the lordes wyerdrawers to drawe the matter styll into lenghe[29] wythowt cause, he dothe me gretere wronge then ever he can be hable to recompence. I dyd yt I proteste before God as beyng moste desyrous to understand everye man's opynyon whereby to perceave what was fytteste for me to do, wherein my mynde was that everye one of mye lordes shold franckye[30] utter hys conceyte, eyther publyklye in the Howse or pryvatlye to my self, lest sum of theym beyng suspected myght for that cause be sylent. And thys I wylled mye lordes my comyssyoners[31] to sygnefye, whyche yf they dyd not they dyd me the more wronge, ffor I am not so unwyse but that I know that althowghe by / caulynge I go before a great p.316 manye, yet manye partyculere persons for wysedom and other respectes are to be preferred before me.

'But nowe for aunswere unto yow, yow muste take an aunswere without aunswere at mye handes. For yf I shold saye I wold not do yt I shold peradventure saye that whyche I dyd not thynke, and otherwyse then yt myght be. Yf I should saye I wold do yt, yt were not fytte in thys place and at thys tyme, althowghe I dyd meane yt. Wherefore I must desyre yow to hold your selfes satysfyed with thys aunswere aunswereles. I know there ys none of yow but ys wyse and well affected towardes me and therefore wyll consydre what ys moste fytte for me to do. Theye muste be deedes and not wordes which must satysfyce[32] your demaunde. I praye yow therefore lett this[33] aunswere aunswereles content yow for thys present, assuryng yowr selfes that I am nowe, and ever wylbe, moste carefull to do that which shalbe best for yowr preservacion. And be not to erneste to move me to do that whyche maye tende to the losse of that which yow are all moste desyerous to keepe.'

The Fryday the ix[th][34] of December the Lord Chauncelor, declaryng the prorogacion of the parlyament untyll xv[th] of Februarye foll500wyng, delyveryd thankes from here Majestie to the whole parlyament for theyre greate and dyllygent paynes taken in the forseyd matter, promysyng that she wold never forget the same as long as she shold brethe.

Afterwardes the Speker desyred the comyssyoners in the name of the Comon Howse that theye wold yeld unto here Hyghenes in theyre behalfes

22. Harl. 158: 'temperaunce' (and below).
23. *Sic.* (and below).
24. *Sic.* Harl. 158: 'anie'.
25. Lansd. 94 (Doc.10) has 'Alcibiades' at this point.
26. *Sic.* Harl. 158: 'judgmentes'.
27. *Sic.* Harl. 158: 'misconster'.
28. Harl. 158 omits 'often tymes'.
29. *Sic.*
30. *Sic.*
31. Harl. 158 omits 'my comyssyoners'.
32. *Sic.* Harl. 158: 'answere'.
33. Harl. 158 adds 'my'.
34. *Sic.* 2 December.

theyre most humble thankes in that yt had pleysed here to caule theym to here counsell in that weytye cause. And that also the sayd comyssyoners and others

p.317 the lordes of here Hyghnes' Counsell that shold have accesse to her Maiestye ernestlye to move here Hyghenes for th'execucion / of the sayd ladye of the northe accordyng to here iuste desertes.

Also the Speker in the name of the Comon Howse desyred the comyssyoners and the rest of the lordes that the petycion delyverd before to here Hyghnes for th'execucion of the sayd ladye myght be enacted and inrolled in the Lordes Howse for a memoriall to theyre posterytyes of theyre carefull travell and delynge for the preservacion of theyre sovereygne, the trewe relygyon of God, and of the comon welthe; which assented unto presentlye, and iiij[or] lordes with vj of the Comons to see the same don.[35]

---

35. There are several marginal notes in this MS, probably in the same hand as the pedigree at the end of the volume, which pedigree is said by another later hand to have been written by James Gresham of Fulham in Middlesex, esquire. The notes simply act as marginal signposts to the text, though on p.307, against mention of the Bond of Association, the writer records 'Assotiacion, the coppy of which instruccion [sic] I have.'

2. *Anonymous journal,*
23 *February–8 March* 1587

Text from [BL Harley 7188, original.

Harley 7188, fos.89–103

[Entitled, (f.88), 'A Book of Parliament notes'.]

23° Februarii 1586.

A bill first read for the bringinge in of fishe.

Mr Job Throgmorton spake sharply of princes, and after rebuked coverdly[1] by Mr Vichambrelayn.[2]

Francis Alforth. Good to mayntayne the action we have taken in hand for the Low Contries. That it was lawfull and good, not to be left of. The contry opposit; havinge it free from all the world. Farre from Spayn, neare to England. To be on the hill to judge on the vale or playn; and contrary. That other kings[?] had wonne and that wee had lost. Cowardes and covetous never good warriours. Wher the honors be, ther the burthens should be. That men should find men and pay no subse[dies]. Wisshinge the confiscations of landes and goodes should be sould and kept to supply other needes. Last against corporacions.

Mr Vichamberlain. Commendinge *liberum suffragium* in makinge lawes. Ij thinges: the justice to undertake and the continuance of it. For the justice, the auncient leages with the princes and the people and with bothe. That the Queen refused it first. Conscience and policy. King Philip greater then Alexander the Great. That to furnishe in all places her Majerty had nede of to do, x^{li} will not serve.

Francis Alford. Mr Alford.[3] Upon excuse, Tully *in re incerta justificas* is *necnon audeam.* That he did not enter into *arcana imperii.* /

24 February 1586. Friday.   v.

1. A bill read touchinge fisshinge in Oxford[4] haven for smeltes.

A bill redd for the mayntenance of the bridge and streetes of East Retforthe, that it may take toole.

A bill redd for the trew pay[i]nge of tythes as of xl years before.

Articles of ij fifteens and one subsedy redd and consented unto.

Sir Thomas Scott. The dangers inward and outward. More danger by advancinge papistes into place of trust and government then by any thinge.

---

1. Corrected from 'openly' in the same hand.
2. Sir Christopher Hatton.
3. *Sic.*
4. *Sic.* i.e. Orford.

A favorable reomedy for them: that it may be enacted, all grantes to known papistes shalbe voyd and that they may inioy no place hearafter.

2. The means to withstand forraygne enimis: treasure, which is alowed by sub[sedy]. But slow payment. He wisht it soner. Nether intelligence nor ought els done without money. The sinew of warres.

3. For defence by for[ce] of shippes. Only desierous t'utter this, that wee must resist the enimy at landinge; to make ready our wache, beakons and men expert before th'enimy land, for consultacion then to longe stay. Examp[le] of Caesar: landinge was resisted and mad retire. The saffest way, t'incounter the enimy in

f.90   the water or landinge, and to prepare all thinges ready before. / A good alarum of the waches at the cost and of beakons the next the sea to be fierd first in tyme of invacion by sea. Wishinge amendment of weapons to be as ready as the [MS blank].

Mr Wroth. Many thinges well spoken of dangers. Nothinge more profitable then to take the Low Contris. If Dunkirke have done us so great harme, what would all the rest do, as Flushing, Brile, Holland, *et cetera*. To take the soveraygnty of it. Loth to troble our selves now after so longe peace. Good to give a large subsedy; and that the good wills of the good subiectes may be tried. That for his own part he would give a C[li] by yeare towardes the mayntenance of it[5] thos warres.

Mr Bakon.[6] All speaches placable and good. Not likinge a committy, but to leave it to her Majesty. But if her Majesty sticke to take it for want of treasure, then to put it to committys. Preposterus the vayle to judge of the hill, *et cetera*.

Francis Alforth. A committy t'agre on a bill to move her Majesty t'undertake the Low Contries.

Mr Grice and Mr Beale. That all papistes' weapons and furniture for warres might be taken from them, *et cetera*.

Doctor Turner. That by some token a papist may be known.

Mr Beinbrick.[7] That detractinge papistes may be loked to. /

v.   Mr Topliffe.[8] That weapons and all massinge trumpery with bookes papisticall weare fownd in the very next howse ioyninge to the Cloth of Estate by the Parlament Howse. Th'owner's name, one Mr Ingam of Kent, a principale of an Inn of Chauncery. He offered him money in the search of his howse, to spare him. Prayers for King Philippe, *et cetera*.

Mr Wentworth. That he myght be sent for and Sir Thomas Scott willed to bringe him in.

25 February 1586.[9]

Mr Vichamberlain. That it is a good course to take the Low Contrye by commen pollicy[10] of the realme, but that her Majesty's Counsell had delt in before and considered of it at large. And her Majesty of present[11] with them. That so many caucions had ben fownd as no moo to be fownd. An enterprice of necessity and justice. An action most benevolent and of the highest reverent course. Warrantable before God and men. She taketh nought from the King of

Spain, nor impeacheth him. Lawfull *inire bellum ut pax inde sequatur.* The commiseration of the poore people of our owne blod and many mached ther. *Regium succurrere miseris.* /

That it will uphold peace on th'one side, and bringe plenty on th'other. *Cum proximus ardet.*[12] To cutt of also his purse of the Indies.   f.91

Defendinge them wee have all vent open, and losinge them wee lose our selves. That wee have vent; by it, profitt. Necesity and justice. Not fitt the King of Spain showld have a monarky of the Low Contries. Question heartofore which part the Frenche should defend and which wee.

The acceptacion of the suveraygnty: the case that withowt us they can not be preserved. That it cost Sir Thomas Cicell 5000[li] in service in the Low Contries.

The Crowne of England not able t'undertake the Low Contries without an extraordinary helpe for holdinge it. Wee must hold continuall warres. The Queen would reserve nothinge of her owne. Defence belongeth to the soveraygnety. 5000 foot men and 1000 horse fownd ther by the Queen. /

Sir Walter Myldmay. That wee are only to thinke *de modo*, how we would   v. have her Majesty enter into the matter of execucion.

Mr Alforth. That the soveraygnty is to be taken.

Doctor Lewin. Whether more just or more honorable *in deliberati[o]nis racionatur, an possit fieri, an expediat?* If easi and necessary, then to be done. Deliberation how it shold be mayntayned. All the vayn charges of the land to be bestowed on this. Rather to be wished then possible to be brought to passe. /

February 26 1586.[13]   f.92

A bill reed for givinge of force to exemplificacions of fines and recoveries.

A bill read agayn for limitacion of tyme towching writtes of error growinge by frawd.

A bill read agayne for th'attaynder of Thomas Lord Pagitt, Sir Francis Inglefeld, Salsbury, Throgmorton, Jones, Shelley, Babington, Tillney, Tichburne, Barnwell, Charnocke and Travars.

Not to reverse a judgment in a writ of error upon treason.

Mr Vichamberlain. A mocion t'admonishe, *et cetera.* That this other day in proceadinge divers spake very well, *et cetera.* But one, a gentleman of noble

---

5. Inserted in the same hand.
6. The half brothers Francis and Edward both sat in this parliament.
7. Robert Bainbridge.
8. Richard Topcliffe.
9. The following passage (to the end of f.94) appears to be a report of proceedings of the committee on the Low Countries and probably belongs to 24 February.
10. Corrected from 'consent' by the same hand.
11. *Sic.*
12. Horace, *Epistulae*, I, 18, 84.
13. This heading, in the hand of the text, is in error as the proceedings seem to be those of 25 February.

blod, zealous in religion, *et cetera*. This escaped him, that he spake sharply of princes and layd indignities on them. The reverence to princes is dew by God. That wee are bownd t'obay good princes. God doth correct by ill princes. That wee should use great regard of princes in free speache. Hard and intollorable to use ill speches of the King of France, continuinge in leage and frendshippe with us. Nether ought wee t'ubbrayd him with his auncestours. God is to judge. Matter nearar then this glanced at also, ye, and towched a litle against the King of Scotland, a prince yonge, of good religion, a frend, and in leage with her

v.   Majesty both offencive and defencive. Sinne then to speak ill of him, / and shame to detract him. Rather to pray for him, *et cetera*. A king presentinge *figuram dei hominis. Soli deo minores; aliis omnibus maiores.* To take good [?] heed in causes of princes [?] that nought escape us but appertayninge. Lest we offer offence to the preiudice of the peace. Therfore howsoever we procead, to be sure to contayn our selves in circle. And that this mocion may avayle to make some repayre.

27 February 1586.

A bill read once for the repeale of certayn branches in severall statutes concerninge buy[i]nge and sellinge lether.
2. A bill towchinge delay of execucion.[14]

    Mr Cope. A mocion. A bill and booke towchinge some reformacion in religion may be read.

    Spoken unto by Mr Lewkner and Mr Throgmorton.

    Agreed to be read tomorowe.

    The [motion] spoken against by Mr Dalton.

    Whittingham: no good till a church reformed.[15] /

f.93   To the committy for taking of Low Contries.

    Sir Walter Mildmay. Her Majesty did make it knowne to all princes [?] what she ment in takinge the Low Contries. Not to seeke to gett ought to her selfe, but to assist and defend her distressed neighbours, as appeareth in the printed booke put in severall languages to be knowne abrod to all the world.[16]

    The matter we have to do is what we will give toward this and all other her Majesty's so great charges. And how.

    Mr Vichamberlain. The imployment of the money to the mayntenance of the state. Not to be taken if not used. Not fitt to designe or direct the Queen how she shall use it.

    Mr Solicitor.[17] For peace and protection of religion. Money of benevolence brought to Moyses to build the Tabernacle till he would no more. To put in all and referre the distribucion of all [to the] Queen and her wise Counsell. /

v.   28 February.

Mr Speakar. That he had sent the bill and booke bothe to her Majesty by her expresse command.

    Mr DunAley.[18] Of the great idolatry begone againe in Wales to an idole; of the numbre of people that resort to it; of the solitary and closenes of the place emongst bushes, wher the[y] abuse other men's wives; of the service, is said in nether Waylch nor Inglishe tonge; and of the supersticion they us[e] to a springe well in castinge it over ther sholders and head; and what ignorance they live in for lacke of learned and honest ministers.

Mr Topliffe. Of the like supersticious use of Buxton's well and how they brought childeren to christen them in the well; of the ignorance for lacke of learned ministers. And wished every man might give a particuler note of all the disordars in his contry, which he him selfe offered to justifie.

Mr Bainbrick. Also for reformacion, to devart Gode's plages from us. /

Mr Francis Hastinges. At strife with him selfe whether to speake or hold his   f.94 peace; but consideringe his dewty to God, loyalty to the Queen, and love to his contry he could not be silent, but in place of free speach willinge and ready to deliver his conscience. The safty of her Majesty and strengthninge of our contry, the matters. That as we dayly pray for it to God, so that wee now use it in our assembly to do that may be most to his glory. Not to thrust God out at dors. Our ministers blind. The necessity of preachinge. Three hinderances; the wantes and dangers; the end, salvacion. Hinderances: idlenes and duplicity; non residence. Wantes: people untaught, *et cetera.* Dangers: God dishonored, the word contemned, seminaries abownd. To make better lawes, her Majesty may be better obayed.

Mr Aldred. Speakinge as a poore laborar in the buyldinge of the temple. Somthinge wantinge wee wishe to be amended. With many examples out of the Bible.

Francis Alforth. That he will not speake Laten: too scoller-like. Prosecutinge for the learned ministery. Wisshed the busshoppes to be complayned on. That ther was reomedy by course of law. To open impropriacions the best reomedy towardes a learned ministery. To lay a plat how, *et cetera.* /

The bill of subsedy redd with ij fifteins and tenthes. A first of March, Ash   v. Wensday.

I was at Court t'heare dean of Powl's.[19]

2 *Marcii* 1586.

Our Speaker. That her Majesty had sent for him and noted great negligence in him that he suffered so great disordar in the Howse. That for matter of reformation, at the beginnynge of this parlament she charged my Lord Chauncler nought should be sayd of religion, but to be first mad privy. That

14. Committed, according to D'Ewes, p.410.
15. Whittingham was not a member. It may be that this line refers to a reference to Whittaker by Job Throckmorton on this day: see Doc.16.
16. A declaration was published in English, French, Dutch and Italian in November 1585.
17. Sir Thomas Egerton.
18. Edward Donne Lee, alias Downlee or Dounley.
19. On this day the Speaker was summoned by the Queen and the house 'departed' (D'Ewes, p.411).

he had before told her pleasure to the House. That, notwithstanding, they had broken it. That againe she commanded no more should be sayd.

Mr Vichambrelayn. That they did great hurt to the good and ordarly proceadinge in reformacion to meddle now so busily in it.

Mr Hare.[20] That wee had all now given our good wills to a subsedy. That we may pay it with like good wills. People loth to have many paymentes. A search yerly hinders willingnes. Preferringe a bill to procure willinge payment. *Execucio legis preservacio regis.*

A bill reed against forstallers, ingrossors and regraters, providinge that all men may not b[u]y barly to malt it. /

f.95   A bill reed third tyme for explanacion of a lawe towchinge fines and recoveries wherin the judges themselves be parties.

A bill read first tyme concerninge the great abuse of purveyars, to take as the statute doth alow or fo[rfeit] 20[li].

Sir Walter Mildmay. Execucion and vexacion of the subiectes for subsedy. Exaction of the purvayars to be well punisshed wher cause proved, but some would complayn for private displeasure. Reason the Queen's people should be free from vexacion and so to offer the bill.

My Lord Lumney his counsell, Mr Walmsley, at our barre for to preserve his right to the goodes of William Shelley in the bill of attaynders. That he had shewed his grant from Queen Mary, *et cetera.*

A bill redd for continuance of divers statutes.

3 Marcii 1586.

The subsedy redd 2 tyme. That it differs from former subsedies in longer daies of payment, and that the commissioners may better sesse thos [that] be not well-assessed. And a proviso to it for the Queen's moniars and officers of the mynt. The proviso dasht by the question to the Howse.

A bill redd for confirmacion of letters patentes since the 15th Elizabeth.

A bill reed for the good makinge of clothe in Suffolke. To be a trew color; lxiiij[li] wayght undrest; drest, but lx[li]; the cloth lxvij yardes longe; the tonynter[21] lxj foote. First readinge. /

v.   The bill 2 reed[22] for reformacion of th'excescive taking of purvayars. None to be caried up upon complant of the purv[ey]ors but upon the informacion and justificacion of ij of the next justices of peace upon payn.

Mr Tasborow.[23] That contrary to law the purvears command the constables and pety constables to bringe so many pultry unto a place. The contry forced to cary them to ther great charge. Not gatheringe in grosse as the[y] should, but by parsels of many which the[y] should pay ready money for under xl[s]. Not satisfied at the justices' handes as the statutes alow, but complayn to the Lords, which cost greatly in attendance or they can gett againe dispatcht from Court. To provid for this.

Recorder.[24] Not to committ it. *Multi impediunt non factum, quae semel factum non impediunt.*

Yet committed by the question.

4° Marcii 1586.

A proviso redd to cut of ingrossors, regraters and forstallers.

    Mr Tasborow. No man that hath neid abbridged.

    Committed.

    Sir John Higham. That he would not, nor thought none of the Howse would, once open his mouth for any disloyall subiect such as Pary was, that was taken out from emongst them and worthely committed. But incoraged by the liberties of the Howse, he was more bold to beseach the Howse to joyn with him as humble sutors to her Majesty for the inlargment of / some of the   f.96 Howse he hard to be latly committed to the Tower for speaking of ther conscience, not well seinge how the Howse could further procead well in matters of so great importance without his members. That a Suffolke pap[ist] said he thought he should do God good service to be hanged for that religion. 3000 parishes in Suffolke, few preachars. Ignorance of the ministry not to infect [?] the numbre of them. Good to instruct them. To joyne with me in most humble sewt for ther delivery.

    Mr Vichamberlayn. 'Methinkes necessary to speake somwhat conserninge this last speache, not hinderinge the liberties of the Howse, as I and my posterytie trust to serve for ever in the same. Of theis gentlemen committed I assuere yow I know nothinge, but knowing her Majesty['s] princly disposition, favoringe all men, I stay at the matter and thinke it necessary wee all stay to be first informed further before we presume to sewe. If it grow of that wee inherite, then to sewe; but if the committment be strange from us, then appertayninge to her justice, we may not medle. Therfore I presume to move yow to learne further before wee procead, as standinge more with our dewty to her Majesty. But out of this I will borow a few speaches, which I will deliver yow truly to my understanding, concerninge the bill and booke of reformacion in religion. / In this great cause her Majesty hath had so honorable   v. consideracion, as she hathe thought good to suppresse it. But yet she yealdethe causes. It is her princly care wee content our selves. Mr Chanclor,[25] Mr Solicitor and my selfe had the booke delivered us from her Majesty.

    'To the pollicy of it. For matter of divinity it hathe no study but as proceadinge from our zeales to the glory of God. For the booke, I fownd my selfe satisfied in government. The Queen's father begone this holy worke. Stricke a great blowe. Abolished the Pope, his lawes, his Peter pence, *et cetera*. He gave a tast of Gode's word first translated. Kinge Edward, he religiously followed to make perfitt his father's worke. His course was open; all men might speake, fyne it and refine it. But notwithstandinge, great change was mad by Queen Mary. But since her Majesty['s] tyme what care to shutt out the Pope agayne, I doubt not but yow all remember it with thankfull hartes. Now all this nought worth, but erronious and more, repugnant to the word of

20. John or Nicholas (*Commons*).
21. *Sic.*
22. i.e. second reading (D'Ewes, p.412).
23. Thomas Tasburgh.
24. William Fleetwood.
25. Sir Walter Mildmay.

God.[26] To procead in generality, bold and presumptuous proceadinge. No other means to reforme religion or commend[27] what is amisse, but take all away. This a hard course. Shall we say we have lived thus many years in so great error? Rather to have told us what had ben amisse then to tell us all is f.97 nought. This bill as a peticion prays a lawe / to be made to make this booke lawfull. Trust me, yow shall know it fitter to be supprest then to be debated. And this I deliver yow from her Majesty, that no further argument be used in it.

'But in this offered reformacion many consequences follow, unknowne to the devisers, which if *et cetera*. This bill and booke offer theis wronges: first to her Majesty, to us her subiectes, to the whole clargy and the mynisters of the Chur[c]he.

'To us, to be disinherited of all patronages, all impropriations, abbay landes, and all belonginge to the Church. Loke upon the booke of ecclesiasticall government: to pull all our landes away under pretence of reformacion of religion; the clargy would have a new calinge; nothinge but equality, the 3 part (the Lords spirituall) cutt away. I will tell yow a pretty story. Ther was in Carthage great murmuringe against the governors; sayd not worthy to live. The tribune of Grece went to pacify them. But at his commynge, thought fitter to give way then deale with them, such was ther fury against them. But found the means to locke up all the governours fast, and told them what he had done. They cried, "Crusify them". But moved first, or they toke theis away, good to provid others. They weare content. But in search non so good could be fownd, as they weare glad to let them alone. /

v.   'I speake not this to excuse all, ther be defectes and disordars. And if laws eclesiasticall weare well executed ther would not be so many.

'Lastly, her Majesty['s] supremacy is also cut away and her prerogative to have only *potestatem in causam, non in personam*. Also all first frutes, tenthes, subsidis, all gone, yet the Crowne still bownd to defend the realme. What burthen lieth upon it is knowne. Then, havinge no other helpe, it must all come out of your owne purses. And yet more. Mislikes the Queen of all lawes ecclesiasticall supream head and governor. What in that, I referre it to Mr Chauncler and Mr Solicitor. Laws also of her prerogative landes. Thinke you this good? To conclude, out of my hart I thinke the honest, zealous gentleman[?] of this House hath ben slyly ledd into this action. And worse then all this, by ther devise the Queen her selfe is to [be] drawne under chayre of ther excommunicacion: so 10,000 Popes in England. Many other causes more largly to be delt in. Abruptly, this I have fownd in it. But by more discret parsons yow shall heare more. And hope yow will conclud with me against the bill and booke; and this is my consent.'[28]

sermonis finis. /

f.98   Sir Walter Myldmay, against the bill and booke. 'I will tell yow what I have noted and what inconvenience'. The bill a longe preamble but the act in few lines; the booke longe, not able to remembre all. By the generall wordes of the bill: to repeale and cancell all laws ecclesiasticall whatsoever before. Ij thinges noted in generall and perticuler. That he never saw the like to that: all to be repealed, the word so generall it may reach to Magna Carta. To repeale all laws or thei[29] be seen? It strecheth to th'old laws we take hold of against the Pop[e]. To the lawes of the Queen: wee recognize she hath power to reforme all concerning the government of the Church. Laws to punishe men: shall we conteme theis lawes? Laws that all men shall take an othe to abandon the Pope: no man of the mynistery to take this oth. Cuttes of all the Queen's jurisdiction and government. A law how ministers should be accepted: a good lawe, if well excecuted this now devise had not comed. Also a law, xx^li a man that commeth not to the Church: this also cut of, with the Booke of Common Prayer. Many mo laws without my profession. If we disanull spiritual jurisdiction then all testamentes and wills, what in tithes, contractes of mariage, questions of bastardy? Leave the religion voyd all theis. But the devisers of this of small judgment, small experience. He honest, but put into his handes.[30]

    Also, what should become of the busshopes' landes? / The Parlament   v. consisteth of iij heades: to cutt of one. Hard unles to bringe in one of theis Popes. What shall become of cathedral churches, deanris and prebendaries, all for learned men? What of ther landes, at one cast gone? Busshops, archbishops, deans, prebendaries and all. Perhappes also they mean to dissolve the parisshes too.

    Pastors, deacons and elders only remayne. 'I thinke all the incumbentes also be gone'. Collegis in bothe th'universites voyd. Good the patrons bestow ther benefices well, and the busshoppes to be carfull in alowinge. An assent or dissent in the vulgar people: this I noted in the booke. 'Thinke yow the lord of any towne would not have such one as he liked?' In the government of a realme, policy of the religion and goodes[31] word to go together. Many faultes to be reformed. No provision in the booke how they should live. A weake ministery to live only of the devocion of the people. No lawfull cause of sewte for tythes. And all the judgment of excom[munication] to ly in the common people. The pastor to minister and preach, the doctors to teache, the deacons to gather the almes. The Queen should lose 2000^li by year. A subsedy also now granted: take away the busshops, a 3 part. A sore blow. Also what sklandor should we leave to the Papistes, Jesuites, and seminaries / and recusantes when   f.99 we can not agree amongst our selsves. All the other churches of the east contries and Scotland thinke them selves well reformed. Yet more reasonable if we might have chosen; and a longe tyme or wee could have judged and determined so great thinges. Busshopp Cranmer, Ridley and the rest toke great

26. The MS is uncertain here: 'more' is written over ?'word' and seems to end the sentence. A new sentence then starts with 'Repugnant'. This probably reflects the note-journal formal adopted by the journalist, and though the punctuation differs from above, the sense is the same.

27. *Sic.* ? 'amend'.
28. Or 'conseat'?
29. *Sic.*
30. See Doc.21 for this section.
31. *Sic.* presumably 'God's'.

advise in the last chance and reformacion. This on a soden. No doubt but we have a Christian Church: the markes – trew doctrine and trew administracion of sacramentes – we have them. But is all well? No. As longe as the Church is militant ther grow disordars to be reformed. Then wee need not doubt our good and gracious Queen in this reformacion.

Mr Solicitor. 'I note thes wordes in the booke: all laws ecclesi[astical,] customs, *et cetera* to be voyd before. So generally did I never heare of before.' But neare it said Queen Mary: all in her brother's tyme to be voyd. But this more generall. Incurable inconveniences. First, the Queen's inheritance and subiectes[32] gone. Queen's prerogative royall, lawes against Popish recusantes, mass, statutes, customs, usages. Impropriacions. Payment of tythes, takinge away of tenthes. But a new law to restrayn tythes, a man's almes at the Counsell of Lateren. The parisshes devided, stricken away. No law for capitall offenders. Busshoppes gone. Questions in faith gone. No executors, any lawfull action. No law to administrators. The revenew of the Crown and subsedy. A caucion: subiectes to be carfull the pipes of the tresury be not cut of. Prerogative also cut of. /

v.   Also convocasions and sinodes cut of from the Queen. The othe of recognision cut of, all lawes against Pope and Papistes taken away. Then, alowing the Pope, recusantes mas[s] at will. Pretence to have a learned ministry. No Church but errors may arise. Then proper the Queen only should reforme, since God hath given us a Josias.

Mr Vichamberlain. It is her Majesty['s] pleasure yow conferre with the booke intycled *Of Ecclesiastical Government*[33] and this new booke, and with the *Supplicacion to the Parlament*[34] and other bookes.[35] A mocion that the Papistes may have an interim to stay till her Majesty['s] pleasure be knon.

Solicitor. To apply our seut to the Queen and no other.

5° Marcii. Sonday.

6 Marcii. 1586.

A proviso put into the bill of continuance of statutes.

The bill redd 2 for takinge of heringes, sprattes and smeltes in Orford Haven; and committed.

Doctor Turner. For the liberty of the gentlemen committed to the Tower. Pleading the libertis of the Howse.

Sir Henry Knevitt. Thinking our knightes weare sent for for that purpose; to stay till they returned.

The bill redd for bringinge in of fishe, 2.

f.100   A fishmonger to this bill. / Sainge fisshinge for heringe at beginnynge of August in the northe. In Suffolke from [the] beginnynge of September to November fisshing sayle sett out CCCC, commonly of 20 tunne; some 20[36] last of heringe more and lesse, 1 and lx myles from land. Pity this should be decayed. Fisshers in saten dobletes with gold and silver. Most rom[37] fisshinge caled thither about Lamas. A last of heringe under xl[s]. One towne, Yarmouth, offered London a 1000 last of heringes. One shipp bringes out of Island 20000 fishe, some 30000. In tyms past some religious howse provided 5000 lynges and 6000 loodes. Not to repeale this lawe.

Recordar. To committ it because matter of fact in it.

Mr Grice and Mr Dalton against the bill.

But 8 last of heringes for the whole salt s[t]ore in London bringing of this least.[38]

Mr Alford. To debat it and all bills well at second readinge, or it be committed.

Mr Sandes also.[39]

Committed by the question.

Sir Walter Myldmay. To make a new bill of purvayars. And more, wheras it was moved by a gentleman, and good hold taken of it, for benevolence above the subsedy; many metinges, no good. Pity it should dy. To meet this Monday after noon about it in the Checquer Chambre. /

A jest. Mr Recordar. A statute, who disturbes a judgment to be in case of premunire. To make also this lawe, that who hinders the bill of purvayars to be in case of premunire.   v.

Whit[e] caled to the barre for arestinge Martyn, a burgis of the Howse, for 500 markes on a recognizance, bownd in 700[li]. Whit[e] commanded forth till the Howse had resolved; then Martyn commanded out. When Martyn came in.[40]

Solicitor. The liberties to be preserved. To see the auncient presidentes of the House, and then to give resolute answar.[41]

Upon the committy for benevolence into the Low Contries, *6 Marcii*, Checquar Chamber.[42]

First in the bill of purvayars. Mr Coferar[43] to take purvayars bownd with good suerties.

For benevolence.

32. MS repeats 'and'. Presumably the meaning is that the subject's inheritance is threatened.

33. The reference is presumably to *A Learned Discourse of Ecclesiasticall Government* (1584), also known as *A Briefe and Plaine Declaration*, and attributed to William Fulke. It was answered by John Bridges' *A Defence of the Government Established* (1587). See *STC*, no.10395 and BL Catalogue *sub* 'England, Church of'.

34. i.e. *A Lamentable Complaint of the Commonalty by Way of Supplication to Parliament for a Learned Ministry* (1585): see *STC*, no.7739.

35. Presumably the speech ends here and a new paragraph begins. The journal here

suggests that Hatton made two speeches, though Doc.20 includes this material (apparently) in the attack on Cope.

36. Or '70': the MS has been altered.

37. *Sic.* one word in MS.

38. *Sic.*

39. It is hard, if not impossible, to differentiate between Edwin, Miles and Samuel Sandys, and Michael Sondes.

40. For White see D'Ewes, pp.410, 412, 414.

41. 'A prorogacion or continuance of a parliament' has been inserted before this speech in the same hand.

42. See D'Ewes, p.412.

43. Apparently John Abington: see *CSPD 1547–80*, esp. p.668, *CSPD, 1581–90*, p.668.

Mr Vichamberlain. That the Lords busshoppes have inlarged ther subsedy one halfe.

Mr Wroth. That to take the soveranty he offered a C^{li}, and that notwithstanding her Majesty would not take the soveraygnty, yet he would mend his subsedy. /

f.101   Mr Vichamberlain. That her Majesty's charges is in many places. The cause remayns, tho wee may not medle with soveraygnty; therfore to thinke on it. The subsedy but litle. If anythinge or nothinge, what yow shall thinke good.

Sir Walter Mildmay. Good to falle to good consultacion heare, how more should be levied. First t'agre on the contribucion and after to rate it.

Mr Whitton. Offeringe the findinge of a man into the Low Contries, valuinge it at xij^{li}.

Mr Morris. That this is not the best course. We may promis for our selves but not for our contrys.

Mr Vichamberlain. That this benevolence should grow volentary without constraynt; but cheifly from the welthiest and moste zealous, well-affected to her Majesty.

Solicitor. Necessary to defend the Crowne. The dangers Ruowne,[44] cares to kepe Barwicke, Irland to defend invacion. Not to deale with soveraynty: to leave that to her Majesty. To give of our abondance. Edward 3: the 9 fleece and the 9 sheefe given. Now not to be a pray to forrayn enimys. And the thing beinge moved, to prosecut it and bring it to some good passe. According to expectations[?]. /

v.   Mr Wroth. By lawe, from x^{li} upwardes to give ij^s in the pownd more.

Mr Vichamberlain. That the recusantes had offered largly for the defence. And that it should be told her Majesty. That the Queen may not leave it. To contribut to bring peace as before.

Sir William More. Good to grant commissions as in King Henry 8 tyme: muche money that way gotten. To doe the like now. To deale with the Low Contries.

A stranger: I know not his name. Theis ways to make men and money. Lij provinces in Ingland; 10 or 12000 parishes.[45] Every parishe to find ij men. And for money ij or iij waies. One, that the seas may be open, cates that cates may. 2. That recusantes may be put to ther pensions, and take ther landes. 3. Usurers; a canker eates men out of ther boones.

Mr Harbert, Master [of] Requestes. Yow have hard all the means. If commissions may be sent, methinkes it's the best course.

Francis Alford. The men that possess inclosures, great sheepe masters, ij^d an acre; rich marchantes *et cetera* to beare the burthen.

Doctor Dale. To agre on a peticion to the Queen. /

f.102   Mr Tasborow. Good to inact that all thos above x^{li} should give so much, *et cetera*.

Mr Morris. That the subsedy, fifteins, and musters wilbe such charge to the contries as benevolence wilbe slowly granted; and that the busshoppes may better do it then wee, they beinge free from musters. To consider on it.

Sir Henry Knevitt. That all thinges be skant, money especially. Rather to give a new subsedy hearafter as neid shall require.

Mr Vichamberlain. That this subsedy will not serve her Majesty 16 monthes.

Agreed to have peticion drawne to persuad commissions may go downe for benevolence.

7° Marcii.

Subsedy redd, past, and caried up to the Lordes.

The bill of purvayars reformed and delivered into the Howse by Mr Vichamberlain. And the bill of attaynders of Thomas Lord Pagit and others.

A bill redd for prohibicion of strangiers born [to] use retayle.

A bill brought from the Lords for horse stealinge and other felonies.

The bill of purvayars redd 2 tyme.

Recorder. That Fissher's evidence was stoln out of the custody in the Fleet to defraud the Queen and all his other creditors.[46] /

8 Marcii. Wensday.

A bill red for the performance of the last will of Sir James Harvy, citizen of London.

1. A bill preferred by Mr Fynes for the payment of the debtes of Sir Gerrat Croker.[47]

2. A bill reed for the naturalizinge of certayn strangers.

The bill reed 3[48] for th'attaynder of Thomas Lord Pagitt and others.

Mr Bacon not satisfied concerninge clayme of strayngiers before this estatute.

Replyed by Mr Tresorar.[49]

Mr Crumwell. But usuall and reasonable requiered by this lawe.

Mr Hwse.[50] Some further salvo in the proviso as Mr Bacon moved.

Mr San[d]se. The Queen t'have all since th'attaynders. Therfore well pend.

Mr Morris. To consider what's given the Queen all before the committment at[51] the tyme. Saved all to strangiers devised before. To provid for strangiers what they had at the tyme committed. A right before risinge after alowed that so the wordes may stand.

Sergiant Snagge. An use no right till the use come.

Solicitor. That for that may hape, can not be provided for. As carefull of the prince and common welth before as now. The sam proviso now put in. 23 Henry 8 the statute of attaynders. 23 to be withowt office. That the wordes will helpe. Right and possession both saved at the tyme of the treason

v.

44. *Sic.*
45. The same hand adds '13,000 parishe churches in England', perhaps in the light of information gathered after taking this note.
46. See D'Ewes, p.413.

47. D'Ewes, p.414 places this bill under 9 March.
48. Cf. D'Ewes, p.413
49. Sir Francis Knollys.
50. Presumably Thomas Hughes.
51. MS repeats.

committed. Generall wordes dangerous in savinges. Rather wisshinge the committies go alter, then now upon the soden.[52] /

f.103   Mr Topliffe. To prove how crafty counsell the traytors have to defraud the Queen. Example of Norton that antedated deedes, and that one of theis last traytors sayd he had made certayne conveances of trust by which he could do his frend a good turne. And that some gayne more by givinge of counsell to trayors the[n] many others by giving good consell.

Joons [the] Lawier.[53] Not possible to make a law *qui omni parte prospicit*, but t'have this proviso reformed to be mad more playne, returned to the committy.

Sir Henry Knevitt. An inconvenience to be saved.

Harris.[54] To have generall savinge.

Mr Vichamberlain. 'To tell my opinion and what I have red, theis matters of treasons hatch up every day.'

---

52. See 23 Hen VIII, c.34 (1531–2) in *SR*, iii.415–16, esp: sect iii, and *SR*, iv.766, sect ii.

53. Probably Thomas, rather than Sir Thomas or Walter (*Commons*).

54. Robert (II), or Thomas (I or II) (*Commons*).

THE SEVENTH PARLIAMENT:
4 FEBRUARY–29 MARCH 1589

Documents

This parliament eventually assembled on 4 February 1589 only months after the Armada threat had passed, though writs had originally been issued in September 1588. It was the only occasion on which Hatton presided as Lord Chancellor, and we are fortunate to have one of his speeches here, though full accounts of the formalities of opening and closing proceedings have not survived. There is no first-hand account of the speeches made by the new Speaker, Serjeant Thomas Snagge, at the beginning or end of the session, of Hatton's reply, or indeed, of any speech which Elizabeth herself may have made.[1]

A version of Hatton's own opening speech (Lords 2) on 4 February demonstrates perhaps the 'natural excellence of speech' with which he was apparently blessed, and which drew praise from some contemporaries. This was even apparent in the notes (Lords 3) for a speech clearly intended to reply to the Speaker's formal attempts to excuse himself from serving, a mundane enough task which would not ordinarily offer much scope for imaginative eloquence. This may be Hatton's work for this occasion (6 February), though the MS bears no descriptive title and is unendorsed. If Hatton followed these notes, however, a largely businesslike speech may have been enlivened by observations about the paradoxical relationship between diffidence and confidence on the one hand, and varying levels of ability on the other, as well as a sprinkling of images and metaphors. All this was designed to convey the simple traditional message that the Speaker-elect had to comply 'with humilitie' with the Queen's acceptance of his election by the Commons. There appears to be no basis for the assertion that warnings about freedom of speech were given in conjunction with a strict ban on religious discussion.[2]

The message to be delivered on 4 February was plain, according to a draft of Burghley's, perhaps offering suggestions for Hatton's speech itself. Recent dangers had been averted by God's good grace, but the realm which had been under various threats from the beginning of Elizabeth's reign had to be further protected. England's enemies had to be persuaded to change their 'desynes of hostillitie into honorable offertures and conditions of peace'. In this way would the gospel and God's blessings be enjoyed by all in freedom and voluntary loyal obedience to the Queen. So good advice and aid was necessary from 'yow representyng the whole realm whose cause this is' (Lords 1). The account of

---

1. *EP*, ii.201–2, 237–9.   2. *EP*, ii.201–2.

Hatton's speech itself is far more eloquent than Burghley's competent, though prosaic, effort (Lords 2). No less a plea for help to preserve all that was dear, it catalogued plots and plotters against the Queen, including some of those Hatton said he would not talk about. Even Gregory XIII's bull, allowing the Queen's Catholic subjects to acknowledge her, was a stratagem, and Rome's evil intent had culminated in the 'Pope's bridge of wood made on the seas'. Despite threats the Queen was determined to cling to true Christian religion, and to preserve England in peace, plenty, and justice: Popish superstition and idolatry were shunned. But 'we maie not stande beholdinge these daungers a farre of', and it was necessary to seek means for our defence. It was a holy, just, honourable and necessary cause. Though this powerful speech was designed primarily to excite passions against the foreign foe, Elizabeth was apparently keen to demonstrate through Hatton her antipathy to enemies close to home who posed threats to the same precious characteristics of life in Elizabethan England. Critics of the present Church and their intemperate humours were disavowed, as were 'platformes and devises' and the 'unspeakable tyrannie' they would herald.

A few days later, on 11 February, Chancellor of the Exchequer Mildmay introduced the question of taxation. D'Ewes comments that there was no certain record that he spoke for supply, though a committee was appointed that day to frame the subsidy bill, and eventually a double subsidy was granted.[3] There are some notes, however, among the Fitzwilliam papers dated 11 February, and presumably of Mildmay's speech, though they may not have been written by his son-in-law William Fitzwilliam, let alone Mildmay himself (Doc.1). They are set out in such a way as to emphasize the systematic development of the argument that taxation was essential for defeating Spain's threat. Again the long-standing character of that threat, and Rome's support for it, was stressed. Again the threat to God's true religion in England was demonstrated: wise mariners must take guard against the second storm, which might be worse than the first.

It may have been at the third reading of the bill that opposition to the subsidy was voiced (10 March), though this parliament broke new ground by agreeing to pay a double subsidy.[4] There is an undated speech in the Lansdowne collection, again with no descriptive title, which was attributed by Neale to Henry Jackman (Doc.5). It is concerned with the subsidy and refers to the proposal to raise two subsidies in four years. Its significance is perhaps not that it is an example of opposition to taxation demands as such: indeed, the author was at pains to stress the Crown's right to demand money, and even invoked a civil law dictum that *omnia regis sunt*. But he was also keen to establish that every subject had his own possessions until the Queen commanded otherwise. More interestingly, it was argued that the fear of invasion – on which Hatton and Mildmay had built their case – was not apparent. On the contrary, the enemy's teeth and jaws have recently been broken, he said, so that a subsidy would not be of any practical use, especially as the first part was not due for three years. Concentrating his gaze on the domestic, rather than the international, scene, the author claimed that the common people in particular had been heavily affected by the various demands in the summer of 1588. Demands came upon them like waves one upon another, he said, resorting to the imagery Mildmay had used in 1586 to justify taxation. It would be dangerous to tax subjects unnecessarily, and reference was made to Hatton's comment about the Queen's ruling by faith rather than by iron. Concern was professed for the 'poor and needie countryman', among others, 'for whom we sit here more principally then for ourselves'; and as members were often assessors for the subsidy, the author said they knew well enough about subjects' complaints. In the context of possible food-price rises and trade disruptions care was needed lest the flames of discontent were fanned by malicious whisperers.

Doc.10 is apparently a copy of part of the lost journal of the Commons relating to the last day of the session, and must be seen in conjunction with a draft of Burghley's summarizing the Lords' willingness to offer lives, lands and goods in the struggle against Spain (Lords 6). This latter was probably written before the Upper House decided to call upon the Commons' support in petitioning the Queen to take action against Spain. Indeed in composing it, Burghley seems to have thought it advisable to note that it was the Commons, as well as the Lords, who had granted the subsidies. Doc.10 simply records that subsidies had been granted for defence of the realm, that the Lords also had ventured lives and bodies, and that the Commons agreed to join the Upper House in petitioning the Queen to adopt offensive, as well as defensive, means to defeat Spain's schemes. There is no positive evidence that the petition, to be made by the Speaker, included the words about bodies and lives as well as their lands.[5]

The Martin Marprelate tracts and Bancroft's famous St Paul's Cross sermon on 9 February are significant parts of the background to this parliament's proceedings. Despite anything Hatton may have said on 4 February, religion was to surface within a matter of weeks. The general tenor of the lengthy document entitled 'Certayn motions . . .' is clearly associated with the young lawyer Humphrey Davenport's attempts, as recorded by D'Ewes, to secure 'a due course of proceeding in laws already established'. As we know, this initiative was suppressed (Doc.2).[6]

A number of copies of these motions exist, though only the Thynne MS – John Thynne sat for Wiltshire – carries the comments written around the text itself which Neale assumed were Whitgift's own. The manuscript clearly passed through his hands at some point as it bears his endorsement, though the commentary itself is in another's hand, probably that of one of his clerks. There can be little doubt that these comments represented Whitgift's position, and there are indeed signs of the haughty attitude which helped to make him unpopular with many contemporaries. The motions called for the discussion

3. D'Ewes, p.431, and see *EP*, ii.204–5.
4. *EP*, ii.206.
5. *EP*, ii.234.
6. D'Ewes, pp.438–9.

and ending of what were seen as 'abuses' of bishops through a conference in Parliament, involving Lords and Commons and in the presence of the bishops and the judges of the land. There was no intention, it was said, to impugn Elizabeth's supremacy, or current ecclesiastical law. The bishops' shortcomings consisted in acting contrary to statute, law or custom, and Parliament was therefore to be given a role in remedying shortcomings.[7] There was much discussion throughout, both in the text and the comments on it, about the meaning of laws passed in Henry VIII's and Elizabeth's time, and not surprisingly Whitgift was forced to confront the argument that the *intent* of the lawmakers in 1559 had been anti-Catholic, and that their laws should not therefore be used against Protestants.[8] Moreover, Whitgift clearly feared – and was anxious to stress – the existence of wider, more radical issues. In this he was undoubtedly assisted by the attacks made on Bishop Aylmer in the recently published Marprelate tracts.

The Archbishop constructed a massive refutation of these petitions. Custom and statute were called on to defend the conduct of bishops and of himself, and the gulf between him and his critics appears unbridgeable.[9] Appealing to Parliament to remedy matters would transform it into a *parlement*, he said, and he could not agree to what would be the exclusion of the bishops from questions concerning the word of God. Elizabeth, who had been entrusted with control of the Church in 1559, should not be pressurized on these matters. Whitgift's responses also reveal a defiant, even sarcastic, aloofness. Defending the use of the *ex officio* oath he said he wanted to avoid the intervention of lawyers who would allow ministers to wriggle out of charges: 'A man's owne facte may be aunswered withoute counsell'.[10] The Lords and Commons were unfit to determine matters of this sort, and he said that he would answer only to the Supreme Governor. Behind this was the fear that despite the apparent moderation of the proposals, larger issues were at stake. If what was asked were granted, then men of 'all sectes and badde opinions' would be allowed into the Church.[11] He further asserted that others would be keen to go further. Many of the ministers who had been disciplined were anabaptists and schismatics,[12] and he wondered if the author would be satisfied if his requests were met. 'Can they live without their elderships?'[13] His parting salvo suggested the document was part of a more extensive strategy: 'It seemeth therefore this is but a colourable dissembled kinde of dealinge, to shake firste one or two stones in the buildinge that the rest may followe'.[14]

Though Henry Apsley subsequently produced a bill on pluralities,[15] the subject was an important part of 'Certayn motions . . .'. Despite Elizabeth's known antipathy to activities of this sort, a bill was sent to the Lords. An account of three speeches in the Upper House on this bill presumably belongs to 13 March when it was debated on its first reading, though it went no further.[16] It is not surprising that the bill, which may have been 'hopelessly visionary', did not escape unscathed, even from those who saw merits in it.[17] Burghley expressed some criticism of the bishops, though his support for the bill could not be wholehearted; and Grey's response to Whitgift's own answer to Burghley place him among the ranks of Whitgift's critics. The Archbishop, however, seems to have been able to count on the support of Lord Chamberlain Hunsdon.[18] The general drift of these contributions to the debate is clear enough, though the note-form of the MS does not make for easy reading and comprehension: it shows all the signs of being made up of notes taken on the spot, possibly to act as an *aide-mémoire* for further embellishment, or as a basis for verbal reporting.

Neale argued that 'Puritan' activity in and out of Parliament continued and that the pluralities bill may have encouraged it.[19] Otherwise Beale and Morice may have been busy preparing or encouraging further attempts to curb the Bishops' proceedings about which the 'motions' had been concerned.[20] A document among the Petyt MSS and probably belonging to the later part of March, as the end of the session seemed near, may have been the work of a committee of the Commons, though this copy bears no title which could reveal its precise origins.[21] Grounding itself on hardships to which Jackman's speech on the subsidy had drawn attention – namely problems members faced as tax gatherers asking their people for a double subsidy – it asked the Queen to rescind certain statutes pending their full statutory repeal by the next parliament. The main burden of the document, however, was to state that complaints voiced many times to the Queen 'touching sundry ecclesiastical disorders' had not been rectified. As a result subjects were turning their allegiance to Rome for lack of 'good instruction'. Disavowing any intention to encroach upon the Supreme Governor's prerogative, the petition nevertheless insisted that parliament had been called to deal with the Church, and that the Commons were spokesmen for all the people of the land. It was important that effective remedies be implemented. Claims were made about the unacceptability of parts of canon law and the abolition of the *ex officio* proceedings in Henry VIII's time, as well as the need to ensure that her Majesty's ecclesiastical commission was 'abused' no more. The concluding paragraphs are, perhaps, the most poignant. Here all charges of being traitors and anarchists are stoutly denied; the wish to make new laws concerning religion is disclaimed; and what is upheld is the longstanding desire, shared by many, for a preaching ministry and a 'peaceable toleration' of ministerial practices, which it was claimed existed in Edward VI's reign, and even in the early days of Elizabeth's.[22]

In many ways the petition seems to represent an endorsement of John Stubbs' own supplication (Doc.9), though D'Ewes says nothing about this or

7. F.6.
8. F.6v.
9. F.6v – imprisonment and deprivations.
10. Fos.6v, 9v.
11. F.10v.
12. F.8.
13. F.9v.
14. F.12.
15. *EP*, ii.224–5.
16. Lords 5; *LJ*, ii159.
17. *EP*, ii.226.
18. *EP*,ii.227–9.
19. *EP*, ii.229–30.
20. *EP*, ii.234-5.
21. Doc.8; *EP*, ii.235–7.
22. See Doc.2.

the petition.[23] This supplication is also a study in moderation and goodwill, a denial of extreme intentions. Stubbs wanted a mild exposition of the laws governing the Church – 'we crave noe innovation' – though he requested that bishops should not be the 'onelie judges' of men's offences. But in his quest for a resident and learned ministry, Stubbs also stressed the benefits which would accrue for the safety and unity of the realm against Catholics, and he protested that those who fell victim to the bishops were not to be condemned with Jesuits, anarchists and others. Stubbs had no sympathy for the idea of separation from England's Church, and from its prayers and sacraments.

The two bills introduced on 14 February on purveyance and the Exchequer also constituted threats to Elizabeth's prerogative powers. By 27 February it had become clear that the Lords had refused to allow further progress because of Elizabeth's intervention, and the Commons' response was to set up a committee to consider reasons for proceeding, despite her antipathy (Doc.3). Privy Councillor John Fortescue reported these to the House on 4 March. It was duly agreed that the Speaker should present them to Elizabeth, and the Lords were also told, presumably in the hope of support from the Upper House.[24] On 7 March the Queen met ten members and Speaker Snagge reported on their audience with the Queen on the following day. Neale's view was that the answer to Elizabeth's objections to these bills show that the 'constitution was by now standing on uncertain foundations'. The Queen clearly felt herself to be under pressure, and the Commons' argument that petitioning about grievances was an ancient means of seeking remedy took no apparent account of her objections to proposals made in the form of bills. But it is important to stress that the committee's statements are couched in practical terms and concentrate on the best way, as they saw it, of dealing with longstanding problems where previous answers – including statutory ones – had not been completely successful. They wished to emphasize that neither the prerogative or the system of purveyance was under attack here, only the abuses. It was difficult for them, they said, to see why legislation could not be used to deal with the Exchequer in particular, simply because there were already laws on the statute books which dealt with Exchequer officials. No innovation was being offered, and the proposed remedy provided a speeding up of over-long proceedings in the Exchequer Court.

Doc.4 is (part of?) Burghley's response to the Commons' rebuttal of Elizabeth's objections, though it is not clear if any of his arguments were presented to the Lower House. Perhaps these are notes, for, or of, his response to the Commons' notification of their request for a meeting with the Queen; they might even be a marshalling of his thoughts for the Queen herself in readiness for the audience on 7 March. Their striking characteristic (beyond the fact that they reflect his mistress' rejection of legislative action) is their practicality: they comment on the form of the purveyance bill rather than directly on its constitutional impropriety. Burghley attempted to demonstrate inconsistencies between the purveyance bill itself and what the Commons had said about it in their first answer. He also claimed that existing laws against purveyors, couched 'in form of complaynt and a request to have the abuses reformed', differed wholly from what was now offered. He argued that the severest of penalties against purveyors already existed, so that it was not true to assert that current laws lacked teeth.

One of the central concerns of these two documents was how to make laws effective, and they thus draw attention to a constant problem for the lawmakers at Westminster. Other documents printed here also reflect their preoccupations, the first of them (Lords 4) concerning the bill against informers. It was not used by Neale in his account of this parliament. The arguments against the bill provide a good illustration of the scrutiny measures might provoke. The bill's drafting was said to be uncertain and its proposed penalties harsh. This criticism was accompanied, however, by constructive proposals for amendment. The document may be an account of a speech written for Parliament, and the endorsement, which dates it 10 March 1589, means that it was intended for the Lords. However it must be stressed that there is no certainty that it was delivered, neither is there any obvious indication of its origin. And it may, in fact, be a summary of various contributions to debate on that day.

On 24 March the Vice-Chamberlain reported about committee deliberations on a Lords' bill on soldiers, and how it compared with acts already in force for the provision of horse, armour and weapons and for the mustering of soldiers. Imperfections had been found in both, he said, and he produced a 'note collected of the same imperfections'. The Lords asked for a conference on the matter, and the next day it was reported that the Lords had answered these objections.[25] The notes in Doc.7 are brief, even cryptic, though the MS bears Burghley's own answers and denials, which are clear enough, in the margin. The Commons were concerned about the harshness of the new measure, and whether it actually made improvements on the existing laws: they also complained that it lacked clarity, especially where it spoke of those who sought to 'defraud the service'. To this last complaint Burghley responded that fraud was a common and triable legal concept. Nothing more was heard of this bill.

The third example is a speech – again, we cannot know if it was delivered – on the bill against foreigners (Doc.6). This is one of the speeches attrbuted to Henry Jackman by Neale, and is said to demonstrate that he was of a 'liberal cast of mind'.[26] The author addressed the problem of immigrant traders whose activities were causing concern among their native rivals. A bill had therefore been produced which tried to limit the foreign retailers' freedom of trading. Jackman deplored the distinction between native and foreign on which the bill was predicated, and in any case, he said, God loves the stranger. He also doubted the harmful effects of tolerating foreign traders: was it really tantamount to 'takinge the children's bread and castinge it to the dogges'? Competition was not that much greater in practice, he said. If it were true that

23. *EP*, ii.235.
24. D'Ewes, p.442.

25. *LJ*, ii.147, 148, 149, 151, 152; D'Ewes, p.452.
26. *EP*, ii.207.

they undersold English retailers, this should be counted a benefit to the commonwealth: and if it was not true, then the bill's basis was destroyed and it would be unfair to proceed with it.

The 'journal', also attributed to Jackman, is in fact a record of some of the bill readings occupying the Commons during the first two weeks of the session. A brief account of the discussion on 8 February about members and absence through sickness is the only exception to this. It is a factual listing of readings and summaries of the contents of bills, so none of the colour of debates emerges. It is again a clear reminder that Parliament was about the business of making and reviewing law, even though representation of the broad scope of the purveyors bill betrays nothing of its contentious nature. If 'Jackman's' journal and the speeches printed here are in fact the work of one man then we are fortunate in having an interesting example of a business-like and undramatic parliamentary mind actively employed about its everyday work.

1. [House of Lords] Lord Burghley's brief for Sir Christopher Hatton's opening speech, 4 February

Text from BL Lansdowne 104, original draft in Burghley's hand.
Other MS. BL Lansdowne 60 (later copy of Lansdowne 104).

Lansdowne 104, fos.62–3

A somme of that may be declared to the 3 states assembled.

Uppon the first poynt in my Lord Chancellor's memoryall.

That the warrs of late yers prepared and made ageynst hir Majesty and hir realm, and now contynuyng, ar different greatly from the wars of former tymes moved ageynst this realm, for both from France and Scotland the warrs hath grown many tymes only for quarrells of iniuryes doone to the people [of one][1] syde sometyme by [land][2] and sometyme by sea, and ether party hath by wars sought to mak reveng, and yett in a short tyme the princes on both sydes have bene so well weared,[3] as peace hath followed, with consent of all partes. But these late wars ar seene manifestly made specially from Spayn, the Pope and ther confederates, not uppon any such quarrells but first to extyrp the truth and profession of the Gospell, secondly, to deprive hir Majesty, our undowted soverayn lady and Quene, both of hir liff and hir Crown. And both those to be doone directly with all violence possible by conquest of the whole realm and subduyng it to servitud of the conquerors. And whan a conquest is duly considered, and the effectes therof, ther is no savety can be assured for any person of any degre, nether for old, nor yong, for woman, nor child, for any famyly or blood what so ever secret offers may be made to tempt sondry persons to disioyn them selves on from an other to weaken our selves. And though all men in reason may judg this warr ageynst this realm to be iniust – as it is – and the defence ageynst it most just and necessary in sight of God and of all good men, yet for more clearnes therof God hym self hath so manifested it by many notable argumentes even from the begynning of hir raygn to the very end of this last sommer, yea, by some other extraordinary actes of dissipatyng of some heades hir coniured enemyes within these few wekes on the other syde of the seas. / And to run over many yers blessynges in a few wordes, because   v.

---

1. MS damaged here. The much later copy in Lansd. 60 has 'either'.

2. As supplied in Lansd. 60.

3. *Sic.* Lansd. 60: 'wearied'.

the particularetyes of every yere'[s] good successes to hir Majesty this may suffyse for a short recitall.[4] It is sene how God hath blessed hir Majesty in all hir actions contynually used for hir defence. First, whan hir title was impugned by the French sekyng by way of Scotland to have recovered this realm, and knytt both this and Scotland to the Crown of France, God blessed hir Majestie's attemptes, to mak irritat ther attemptes. He tok awey ij kinges, both father and son, that sought it.[5]

He blessed Scotland with knolledg of his Gospell, wherby in stead of enmyte a strayt amyty followed betwixt both the realms and at this day ther is good amyty between hir Majesties[6] and that Kyng, notwithstandyng the contynuall sollicitations from the Pope, from the King of Spayn and all ther confederates. Hir Majesty also hath so preserved hir realm by Gode's goodness as nether rebellions styrred by hir forrayn adversaryes hath long contynued unsuppresse[d], nor outward forces provyded abrod hath yet to this daye had power to invade this realm, or so much as to spoyle any the lest fishyng town of hir realm. The prooff wherof was most notably seene by Gode's miraculous favors this last sommer. And seyng God hath shewed that hir Majestie's quarrell of defence is just, by his favors, it is also a just cause /

f.63   of comfort for hir Majesty, and for all yow hir good people, to persist in the defence therof ageynst such tyrannooss attemptes by them that ar the professed ennemyes of God.

For which purpousses hir Majesty hath thought mete to assemble these hir 3 estates of Parlement to communicat this great weighty cause with them, to the end it may be by th[em] well and gravely considered how hir Majesty may with the help of hir good subiectes be habled to contynew this just defence of hir realm and people, and how hir enemyes' uniust enterprises may be also made voyd and frustrat by propulsyng or divertyng therof, so as by Gode's goodness, and by hir Majestie's and hir people's forces, hir self, hir realm and people may be not only preserved ageynst all invasions and violences, but also recover peace betwixt hir and all hir neighbors, and restore hir realm and subiectes to the use and fruition of Gode's blessynges to lyve in profession of devout religion towardes almighty God, and of a voluntary loyall obedience towardes hir Majesty; and to contynew this noble kyngdom and the subiectes therof in the auncient fredom and dignite, as on of the principall kyngdoms and monarches of christendom. /

v.   And whan uppon conference amongst your selves uppon due information to be gyven yow it shall appeare what war the great charges allredy expended for the defencees made both by land and sea this last yeare, and what may be by wisdom considered aforhand what greatar preparations the ennemies ar lyk to mak this yere now coming, as well to satisfye ther ragyng myndes of revendg for recovery of ther honor and rychess lost as for the prosequutyng of ther formar long digested enterprise of conquest, hir Majesty hath no dowt, but to receave from yow representyng the whole realm whose cause this is, both good advise, and ayd convenient to enhable hir Majesty to contynew the just and honorable defence of hir realm ageynst any power what so ever of the enemy. Wherin as hir Majesty hath not spared any care of hir mynd, no nor of hir own body nor any pece of hir treasur, both to withstand, and in good pollycy to dyvert, the enemyes' forces, so what so ever hir lovyng subiectes shall, uppon consideration had, offer of ther abundance towardes this most important necessary service, the same shall be imployed with all good wisdom and care for the contynuance of the Gospell in this realm, and for the preservation, of all the subiectes with ther substance and ther posterites;[7] and by Gode's favor so to repulss the enemyes, as they shall chang ther deseynes of hostillite unto honorable offertures and conditions of peace, wherof God by hir formar blessynges gyven to hir Majesty doth also gyve hir and us all fyrm hope to have a long fruition.

---

4. *Sic.*
5. i.e. Henry II and Francis II.

6. *Sic.*
7. *Sic.*

2. [House of Lords] Sir Christopher Hatton's opening speech, 4 February

Text from Lambeth Palace 178, copy in the hand of Michael Murgatroyd(?), secretary to Archbishop Whitgift.

Lambeth Palace 178, fos.75–81

[Headed in a later hand

'The Lord Chancellor Hatton's speech at the opening of the parliament in February 1588'.]

'My lords and masteres all. It hath pleased the Queen's most excellent Majestie to commaunde me accordinge to the auncient custome of this place to deliver unto you the especiall occasions which have principallie moved hir to summon at this time this honourable assemblie and high courte of Parliament. For the performance of which dutie, howe unable I am either in respecte of hir Majestie's direccions unto me, which were most princelie and singular, or of this place, which heretofore hath bene supplied with grave and learned men, I myself doe best knowe it; neither can hir Highnes or anie here present, whoe shall consider my bringinge up, be ignoraunte of it. Notwithstandinge, seeinge that through hir Majestie's most roiall and gratious favour towardes me I am called to this roome, *nescio quo fato*, but since I am not of anie deserte, and that therfor your expectacion of me for learninge can be none at all – for experience it must nedes be almost as litle, and for anie thinge else in me it can not be great – I trust you will beare at this time with my wantes, especiallie the cause I have to handle beinge so manifeste as that it lacketh but a tounge, for otherwise it speaketh plainelie enough for itself.

'It is concerninge the happie continuance and preservacion of this state, of this kingdome, of this realme, of us all, religion, hir Majestie, your countrie, your wives, your children, your freindes, your landes, your gooddes, your lives. A matter so honorable, so honest, so profitable, and so necessarie as I am well assured all the worlde besides is not so acceptable to you all, or so much desired and wisshed for of you all.

'That which I have farther to saie hereof I have comprehended under these 3 pointes. First, because evills before thei be seene can hardlie be prevented, I have thought it expedient to call to your remembrance what mischeifes have bene devised against us, put in practise, and by whome. Secondlie, it shall appeare that the like mischeifes or greater are still intended. Thirdlie, howe necessarie it is that as heretofore there have bene no meanes neglected for our defence, so at this time especiallie that our care be continued; naie rather, in such sorte everie waie increased as that we maie be able through God's assistance (our adversairies multipliinge their malice) by good foresight to redouble our forces to withstande them. /

'It is not unknowen to all the worlde what great dishonoures and indignities, v. what cruell exaccions, oppressions, and iniuries manie emperours, kinges, and countries have sustained of later yeares at the Pope's handes; and especiallie this croune and realme of England, in so much as in respecte thereof it hath bene termed abroade in other landes the Pope's asse. And although diverse of hir Majestie's predecessours, as Kinge Jhon, Henry the 3, Richard the 2, Edward the 3, and Henry the 8 of famous memorie, hir Highnes' father, indevouringe in their severall times upon sundrie occasions to be delivered from such usurped tyrannie and to have recovered the auncient libertie, authoritie, and honour appertaininge unto them, have bene manie waies despightfullie dealte withall; yet notwithstandinge, there was never anie of them all so diverselie attempted, so malitiouslie persecuted, or so greatlie indaungered, and that in the highest degree, as hir Majestie hath bene through the infinite lewde, cruell and barbarous practises of those most proude and shamelessse preistes.

'You cannot forget howe Clement the 7 and Paule the 3, breakinge out into furie against hir Majestie's father, spared not even then to smite at hir honour. Afterwarde, hir Highnes beinge possessed of the croune, what a raginge bull did that monster Pius 5 bringe forth, whereby he laboured everie waie to wounde hir: in hir soule by denouncinge hir an hereticke, in hir honour by his slaunderous calumniacions[?], and in hir most roiall dignitie by deposinge hir, by absolvinge hir subiectes from their duties of obedience, and by cursinge of all such as shoulde anie waie acknowlege their alleageaunce unto hir. Not thus satisfied, he procured the said bull to be published in this realme, and for the better execucion of it did thereupon likewise sollicite and stirre up the northren rebellion: as also immediatlie after him Gregory 13, beginninge where he had lefte, attempted to the same purpose an invasion in Irelande.

'In both which interprises, perceivinge thei wanted number to effecte your[1] designmentes, and that their instrumentes wherby thei wrought, through the providence of this government were intercepted and cut shorte, as a generation verie pregnant to bringe forth newe mischeifes, thei devised another most pernitious and daungerous complot. And it was that the litter of the seminarie preistes, from 9 daies olde[2] and upwarde, tag and rag, shoulde be sent hither, / pell-mell, thicke and threefolde, under pretence of plantinge of poperie to f.76 increase this[3] number and to reconcile such againe to his Holines as had neglected their duties in not assistinge of the foresaid rebellions. Order was also in like maner then taken by a mitigacion of the bull obteined from Gregory the 13, that the better to cover their stratagems and to avoide the daungers which otherwise thei might have incurred, it shoulde be lawfull for them to

1. *Sic.*
2. *Sic.*
3. *Sic.*

acknowlege hir Majestie in verie large termes to be their lawfull soveraigne and themselves hir dutifull subiects, marie, *rebus sic stantibus*, that is, until they shoulde be able by force to depose hir.

'Whilest this number was thus in preparinge, but not with such successe as was expected, diverse other waies far more compendious were greatlie urged and commended. And hence it was that diverse pictures were made and sundrie inchauntementes used, you knowe to what purpose: that Somervile undertooke that villanie against hir Majestie's person with his dag; that Parrie was set on by the Cardinall of Como with the Pope's consente to have committed the like unnaturall crueltie with his dagger; and that both Savage and Babington with the reste of those traiters (all the former designmentes beinge prevented) shoulde have accomplished the same, as the fittest opportunitie might have bene agreable to that purpose.

'All this while you must remember that these 2 former popes, havinge hope by hir Majestie's fall of another's advauncement answearable to their desire, did still direct their mischeifes principallie against hir Highnes. But nowe that their expectacion therein, and that thei grewe wearie of anie longer delaies, the Pope that nowe is (Sise sinck),[4] exceedinge all other that wente before him in tyrannie and crueltie, he will needes have a bridge of wood made over our seaes; he will no more bende his wittes onelie against hir Majestie (although in dede as in the harte is conteined the life of the bodie, so is our happines in hir Highnes' safetie), but nowe he voweth the utter subversion and destruccion of us all, Queen people, and countrie, and to make our lande a praie to foren enemies.

'To this ende he hath renued the bull of Pius 5[us], fraughtinge the same with most villanous sclaunders; he hath abrogated his predecessours tolleration; he hath cursed us all and blessed our enemies; he hath taken upon him to geve and dispose of the croune of this realme as it pleaseth him beste; he hath sollicited diverse kinges and princes, accordinge to their oathes in the Holie League to be the executioners of this intended crueltie; and hath at the length, with his charge of 2 millions, found a man accordinge to his owne harte and disposition, v.   whoe hath bene content to be so wickedlie imploied. / This mercenarie souldier and preistlie champion is the King of Spaine, one of all the kings of Europe that had least cause so to doe; were it not that like a most ambitious tyraunte, forgettinge all the honour he hath received amongest us, he thought like a conquerer to take this occation for our utter subduinge: and accordinglie you knowe he hath proceeded. For what preparacions he was able to make either by sea or lande, what forces he coulde procure from all his confederates, the Venetians, the Florentines, the Gennaens,[5] the Bavarians, and the Germaines, he hath assailed us with them. He hath came[6] late against us like thunder. In deede, God be thanked he feared moe then hurte us: but *in rebus malis est voluisse satis.*

'These thinges, as thei are in themselves by our experience most evident, so are thei sufficient to shewe to all posteritie the unchristian furie both of the Pope, that woolvish bloodesucker, and of the Spaniarde, that unsatiable tyraunte, in that thei never bente themselves with such might and resolucion against the verie Turke or anie other infidell, as thei have done against a virgin Queen, a famous ladie, and a countrie which imbraceth without corruption in doctrine the true and sincere religion of Christe. But yet that which moveth hir Majestie most is this: to thinke that ever anie of hir owne subiectes, mere English men, borne and brought up amongest us, should combine themselves, (as somehave done) with hir so deadlie [enemies]. For thinke you that anie of these horrible and heathenish treacheries, of these villanies, treasons, and barbarous intended cruelties were ever devised or attempted without some of their sollicitation and persuasion? I tell you naye.

'What was done against hir honour in hir ffather's daies, it was wrought by the malice of that proude Cardinall Poole. The calamities she sustained in hir sister's time were inflicted upon hir by Gardiner's suggestions, whoe, together with that traitor Storie, foreseeinge that hir Majestie was like to prove (as in deede she hath done) the tree of life in this our earthlie paradise, was evermore insistinge to have it chopte of and cut doune by the rootes. Dr Hardinge was the man that procured the first bull and Felton did publish it. Dr Morton was the cheif instrument for the northren rebellion; and so was Dr Saunders for the Irish invasion. / Campion for a farther mischeif obteined Gregorie's mitigacion;   f.77 Hall the preiste set Somervile on woorke; and although the Pope with the Cardinall of Como thrust Parrie forwarde, yet he confesseth that Allen's writings did cheiflie confirme him. Gifforde incouraged Savage, and Ballard was the meanes that Babington and his companie ffell to that wickednes.

'I omit here to speake of Morgan, Charles Paget, Throckmorton, and diverse others whoe have bene longe practitioners; but yet, of all the villanous traitors that I thinke this lande ever bred or brought up, that wicked preist, that shamelesse atheiste and bloodie Cardinall Allen, he in deede excelleth. Looke what late daungers have bene anie waie towards us and you shall finde him a cheif dealer in them. He especiallie by his false libells hath sought to bringe this state with all the worlde into perpetuall hatred. He greatlie commendeth Stanlei's treasons and persuadeth others to followe his example. He was the procurer of this last bull, and, it is verie apparaunt, the penner of it. He like a proude and an impudent verlet dareth by his letters to sollicite the nobles and comminaltie of England to ioine with the enemie. He is not ashamed to confesse, and that in writinge that the memorie of his villanie maie never die, howe this Spanish hostilitie hath bene greatlie farthered by his and the reste of these ffugitives indevers. His woords are these. His Majestie (meaninge the King of Spaine) was not a little moved by my humble and continuall suite, together with the afflicted and banished Catholickes of our nation of all and everie degree, to take upon him this holie and glorious acte: that is, the destruccion of this land, the overthrowe of religion, the ruine of hir Majestie and the death of us all. O savage and barbarous preiste! It is much to

4. *Sic.* Sixtus V must be intended.   6. *Sic.*
5. i.e. Genoans.

have such crueltie attempted by anie foraine enemie: it is more that preists shoulde so delight in bloode. But that English subiects, beinge preists, shoulde take upon them to be the woorkers of such an extremitie, and that against their owne native countrie: before this devilish broode was hatcht, I thinke it was never hearde of amongst the verie Scythians. It is said that the snakes in Siria will not bite nor stinge the people that are borne there; but these most venemous snakes you see doe not onelie labour to bite and stinge us, but, as a generation of cruell vipers, to teare us in peeces and to feede themselves with our bloode.

'The consideracion, my lords and masteres, of these unnaturall dealings proceeding from our countrie men, together with their promises touchinge the
v.   practises of the Pope, and / the late attemptes of the ravenous Spaniarde, forasmuch as thei are past, peradventure it doth not so greatlie move you; but as I noted in the seconde place, yf the like hatred be still lodged in our ffugitives' hartes, yf the Pope have ingaged his triple croune for our destruccion, yf the King of Spaine have pawned his honour either to conquere us or to be subdued by us, howe ought we then, my Lords, to be affected?

'First therfore of the cause. Whatsoever our enemies doe inwardlie meane, yet in apparance thei confesse, and that trulie, that hir Majestie's abandoninge of poperie is the verie roote and grounde of all their malice; a cause which ever shall tende to the perpetuall fame and admiration of hir Highnes' most rare and princelie magna[ni]mitie. For notwithstanding hir experience of the manifolde daungers which she had escaped in hir private estate for the profession of religion, and albeit she was not ignoraunte what untollerable iniuries hir father of most famous memorie, Henry the 8, in the like case had sustained by the tyrannous attempte of Clement the 7 and Paule the 3, and howe even then thei had sought hir dishonour and by the course which she intended woulde never leave of their villanie towards hir; yet, I saie, all these things notwithstandinge, her Highnes, havinge received the croune of this realme and foreseeinge before what since is come to passe, did first and principallie in spite of all gainesayers seeke to roote superstition out of hir peoples' hartes and to plante in their consciences a right and true feelinge of Christian religion.

'Since which time, yf hir Majestie woulde ever have bene wrought to have altered hir religion and to have imbraced the popish superstition and idolatrie, whereas nowe thei charge hir with great dishonour, defame hir government and seeke hir destruccion, then thei woulde have confessed that to be which we finde to our benefite and hir perpetuall commendacion – that the realme of England did never so longe floorish with so honourable a peace, with so great plentie, and with so directe a course for iustice, to the generall content-ment of all estates, as it hath done in hir most noble and provident government. Then woulde thei (as we doe) have acknowleged in hir Majestie the verie livelie example of Kinge David's righteousnes, of Salomon's wisdome, of Jehosaphate's zeale, and of Augustus' clemencie, or of anie other vertue
f.78   whatsoever that hath bene in anie of hir predecessours / or might be looked for in anie kinge or queene. But now that thei finde, and therein thei are not

deceived, hir resolute determinacion in hir course of Christianitie to be everie waye answearable to their experience of hir magnanimitie, and that notwithstandinge all their allurementes, promises, persuasions, pollicies, and cruell practises, which have bene infinite, hir Majestie, as she did begin, so she doth continue, and will never be driven, whilest she maie keepe the croune, to forsake or alter the reformed estate of religion as nowe it is established in hir Highnes' dominions; ffindinge this, I saie, thei behave themselves as partelie you have hearde, thei rage, thei raile, and whilest this cause remaineth (which I hope shalbe till thei be all destroied) thei will never, most assuredlie to their powers, geve over their wicked and develish devises. And yet herewithall hir Majestie is not so much greived — because she ever accounted them hir enemies and never looked for anie better at their handes — as she is that ther are diverse of latter daies risen up, even amongst hir freinds, whoe beinge men of a verie intemperate humour doe greatlie deprave the present estate and reformacion of religion, so hardlie attained to and with such hir daunger continued and preserved, whereby hir lovinge subiectes are greatlie disquieted, hir enemies are incouraged, religion is slaundered, pietie is hindered, schismes are maintained, and the peace of the Church is altogether rente in sunder and violated.

'These thinges hir Majestie confesseth doe in deede verie greatlie trouble hir, and hath geven me particularlie in commaundement touchinge those maner of persons and their dealings with their causes, to intimate this hir pleasure unto you: that forasmuch as hir Highnes upon certaine triall doth knowe most assuredlie that those kindes of platformes and devises which thei speake of are most absurde, that thei tende to intollerable innovacion, that thei wante all groundes of authoritie but such as thei wreste to serve their purpose, that they affecte an unspeakeable tyrannie, and that they are most daungerous to all good Christian government; and is withall most fullie and firmelie setled in hir conscience by the woorde of God that the estate and government of this Church of England as nowe it standeth in this reformacion maie iustlie be compared to anie church which hath bene established in anie Christian kingdome since the apostles times; that both in forme and doctrine it is agreable with the scriptures, with the most auncient generall councells, with the practise of the primitive church, and with the iudgementes of all the olde and learned fathers. And for that herein also hir Majestie hath bene confirmed by letters of congratulacion from the most famous men in Christendome, / from manie other reformed churches, and by sundrie bookes written as well against the papists in defence thereof, as also against these sectaries, hir Highnes therfore, in respecte of your lovinge affeccion towardes hir, doth as a most gratious ladie verie hartilie desire and intreate you, but yf that will not serve, then doth she as your prince and dread soveraigne most streightlie charge and commaunde you upon your allegence, that, the premises considered and seeinge that all authoritie for dealinge in these causes is by all your consentes (as by right it ought to be) invested into hir imperiall croune, you doe not in this assemblie so much as once meddle with anie such matters or causes of religion, excepte it be to bridle all those, whether papists or puritanes, which are therewithall discontented; assuringe you farther in the woorde of a prince that as better opportunitie shalbe offered and occation shall require, there shall such order be taken for the reformacion of anie abuse as to equitie, conscience, and good religion shall anie waie appertaine.

'This hir Majestie's pleasure it is reason we should accomplish, and because I knowe your great wisdomes and loialtie, I doubte not of it. I will therfore leave the presente estate of our religion, as a stumbling blocke I truste onelie to hir enemies, and proceede accordinge to my instruccions more particularlie touchinge the continuaunce of all their intended mischeifes and cruelties against us.

'And here I maie not forget those vile wretches, those bloodie preists and false traiters, here in our bosomes, but beyonde the seaes especiallie. Thei will not cease to practise both at home and abroade, as they have done. For, besides that the cheif cause of their furie (as thei pretende) remaineth, it is verie well knowen that thei growe verie odious in the countries where thei are fostered, and thereby are verie wearie of their exilement. Thei are intituled to the greatest promotions and honoures in this state, and doe thirste after them with all kinde of grediness. Thei have incorporated themselves into the bodie of all mischeif, and are accordinglie to be imploied by the heades of the same. But to make this thinge out of question, Allen himself hath set it doune as a pointe of the Romish religion that all preistes and catholickes are bound under paine

f.79   of damnation (as thei saye the case / standeth nowe in this realme) still to sollicite the Pope and the Spaniarde, and never to geve over their former or the like attempts untill (yf it maie be) the before mencioned designmentes be fullie accomplished. And to that purpose likewise he hath made a newe tolleracion of this last bull, assuringe all catholickes of the Pope's meaninge, that untill thei maie be able either by strength at home or by assistance from abroade to playe the roaringe lyons, to resist hir Majestie (the usurper, saith the traiter) and to execute the Pope's sentence, it shalbe laufull for them to playe the wilie ffoxes, to confesse their alleageaunce unto hir in all temporall matters. So as it is most manifeste what we maie expect at these men's handes.

'And concerninge the Pope in like maner maye we looke for anie better dealinge from him? It were madnes to thinke so. *Venti desituri vehementissime spirant*: windes, a litle before thei fall, are ever most boisterous. He seeth his ruine at hand excepte he bestir him. Pius 4 was a man of great furie; and Gregory the 13, though in shewe he was more temperate, yet in his devises he was of as cruell a harte. But thei were both but lambes in respecte of this tigre. Thei no doute foresawe what ignominie and desolacion was like to fall upon that sea[7] yf England were not reclaimed unto their subieccion. Thei coulde not but remember howe like gods in times paste thei had sit in our harts commaundinge us and howe lyke tyrantes they had dealte with us, oppressinge us; which pinched them with sorowe in their verie soules and caused them to curse, to practise, to procure the bloodie league,[8] and to sollicite manie great potentates to have undertaken in their times this unchristian war and crueltie.

But this Pope, he is as provident as thei were, he is as proude as thei were, he is possessed with as great hatred both of us and our religion as thei were, and beinge of nature more furious, more cruell, more savage withall then thei were, can we imagine but that nowe he hath got the oportunitie which thei sought for, he will followe it to his uttermost power and abilitie, especiallie seinge he confesseth in his bull, and that in plaine termes, that excepte this attempte of the Spaniarde take good effecte, all Christendome is like to fall from his Holines? He hath bene at the charge of one million alredy, but when I consider together with the premises with what villanous furie he is inflamed in his said bull, howe he rageth, howe he fometh, howe he lieth, howe he sclaundereth, howe he thundereth against hir Majestie and / this estate, not- v. withstandinge that he blasphemouslie alleges for himself that he is moved therunto by the Holie Ghoste, I am fullie of opinion that rather then this invasion shoulde not goe forwarde, if that might serve the turne he woulde geve his soule to the devill. What maye be done by him, it shalbe done, we maie assure ourselves.

'And lastlie for the King of Spaine. He doth not either knowe or sufficientlie consider what he purposed, or howe he hath intangled himself in this attempte that can once conceive he shoulde nowe geve us over. For although the Pope in his bull, and that traiterous villen Allen in his booke,[9] doe geve it out that he undertooke this accion for the good will he bore to our nation, havinge bene our king, for the olde love and league betwene this kingdome and the house of Burgundie, and for his especiall zeale unto the sea apostolicke, yet in truth it was his ambitious nature, which is like a vessell with the botome upwarde and will never be full. It was because we stande in his light, that he cannot as yet see the fullnes of his desired monarchie. It was the good occacion offered him under the shewe of zeale to procure such assistants as he did, and to hope for aide from amongst ourselves. It was the love and good will he beareth to our landes and to our gooddes, and his hatred to hir Majestie, of our health and of our prosperitie, that hath thruste him into this open hostilitie and that must needes (as he resteth affected) continue him in the same.

'Besides it is well knowen what good offices hir Majestie hath taken upon hir on his behaulf, and howe from time to time notwithstandinge he hath dealte most dishonourablie with hir, howe as occacions have bene offered of anie unkindnes he hath bene sent unto with sufficient meanes of reconciliacion, and howe, unlike such a king as he woulde seeme to be, he hath contemned the same with great reproch and uncivill disdaine. Hir Majestie's enemies he hath ever favoured, countenanced and incouraged them from the beginninge of hir raigne, and woulde never be brought to anie equall intercourse of brotherlie freindship, but hath ever bene plottinge and devisinge by his ministers some mischeif against hir. These thinges hir Majestie deepelie consideringe, and withall foreseeinge his secret preparacion and intencion which nowe is evident,

7. i.e. 'see'.
8. The Holy League.

9. *Defence of the English Catholics.*

f.80   she hath in deede as a wise and provident governor somewhat of late crossed his purposes and pruned a litle / that more then ranke vine of his most ambitious humour, that it might not spreede so far as hastilie it shoulde blemish or indaunger hir croune and countrie. This providence for defence he taketh for matter of offence, and because he was not suffered without anie resistaunce to woorke his pleasure upon us, he nowe standeth upon it that he wilbe revenged.[10]

'Farthermore, it cannot be denied that he is a great and mightie Prince, but yet as Briareus[11] had 100 handes so had he to feede with them 50 bellies. Though the Spaniarde hath under him manie kingdomes and countries, yet is he therby drawen we knowe not to what exceedinge charges. His successe of late yeares in manie places hath wrapped up his estate in darkenes; but as it is in men's bodies, whilest thei are in health thei feele no paine in anie parte, but yf thei growe to be sicke all infirmities and weakenesses of everie member doth shewe it self, so fareth it with him. For consideringe his oath in the League, his promise to the Pope, his bragges throughout the worlde, his peremptorie distribution both of this croune and countrie, his vowes, protestacions, attemptes, and invincible preparacions (as he termed them) for our utter extirpation; yf now notwithstandinge, either through wante of power and abilitie or upon anie other consideracion, he shoulde be driven to put up such great losse, so open a foile, so publicke a shame, and so great a dishonour as to the admiracion of all Europe he hath received at our handes and toucheth him (no question) in the highest degree of his princelie and kinglie reputacion, assuredlie he shoulde make himself a bywoorde to all posteritie; his weakenes or cowardlines must needes be manifeste, and the provinces under him, which are in tyrannous subiection and doe hate him with a deadlie hatred, as the Indians, the Neapolitanes, the Millanes, and such other, thei will begin to examine their strength and to shake of the yoke of their servitude and subieccion. So as we are all fullie to assure ourselves that what he is able to doe, either by the ffreinds, by his credit, by his monie, or by his uttermost force, power, and strength; what the Pope or anie English traiter can anie waies woorke by sorceries, cursinge, practises, crueltie, or anie maner of persuasions; what thei can severallie everie one of himself, or iointelie altogether devise to bringe to passe, all shalbe imploied to our invasion; a mischeif which comprehendeth in it all the miseries and calamities which can possiblie fall upon anie estate or countrie. /

v.   'It maie therfore please you, my lords, if these things which hitherto I have touched be apparaunte unto you, that nowe in like sorte I maie proceede to the consideracion of such care and regard as it is fit to be had of us all in so weightie a matter and of so great importaunce. For we maie not stande beholdinge these daungers a farre of, as men looke upon a storme of haile: everie one praieth it maie not light on his corne, but no man seeketh to staie it. We nowe are in case as he that is sicke of an ague, one fit is paste and we have evident signes of another. Though a man be never so well on his good daie, yet he will not forget the sharpe fit which is cominge. The Spaniarde hath nowe experience of his owne wantes and of our forces; and so his seconde assaulte must needes prove more daungerous then the firste. His malice is increased and therfore he will double his strength.

'It is true that God hath mightilie hitherto defended hir Majestie and this realme from the hands of hir enemies by detectinge their conspiracies and makinge the verie birds of the aire as it were to reveale them. He hath blessed where thei have cursed, and multiplied his innumerable benefits upon us. Their bulles he hath caused to goare themselves and geven us of late a most notable victorie. But yet notwithstandinge, we maie not be secure. Meanes for our defence must diligentlie be cared for. An enemie is never so much to be feared as when he is contemned. *Arbor excisa pullulat*: we have lopte of some of his boughes, but thei will sooner growe againe then we thinke of.

'If those things coulde be iustified wherewithall the Pope, the Spaniarde, and our fugitive traiters doe charge hir Majestie and this state, then surelie our care ought principallie to be directed howe we might by our submission, though it were with most unequall conditions, seeke and procure their favours. But nowe it is far otherwise. Their pride, their ambition, their malice and their gredines, wherein thei are insatiable, implacable, and most intollerable, hath caste them into this furie and enmitie against us. And herein surelie we maie reioice, that as in buildinge *infimae partes debent esse firmissimae*, / so it is with us. The beginninge and foundation of all their quarreles is on our side most glorious. And therfore it were their partes to looke unto us. But thei will not; and yet I hope thei shalbe compelled, yf not by us yet by God himself. For we are bounde to defende our selves, our wives, our children, our freindes: it is by an instincte of nature. We are bounde to defende our countrie, our prince, our state, our lawes, our liberties: it is agreable to the lawes of all nations, and toucheth us all in honour. We are bounde to defende our possessions, our liberties, our gooddes, and our landes: it whollie concerneth our profit. Without this defence we shalbe nowe deprived of all these benefites. It is then most necessarie, howsoever you consider of it, by all lawes of nature and of nations, of God and of man, this defence that we are driven unto. It is holie, iust, honourable, and necessarie.

'If then, my Lords, our enemies, so manie and so mightie, in so lewde a cause as theirs is, have combined themselves together against us, yf in the respects before mencioned thei are fullie resolved to set up their rests either nowe or never to subdue us, either nowe to conquere us or to lay themselves open to be conquered of others, yf accordinglie thei ioyne together and are in devisinge all the waies and meanes whereby thei maye be able to execute their furie upon us, to overthrowe our religion, to depose hir Majestie, to possesse our lande, and with all kinde of crueltie to murther everie one of us; what care then I say, my Lords, ought we to have in so holie, so iust, so honourable, so profitable and so necessarie a quarell to ioine together, to foresee these

f.81

---

10. This paragraph is marked by a line   11. See Homer, *Iliad*, i.403.
    drawn down its whole length, possibly
    indicating that it was to be deleted.

daungers, to provide for them, and to set up our rests either nowe or never to be able to withstande them. In times past our noble predecessours have bene able to defende this realme, when they wanted such meanes as we maie have; and shall we nowe disable ourselves and through our negligence loose it? They upon occations offered have bene, you knowe, most worthie conquerers; and shall we nowe suffer ourselves with all dishonour to be conquered? England v. hath bene accounted hitherto the moste / renouned kingdome for valour and manhood in all Christendome, and shall we nowe loose our olde reputacion? Yf we shoulde, it had bene better for Englande we had never bene borne.

'I am persuaded there is none here present whoe woulde not sweare it yf he were asked, that yf he had an hundreth lives he would spende them all rather then anie soch matter shoulde come to passe. Marie, our cares and indevours for good meanes of defence must be therunto agreable; or else where deedes are necessarie it is but vanitie to stande upon woords. Our ship is yet safe; and therfore, as one said once in the like case, "Looke mastere, looke mariner, looke everie bodie, that it be not overthrowen by wilfullnes and negligence; for yf the sea get the masterie then is it too late." God forbid that we shoulde ever come to these woords: Lord, whoe woulde have thought we shoulde have come to this? Alas, alas, yf we had done thus and thus all had bene well.

'And therfore, my Lords, whilest the time serveth let us provide for our selves. Our enemies make great preparacion to assaile us by sea: our navy must be made fit to incounter them. Thei have great strength to invade us by lande: a correspondency of force must be had to withstande them. Thei are caringe for meanes to continue their offence: we must likewise consider of good meanes to continewe our defence. Our duties towards God, hir Majestie, and our countrie, doth require all this at your handes. The question then is, howe this maie be performed; and that hir Majestie, forasmuch as she knoweth your honoures, your hartes, your courages, your affeccions, your iudgementes, and that this cause doth principallie concerne you all; hir pleasure is not to preiudice your wisdomes, but doth refer the same at this time unto the most grave advise, deliberacion, consultacion, and care of you all. And so I ende.'

Finis.

3. [House of Lords] Reply to the Speaker's disabling speech, 6 February

Text from Lambeth Palace 178, copy in the hand of Michael Murgatroyd(?), secretary to Archbishop Whitgift.

Lambeth 178, fos.88v.–89

The effecte of your speech $\begin{cases} \text{to disable yourself} \\ \text{to be dismissed.} \end{cases}$

The wisest men doe most suspect themselves, and none are more confidente then those of leaste abilitie. The ice when it is the strongest will crak as yf it were then weakest. The weakeninge of yourself by your woordes doth argue your strength for your deedes.

As he that hath passed the sea often under a guide beinge no idle observer will soone become able to be a guider of others; so your often presence and diligent observacion of such men as have gone before you in this course cannot but make you fit to directe others yourself.

Although hir Majestie hath had some experience hirself of your gravitie, wisdome, and fitnes for this place, yet nowe that she seeth the generall consente of hir knights and burgeses to concur with hir opinion of you, she can in no sorte dislike of their choice.

For your wisdome, learninge, courage, and integritie, hir Majestie knoweth that you well understande not onelie what is to be done, and howe to performe the same, but also that you dare doe it boldlie without feare and will doe it sincerelie without corruption and partialitie.

In fliinge from your shadowe, yf you fall upon it you apprehende it: by your modestie in refusinge this place you have the rather attained it.

Why you are not to be dismissed.

A wise builder knoweth for what use everie peece of timber is fittest, and geveth direccion for placinge of it accordinglie. And even so hir Majestie, beinge the builder and upholder of this common wealth, findinge you at this time the meetest to be imploied in this service, hir pleasure ought to contente you for the undertakinge of the same.

Besides this dutie nowe required at your handes, it tendeth to the benefit of your countrie (to whome you owe yourself and all your indevers) and therfore will not permit you to withdrawe yourself from so necessarie an office imposed upon you: especiallie beinge so well furnished with singular guiftes for the discharge thereof. /

f.89   As yf you had of yourself, through some great conceite of your owne worthines, aspired to this place it might well have bene misliked: so on the other side to seeke your disburdeninge of the charge laide upon you by so honourable an eleccion maie no waie be allowed of.

When men have bene knowen woorthie of anie places of service in the common wealth, and beinge called to the same have of purpose withdrawen themselves; of aunctient times by mulctes[1] thei were therunto compelled. *Necessitatem poena advexit.*

Epaminondas,[2] beinge chosen in Thebes to a verie meane office in waie of disgrace, did yet to his great commendacion accept of the same with these woordes that as *magistratus* did *iudicare virum*, so sometimes *vir* did *iudicare magistratum*: and accordinglie he so used himself in it as that the place was of greater accounte ever after. But you are chosen to an office of so greate accounte and credit alreadie, as hir Majestie douteth not but that through your wise and discreete dealinge therein you shall by the same increase your reputacion, and therfore you maie not well refuse it.

What prerogative the mynde hath over the bodie, the same hath a good Prince over hir subiects. In a wise man when reason commaundeth, the will and affecc[i]ons doe redilie obeie. In like maner, hir Majestie thinkinge you a fit man for this service, you are with humilitie to conforme yourself to hir pleasure.

1. i.e. fines.   2. Theban general and statesman.

4. [House of Lords] Exceptions to the bill against informers, 10 March

Text from BL Lansdowne 58, ? original.

Lansdowne 58, f.138

[Endorsed by Burghley's secretary '*10 Martii 1588*.[1]
  Exceptions to the bill against informers']

Towchinge the bill that common informers shold putt in sufficient suerties for the answeringe of costes and damages accordinge to the statute of *xviij°*.[2]

Incertenties and imperfections in the bill.

Where it is enacted that no person or persons as 'a common informer' shalbe admitted or received to preferr or have any suyte or informacion againste any other uppon any penall statute, except he first putt in twoe sufficient suerties, etc. There may be question whoe is 'a comon informer' bounden by this lawe to putt in suerties, for the trouthe is noe person is admitted in any courte to be a common informer, nether is there any mencion made in any informacion that any informer doth preferr or have his suyte or informacion as a common informer but all that doe informe for the Quene and them selves, whether they be officers or others, or whether they doe exhibite one or many or fewe informacions, doe sue and preferr informacions after one and the same manner and forme. And yf the meeninge be that he is a comen informer that is noe officer or partie greived to whome onelie action is given by the statute, then yt would be so declared; and yf it be ment that he is commen in respect that he preferreth many informacions then yt would be declared for howe many suytes he may be accompted a common informer, for otherwise the court receavinge the informacions by one and one and not knowinge howe longe the informer will contynewe that trade cannot understand when to demaunde bondes.
  The hardnes of the bill is
That an informer that hath many suytes shall putt in twoe sufficient suerties for every suyte.
  The amendementes and qualificacions

---

1. This was the day of the 2nd reading and commitment of this bill, brought up from the Commons on Tuesday 4 March (*LJ*, ii.156–7, 159).

2. 18 Eliz., c.5 (1576) in *SR*, iv.615–16.

To specifie plainelie and certenly the informer that is ment to be towched by this lawe.

To make the lawe that the informer shall putt in but one bond with two sufficient suerties to answere the costes of all his suytes that he shall preferr, where nowe as the bill is he must putt in twoe suerties for every severall suyte. /

v.   A proviso that, if by reason of this act the execucion of any penall lawes shalbe more hindred then shalbe good for the common welth, then her Majestie by the advise of her Privie Counsell may by her proclamacion dispense with this statute for such statutes as in the same proclamacion shalbe specified.[3]

3. Cf. *SR*, iv.801–2 for 31 Eliz., c.5.

5. [House of Lords] Lord Burghley's speech and debate on the bill against pluralities, March

Text from Lambeth Palace Library 2007, fos.119–20 copy in the same hand as 1593 Commons' speeches in these MSS.
Other MSS. BL Lansdowne 396; Inner Temple, Petyt 538/52.

Lambeth Palace Library 2007, fos.119–20

[Endorsed by Whitgift 'The some of the Lord Treasoror's speach in Parlament against pluralities.']

Moved to speak for his
$\begin{cases} \text{conscience} \\ \text{countrey.} \end{cases}$

Extolled the bill
by the preamble
$\begin{cases} \text{divine service} \\ \text{preaching} \\ \text{hospitalitee} \\ \text{poore } etc, \\ \text{learning.} \end{cases}$

Thinges well provyded
for *21° Henrici* 8^i in
2 poyntes.[1]
$\begin{cases} \text{pluralitees not above viij}^{li} \\ \text{non-residence taken away} \end{cases}$
Both corrupted after
etc, and againe *31°*.[2]

Theis corruptions and qualifications for Masse to bee sayed: which being a hawking or hunting Masse was verie shorte, *etc*, and more needfull then.

    Then followed a recytall of qualifications from archebishoppes and dukes to the lowest sort[3] of the judges, attourney, sollicitor, Master of the Rolles, and Masters of the Chauncerie, *etc*.[4] And yet the chaplens would take their advantage of the statute, and doo no service in their lordes' houses, but putt all in their pursses, neither yet any service to the common weale, which were to bee allowed, as *articuli cleri anno 1° Edwardi 2^i, qui absunt a republica in servitute ecclesiae*.[5] There was a good proviso annexed to the sayd statute, yf it had bene

1. 21 Hen VIII, c.13 (1529) in *SR*, iv.292–6, esp. 293, 294–5.
2. The reference is not clear here: perhaps the Six Articles Act?
3. Petyt has 'lower house' rather than 'lowest sort'.
4. See *SR*, iv.294.
5. For *Articuli cleri* see 9 Ed. II in *SR*, i.172, and clause viii for clerks in the King's service.

observed, *viz*: that no dispensation should bee graunted agaynst the worde of God, but onely for the mayntenaunce of good gouvernement and to represse vice. And therefore more attributed to the Quene then the statute would seeme to allowe her.

Then folowed a rehersall of diverse constitutions of Octobonus, Otho, *etc.* and the articles in synod London, under Dr Parker, 1571, wherein the absence of shepeheardes is to bee abhorred, and lx dayes to bee resident, and no moe but 2 benefices, and those within xxvj^ty miles.[6]

Then was alleaged certen canons of the Tridentyne Councile *sessione 6ᵃ, cap. 1 et 2, et 23 et 24.*[7] *Ecclesiasticus ordo pervertitur etc.* And an othe taken of vicars for personall residence. *Omne[8] beneficium curatum, de jure communi exigit residentiam.*[9]

Bishop Grindall cutt of many facultees in tryfling causes, and so he thought my Lord of Canterbury nowe did, and would doo more.[10]

Then a merie tale of Dr Chambers, a physitian, and Dr Buttes but he thought it was not now so.

Then all the bishops were charged and coniured with some hard termes: and that it was not to bee suffered to have no presence, no service, no hospitalitee, but all the fruites gathered and putt in the purse.

Afterwardes it was signified that her Majesty was acquaynted with the matter, and that shee was verie forwardes to redresse the faultes; and therefore requyred the bishops not to hinder her good and graciouse purpose, for that her Majesty would conferre with them *etc.*

An aunswere to the bill of purveighors, that it was but touching the food of the body, but this concerned the food of the soule, *etc.* /

f.119v   The conclusion was that hee was not so scrupulouse absolutely to lyke of the bill without any exception: for he did favour both learning, and wished a competent reward to it, and therefore could lyke and allowe a learned man to have *ij°* benefices, so they were bothe in one parish. That is to say in one dioecese; and not one in the dioecese of Winchestre and another in the north, where the severall dioecesanes could have no regard of them: whereas being both in one dioecese, the bishop would look unto them.[11]

The Lord G[ray] notwithstanding the Archebishop's aunswere, rather persuaded to assent to the Lord T[reasurer] his opinion then before.[12]

His aunswere to the impossibilitee was that lerning would rather encreasse when there should bee more preferrementes, *viz*: 2° for one.[13]

His aunswere to the assertion of more learned ministres in the Churche of England then ever heretofore, nay then in all the reformed churches in Christendom, was this, that it was not to bee attributed to the bishops or their actions, but to God, who nowe opened the hartes of many to see into the trueth, and that the schooles were better observed.

Then hee seemed to wonder greately at her Majesty, that shee would make choyce to conferre with those who were all enemies to reformation, for that it nerely touched their freeholdes. And therefore he thought it good the House should make choyce of some to be ioyned with them.

Last of all hee wished the bishops might bee served as they were in King Henry the 8 his dayes, when as in the case of praemunire they were all thrust out of the dores.[14]

The Lord T[reasurer] sayd that the bishops yf they were wise would themselves bee humble suiters to her Majesty to have some of the temporall lordes ioyned with them.

The Lord Chamberlen[15] utterly dislyked the lord G[ray's] motion, alledging that it was not to bee well lyked of that the lordes should appoynt her Majesty any to conferre withall, but that it should bee lefte to her owne election. /

1. The preamble of the bill not performed, but the contrary.   f.120
2. *Commodum non per se, sed quatenus*[16] *subsidium ad virtutem.*
3. The division of benefices *non de iure divino, sed etc.*
4. The inaequalitee[17] of guiftes must have a difference in rewardes: elles if all bee equall there will bee no distinction.

6. See Wilkins, *Concilia*, i.649–56; ii.1–20; iv.267 (*de residentia* and *de pluritate*) for Otto (1237), Othobon (1268), and Parker.
7. *Canones et Catechismus Concilii Tridentini*, (1846), pp.39–41 for caps 1, 2 of *Decretum et Reformatione* of the 6th session.
8. Petyt: '*omnium*'.
9. Petyt: '*residentia*'.
10. Strype, *Grindal*, (1821 ed.), p.300; cf. P. Collinson, *Archbishop Grindal, 1519–1583: The Struggle for a Reformed Church* (1980), p.229.
11. A small space is left before the next paragraph.

12. 'Grey' and 'Treasurer' appear as 'G' and 'T' here, though Petyt has the names spelled out. Grey is probably Lord Grey of Wilton.
13. This paragraph appears in Petyt and Lansdowne as a marginal note against the paragraph 'The conclusion was . . .', though it reads '. . . the preferments etc. two or one'.
14. A small space is left after this paragraph.
15. Lord Hunsdon (Henry Carey).
16. Petyt: '*quantenus*'.
17. Petyt: '*maequallitie*'; Lansd.: '*mequallitie*'.

5. Mayntenaunce of lerning and hospitalitee taken out of cathedrall churches, and learned men taken away out of the universitees.

6. It is not thought hurtefull for one man to have diverse offices in the commonweale: and why then rather in the Churche?[18]

18. The manuscript accounts of these proceedings present problems. They are not dated, though the title and endorsement leave little doubt that this item is a representation of the Lords' discussion. We also know that the bill on pluralities which was introduced in 1589 reached the Upper House. There are many other papers in the Lambeth MSS relating to the vexed problem of pluralities, though they are not *clearly* intended for Parliamentary use. The Petyt and Lansdowne versions of this document (Lansdowne is probably a copy of Petyt made later in the seventeenth century) continue with further material at this point, though Lansdowne begins it on a new folio, possibly suggesting (as this Lambeth MS does) that what has appeared to this point is a separate item. Though what follows in Petyt (and Lansdowne) relates to pluralities, there is nothing which gives a certain indication that it is an account of a *parliamentary* argument, and it is therefore not printed here. Neale, however, assumed that the Lambeth MS was an incomplete account, and that a reference in Petyt to 'Mr Forscue his speech' helped to make the whole document an account of parliamentary debate in 1589 and of John Fortescue's contribution to it (*EP*, ii.226, 229, n.1). In a section headed 'Touching the Court of Faculties' there is a reference to 'this bill', which *may* link it with the pluralities bill, though the material could easily form part of a debate which clearly had a life outside and beyond the brief parliamentary session. Petyt and Lansdowne also assemble a number of other items with headings which proclaim that their intention is to argue against the bill of pluralities, though dating is again a problem. Many of these appear as separate items in Lambeth MSS 2004 and 2007, though they are run on in Petyt.

6. [House of Lords] Lord Burghley's brief for Sir Christopher Hatton's speech, 29 March

Text from BL Lansdowne 104, original draft in Burghley's hand.
Printed. Strype, *Annals* 3. ii.55–6 (from Lansdowne).

Lansdowne 104, f.55

[Endorsed by Burghley's secretary '29 *Martii 1589.*
The declaration of the Lordes to assist hir Majesty with their lives, landes, and goodes in the quarrell against the King of Spaine.']

The heades of the declaration and offer to be made by the Lords spyrituall and temporall to hir Majesty, of ther redynes to serve hir Majesty in this sort followyng: to be delyvered by speche of the Lord Chancellor.

Although uppon great considerations appearyng to them of the mighty and resolut determinations of the King of Spayn in makyng of open warrs ageynst hir Majesty and the realm for Gode's cause, and to extirp the Christian rellegion in this [realm], and specially uppon the sight [of] his last yere's oppen invasion attempted ageynst this realm with intent to have conquered the same, the Lords and the Commens of the realm[1] have most willyngly yelded to a kynd of subsydye, though in ther opinions not so sufficient to answer hir Majestye's chardges to be susteaned, as war requisit;[2] yet for a furder manifestation and declaration of ther most bounden dutyes both towardes the defence of hir Majesty and the realm ageynst so mighty attemptes, and also to offend hir sayd enemy, they do offer with all manner of dutye and willyngnes to hir Majesty, that whan so ever she shall fynd it mete and proffitable for hir realm to denounce any oppen warr ageynst the sayd Kyng and his adherence,[3] they shall be red[y] with all ther powers, ther bodyes, ther lyves, landes and goodes to serve hir Majesty therwith, aswell by offensyve warrs abrode as defensyve at home, ageynst the sayd Kyng and all his adherentes.[4]

---

1. The words 'and the Commons of the realm' are added.
2. The words 'to be susteaned, as war requisit' replace 'of defence as they seam'.
3. *Sic.*
4. The words 'and therwith shall contynew' have been deleted.

1. [House of Commons] Notes of Sir Walter Mildmay's speech for supply, 11 February

Text from Northants Record Office, Fitzwilliam of Milton Papers 147.

Anno Undecimo Februarii 1588

In the Common Hous { Notes towching the Spanishe entreprise against England.

The fire { kindeled long and carfely nourished } by { the Pope and his minestres.

It now broke forth into { a terrible and daungerous flame.

provoked and grounded { uppon the Holy League ordeyned long sithence in the Councell of Trent which now they wold put in full exequution.

general: { [Restitution of popery][1] Malice to the Gospell.

1. The causes

particuler: { Coveting to overthrow this realme, as there greatest impediment, and that hath most shaken the Pope's chayre.

Suppression of the religion of the gospell here, and in all other countryes. Deposing of our Quene.

2. The end: Conquest of this land with all cruelty which they use in all places. { religion liberty landes lyves

Example
{
Naples
Scicol
Milleyn
Flaunders
West Indias.
}

Secreate:
{
Jesuytes
seminaryes
fugityves
home papistes
traitors
}

The meanes
they have
used against
us.

Open: 2 bulles[2]
{
rebellion in the North
rebellion in Ireland
invasion there
the greate king, as they call hym,
   of Spayn his last greate navy sent
   hether this sommer with fforces
   from the Duke of Parma owt of
   Flaunders
ayde from the Duke of Guise owt
   of France
hope of a party here, publishing
   of a late Bull against the Queen
   wherin are named the King of Spain
   as chief and Parma as generall
hope that the Queen had but few
   adherentes and frendes here as
   the bull saieth.
}

The meanes
we had
against
them:
{
The mightie hand of God
The providence of the Queen's majestie; hir
   invincible courage
The magnanimitie and constancy of the nobilitie
The fidletie and readynes of the people
The Queen's forces by sea
Hir forces by land
The goodnes of he quarrell
The defence of the gospell and the realme
The prayers of good people
The honorable and good dealing of the King and
   realme of Scotland, tyed unto us with the band of
   religion.
}

1. Deleted in MS.

2. The words '2 bulles' have perhaps been
added on a different occasion.

Their losses in $\left\{\begin{array}{l}\text{narrow seas}\\ \text{cost of Ireland:}\end{array}\right.$

shippes
men $\left\{\begin{array}{l}\text{shipps xxxij.}\\ \text{men x m}^1.\end{array}\right.$
munition
money

The
Estat:
$\left\{\begin{array}{l}\text{Their hole entreprice disappointed and that so sone}\\ \quad\text{as hir Majestie may say as Caesar did}\\ \quad Veni,\ Vidi,\ Vici.\\ \text{Their pride abated}\\ \text{Their shame and dishonour increased}\\ \text{The Queen's victory against them}\\ \text{Hir honour and fame therby}\\ \text{Not one ship of hirs lost, and veary few men.}\end{array}\right.$

So as now:
This storme is $\left\{\begin{array}{l}\text{greate and}\\ \text{daungerous}\end{array}\right.$
over being

And therby $\left\{\begin{array}{l}\text{all calme}\\ \text{and sauffe}\end{array}\right\}$ for this tyme.

The clowdes
nevertheles $\left\{\begin{array}{l}\text{darke}\\ \text{over}\\ \text{our heddes}\end{array}\right\}$ and threaten an other tempest.
remain still

Wise maryners $\left\{\begin{array}{l}\text{aftre a daungerous storme provide to}\\ \text{resist an other that may follow,}\\ \text{dowbtinge the second may be worse}\\ \text{than the former.}\end{array}\right.$

So we
having overcome
this first attempt $\left\{\begin{array}{l}\text{by hir Majestie's forces, assisted}\\ \text{and conducted by the powre of God,}\end{array}\right.$
of our enemyes

we are to
thinke uppon
a second from $\left\{\begin{array}{l}\text{enemyes so greate}\\ \text{so malitious}\\ \text{so covetous}\\ \text{so cruel}\\ \text{so prowde as they will seeke to repaire}\\ \quad\text{the credyt they have lost}\\ \text{and not like to leave the prosequution}\\ \quad\text{of the Holy League.}\end{array}\right.$

And therfore provision is to be made in tyme:

Of fforces $\left\{\begin{array}{l}\text{by sea}\\ \text{by land}\end{array}\right.$

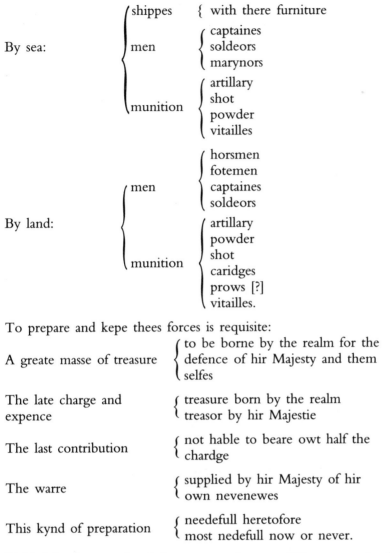

By sea:
- shippes — { with there furniture
- men —
  - captaines
  - soldeors
  - marynors
- munition —
  - artillary
  - shot
  - powder
  - vitailles

By land:
- men —
  - horsmen
  - fotemen
  - captaines
  - soldeors
- munition —
  - artillary
  - powder
  - shot
  - caridges
  - prows [?]
  - vitailles.

To prepare and kepe thees forces is requisite:

A greate masse of treasure { to be borne by the realm for the defence of hir Majesty and them selfes

The late charge and expence { treasure born by the realm / treasor by hir Majestie

The last contribution { not hable to beare owt half the chardge

The warre { supplied by hir Majesty of hir own nevenewes

This kynd of preparation { needefull heretofore / most nedefull now or never.

[Added in the same hand, but apparently on a different occasion:]

Henry 8 {
- Tornay and Tirwyn
- Boluigne[3] {
  - subsidies
  - lones
  - benevolences

---

3. i.e. Tournai, Thérouanne and Boulogne.

This cause toucheth
{
the Queen
hir realmes { England / Ireland
hir hole people.

2. *Certain motions for a conference on religion, 25 February*

Text from Longleat, Wilts: Thynne Papers lxxvi, copy with
marginal answers probably in the hand of a secretary of
Archbishop Whitgift.
Other MSS (without the answers). London: BL Lansdowne 119,
Add. 21563, Add. 48064 (Yelverton 70); Inner Temple, Petyt
538/36.

Thynne Papers lxxvi, fos. 5–12

[Entitled, f.5]   'An aunswere to certaine motions moved in Parliament.
Anno 1588. Februarii mensis.'
[Endorsed by Whitgift, f.5v]   'An answere to certanine[1] motions moved in
Parlament *Anno* 1588.'

1588
Feb.

Certayn motions wherupon a
conference is humbly to be desyred
before the lords of the Higher
House and a committie of the
Lower House, in the presence of the
lords bisshops and all the judges of
the lande, to the honour of God,
and for the mayntenaunce of her
Majestie's prerogative royall, the due
observation of her Highnes' lawes,
and the quyetnes of the Church and
estate of this realme of England.

f.6

*Protestatio cum contrario actu non
relevat.*[2]

Inprimis, it is not meant that ether
her Majestie's supreme autoritie or
any ecclesiasticall law of this realme
should be called in question, but
remayne in such sort as they are and
lawfully may be.

This is a generall sclander except
some will take upon him in
particuler to avowe it.

It is onely required that the
abuses of the bisshops and
commissioners ecclesiasticall ageinst[3]

1. *Sic.*
2. The marginal answers are probably in the
   hand of a secretary of Whitgift's: they do
   not appear in the other MSS.

3. Add. 48064 omits.

the worde of God, the prerogative of the[4] crowne, the lawes, liberties, and customes of this free[5] realme of England, ageinst the auncient canons and counsells and her Majestie's commission ecclesiasticall, should be reformed and redressed.

And for that by sundry statutes and lawes of this realme we be assured that no ecclesiasticall law or canon is to be executed in this realme that is repugnant or derogatorie to any statute, law or custome of the same, and that the sayd commission and all others are to be expounded to be *stricti iuris,* according to the letter: it is to be consydered whether the bisshops have not offended, both in the manner of their proceedinges and the causes by them pretended, both ageinst law and the sayd commission.

Yf every man at the suite of another shulde be now broughte to answere any pretended breache of lawe, in Parlement, it muste be made a sette courte, as it is in Paris: which how inconvenient it were, is soone iudged. And yet I see no partie made in all these accusations.

This high court of Parliament is the place where remedy is to be sought, as appeareth by the statute *15° Edwardi 3 cap.* 3,[6] where it is ordeyned that yf any minister of the kinge's, or other person of what condicion he be, doe come ageinst any poynte of the Great Charter or other statutes or lawes of the lande, he shall answere to the parliament aswell at the kinge's sute[7] as at the sute of the partie,[8] whether it was done by commission or commandement of the king, or of his owne autoritie.

The parlament allready hath trusted her Majesty to reforme suche mischiefes as now be surmised in the state ecclesiasticall: will then this penner take away againe this autority, against her prerogative acknowledged and his owne protestation?

And in the statute *de provisoribus 25°*[9] of the sayd king made upon complaynt of the commons ageinst the clergie, as appeareth by the printed booke, it[10] is sayd that the right of[11] the Crowne of England and lawe of the realme is such, that upon mischeifes and domages which

It is offered by some of the Commons to have all them allowe of it, and so to be parties; shall they allso be iudges? And shall not her Majesty be trusted with appointyng hearers of this conference?

In steede of charging ecclesiasticall persons with breache of lawes, here be certaine doubtes offered to be resolved by some temporall lords and Commons, as yf they satte and were assembled to assoile questions and not to make lawes. But, being *quaestiones iuris*, why are the lordes spirituall debarred from the resolution and consultation, especially where it is surmised some course to be against the worde of God?[13]

Yf it were understoode what proceeding *ex officio* meaneth this doubte were frivolous. It is when by fame or credible relation some enormiousse and secret crime not

may happen to this realme, the king ought and is bounde of the accord of his people and in Parlyament to make remedy[12] for the avoyding of such mischeifes and domages which weare attempted by negligence and sufferance, contrary to the lawes.

It is also desyred that the lords temporall and Commons may be only judges in this cause, for that the lords spirituall are parties, and in former tymes the auncient statutes ageinst the *premunires* were made by the king, the lords temporall and Commons, notwithstanding the clergie did not only not assent therunto, but also protested to the contrary.

The poyntes wherupon the conference is desyred are these:

1.[14] Fyrst, touching their manner of proceeding, it is to be considered whether their proceeding *ex officio* be not ageinst the worde of God, and the canons, and abrogated by the

4. Add. 48064 omits 'of the'.
5. Lansd. 119 omits.
6. 15 Ed III, c.3 (1341) in *SR*, i.296.
7. Underlined, apparently by the writer of the marginalia.
8. The words 'of the partie' are underlined, apparently by the writer of the marginalia.
9. 25 Ed III, stat.4 (1350–1) in *SR*, i.316–18.
10. Lansd. 119: 'that'.
11. Lansd. 119 omits 'the right of'.
12. *Sic* in all MSS. The act says that the

King 'ought and is bound by his oath, with the due accord of his people in his parliament, thereof to make remedy . . .'.
13. This paragraph appears against the section starting 'The poyntes . . .' and ends at 'commission ecclesiastical'. The paragraph beginning 'Yf it were understoode . . .' runs along the bottom of f.6.
14. The numbers have been inserted by the writer of the marginalia: they do not therefore appear in the other MSS.

easily to be discovered or refourmed by ordinary iurisdiction, is for the publicke interest of the Churche or common welth sought to be boulted furthe, thoughe no particuler person doe prosecute. Why is this more unlawfull then when the Queen's counsell dothe the like, or the iudges by examinations, or when generall inquistions are made by the graund enquest in assises or quarter sessions, or at bishops' visitations; a course not onely permitted but commaunded even by olde canons? And the statute *1° Elizabethae* warranteth suche ecclesiastical proceding as heretofore hathe bene used.[15]

lawes of England, and not warranted by the commission ecclesiasticall. /

v.   Yf an acte of Parlement that warranteth the commission according to the purporte of it be lawe sufficient, then is this warranted by lawe. And why is it not as convenient for a crime to be called from a remote place, as for a civill matter as of dette *etc*, to be called from Carlile to Westminster Hall?

2. Whether the cyting up of ministers from remote places to London and Lambeth be not ageinst the canons, the lawes of England and commission ecclesiasticall.

Before they answere they knowe to what they aunswere: they are not suffered to have copies afore leste they seeke through counsell by evasions to delude theire oath. A man's owne facte may be aunswered withoute counsell.

3. Whether the swearing of them to answere they know not to what, be nor ageinst the canon lawe, the libertie of England, and commission ecclesiasticall.

A proper course by way of question to sclaunder and revile a man in autority. He was an ecclesiasticall person and therefore the bishop in any place of his diocesse might tender it to him. *5° Elizabethae.*

4. Whether the Bishop of London might by the statute of 5to[16] tender in his chamber the oath unto Benison,[17] having no ecclesiasticall living nor doing any act contrary to the Booke of Common Prayer or statute of uniformitie, untruly pretending that he had bene at Geneva, who never was out of her

Majestie's domininions: and whether
the committing of him so long a
tyme to pryson, and the untrue
certificat to bring him within the
daunger of that statute, weare not a
most tyrannicall action, contrary to
the lawes and liberties of England.

The firste parte hereof is the same
with the thirde.[18] It is absurd to
imagine that diverse factes (being
crimes) may not be obiected in one
sorte of articles.

5. Whether the refusing to shewe
unto the ministers the articles
wherwith they be charged, and
wherto they should answere, and the
ministring of other articles, not
incident to the present fact, be not
ageinst the canons and lawe of
England and commission
ecclesiasticall.

Suspension is a censure allowed by
canon, by statute law and by
commission autorized by statute. Are
not they most fitte to be censured
herewith that refuse to testify theire
conformity with the Churche of
England, or to aunswere upon theire
othe to matters with the which they
are charged?

6. Whether the putting of men to
sylence for not subscribing or
swearing, having a lawfull calling in
the Church and maynteining no
false doctrine contrary to the articles
establsshed in Parliament, be not
ageinst the canons, the lawe of
England and commission
ecclesiasticall.

None are imprisioned for trifles and
theire imprisonment is warranted by
commission.

7. Whether the ymprisoning of
them without a lawfull cause for
such tryfles be not ageinst the
canons, the lawe and libertie of
England and the commission
ecclesiasticall.

When imprisonment is the penalty
of the misdemeanoure and not for
safe custody onely no lawe alloweth
baile.

8. Whether the refusall of bayle in
such cases be not ageinst the lawe
and libertie of England.

We know no suche deprivations
used. Why shulde any be a minister
of the Churche of England that

9. Whether their deprivacions of
men for causes not expressely
appoynted by lawe be not ageinst

---

15. *SR*, iv.352, sect.viii of the Act of
    Uniformity.
16. *SR*, iv.403, sects.iv, v of the Act for the
    Assurance of the Queen's Power.

17. See W. Pierce (ed.), *The Marprelate
    Tracts, 1588, 1589* (1911), p.93 & n.2 for
    Aylmer and Benison.
18. i.e. the third point.

depraveth it, and thinketh the government antichristian and unlawfull?[19]

That statute appointeth allso the use thereof, and in suche manner and fourme. I knowe none that extend it farther then lawe will.

This question implieth a very strange and dangerous position, as yf any other then papists (becausse they were chiefely shotte at, puritans being sence hatched) might lawfully omitte the use of the Booke, or not use it in suche manner, or use another fourme or deprave it freely: so that (yf a man wolde saie he doth it not as a papist) he might say a Masse *etc*, and as yf the paines that papists incurre hereupon are iust, but upon others violating the lawe as well as they, uniuste, by this interpretation. A lawe conceived in generall wordes dothe include all within that generality, howsoever the lawe-makers in theire entent doe meane but to touche some. And yet no doubte theire meaning was to enclude all that shulde offende it, upon what perswasion soever. Yf any in England wolde sette up the publicke exercise of Mahomet's religion, shulde not this statute reache them, and yet the parlement propounded not this case before theire eies.

the lawe of England, the canons, and commission ecclesiasticall.

Now to the causes pretended and inserted in divers of their sentences of depryvation.

1. Wheras the statute of *primo* touching uniformitie appointeth three offences: for not using the forme of prayer prescribed, or usyng any other[20] forme, or depraving of the booke, the law being penall and *stricti iuris*: whether it is agreable with the iustice and aequitie of the lawe of England, to extend it further to any other causes or offences.

2. Seing the Booke of Common Prayer was fyrst authorized in the Lower House, and after assented unto by the lords temporall of the Higher House, and then confyrmed by her Majestie, without any convocation or bissops, which then were all popish, and it is a maxime in lawe, that the makers of the lawe are the best expositors of the same: it would be understood in Parliament, whether the principall meaning was not then ageinst the papistes, and not ageinst others, whom the bishops now most persecute contrary to the meaning of the lawe makers. And so *ordinata in unum finem, contrarium finem operantur*, which is ageinst the rules of all lawe and aequitie. /

Th'execution of that statute committed to ordinaries, to punishe by censures at any time after, and deprivation named, with relation to former usage as in like cases by ecclesiasticall lawes. And so the statute aunswereth these two questions.[22]

3. When as[21] the sayd statute appoynteth deprivacion upon conviction of an offence the second tyme, whether it standeth with the lawe of England that the ordinary or commissioners may deprive for the first tyme of offending or no.

4. Whereas the sayd statute appoynteth that no person shalbe impeached or molested for any offences commytted ageinst the sayd act, unles he be therof indyted at the next generall sessions before the justices of oyer and determiner or justices of assise next after the offence committed: whether it standeth with the law of England to have the ordinary or commissioners to proceed without any such enditement, or respect of tyme, at their pleasure.

By the preamble of this doubte the question shulde have bene whether we have any booke established. And whether papists and others have not had wronge to be punished.
Yf any thing withoute warrant have bene altered, yet that which agreeth with King Edward's booke is lawefull. *Utile per inutile non vitiatur.* Let him accuse those that of theire owne autority have altered it.

5. Seing the statute requireth a Booke of Common Prayer with the three additions only, and not otherwise differing from the booke of 5 and 6 Edward 6: fforasmuch as themselves in their advertisementes and articles confesse an alteration in the calender syth the vth yeare of her Majestie's reigne: whether the prelates have by the law of England any autoritie to alter the Booke at all.

The taking of the oathe is not commaunded as a penalty, but for

6. Seing the statute of 5[to] appoynteth the oath and penaltie of that act to

---

19. This sentence appears against 'Now to the . . .' but clearly refers to point 9.
20. Other MSS have 'another' rather than 'any other'.
21. *Sic* (+ Petyt); Lansd.: 'whereas' (+ Add. 21563, 48064).
22. The Act of Uniformity says that the accused may be 'lawfully convicted according to the laws of the realm by

verdict of twelve men, or by his owne confession, or by the notorious evidence of the fact.' Section iv however charges the Archbishops, Bishops and other ordinaries to execute the law, and gave them 'full authority to refourme, correcte and punishe by censures of the Churche' (*SR*, iv.356–7).

better assurance. Yf it were, the former penalties are not thereby abrogated, but the magistrate at liberty to inflicte either.

be executed toward such a person that shall not observe the ceremonies and rites of the Church of England, or shall deprave the same: whether it take not away the penaltie of the former statute of *primo*, or whether both penalties are to be inflicted for one offence, or which of them, *viz*, ether the statute of *primo* or the latter of *anno 5to* be to be[23] observed.

They are no new lawe, but an execution of the olde. They were not published in any man's name. Hathe this penner learned of Martin that her Majesty did not assent? When her Majesty requireth his aunswere, he will yelde it.

7. Wheras by two statutes made in the tyme of King Henry the Eight, and revived *primo* of her Majestie's reigne,[24] the bishops be inhibited to put in ure any constitution or article synodicall or otherwise without the kinge's royall assent, under payne of fyne and ymprisonment: seing the articles of subscription which have troubled the Church were publisshed in the Lord Archbisshop's name and not her Majestie's, and without her Highnes' hand: it is to be understand,[25] what autoritie he had to promulge and enforce[26] the same.

Continuall omission is a very dispising of the Booke by suche as shulde use it.

8. Whether the omission of some parte of the service, especially in respect of a sermon, be ageinst the canons or lawe of England.

No. But are the lordes temporall and Commons fittest iudges hereof? '*Legit quidem ecclesia, etc*', saith Hierom.

9. Whether the reading of the Apocripha in the Church be not ageinst the worde of God, the auncient canons and counsells, and lawes of England.

Many thinges well commaunded by lawe, which without repugnancy to scripture might be omitted. Shall no civil lawe or ecclesiasticall for order be retained, yf the omission be not sinne?

10. Whether the omission of the crosse in baptisme may not be tolerated by God's booke and the lawe of England.

The demaunde is to the godfathers, but in the name and behalfe of the

11. Whether the wordes in baptisme oughte to be pronounced to the

childe, who promisseth by them his sureties.

The wordes of the Booke are: 'it is expedient that he be brought to the churche'.[27] Suche parents are proceeded against by the penalties provided, for theire obstinacy in them selves and theire children. Yf those penalties cannot bringe them selves, as imprisonment and fine, is it likely that they will sende theire children? This cannot be done, except you will take theire children away by force, and then shall you not learne of any of theire baptizinge or not, and so may happely rebaptize them. Yet diverse have bene punished for this contempt as Wrenford, Timperley *etc*.

The lawe is dispositive, 'the man shall gyve' and 'the priest shall deliver'.

The words are: 'the woman shall come, shall kneele downe', and 'the priest shall saye'.[28] All ordinaries by the statute are charged to see the execution of that statute, and to punishe the breaches. The

godfathers (Doe yee beleve?) and not to the childe (Doest thou beleeve?) by the Booke of Common Prayer and lawe of England.

12. Wheras the Booke of Common Prayer no otherwise tolerateth pryvate baptysme, but that the childe should afterwardes be brought to the church to have that supplied that was fyrst wanting in the case of necessity, as was also accustomed in poperie: seing it is notoriously knowen that the children of papistes and recusantes are pryvately / baptyzed, it would be understood   v. what one of their children hath bene so brought unto the church according to the Booke, and what punishment hath bene extended for the default, by any ordinary or commission[er] ecclesiasticall upon them; and whether it hath bene required of them to have the contentes of the Booke performed.

13. Whether in the celebration of mariage the omission of the ringe may not be tolerated by the law of England.

14. What lawe, ether English or canonicall, or warrant in their commission they have to punish any woman for not being purified or churched. And whether the Bishop of London, committing by his sole

---

23. Lansd. 119 has 'oughte' rather than 'be' (+ Add. 48064).
24. The relevant laws are the Act of Submission (1534), and the Act which provided for the appointment of 32 persons for making ecclesiastical laws (1536): while Elizabeth's Act of Supremacy revived the former, the latter seems to have remained repealed according to the Marian legislation of

1554–5 (*SR*, iii.460–1, 548–9; iv.247, 351, sects ii, iv.
25. *Sic*.
26. Lansd. 119 omits 'and enforce' (+ Add. 48064).
27. The words 'it is expedient . . . the churche' are underlined, apparently by the writer of the marginalia.
28. The quoted words here, and immediately above, are all underlined.

commission alloweth besides censures, fine and imprisonment. The Bishop of London can well aunswere what and by what warrant he hathe done. It is ridiculous to demaunde of the parlement how the Bishop of London can defende his facte.

autoritie the wife of[29] one Marion, a twelve moneth after the offence done, where she was for a certayn space kept in fetters and yrons from her sick husband and yonge chylde, which she nursed at that tyme, and could not be bayled, can defend his so unreasonable and execrable a fact by any lawe, canon, or commission of England. And whether the poore man weare not contrary to the meaning of the lawe of England barred from his remedie of action of false ymprisonment.

Surplesse is commaunded by statute by reference to the 2 yeare of King Edward. The Advertissements were published by her Majestie's autority which commaunde the other. To this she is waranted by the statute *1° Elizabethae*. The very canons *pro clericali habitu* are not abrogated.

15. Whether there be any lawe canonicall or English to punish a man for not wearing a surplesse,[30] a[31] cap, tippett, or formall gowne; and whether the lawes that were sometime made for that purpose, be not ether wholly now in England abrogated, or ells without any penaltie at all.

How true this reporte is I referre to those can remember. I am sure Bishop Hooper was urged to rochet. What booke he meaneth (except Dr Bridges)[32] I cannot coniecture. How tolerating the breache of lawe may breede unity, or why the urging of this order shulde gyve causse of division betwixt clergy and temporalty I cannot see, except some temporall men will be offended with any that observeth order.

16. Seing in the time of King Edward the 6 there was a toleration used by the godly bisshops concerning apparrell and other rites now urged towardes divers, as Mr Rogers,[33] by their own confession in their booke intituled, *The Defence of the Ecclesiasticall Government of England*: item towardes Mr Bradford, Saunders, Philpott, Samson, Haddon, as is notoriously knowen, and many others: whether it be not better for th'estate of the Church and realme to have such a toleration nowe also, to maynteine peace and unitie, rather then by enforcing the contrary, to geve cause of hatred and devision betwene the temporaltie and clergie of this realme, wherby the services of God and her Majestie are mightily weakened and hindred.

A strange question of facte for the parlement to resolve. It may be they have mantained (as I am sure) and yet the parlement knoweth it not.

17. Whether the ministers that have bene so hardly used have maynteined any errors or heresie contrary to the statute and commission.

I thinke none have: they have not bene complained of, and wise men cannot yet finde suche errors. There was but one authoure of that booke. He hateth the Masse and is able to say more against it then any or all these preferrers. The surmise of being reconciled (which is treason) is a most villanous sclander to be imputed to any except it be true and to be proved.

18. Whether some that have oppugned them have not openly sett forth in their bookes[34] doctrine tending to induce manifest errors, ageinst the lawes and doctrine heretofore professed and publisshed in this realme, and whether one of the authors of the sayd bookes intituled *The Defence of the Ecclesiasticall Government of the Church of*[35] *England*, hath not bene synce at Masse, and as it is supposed, reconciled to the Pope, and had a superaltare found in his chamber.

A superaltare taken in some serche may be founde in a more honest man's chamber then the penner of these is.

Ad 19.
Yf the Churche of Rome have erred in faithe and ceremonies, dothe it hereof followe that we may holde nothing which they helde withoute dishonoure to our Churche? Why, they helde 3 persons in Trinity. The imitation of them in matters not impious (lest we shuld have seemed rather to have detested theire persons then theire errours) to be dishonorable or apishe, is onely

19. Seing in the 19 article establisshed in Parlement we professe that the Church of Rome hath erred not only in matters of fayth but also in manner of ceremonies: whether it be not a great dishonour to the Church to have our adversaries to write that in our service or any / where els, we have not any thing to be commended, but have it as apes taken from them by imitation, as (they say) may appeare[36] by the

f.8

29. Lansd. 119 adds 'a poore man' (+ Add. 21563).
30. Lansd. 119 omits.
31. Lansd. adds 'forked' (+ Add. MSS).
32. John Bridges' *A Defence of the Government Established in the Church of Englande for Ecclesiastical Matters* appeared in 1587.
33. Richard Rogers was actively critical of Whitgift's disciplinary regime.

34. Add. 21563 adds 'and'.
35. Add. 48064 omits 'the Churche of'.
36. Petyt: '. . . but like apes we have taken from them by imitacion (as they say) as may appeare'; Lansd. 119 as above but omits 'taken' (+ Add. 48064); both Add. MSS have '(as they say)' rather than as above.

theire collection and the puritans who are bothe alike enemies to the Booke of Common Praier, thoughe in diverse respectes. The meaning therefore of this question was, under the persons of the papists to deprave the Booke. And is not this to call an ecclesiasticall lawe in question?

No degradation which is reall deposition ever used by our bishops.

It seemeth this man knoweth it allready. Why then doth he aske the parlement what hath bene written? That which the papists perverte for the Pope that dothe the Deane of Poule's and others truly shewe to be meant of every bishop and archbishop in theire territories. But T[homas] C[artwright] useth diverse times very popishe arguments and to the same ende, and being therewith charged he saith he tooke it not oute of them, but marked it by his owne readinge: and so either condemneth himselfe of calumniation or iustifieth the goodnes of popishe reasons.

Yf those bookes of his teache any false doctrine, the Bishop of London is not of suche meane iudgement but he coulde have espied it.
A wise question to aske an account of the parlement what the Bishop of London hath done in his diocesse.

Communion booke, comparing it with the Masse booke. Item in the spirituall courtes, visitations, convocations, excommunications, burning of heretiques, deprivations, degradacions, used by our bisshopps.

20.   Whether a notable papist and adversary to the Church[37] and estate of England, hath not long synce written of our prelates, that *responsionem quam in pontificiis non ferunt contra suos symistas in regimine ecclesiastico ab ipsis dissidentes audacter adhibent*: meaning that the same argumentes which the Church of England and themselves have misliked in the Pope and popish bishops for the mayntenance of their usurped authoritie, are now used by themselves to maynteine their pretended jurisdiction, as his playne wordes be, '*respondent idem quod nos*': and that the same argument that they use for the mayntenance of the archbisshop's authoritie, *respondemus et nos de summo Pontifice*.

21. Whether the Bishop of London did not openly in printe inioyne the schoolemasters of his diocesse to reade unto their schollers a dialogue of fayth conteyning unsounde or suspected doctrine: which booke was first made in Latin by Sebastianus Castalio,[38] a man notoriously knowen to be addicted to the heresie of the Arrians, to maynteine the having of two wives at once, and an enemy to the doctrine of God's eternall providence and

predestination, professed in this Church of England.

Neither I nor any of the parlement I thinke can tell this, besides the penner. Belike he sawe it in his travail in Germany.

22. Whether the more cunningly to insynuate the same booke, the sayd Castalio's name was not changed into an other disguised name, and whether the sayd bookes were not burnt by the magistrates of Basill and Franckfort as hereticall and erroneous, and the publisshers fyned for publishing the same.[39]

Yf suche booke were erronious, why is the autority for suppressing it called in question?

23. By what authoritie the same booke was suppressed, and whether there was any punishment[40] taken of the parties by the sayd bishops or no.

A man may have a preeminence in order and dignity withoute iurisdiction over other: as *princeps senatus*, and your moderators or presidents in your councells and synodes. Is not St Peter in the number called πρῶτος in the gospell?[43] *Aetatem habet respondeat pro seipso* yf he have so written as I thinke he hath not.

24. Whether Dr Bridges hath not[41] in his booke maynteined popish doctrine by attributing unto the apostle Peter a preheminence above the rest of the Apostles: and wheras he writeth that a priest may be chozen to be head of the Church in a realme or cuntrie, it is to be considered:[42]

You wolde gladly wrappe us in danger of disloialty. But why doe your godly ones seeke now to refourme against her expresse commaundement, teache how subiects may excommunicat and depose her, gyve away all iurisdiction ecclesiasticall from her unto others, making of ecclesiastical lawes, callinge of synodes, proclaiming of fastes, the last appeale *etc*?

25. Whether this be agreable with the statute and his oath of supremacie, that recognizeth this prerogative only in her Majestie, as in the right of her Crowne inseperably: what the offence of the sayd doctor is, and of such other as sawe the booke before the printing, and allowed therof, and yet[44] stand in defence of the same, by the lawe of England.

37. Petyt omits.
38. Sebastian Castellio had quarrelled with Calvin and Beza over *De Haereticis*. He died in 1563.
39. Petyt runs this and the following paragraph together.
40. Add. MSS: 'publishment'.
41. Lansd. 119 omits 'hath not'.
42. Petyt runs this and the following paragraph together.
43. Mat 10: 2.
44. Add. 48064: 'it'.

Some of them be all these and anabaptistes too, and many of them be schismatikes.

Yf by the *other side* you meane presbytery patrones it is true.

v.   The resolution of this standeth in the lawfullnes of that which is required: for yf it be lawfull and honest, then doe they forget their obedience canonicall.

Willfull breache of lawe, yea, and suche lawe as this party doth proteste he will not impugne, is a crime deserving any proceeding that hathe bene used, especially being ioyned with a willfull purpose of continuance.

Either these men must derogate from the Queen's supremacy, allready graunted and allwaies due, and from the statute which autoriseth the commission, or els this clausse must have some effect. But yf it shuld worke nothing, yet must it be *ad delegantem* and to none other. The truthe is, if any iniustice do appeare flatte contrary to lawe, *delegans adermdus*[48] *est per viam querelae*. So that this course is more equall then theire new platte which admittes none appeale from a nationall synode, no not to the prince.

26. Whether any of the sayd ministers be schismatikes, or donatistes, or novations, or puritans?

27. Whether some of the other syde have not openly in their bookes maynteined some of the opinions[45] of Donatus and Novatus, and puritanes, heretofore disallowed by the auncient ffathers of the Church at those[46] tymes. /

28. Whether the sayd ministers by refusing to subscribe or sweare at their pleasure, or refusing to obey their commandementes not warranted by lawe, may be sayd to have committed any contempt or breach of the pretended canonicall obedience, contrary to the canons and lawes of England.

29. Whether the sayd ministers can be charged with committing any enormities, crimes, or abuses, which by the canons or law of England doe deserve such hard proceeding ageinst them.

30. Whether the sayd ministers may not by the sayd[47] canons and lawe of England appeale from their most uniust sentences of deprivation and otherwise, notwithstanding the clause in the commission of *omni appellatione remota, viz*, to the Queen's Majestie, the lords of the Councell, and to the high court of Parliament: and whether the sayd court have not authoritie to procure a remedie for such ecclesiasticall iniustices[49] and incrochmentes, as in former tymes it hath done.

It cannot be in dutifull manner which is contrary to an expresse commandement: neither is every thinge worthy reformation that a few doe fansy.

31. Whether the desire of a further and better reformation in the Church of England in dutifull manner be not warranted by the word of God and the lawe of England.

It is not made necessary by the Booke, but meete for the ends there sette downe. The defect herein is not in the bishop but in such factious heades as both contemne to bringe theire owne children, and disswade others. There is no coloure of pretext when the fault of not being confirmed is in themselves or parents. Yf this in the Booke be a faulte to be amended,[51] how is the protestation observed? And why is the neclect of it obiected as a faulte to the bisshoppe?

32. By what warrant the bishops commonly neglect confirmacion of children, if it be so necessarie as the rubrick of the Booke pretendeth, and seing it is sayd that no man is to be admitted to the communion, that is not confyrmed: whether this may not[50] be a pretext to the backsliding youth not to come to the communion, unlesse the fault be amended.

It is not obtruded: bothe are by law, and therefore either may be observed; but for avoiding of offence most meete to retaine that which every severall churche hathe of longe time observed. We might obtrude it as well as Geneva dothe.

33. By what autoritie they obtrude[52] in the communion the use of wafers, directly contrary to the Booke of Common Prayer.

They that are to receive it in theire hands must be kneeling: but the people must so receive it, by the wordes of the Booke, and therefore not indifferent in use, thoughe in nature indifferent.

34. Whether the lawe of England doe not leave it a thing[53] indifferent to receive the communion ether kneeling or standing.

45. Add. 21563: 'opinion' (+ Lansd. 199, Add. 48064).
46. Add. 48064 has 'theise' rather than 'the Church at those' (+ Lansd. 119, Add. 21563). Petyt: '. . . fathers of those tymes'.
47. Other MSS omit.
48. *Sic.*

49. Add. 48064: 'ministers' (+ Add. 21563, Lansd. 119).
50. Lansd. 119, Add. MSS omit.
51. The words 'faulte to be amended' are underlined, as is 'fault' at the end of 32, probably by the writer of the marginalia.
52. Add. 21563: 'obtende' (+ Add. 48064).
53. Other MSS omit 'a thing'.

Yf this were a faulte in the bishops this is none excuse to the ministers. But the rites he speaketh of reacheth not to bishops, but only other ministers: see the rubricke of the communion booke.

Yf any have of late done it, it is withoute warrant. All may not be charged for one or two men's faultes. Yf any before time have done it, either they are pardoned or deceassed. But the greatest occasion of takinge this liberty for small cures is the disiunctive (or) used in the statute, whereby the ability in the Latin tongue is not absolutely required.

1. This sorte of men are so used to disobey, that they counte disobedience but a trifle. Yf theire presbyteries were up, shulde not willfull refusall to appere or to doe as is enjoyned be censured with excommunication? Apparance is *extremum in iurisdictionae* withoute which no proceeding can be. Yf the originall causse be but small yet is not the contempt lessoned: *in minori re maior est contumacia*. Neither lawe nor divinity alloweth a penitent sinner (but an obstinate) to be excommunicate.

2. Touching the second parte hereof: to pronounce a man *contumax* is in effect to pronounce him worthy to be excommunicate. *Omnis innovatio periculosa*. It wolde have gyven occasion of quarrell, that

35. By what autoritie the bishops omytt the use of copes, and the bearing of their pastorall staff, which the booke of 2 and 3 Edward 6 prescribeth, whereto the statute of *primo* referreth them for rites, aswell as the minister for ornamentes?

36. Wheras[54] the booke of making ministers, and especially the statute of 13,[55] require the clerke to be learned in the Latin tongue, to have orders geven *in facie ecclesiae*, before the congregation, with a communion: by what warrant[56] of God's booke, canons and lawes of England, they have made unlearned and insufficient ministers, in their closettes and other prophane corners: and whether the Bishop of London's porter[57] were a person so qualified, and made minister as the law requireth?[58]

37. Whether the use of excommunication[1] for trifles (as it is now used) be ageinst the word of God, the prerogative of the Crowne, and the lawe and libertie of England, and articles publisshed upon the suppression of the Pope in the tyme of King Henry 8, and 2[59] whether the remedie that was offered unto them for the mayntenance of their ecclesiasticall jurisdiction by establishing a writte *de contumace capiendo*, was not more agreable both with Christianitie and law, then the custome still used. /

we had devised new censures ecclesiastical not knowen to the primitive Churche.

The Booke is after the accustomed manner, which was to have banes where there was no licence. The statute for dispensations (*Henrici 8ⁱ*) revived by her Majesty dothe in expresse wordes allowe these licences.[60] And many weighty occasions may happen to omitt the banes. A lawe generally sette downe doth not repeale another lawe allowinge of dispensation with such lawe. It is very like the deviser of these was not married with banes.

38. Whether their dispensation of banes in mariages be not ageinst the lawe of England.

f.9

Looke *articulos cleri*, whether commutation be not allowed.[61] Who doe use it more then precise justices of peace where they favour those that have begot bastards?
Her Majesty may call for suche accounte. But the Parlement can no more doe it then they may [c]all civill officers for theire accountes and extortions.

39. Whether the commutation of penance be not ageinst the law of England, and whether it is not meet to call them to accompt for that which they have received: and to what *pios usus,* or rather prophane, the same hath bene ymployed.

The statute for dispensations doth allowe them, and there is no coloure of abrogation by any other lawe.

40. Whether the licences for celebration of mariages, in times heretofore prohibited by the popish law, be not ageinst the law of England.

54. Add. 21563: 'whether'.
55. 13 Eliz, *c*.12 (1571) in *SR*, iv.546–7.
56. Lansd. 119: 'authoritie'.
57. See W. Pierce, *The Martin Marprelate Tracts, 1588, 1589* (1911), pp.46 and n.2, 278.
58. At this point Add. 21563 has the following additional clause: 'And whether Mr Harris Butler, made a minister by the Bishoppe of Peterburowe, and not able to give an accomte in Englishe how many sacramentes there were, being examined by Horne, Bishoppe of Winchester, in

whose diozes he required to serve, were a minster well-qualyfyed or not'.
59. The writer of the marginalia has inserted this number and the '1' over 'excommunication' at the beginning of the paragraph. See T. Fuller, *Church History* (1837), ii. esp. 78–9 for the Ten Articles.
60. The Supremacy Act revived Henry VIII's Act of Dispensations (*SR*, iv.351) which spoke in general terms of archbishops' and bishops' powers (*SR*, iii.672–3).
61. 9 Ed II, stat 1 (1315–16) in *SR*, ii.171–4 does not prohibit commutation.

There is no law nor practise of autority to tolerate suche.

41. Whether the toleration of lawles churches without seeking any reformacion at all, be not ageinst the word[62] of God, and all lawe and honestie.

Let those who have done so be blamed, and suche allso as for money have procured letters and suites for unreasonable leasses by untrue suggestions.

42. Whether for their excessive dilapidacions, spoyles of their woodes and lyvinges contrary to her Majestie's inhibition and all lawes and the estate of the realme, divers of them have not merited to be deprived, according to the canons and lawes of England.[63]

None have bene so inhibited proceeding orderly. No laye person but in causse of bastardy can punishe them. They have none autority to trye who is reputed father. The statute *1° Henrici 7ⁱ* dothe gyve the punishement of incontinent priests by imprisonment unto ordinaries.[64]

43. Whether the sayd commissioners may inhibitt, by vertue of their ecclesiasticall commission, seculer and lay persons to proceede to the punnishment of adulterous priestes, having warrant ether by law or commission under the great seale of England.

He that hathe bene dealte with by one, is not troubled by another. A particuler is no *supersedeas* to a generall.

44. Albeit the high commission ecclesiasticall be extended through the realme of England, in places exempt and not exempt: whether if a speciall commission for the same matter be gotten for the other province or any other dioces; whether both may proceed, ether together or one after an other, to the great vexation of the subiectes of the realme. Or whether the latter commission be not in nature a *supersedeas* to the fyrst.[65]

Let him name those which so hath done. Smithe was convented for usury above 10 in the hundred, which is a causse ecclesiasticall as well as civill by the statute.

45. Seing the commission ecclesiasticall is by the statute ordeyned only for spirituall and ecclesiasticall causes, and by the law of England no ecclesiasticall judge ought to hold plea for causes appertayning to other courtes: what offence it is to call men before the commissioners ecclesiasticall for

meere lay causes, as the Bishop of London did one Smith for a debt owing unto him by Dr Squire his sonne in law.[66]

A greate matter when a thing is concluded of afore, to sette handes severally to it. Is not this done daily at the counsell? And doe they therein contrary to lawe?

46. Whether it be not agreable with law and justice that the warrantes of the ecclesiasticall commission should be made at a sytting, and handes not procured from one to one, contrary to the common lawe and intention of the commission.[67]

Yf they be no more then ordinary they are not. The pursivants are the Queen's men and have allowaunce as others have of like sorte, thoughe the precise sorte for the most parte pay nothing.

47. Whether the fees of their registers and pursuivantes be not extortions ageinst the lawe and commission ecclesiasticall.

None is warranted to take away any thinge but forbidden bookes and popishe stuffe, *etc.* The commission alloweth taking of recognisances, yet for the most parte bondes are taken.

48. What warrant they have by lawe, or in their commission,[68] forceably to enter into mens houses, to search and cary away what pleaseth them, or to take recognisances or bandes, seing by lawe themselves have no autoritie to take recognisances[69] but in cases of matrimony and testamentes.

Here is a charitable question as charitably aunswered by an unchristian surmise.

49. Whether the Bishop of London did not admitt one a pursuivant to attend upon the High Commission that was a notorious papist and recusant, and that received Campion the Jesuite and traitor[70] in his house

62. Petyt: 'law'; Lansd. omits 'of God' (+ other MSS).
63. Lansd. 119 (+ other MSS) has an additional clause here: 'Whether the commissioners ecclesiastical have any authoritye to subdeleague or give commission to their pursuivantes or others, contrarie to the cannons or lawes of Englande'.
64. 1 Hen VII, c.4 (1485) in *SR*, ii.500–1.
65. Lansd. 119 runs this and the next paragraph together.

66. Cf W. Pierce, *The Martin Marprelate Tracts, 1588, 1589* (1911), p.78 and n.1.
67. Lansd. 119 (+ Add. MSS) adds 'and whether one commissioner, in the absence of a nother, maye subscribe his hande, or noe'.
68. Lansd. 199 (+ Add. MSS) adds 'to authorise their pursuivantes'.
69. Add. 21563 omits 'or bandes . . . recognisances'; Add. 48064 has 'or bringe them' rather than 'or bandes'.
70. Petyt omits 'and traitor'.

within the citie of London, belike for that he was a fitt man to plague those that weare zealously affected in the service of God and her Majestie.

I cannot finde by any statute suche oathe required. Yf any other can finde it they willbe ready to doe any thing required of good subiects, but not at every fantastique's call and motion.

v.

50. Whether it be not meant[71] to have the sayd ecclesiasticall commissioners, and all other ecclesiasticall judges, sworne to maynteyne the lawe of England and to iudge accordingly as the statutes require, and as the bishops were sworne in the time of King Henry 8: and whether besides the oath of / her Majestie's supremacie,[72] they ought not to take an other othe, as all other judges and justices doe: and whether this be not the meaning of the statute of 25 Henry 8 concerning their oath of fealtie there mentioned.[73]

In the olde churches all be elective, in the new churches her Majesty presenteth or gyveth; yet are they ecclesiasticall, becausse without dispensation a laye man cannot holde them, and they shulde be instituted to them. Churches donative are ecclesiasticall livings, and so are deaneries called in statutes.
Yf to deprive suche as holde by donation be against lawe, as was iudgd in Barlow's case, yet is it not further then a *premunire*.

There are no such iniustices laied here otherwise then by way of question, much lesse proved.

51. Seing the lawes of this realme esteeme a deanery or other like ecclesiasticall living, being a donative, to be a meere[74] lay thing, not subiect to any ecclesiasticall jurisdiction: whether the commissioners ecclesiasticall, depriving such a one, doe not offend in the highest degree ageinst the prerogative of the Crowne and lawes of England.

52. Whether by such manifold iniustices and contemptes, and other such like proceedinges without sufficient and lawfull warrant, the commissioners ecclesiasticall and bishops be not fallen into the high offence of the *premunire*, together with all their doctors, proctors,

chancellours, officialls, registers, apparitors, *etc.* as in the tyme of King Henry the 8.

O greate kindenes and charity: he which so spitefully belieth them willbe a colde suiter for theire pardon in case they needed it.

53. That if it be so (as there is vehement presumptions so to thinke) we may be humble suters unto her Majestie for their pardons: and for some better order to be established for the quietnes of the Church and realme, that the like inconveniences[75] doe not happen hereafter, which the Lord for his sonne Christe's sake graunt unto us.

54. Fynally, wheras the sentences geven in the time of King Edward 6 for depriving of Stephen Gardiner from the bisshoppricke of Winchester, Bonner from the bisshopprick of London, Heath from the bisshopprick of Worcester, Day from the bishopprick of Chichester, Tunstall from the bisshopprick of Durham, Vessie from the bisshopprick of Exeter, wherin many grave and learned commissioners were ymployed, as the Archbisshop Cranmer, Ridley Bisshop of London, Goodrick Bisshop of Ely, Sir William Peter and Sir Thomas Smith, the Kinge's Secretaries, Sir James Hales, one of the judges of the lande, Mr Gosnoll, Mr Goodrick, Mr Lisle, Mr Stamford, men notable learned in the common lawes of this realme, Mr Leveson and Mr Olyver, doctors of the civill lawe, nevertheles were in the time of Quene Mary revoked and disanulled without Parliament, within the space of three dayes, by

71. Add. 21563: 'meete' (+ other MSS).
72. See *SR*, iv.352 (sect ix).
73. Petyt omits 'there mentioned'; see *SR*, iii.474 (sect ix).

74. Lansd. 119 omits (+ Add. MSS).
75. Lansd. 119 omits (+ Add. 48064).

Quomodo hoc constat? Some of the other here touched being materiall pointes of iustice might happely be alledged of course, howsoever the processe afore were made. But the maine grounde was for that it was supposed to be done in a schisme and so voide.

A very grave consideration, as yf religion shuld change, they wolde allow of any thing done under her Majestie's autority how orderly soever it were. But perhapps he meanes the erecting of theire presbyteries. Truly then we looke for as little moderation or course of iustice. They will reverse all, becausse they holde the government now antichristian and unlawfull, and

f.10   are so farre oute of charity even with the sounde parte of the canon and civil lawe, that they willbe tied in theire consistories to holde no course of justice, but condemne men standing in deniall withoute any proofe upon the bare secret surmise of any sycophant. 'Oh (they say) we must beleve a brother, *etc*', but the party charged shall never see him brought in as accuser or as witnes. And doe they not use to censure men by way of retent, not expressing any causse but *propter caussas nobis cognitas*?

vertue of other commissions for defaultes found in the processes, *viz.* that sometymes the former commissioners had proceeded[76] *ex officio* without autoritie, contrary to the Kinge's ecclesiasticall lawes, sometimes *quod iuris ordo non fuerit servatus etc*: that the articles of the generalitie were of no force,[77] that the interrogatories were ministred to divers persons without knowledge of the deffendants *etc*: that some of the witnesses were examined privately without oath *etc*: that their exceptions and appellations were not admitted, but their persons committed to pryson, *pendente appellatione*: and for these causes, the sayd bishops were restored, and the[78] others put out. It is to be consydered[79] whether if ever the world should change (which the Lord defend) the judgementes and sentences of the commissioners, made by a trialitie[80] of a bisshop, doctor and chaplein, all ignorant of the lawes of England, and most of them unskilfull in the canon[81] lawes, may not[82] be revoked for many / more notorious defaultes and nullities, both in the manner of the proceedinges and the matters, then were in those dayes, to the great and infinite trouble and confusion of the state, and the dishonour of her Majestie's godly and iust government, as her Highnes' syncere meaning is, whatsoever others have of them selves done, or shall doe, without lawe or warrant to the contrary. /

I knowe no one suche triality, but every of them have more skill and experience in the common and canon lawes then this wise penner dothe declare him selfe to have. But yf they were twise as unskillfull as they are, yet the meanest suche triality may compare in ripenes of iudgement with any theire tetrarchy of pastor, doctor, laye or mechanicall elders and deacons of base craftes, yea thoughe they make up a baker's dosen in a parishe. But I cannot see whereat this last consideration driveth, except the meaning be that there shulde be no proceeding in ecclesiasticall causses, lest at a change all be chaunged againe with great confusion.

Yf any have bene since made to the contrary, the bishops are subiect to the penaltie.

f.11

Meanes of Unity.

1.[83] That it would please the reverend ffathers that according to the booke establisshed for making of ministers, their own canons and the statute of 13 of Elizabeth, no ministers be made that are not so qualifyed as is by them required, and[84] that all admissions to benefices, institutions, inductions, tolerations and dispensations be voyd, according to the meaning of the sayd act.

The acte maketh them voide, and is daily as occasion is offered practised.

No reason that he which receiveth orders shulde be punished. Every

2. That some punishment[85] may be inflicted upon such as shall geve and

---

76. The words 'had proceeded' have been underlined, probably by the writer of the marginalia.
77. Other MSS add 'etc'.
78. Land 119 omits (+ Add. MSS).
79. The words 'It is to be considered' have been underlined, probably by the writer of the marginalia.
80. The words 'by a trialitie' have been underlined, probably by the writer of the marginalia.

81. Lansd. 119: 'comon' (+ Add. MSS).
82. Lansd. 119 omits (+ Add. 48064); Petyt: '. . . canon lawes also may not . . .'.
83. The first 4 numbers are in the hand of the text, the rest in that of the writer of the marginalia.
84. Underlined, apparently by the writer of the marginalia.
85. Add. 21563: 'penaltie' (+ other MSS).

man is a partiall iudge of his owne sufficiency.

By the auncient lawe of England the bishops and archbishops are triers of the ministers' sufficiency and not laye men appointed by others. And it must be suche as may be streined by his temporalties, yf he disobey.

This is convenient: but the booke doth not say that none shallbe otherwise gyven, and therefore being omitted maketh no nullity, but dothe subiect the bishop to punishement, being duly proved to have bene done withoute good causse.

Answere to the 5 partes of the 4 article for meanes of unity.[88]

Ad 1. The Queen's supremacy, the Booke of Articles by lawe established (as this penner confesseth), the bookes of Common Praier and ordering of bishops, priestes and deacons, established by Parlement, are no newe matters. These conteine the substance of faithe professed, manner of administration of sacramentes, and government ecclesiasticall of this Churche of Englande. It is very absurde for a man to be a publick minister in that Churche that will not by his hande writing testify his liking of it in these pointes. No man in any other reformed churche is admitted to function ecclesiasticall but he dothe the like: why shulde any in oures have an exemption? Or why shulde we thinke more meanely of our reformation then they doe of theires? Or have lesse care of uniformity, then they? This is no meane of unity to suffer men of all

receive orders otherwise: and that some order may be establsshed for the tryeng of the sufficiencie of the minister by 4 persons, wherof 2 to be chosen by the ordinarie, and two other learned men by the judges before whom the action may depend.[86]

3. That according to the booke of making ministers, no orders be geven but openly in the church, after examination, and in the presence of other ministers, *etc.*[87]

4. That such as be by the law of England admitted to the office of a minister or pastor,[89] and likewise licensed by the universities or other lawfull authoritie to preach, be not without warrant of lawe:
1.[90] urged to the subscription of newe articles:
2. sworne to answer upon articles not fyrst imparted to them:
3. imprysoned without bayle:
4. put to sylence:
5. proceeded against *ex officio*, suspended or deprived, unles upon a lawfull cause, an accusation, information, or presentment, upon oath of 2 lawfull and honest witnesses, according to God's lawe and the law of this lande: and that the partie accused may be admitted by other as many and more witnesses to prove his innocency.

sectes and badde opinions to possesse
churche roomes.

Ad 2. When secret crimes or
publicke misdemeanoures are to be
founde oute, there is no reason that
they have the articles afore they be
sworne, that they may have advise
how to elude and evade them in
aunswering, or yf they cannot to
refuse to sweare. But they heare and
consider of them sufficiently when
they make theire aunsweres before
th'examiner. And they are but
examined of theire owne factes.

Ad 3. When imprisonment is for
safe custody baile is admitted, when
it is for punishement no reason it
shulde be. Is it not so in the Starre
Chamber, Chauncery, *etc.*

Ad 4. He that once breaketh the
orders of the Churche and will not
acknowledge his offence nor promise
reformation after: shulde suche an
one be still suffered? Is this a meane
of unity? Doe they so at Geneva
and other churches?

Ad 5. Touching proceeding upon 2
witnesses, the lawe of the lande is
misreported. For the iury may endite
yf upon theire, or any of theire
conferences, they finde it, or yf one
witnesse be sworne afore them: yea
a triall against a man may passe even
withoute witnesses upon the
knowledge of some of the jury.
But why shulde not proceeding *ex
officio* when a thing is discovered *per*

86. At this point Lansd. 119 has item 10,
and part of item 11, all crossed through.
They were clearly transcribed
erroneously for the second time by the
copyist.
87. Add. 21563 omits.

88. This answer fills f.10v.
89. Add. 21563: 'preacher' (+ Add. 48064,
Lansd. 119); Petyt: 'priest'.
90. Petyt runs paragraphs 1–5 together, with
'nor' between each of them and before
'suspended' in paragraph 5.

clamosam or *credibilem insinuationem* to the iudges, or *per viam denunciationis* when a man hath bene admonished all will not desiste, be accounted the lawe of the lande, seing the statutes call them the Queen's ecclesiasticall lawes and the Queen's ecclesiastical iudges? And being agreable to equity and the lawe of nations, yea and to the daily practise of theire presbyteries?

He that penned this sheweth great skill (no doubte) in rules of justice. When two witnesses have deposed and so knowne to have done one waye, shall other witnesses be produced upon the flatte contrary afterwarde? Must not the one party then be assuredly periured? And why may not the two be the true witnesses as well as the twenty on the other side? Is not this a ready way to subornation of periury? Witnesses shulde be indifferent, and the wante hereof is to be discovered by theire aunsweres to the defendant's interrogatories, and not by examination upon the same or flatte contrary articles after some are knowne to have deposed one waye.

This is so generall that I knowe not what it meaneth.

5. That these may be only adiudged[91] lawfull causes of such proceeding, *viz.* heresy, schisme, abuse, offence, and enormitie according to lawe,[92] and the commission ecclesiasticall and the true meaning of the same.

Yf the lawe commaunde it, who can tolerate? Dothe not the penner urge this him selfe? And how agreeth this with his protestation that onely execution of lawe is sought, and not breache? Belike bishops shallbe

6. That the sayd preachers and ministers be not forced to the use of the surples, cap, tippet, and that with the assent of the sayd[93] reverend ffathers, a charitable and freindly toleration may be by them permitted,

urged for theire breaches of lawe and commissioners thoughe they be onely oversights: but willfull breakers (that thinke lawes to be ungodly) they shallbe gently tolerated?

Onely continuall omission is punished.

Yf this be a good reason then may all the common praier saving the very wordes of institution be omitted.

I take it that apocrypha there were suche bookes not as we call now so (which were then called hagiographi), but Nicodemus' gospell, *Protevangelium Jacobi* and suche like. For yf the iudgement of these councells may be received, then (as I remember) shall the booke of Maccabees and some others not in the Hebrew canon be reade and holden as canonicall.

No man is called, for the lawe alloweth either. Yet for Geneva's sake me thinke they shulde like better of unleavened breade.

as was both in the tyme of King Edward and sometymes in her Majestie's reigne. Nevertheles that any person of that calling, using any undecent and unseemely apparrell, may be punished accordingly.

7. That the omissions of any parcell of the service, being not of the substantiall partes of th'administration of the sacramentes, be not accompted an offence or cause of imposition of sylence, ymprisonment or deprivation *etc.*,[94] especially at such tyme as there is a sermon.

8. That the omission of the crosse in baptisme, questioning with the childe contrary to the rubrick, be not a cause of like offence and proceeding *etc.*,[95] seing they are no essentiall poyntes of the said sacrament.

9. That no man be called in question for not[96] reading the apochrypha contrary to the Councile of Laodicea and fourth of Carthage, the Booke of Common Prayer, the articles, and especially not being in the calender of King Edward, and the booke of *primo* of her Majestie's reigne. /

10. That no man be called in question for celebrating the holy[97] communion in common fyne bread according to the Booke of Common Prayer, nor forced to follow the iniunction confyrming the manner

v.

---

91. Add. 48064: 'adiuged onelie' (+ Lansd. 119, Petyt).
92. The words 'and enormitie according to lawe' have been underlined, probably by the writer of the marginalia.

93. Lands 119 omits (+ Add. 21563).
94. Add. MSS omit.
95. Add. 48064 omits.
96. Lansd. 119 omits.
97. Petyt omits.

of King Edwarde's first Booke for round wafers.

The communion booke is lawe sufficient.

11. That it may be indifferently left,[98] whether weemen wilbe churched or no, seing ther is no law to enforce it, ether canon or English.

Yf any deale otherwise it is colore but not *virtute commissionis*, and so voide.

12. That according to all lawes, the commission ecclesiasticall be not extended to any other statutes or offences then are mentioned in the sayd commission, seing that a statute sayth that ecclesiasticall jurisdiction hath no autoritie to deale where the kinge's other courtes ought to hold plea, and the commission is in all law *stricti iuris*: and that no letters in nature of *supersedeas* be graunted to the contrary.

There is a proviso put in dispensations that yf the living will beare it, a man able to preache shallbe curate.[99]

13. That some good order be taken for non residences and pluralities, so as the cures may be duly served, and the people taught by preaching.

The ordinary course is by banes yet there is great occasion of the other, and the statute expressely alloweth these dispensations.[100] Thoughe neither banes nor licence be had, the marriage willbe perfect.

14. That secrete licences of mariage may be inhibited, seing the lawe of England, that is, the Booke of Common Prayer, requireth banes, and no bisshop may (as we take it) dispence ageinst the lawe of England, and hereupon great inconveniences[101] have ensued.

It is provided for by the late canons.[102] But for murder and other crimes meere civill, no censure may be used without danger of *premunire*, which now he wolde have us incurre, thoughe he terrify us with it elsewhere.

15. That seing the Booke of Common Prayer and the Iniunctions prescribe a publick confession of a publick and notorious offender:[103] that in great faultes of adulterie, incest, notorious fornication, murther, manslaughter *etc*, no commutation of penance be used, but that the parties may[104] make satisfaction openly in the church, before they be admitted to the Lorde's table according to the Booke.

This is not forgotten when neede is: but the waiwarde sorte will neither beleeve one nor other, they are so wedded to theire owne wills.

Contumacy and disobedience to autority is no trifle in St Paul's and St Jude's iudgement.

They are shewed the contrary. Why may not any violater of other lawes seeke the like favoure?

16. That seeing the subiectes of this land are to be ruled by the lawes of the same, and the commission ecclesiasticall is grounded upon sundrye statutes: that in every sentence ageinst a minister lawfully admitted and autorized, the presence and advise of 2 common lawiers in commission be at the least to geve his[105] advice, that nothing be done contrary to the lawe of England.

17. That the high censure of excommunication be not used for trifles, but for great and notorious offences ageinst God's booke, according to the articles of King Henry 8.

18. That, seeing in the preface before the Booke of Common Prayer, the lords bisshops and archbisshop are sufficiently autorized in matters of ambiguitie and doubt to sett downe such order as they shall thinke good, so as it be not contrary to the Booke:[106] seing these peticions of the libertie of the ministers be not contrary to the Booke, nor detract from them any living,[107] lawfull jurisdiction, or praeaeminence: it would please them for unitie's sake, peace of the Church, and advancement of Gode's glorie, to release and restore all such ministers as have bene heretofore put to sylence, suspended or deprived for

98. Add. 21563: '. . . indifferently may be lefte' (+ Add. 48064, Lansd. 119).
99. Cf. *SR*, iii.672–3.
100. Cf. *SR*, iii.672–3.
101. The words 'great inconveniences' have been underlined, probably by the writer of the marginalia.
102. See E. Cardwell, *Synodalia* (1842 ed.), i.139–46 for the canons or articles of 1585.

103. Lansd. 119: 'offence'.
104. Lansd. 119 omits (+ Add. MSS).
105. *Sic.*
106. The words 'be not contrary' have been underlined, probably by the writer of the marginalia. Petyt omits the following words, commencing again at 'seing these peticions . . .'.
107. Lansd. 119 omits 'living', as well as the earlier 'them'.

Why shulde a learned man be suffered to breake lawes more then another? *Justum est aequabile.*

The preachers he most favoureth will doe it in words being urged, but never in pulpitte. And theire doctrine in many materiall pointes doe abridge it no lesse then papists doe.

f.12   Who made this rent? Dothe not this man seeke to nourishe it still, except every man may be permitted to doe what he liste?

Is not this to maintaine a rent?

such causes, and not to proceed with[108] any learned and sufficient[109] ministers in such sort hereafter.

19. That order may be taken, that the sayd ministers shall dutifully agnize[110] her Majestie's supreme autoritie[111] in all Christian modestie, by their preaching seeke to beat downe synne, and to maynteyne true unitie and obedience:[112] / so as the rent[113] which is now in the church and estate may be frendely compounded, to the pleasure of almighty God, encrease of vertue, and conservation of the peace and unitie of this realme, as the statute of *primo* speaketh, and so as her Majestie may be obeyed and served even for conscience sake by all her subiectes being thus duly taught on both sydes,[114] and all poperie and atheisme suppressed and rooted out of men's hartes, which is the only meanes of true and assured obedience, ageinst which all the threateninges and attemptes of the devill, and such our enemies as he mightely possesseth, shall never prevayle. For yf the Lord be with us, who shalbe ageinst us? Otherwise, a terrible wo lyeth upon them that take counsell without him, and unlesse we first seeke the kingdome of God, and thinges that appertayne therunto, the mouth of hym that never lyed nor can dissemble, and whose arme is not shortened, hath assured us that other good thinges can not be yeelded unto us. And therfore for the default hereof, greater inconveniences are like to ensue, which it is our dutie to prevent by all the good meanes we may.[115]

Yf a man shulde aske the question
of these penners and preferrers,
whether yf all these theire meanes of
unity were graunted, will they reste
for ever here? And yf they will, shall
others doe the like? Can they live
withoute theire eldershipps? Can any
churche be withoute them? Doe
they not remember what theire
complices saye of this present
government and what resolute
pointe they are at that they must
and will have their presbyteries
(I thinke) thoughe God and man
shulde say naye? It seemeth
therefore, this is but a colourable
dissembled kinde of dealinge, to
shake firste one or two stones in the
buildinge that the rest may followe.

108. Lansd. 119: 'against'.
109. The words 'learned and sufficient' have
    been underlined, probably by the writer
    of the marginalia.
110. Lansd. 119: 'against'.
111. The words 'Majestie's supreme
    autoritie' have been underlined,
    probably by the writer of the
    marginalia.
112. Petyt starts a new paragraph here
    (+ Add. MSS).

113. The words 'the rent' have been
    underlined, probably by the writer of
    the marginalia.
114. The words 'both sydes' have been
    underlined, probably by the writer of
    the marginalia.
115. Lansd. 119 adds 'And that they be
    hereafter executed in suche sorte onely,
    and none otherwise, then as the plaine
    meaninge and intente of the said statute
    ys' (+ other MSS).

3. Reasons for proceeding in the bills touching the exchequer and purveyors, 7 March

Text from BL Lansdowne 86, copy in the hand of a secretary of Lord Burghley.
Printed. Woodworth, *Purveyance* 24–25 (from Lansdowne; section on purveyors only).

Lansdowne 86, fos.144–5

[Endorsed 'Reasons for proceding in the bills towching the Exchequer and purveyors.']

Purveyors.

That hir Majestie was not, before the bill exhibited, informed *etc.*
That the bill doth presse an understandinge or knowledg in hir Majestie of the grevaunce.

The aunswere.

The informacion to hir Majestie intended by this bill is not untill the same be passed both the Howses of Parlyament, and then hir Majestie hath understanding of the truthe of the grevaunce by the whole bodye of the realme.

The preamble also of the bill importeth hir Majestie's understanding to be by the peticion and complaint of the Commons in this present parlyament, and so no understanding pressed in hir Majestie but by complaint of hir subiectes.

This forme of proceding is and hath bene in all tymes verey usuall that the king by the peticion of his commons assembled in Parlyament provided remedy in Parlyament for the grevaunces of his subiectes, which is moost agreable to his pryncely authoritie and moost acceptable to the subiectes.

That hir Majestie hath skill, will, and abilitie to reforme hir owne howshold.

Aunswere.

Hir Highnes we confesse hath power to punishe hir officers offendinge. Nevertheles, hir Majestie's lawes do not permitt any recompence to be geven to the subiect wronged, by accion or otherwise, or pecuniary punishment to be imposed uppon the offendor but by act of Parliament: which course of punishment by act of Parlyament hath bene allwayes used in the tymes of hir Majestie's moost noble progenitors even from the raigne of King Henry the 3 in this case of purveyors.[1]

Furthermore, a lawe or ordenaunce to have contynuaunce and to bynd, requireth an act of Parlyament.

And necessary it is to have a lawe by act of Parlyament for that the wronges committed by purveyors are so manye, and often donne in places remote, that by reason thereof hir Majestie without greate charges and trobles to hir subiectes can not have understanding of the same.

Before the Commons proceded to the ingrossing of this bill they had care to conferr with Mr Cofferer[2] and the clarkes of the Greene Clothe, and harde their reasons and obiections. /

That hir Highnes' prerogative is towched in this bill.   v.

Aunswere.

The abuse onlie of purveyors is restrayned by this bill, and hir Majestie's purveyaunce or prerogative therein nothing thereby impeached.

The untrewe informacions of purveiors and their deputies is only restrayned by this bill, by which untrewe informacions and suggestions hir Majestie's poore people are many tymes uniustly molested to their greate travaile and expences, and the prerogative of hir Majestie by them greatly abused.

But the authoritie of the Lord Steward, the Threasurer and Comptroller[3] of hir Majestie's honorable Howshold doth remayne in such state as that they, and everie of them, may at their discretions send for any offendor, as before tyme.

To sweare a purveyor that his informacion is trewe semeth to be agreable with like former ordenaunce, whereby it is provided that every purveyor should take an othe for the due execucion of his office. /

Th'Exchequer bill.   f.145

That the Exchequer is hir Majestie's courte concerninge the revenues and prerogatives of hir crowne, and therfor in hir Majestie's power to reforme the same. And that this bill is in preiudice of hir Majestie's tenures, wardshippes and revenues.

Aunswere.

There are many presidentes by act of Parlyament wherby it appeareth that diverse lawes have bene made concerning the order and officers of the same court in releif and ease of the subiect. And therfor this bill importeth no straung or rare matter.

The long pleadinges sought by this bill to be shortned is to the benefitt of the subiect and no preiudice to hir Majestie, and can not be donne without them but by provision in Parlyament.

---

1. The first statutory regulation of purveyors came in 1237 (*Close Rolls, 1234–37*, p.522).
2. This was apparently John Abington: see above, p.66n.9.
3. The earl of Leicester, Sir Francis Knollys, and Sir James Croft respectively.

This bill doth not preiudice hir Majestie concerning hir revenues, wardshipps or tenures any wayes.

Hir Majestie's counsell learned were called to conference and gave advise concerning this bill; with the assent also of the officer (whom it cheiffly concerneth) this bill was framed.

4. Lord Burghley's answer to the Commons' answer on purveyors, 7 March (?)

Text from BL Lansdowne 56, original in Burghley's hand.

Lansdowne 56, f.87.[1]

Answers abruptly to the answers of the Commens.

1. The very wordes of the bill purport that hir Majesty did know at the tyme of the exhibityng of the bill to the Howss, of the misusadg of the officers of the Howshold in molestyng the subiectes uppon complaynt of the purveyors. And all other laws made ageynst abuses of purveyors have bene in form of complaynt, and a request to have the abuses reformed.
2. It is not truly reported that hir Majesty understandeth the abuses by the complaynt, but that she did understood[2] it befor the complaynt; and therby is inferred a lack to hir Majesty that she did know the abuse of hir officers and wold not reform them.
3. Answered in the first. And all laws made for purveyors vary from this form wholly, as [illegible], *28 Edwardi 1,* [MS blank][3] *Edwardi 3, 25 Edwardi 3, 28 Edwardi 3, 36 Edwardi 3, 20 Henrici 6ᶦ, 23 Henrici 6ᶦ, 28 Henrici, 6ᶦ,* and no such form in the last statute, *2 et 3 Philippi et Mariae.*[4]

Ther ar many laws to punish purveyors by deth, and many laws to inquire of them by the justices of peace and to hang the purveyors. *Second answer.*
Ther ar laws also ageynst any that will trouble any person for resistyng of purveyors.

---

1. There is an endorsement on f.87v. Though its heading is damaged at the begininning, it continues 'mentioned in the statute. 1588'.
   There is then a list of items:
   'All kindes of spice and wares
   wyne
   butter and egges
   All kindes of wild fowle
   checkins
   stockes [?]
   [blank]
   wood and cole
   [blank]
   haye and wettes [?]'
   This may refer to items covered in the bill.
2. *Sic.*
3. There are several statutes: see *SR*, i.262, 265–6, 276–7, 288, 301.
4. The statutes cited are in *SR*, i.137, 319, 347–8, 371–3; ii.320–1, 339–40; 354–5; iv.282–3.

5. Henry Jackman's speech on the bill of subsidy, 10 March

Text from BL Lansdowne 55, original draft.
Printed. Strype, *Annals* 3. ii.561–8 (from Lansdowne, somewhat rearranged).

Lansdowne 55, fos.180–3.[1]

[The first three lines are crossed out and virtually illegible; then the speech goes on:]

'in respect wherof, together with the consideracion of my manifold defectes, I maye iustlye feare once to open my mouth in this honorable and grave assemblye, and to offer to speake to this bill which maye seeme to have had so generall and currant a consent it maye seeme superfluous; and especially att this tyme after the ingrossinge therof, after the resolution theron by a greate grave and wise comittee, I maye be deemed presumptuous, but to speake agaynste this bill whereby the service of her Majestie and the whole realme maye be suppposed to be hindered it maye be thought impious, it maye be thought daungerous. The consente of the greater parte of this House as I take it concludeth all the reste att the question, but excludeth none in the arguinge, this tyme indeede I confesse to be somwhat unseasonably chosen, but yet it is nowe tyme to speake or elles for ever hereafter to be silent; and herein I do somwhat relye upon the authoritye of an honourable parsonadge who att the puttinge of this bill to engrossinge affirmed it in his experience not to be unusuall to have a bill argued unto betweene the third readinge and the question ij or iij dayes.[2]

'The matter likewise wherof I am to speake I must needes acknowledge to be of far greater depth then my shallowe brayne is able to sounde, and my selfe also to be incomparablye unequall both to the meaneste of the comittees who have taken paynes therin as also to as many as before me have spoken therunto; so that of the one and the other, *scilicet* matter and men, I maye well saye with the poet, "*Quis tantae pondera molis sustineat? Tantisque queat se opponere viris?*"[3] As for the service of her Majestie and my countrie unto which two I owe all subiection and dutye, I am so far from withdrawinge eyther my selfe or others therfrom that my speach shall have none other ende then the advancement therof, neyther as I hope shall in that behalfe neede any other apologie then it selfe. /

v.   'The principall cause which moveth me to speake at this tyme is that whereas I am, thoughe unworthyly, a Member of this House, and therefore

desirous to conioyne my selfe by consent in all good proceedinges with the
bodie therof, I have hitherto in this gret matter of the subsidie receaved so
small satisfaction for the direction of my iudgment, that unles I should manifestly dissent from myne owne conscience, which neither this place requireth
nor Christianity alloweth, I cannot consent with the bill therin: as one therefore rather desirous to be satisfied and drawen to consent with the reste, then
to persuade or drawe others to consent with me (which is a burden far unfitt
for my shoulders).[4] Thus have I presumed to deliver myne opinion, hopinge
that if any thinge have escaped me worthye reprehension throughe ignorance,
it shalbe excused by reason of myne infancye in this practise of speakinge.[5] Or
if any parte of my speech maye receave a double construction, it maye be
defended by your beste and most favourable interpretation.

'My meaninge is not to dispute whether it be lawfull to graunt a subsidie or
no, for then our saviour Christe him selfe would stop my my[6] mouth with his
answer to the captious questionistes in the 22ᵗʰ of Mathewe, for sure the very
impression and superscription of our monie putteth us in minde to whome it
doth appertayne. Neyther will I argue whether it be necessarye to graunt a
subsidie or not, but therein content my selfe with the example of our Saviour
who in the 17ᵗʰ of Mathewe payde his xxᵈ out of the fishe's mouth for himselfe
and Peter.[7]

'Nor yett whether it be convenient to contribute towarde the necessarye
expences of our lawfull princes, for St Paule teacheth me in the 13ᵗʰ to the
Romaines[8] that tribute appertayneth unto them of dutie as unto governors sent
by God for the well orderinge and guidinge of his people. /

'But the question wherin I desire to be resolved is whether it be necessarye   f.181
or convenient for us at this tyme to tender unto her Majestie suche a Subsidie,

1. Lansd. 55, fos.186–7 contains a collection of notes, mainly quotations from biblical and other sources, relating to foreigners and the subsidy, the subjects of two speeches prepared for this session and attributed to Henry Jackman. The document bears no heading and its format suggests that it was a preliminary gathering of thoughts on the subjects. A high proportion of the quotations are from Latin sources; and some of them are employed as supporting quotations in the two speeches which are printed here. As far as the subsidy was concerned, these included references to two parliaments of Henry III and Henry VIII (the former was described as 'much like unto this', though the words were deleted).

2. This paragraph is marked with a vertical line in the margin. Its beginning and ending are also marked with 'o', which mark appears again on the same side of the folio, after '*viris*'. The opening section on f.180v is also marked by a marginal line. These markings seem to be related to the arrangement of the text as printed by Strype, which starts 'Whereas I am, tho' unworthy . . .'.

3. The mark 'o' appears here. Cf. Ovid, *Metamorphoses*, 5, 1–2.

4. The passage 'The principall cause . . . for my shoulders' is marked with a vertical line in the margin. 'Epilogue' also appears in the margin, though Strype links it with 'Thus I have presumed . . .' and moves it to the end of the speech.

5. At this point 'place' has been deleted, and 'practise of speakinge' inserted in the same hand as the text.

6. *Sic.*

7. Mat 22: 17–18; Mat 17: 27.

8. The words 'in the 13ᵗʰ to the Romaines' are underlined. Rom 13: 1–7.

and in such maner and forme as the purport of this bill offereth unto us⁹ hath
bin by divers heretofore moved.¹⁰ That is in breefe a double Subsidie to be
payde in fower yeres. And firste for the necessitie therof. I cannot denie but,
(if it were a charge imposed upon us by her Majestie's commaundment, or a
demaunde proceeding from her Majestie by waye of requeste,) that I thinke
there ys not one amongste us all eyther so disobedient a subiecte, in regarde of
our duty, or so unthankefull a man in respect of the inestimable benefites
which by her and from her we have receaved, which would not with franke
consent both of voyce and harte moste willinglye submitt him selfe therunto,
without any unreverent inquiry into the causes therof. For it is continuallye in
the mouthes of us all that our landes, goodes, and lives are att our Prince's
disposinge, and it agreeth verye well with that position of the civill lawe which
sayth, "*Quod omnia regis sunt.*" But howe? "*Ita tamen ut omnium sint, ad regem
enimque potestas omnium pertinet, ad singulos proprietas,*" so that although it be
moste trewe that her Majestie hath over our selves and our goodes *potestatem
imperandi*, yet it is as trewe that untill that power com[mand], which no doubt
will not com[mand] without very iuste cause, every subiecte hath in his owne
proprietatem possidendi. Which power and commaundement from her Majestie
because we have not yet receaved I take it (savinge reformation) that we are
freed from that cause of necessitie. An other cause of necessitye is the
daungerous estate of our common welth in respecte of invasion by our
common and mightye enemies which reason because, in my heareinge, it hath
bin the principall and almost onely perswader for the bill requireth a more
sufficient and exquisite answer then perhaps I shall make unto it. I have before
acknowledged it to be a necessarye argument to move all men to unwonted
and extraordinary contribution, and I muste herin needes subscribe to a wise
and lerned man of our age who sayth that they be "*pia quae civibus imperantur
tributa sine quibus civitas ipsa funditus sit interitura.*" But as I doe assuredly hope
that our countrye is att this present in no such desperate or daungerous case,
the very / teeth and iawes of our mightieste and moste malicious enemye
havinge bin so latelye broken, and the sworde of his greateste confederat more
latelye sheathed in his owne bosom, besides the hope which maye iustlye be
conceaved of the expedition nowe setting forward¹¹ for the defeatinge of all
their plottes and disapointing of all their devises: as I saye, I do assuredlye hope
that our country for these reasons is in no suche great daunger as is pretended,
so may I constantly affirme that althoughe by waye of concession I shoulde
graunt it so to be, yett the subsidie required by this bill to be graunted coulde
geve little or no relefe therunto. For as a pardon cometh unprofitablye to an
offender after his execution, or a potion to a patient after his death, or
recoverye to health, so if the stroke of Gode's enemy and ours be likely to lite
upon us eyther this yere as it hath bin heere affirmed, or the next as it is in my
smale iudgment more likelye, I doubte not but you will all consent with me
that a subsidie, the firste parte whereof is not to be payde till the end of three
yeres (for unto that onelye my speech hath relation), can serve neyther for paye
nor provision in defence therof. "*Utilis est medicina suo quae tempore venit,*" sayth

a poet, and *sapientia sera* is sayde to be *proxima stultitiae*. And thus havinge breefelye sett downe myne opinion againste the necessitie of this graunt I will by your favourable pacience with like brevitie declare such inconveniences as I have conceaved maye ensue therby. It is not unknowen to you all, but moste sensiblye felt throughe the whole realme what charge and expences the commons therof were this laste sommer driven unto by preparation and provision of armour, horses, apparell and other necessaries for their iuste and naturall defence againste the pretended invasion. You knowe that since that tyme a paymente of the subsidie laste graunted hath bin made unto her Maiesty. There is none of us ignorant what nombers of privie seales are even nowe dispersed throughe the whole realme to the emptyinge of men's cofers and impayringe of their stockes, with what redines, dutye and good will these thinges have bin and shalbe perfourmed by the subiectes no man heere may doubte. /

'Nowe then to bringe in a newe and unacustomed continuation of f.182 paymentes one to rowle in the necke of another, *sicut unda supervenit undam*, I knowe not by what warrant of reason or conscience we maye do it, especiallye consideringe that it is not a matter necessarylye imposed upon us as I sayde before, but voluntarylye to be offered by us. Surely one speaketh verye playnelye and sayth, "*Asini est clitellam ferre libentur*"; but I will as it becometh me use more reverence in this honourable place, and saye that I thinke it not convenient that we should laye burdens on our owne shoulders, or put shackles on our owne feete. But it is still urdged that the service of her Majestie and safegard of our owne selves is provided for hereby. Surelye by your favourable pacience I will attempt to prove that by this course, her Majestie's service shall rather be hindered then furdered, and our selves rather indaungered then secured. It was very gravelye and wiselye delivered unto us in her Majestie's presence att the begyninge of this Parlament by my Lord Chauncelor *quod tutius fide quam ferro regnant reges*, and surely if *auro* were put in the place of *ferro*, the sentence notwithstandinge were never the lesse trewe. For it is not the abundance of Treasure, nor the multitude of possessions, neyther the infinite nombers of men which mayntayne and establishe a kinge in his throne, but the fayth, love, loyalty and contentment of his people and subiectes: which as her Majestie hath hitherto from her firste inauguration moste deservedlye had, and that as fullye and amply as ever had anie prince in Europe, so were it greatlye to be lamented that nowe throughe our defaulte any such discontentment should be bred in the mindes and hartes of her people whereby their accustomed affections towardes her might receave the leste diminution. And surelye whosoever they be that by newe and strange exactions on the people shall go about to fill up the Prince's cofers, may perhaps please the Prince by servinge his tourne for the tyme but shall in the ende be founde to have don him but

9. The words 'the purport of the bill offereth unto us' are underlined (for deletion?).

10. The words 'hath bin by divers heretofore moved' are inserted in the same hand as the text.

11. Drake's Portuguese expedition.

bad service. The answer of the Emperor Tiberious unto his questors or tresurers which perswaded him for the repayringe of his Tresurye to lode the provinces with tribute is worthy eternall memorye, which was that it is "*boni pastoris tondere oves non autem deglubere.*" And the practise of the Romanes, wylles Annibal besieged their citie, is of all mations worthy to be imitated, /

v.   ffor beinge hardly pressed by the siege and their common tresurie quite exhausted, the Senate tooke counsell together for the redresse of these mischiefes, som of them persuadinge like Tiberius his treasurers that the people were to be charged with a subsidie or imposition, but the greater and wiser sort (whose authoritie also prevayled) would by no meanes assent therunto, thinkinge it especially in that tyme of extremity moste inconvenient by new taxes and impositions to discontent the people, in whome the strength and defence of their citie consisted. But what did they? Mary, they decreed that a contribution should be made by waye of a benevolence, and they them selves would firste go unto the Triumviros Mensarios which were officers apointed for that receipt, and there bestowe so liberally of their owne that the inferior people should by their example be incited to a large and bountifull Contribution. But what followed? The people (as the story sayth) cam in so faste, and the monie in such aboundance, "*ut nec Triumviri Mensarii accipiendo, nec scribae referendo sufficerent.*" It is written by Livy in his 26th booke, and needeth no application.[12] Onelye this I would wishe to be considered, whether if we shoulde by extremity be put to the like shifte for a benevolence before the payment of this latter subsidie, the graunt of this woulde not doe greater hurt to that contribution then it selfe could do good when it shalbe payde. I could with enumeration and amplification of the inconveniences which maye growe by this double subsidie deteyne you longer then eyther it is fitt for me to speake, or pleasinge to you to heare. But I will hasten to an end.

'It maye by obiected that this subsidie cannot be an occasion of any such greevans or discontentment as is spoken of, or if it were, that the sharpnes therof is well alayed and tempered by the prolonginge of the payment. Surely it maye be that to all or the moste parte of this honorable House, who both in respecte of their abilitye maye, and by reason of their liberall education and great wisdom will submitt them selves unto it, it is a light and easie burden and accounted but for a fleabytinge. But unto the poore and needie countryman, to the artificer whose tresure is alwayes in his hande, for whome we do sit heere more principally then for our selves (under correction) it cannot be accounted but for a punishment. Samuell in his oration which he made to the

f.183   Israelites when they would needes have a kinge, amongeste / other burdens which he toulde them they should beare under that kinde of of government, accounteth the payment of the tenth of their seede, their viniardes, and their sheepe.[13] Which maye prove that then it was reckoned for a payne; and the sutes, exclamations, complaintes, and lamentations of the comons of this realme, well knowen to the moste part of this House, which they make eyther att the assessinge or collection of these subsidies or both, do sufficientlye testifie unto us that they account it nowe a punishment. And as for the prolonginge of the payment, I am so far from thinkinge that it is any mitigation of the punishment that I am rather persuaded that it is increased thereby. For as it is well sayde of Seneca in the bestowinge of benefites "*quod bis dat qui cite dat*"; so is it as truely spoken of another in the inflictinge of punishmentes that *dilatio poenae* is *duplicatio poenae*; and of another that the irrevocable sentence of death beinge once pronounced it is *misericordiae genus cito occidere*. Neyther have I heard any greater reason why the paynes of hell are intollerable but because they are perpetuall, ffor *malorum sensus accrescit die*, and *leve est miserias ferre, perferre grave*. Seinge then that it is apparant that this imposition by howe much the greater it shalbe by somuch the more greevous it wilbe to the meane, ignorant, and untaught commons of this lande, who bende all their thoughtes and actions to the procuringe and maintayninge of their private commoditie; and seinge that their longe meditation theron will increase and double this their greefe and punishment, and that no man howe well natured or nurtured soever he be can well content himselfe with payne and greefe, I hope you see as cleerelye as you heere that the subsidie required by this bill to be graunted muste of necessitie breede a discontentment in the mindes and hartes of her Majestie's people. Of which their discontentment what might ensue and followe I woulde be very loth to divine. What if a dearth of vittayles? What if restraint of traffique by meanes of wars? Whatt if therby occasion should be geven to seditious and trayterous whisperers to augment and increase it? Sure I am that hereof could followe no good service to her Majestie, no great safetye to our selves, no benefite to the common welth. But we should then all to late crie, "Woe be to them that brought the firste sparke to the kindlinge of this fire". And it hath often bin proved heretofore by experience that monie in this sort obteyned from the people hath bin spent in greater measure in the pacyfiing of them of whome it was collected. /

'The president besides maye be daungeros both to our selves and our posteritie, for we comonly see that in all counsells and deliberations a president is a forcible and perswadinge argument, and it is a wise and true sayinge that "*Diuturnitas temporis efficere potest ut quod pernicioso more et exemplo convaluit potentius ipsa lege dominetur*". And althoughe I have before graunted you by waye of concession that her Majestie's will and comaundment is a necessarye argument to perswade us to the passinge of this bill, yet leste it maye be thought of more absolute necessitie then perhaps it is requisite it shoulde, I will sett downe a president or two wherin the like cases have in this House bin determined hertofore. In the 39ᵗʰ of Hary the 3[14] a parlament was somoned wherin was required an extraordinary reparation of the kinge's tresurye by a subsidie, the Commons because the demaunde was greater then usually had bin payde would graunt no subsidie at all.'[15]

v.

12. Livy, 26, xxvi, 11.
13. 1 Sam 8, esp. 15–17.

14. Cf. S. K. Mitchell, *Taxation in Medieval England* (1951), pp.194, 214–18 for 1254.
15. *Sic.*

6. Henry Jackman's speech on the bill against foreigners, 12 March (?)

Text from BL Lansdowne 55, original draft.
Printed. Strype, *Annals* 3. ii.568–73 (from Lansdowne, omitting opening paragraphs).

Lansdowne 55, fos.188–9

'I am not ignorant how trewly and wisely it is said by the orator that itt is *magnum quiddam onus atque munus suscipere et profiteri se esse omnibus silentibus unum magno in conventum hominum maximis de rebus audiendum.*[1]

'In regard wherof, together with the consideration of my manifold defectes and disabilityes both in nature, arte and exercise of speaking itt might better beseeme me to lende myne eares to receave instruction, then to bende my tongue to geve information.

'Notwithstandinge, the regard of the person which most unworthely is imposed upon me, and the care which I take of my conscience and duty in this place have so far pevayled[2] with me that I have by the advise of a wise writer rather resolved *prudentis viri nomen amittere quam boni conscientiam non retinere.*[3]

'Of my selfe no more, as beinge an obiect most unworthy the attentive eares and mindes of this grave and reverend counsell, and a subiect most unfitt to consume their pretious tyme.

'But to the bill now red and the matter therin conteyned a word or two and that breifelye.

'This bill as I conceave offereth to the consideracion of this honourable House a controversie betweene the naturall borne subiect of this realme and the stranger inhabitinge amongst us.

'Surely before I proceede any furder I finde my selfe doubly affected and doubly distracted.

'For on the one side the very name of my countrye and nation is so pleasaunt in myne eares, and so delitefull to my hart that I am compelled to subscribe unto him who, havinge rehersed all the degrees of coiunction[4] and societye, in the end concludeth thus that *omnes omnium charitates una patria complexa est.*[5] In somuch that in this case wherein my country is a party, and especiallye that parte of my country which as itt is the head of the bodye, so ought itt of me for speciall respect to be most honoured and loved in this case I saye mee thinkes I must needes iudg my selfe to be no competent judge.

'But on the other side, when in the person of the straunger I consider the miserable and afflicted estate of these poore exiles, who together with ther countries have lost all or the greatest comfortes of this life, and for want of frendes lye subiect and exposed to the wronges and iniuryes of the malitious and ill-affected (for that the condicion of straungers and travellers is that they have *multa hospitia* but *paucos amicos*), in these repectes I saye I am moved with an extraordinarye commiseration of them, and feele in my selfe a sympathie and fellow sufferinge with them. In the thirde place I looke on my selfe, or rather into my selfe, not as I am of my selfe which is nothinge, but as I am intended heere to be, which is more then I can be, thoughe no more then I ought to be. *Judicis est in causis verum sequi, seponere affectus, admittere rationem ex rebus ipsis non ex personis iudicare.* And therefore I pray you that I may with like brevitye lay before you my judgment in the matter, as I have declared myne affections to the parties.

'The bill requireth that it may be inacted that no alienes borne, not beinge denizens nor havinge served as apprentises by the space of 7 yeres, should sell any wares by retayle. /

'Because it is required that this may be made a lawe lett us first consider how   v. itt may stande with the groundes and foundations of all lawes which are the lawes of nature and the lawe of God; and secondly, with the profit and commoditie of the common wealth.

'I will not detayne you with mathematicall or philosophicall discourses to shew that the whole earth beinge but a pointe in the center of the worlde will admitt no division of dominions, for *punctum* is *indivisibile,* or that man (as Plato sayeth) is no earthlye but a hevenly creature and therefore hath *caput tanquam radicem infixum caelo.*[6] Neyther will I stand upon itt that the residence or continuance of one nation in one place is not of the law of nature which beinge in itt selfe immutable would then admitt no such transmigration of people and transplantation of nations as in dayly experience we see. But I will onelye propose unto you two groundes of nature as more proper to this purpose: the one that we shoulde geve to others the same mesure that we would receave from them, which is the goulden rule of justice; and the other that we ought by all good meanes *tum artibus, tum opera, tum facultatibus devincire hominum inter homines societatem* but *qui civium rationem dicunt esse habendam, externorum negant hi dirimunt comunem humani generis societatem.*[7]

'The law of God is next which in infinite places commendeth unto us the the[8] good usage and enterteynment of straungers.

'In Deuteronomy God loveth the straunger, geveinge him ffoode and rayment, therefore love ye the straungers.[9] In Leviticus, if a straunger soiourne with you in your lande ye shall not vex him; but the straunger that dwelleth with you

1. Not in the notes on fos.186–7.
2. *Sic.*
3. Not in the notes on fos.186–7.
4. *Sic.*
5. Cf. Cicero, *De Officiis,* I, 57.

6. The notes (f.186) attribute this to 'Plutarch 549'.
7. Cf. Cicero, *De Officiis,* III, 28 (f.186: 'Cicero, *Officiis,* 3°. 212'.
8. *Sic.*
9. Deut 10: 18 (as in f.186).

shalbe as one of your selves, and you shall love him as your selves, ffor ye were straungers.[10]

'In Ezekiell itt appeereth that the land of promise was by Gode's appointment alotted aswell to the stranger as to the Israelite, ffor "they shall part inheritaunce with you in the middest of the tribes of Israell", sayth the text.[11]

'And the comaundement which is geven for the observation of the Saboth forbiddeth the straunger on that day to labour, whereby itt may well be gathered that att other tymes itt is lawfull fer him to exercise his lawfull trade or vocation.

'So that for this point I may well conclude with Mr Calvin who saith that itt is "*Barbaries et immanitas inhospitalis miseros advenas opprimere qui in fidem nostram confugiunt.*"[12]

'It hath byn confessed that the argumentes used against this bill do carrye with them a greate shew of charytye, which (saye they) beinge severed from pollicye is now no charitye but folly.

'I will answer that if itt be a good rule and principle in divinitye that in comparison betweene the lawes morall and ceremoniall *moralia sunt anteponenda ceremoniis*,[13] it ought much more to be overluled[14] in all Christian consultations that *humana sunt postponenda divinis*,[15] and therfore that pollicy without charity is impiety. But lett us consider how this charitye overthroweth our pollicye: forsoothe it is said generally by impoverishinge the naturall subiect, and enrichinge the stranger, by nourishinge a scorpion in our bosomes, by takinge the children's bread and castinge itt to dogges. /

f.189   'And this is more particulerly as they say effected by 2[16] meanes. First by the multitude of retaylers, for the more men exercise one trade the les is everye one of their gayne; secondly by the straungers' pollicye, [which consisteth eyther in providinge their wares in such sort that they may sell better cheape then the naturall subiect, or els by perswadinge our[?] people that they may so doe; and thirdlye by their frugalitye in diett and apparall, by meanes wherof they may apportion their gaynes to their chardges.][17]

'To the generall accusation, if I should use none other defence but this that these people, (the denizens I meane, for of them and for them onely do I speake) havinge renounced their obedience to their naturall governors and countries, and subiected them selves even by their othes to the obedience of her Majestie, her lawes and aucthority, are nowe to be accounted of us thoughe not naturall yett naturalized subiectes, thoughe not spronge up from our rootes, yett firmlye ingraffed into our stocke and body, thoughe not our children by procreation yett our brethren by adoption; if (I say) I should use none other defence but this, I doubt not but I might in the opinions of all or the moste parte of this honourable House cleere them of the envious title of the rich stranger, of the odious name of the venemous scorpion, and of the uncharitable terme of contemptible doges. But because the strength of the generall accusation consisteth in the validity of the particuler obiections I wil, by your good favours, in a word or two make answer unto them.

'It cannot be denied but that the number of retaylers is by these denizens somwhat increased, but yet not somuch that the burden of them is so insupportable as is pretended, for by the confession of their adversaries they[18] are not in all, denizens and not denizens, in and about this Citye, of all maner of retaylers above the number of 50 or thereaboutes. Wherof it is probable that the denizens whome onely my purpose is to maintayne exceed not the nomber of 30, who, beinge devided into many trades and compared with the infinite numbers of retaylers of all sortes in the Citye of London and the suburbes therof, cannot in common reason somuch impoverish any one trade or company by their number onely as is suggested. As touchinge their pollicy which consisteth in drawinge of customers to their shops or houses, eyther by sellinge cheape indeede or ells by perswadinge us that they sell their wares more cheape then our nation can doe, I take it (savinge reformation) very easy to be answered. For if the first be true that they do indeede sell better penyworthes then have we no cause to punish but to cherishe them as good members of our common wealth, which can by no meanes better be enriched then by keepinge downe the price of forren commodities and inhaunsinge the value of our owne. Besides, the benefite of cheapnes of forren commodities by somuch exceedeth the benefit of deare prises, by howmuch the number of buyers of them exceedeth the number of sellers, which is infinitely.

'But if the seconde be true, that itt is but our error to beleve that they sell their wares better cheape then our nation doth, then surely I cannot but thinke itt very greate iniustice to punishe them for a fault committed by us.

'It hath bin furder obiected unto them in this House that by their sparinge and frugall livinge they have bin the better inabled to sell good peniworthes. It seemeth we are much streightned for argumentes that are driven to accuse them for their vertues.'

10. Lev 19: 33–4 (f.186: '33').
11. Ezek 47: 22 (as in f.186).
12. The notes (f.186) attribute this to 'Calvin 343'.
13. This quotation does not appear in the notes.
14. *Sic.*
15. This quotation does not appear in the notes.
16. Altered from '3'.
17. The first part of this section is crossed out by an oblique line, and the end of it is scored through.
18. MS damaged: ? 'they'.

7. *Committee on the bill for soldiers, 24 March*

Text from BL Lansdowne 58, ? original.

Lansdowne 58, f.164.

[Endorsed in same hand as text 'The obiections and answeres touchynge the byll for musters, captaynes and souldyoures. Marche 24, 1588.']

The preamble.[1]
A new proviso
therefore to
amend the
former.

The commytty for captains and soldyors, *Mar[c]ii* 24, 1588.

No defect in the new law lyk to the old.[2]

1. This byll as imperfecte, and defectyve, and more penall.

No such use.
Yet not
unprovided.

2. Noble men not to be exempted for example.[3]

The old lawe
more streyt. *for
all ther armur.*[4]

3. Suche armor as they have or oughte to have, for his owne person: no lawe, and some speciall armor.

By this the
service may be
defrawded. And
the lords
constrained to
provide remedy.

4. Armor to be borowed: if perhaps a man save yeanoughe for hym self or his frend.

*It is an usuall
word in many
laws, and fraud is
tryable.*

5. To defrawde the servyce: the meanynge thereof not knowne.

The old
lawe.*Without
chang.*[5]

6. A pretence for the benefyte of corporacions, and this contrary, for that the townemen may be drawen farre out of there libertyes.

No suche lawe
or custome.

7. Armor to be the souldyors' owne, *jure belli, post commissam pugnam.*

8. The chainge for a better, or to be sold for necessyty.

The old lawe is harder.

9. The armor may be taken away from any person, by reason of a lyberty reserved to the generall.

4° et 5° *added new* upon reasonable respectes.

10. The penalty to great, *yz.* 10 tymes the valewe and triple damages.

The old lawe 4° et 5° imbeselinge hurtefull by experience.[6]

11. The burden to great to certyfye the deathe or departures of the souldyors.

The old lawe *bound to do it every month.*[7]

12. No fellony, the armurye beinge in there owne custody *etc.*

Servantes fellons for xl s *by a li* and great harme by imbesyllynge of powder.

---

1. Marginal notes are in the same hand as the text, though the italicised words are in Burghley's hand.
2. The acts principally concerned are those for horse, armour and weapons, and for musters, 1557–8 (4 & 5 Ph & Mary, cc.2, 3 in *SR*, iv.316–20, 320–2), though Henrician and Edwardian statutes are cited there.
3. Noblemen had to provide horses and armour according to the law of 1557–8,
though allowance was made for horses lost on service abroad.
4. Cf. *SR*, iv.316 (sect. i) where individuals were liable to provide armour for more than one horse.
5. Cf. *SR*, iv.322 (sect. x).
6. Cf. *SR*, iv.321.
7. Cf. *SR*, iv.40 for sect. vi of 2 & 3 Ed VI, c.2, the 1548 act for captains and soldiers.

8. *Petition for the suspension of penal laws, March*

Text from Inner Temple, Petyt 538/36, copy.

Petyt 538/36, fos.327–9

To the Queen's most exellent Majestie, our most dread and Soveraigne Ladie.

In most humble manner sheweth unto your most exellent Majestie your most humble faithfull and obedient subjectes the commons assembled in the high court of Parliament, that wheras we have for divers good consideracions willinglie and freelie yealded unto your Highnes a double subsidie, otherwise then hath bene in former times accustomed, which we beseech the Lord to blesse for your Majestie's contentment and the service of the whole realme: fforasmuch as we the knightes and burgesses are to be imployed in the assessinge and levying of the same; seeing it may be that the people in our cuntries, who have bene very lately charged with subsidies, loanes, finding of shipps, and other services, and which are now in a manner destitute of all manner of forreyne trades and meanes of gaine, wilbe aggreived with our doings; to the intent we may be the better able to satisfie and content all men, franckly (as we have done) to condescend therunto, we have thought it convenient most humblie to beseech your most royall Majestie, that according to your gratious pleasure delivered unto us from the Lord Chauncellor and others, touching your gratious disposition to unburthen the realme of a heavy yoke of divers unnecessary and penall Lawes, if your Highnes shall see cause to end this session of Parliament before the same may conveniently be done by actes, as is to be feared – considering what time hath bene already spent, and how few bills have passed both Houses – it would please your Majestie, of your aboundant goodnes, before our departure from hence to give order that th'execucion of the sayd penall statutes and bills lately desired to be enacted for the benefitt and ease of your sayd subjectes may be, by your Majestie's royall authority in the best and most effectuall manner that may be in lawe, suspended untill the next parliament or session of Parliament; and soe by open proclamacion before th'end of this session signified to all the realme, to th'entent we may be the better able to content all persons, and to doe your Majestie such further service as our desire is in that behalfe. And wheras (most gratious Soveraigne) by the space of many yeares we have made divers complaintes in this honourable and high court of Parliament (as in all former times hath bene accustomed) touching sundry ecclesiasticall disorders, which your Highnes heretofore referred to Lords Bishops, to th'intent the same might

be by them redressed: but nevertheles continue / still, to the great displeasure   v.
of almightie God, and breach of the peace and unitie of this realme, wherby
Poperie and atheisme are marvailouslie increased, and many of your naturall
subjectes for lack of good instruction (being th'only meanes to worke godly
and dutifull obedience) have bene and are daily withdrawen from their
bounden allegiance to favour your mortall enemie the Antichrist of Rome, to
the subvercion and perill of your Majestie's person and estate. Albeit our
meaning be not to intermedle any whit with your Majestie's prerogative royall,
to whom it appertaineth to reforme and redresse such causes; yet seeing we
have bene called hither by your Majestie's writt, which hath declared your
Highnes' gratious meaning to the whole realme to consult of matters even
concerning the Church, and to serve as eyes to represent and lay before your
Majestie the lamentable wantes and disorders in the same, and as mouthes in
the name of all the people of this land to crave and desire a reformacion at your
Majestie's handes, both for the discharge of your Majestie's dutie towardes
God, and for the ease of your poore and obedient subjectes; yea, and for the
assurance of your Highnes' owne estate and peace of the realme, by preventing
such inconveniences as by increase of atheisme, Popery, and divisions may
happen, we most humblie upon the knees of our heartes beseech your
Majestie, as the Lord's anoynted and our only soveraigne, to provide some
better remedies for such disorders then hitherto we have fellt by such persons
as your Majestie heretofore committed that charge unto. And wheras by
certaine statutes made in the tyme of your Majestie's ffather of famous memory,
upon the suppression of the Pope's usurped and tyranicall government, and also
confirmed and revived in the begining of your Majestie's blessed raigne, we be
taught that in the lawe (which men commonly call canon) divers things are
contained which are repugnant to your Majestie's prerogative royall, and the
lawes and liberties of this your highnes' realme of England which hitherto
never acknowledged any other lawes then such as either were made in the
same, or ells only soe farr forth tolerated as that they were not contrariant or
derogatorie unto the same. Seing of late yeares under colour of that canon law
divers of your Majestie's true and faithfull subjectes, ministers, and others have
bene proceeded against *ex officio*, which was in your Majestie's ffather's tyme
abolished, and is (as we take it) by the lawes revived in the first yeare of your
Majestie's raigne, likewise abrogated, and hath noe warrant in your Majestie's
high commission ecclesiasticall, and besides is otherwise used then the sayd very
canon law prescribeth; and other your Highnes' subjectes have bene cited and
sent for up from very remote places, and out of the diocesse where they dwell, /
contrary to an espetiall statute made in the 23th year of the raigne of your   f.328
Majestie's most noble ffather, and revived in your Majestie's first parliament:[1]
which manner of proceeding overthroweth all ordinary jurisdiction, contrary to
the meaning of divers lawes of this realme. And wheras most of them upon

---

1. 23 Hen VIII, c.9, revived by 1 Eliz, c.1
   in *SR*, iii.377–8; iv.351.

their appearance cannot gett the copies of such matters wherwith they be charged, contrary to an old acte in the second year of King Henry the 5,[2] but are sworne to answere they know not to what, contrary to the lawe and libertie of England which heretofore graunted prohibitions against ecclesiasticall judges that should demaund an oath in any cause unles it were for matters of mariages and wills: and nevertheles, divers for refusing the sayd oath and certaine new subscriptions contrary to lawe have bene put to silence, imprisoned without bayle, and deprived from their freeholldes (as the law of England holdeth them) for trifles (as themselves confesse), both contrary to the lawes of your Majestie's realme, and also the Popish canons. For asmuch as (O most dread and gratious Soveraigne) we be taught by the sacred and infallible word of God[3] that plagues and destruccions upon kingdomes come for nothing more then for iniustices in partiall magistrates, and ignorance and contempt of his word in the common people, we most humblie beseech your Majestie to take order that your Highnes' commission ecclesiasticall may not be soe abused as hitherto it hath bene, and might be more particulerly declared unto your Majestie, if it might stand with your Highnes' good pleasure more particularly to heare the manyfolld complaintes of your poore subjectes. It may please your Majestie to call to remembrance how Joas and Josias, two notable and good Kings of Juda, were by the space of many yeares likewise deceaved by the priestes, to whom they had committed the repayring of the breaches of the house of the Lord, and therfore were forced to take another course.[4] And wheras we your Majestie's humble and loyall subjectes have bene heretofore openly defamed by seeking of redresse in this place, to follow Jesuites and seminary preistes, being odious and detestable traytors; to seeke anarchies and confusion of th'estate; to overthrow and goe against or before lawes established; to mayntaine conventicles and factions to the perill of your Majestie's estate and disturbance of the common quietnes of this realme; we most humbly beseech your Majestie, that whensoever any such uniust suggestion shalbe brought to your Majestie's eares, to continue that good opinion of our loyalties which it hath pleased your Highnes to signifie unto us since our assemblie in this place, and to assure your self that nothing can draw us to committ any thing in thought, word, or deed that may be displeasing to your Majestie, if our myndes be well /

v.   conceived, much lesse any wayes tend to your Majestie's hurt, as we trust by our forwardnes in all your Majestie's services, both heretofore, now, and hereafter, hath, doth, and shall appeare. We desire not anything to the preiudice of your Majestie's supreame authority and prerogative royall, or taking away of any lawfull jurisdiction or member of this estate, nor innovacion or making of new lawes. We are noe schismatikes, noe libellers, rebellious or disordered persons, as some would mingle and couple us with recusantes, sectaries, and other like offendors. We holld no conventicles or unlawfull assemblies, but detest them. We desire to live under your Majestie's lawes, and not the lawes of the Pope, or innovacions of private men's opinions, who (under colour of your Majestie's prerogative) may perhapps rather seeke to revenge particuler passions, and to sett out themselves, then to advance either the service of God or your Majestie. We desire that by a preaching ministery all the people of your kingdome may be taught to obey and serve your Highnes, not with eye service, but from the hart in the feare of the Lord, who only seeing the heart, can discerne hipocrasie, and will punish the least conceipt that may rise to the contrary. And seeing it is by the lords of the cleargie confessed that the disagreement betwene them and many good and learned ministers is not in any substance of doctrine, but only in some ceremonies and indifferent things, wherto the Apostle teacheth us that every man's conscience is not to be forced,[5] till such time as the Lord shall have informed him better: we most humblie beseech your Majestie that without any breach, offence, or new making of lawe, according to the authority of your Highnes' supreame government, yea and the power graunted already by lawe unto Lords Bishops and Archbishops to take order in such controversies as might arise in matters ecclesiasticall as they should thinke good, soe as their new order were not contrary to th'order prescribed by lawe; your Majestie would gratiouslie permitt and establish such a Christian and peaceable toleracion not contrary to the lawe, towardes divers good and dutifull preachers, as was used in the time of your Majestie's blessed brother King Edward the 6 and also somtimes in your Majestie's happie raigne, the want wherof by experience hath bene allwaies found to be the cause of the breach of the peace of the Church. And as we seeke not to excuse or except any man offending the lawe from suffering the penaltie due by the lawe of England, soe we most humblie beseech your Majestie that (in your most godlie and milde goverment towardes most haynous offendors) good and peaceable men which daily pray for your Majestie's preservacion, and are ready to leese all for your Majestie's weale, be noe otherwise iudged nor proceeded against then according to your Highnes' lawes of England. / And soe we doubt not but that your Majestie shall long f.329 enjoy a most peaceable and happy raigne over us in all honour and felicitie, and be able to withstand all th'attemptes of your enemies, which we most humblie from the bottomes of our heartes crave of almightie God: and with an unfayned and most humble presentacion of our bounden obedience and loyaltie, beseech your Majestie to accept in good parte this our humble and necessary peticion, proceeding from the very consciences and soules of true subjectes, for the discharge of their duties towardes god, your Majestie, and their cuntrie; who shalbe alwayes found willing and ready to imploy their lives and all that they have for your Majestie's service and safetie.

---

2. 2 Hen V, stat. 1, c.3 (1414) in *SR*, ii.176.   4. 2 Kgs 12; 22; 23.
3. e.g. 2 Chr 21: 12–15.   5. ? Heb 9, esp. 8–14.

9. *John Stubbs' supplication, March*

Text from BL Add. 48101 (Yelverton 110), copy.

Add. 48101 (Yelverton 110), fos.136–7

[Noted at the end in Robert Beale's hand: 'This supplication was drawn by Mr Stubbes to be exhibited in parlement March 1589.']

To the Queene's most excellent Majestie. Most gracious and dread Soveraigne.

Haveing nowe one and thirtie yeres' most happie experience of Gode's tender and watchfull eye over your princelie care and studie to protect and governe us in pietie, peace, and iustice, thereto receiveing lately by our Speaker your good pleasure aunswereable to your wonted clemencie, and forasmuch as for most reall accomplishment of your word, and whatsoever may be expected from a good prince your Majestie is renouned above all princes of the earth; hereupon we repose our selves more confidentlie and securelie, in our comon griefes, then upon any bill[1] by us here to be preferred. Namelie in a particular more nearely toucheing us then either purveyors, *Quo titulo*, or any penall lawe (for it goeth even to our soules), we the comons in this present parlament assembled doe in the name of all your humble and faithfull subiectes, the third estate of this lande, most lowelie beseech your Highnes that, whereas we are not onely burdened with more then a pluralitie of unprofiteable ministers, many non-resident, and more not learned, against whom any manner accusation is hardely received to remoove them; but alsoe whereas our ministers of better conscience and more profiteable learneing in their pastorlike care lyeing resident with their flocke, as becometh lawfull incombentes as well for bodilie hospitalitie accordeing to their habilitie, as also for instruction in Gode's holie feare and an inviolable allegeaunce to your Highnes, whereby the Jesuites, seminaries, and other traytors, hatefull enemies to Christe's eternall truth and your royall state, may neither worke nor lurke to destroye this Churche whereof you are the sacred defendor, nor interrupt our marvelous prosperitie and peace whereof you are the blessed meane, are neverthelesse right greivousely intreated and proceeded against, ascited from farre, suspended and deprived both from their spirituall function and from their freeholde, absolutely and *ex officio*, sometyme by othe to accuse themselves before they can have copie of that whereto they must aunswere, contrarie to lawe, (then the which – torture excepted – we knowe noe higher inquisicion leafte for most heynous offences), and sometime by subscription urged beyond lawe, when the poore men offer to subscribe as farre as lawe requireth, and by diverse other wayes contrarie to lawes, olde canones, and late iniunctiones, all this not for contempt of your Majestie's lawes, which they reverence, and which conteine sufficient provision within them to punish all offendors against them, nor for matter of faithe, in the / opinion of themselves that soe intreate them, but of ceremonie   v. and ordre, nor for matters perilous to your state, which they recommend to God by fervent prayers and commend unto men, teacheing their congregationes soe to doe, but for pointes offensive to some degree and sort of men, to whom though upon like complaintes these matters have ben committed yet finde we noe remedie. It may nowe therefore please your Majestie, either to reserve these thinges to your royall equitie, counsance,[2] and wisedome, whereunto we appeale, and that those persones whom we had rather call ffathers then complaine against or challenge as parties, may not still be the onelie iudges; or else that your Highnes wold vouchesafe informacion of these matters by such most honorable lordes and counsellors as the same shall please to appointe, that soe either by more mylde exposition of lawes, or by alteracion not against equitie, such as in the dayes of your Highnes' religious brother and dureing your owne most gracious raigne hath beene happilie practised, the necessarie course of preacheing faith and true obedience may not be stayed.

And because, being dispersed or dissolved from this corporation into the common bodie of your subiectes we shall not be present to explane and approove this our iust and dutifull complainte against their insinuationes whoe may finde themselves hereby provoked; and seeing heretofore, that whoe soe did accompanie, releeve, and reverence those ministers which are more painefull then their fellowes, were straighte wayes by certeine indiscreete men's sermones and writeinges coupled with Jesuites, recusantes, rebelles, and traytors, infamed as puritanes, schismatikes, platformers, enemyes to governement, freindes to anarchie and such like:

We humblie praye that your most gracious integritie and goodnesse may be the continuall interpretor of this which we offer without anie contempte of them, or stomach to them, whom we professe to love as contrymen and brethren, as fellow servantes and subiectes to God and you, and as fellowe citizens and coheires as well of this eartheley inheritaunce in your kingdom as of that everlasting inheritaunce in the kingdom of heaven. Our faith is that which this Church professeth, we reverence this Church and deeme them for excommunicate that doe condemne it, we crave noe innovation, but observation of olde lawes, with freedom from canons and customes abrogated, and that all causes may be determined by the lawes and liberties of England, and not by men's passionate opiniones. /

We abhorre all traytors and all sedicious persones, we detest all heretikes,   f.137 schismatikes, and fantasticall sectaries separateing themselves from the prayers and sacramentes of this Churche, we renounce all fellowshipp or parte with anie sedicious and rayleing libellors, and whatsoever tending to faction or schisme. Such we are and such we pray to be accoumpted especiallie by your

---

1. Inserted in another hand.   2. *Sic.*

Highnes, into whose sacred handes we deliver up this not in anie diffidence of your wonted mindfulnes to doe us all maner good, but as a recorde of our verie thoughtes seekeing onelie those meanes of releife which may best stand with your good pleasure and with our dutifull recognition of all your highe prerogative, dignitie, preeminence, and royall powre, in causes aswell ecclesiasticall as civill, for honoureable continuaunce whereof many yeres in love of your subiectes, in health of your person, in honour of your name, in ioye of your harte and in all flourisheing happines thorough Gode's mercie we shall not onelie make unfeined praieres, but employe the services of our goodes, bodies, lyves, and all other our meanes whatsoever aswell in regarde of our natureall allegeaunce, and for the infinite graces which we inioye by you, as alsoe in our soule and conscience towardes almightie God, who still and ever blesse all them that blesse your Majestie and curse all those that saye not thereto. Amen.

10. *Proceedings, 29 March*

Text from PRO SP Dom.Eliz. 223 / 34, corrected copy.

SP Dom.Eliz. 223/34

[Endorsed '*29 Martii 31 RR Elizabethae.* Touching a proclamation of war against Spaine'.]

Anno 31° Elizabethae Die Sat: xxix° Martii 1589.

Mr Threasurer, in the name of the rest of the committees appointed for conference with the Lords this present forenoone, sheweth that their Lordshipps have ymparted (by the mouth of the Lord Threasurer) unto the committees of this House the effect of a conference which their Lordships have had amongst them-selfes, and of their resolucion therin, which is, that (considering the great practizes, treasons, invasions, and attemptes lately intended and pursued by the Pope, the King of Spaine, and their adherentes for the subverting of true religion, her Majestie, and the whole state of the realme) as their said Lordships together with this House have yealded, and granted unto her Majesty an extraordynary and most liberall supply of theire treasure for the necessary defence of her said Majesty state[1] and kingdome against the like daungerous attemptes of such mighty enemyes: So likewise (for the causes aforesaid) have their said Lordships not only upon the said conference resolved to offer unto her Highnes the expence, and ymploying of their landes and handes, but also of their bodyes, and lyves. And likewise for the more honorable performance of the same defence to become humble sutors unto her most excellent Majestie (yf yt so shall seeme good unto her said Highnes) for denouncing of warre, and for preventing of like attemptes, to use all honorable meanes, aswell offensive as defensyve, against the said King of Spaine and his adherentes, at such tyme and occasion, as to her Highnesses[2] wisedome and princely good pleasure shalbe thought convenient. And that if yt stand with the good likeing of this House, to ioyne with their said Lordships in peticion unto her Majestie for the same: and also that Mr Speaker doe delyver the same peticion in the name of the Lords and of this House in his oracion to her Majestie in the Upper House this afternoone ymmedyately after the offering and deliverie of the graunt of the fifteenes, and subsedyes. And this upon the question was resolved to be accomplished accordingly.

1. *Sic.*   2. *Sic.*

[Journal: House of Commons] Henry Jackman's Journal, 7–19 February

Text from BL Lansdowne 55, original.

Lansdowne 55, fos.184–5

Februarii 4° Anno Reginae Elizabethae 31° the Parlament began.

7°   A bill concerninge informers and informations was red, and comitted. The partes:

> That none should be admitted an informer that is detected for any crime in a court of recorde. That he bringe testimoniall of his good behaviour to the judges of the court where he shall informe. That he be assessed in the subsidie att xl^s lande or v^{li} goodes.
>
> That he shall sue his information in the county where the offence was comitted, within one yere after the offence. If he discontinue or be nonsute[d], barred for ever.
>
> A repeale of a statute *anno* 7° Henry 8 for the tyme of bringinge information.[1]

8°   A bill for disorders in innes and alehouses. Partes:

> Repeale of all other lawes[2] concerninge that matter. 4 in a market towne beinge a borowe, 3 in other markettes, j in any other towne: to be appointed by the iustices of peace.
>
> Licence to continue but for a yere.
>
> Offences inquirable att the quarter sessions.

For the justices   5^{li} fine for not retourninge the bondes taken to the assises.

> 10^s for the vittlers that shall admitt comon haunters, especially on the Saboth in tyme of service. Common haunters sett in the stockes.
>
> A clause for the gaginge of bruers' vessels.[3]

A bill concerninge the priviledge of clergie.[4]
Partes:

> Repeale of all lawes concerninge that matter. That a witnes without the recorde shall suffise to testifie that a felon hath once had his clergie. That he had that had[5] his clergie shall not answer to former offences.
>
> Clergie denied to som who might before have it, but granted to none to whome it was before denied.

Whether a burgesse retourned not sworne maye have another put in his place in case of sicknes: moved by Mr Wroth for a gentleman and affirmed.[6]

A bill that intayled and copihold landes should be lyable to the payment of debtes. Red and reiected.

A bill for pursute of hue and crie.[7]

Partes:

Repeale of all former lawes concerninge that title.[8] The hundred where the offence was don with 3 other next adioyninge to satisfie the partie, to be rated by ij justices of peace, and levied by the constables and hedboroughe. /

A bill for Orforde Haven twise red.

A bill for Ugnall against Trussell, for the assurance of the land againste Trussell, Ferris, and the lord by escheate.[9]

Pilson[10] served by subpoena into the Starchamber by Aylmore complayneth, Aylmore is called and acknowledginge his faut is pardoned payinge Pilson's charges and the Seriante's fees.

A bill for proclamations for fines.[11]

A bill for fforstallers, regraters, and ingrossers.

A bill for the Curriers, wherin is required the repeale of ij former statutes wherin they are prohibited to buy lether.[12]

A bill for the repeale of these statutes, *videlicet*,[13]

for the preservation of grayne,
for wearinge of capps,
ffor sowinge of flax and hempe,
for breedinge of horses,
for clogges and patens,
for ffylesters of the recordes.[14]

The bill for inkeepers and alehouses 2[dly] red.

1. 7 Hen VIII, c.3. (1515) in *SR*, iii. 177–8. 31 Eliz c.5 (1588–9) in *SR*, iv.801–2 repealed the Henrician statute 'utterly'.
2. See 5 & 6 Ed VI, c.25 (1551–2) in *SR*, iv.157–8, D'Ewes, p.429 does not mention this bill on this day.
3. See 31 Eliz, c.8 (1588–9) in *SR*, iv.805–6 for the act concerning vessels. The scope of the bill as recorded here was narrowed (D'Ewes, p.440). D'Ewes, p.430 does not mention this bill on this day.
4. D'Ewes, p.430 does not mention this bill on this day.
5. *Sic.*
6. See D'Ewes, p.430 for 8, 10 February.
7. Read the first time on 11 February, according to D'Ewes, p.430.
8. 27 Eliz, c.13 (1584–5) in *SR*, iv.720–2 cites statutes of 13 Ed I and 28 Ed III,

and amends their working. 39 Eliz, c.25 (1597–8) enlarged that statute in the interests of a small hundred in Berkshire.
9. D'Ewes, pp.431–2 does not specifically mention this bill on this day.
10. Cf. D'Ewes, p.431: 'Puleston'.
11. D'Ewes, pp.431–2 does not specifically mention this bill on this day.
12. D'Ewes, p.432 does not specifically mention this bill on this day. See ? 1 Eliz, c.9 (1558–9) and 5 Eliz, c.8, sect. vii (1562–3) in *SR*, iv.369–70, 429–36.
13. D'Ewes, p.432 does not specifically mention this bill on this day.
14. See 14 Eliz, c.11 (1572) for grain, 13 Eliz, c.19 (1571) for caps, 5 Eliz, c.5, sect. xix for flax and hemp, 27 Hen VIII, c.6 (1535–6) for horses, 4 Hen V, stat. 2, c.3, and 4 Ed IV, c.9 for clogs and pattens in *SR*, ii.196, 416; iii.535–6 iv.425–6, 555, 601–3.

14th   A bill againste th'officers of th'Exchequer.
Partes:
1. A tenure appeeringe upon record no *quo titulo* awarded for the findinge of it.
2. A recorde to prove a tenure in soccage etc, no *quo titulo* to enquire for a tenure *in capite*.
3. Debtes answered upon recorde no proces to be awarded.
4. No proces but grounded upon recordes of the court.
5. Longe pleadinge both upon *quo tituloes*, and of the pardon generall provided for.
A bill for the sale of one Hanforde's lande for debte to the Queene.
A bill brought in againste purveyors.
A bill for the dissolvinge of a conveyance made by Mr Henry Nevell.
The bill for abridging of proclamations upon fines 2dly red.
A bill [for] confirmation of leaces made by corporations, thoughe they want the woorde of the firste foundacion.[15]

15th   The bill againste purveyors red.[16]
Partes:
1. Execution of all former lawes.[17]
2. No takinge on the highe waye or comon passage.
3. The purveyor shalbe no butcher, poulter, grasier, etc.
4. No man constrained to appeere before the Greenecloth upon complaint of the purveyor unles the complaint be testified to be juste under the handes of ij justices dwellinge where the offence is supposed to be don.
5. The purveyor's payne falslye compleyninge 20^{li}, and losse of his office. /

f.185   6. Februarye 1588
The justices bounde to reade the statute att every quarter sessions upon payne of 5^{li}.

17th   A bill for abridginge of sutes att the comon lawe.
Partes:
1. Smale accions of trespas not touchinge the ffreehould to be sued in courte barons.
2. A sufficient recompence offered for a trespas before ij justices of peace and ij other wittnesses and refused, the same beinge afterwardes founde by verdicte: the jury shall pas for the deffendant.
3. 14 attorneyes onelye in Norffolke, 8 for the sheir, 2 for Norwich, 2 for Lyn, and 2 for Yarmouth: to be assigned by the Cheife Justices.
Committed.
The committees reporte for the subsidie, *videlicet*
4 15^{thes} and 10^{thes} payable in 4 yeres, the 20th of November yerelye.
2 subsidies likewise in 4 yeres the 12th of Februarye yerely.[18]
A motion for the continuance of statutes.[19]

18th   A bill for disposinge of lande in socage without licence of mortmayne.
A bill for clothworkers, *videlicet* the repeale of the wordes 'Kent' and 'Sussex' in a former statut which they require may be generall.

A bill for the ffishmongers.

A bill to reforme the deceipt of Thomas Drurye toward one Haslewrigge.[20]

A bill delivered from the Upper House.[21]

The purveyors bill discussed and amended.   19th

15. The bills for Hanford, Nevell and leases made by corporations are not specifically mentioned by D'Ewes, pp.432–3 on this day.

16. D'Ewes, pp.432–3: two readings and committed.

17. Note that the continuation statute of this session (31 Eliz, c.10 in *SR*, iv.808–9) continued the act of 1571 relating to grain near Oxford and Cambridge.

18. Cf. *SR*, iv.818–34 for payment details.

19. D'Ewes, pp.433–4 does not mention this.

20. D'Ewes, p.434 only specifically mentions this last of the four bills. 8 Eliz, c.6 (1566) in *SR*, iv.489 specified that Kent and *Suffolk* cloths should not be exported unwrought.

21. Writs of error in Exchequer and King's Bench (D'Ewes, p.434).

Indexes

This index is divided into three parts: a general section covering main subjects; bills, arranged by session; and persons (and principal officers). Unlike in Volume I matters covered by entries in the index of bills do not appear again as main entries in the general index. Identification of some of the parliamentary figures remains problematic in some instances, and these have been indicated. Abbreviations may be used where more than one journal covers the same material (see below). Otherwise, references to the separates are rendered in the usual way. References to the translation of proceedings in the Low Countries committee appear in brackets, e.g. 292(299). The numerous indications of antipathy to, and anxiety about, the realm's religious foes at home and abroad means that it is not practical to avoid all long undifferentiated entries.

An = Anonymous journal (1584–5 or 1586–7)
Com jnl = proceedings on Mary Stuart
Cr = Cromwell (1584–5)
Fl = Fleetwood (1584–5)
Fz = Fitzwilliam (1584–5)
Lds roll = Parliament roll (1586–7)

GENERAL INDEX

INDEX OF BILLS

INDEX OF PERSONS

(including principal officers)